MODERN GREEK POETRY

TRANSLATION,

INTRODUCTION,

AN ESSAY

ON TRANSLATION,

AND NOTES

by

KIMON FRIAR

SIMON AND SCHUSTER / NEW YORK

First printing

SBN 671-21025-4
Library of Congress Catalog Card Number: 70-171604
Designed by Edith Fowler
Manufactured in the United States of America
by American Book–Stratford Press, Inc.

The publisher is grateful to the poets whose work appears in this
collection for permission to translate and include those poems selected
by Mr. Friar.

TO MY COLLABORATORS
THE GREEK POETS

CONTENTS

[A date alone indicates date of composition, whether first or final draft; c. indicates an approximate date, p. the date of first publication in book form.]

INTRODUCTION

I | THE HISTORICAL BACKGROUND

In his Introduction to *Medieval and Modern Greek Poetry* (1951), an anthology in the original Greek covering the centuries from A.D. 330 to 1949, the poet and scholar Constantine A. Trypánis refers to Greek poetry as that "with the longest and perhaps noblest tradition in the Western world," and concludes that "in the last hundred years greater and more original poetry has been written in Greek than in the fourteen centuries which preceded them," and that "in the last fifty years it has at last . . . achieved universal validity." In the very year Professor Trypánis published his anthology, I also coedited and published, with John Malcolm Brinnin, another anthology, *Modern Poetry: American and British*, the result of intensive reading and teaching at various universities in the United States and in directing the Poetry Center in New York City. I began reading and translating the modern Greek poets after my first visit to Greece, in 1946; my subsequent work in this field over some twenty-five years, and comparative readings in other literatures, have led me to substantiate and indorse Professor Trypánis' observations. Such long dedication on my part indicates, at least, my own personal belief in the validity and achievement of modern Greek poetry.

Most educated persons have some awareness of ancient Greece as the cultural wellspring of the Western world, or some appreciation of contemporary Greece as an enchantment of sun-washed shores and ruins, but the more-than-two-thousand-year interim between these two worlds often is, to them, a blank or blurred page of history. Yet, to understand any aspect of modern Greek culture—in this case modern Greek poetry—a reader should have some slight knowledge of what happened to Greece and to the development of its language and literature between 146 B.C., when the Roman consul Lucius Mummius sacked Corinth and Rome began to exercise a suzerainty over Greece proper, and A.D. 1830, when part of Greece was freed from Turkish domination and declared an independent nation.

In A.D. 285, Diocletian divided the unwieldy Roman Empire into an eastern and a western half, and in 395, Theodosius I made the separation irrevocable by dividing the Empire between his two sons. Greece had become part of the Eastern Roman Empire, but from earliest days of Roman domination Greek culture and language had pervaded the Romans, and the eastern half remained Greek-speaking. The Greek language played a significant role in the diffusion of Christianity. The Old Testament had been translated into Greek by the first century B.C., and St. Paul had visited Thessaloniki, Athens, and Corinth by the middle of the first century A.D. Although Christianity was being persecuted in both halves of the Empire, Christian churches were flourishing on Greek soil. The Christian Church became recognized as a legal entity by the Edict of Milan in A.D. 313, and in 330 Constantine inaugurated Byzantium, an old town on the Bosporos, as "the New Rome that is Constantinople," thus transferring the balance from the West to the East and making Constantinople the new center of Graeco-Roman and Christian culture. Constantinople also became the capital of the Byzantine Empire, as the eastern half of the Roman Empire came to be known. Although Hellenistic tradition throughout these years remained strongly pervasive, it was gradually assimilated by the Christian ethos and finally suppressed as pagan idolatry by Justinian in 529, when he closed the schools of Athens. Hesitating to call themselves "Hellenes" because of the word's pagan connotations, the Byzantines now called themselves "Romaioi," that is, citizens of the Roman Empire, a term still in use today to designate a Greek of more than national scope or boundary.

The Western Empire crumbled under sporadic invasions by northern barbarians until, in 476, the German Odoacer overthrew the last of the Roman emperors and proclaimed himself king. The far-flung Byzantine Empire expanded and contracted spasmodically under the invasion of Goths, Ostrogoths, Huns, Slavs, Bulgarians, and finally Ottoman Turks. To obtain the assistance of Venice against Norman invaders, a Byzantine Emperor in the eleventh century granted to Venice the right of free trade throughout the Empire. The raids of Western princes now began.

Venetians and Genoese made many inroads into the Eastern Empire, first establishing coastal cities and ports, and eventually conquering and dominating most of Greece proper and its islands. In 1202 Venice helped organize the Fourth Crusade, ostensibly to fight the infidel, but in reality to crush its commercial rival, Constantinople.

The sack of that city by the Fourth Crusade in 1204 marks the beginning of a new period in Greek history, for although this particular occupation lasted only fifty-seven years, and although the revived Byzantine Empire was to last another two hundred years, the Fourth Crusade prepared the way for the complete dissolution of Byzantine civilization by the invasion of the Ottoman Turks, climaxed by the fall of Constantinople to them in 1453. Franks, Venetians, Genoese, and Turks contended for centuries over various parts of Greece, splintering it into many small feudal states composed of principalities and duchies. Venice possessed parts of Greece from 1202 to 1699; the Franks occupied Rhodes, Cyprus, and parts of the Dodecanese, from 1309 to 1522, and for almost four hundred years, from 1453 to 1830, most of Greece was subjugated as part of the Ottoman Empire.

Although liberated in 1830, Greece was granted only a small part of her former territories by the Great Powers. She then had a population of about 800,000, while 2,500,000 lived in unfreed territories. The Ionian Islands, Thessaly, Macedonia, Crete, Western Thrace, a part of Epiros, and the eastern Aegean islands were annexed at various times much later, the Dodecanese Islands as late as 1947. Cyprus is still an issue. In the brief 140 years since her liberation, Greece has repeatedly suffered intervention by the Great Powers, two world wars, two Balkan wars, a German-Italian occupation of almost four years, a vicious civil war, and many military coups. During periods when such countries as England, France, Italy, and Germany were blossoming into renaissance (much of it triggered by a revival of classical learning abroad), the Greek creative imagination was shackled and stunted. My purpose, however, in detailing this horrendous chronology of subjugation, exploitation and inundation by foreign populations is to emphasize that throughout these long centuries the Greek character has miraculously preserved its original vigor, and that the modern Greek language is still the heir of the classical Greek tongue. I know of no other country, at least in the Western

Hemisphere, which has retained such identity and integrity under such crushing odds.

II | LANGUAGE AND LITERATURE

When the multiple city states of ancient Greece lost their independence by merging into greater political unities, and with the ascendency of the Athenians in the fifth century, their dialects were gradually absorbed into a spoken language which in time became the Hellenistic Koine, or Common Greek, based on Attic Greek but transformed in morphology, diction, and pronunciation by those who spoke Greek in Asia Minor, Syria, Persia, and Egypt after the conquests of Alexander the Great. It is in forms of this Common Greek in which the Septuagint and the New Testament were written, and from which the modern Greek spoken language, the demotic, has gradually evolved over the centuries. But it was also in the Hellenistic period, particularly about the time of Christ, that scholars and pedants, scorning the contemporary spoken language, tried to imitate and revive the language of "classical" times, hoping that by emulating the letter they might incarnate the spirit, but forgetting that in the "classical" period no dichotomy of importance existed between the written and spoken language. Thus the bilingual problem was born, one that has plagued Greece to the present day. Periodically, those who looked back nostalgically on the language of Greece during its apogee have striven to write in some form of "Atticism" until, in the late eighteenth century, and in the nineteenth century before and after the Greek War of Independence, such linguists constructed a compromised tongue, the *katharévousa*, or "purist," adapting words, grammar, and syntax in a purification that hoped to approach the archaic language and literature. Like Caváfis, they preferred artificial to real flowers.

Although Latin remained the official tongue of the Eastern Roman Empire until the early part of the seventh century, it was never the spoken language of the Greeks themselves. By the eighth century it had been all but eliminated, leaving behind a few words for several objects of daily life. The pervading influences in literature, however, during the transitional three centuries of the Eastern Empire, were Hellenism and Christianity, until gradually a Hellenized Christianity evolved into a Christian Byzantine culture. Scholars and poets at first strove to write in the manner of the ancient Greeks in an Attic dialect of varying degrees of purity or impurity, and hoped to protect quantitative measure from the inroads made by the transition of the language from pitch to stress. Striving to keep alive their sense of racial and linguistic continuity, they wrote artificed religious poems, some of great beauty. During the fourth and fifth centuries, *tropária*, or short hymns, dominated; during the sixth and seventh centuries, *kontákia*, or long and elaborate metrical sermons; from the seventh to the ninth century, the *canón*, a form of hymn cycle. Lyric poetry of a sort and the epigram reached their height from the eighth to the eleventh centuries. There was no drama, but many dramatic elements were to be found in the dialogues and antiphony in the liturgy of the Greek Orthodox Church. The Byzantines recognized Attic Greek as the official tongue, and the gap between it and the spoken language grew wider and wider. By the time of the eleventh century, the demotic had closely approximated its present form, which in grammar today varies but slightly from that in use during the downfall of the Byzantine Empire in the fifteenth century. Secular poetry, written in the stress language and various dialects of the demotic, attained its fullest expression in various versions of the romantic epic poem *Dhiyenís Akrítas*, compiled in the tenth century from many previous sources.

It was probably in the fourth century, or perhaps even earlier (its origins remain obscure), that the most popular measure of Greek poetry first appeared, the stressed iambic line of fifteen syllables, written usually with a pause after the eighth syllable. It was used in many ecclesiastical hymns, and is the measure found in the poems of the Akrític Cycle, in most folk songs and in long narrative poems such as *Erotókritos*. Indeed, it bears a remarkably close relationship to the rhymed couplet division (a combined tetrameter and trimeter of fourteen and often fifteen syllables) of many English and Scotch popular ballads. I refer to such folk poems as "Sir Patrick Spens," "The Wife of Usher's Well," the Robin Hood cycle. Here, for instance, is the last stanza of "Bonny Barbara Allan":

> O mother, mother, make my bed!
> O make it saft and narrow!
> Since my love died for me today,
> I'll die for him to-morrow.

As a medium for long narrative or dramatic poems, it has analogies in the use of iambic pentameter in English, as in *Paradise Lost*, Elizabethan plays, Pope's "The Rape of the Lock" and his translations of Homer.

From the conquest of Constantinople in 1453 by the Turks until the beginning of the Greek War of Independence in 1821, Greece remained for almost four centuries in a dark twilight during a period when other European countries were fermenting with renaissance. Only the Greek Orthodox Church kept alive a few smoldering embers of language and education. It was in lands under Frankish rule that Greek learning began to achieve an independent life: in Khios, Crete, Monemvasía, the Ionian Islands, Rhodes, Cyprus, and even in Venice itself, where Greek scholars immigrated and where the Greek classics began to be published during the fifteenth and sixteenth centuries. The demotic and Attic traditions continued to contend with each other and developed in their own way, dominated now by French and Italian influences. But in Crete, under Venetian rule for almost four and a half centuries, from 1204 to 1699, a masterpiece was composed in the Cretan demotic tongue, *Erotókritos*, which was written by Vikéntios Kornáros about the middle of the seventeenth century, an epico-lyrical poem of 10,052 fifteen-syllable lines arranged in rhymed couplets that has since greatly influenced all modern Greek poets in vocabulary, tone and syntax. It was in Crete too that the drama flourished in such fine religious plays as *Abraham's Sacrifice*, which was also probably written by Kornáros, and the blood-and-thunder melodrama *Erophíli*, written by the poet Yeóryios Hortátzis before 1637. Had Crete not fallen to the Turks in 1669, the Cretan variant of the demotic, as developed in works such as these, might have become the basis for a common literary idiom throughout all of Greece. Modern Greek Cretan authors such as Níkos Kazantzákis and Pandelís Prevelákis have utilized their native dialect to great advantage.

But it is to the popular ballads and folk songs, arising primarily in the early Middle Ages (though some may be traced back to Homeric times) and reaching their climax in the brigand songs of the eighteenth century, that the true source of modern Greek poetry is to be found. Written, like the folk poetry of all lands, in a demotic tongue of fresh and rich expressiveness, they are short and simple, and contain few decorative adjectives. Lyrical, narrative or dramatic, they are imbued with a deep but restrained emotion and deal directly with basic experiences but without mysticism, singing of the joy of life and nature, exulting in the gallantry and pride of youth, mourning the death of heroes in the *mirolóya*, or laments, narrating myths and tales in the *paraloyés*, or ballads, defying oppressors in the *kléftika*, or brigand songs, of the guerrilla mountain chieftians. Even today, in the Cretan mountains, shepherds have composed long epical poems in rhymed couplets about the German paratroop invasion of their island in 1941. The present-day tourist who delights in the modern *rebétika* songs, as he watches the Greek worker or peasant dance in his tavernas today, should understand that these are the urban heirs of the folk songs. Originally the expression of the *rebétis* (the idle one, the wretched one, the habitué, more than likely, of the underworld), these songs are individualistic, avoiding more often than not sexual or pornographic innuendos, concentrating on the beloved mother or the betraying mistress. The tough young man of the lower classes, the *mángas*, dances these songs at night in tavernas, either with lonely introspection in the *zeïbékiko*, or by linking arms with a friend or two in the ritualistic *hasápiko* or the *hasaposérviko*. The modern *rebétika* songs rose primarily out of Smyrna and Thessaloníki and lasted for about thirty years: the Smyrna style of 1922–32, the golden period of 1932–40, and the last period, 1940–52, of great individual composers who wrote their own words and music. The chief instrument used is the *bouzoúki* (a kind of mandolin) accompanied in more recent times by guitar, clarinet, drum and piano. Almost impossible to translate, because of the predominance in them of slang, local references, argot and foreign phrases, they may be divided into some twenty-four categories, such as songs of derision, poverty, hashish, the underworld, eroticism, bravado, anguish, jail—all reverberating with the "dying fall" of a nostalgic epoch in Greek urban life. If the demotic songs and dances are the romantic and heroic expression of the Greek mountaineer and shepherd, the *rebétika* songs are the anguished existentialist poetry of the Greek lower classes in city and village.

During the Turkish occupation, the language of learning was written primarily in an Attic Greek in various stages of corruption. In the development of the Greek language, with its rich resources, the chasm between the cultivated and the vulgar tongue had been constantly widening: the demotic of the people evolving in morphology, syntax, grammar and vocabulary, splintering off into many dialects under ceaseless historical and phonetic changes; the purist of the educated revolving more or less statically around Attic Greek and the Hellenistic Koine. By the end of the eighteenth century, the demotic tongue had found champions even among the educated, and the more modern aspects of the "language problem" was born. In 1804, Adhamándios Koraís, living in Paris, and the first Greek philologist with European authority, recommended a "beautification" of the demotic tongue of the educated middle classes, a restoration of common words to ancient forms, a compromise that would recognize modern vocabulary but retain ancient grammar and syntax, a concept that greatly influenced the progress of modern *katharévousa*. It was the hope of these scholars and men of letters that, with the rivivification of the new Greek nation, its ancient glory and language might also be reborn.

The Greeks were gradually beginning to think of themselves now not only as members of the Byzantine Church and Empire under feudal Frankish or Turkish rule, during which their national consciousness had become dimmed, but as the awakened heirs of a classical and glorious past. They were beginning to rediscover their long-lost classical heritage. But unknown to all, an illiterate hero of the Greek War of Independence, General Yánnis Makriyánnis, taught himself to read and write in his thirties that he might set down his *Memoirs*, written between 1829 and 1850, then hidden and lost, and not published until fifty-seven years later, in 1907. The simple, sincere, unadorned demotic style of Makriyánnis, who wrote as he spoke, has so much become the touchstone of purity in demotic usage for many sophisticated Greek writers of burdensome education that George Seféris could refer to him as "this illiterate, my master in Greek."

The literary reforms of Koraís were opposed by Yánnis

Psiháris, who in 1888 published a travel journal, *My Journey*, written in an untrammeled demotic tongue. The battle now began to take on more definite form. From now on literature was to be written in the purist on the one extreme, in the demotic on the other, and in a bewildering variety of hybrid forms in between. The language problem also began to take on a sociological and political flavor: the purist tongue became that of the conservatives, the aristocrats, the pedants; and the demotic that of the liberals, the democrats, the proletariat. The purist was then declared to be, and is still today, the official language of Greece, that used in Parliament, in courts of law, in the schools, over the radio and television, and in many of the newspapers. Depending on their political coloring, some newspapers were written in extreme purist, some in extreme demotic, but most in an inelegant mixture of the two, a *kathomilouméni*, or "daily tongue," a middle-class Greek without much grace or coloring, neither demotic nor purist.

The purist tongue is condensed, inflectional and synthetic, an artificial language bristling with pride in its derivative ancestry, precise yet abstract. The demotic is periphrastic, rich in many concrete words and phrases, often retaining words in living form in use thousands of years previously, but poor in those abstract words which were not the concern of the common peasantry who have kept it alive. Today such lack of abstract words in the demotic is the despair of the modern poet who may wish to express a thought of metaphysical nicety. Although Seféris with much difficulty had succeeded in translating Eliot's *The Waste Land*, he found that such lack of abstract words in the demotic made it impossible for him to translate the more metaphysical *Four Quartets*. And yet, today the contemporary Greek poet may mold his expression on a living language of great antiquity and borrow his vocabulary from ancient, Hellenistic, Byzantine, medieval, and modern Greek and its dialects. The fact of the matter is that the Greek language is at once very old and very new. The Greek poet has at his disposal a vocabulary of overwhelming wealth, strangely lacking in foreign borrowing of much importance, for the Greek language has the unusual capacity and unrestrained power of creating words for any new shade of meaning or invention. Many new words formed from Greek roots in foreign lands have returned to their root source in this circuitous way. Often a Greek may use two different words which are more similar in meaning for the same thing than synonymous, though they differ in tone, in quality, in formality or informality. Such are the two words *ártos* and *psomí* (both meaning bread): *ártos*, the word used by the purists, is taken directly from the ancient Greek, although today it has attained an early Christian aura because it has most often been used to denote the bread taken during communion. It is etymologically significant to point out, however, that *psomí*, the word in daily conversational use even by those who write in the purist, also derives from an ancient Greek word, *psomós*, meaning "morsel," and that many other demotic words have as ancient a heritage, although they have undergone morphological change. And yet, as though to emphasize the dichotomy that is a living reality in Greece today, the word over a bakery shop is always *artopiíon*, although the baker himself is referred to as the *psomás* or as the *foúrnaris*, another demotic word with its source in the ancient Greek word *foúrnos*, meaning "oven."

The English language enriches itself by constantly borrowing and adapting, the Greek language by a constant ferment of reformation. Since no poet or man of letters can proceed much beyond the capacity of a people to assimilate, the new living language in its vocabulary and grammar must be formed gradually by a continual interreaction between writer and people, the two creators. If in all this confusion of poverty and superabundance the modern Greek poet sometimes despairs, he may remind himself that poets are most free in their expression and imaginative flights when the language is still plastic and in ferment, that in periods of language reformation great poets have risen, a Chaucer, a Dante, even a Shakespeare. The question facing any author in Greece today is no longer whether the demotic or the purist should be the language of literature (for the demotic, with its many setbacks, always wins the battle), but rather how much borrowing from contemporary vulgar sources and from purist and other historical modes a writer may impose on his demotic base. To a temperament such as Kazantzákis, which delighted in constant change, in revolution and evolution, this state of the language was exciting and an opportunity to help shape and create it. His Odysseus exclaims, "Blessed be the fate that gave me birth between two eras!" But to such a temperament as Seféris, which relies heavily on precision, nicety and purity of taste, such fermentation is a cause of frustration.

Although the Greek language has been developing for over three thousand years, it reveals a unity for which no analogy may be found in the history of any other Indo-European tongue. There are more discrepancies between the Koine and Homer than between the Koine and "modern" Greek. Although the phonological, morphological, and syntactical systems of classical, Byzantine, and modern Greek are not the same, the Greek language, nevertheless, discloses an entity which Latin, for instance, and its derivative languages do not possess. In our universities the departments of classical Greek should truly become departments simply of "Greek," in which the language, throughout its historical development, may be taught as one entity. A classical scholar from the United States or Europe can, in a few months, read a modern Greek newspaper without much difficulty. The *Iliad* and the *Odyssey* are more intelligible to an educated Greek today than *Beowulf* to a comparable English reader, although in the first instance some 2,770 years have intervened, and in the second less than half that interval. "Despite many racial, cultural, and political changes, and various forms of occupation and suppression during the past two thousand years," writes the scholar of Greek, Nicholas Bachtin, "more than any other language, Greek, in the entire extent of its development, is a living whole."

III | THE SCHOOLS

The Old School of Athens

Western influences began somewhat to infiltrate Greek letters after the Fourth Crusade of 1204, when Frankish romances and popular songs began to be adapted and imitated. During the Ottoman Empire, educated men and scholars living in the Phanar ("Lighthouse") district of Constantinople attained to the highest positions in the Ottoman government, becoming dragomans (interpreters) of the Porte and ambassadors to Western courts. They wrote mostly in the purist forms but, since French was the language of diplomacy, tempered their language with a sensibility steeped in French literature. Their influence was to last until the

Greek War of Independence, and beyond, with those for whom the rebirth of the nation meant also the rebirth of the classical language. Although they wrote at times in a simple style and were influenced by folk songs, their spirit was that of the Phanariot tradition, imitating not so much classical Greek bucolics as those fashionable in French drawing rooms of the eighteenth century, or singing rhetorical songs of freedom inspired by the French Revolution.

Immediately after the formation of the Greek kingdom in 1830, it was these Phanariots who brought to the new capital their romantic enthusiasm for a rejuvenated classical Greece, the French influence, and the purist tone, and thus helped to form the first definite literary group, the Old School of Athens, which flourished from about 1830 to about 1880. The idols of this romantic school were Hugo, Lamartine, Byron, Schiller, Leopardi. They wrote poetry of rhetorical patriotism, fraternity, and satire in the spirit of Hugo and Byron, sometimes in the purist, sometimes in a demotic heavily tainted with the purist. Because of his poetic stature and the adventurous cut of his life in the cause of Greek freedom, Byron became the hero and model of these poets well into modern times. On the whole, their poetry was an exaggerated distortion of European romanticism expressed in a nostalgic re-vamping of classical myths, in a rhetorical eulogizing of heroes, in a preoccupation with death and disease, in an unrelieved patrio-tism, in sentimental love poems and heart-rending threnodies, and in some political satires of power.

The School of the Ionian Islands

Another school of poetry was being formulated in the Ionian Islands of Zákinthos and Kérkira (Corfu). Both schools belonged to the romantic tradition, both idolized Hugo and Byron, but whereas the Athenians, with some exceptions, looked backward toward ancient Greece and forward to Paris alone, the poets of the Ionian Islands, again with some exceptions, looked closely at their country's folk songs and westwards not only to Paris but also to England, Germany, and in particular to Italy. Although the Ionian Islands had never been under Turkish domination, they had been occupied by the Venetians and the English from about

1482 until 1864, when they were finally ceded to Greece. The romanticism of these poets, in contrast to that of the Athenians, was quieter, more refined and restrained, imbued with the tender melancholy of the Italian style, and their patriotic declarations were more humble and sincere, befitting a region that was still not a part of the new Greek nation but that, with an ardent nostalgia, aspired to unity.

The greatest of the Ionian poets, and among the greatest poets of modern Greece, were Andréas Kálvos (1792–1869) and Dionýsios Solomós (1798–1857). Both were born in Zákinthos, both were educated in Italy, both wrote their first poems in Italian, both were zealous patriots, but here the similarity ends. Although both lived in Kérkira at the same time, they were never friends nor even, so far as is known, acquaintances. Kálvos lived most of his creative life abroad, not only in Italy but also in France, Switzerland, and mostly in England, where he died and was buried. It was among the Philhellenes in Italy and Switzerland that he tried to coordinate a revival of ancient Greek culture with the rebirth of the modern nation. He published ten odes, in *The Lyre*, in Geneva in 1824, ten more, in *Lyrics*, in Paris in 1826, all imbued with the fervor of patriotism, ancient and new, all written on exalted themes of death, liberty, victory, glory, country and heroic warriors. But disillusioned by the savagery and bickering of the guerrilla leaders he met in Náfplion during the War of Independence, embittered by lack of recognition during his years in Kérkira, he seems never to have written poetry during the remaining forty-six years of his life. It was not until the transitional years ushering in the twentieth century that his works became tolerably well known in Greece. In a sense, Kálvos epitomizes whatever virtues the Old Athenian School embodied, but as expressed by a man of genius. He wrote in one style and structure only, in an unrhymed stanza composed of four roughly seven-syllable lines (which, if broken into couplets, reveal the essential structure of the traditional fifteen-syllable line) and a last line of five syllables modeled on the Adoniac last line of the Sapphic ode, a severely simple and classical conciseness. He wrote in a curious diction which, mixed with elements of demotic, was overladen with ancient words and phrases taken from dictionaries, grammars and old texts set in a neoclassic rendering. But what is important in Kálvos is that this rigid form and technique are informed by an untrammeled romanticism, a sincere emotion, a genuine lyricism, and a modern sensibility to nature around him. He may be likened to Gerard Manley Hopkins or Dylan Thomas, for in all three a highly artificed technique in structure, meter and vocabulary is vitalized into spontaneous expression, a pulsing yet sincere emotion, an outpouring of lyrical frenzy within the straitjacket of rigorous verse patterns. Kálvos brought together classical form and romantic emotion not in harmony but in tension, and herein lies his worth and great contribution. Unknown for many years, too eccentric and unique for imitation, it was only in the thirties that modern Greek poets, such as Odysseus Elýtis and Alexander Mátsas, began to discover what they may learn from him in terms of tension between technique and warmth of expression. In 1960, decreed as the Year of Kálvos, his bones were disinterred in England and reburied in Zákinthos.

Kálvos lived obscure and unknown, but his compatriot Dionýsios Solomós, whose father was a count and mother a family servant girl, became renowned almost at the outset and may be considered to be the father of Greek demotic poetry. His influence on modern Greek poets has been all-pervasive from the beginning. He was immediately drawn to Greek folk poetry, and it may be speculated on whether his early foreign education and his limited knowledge of Greek at first was not in part responsible for his writing in the easiest and most enchanting living form of Greek, unburdened by the purist, a language he did not know. Three of the greatest of Greek poets, Kálvos, Solomós, and Caváfis, and a poet who died too young to fulfill his great promise, George Sarandáris, all had an imperfect knowledge of Greek, a condition which may have freed rather than hampered their taste and imagination.

Solomós seems never to have visited the Greek mainland; he lived the first ten years of his life in Zákinthos, the following ten in Italy, and the rest of his life in Kérkira. Just as Dante had chosen Florentine Italian, and not Latin, in which to write with pellucid clarity, so Solomós chose demotic instead of the *katharévousa*. After a first essay in lilting, almost sentimental lyricism, his lofty personality, drawn to German romantic philosophy, especially to that of Schiller, found more and more need to express its ethical concerns and its love of liberty in poems that became progressively more difficult for him to write the more he became obsessed with perfection of theme and technique. Modern Greek poets and critics have become fascinated by fragments of unfinished work he left behind, not only perhaps for the workmanship itself, as of the limbs of a lost statue, but also for the totality of perfection the fragments imply might have been attained. If the lost limbs of the Venus de Milo were ever found and restored to the torso, our disillusion might be great; the uncompleted whole of Solomós' fragments lies in the realm of the unattained and not the lost, but will forever be deeply moving as indication of a perfection always longed for but rarely achieved.

Early in 1823 Solomós wrote his *Hymn to Liberty* in 158 quatrains, the first few of which have become the Greek national anthem, and in 1824 he wrote *On the Death of Lord Byron* in 166 quatrains. In a departure from the predominance in Greek poetry of the fifteen-syllable line, he was chiefly responsible for introducing into Greek several Western meters, and such stanzaic forms as the terza rima and the ottava rima. But beyond and beside the greatness of his poetry, Solomós is the fount and source of demotic resurgence, for his use of a pure and tasteful demotic marked the turning point in the battle between purist and demotic, and all subsequent Greek poets have gone to him as to a fountainhead or touchstone. He wrote poetry of exquisite refinement, but as his work matured it became more and more concerned with life as an ethical struggle, with the meaning of innocence and liberty, with the essence of the spirit, with a refined romanticism. Yet he had a deep classical sense of form, which he tried to express not by imitating ancient modes, as did Kálvos, but by struggling to bring it to birth out of the raw and fresh materials of his demotic sources. This conflict within him between his romantic ideals and his need of a form which would in itself be part of the ideality of his meaning, was in him a conscious struggle. He wrote, in a note to himself, "Consider well whether this will become romantic or, if possible, classic, or a mixture of both, but legitimate. The extreme example of the second is Homer, of the first Shakespeare; the third I do not know." It was the third example for which Solomós sought all his life and that would lead not, as in Kálvos, to a tension between classical form and romantic content, but to a harmony in which form and content lose their antagonism and their separate identities and meanings. In this he often succeeded, and perhaps it is also because of this struggle for such a harmonious

ideal that he left most of his later poetic works in isolated frag-
ments, like the moss-covered ancient monuments in ruins through-
out the Greek countryside. But perhaps it would be best to think
of some of the greatest of these fragments—*The Free Besieged*,
Pórphyras, *The Cretan*—as promissory notes which modern Greek
poets, ever since, have been striving to pay in full, with honor.

The New School of Athens

Meanwhile, in France the poets born around 1840 to 1850
reacted against the excessive romanticism, sentimentality, rhetoric
and introversion of their predecessors, and formed what is known
as the Parnassian school of poetry, centered around Leconte de
Lisle and named after the first of three anthologies they published
between 1866 and 1876. Although they still clung to traditional
forms, meters and rhymes, and were conservative in their ethical
codes, they set up the dedication to, and the writing of, poetry as
a cult, lived in spiritual ivory towers, devoted themselves to the
formal aspects of technique, and were often conscious Hellenists,
utilizing in their poetry many of the myths and forms of ancient
Greek verse.

Around 1880 a group of young poets in Greece formed the
New School of Athens, in revolt against the Old School, in imita-
tion of the Parnassians, and in an attempt to bring back objectivity
and restraint to their art. Their influence was to last until about
1895 and prepare the way for the even greater influence of sym-
bolism. The central figure at the outset of this movement was
Kostís Palamás, 1859–1943, who in his long reign of sixty years
went far beyond this movement, influenced all of modern Greek
poetry, and launched it into synthetic and philosophical specula-
tion. He continued the battle of Psiháris for the demotic tongue,
emphasized the inspirational source of Greek folk songs, which
had then begun to be collected in anthologies. He denied nothing
of the long Greek tradition, but contended that all aspects of
Greece's long history and literature were constantly to be referred
to the universal scene and the burgeoning importance of science.
He is the true heir of Solomós and consolidated what the Ionian
poet had begun. What was inspiration in Solomós became con-
templation in Palamás; what was fragmentary in Solomós became

in Palamás long works that aspired to embody the entire Greek consciousness in an assimilation of all experience, of East and West, of philosophical thought and lyrical expression. This all-embracing attempt at unity may best be seen perhaps in two of his most important long poems, the epico-lyrical *The Dodecalogue of the Gypsy* (1907) and *The King's Flute* (1910). He is perhaps the most varied of the Greek poets. In the formation of the demotic tongue and the Greek national consciousness, he marks a partial fulfillment of what had long been a promise. Living in a transitional period between the first and the new forms of modern Greek poetry, he could as well end an anthology of the first period, beginning with Solomós, or begin one of the second period to contemporary times. Perhaps because he has more elements in his thought, outlook and technique that relate him to Solomós and traditional modes, and because during his lifetime there lived a poet who more properly may be considered the father of the second period of modern Greek poetry, Constantine Caváfis, this anthology does not begin with his work, which in effect straddles both periods.

IV | FORERUNNERS AND TRADITIONALISTS

The end of the nineteenth century and the beginning of the twentieth was a period of great ferment and transition in Greek life and letters. Two humiliating defeats by the Turks caused a deep and traumatic upheaval in Greek national pride and character. The first was the Catastrophe of 1897, when Greece was badly defeated in only thirty days and forced to cede territory, and the even greater defeat and disaster of 1922, after Greek troops had reached within a few miles of Ankara. Humiliated and dispirited, the Greek people finally gave up what they had once again nourished as *I Megháli Idhéa* (The Great Idea)—that is, that the Asia Minor coast would once more become part of a greater Greece, and Constantinople the capital of a reborn Byzantine Empire. In this period of transition and frustration, ferment and change, in literature as well as in national character, the Greek poets had to face up to reality. This was also the period of a heroic demoticism. Athenians rioted in the streets when a troupe of actors tried to stage Aeschylos' *Oresteia* in a modern translation, several students were killed protesting, and a government was toppled in 1901 during a battle over Alexander Pállis' translation of the New Testament into demotic Greek. Important literary magazines espousing the cause of the demotic were founded, and grammars of the demotic tongue were published, although no complete dictionary of the demotic tongue exists even today. Under the government of Venizélos in 1917 the demotic was officially recognized by the Ministry of Education, the first of a series of recognitions and rejections, depending on whether the government in power was liberal or conservative.

But the most pervasive influence in Greek letters and thought during this period was the importation, again from France, of symbolism. In France the movement had first come into consciousness about 1880, when a Greek poet living in Paris and writing in French, Jean Moréas (the pseudonym of Yánnis Papadhiamandópoulos), first gave it its name in 1885. Baudelaire, the single most pervading influence in Greece during the first part of the twentieth century, was in a sense the father of symbolism, the precursor of the "damned poets," the image of the dandy and the cosmopolite, the dissector of that "delicate monster," ennui. Mallarmé, Verlaine, Rimbaud, Lautréamont, and Corbière changed the course of Greek poetry and mark the zenith of French influence on Greek letters, although Belgian and German symbolism and philosophy added their darker and more brooding colors to the Greek palette. Poetry was to be apprehended intuitively, symbolically, through the senses, and not through the mind. Inevitably, poetry from now on took its distinctive "modern" tone, became difficult and hermetic, for Mallarmé thought that "to name an object is to suppress three fourths of the delight of a poem which is derived from the pleasure of divining little by little: to *suggest*, that is, to dream." Valéry refined symbolism to a "pure" poetry but with an exactitude of diction that was greatly to create in his poetry a curious and exciting rapport between suggestive content and precision of technique.

Basically, of course, in symbolism one thing represents another, as, to refer to Christian symbolism only, the unwithering rose represents the Virgin Mary, a closed garden gate her Virginity, the cross all of Christianity. But essentially, in symbolist poetry, the music and orchestration of words, rhythms, and cadences become an integral part of the meaning until they *evoke* rather than *disclose* a mystery. Disillusioned with the hypocrisy, sham and unreality of the common-sense world, the symbolists tried to hasten the disintegration of the modern world by a further "derangement of the senses," in order that, by recombining the exploding elements with little or no relation to their former structures, they might construct a truer world of inner reality. Since grammar and syntax are also logical structures related to the semantics of their culture, the symbolists discarded or concentrated traditional usage in order that their symbols might not be related to a dispirited order. "We must take rhetoric," Verlaine wrote Rimbaud, "and wring its neck." For some symbolist poets, words became so disassociated from that which they originally represented that they were used less and less for what they denoted than for what they connoted; they began to take a complete *phonetic* reality of their own almost devoid of semantic reference, and to evoke a pure poetry of absolute musical abstraction. They were no longer *representations* of anything but were in themselves *presentations* of their own self-contained, self-creating universe. In Greece this never reached the severe abstraction brought to this method in France, or in English literature by Gertrude Stein, in whose poetry every word is disassociated from its meaning, a separate chord of sound invoking some entity never named. The Greek purist tongue might tend at times toward such refinement, but the demotic tongue, in a constant state of fermentation, has never been exhausted into abstraction.

Symbolism, which lasted in France from about 1887 to 1902, was to spread throughout the world and change the course of modern poetry. It had its greatest influence in Greece from about 1892 to 1902 and then on to 1930, when it had begun to take on a metaphysical and existentialist cast in a postsymbolistic reformation. The first book of symbolist poetry in Greece was published in 1892, a middling book by a middling poet, *The Dreaming Roses*, by Stéphanos Stephánou; but one of the first good symbolist poems was Palamás' "Greetings to a Sunborn Lady" (1900), chronologically perhaps the first "modern" poem in the widest sense. The richest resources of symbolism in Greece, however, are not to be found in its purest symbolists, such as Kóstas Hadzópoulos (1868–1920) and Apóstolos Melahrinós (1883–1952), but in those who, like Caváfis, Sikelianós, Papatsónis and Seféris, adapted it to their own aesthetic orientations. With symbolism also—primarily through the influence of Baudelaire's prose poems and Rimbaud's *A Season in Hell*—free verse, which had made its first tentative appearance with the Greek Parnassians, broke from metrical and rhyming shackles completely. Walt Whitman's third edition of *Leaves of Grass,* published in 1869, was not translated into Greek (but for a few poems) until 1956.

Cónstantine Caváfis

Kostís Palamás was to cast his shadow over most Greek poets during the first decades of the twentieth century, but it was his younger (by four years) contemporary Cónstantine Caváfis who, although not very well known in Greece proper until the middle thirties, was ultimately to challenge and overwhelm him as the true predecessor of modern poetry. Caváfis was born in Alexandria, Egypt, in 1863, and died there in 1933. But for seven formative years (between the ages of nine and sixteen) spent in England, two years in Constantinople, four brief visits to Athens lasting, all told, less than a year, and one visit to Paris, he spent his entire life in that mythological and mysterious Greek-Egyptian, Arabic, English city of polyglot tongue, Alexandria, where in Hellenistic times great poets of learning had flourished and filled its great library to overflowing, battening on rich classical meadows and forcing into bloom their cultivated and artificial flowers. He did not publish a book of poetry until he was forty-one, and then issued a slim volume of only fourteen poems, privately printed and not for sale; when he reissued this volume six years later, he added only seven poems, and never published another volume in his lifetime. The poems he wished to preserve, published after his death, are only 154 in number, averaging about fifteen lines each. Of these, only twenty-four were written before his forty-eighth year. Caváfis matured late as a poet and, on the whole, was his own severest critic, for only a handful of his previously unpublished poems rank among his best work. Most of these show no special talent, are written in traditional modes and meters, and in contrast to his later work have somewhat the same relationship that such early poems of Walt Whitman as "O Captain! My Captain!" have to the poems of his maturity.

From this account of his publishing habits, it can be seen that Caváfis was fastidious and secretive, qualities that were abetted, most probably, by his homosexual nature. Although he would be conservatively dressed on the whole, befitting a man who worked as a clerk in the Egyptian Department of Irrigation for thirty years, some detail might give him away, some cut of the collar, some angle of the hat, his gold-tipped cane, perhaps, or his too-bejeweled fingers, the peculiar way he had of carrying his body, something of the affected in his greeting, in his manner or his walk, in the proffering of his hand, something artificial in his character, as ritualistic as that of a cardinal or as contrived as that of a consummate actor. A brilliant conversationalist, he would speak his Alexandrian Greek with a trace of English intonation. E. M. Forster has summed him up deftly by describing him as "this Greek gentleman with a straw hat, standing absolutely motionless at a slight angle to the universe." When in "Morning Sea" the poet pauses to look at nature, he finds himself instead gazing inwardly at his "memories, the illusions of sensual pleasure." He would agree with Oscar Wilde that nature imitates art, and he preferred artificial to real flowers, for these do not sprout unclean from dirt and mire, they will never wilt and rot, but are "trustworthy gifts of a trustworthy art." Like Yeats, he longed to be metamorphosed, during one of his beloved periods of history, the Byzantine, into "such forms as Grecian goldsmiths make / Of hammered gold and gold enamelling." Poetry, for Caváfis, was an aesthetic salvation, the only immortality life could bestow, the only "artifice of eternity." When a Greek divinity in "One of Their Gods" descends to the bystreets of Seleucia to indulge in debauchery, the poet envisages him as an adolescent of perfect beauty, but with "the joy of incorruption in his eyes"; for, unlike the Syrian student in "The Dangers," a god may give himself up "to the most daring and erotic urges" and yet retain his purity of soul. Caváfis understood with profound irony that such purity may be found only in divinity and art, never in life. Unlike Kóstas Várnalis in his sonnet "Aphrodite," Caváfis depicts this incorruptibility of the gods with sympathy and not with satire.

In early youth and manhood, suffering from qualms of conscience and guilt, he cautioned himself not to reveal too much of his obsession in his verses. Like the adolescent in "Two Young Men, 23 to 25 Years of Age" (his handsome youths never go beyond their twenty-ninth year) impatiently waiting for his friend, Caváfis too was seized by irksome thoughts of a life misspent. It was primarily in old age, that "wound from a hideous knife," when his emotions were recollected in nostalgia, that he understood the meaning of a "life of lust," for now he saw that "in the dissipations of my youth / were shaped the volitions of my poetry, / was laid the groundwork of my art." After describing a young man slinking away from the consummation of some unlawful pleasure, the aged poet realizes "how greatly was the artist's life enriched. / Tomorrow, the next day, after many years, / the strong verse shall be writ that here had its beginning." Freed finally of restraint and guilt, he wrote candidly, sensuously, longingly, often in the first person now, poems about homosexual youths which are not the romantic love poems in the tone of Shakespeare's sonnets, but frankly erotic poems of nostalgia and reminiscence depicting the guilts, neuroses, anxieties, as well as the pleasures and voluptuousness, of "illicit love." Here are to be found the gross and lawless lusts of early youth in bars and suspect taverns, the bought or stolen loves in lonely hotels or shabby rooms, the pick-ups, the hustlers who sell their bodies for a gaudy necktie or villas on the Nile, the anguish and sentimentality. One must go back to the Greek Anthology to find erotic poetry of comparable kind and quality. Caváfis' open amorality in these poems, his refinement of technique, his fussy concern with detail and minor perfectibilities, his tender compassion for shady characters and opportunists of history all had their source, no doubt, in his own "illicit" nature. The voluptuary in Caváfis is revealed also in his lingering descriptions of dress, jewels and perfumes in such poems as "Alexandrian Kings," "Waiting for the Barbarians," and "Ithaca," but which are, nevertheless, rigidly controlled with a style whose overriding tone is one of dry precision, even in the depiction of hedonistic detail.

Few of Caváfis' erotic poems rank among his best work, with those of a contemplative or historical cast. Although he has written some poems set in the classical world, he found his personal mythology in the Hellenistic, Greco-Roman, and Byzantine ages, in ambiguous and transitional periods when Jews were being

Hellenized or Hellenes were being corroded by the inroads of Christianity, in the twilight decadence of great civilizations of which his native Alexandria was heir. Yet even in these periods he was interested not in great events or personalities but in minor actions and ravaged figures, such as the abandonment of Antony by his patron god, Dionysos, or the substitution of glass for real jewels in the coronation of an impecunious Byzantine emperor. If he chose some great event, such as the destruction of Antony's and Cleopatra's fleet at Actium, it was to glance ironically at some insignificant detail that deflates pomposity and reveals human vulnerability. What interested him were not the heroic deeds of the Greeks at Thermopylae but their betrayal by the inevitable Ephialtes. Nor does joy or triumph endure, for at the height of any delectable moment some Theodotos is preparing to betray and behead a Pompey, and to bring in his head on a tray.

There is an element of didacticism in many of Caváfis' contemplative poems, a moral rarely stated but often implied. In "Waiting for the Barbarians," he reveals the secret temptation in the hearts of free men to cast off their responsibilities and yield themselves to directing power. The suppressed desire to be ruled, to be told what to do, to give up onerous responsibilities of choice and decision has rarely been so dramatically, so ironically, so cynically expressed, for the barbarians were "some sort of a solution." His "Ithaca" is the perfect complement to Tennyson's poem, for he reminds us that Ithaca is the perfection never attained, the ideal always striven for though never reached, that the true meaning of our eternal quest lies not at journey's end but in the journey itself, that Ithaca has given us the lovely voyage and that she has nothing more to give. Caváfis truthfully said of himself that if he were not a poet he would have made a good historian, but no doubt one who would have avoided the great catastrophes of "world-shaking" events to ferret out underground seismic faults that topple temples and the pediments of gods and heroes. One of Caváfis' great abilities was to interpret characters or events in the past out of his personal knowledge of like circumstances in the present, and to imbue these with universal meaning beyond time or history.

His characters often show courage and heroism, but more often frailty, egoism, opportunism, cynicism, cowardice, bewilderment and worldliness, all of which he depicts with indulgent

tolerance, with amusement, with tender sympathy and under-
standing. The knowledgeable young man in "They Should Have
Provided" would have been delighted to serve some honest poli-
tician, but since the Establishment or the gods have provided him
only with fools or idiots, what is the poor devil to do? What
interested Caváfis were inconsistencies of character, the compro-
mises of those who vaguely feel they should be moved by great
ideals but are unable to maintain them, the indecisions, hesitancies
and pretensions of the self-deluded who are impelled to rationalize
their natural tendency toward debauchery or opportunism.

His poems are neither emotional nor lyrical, but narrative,
dramatic, objective, realistic, learned and witty, a recounting of
events and episodes with subtlety in a tone of voice that is precise,
dry, and deliberately prosaic. They are, above all, ironic, especially
when he describes abortive desires or the discrepancies between
fact and illusion, perfidy and promise. Little influenced by Euro-
pean modes or the work of his compatriots in Greece, his poems
belong to the tradition of the Greek epigram of the fourth century
B.C. and later, to those of Simonides, Callimachus, Asclepiades of
Sámos, to the polished verse of Alexandrian and Byzantine intel-
lectuals of that period. His diction and syntax are based not on the
Greek of the educated Athenian of his time but on that of the
Greek of the Diaspora spoken with the accents and intonations of
Constantinople, Alexandria or Asia Minor. On this foundation
Caváfis embellished his façade with words, idioms, and turns of
expression borrowed from the entire range of the Greek language
from classical times, delighting to set an archaic word next to some
contemporary colloquialism, to demonstrate a pedantry of modern
argot as well as of some ancient text. The result is an idiom
peculiarly his own, an individual amalgam which identifies his
line at once, an artifice suited to and made integral by his tempera-
ment, and which, by its very nature, is lost when translated into
the English language, whose shorter historical development and
lack of dichotomy do not permit such amalgamation. In his
early verses he prided himself on his correctness in meter, his
adroitness in rhyme, but as he progressed he experimented with
homonyms and half-rhymes, or he discarded rhymes altogether,
relaxed his meter and often broke it, though still keeping to an
iambic-anapestic base, sometimes departing into free verse, yet
always hovering about an innate sense of structure. His poems are

contracted into their greatest density, yet with a clarity unimpeded by simile or metaphor, revealing the larger tropes of events, situations or character analyses. No superfluous word is permitted, everything is premeditated and exact, emotions are under control, although occasionally, when he recalls his nostalgic lusts, a surprising sentimentality intrudes. These devices and techniques, coupled with his dry, almost prosaic incisions, his ever present irony, make him the true forerunner of modern Greek poetry.

Ángelos Sikelianós

Born on the Ionian island of Lefkádha in 1884, Ángelos Sikelianós was the heir of a rich Ionian tradition in politics, literature and religion, all of which were to play an impelling role in the formation of his character, his thought and his writing. His paternal uncle served as Minister of Justice in the newly formed Greek nation under Kapodhístrias; another uncle fell heroically in the siege of Missolóngi; his paternal grandfather was the mayor of Kérkira and a member of the Ionian Tribunal. On his mother's side he was related to Saint Dionýsios, the patron saint of Zákinthos. As a patriot, he was to remain an ardent democrat his life long, supporter of the poor and oppressed, protector of the Jews during the German-Italian occupation. Moved by a religious sense of the beauty and mystery of life, he was to write of it with a mystical exaltation. From Solomós and the Ionian poets, he derived his love for the demotic tongue, of which, by living only briefly abroad and roaming the length and breadth of Greece, he was to acquire one of the richest vocabularies of any Greek poet.

As an adolescent, between the ages of eighteen and twenty-one, he wrote some twenty poems which he never admitted into the canon of his collected works. Written in meter and rhyme, they show the influence of the New School of Athens, and in particular that of symbolism, for they are filled with mirrors, mysterious voices, legendary woods, swans, and all the paraphernalia derived not from Greek but from French and Italian sources. Then, at the age of twenty-three, in 1907, he retired for a few months to his brother's home in the desolation of Libya, where he wrote a long epico-lyrical poem, sporadically rhymed in free verse, *The Visionary*, which was similar in theme and structure to D'Annunzio's *Laudi*, and which established him at once in the front rank of his generation. Eight years later he was to write, between 1915 and 1916, the greater portion of his only long work in free verse, the book-length *Prologue to Life*, whose five parts are devoted to the poet's consciousness of his Greek landscape, his race, woman, faith and personal creativity. With lyrical passion and intensity of thought, the young poet attempted in these two books to fulfill the endeavors of the generation of 1880 and his own to synthesize elements of Greek tradition with the intellectual and spiritual attainments of the East and the West. Most of his main themes, developed with greater depth and dexterity in his later work, were first announced in these exploratory poems: the autobiographical and romantic role of the poet as prophet and visionary, the celebration of the Greek landscape and language, the combination and identification of pagan and Christian mythology, and more, the immersion into the collective memory of his race, the adoration of Eros and woman, the intuitive formulation of a cosmology that would be all-embracing. Palamás had striven for a similar all-inclusiveness, but with a more intellectual and historical approach; Sikelianós called on the divinity of life to guide him in his inspiration, and trusted in his genius.

In contrast to most poets of his generation, who began with traditional meter and loosened into free verse, Sikelianós was rarely to write in free verse again. Even during this period, although romantically disclaiming any knowledge or interest in technique, he wrote some of the most adroit stanzaic forms and rhythms in modern Greek poetry, bringing the normal meter almost to the breaking point with expert variations and counter-pointing, much like Yeats in his later period, with whom he may best be compared in character and mastery. The lyrics he wrote during this period are sensual, dramatic, and narrative in an unstinted celebration of life, even when he delineates self-destruction in "The Suicide of Atzesiváno." He depicts Aphrodite rising from the sea and falling into the erotic arms of the sun in "Anadyomene"; primeval, atavistic symbols of fertility in "Pan"; the fragrance of nature, the beauty of youth, the serenity of the artist in "Pantarkis"; the vigorous and bursting health of country lass and life in "Thaleró." And he has written among the best sonnets in Greek literature, sonorous, vigorous, impetuous. All these poems arise from a free-flowing and enraptured vision of life.

In 1906, when he was twenty-two, the young poet met a wealthy heiress, Miss Evelyn Palmer of Bar Harbor, whose sister Penelope was to marry Raymond Duncan, brother of Isadora Duncan. They were married in 1907, on his return from Libya. Eva Sikelianós was to devote the rest of her life to espousing her husband's ideals; she wore ancient Greek chitons and sandals, studied the transcription and playing of ancient Greek and Byzantine music, revived the art of weaving and of Greek choral movement and chant, helped and supported her husband when he founded the Delphic Festivals of 1927 and 1930. At Delphi, where the Amphictyonic Council used to meet in ancient days (the oldest known confederation of Greek states, a precursor of the League of Nations), Sikelianós hoped to establish a cosmic center where, through a dedication to a religious view of life without dogma, and through a cultivation of the arts, the nations of the world might meet to ensure peace and justice. The *Prometheus Bound* and *Suppliants* of Aeschylos were sumptuously produced, Olympic Games were held in the stadium on the Delphic heights of Mount Parnassos, Byzantine music was played, Greek demotic songs were danced and mounted, and an International University was planned. Although the enterprise was ratified by the Greek government, Sikelianós could not agree to the stipulations set, and the advent of the Second World War destroyed all plans and preparations. When she died, Eva Sikelianós was buried at Delphi among the ruins of ancient monuments and her hopes.

During the German-Italian occupation, Sikelianós risked his life often to save those of others. Especially outraged by the treatment of the Jews, he made many efforts, through the press, in speeches and through personal intervention, to alleviate their plight. During this period he wrote the *Akrític Songs* (named after Dhiyenís Akrítas, border guard of the Byzantine Empire), poems of resistance and rebellion, veiled from inimical eyes in allegory and symbolism, magnificently copied in hand and illustrated with woodcuts by Spíros Vasilíou and distributed by the underground. In "Greek Supper for the Dead," the poet vows eternal faith to the dead of the heroic resistance and calls on them to rise up and join the living for the "divine onslaught." In "Unrecorded," every Greek reader during the dreadful winter of 1941, when people were dying of hunger in the streets of Athens, recognized the carcass of the dog cast on the garbage heap beyond the walls of Zion as a symbol of gutted Greece herself. But like Jesus, who gazed upon that carcass, the people of Greece stood and marveled at the gleaming teeth of that dog in the setting sun, a "reflection of the Eternal, but still more, / the hope and the sharp lightning bolt of Justice."

In his last poems, Sikelianós returned to the rapturous vision of his early years and tried to embrace all the universe in a cosmological vision. These poems are written in a highly intricate and subordinated syntax, sonorous and rhetorical, often with the lengthy elaboration of the Homeric simile. They are not to be read analytically or intellectually, but are to be apprehended intuitively with a Dionysian empathy. Andréas Karandónis has described Sikelianós' poems as huge trees rooted deep in earth but with bare branches extended amid the freezing winds of death. All his life, but primarily in his old age, the poet longed to feel on his lips "the virginal kiss of the Abyss," to plunge deep into himself and his country's ancient traditions, and through both communal and individual roots to find the essential Self in a mystic and passionate identification with the cosmos. He swept into his vision the Eleusinian and Orphic mysteries and merged them with Plato's philosophy and Christian reinterpretations of pagan ritual. He identified Dionysos with Christ and the Word as vegetative gods of fertility, death and resurrection, incarnations of the central mysteries of the universe. As Eros, Dionysos became the portal through which man leaves behind him the dualities and shadows of the outer world and enters into Ultimate Reality, "trampling on death with death," for "the only method is death." Both Eros and Hades become mediums through which Sikelianós attains a mystic communion with God. Through the sensuous body of woman as the fertile and potent receptor—whether as Astarte in "Rehearsal for Death," or as Ariadne in "Supreme Lesson"—the poet dies erotically into fulfillment where dualities, such as man and woman, become one, as once they were.

Sikelianós celebrated that mystic identification with divine nature which the followers of Dionysos and Orpheus sought with orgiastic ecstasy. He inquired into an Orphic sense of evil which, according to J. E. Harrison, involves the "need for purification, the idea of a man-god incarnate and suffering and, closely connected with these, the idea of man's immortality, of his ultimate escape from evil by renewed purgation in another world." In

"Rehearsal for Death" he transforms his terrestrial fever into a "mystic fever," that "perfect and noble practice for death," which breaks through barriers of time as we know it here on earth and goes beyond the "stubborn strifes of all creation" until the poet finds his liberation by plunging beyond the flaming stars and into the very rhythm of creation itself, into the fire within the Creator's mind. In "Supreme Lesson," Ariadne is that feminine form that prefigures the eternal Platonic Form which must be worshiped in an "unrestrained desire to join / the Mystery," in an ecstasy that exalts "life above life, with the first touch of Death." The turbulent commotion of the ocean is here an image of Dionysian intoxication that, by giving priest and neophytes both a taste of mystic death, may teach them "how all Eternity proceeds from Time alone."

Sikelianós was essentially a psalmodist, a priest and prophet, and all his last works and poetic plays are dramatic extensions of these themes. An extremely handsome man, an impetuous lover, chanting his verses in sonorous tones, striding through the streets of Athens later in life in a long flowing black cape, his white hair waved and shining, with a touch of blue, his feet bare and sandaled, holding in his hand a walking stick of black ebony inlaid with ivory, he embodied his life long the romantic concept of what a poet should look like and be. He was a poet in the grand tradition, a man of great concepts and noble actions, one who tried to assimilate the cultural heritage of his own nation and those of the modern world, a revolutionary democrat and mystic who acted beyond the political and religious creeds of the world.

Nikos Kazantzákis

Níkos Kazantzákis was born in Iráklion, Crete, in 1883, a year before Sikelianós. When in 1914 they met for the first time, the two young poets recognized each other as kindred spirits, although differences as basic as their similarities were later to reveal themselves. They spent forty days together that year on Mount Athos, that Mecca of Greek monastic life, toured the Peloponnesos the following year, and in 1942, two years after Kazantzákis had stood as best man to Sikelianós' second marriage, lived in adjacent homes for six months on the island of Aegina.

They had the same lofty and grand concepts of life and poetry, both based their inspiration primarily on a Dionysian vision of life, both longed to embody their vision in poems of length that would unite their Greek world and heritage, both loved and hoarded the Greek demotic tongue of the common people, but here the similarities end. Both bent over and stared into the gaping abyss, but whereas Sikelianós smelled the fragrance of an unknown flower and in a mystical trance of joy and hope embraced death and the universe, Kazantzákis gazed clear-eyed and without mysticism at the gaping abyss and acknowledged it, in necessity, as the devouring maw where every individual and unique identity is again reduced to its elemental parts in one great churning energy and rhythm. Sikelianós spent less than two years abroad, but Kazantzákis lived over a third of his life in foreign lands. Sikelianós wrote in long, complex sentences in which cadences rose and fell with the majesty of contrapuntal music; Kazantzákis wrote in compound, almost staccato sentences laden with adjectives and tropes. Sikelianós, other than writing a few essays, was interested only in capturing his vision in poetry, whereas Kazantzákis, with voracious appetite, found words almost an impediment to his vision and tried to capture it not only in poetry but also in a flood of novels, dramas, travel books, philosophical essays, translations, newspaper articles, scenarios, and even in political action.

A revealing parallel may be drawn between Kazantzákis and D. H. Lawrence. Both were Dionysian, demon-driven men, placed instinct and the promptings of the blood above the ordered deductions of the mind, celebrated the primitive and atavistic origins of the human spirit, were insatiable travelers who in landscape and inscape discerned the contours of God's or Nature's purpose, turned to the physical universe for their imagery and away from urban mechanics and subtleties, extolled strife and crucifixion as the unavoidable and necessitous law of life and even of love, were impatient with refinements of craft and entrusted themselves to the demonic outpourings of creative inspiration, placed the prophet above the man of letters, were obsessed with messianic drives and dreams.

Kazantzákis' major attempt to embody his vision of life was in daring to write a sequel to Homer's *Odyssey*, and at a time when all scholars were agreed that it was no longer possible to compose a long narrative poem based on traditional myth. Cut from his original draft of 42,500 to 33,333 lines, his *The Odyssey: A Modern Sequel* is still three times the size of Homer's original poem. Kazantzákis always referred to it as his *magnum opus* with which he might perhaps live on in the memory of man. In the "Prologue," the poet announces his main theme, that of the transubstantiation of matter into spirit: "stones, water, fire, and earth shall be transformed to spirit, / and the mud-winged and heavy soul, freed of its flesh, / shall like a flame serene ascend and fade in the sun." He then boldly grafts his epic on that section of Book XXII in Homer's poem where the hero has killed the suitors of his wife, Penelope. As though his sequel were a direct continuation of Homer's poem, Book I opens impetuously with Odysseus going to cleanse his body of the suitors' blood. But finding himself estranged from his wife, his son, his people, Odysseus gathers a motley crew, sails to Sparta, and there persuades Helen to abscond once more. They sail to Crete, where they join an uprising of workers and slaves against the palace of Knossos and destroy its decadent civilization and its bull orgies. Leaving Helen behind, he then floats up the Nile and engages in an unsuccessful socialist revolt against the exploiting Pharaoh and his priests. Although he had long since abandoned the Olympian gods, he sees that in Egypt the gods have not as yet outgrown their bestial origins, for here they are still half beast and half man and not, like the Greek gods, half man and half god. In dream, he sees a vision of a new, tormented and suffering god. Cast out of Egypt, he gathers a company of adventurers, of the dispossessed and the driven, and discovers the lake source of the Nile, where he plans to found a new civilization far from the contaminations of his times. Ascending to the summit of a mountain by the lake, he communes with his god for seven days and seven nights, then descends with new commandments on which to build an Ideal City, a Utopia.

Odysseus has been slowly changing from a pagan into a Hebraic figure resembling Moses. On the inauguration of the Ideal City, however, the mountain erupts, the earth gapes wide, and his entire city and most of its inhabitants are swallowed up. After this traumatic experience, Odysseus abandons all hope and turns into a brooding ascetic searching for the meaning of life. As he treks down the heart of Africa toward its southernmost tip, he meets on the way representatives of various ways of life: the young Prince Motherth (Buddha), terrified by death; the courtesan Margaro, for whom sexual union is the unifying force in the world that merges opposites, the male and the female; an ascetic who renounces his abstemious life as he is dying; Captain Elias, a tragic poet who discovers that creativity can only arise out of suffering and sacrifice; Captain Sole (Don Quixote), an impractical idealist; an old Negro chieftain who, murdered and eaten by his twelve sons, symbolizes the atavistic origins of man; a fat and sluggish hedonist, Lord of the Tower; and finally a young black fisherman (Jesus Christ), who expounds a new philosophy of returning good for evil, love for hate, of an ultimate realm wherein man and God merge into a one-and-only reality.

Odysseus listens to all with compassion and understanding, but rejects or adapts their points of view. At the southernmost tip of Africa, finding that his reputation has preceded him and that he is being worshiped as a god, he exclaims: "I've been reduced to a god and walk the earth like myth! / O wretched soul of man, you can't stand free on earth / or walk upright unless you walk with fear or hope. / When will companion souls like mine come down to earth?" Building a small skiff, something like a kayak, he lives for a winter season among primitive people in a land of ice where the gods are once again the primordial deities of Fear, Hunger and Cold. As he sails away in the spring thaw, he watches from afar as the ice gapes wide and swallows the entire tribe, much as his own ideal city had been gulped down. As Odysseus now sails toward the South Pole and his skiff crashes on an iceberg, he clings to it with bloodied fingernails and toenails. His spirit, his consciousness, leaps like a flame from its wick, and for an eternal moment glows, disembodied in the air, before it vanishes forever. It is in this eternal moment of the suspended candle flame that the entire action of the twenty-fourth and last book takes place, as Odysseus dies surrounded in imagination by all those with whom in life he had lived through some intense or meaningful experience.

In Odysseus' conversations with the representative types, but particularly in Books XIV and XVI, where he communes with his god on the mountain top, Kazantzákis has embodied his philosophy, or rather his vision of life, which just before beginning *The Odyssey* he expounded in a work half prose and half poetry, *The Saviors of God: Spiritual Exercises*. This book is the philosophical key not only to *The Odyssey* but to all his work, for Kazantzákis was a man of one overwhelming vision, which he strove to give shape in all the literary forms he could master. A man, he writes in *Saviors*, has three duties. His first duty is to the mind, which imposes order on disorder, formulates laws, builds bridges over the unfathomable abyss, and sets up rational boundaries beyond which it dares not go. But his second duty is to the heart, which admits of no boundaries and yearns to pierce beyond phenomena to merge with something behind mind and matter. His third duty is to free himself from the hopes which both the mind and the heart offer—from the hope that the mind can indeed subdue phenomena or the heart penetrate into the essence of things. A man must then embrace the annihilating abyss without hope of any kind; he must say that nothing exists, neither life nor death, and must accept this necessity bravely, indeed with exaltation and song. He may then build the affirmative structure of his life over this abyss in an ecstasy of tragic joy.

A man is now prepared to undertake a pilgrimage of four stages. At the start of his journey, he hears an agonized cry within him shouting for help. His first step is to plunge into his own ego, his own unique identity, until he discovers that it is the endangered spirit of God within each man that is crying out for liberation. In order to free it, each man must consider himself solely responsible for the salvation of the world, because when a man dies, that aspect of the universe which is his own particular vision and unique play of his mind crashes into ruin forever. In the second step, a man must plunge beyond his ego and into his racial origins and traditions; yet, like Odysseus in Homer's Hades, he must choose only those ancestors who can help toward a greater refinement of spirit that he may in turn pass on his task to a son who may surpass him. The third step is for a man to plunge beyond his own particular race and into the races and traditions of all mankind, as one belonging to the species *man*, and to suffer their composite agony in the struggle to liberate God within himself. The fourth step is to plunge even beyond mankind and to become identified with all of nature, with animate and inanimate matter, with earth, stones, sea, plants, animals, insects, birds—with the vital impulse of creation in all phenomena. Each man is an unfathomable composite of atavistic roots that plunges deep into obscure and primordial origins. A man is then prepared to go beyond the mind, the heart, hope itself, beyond his ego, his race, even mankind, beyond all phenomena, and plunge further into a vision of the Invisible permeating all things visible and forever ascending.

The essence of the Invisible is an agonized ascent toward more and more purity of spirit, toward more and more light. The goal is the struggle itself, as in Caváfis' "Ithaca," since the evolutionary ascent is endless. "My soul," Odysseus exclaims, "your voyages have been your native land!" God is not a perfect Being toward whom man proceeds as toward a terminal, as in Christian dogma, but a spiritual concept which is always evolving toward purity as man himself evolves on earth. God is not Almighty, for He is in constant danger, lacerated with wounds, struggling Himself to survive. He is not All-holy, for he is pitiless in the cruel choices he makes, caring nothing for men or animals, neither for virtues nor for ideas, but making use of them for a moment, then smashing them in an attempt to pass beyond them and shake Himself free. He is not All-knowing, for His head is a confused jumble of light and dark. He cries out to man for help, because man is His highest spiritual reach in the present stage of His and man's evolution. He cannot be saved unless man tries to save Him by struggling with Him; nor can man be saved unless God is saved. On the whole, it is rather man who is the savior and who must save God. When a man has had this vision of the ceaselessly unsated and struggling spirit, he must then attempt to give it shape in works of every nature, realizing, of course, that any embodiment must of necessity pollute the vision, yet accepting and utilizing such imperfect instruments in the never-ending and ever-ascending struggle.

Central themes in *The Odyssey* are: What is freedom? What —not who, but what—is God? The essence of God is the attempt to find freedom, salvation. Our duty is to aid Him in this attempt, and to save ourselves from our final hope: that freedom and salvation do indeed exist. They do not. There remains only the attempt to find freedom, to achieve salvation, knowing that neither exists, and to accept this with tragic joy. Love is the force that drives us on, that descends upon us as a dance, a rhythm. Injustice, cruelty, hunger, war are forces that urge us on. It is man's great glory and nobility that he has himself created such concepts as justice, kindness, plenty and peace. God is never created out of happiness and comfort, but out of tragedy and strife. The greatest virtue is not to be free, but to struggle ceaselessly for freedom. The universe is a creation in the meeting of two opposite streams, one male and the other female, one ascending toward integration, toward life, toward immortality, the other descending toward disintegration, toward matter, toward death. It becomes a blossoming Tree of Fire whose summit bears the final fruit of light. Fire is the first and ultimate mask of God. One day the universe will vanish into the deepest and most distilled essence of the spirit, that of Silence, where all contraries will at last be resolved, for as Horatio said of Hamlet, "The rest is silence." "Death," says Odysseus, "is the salt that gives to life its tasty sting."

Because Kazantzákis so castigates "rotten-thighed Hope," and so strongly insists on the ultimate annihilation that awaits us all, individually or as a species, he has been defined as a desperado, a nihilist. Although negative emotions have been violent and pervasive within him, he ultimately pronounced the almighty Yes over the almost equally almighty No and insisted that it is exactly over the gaping abyss that man must build the affirmative structure of his life. He gives value and dignity to the human condition by insisting that such life and structure are more worthy, more precious, more noble than those built on illusion, hope, or dream or fear. Over his grave in Iráklion are engraved these words: "I do not fear anything, I do not hope for anything, I am free." He transformed the Great Negation into affirmation by embracing it with fierce exaltation. "My son," Odysseus tells the faint-hearted Prince Motherth, "I too watch Death before me night and day; / . . . yet you sink nerveless to the ground / . . . and freedom cleaves your head in two. / But I hold Death like a black banner, and march on!" Life became for Kazantzákis a series of conquered negations in a blood-spattered ascent toward ever-shifting and higher summits, in a rapturous though painful knowledge that there was no ultimate summit to be reached. "There is no summit," he wrote in *Report to Greco*, "there are only heights." Life is a powerful, onrushing, amoral force, utterly indifferent to man's fate, using atoms and men *as though* it had a purpose.

In the first analysis of this Bergsonian *élan vital* Kazantzákis saw that good and evil were enemies, in the second that they were fellow workers, in the third that they were identical and One, and in the final that *even this One does not exist*. Bergson gave him the metaphysical key, but Nietzsche gave him the Antichrist, the hero-saint who was to be his ultimate standard of greatness until

he created his all-inclusive hero in the likeness of his heart's desire
—Odysseus. "The moment I want to paint," Greco tells Kazant-
zákis, "is the moment when God's creations are burning, just
before they turn to ashes." This was Kazantzákis' long agony in
life: how to define God and Freedom, how to transubstantiate
flesh into spirit and, further, how to wring from flame its final
fruit, that of light. "Take the flames that are burning you, take
them and turn them into light. Then blow out the light." Although
he was never consciously to use the trappings of existentialist
philosophy, Kazantzákis, like his favorite saint, Francis of Assisi,
bore the stigmata of his vision, and in his life and work revealed
the existentialist agony.

Kazantzákis wrote his *Odyssey* in about four years, over a
period of fourteen years, from 1924 to 1938. When it was pub-
lished, it was primarily either ridiculed or greeted with silence.
Where his readers had expected a work of classical proportion
and nobility, they were confronted, on the contrary, with a work
which is anticlassical, anti-Hellenic, and passionately romantic and
baroque. They were confronted with an adjectival cataract of
rich epithets, a gothic profusion of metaphors and similes, of
allegorical and symbolistic characters and episodes, of fables and
legends that seem to digress and never return. Furthermore, the
poem was filled with disturbing innovations, for he had published
it in a form of simplified spelling and syntax which he had long
advocated, and had discarded all accentual marks but one. But
worst of all for the educated was to be burdened with a lexicon
of two thousand words appended to the poem, for Kazantzákis
had written his epic in the dialect and pronunciation of shepherds,
goatherds and fishermen, words and expressions which still have
not been collected in dictionaries of the demotic tongue. He had
even discarded the hallowed fifteen-syllable line, always used
hitherto for works of narrative length, and had written in an
extremely long and little-used line of seventeen syllables with eight
stresses which, to the traditional, seemed rude and ungainly.

Kazantzákis consciously modeled his thought and character
in imitation of persons he admired throughout history, and in his
only other book of poetry, *Terza Rimas*, written between 1932 and
1937, when he was putting the final touches to *The Odyssey*, he
wrote invocations to Dante, Greco, Genghis Khan, Psiháris, Saint
Theresa, Lenin, Don Quixote, Mohammed, Nietzsche, Buddha,

Moses, Shakespeare, Da Vinci, Hideyoshi, Alexander the Great, and others. To these he might have added Bergson, on whom he wrote a treatise; Zorba, about whom he wrote a novel; and Homer, to whose *Odyssey* he wrote a sequel.

In his book *The Ulysses Theme*, in which he traces the permutations of the Odysseus myth from Homer to the present day, W. B. Stanford concludes that Kazantzákis' *Odyssey* and Joyce's *Ulysses* are "the most elaborate portraits of Odysseus since Homer," that they are "unusually comprehensive symbols of contemporary aspirations and perplexities," and that in Kazantzákis the episodic and spatial enrichments of the myth have been "augmented on a scale, both physical and imaginative, far beyond any contributions since Homer."

Kóstas Várnalis

Because Kóstas Várnalis was born in Bulgaria (in 1884) and there as a student steeped himself in the classics and did not come to Greece until he was nineteen, he not only romanticized and idealized Greece with the nostalgia of an exile, but also wrote his poems in the purist with traditional stanzaic forms, meters and rhymes. When he went to Greece for university studies, however, and confronted his dream, a conflict raged within him for some time between Greece as an ancient ideality and Greece as part of the modern world of catastrophe and exploitation, a dualism he was to retain in some form or another throughout his life. When he arrived, the battle for the demotic had more or less been won. Under the influence of Palamás, Sikelianós and of the Parnassians of the New School, he wrote his poems in the demotic and was never again to permit the slightest influence of the purist. Nevertheless, in keeping with his dichotomy, he still retained traditional techniques and was rarely to write in free verse even in his later years.

In the decade that followed, Várnalis wrote poems—such as "Orestes," "Aphrodite" and "Alcibiades"—which were primarily an aesthetic reconstruction of the classical world, evoking his nostalgia for a vanished glory. Although written in the demotic, they are highly wrought poems in the strict forms of sonnet or quatrain. In "Orestes," he still sees man as a slave to his destiny, pursued by the Furies, unable to attain his own salvation. In a Caváfian mood, he celebrates in "Alcibiades" the myrrh-scented youth who always seems to be twenty-one, the enchanting playboy, rogue and opportunist. But in "Aphrodite," although the theme is embellished with sonnet form and classical imagery, a note of sarcasm and irony creeps in, which in his later poetry was to turn to savage satire. After her adulterous episode with Ares under the raucous laughter of the gods, Aphrodite regains her virginity simply by bathing in the waters off Páphos in Cyprus until not even one drop of scandal clings to her. Like the divinity in Caváfis' "One of Their Gods," she too enjoys incorruptibility. Várnalis was never to abandon his interest in the classical world, later evidenced primarily by his magnificent translations of Aristophanes.

The First World War, his literary and political experiences in Paris, where in 1919 he went to study for a year, the outbreak and outcome of the Balkan Wars and the Disaster of 1922 awakened Várnalis to political issues and caused him to turn more and more to an espousal of Marxism. Even in the sonnet "The Chosen One," written in 1913 and set in classical times, he sneered at the aristocrat who passes among the gross crowd, primped and perfumed, unable to comprehend the strange tongue of the masses. From now on Várnalis' poetry was to become increasingly polemic, satirical, propagandistic. He turned away from the small group of the "chosen," and as once he had passed from purist to demotic, he now passed from the aesthetic to the political. In Paris he wrote his second book, *The Burning Light* (1922), a series of lyrical poems in three parts, with one uniting theme. It presents man's fight for freedom from ancient times through the figures of Prometheus, Christ, and a modern proletarian leader. The reactionary powers of darkness against the Burning Light are represented by the Aristea (the oligarchy), the Monkey (the bought intellectual), and the Archon (the nobleman) who use the Republic of Bosses (the Establishment) to repress Mómos (the mocker), the Nightingale, the Nereids, the Seraphim, and the People. Here, in the first thoroughly left-wing poem to be written in Greece, Várnalis exposes, with compassion, those vulnerable weaknesses in the forerunners of mankind which make them dupes as well as saviors. Against these, as an example, he posits the Leader, who is not the son of God but the "child of Necessity," born of the myriad oppressed dead and living, and who comes with sword in hand to found the "Kingdom of Work." He is the proletarian leader, in short, who fights the three weapons which those in authority have historically used against the people to exploit, intimidate and deceive: The Republic of Bosses, Religion, and the idealistic notions of intellectuals who mislead the people from the paths of revolution. In the Monkey, Várnalis castigates his own colleagues in arts and letters who, by proffering their pens to the service of those in power, muddy the clear waters of action, loathe and fear the truth, and write whatever their masters dictate that they may insure for themselves personal safety and comfort. As the Aristea and the Monkey embrace, the Leader, with his courageous and apocalyptic words, dispels the darkness and leads the slaves toward freedom. Surely this must be one of the most "classical" of all proletarian poems, as perhaps is evident in "The Leader," and perhaps less evident in "Magdalene" (also taken from this poem), in which the compassionate prostitute knows pure happiness "in giving without fee, / freedom in slavery to a certain true ideal." Such dichotomy was never to leave the poet.

Three years later, Várnalis was fired from his position as teacher of literature in secondary schools, and two years after that, in 1927, he published another long epico-lyrical poem in four parts, Slaves Besieged. The first part depicts the clash between spirit and body, idealism and materialism. The second part interprets war from the point of view of the querrilla fighter, of the skeptic for whom war is a form of economic exploitation, and of the madman who envisages the overthrow of society. In the third and fourth parts, Pain and Hate are personifications of those victims who, oppressed by violence and falsehoods, are unable to discover the truth. The poem ends with the peal of the Liberty Bell. So long as men are "besieged" by Idealism, Várnalis says, so long as their masters oppress them and drag them off to slaughter, men will remain slaves. This is a poem that rose out of the disappointment and despair of Greece's defeat by Turkey in Asia Minor in 1922, expressing a hatred of war, and striking out at several aspects of an ideology that blinds the masses into an acceptance of slavery and fascism.

Himself an idealist by nature, Várnalis has utilized the polemic and the satire as angry whiplashes against injustice and exploitation. His use of traditional meters, rhymes and stanzaic forms is pyrotechnical in dexterity, and he is as capable of delicacy and aestheticism as he is of wrath and indignation. His proletarian poetry, stripped of the language in which it was written, seems naïve propaganda in translation. His tavern poems, written with great verve in argot and dialect, cannot possibly survive transplantation. Poems from his last book, *The Free World* (1965), show an abiding concern for social justice, scathingly point out that the Unknown Soldier is swindled with "a cheap tinsel wreath," and with anger declare that in this dreary and filthy time of ours there is no "greater sacrifice / 'for God and country' now than Treachery."

The life spans of Sikelianós, Kazantzákis, and Várnalis were sufficiently long so that, although as products of their generation they wrote in traditional techniques, they were also alert to various progressive changes that came into being in the period between the two world wars and after. Sikelianós was emboldened by surrealism and democratic ideals, Kazantzákis was permeated by existentialism, and both he and Várnalis were oriented by Marxism. The generation that arose on the eve of the Second World War and most suffered the consequences of the Balkan Wars and the Asia Minor disaster, however, stagnated in ennui, dissolution, negation, hesitation and escape. A spate of new periodicals brought to Greece not only French writers but also writers from England, Belgium, Scandinavia, Germany and Russia—authors such as Ibsen, Hamsun, Wilde, Nietzsche—indication that Anglo-Saxon writers were later to usurp the influence so long held by the French. The ideal of synthesizing all aspects of their Greek heritage, which had so moved Palamás, Sikelianós, and Kazantzákis, meant little to this generation in its corrosion and common disbelief. The minor figures of this period are too evanescent, too ephemeral in their gentle melancholy, to translate well: Napoleón Lapathiótis (1893–1943), with his pessimism, his sentimental idolatry of working-class boys, his themes of death and decay; Mítsos Papanikoláou (1900–1943), with his nebulous and exquisite symbolism; and the strongest of these, Télos Ághras (1899–1944), sensitive and cultivated, living in Greece under clouded northern skies and a monotone of gray.

Kóstas Ouránis

Some indication of their mode and manner may be found in the poetry of Kóstas Níarhos, 1890–1953. When, at the age of eighteen, he began to write under the pseudonym Ouránis (the cognate root of "heavenly," "celestial"), it was as though he were still determined, doggedly, to rediscover the lost paradise of his childhood years, and his ideal Beatrice in it. Estranged from his merchant father, attached to a mother who but vaguely understood him, he created in fantasy a world of escape into many affairs that soon lost zest and meaning, into a restless journey from country to country (his travel books are among his best works) that soon declined from forays of self-discovery to sieges of self-immolation, into a restless opiate for constant change, to be where he was not. Thoroughly egocentric and narcissistic, he soon wearied of affairs and travel, until he noted in a confession, "Let me not seek for anything outside myself, neither in love nor in hate." Yet opposed to his subjectivity was a delight in joviality and comradeship, a fascination in things outside himself but which he felt to be, nevertheless, his prison walls. His poetry and personality developed in a clash between his two egos in which the subjective side seems to have been the stronger.

In his first book, *Like a Dream* (1909), he sought escape; in *Spleen* (1912) he indulged in morbidity, the heir of Poe and Baudelaire; and in *Nostalgias* (1920) he fell into a melancholy symbolism. Rarely have the titles of a poet's books so summed up his personality and mood—dream, spleen, nostalgia. Among the last of the Traditionalists as well as of the Romantics, Ouránis wrote in formal patterns, most often rhymed, yet not too carefully wrought or polished, in which he retained something of the indolent grace of the gentlemanly amateur. In cadences that are lilting and often slack, his poems are windows of escape into the lost paradise of childhood wonders, into memory and nostalgia, into an invocation of dream tinted with elegiac tones of causeless sorrow—"I shall be dying until the day I die." The favorite season of poets of this generation was autumn—not the dry, brilliant season of the Greek landscape, but the pallid and gusty autumn of

Paris, where Ouránis lived for several years and wrote that he might "die one day on a mournful autumn twilight." His verses are flowing, gentle, tender, uncertain, often suffused with a melancholy irony. Stripped of illusions late in life, he wrote in iambic verse of uneven line length what were more notations for poems than realized creations. He found his soul to be now a dark, barren well without echo or sound. A stranger even to himself, he discovered that he had been living in a stillness that had become a stagnant serenity. Toward the end of his life, he wrote with self-awareness: "If Death should come, he will find nothing to take, but much to give." Yet the final impression Ouránis leaves is not one of profound despair but of the vague and twilight zone of those neoromantics whose indefinite aura of undetermined sorrow never explodes into tragedy.

Kóstas Kariotákis

Such an explosion did occur, however, in 1928 in Préveza, a town in northeastern Greece at the entrance to the Gulf of Árta. There, on the night of July 21, at the age of thirty-two, Kóstas Kariotákis, who was born in 1896, tried in vain for ten hours to drown himself, but discovered he was too good a swimmer. On the following day, he bought a pistol, then in the afternoon sat for about three hours in a seaside taverna, The Heavenly Garden, wrote a suicide note, thrust it into his pocket, stretched out under a eucalyptus tree and shot himself through the heart. The note, both serious and sarcastic, reads in part:

"It's time I revealed my tragedy. My greatest faults have always been an unbridled curiosity, an unhealthy imagination, and an attempt to inform myself about all emotions without being able to feel most of them. . . . Every reality is for me repulsive . . . I am paying for all those who, like myself, can never find an ideal in their lives, who remain always the victims of their hesitations, and who consider their existence to be a meaningless game. I see such persons increasing more and more with the centuries. It is to these I address myself. Since I have tasted every joy!! I am now ready for a dishonorable death. . . . P. S. I advise all those who swim well not to try death by drowning. . . . At the first opportunity I shall write of my impressions as a drowned man."

By this act of self-abnegation and self-annihilation, Kariotákis acted out a nightmare many poets of his generation, Ouránis among them, had lived in fantasy only. He is the best and most worthy representative of the generation of the twenties, of the Damned who wrote of an unbearable ennui, of suffocation, of futility, exhausted in emotion and language both. Better than all others, he best expressed the anguish of the poets between two world wars. The title of his first book, published when he was twenty-three, is a grim description of his condition, *The Pain of Men and Things* (1919); the title of his second, *Nepenthe* (1921), is the name of a potion used to dull pain and sorrow, an opium to obliterate suffering. The sentimentality that often infuses romantic and melancholic temperaments is present in "Dedication," balanced by the ever-present self-mockery of "Ballade to the Inglorious Poets of the Ages."

Kariotákis informed a friend that his third book of poems would have for title the drawing of a skull and bones arranged so as to form the algebraic sign for infinity, with the motto: "We shall become reconciled with Nothingness and Infinity." His third and last book, *Elegies and Satires* (1927)—published, however, without skull and bones—keeps an even balance between sarcastic lamentation and mournful satire. Poetry is likened to the slack strings of a rickety guitar, poets to incredible antennae trying to tune in on the infinite, receiving static more often than music; nerves are confused, bodies ache, the senses are deranged, poetry itself is a refuge that offers no solace. In "Ideal Suicides" he is caustic about would-be suicides who pose in self-pity against "the tears, the sweat, and the vast sky's / nostalgia, all the bleak waste lands," leaving their pathetic little notes, but still living on in their self-desiccation. In "March Funereal and Vertical," however, the note turns ominous, the poet contemplates death by hanging from the ceiling with its fretted plasterwork of roses and acanthi, a "vertical" death that would be simply "a matter of height," and a final escape from the "daily struggles for bread and salt, / love affairs, boredom." If he cannot wear the unwithered laurel wreath, at least he can crown himself with a kitsch wreath of plaster flowers and, in a characteristic note of self-conscious sarcasm, be admired by all. But in two poems written before he committed suicide, the impasse he had reached is stark and evident. In the ironically entitled "Optimism," he has reached "the frontiers of silence," "the dark blind alley and the mind's abyss," where the poet is forced into the postures of acrobat, charlatan, clown. And in his last poem, "Prévesa," the small deaths in the banal routine of daily life in a provincial town, the boredom, the death within deaths, finally find expression in phrases that are mocking, slashing, bitter. And yet, characteristically, as in the postscript to his suicide note, he ends on a tone of mockery both toward himself and toward others, deflating even the pretensions of death. He committed suicide not so much in protest against the tragedy of life as against its insignificance, its farce, its musical-comedy strut.

For a while, helped by the mythical proportions of his suicide, young poets tried to imitate Kariotákis' manner if not his substance, but they lacked his lacerations, the deadly impasse of his character. He created no new school, for he was the end of a period and not the beginning of anything new. When he put an end to his life, his poetry also had all but ended, whereas Hart Crane, when he drowned himself in the Caribbean Sea in 1932, only a year older than Kariotákis, found himself unable to cope with a burgeoning imagination seeking not the frontiers of silence but a mystical country beyond all boundary stones. Crane was revolutionary in imagery, metrics, technique, but Kariotákis was conservative in his versification, writing in a metric and a rhythm that nevertheless took very many liberties. He came at a time when not only emotions and inspiration, but also rhymes, rhythms, images, meters and similes were suffering from a form of exhaustion. At times he tried to imbed some purist words in his demotic diction, essayed some prosaic elements in his phrases or took a daring image from familiar life, such as comparing the slack strings of a guitar to dangling watch chains, speaking of women who make love "as easily as they peel onions," or referring to a bank account where he had just deposited "just one dollar."

Tákis Papatsónis

Similarities of style and theme may be found in Sikelianós, Kazantzákis and Várnalis, but just as this group was preceded by a forerunner, Caváfis, whose uniqueness in style and content set him apart, so it may be concluded by another poet, Tákis Papatsónis, in his own way unique, yet utterly different from Caváfis in attitude and dedication, the forerunner of a natural mysticism in Greece. Born in Athens in 1895, he shares with Sikelianós a distinguished ancestry in politics and religion. On his father's side he is descended from a historic family which played a great role in the military campaigns during the Greek War of Independence and in the political affairs of the newly formed state. During the Turkish occupation, members of his family were governors of Emblákion, a large area of Messinía consisting of forty-five villages. On his mother's side he is a direct descendant of the Marquesa di Bartoli of Ancona, an ancient Catholic family which has given many ecclesiastics to the Church. Kazantzákis served briefly in the Greek government, but Papatsónis is among the first modern Greek poets who have served their governments with distinction in posts of high responsibility, a European phenomenon whose only parallel in the United States has been Archibald MacLeish. It is interesting to speculate how much Papatsónis' career in the Ministry of Economics, of which he eventually became Secretary General, and his involvement in the tariffs, custom duties, and economics of his country impelled him toward a poetry of metaphysical nuance, religiosity and mysticism, the exact antithesis of his mundane occupations.

Papatsónis began publishing poetry in periodicals in 1914, but his governmental responsibilities did not permit him to gather them in a first book, *Selections I*, until 1935. Although he published another small book of poetry, *Ursa Minor*, in 1944, he waited eighteen years before publishing *Selections II*, in 1962. Enough poetry for four or more volumes lie scattered in various periodicals and anthologies. Primarily, Papatsónis is a religious poet with an inclination toward mysticism and naturalism, tempered by an erotic strain. He is the only poet in this anthology influenced more by the rituals of the Roman Catholic than of the Greek Orthodox church, in keeping with his family tradition. His poetry is studded with reference to Catholic dogma and its ceremonies, with a liberal use of ecclesiastic Latin terminologies— *mea culpa, de profundis, in plateis oppidi*—some of which, in his earlier poetry, he rhymed with Greek endings. At times dogma and quotation are used with simplicity or naïveté, at other times with an almost doctrinaire precision, as in the prose statements of logical deduction regarding the Pope's infallibility in "Outline of Error." Nevertheless, his God is not the deity of dogma but a metaphysical concept to which he refers as Unseen Wisdom, Mighty Element, Supreme Sun, Third Empyrean, Presence, Equilibrium of Elements, Indivisible Order, Serene Light, Quietude, Tranquillity. In early poems, such as "Before the Advent" or "To a Young Girl Brought Up in a Nunnery," he may lament being locked out of the Garden of Eden because he has lived in the embrace of evil, or he may beg Tranquillity to haul him out of the savage billows of the sea, but in all his subsequent poetry he was to turn his back on Kariotákian despair, characteristic of his generation, and write a poetry of faith and joy which was to presage the Aegean felicity of Odysseus Elýtis. Something sweet and gentle suffuses his thought and his poetry. But his God does have somber powers, often symbolized by the dark and vast night, freezing winter, the north wind, terrors, doubts, escapes, the stone of Sisyphos. The naturalist in Papatsónis recognizes these powers, but the mystic, upheld by faith, as in "Crossways," says "yes in the hour of corruption," exchanging serenity for agitation, and finds communion "in the difficult distinction between Good and Evil." In the realm of relativity, amid the contraries of existence, as he writes in "The Dependence," good hours and joyful days exist, for all are placed in order by "the attractions and repulsions / of a Mighty Element," an Unseen Wisdom. Similarly, in "Self-Scrutiny" the poet fights off the dark powers and understands that the constant struggle to perfect oneself in the realm of action has its parallel in the constant struggle of a poet to control his poem, to revise the many drafts of his life and art, to perfect an order out of chaotic emotions.

On a lower level, Papatsónis derives sustenance and faith through a simple observation of Church ritual and discipline—in the observance of Apostolic law and moderation in "Summer Tourists Go to Mass," in the Canonical Hours of Catholic ritual. In his poetry, Christmas, the birth of Christ as Savior, occurs more often than any other Christian holiday, as in "Before the Advent," "To a Young Girl Brought Up in a Nunnery," "The Inns" and "The Thread." It is a time, a threshold of salvation, when a sinner may be visited by the angels with their joyful caroling, when the Thread, which is Christ, may delicately bind all things together into one body, defying the census takers. But Papatsónis' transcendental mysticism, based on the use of nature as symbol, and his ultimate and irrational affirmation, attain their highest expression in such poems as "Ode to Aquarius," wherein the awesome turbulence of God's roaring cataract in the infinitude of space reaches the troubled and solitary man as "indolent Minor Waters," where "a drop / of water seldom measures / the immeasurable moment of eternity." The unlooked-for theme, in the poem by that name, is the essence of a violet, a plateau of pellucid air and serenity that is antithetical yet strangely similar to the essence of God's roaring cataract erupting out of an unfathomable *De Profundis*. So also, in "Attic Shapes," the dawn of blissful weather brings a premonition of tranquillity wherein everything is immobilized in eternity. And yet, as the critic Kléon Paráskhos has pointed out, nature in Papatsónis can become godlike without being identified with God. Nature is seen through the eyes of a child, pure and fresh, and yet as strangely evocative as a canvas by Rousseau or the Greek primitive painter Theóphilos; such is the description, in capital letters, of the flora and fauna of the Garden of Eden in "Before the Advent." Papatsónis has retained something of the naïve, the primitive, the amateur, but this is strangely combined with a sophistication of tone and an abstract, polysyllabic vocabulary heavily weighted with words taken from the purist and foreign languages, all elaborately interwoven in a syntax revealing a mind that is also logical, didactic, lucid. The ultimate impression is one of having strayed into a sensual yet metaphysical jungle of foliage painted by Rousseau. As in all mystical poets, Papatsónis' description of ultimate revelation is strongly tinged with eroticism, a delight in the senses, an ecstatic certainty that the celebration of sensuosity and animal desire, as in "Rape of the Sabines," is also an approach to God, a transubstantiation of the "nebulae of our ashy earth" into "the purely azure Third Empyrean with its eternal / splendor in the very heart of the Supreme Sun."

A highly cultivated man, Papatsónis has been in constant touch with literary avant-garde movements in several languages. He has translated and been influenced by Hölderlin, Claudel, Aragon, Saint-John Perse, and published a translation of Eliot's *The Waste Land* three years before Seféris published his. He passed through Kariotákian pessimism unscathed, refreshed his imagery with surrealism, enriched it with symbolism, but is primarily the forerunner in Greek poetry of the metaphysical, intellectual and logical statement but with no hint of existentialist agony. From his career in the Ministry of Economics he probably carried over into his poetry a love of deduction and logic, of precise statement, of almost mathematical nicety, as in "Outline of Error," "The Dependence," "Crossways," and "Self-Scrutiny." The prose statement, Pound's dictate that "poetry should be as carefully written as prose," has taken in Papatsónis a direction other than that taken by Caváfis, a lambency of abstract ritual instead of a play of irony and wit. His mixture of purist and demotic is less extreme than that of Caváfis, and this is accompanied by a lack of verbal sophistication, by a metrical and rhythmical simplicity, by something of the unpolished and loose structure of a highly educated amateur. Poetry has been for Papatsónis the almost unprofessional release and natural expression of the inner man who communes with God in the Inner Sanctum not of a bustling metropolitan Cathedral but of a quiet country chapel.

V | TRADITIONS AND TRANSITIONS

Alexander Báras

Greece has always been, from prehistoric times it seems, a triple crossroads between Asia, Africa and Europe, for its classical Apollonian equilibrium has always been tilted by an Oriental Dionysian ecstasy and a brooding African exoticism. Born in 1906 in Constantinople, where he lived most of his life in the service of the Royal Greek Ministry of Foreign Affairs, Alexander Báras has been a wayfarer on these crossroads, combining in his poetry a Hellenic restraint, an Oriental sensuousness, an African indolence. Although he has been preoccupied with many of the themes and atmospheres which obsessed Ouránis and Kariotákis— boredom, disillusion, suicide, and other lacerations of the decadent school—he has never permitted himself the self-indulgence of surrendering to these, but has almost puritanically subjected them to a spare art of wit and irony. Nor has he written with the traditional meters, stanzas and rhyme schemes of the neoromantic school of his generation, but rather with the diction, mixture of language, and dramatic lyricism of another poet who derived from Constantinople, Constantine Caváfis. His poem "The *Cleopatra*, the *Semiramis*, and the *Theodora*," published in 1929, was among the rare poems at that time to be written in free verse, although the basic rhythm is strongly iambic, as in most of his poems, and rhymes are used irregularly in uneven sequence.

Báras sees life as failure, contradiction and disappointment, filled with futile routine and the "tyranny of boredom," with neurasthenics and "their tedium following faithfully after," with a world of "unlucky love affairs, / secret sins, / great failures, one after the other." He longs nostalgically, as do other neoromantics, for the first happy country of innocent childhood, the "vestibule of Paradise," but he knows, in "The Unattainable," that there is no return, that the mountain pass opens to a sea that is "black, endless / without sun, without birds, without fishes, / without shores, and bottomless." His only certain refuge, as for Caváfis, is that of art itself, the practice of his craft, where subversive phenomena and emotions are controlled and subdued. In modest tones of self-mockery and ironic skepticism, with an almost imperceptible half-smile, in a low voice never raised above a whisper, almost disinterestedly, he became rather the compassionate surgeon of decadence and not its victim.

Even voyages for Báras are not open avenues of exploration, as for Caváfis and Kazantzákis, but simply boredom and routine on a larger scale. From his harbor window he watches ships with names redolent of romantic escape—Cleopatra, Semiramis, Theodora—leaving their wharves always and inevitably on the same day, the same hour, nine o'clock sharp, year after year, voyaging in the same cyclical wake—Piraeus, Brindisi, Trieste—no different in kind from white-collar workers, like himself, horribly metamorphosed into time machines. He is no John Masefield longing to go down to the sea again. "When the road is the same always," the poet asks, "what does it matter if it crosses an entire Mediterranean / or goes from one house to another neighborhood?" A widely traveled man himself, Báras circulated in exotic countries with the conscious mockery of one only half involved, whose detachment never permitted him to be immersed in the quicksands of emotion or to withdraw safely into the high branches of the mind. With a "tension adventurous and narcotic," thirsting for something new, like Ouránis, and tired of always living the same despairing life in the same city always, his characters pass before the exotic names of foreign embassies, fascinated by "peculiar and remote" places.

Yet Báras is aware of primordial rumblings in the dark source of the human spirit, where, rising over "prehistoric murky forests," the moon awakens "out of chaos and the deep profound, / slumbering life / and the first rhythms of History." His indolent Ethiopians, their sensuous bodies smeared with oil, watch their native palm trees outlining the crumbling marble columns of ancient decaying civilizations. He is aware of "aromatic insanity," of the Oriental luxury of Asiatics passing by on their "holy pachyderms," with their "sunburnt, / their voluptuous, indolent / and handsome bodies." In "Centaur," the naked body of a youth is lingeringly caressed with the wonder if not the sense of passing time of Alexander Mátsas. Yet Báras is never effusive, never confessional, and his excesses and primordial disruptions are brought under control by a gentle irony, an innate skepticism, a discipline of art and spirit.

Alexander Mátsas

After he had joined the Greek diplomatic service in 1934, Alexander Mátsas, who was born in Athens in 1910 and died in London in 1969, served his country in a variety of posts, lastly as Ambassador to the United States from 1962 to 1967. A highly sophisticated man of wide culture and formal, gentlemanly manners, he had published his first book of poems in French, in 1925, when he was only fourteen, *Le Vieux Jardin*, with a prestigious preface by Palamás. But twenty-one years were to elapse before he published another book, *Poems* (1946), this time in Greek, and eighteen years more before the appearance of his third and last book, *Poems* (1964), selections from his previous book with additional new work. Precocious, precious, disdainful of easy fame yet desiring it, aristocratic in manner and taste, well bred and urbane, his entire being nevertheless vibrated to the sensual responses of the body, the violence and tenderness of the flesh under "the purification of absolute noon." His style, influenced by the metrical neoclassic austerity of Kálvos, is set in formal yet unrhymed patterns, but his content has the voluptuousness of a Caváfis refined into a ceremonious and ritualistic praise of the body and lamentation on its decay. Influenced by Caváfis also in his use of language, and with a native disposition for artifice, he borrowed words from the purist with elegance and style. This combination of an outer concern for form and a content of seductive voluptuousness imparts to his poetry not so much a vibrancy of tension—as in Kálvos—as the pulsation of light in an alabaster urn. Curiously enough, the final effect is one of cool detachment, of ritual, of ceremony, of preciousness, a hermetic poetry in which an ultimate secret is deliberately and cunningly hidden from prying eyes.

Here is a metaphysics of matter, a mysticism of the senses. The multiplicity of human nature, the successive metamorphosis of the individual in character and personality under the stress of circumstance and time (a Caváfian theme) seemed to Mátsas the most striking element in life. Because he believed that communion with life is best obtained through the world of the senses, his poetry is often an exaltation of physical beauty, especially that of the male figure as idealized by classical Greek sculpture, and a lament on the passage of time and the dispersal of the body. The body is perhaps his chief metaphor—"worthy of column and tree"; a "warm statue / carved on the pediment of night"; "the captive prince of imperfection"; "vulnerable and richly corruptible"; "quietly burning toward death." It is a delicate and convoluted shell reclining on the boundaries of sleep and time, the delightful tomb of flesh into which the spirit awakens as it wells up into the body like a tide from the depths of time and sleep to sojourn for a while in this "bittersweet realm / of imperfection." In the body, Psyche (the soul) pursues tirelessly her great adventure, informs the hand that now "completes some movement begun / on the other shore," shapes "the powerful figures / that rule the inexorable firmament of Myth" which is the history of the body as we know it in time. But life is a "trapdoor of myth," which may open suddenly any moment and drop us into the unfathomable abyss. Sleep and love are an escape into a timeless Time. Sleep, the twin brother of death, is the rival lover, seducing the beloved away into Lethe and oblivion, turning the head toward darkness. Death and darkness shatter "the divine vertical" of the sun, the golden burden of noon, and are the Dark Lovers to whom the beloved body finally and passively surrenders, a Ganymede transported and seduced by gods. Poetry, for Mátsas, was a precise art, yet one that was permeated with suggestive disintegrations under which precise meanings crumble away and vague, unanswered questions of death and decay obtrude.

Níkos Kavadhías

Because the Greeks have always been a seafaring nation, it is surprising that not more than two poets in this anthology, Níkos Kavadhías and Dhimítrios Antoníou, make their living on the sea. When Kavadhías' *Marabou* was published, in 1933, and his *Fog*, in 1947, they enjoyed a popularity similar to that of FitzGerald's version of the *Rubáiyát* of Omar Khayyám. Written on the whole in a narrative-ballad measure of rhymed quatrains, they struck a note of nostalgic recollection in old sea salts and swept a whiff of briny air to landlubbers dreaming of escape. The style and vocabulary were an easy and lilting demotic, the subject matter and images were all the popular imagination fancied as the swaggering adventures and forbidden pleasures of untrammeled sailor life, as though to cut off from land were also to cut off from ethical or moral ties in which land creatures were confined. Here was the fascination of long voyages and remote countries. Here were not only the longed-for ports of middle-class fantasy—Madras, Algiers, Singapore—but even more exotic and unheard-of harbors of sin: Sfax, Djibouti, Torkopilla, Akora. Here were the lyric or dramatic renderings of magical encounters, of corrupt, perverted or debauched adventures, of tropical nights, of secret wounds, of lewd tattoos, of life squandered in brothels or seaside bars, of knifings for the favors of Arabian girls, of cargoes of hashish, pot, and white powder. Yet in all this debauchery, washed clean by the salt brine of the sea, the reader feels an inner innocence, the playacting of braggadocio youth, like that of Kavadhías' midshipman who, on the bridge in an hour of peril, brooding on his labyrinthine wanderings in sin and error, still knows that he retains "the pure heart of a child."

We read these poems with the same relish with which in adolescence we read dime novels and penny dreadfuls, delighting in and accepting coincidences and sentimentalities we could never accept elsewhere, as in the more adroit of soap operas. The longed-for lady of the heart's desire, Beatrice, has now been turned into a harbor whore, but ultimately she is only to be attained in reverie, a ghostly wraith, hovering in the steering cabin, her white dress drenched with spray. Here is the brooding on death and suicide, as in Ouránis and Kariotákis, the same desire for escape, whether from land or life. Like A. E. Housman, Kavadhías has published only two slim volumes of poetry separated by a long stretch of silence. Both poets are limited in range and idea, in the work of both the men cheat and the girls betray, courage is dominant, and a sweet pessimism gives to life the misty vapors of a tropical night at sea. It is simply a matter of poetic justice that Níkos Kavadhías should have been born (in 1910) in the exotic remoteness of Harbin, Manchuria.

D. I. Antoníou

Poetic justice was twice mindful of romantic amenities in that our only other seafaring poet, Dhimítrios Antoníou, was also born in an exotic land, this time Beira, Mozambique, in 1906. On both sides of his family, Captain Antoníou is descended from generations of sea captains based on the island of Cássos, in the Dodecanese. The entire corpus of his published work consists of about forty-three short poems written over an interval of thirty years, published only in periodicals and reprints. In 1934 he began a long poem, *The Indies*, completed in 1944 but not published, except for a few tantalizing fragments, until 1967. The impression given by the scarcity of his compositions and by the poems themselves is of a man breaking granite barriers of silence reluctantly, whittling away on blocks of remembrance until memory is captured in a language lean and sparse yet capable of slanting suggestivity, nebulous half-meanings, disturbing overtones. He seems to have found his own voice and owes allegiance to no school.

Captain Antoníou's poetry is that of a man voyaging, scrutinizing the stars at night during long watches on the bridge, scribbling his drifting nuances of thought on the backs of innumerable Greek cigarette boxes and scraps of paper, but always in recollection, whether of the beloved whom in self-imposed exile from his native land he has left behind, or whether recalling the exotic contrasts of landscape and civilizations in regions he has visited throughout the world. Terse and precise in a pure demotic style as though written in shorthand, his poems are crabbed and gnarled in diction, like ancient olive trees, in the poet's attempt to arrive at what he terms "the specific gravity of expression." For such a poet the blank paper is an abyss, a mirror to be conquered, "securing in words that fill it this bruised / necessity." Indeed, many of his poems are themselves concerned with craft, with "finding the cry and giving it existence / with a simple and quiet narration." He makes "easy conversation and difficult literature" out of "passions fallen silent and jasmines long past," and agrees with Walter Pater that an artist must burn always with a hard, gemlike flame, for in "This Meager Grass" he writes that "what is needed for your art is this: / *to burn coldly / that you may exist.*" It is the cold imagination that such a poet evokes, the crystalline flame of precious stones that purify without destroying, for "Dazzling is a work of art / rising out of the flames that create it, / unalterably serene in the triumph of our eternity."

Trained in music, Captain Antoníou often expresses in his poems melodic states of mind, half-articulated meanings that dissolve in rhythms, as in a series of poems entitled "Of Music." He uses punctuation—dashes, semicolons, colons, diaereses, parentheses, a series of periods—much like musical notation. His poetry is largely an attempt to recollect emotion in tranquillity. "Did he command the past?" he asks; and he concludes, he "has finally under his control the danger of a passion / and sips the unquenchable liquor of memory." Recollection takes on the cold glitter of stars until "Only remembrance remains unwithered," until "the spells of an illusion / are the means of life." The beloved is recalled in a wintry garden, in a chiaroscuro of grays, her ring on the finger of another. The sea voyage is a trial during which one is tested, until in Antoníou's poetry a muted romantic mysticism arises, without sentimentality, honed to an icy precision and glitter by the wide spaces of sea and sky through which he has sailed in a fluid dream of time, trying to net in his consciousness, as in his poetry, that distinction between time as a finite system of measurement and time as an ever-flowing eternity. A deep religiosity, without dogma, often impels this poet, who by heritage is also a mariner adrift on tides and times, to appeal to an Eternal Judge of values.

Antoníou began his only long poem, *The Indies*, as a second officer during the visit of his ship, *Peleus*, to the villages of Masoulipatam and Kalingapatam in the Bay of Bengal during late December of 1933 and early January of 1934. Although written in a clear narrative line that varies with the pulsations of thought, it is still a difficult poem of elliptical meaning and mystical intent embodied in the exotic imagery of the Indies. In the form of a letter to the poet's family, it addresses in particular a girl "brought up in French music of the eighteenth century." The main theme is struck early as the poet relates how on New Year's Eve, while the ship was being loaded with pistachio nuts and castor-oil seed off Masoulipatam, the coolies were tempted to eat pork and drink whiskey, and how they burst into a savage and barbaric dance on the hatch, singing to their god Rama. The young officer becomes aware of the conflict between primitive and mechanized civilizations. Later, when he and his companions visit Kalingapatam, the strange flora and fauna, the outlandish dress and mores of the villagers plunge him into the dark atavistic roots of mankind's origins. In a forest clearing, he sees a primitive god's idol, and then, as in revelation, feels that someone had approached him and vanished. Was it Sita, who dances and sings to him with bells and drums? The last part of the poem is a memorial to the *Peleus*, sunk by a German submarine in 1944. Most of the survivors were machine-gunned; four drifted on a raft for thirty-seven days before they were found. In recalling these incidents throughout the years of composition, remembrance itself turned into a medium of metamorphosis, and the poet became aware of a distinction impossible to translate adequately into English: that between *hrónos* ($\chi\rho\acute{o}\nu os$), time as a finite entity, and *kerós* ($\kappa\alpha\iota\rho\grave{o}s$), the fluidity of time without past, present or future. He participates, as have all saints and mystics, in the nucleus between macrocosm and microcosm and exists simultaneously in both worlds. This poem, with its strange beauty, its organic metrical structure, its sparse language yet exotic coloring, is unique in modern Greek literature, the fruit of long contemplation and an almost agonized dedication to craft.

I. M. Panayotópoulos

Born on an island near Missolóngi in 1901, I. M. Panayotópoulos is one of the most versatile men of letters in Greece today—poet, novelist, educator, critic, journalist, and writer of travel books. His early inspiration was rooted in the generation of the twenties, and his first collection of poems, *Miranda's Book* (1924), shows the influence of the French and German symbolists and post-symbolists, in particular that of the Belgian poet of the twilight, Rodenback. In an atmosphere of musical suggestiveness, elliptical expressions, uncertain lambencies, unfulfilled desires, reveries, melancholy thoughts of suicide, and images lost in mist or melting in sleeping waters, the poet wanders in search of his Ideal Lady, the Miranda of Shakespeare's *The Tempest*, who in all of Panayotópoulos' later books is still longingly sought for in the form of Helen. These poems are written in traditional meter and rhyme, as are the poems of *Lyrical Sketches* (1933). Here the poet passes from faith to doubt, from doubt to despair, in a cycle of ceaseless negation typical of the generation caught between two major world wars. The Ideal Lady is possessed, but the affair ends in catastrophe. Nevertheless, the poet clings to the salvation that art has to offer, realizing that the world has no value other than that which beauty creates.

Sixteen years and the agonies of the Second World War were to pass before Panayotópoulos published his third book of poems, *Alcyone* (1950), a departure from the symbolism and neoromanticism of the previous books. In this work he begins to assert the love and value of life. Although most of these poems are still written in meter and rhyme, the poet has become concerned and involved, within his formal patterns, in the fate of others, in the brutality of the German-Italian occupation. "Eumenides" was written to depict these tragic hardships and yet to express hope for liberation. Perceiving the empty cradles, the shuttered houses, the idle plows, the poor dying in the streets as another part of existence continues on its serene way, the poet asserts that "now it's time to hate," and he awaits the coming of the avenging Furies. In the last third of this book Panayotópoulos throws off the shackles of meter and self-laceration to find a deeper subjectivity that also includes the outer world. He explores dark existential areas, metaphysical inquiries, landscapes half real and half symbolic, where the frozen moon casts a lurid light. The absurd has been confronted and surpassed by a dedication to poetry and creativity that turns everything into passion, although with lyrical irony. Out of futility and nihilism, the poet affirms "the one and only moment," with no past, no future, where one "exists" without illusions but without denial, a humanistic and stoic approach. In a free-verse poem, "Apology of the Small Faun," he tries to make some final choice between two destinies, between the longing for an ideal love, the "deathless contours" of a Helen or an Aphrodite, and the gentle dream of homecoming and hearth symbolized by Nausicaä.

From now on Panayotópoulos was to write in free verse only. In "The Nightmare," in a landscape of far-off places, he poses the questions—in several languages, to emphasize their international futility—which Gauguin wrote as the title to one of his canvases painted in Noa-Noa: "What are we? Whence do we come? Whither are we going?" Our essence is a question, but there are no ears to hear, not van Gogh's severed ear, "a wonderful trophy," a symbol of defiance that is a "contrast to our prose futilities"—nor even the remaining ear, the unmutilated one, equally incapable of hearing. But if the poet confronts such metaphysical agony and dread of futility, he does so only to assert man's essential dignity and to impose on him a ceaseless vigil before death, before nothingness, for Panayotópoulos' final stance is that of the humanist and the stoic. Although he had of necessity accepted Nausicaä and the hearth, he still longs for Helen, whose passing feet the Aegean still remembers with nostalgia, the one and only face behind the protean, myriad faces of women.

In *The World's Window* (1962) the poet has come full circle from the introverted nuances of his first volume to objective concern with the wars, savagery and barbarism of our present time and its Hiroshimas, its Dachaus, where man shapes his immortality with his futility and spills out his entrails and values into worlds of outer space. Hiroshima is the new face of our century, the new poetry, the new beauty. Although each separate poem of this book is an entity, the entire poem is a thematic unit that begins with a clear lyrical aptitude and concludes with disdain and contempt for a world based on blood and hypocrisy. But the poet does not give over. Like Kazantzákis, he has confronted the annihilating abyss and, on this ultimate negation, nevertheless affirms the worth of life as reconstructed by the creative imagination. Poetry, for Panayotópoulos, is the lyrical conscience of the world.

Pandelis Prevelákis

Born in Crete in 1909, Pandelís Prevelákis has become one of the foremost novelists and art historians in Greece, teaching the history of art at the College of Fine Arts in Athens, and publishing to date some ten novels, some five plays, and several books on painting and painters. His prose works, his poetic dramas, and his poetry are all written in a rich demotic vocabulary and diction deeply rooted in his Cretan heritage. When he was only seventeen, in 1926, he met Níkos Kazantzákis, then forty years old, with whom he formed a lifelong friendship. In 1958, he published a study of the man and his epic poem *The Odyssey*. In 1965 he also published over four hundred letters which Kazantzákis had written him, with the best introduction to Kazantzákis as man and author yet written. A year after their meeting, in 1927, at the Delphic Festival, he met the other man with whom he also formed a deep and lasting friendship, Angelos Sikelianós. Both Kazantzákis and Sikelianós influenced the young man not so much in technical matters, although, like them, he was an ardent demoticist, as in their breadth of vision, their noble and daring enterprises. At the age of eighteen, Prevelákis essayed an epic poem of some four hundred lines, *Soldiers* (1928), which, set in a mythological and timeless kingdom, reflects the Neo-Hellenic problems of his country during the Asia Minor disaster of 1922. Written in the fifteen-syllable verse line and in the demotic tradition of Cretan and Byzantine folk epics, it is overladen with embellishments and the overpoetic demotic diction in vogue at that time.

Poetry, for Prevelákis, was associated with the ecstasy of his youth. He was not to publish another book of poems until eleven years later, *The Nude Poetry*, in 1939; and his only other collection, *The Nudest Poetry*, was published in 1941. By now he had abandoned meter and rhyme, feeling that any technical form or construction of artifice would falsify and distort the sincerity and clarity, the nudity, the impetuous onrush of true inspiration which the poet must channel, as though he were molding fire in his hands, and not chiseling into shape, as Théophile Gautier would have it, an objective block of marble. He sought the sincerity of the innate word, to receive the exaltations and depressions of poetic creativity and to make the given moment deathless. He wished instinctive wisdom to take the place of professional consciousness and skill. Love and the heat of poetic energy would find, he felt, the necessary inner expression and place a word with absolute confidence, make a sentence pulsate with a rhythm appropriate to the inner thought, and leave the verse free, unguarded, bare. In short, he wished to write a "nude" poetry, a phrase he derived from Jiménez. Indeed, he would often write some of his poems in Spanish first and then translate them into Greek, simply because his instinct so dictated. Simplicity with passion, integrity with clarity, a flaming nakedness of spirit, "the sincerity of the innate word"—each word like a knife in an open wound—these were the criteria the young poet set for himself.

Prevelákis divided life into dead and living time, and all his work has been a "struggle against dead time." Consequently, creativity and poetry itself have been his main themes, a dead Lazarus who, when resurrected, sings like "a sun / ensnared in an entanglement of stars." The poet climbs in maturity to an Upper Jerusalem, an ideal realm, wherein poetry is to receive, as though the soul were a mirror, "clouds, birds of passage, / air-channeled roads of migration, / falling stars, comets, their glittering trains, / and the dust of burning systems." But the theme of his inspiration lay in the Greek land as well as in the absolute heavens, and like buffaloes beating the barren earth with their hooves, Prevelákis, like Moses, struck the dry earth of his native land to release the wellsprings of water, "the roaring and many-leaved plane tree of poetry." The lover in his poetry is the romantic youth dedicated to virtue, sharing and celebrating with the beloved until love becomes the white rose of kindness and valor, a "green / wild olive wreath."

George Sarandáris

Born in Constantinople in 1907, George Sarandáris felt drawn to that other poet whose paternal and emotional ties were rooted in the Bosporus, to Caváfis, and soon acknowledged his idiom as that of the new poetry. Like Solomós, to whom he was related in spirit, he was educated in Italy, where he lived between the ages of two and twenty-four, and wrote his first verses in Italian and French. Like Kariotákis, he died in his early thirties, for he had come to Greece to fulfill his military service and died, ironically, from hardships incurred in fighting the Italians on the Albanian frontier. But unlike Kariotákis, whose influence, intensified by his suicide, was strongest between 1928 and 1936, Sarandáris spurned the poetry of despair, broke with traditional metrical forms and stanzas typical of the neoromantic movement, and wrote in free verse. Like Solomós, his knowledge of Greek, which he spoke with an Italian accent, was spare, the surface diction of the day, having no deep linguistic roots in the language's rich past and literature. This was for Solomós and Sarandáris both a limitation and a liberation. Unlike Caváfis, Sarandáris could not mix his vocabulary with historical impunity, he could not even use simple words with deep etymological reverberations, but, granted his talent, was thus by circumstance forced to use words of simplicity and translucence, to embody subtlety of thought in a diction at once diaphanous and concrete.

Sarandáris was a person of restless intellectual curiosity, articulate, critical, changing from idea to idea, rich in philosophical nuance, contemptuous of the hedonist and the materialist, seeking for the essence of things, impatient with forms and artifice. He brought with him a European awareness and sophistication, and was one of the first to give a voice to existential unrest in Greece, for he arrived well read in Dostoyevski, Kierkegaard and Proust, and had been a devotee of Ungaretti. Although he published three small books of philosophical speculation, his poetry was for him not a substitute for ideas but rather essences captured in concrete symbols. He influenced the imagery of the young man he was first to discover and praise, the university student Odysseus

Elýtis. Before Elýtis, he was a worshiper of the sun, of the sea, of the magic charm of girls, of all those Aegean objects and images which we know and recognize as the sole property of the younger poet, although for Sarandáris they remained more essences than objects. Because he longed for essence, he neglected embodiment, unlike Gerard Manley Hopkins, a position into which he was betrayed by his love for philosophy. He did not follow the automatic writing or illogical forms of surrealism which were the "new" elements in his day, nor did he take from surrealism the abrupt yoking of images or the elliptical manner of delineating metaphysical niceties.

Like Poe, he did not think a poem capable of lyrical extension, and he even concentrated more on the line itself than on the poem. Just as a straight line is the shortest mathematical distance between two points, he thought, so a line of verse is also the sincerest and most direct line of communication, a "lyrical point of the horizon," whose extension is infinite in the mind and the imagination, a line of limited intensity but illimitable suggestivity. He was among the first to denude his poems of punctuation, perhaps fearing that a comma or semicolon might impede the extension of a line beyond the page and into the imagination. His concentration on the line as essence made him impatient with formal structures or musical orchestration of sound; his shapes are amorphous, his music that of ideas, of the spirit, a "music of silence," for he insisted that the soul of poetry lies not in technical dexterity but in the sincere, impetuous, yet imagistic extension of essence. Toward the end of his life, like Thomas Wolfe, he became more and more aware of form and technique as part of meaning. For this reason his short, epigrammatic poems give one the impression of incompleteness, as though he had set down, with sensitivity, notes for poems and not the poems themselves. He wished to strip himself bare and to write a nude poetry of essence embodied in the most elemental of natural objects. Poetry for him was not a mask to hide behind but a revelation of spirit.

To most of his contemporaries Sarandáris gave the impression of being somewhat of a misfit, an ineffectual angel who had inadvertently wandered into this world and had fallen in love with it—particularly with Greece, its landscape and traditions—but could never become enfleshed with it, finding it beyond the reach of his touch no matter how long and lovingly he tried to fondle it, trying to transform it into the spiritual realm of his own lost origins, discovering in it the innocence of childhood as the closest portal to divinity. Like Henry Vaughan, Thomas Traherne, and other poets of the metaphysical school, he longed to capture the white celestial light of his angel infancy, he saw "bright shoots of everlastingness" in the longed-for objects of nature in whose weaker glories he could spy "some shadow of eternity." This led him toward the end of his brief life from a form of existentialist anguish to a faith in the mysticism of Greek Orthodoxy, to the insistence on man as a spiritual and not a physical object. In the words of Andréas Karandónis, his poetry is "pain and drama metamorphosed into crystalline tears of lyrical joy," for his poetry has a lightness, a joyous elevation, a loss of weight. What he wrote of one of his favorite elements, the sea, is true of his own work: "Whoever takes the sea into his arms / Seems not to suffer from weight." His influence and teachings were not immediately apparent, but he remains among the first though rude exponents of new problems and techniques, a forerunner and a promise.

Andréas Karandónis

Andréas Karandónis was born in Ándros in 1910. In every country, at every period, during every literary movement, such a figure as he appears and raises the question as to the relationship between poet and critic. From 1935 to 1940 and from 1944 to 1945 he edited *Néa Ghrámmata* (*New Letters*), the magazine which was the rallying point for the literary movement of the thirties, that welcomed and encouraged writers in poetry and prose who were breaking new ground, that opened its pages to experiments in surrealism, existentialism, free verse, the prose statement in poetry, the poetic lift in prose, and that for the first time published such poets as Seféris, Elýtis, Sarandáris, Antoníou, Embirícos, Papatsónis, Engonópoulos. At a time when many of these writers were laughed at and derided, Karandónis offered them not only hospitality but also, what was more important, understanding and encouragement. He became their apologist and defender, and has done more than anyone else to explore the field of criticism in a land where no modern methods of aesthetics or appraisal have been formed. Criticism based on organized standards or on such methods as those of the New Criticism in the United States, or on any close analysis of text, does not exist in Greece. Among the first in modern Greece who made of criticism a profession, Karandónis has acquired a firm reputation as an appraiser of prose, but his lasting reputation lies in the field of poetry appreciation. He is not a scholarly critic, nor is he interested in exegesis or in biographical exposition or pedantic analysis. His is the creative imagination at work, presenting and explaining to the public with acumen, force and enthusiasm, often with perspicuity and subtlety, aspects of a writer in such a way that the direction and intention of his work becomes illuminated and understood. Modern Greek writers are not often taught in Greek schools; Karandónis, in consequence, has become a university of modern Greek letters for the generally educated public and student. A cultivated and extremely well-read man, with a wide-ranging and restless intelligence, he offers original and individual observations, reveals semantic correlations, makes fruitful comparisons, and invents felicitous phrases that well up out of an essentially lyrical nature. He may best be compared to such a critic as Louis Untermeyer, as an impressionist appraiser with a sensitivity for the suggestive and apt phrase compatible with a poetic temperament.

For any man who has read so many poets and written so many book reviews in an attempt to elucidate poetry to others, the writing of poems necessarily poses a problem, but it is evident from his verse that Karandónis turned to criticism as a first love and not as a frustrated poet. From the outset he showed himself to be thoroughly at home with traditional forms, and in his first two books published a series of expertly written sonnets. Most of his poetry, however, is written in free verse in which one is aware of a professional acumen at work that knows of the pull of tradition as well as that of innovation, whether in rhythm, in cadence, or in imagery. Karandónis has added his own "sur" to "realism," making use of both worlds, but refusing ultimately to fuse them into the one word and one world of surrealism. In poetry he is a lyrical impressionist controlled by a restless critical understanding that tempers flights of fancy with satire and sarcasm, with point and irony, with common sense. He has written poems in praise of the Aegean, but as a region of refuge and repose, a balsam for the weary mind. He is aware of the pathetic and resigned, as in "Old Horoscopes"; or surrealist suggestivity, as in "A Lady"; of bite and wit, as in the "gay deceiver of women of the third or fourth category" of "A Man." He can even satirize the Apollonian light of Greece as the mechanized and photogenic light dear to tourists. The subtlety of his perception may best be felt in "Availability," for here, with sensitivity and indirection, he indicates that eternal essences, in order to communicate, must make use of whatever is available in specific time or place. His poetry rounds out an integral man in whom the source of inspiration, both in poetry and in prose, lies in the critical imagination.

VI | THE TURNING POINT AND THE SURREALISTS

George Seféris

George Seféris spent the first fourteen years of his life in Smyrna, Turkey, where he was born in 1900. Although in 1914 at the outbreak of the First World War his family settled in Athens, where he completed his high-school studies, he spent his university years at the University of Paris. One year after his return to Athens in 1925, he was appointed to the Royal Greek Ministry of Foreign Affairs. More than any other poet in this anthology, Seféris spent the greater portion of his life abroad, by reason of birth and studies, and by representing his country in various diplomatic posts in Europe, Asia, Africa, and lastly as Ambassador to Great Britain, involved in the fate of nations and that of his own country. It is wandering Greeks such as he, who, in sharing the fate of Odysseus, have the greatest yearning for their own land; who perhaps understand it best after tasting "the bitter bread of exile"; who seek to transform foreign experience within the perspective of their long traditions. Seféris is most Greek when his experiences in Europe and Asia and his involved awareness of the Greek past are related to a nostalgic longing for the homeland in an attempt to define what Greece *is*, under the light of timelessness. "No matter where I travel," he has written in one of his poems, "Greece wounds me still." This is one of the main reasons why Seféris' poetry is at once profoundly Greek and profoundly universal.

Although it has often been indicated that Seféris' first book of poems, *The Turning Point* (1931), was aptly titled because it marked a turning point toward modern modes of Greek poetry, this is only partly true, for all the poems are in some form of meter, and all are rhymed. In their avoidance of rhetoric, however, in their vague symbolism, chaste tone, and restrained demotic diction, they do reveal a modern sensibility nurtured on the French symbolists, particularly on Laforgue's urban orientations and Valéry's striving for a pure poetry within the classical canons of prosody. They presage a cleaner, more metaphysical era. Written primarily in quatrain form, they may be compared in kind to Eliot's poems in quatrain such as "The Hippopotamus" and "Whispers of Immortality" in his second volume, *Poems* (1920). In *The Cistern* (1932), although written in cinquains and in lines comparable to the English pentameter with feminine ending, Seféris experimented extensively with assonantal and half rhymes and announced the leitmotif of his subsequent poetry, that of a dying, a desiccated world, caught in an imagery and symbolism of marble fragments and ancient ruins.

But the true turning point and the wide avenue through which free verse and the restrained tones of modern poetry flowed and spread throughout modern Greek poetry was the publication, in 1935, of Seféris' *Myth of Our History* and Caváfis' collected *Poems*. Seféris is an associative link between Caváfis and Eliot, as he has so perceptively demonstrated in an essay wherein he compares these poets, and in so doing reveals his empathy with both. Caváfis and Seféris belong to the modern metaphysical and symbolist tradition as we have known it in English through Eliot and Pound, although neither is as elliptical as Eliot nor as cryptographic as Pound. Both are subtle, dry, ironic, allusive but not elusive, restrained, implacable enemies of rhetoric, at times didactic. Both use metrical and metaphorical techniques with the slanted irregularity of muted modern cacophony. Both are concerned with disintegration, and in his essay Seféris points out that Caváfis and Eliot warn us "not to be self-satisfied, not to fool ourselves with the belief that our life, our tidy and calculated life, is somehow out of reach of the spectacular and terrible. We are all inhabitants of the 'waste land'—you and I and everybody has some consciousness of evil and catastrophe." Caváfis treats of decadence in historical events and human character with sympathetic detachment, but Seféris in anguish contrasts past glory with modern cultural and ethical corrosion. All three poets have the great gift of being able "to identify the past with the present in a simultaneous moment," as Seféris has written of Caváfis, and to all three appertains Eliot's observation on the English metaphysical poets: that in them there is "a direct sensuous apprehension of thought, or a recreation of thought into feeling."

Seféris' poem "Mythistórima" may perhaps best be translated, from its two component parts, as "Myth of Our History," yet because the word in its totality also means "novel" in Greek, the poem takes on the independent validity of imaginative fiction, history re-created in the mind and emotions of one particular sensibility. As Eliot suggested in his essay on Joyce's *Ulysses*, the mythical method instead of the narrative may be used to expose "a continuous parallel between contemporaneity and antiquity." In these twenty-four short lyrical and dramatic poems may be discerned an Odyssean sensibility drifting amid the broken stones and ruins of the Greek heritage, seeking for its own meaning and that of the world. The protagonist is the poet himself, often identified with Odysseus, hiding in many mirrors, in the many reflections and refractions of his personality as he gazes into the mythological past of his country and her symbols.

There is a physical, acute identification with place—the land enclosed by mountains, the scorched pines, the desire to sink into a kinship with stone, yet surrounded always by the embittering, unexplored, inexhaustible sea with its vast and indifferent serenity. The land is desolate, the riverbeds are dry, there are no wells or springs, the body and love itself become as hollow and stagnant as the empty cisterns. The main references are to the sense of separation, to exiled wandering, to the ache of a Homeric *nóstos*, a desire to return home, to regain the lost paradise of an Ithaca. There is the endless voyaging, symbolized by Odysseus, his companions, and the Argonauts; there is the raging search for Alexander the Great, for "glories buried in the depths of Asia," the drift of the soul on outworn seagoing craft for nonexistent pilgrimages. There is only the reembarking with broken oars, the futile search for water and sleep, the sight not of the soul in the mirror but only of the stranger, the enemy. There is the sense-less shifting of broken stones, the rambling amid fragmented statues and ruined habitations. All of the familiar landmarks are lost, friends have gone never to return, those who remain tire us by not knowing when to die and so releasing us. Even the beloved is unapproachable and inviolate in her sleep, in her separate identity. There is no possibility of communication; no one cares; there are only solitude and silence, the decision to forget and be forgotten. For a while it seems as if there might be some justice to be found on the indestructible road to death, but the final justice is to be forgotten, as the Argonauts were forgotten and buried without name on the strands of some foreign shore, for ultimately all nature, all mankind is indifferent to the fate of the individual man, of Elpenor. The return home finds us broken, with ailing limbs and mouths ravaged by brine and rust. At times, throughout all of Seféris' poetry, there is a momentary glimpse of beauty—a girl plucking a daisy, the multicolored glittering boats tossed in the harbor of some Greek island; always the feeling that the next rise of land may show the breaking sea, the marbles shining in the sun, the almond trees in blossom. But the only assurance is to seek the dark serenity of the dead, who smile with a strange stillness from their timeless abode of serene perfection, symbolized by the still and unprogressing smiles of statues who stand as guardians before dead and past glories. The awaited messenger never comes; the poet holds his marble head in his amputated hands; he is Orestes driven round and round in the struggling arena of life by the dark Furies who, though bored with the eternal cycle of man's fate, are nonetheless relentless and unforgiving. Yet each of these poems, weighed down with hopelessness, exile and despair, is written with such melody and imagery, with such evocative nostalgia, as to give aesthetic value to a life exhausted and desiccated.

If I have lingered long on this early poem, it is because it is the propylaeum to the acropolis and temples of Seféris' subsequent poetry, for all his major themes are here announced, although later given greater depth and extension with maturity of content and technique. Here are the landscapes symbolizing a wasteland of spirit, the dry cisterns, empty wells, heavy stones, ruined marble fragments, inexhaustible sea, the silence in the still center and fury-driven wheel of fate, the betrayal of men and gods, the wandering exile and his nostalgia for return, the descent into the past to learn what the dead have to teach us of living, the evocation of memory as a fluid medium that unites fragmented time into one continuous flow, the alienation and sense of separation in love, the gaping void under golden masks, the obsession with time past and time present. Although his mature poetry shows greater strength and stature, none reveals Seféris so fully or exposes more faithfully the complex nerves that compose the modern Greek temperament.

It is evident from this summation that Seféris and Eliot share a remarkable similarity in theme and imagery. Indeed, Seféris had first read Eliot, including *The Waste Land*, in 1931, and published his translation of this poem in 1936, one year after publishing "Myth of Our History." Even a late poem, "The Thrush," is basically written in the five-part sonata division of *The Waste Land* and *Four Quartets*, and resembles Eliot's elaboration in the "music of ideas." But these are superficial and surface similarities; what should be emphasized is that the vision and techniques of the two poets arise from a surprisingly similar sensibility early nourished in both by a dedication to French symbolist poets. Their differences are equally remarkable and are best discerned in their relationship and approach to tradition. The American poet, lacking tradition, laid siege to the literary and anthropological ramparts of the world as though, by an accumulation of plunder and trophies, he might attain to ancestral modes and mores denied him as a birthright. Seféris, on the contrary, had as birthright one of the richest and longest traditions in the world, so rich, so deep and demanding that it all but overwhelms the creative imagination of modern Greek writers, and is often a burden as well as a privilege and advantage.

One of the main themes in Seféris is the agonized struggle to pass over to that "other" shore, to communicate with the ancestral dead, to compare and contrast, to illuminate and appraise precepts of past glory with the disintegrations and wasteland of modern life. Their contrasting birthrights create a contrast in method and style. Unlike Eliot, whose many literary and pseudo-literary allusions are an attempt to adumbrate a mythology, to find images and touchstones with which to shore up his ruins, Seféris constructed his own personal mythology from the one unit of Greek tradition, heritage, and mythology, especially that of the classical period, and by contrast and comparison with contemporary civilization has bridged the gap of time and made universal statement out of national experience and private emotion. In his later poems Seféris has enriched his classical use of myth by adding new images from lands in which he has wandered, from Jerusalem, Egypt, Africa, and in particular from the ancient and medieval history of Cyprus.

In "The King of Asine," one of his best and most significant poems, the theme is one that has obsessed all poets, that of Shelley's "Ozymandias," or Villon's "Ballad of Old-Time Ladies," with its famous refrain, "Where are the snows of yesteryear?" Nothing remains of the once mighty king of Asine but a gold mask covering a void; his children, as those of all the ancient Greeks, are known to us only as broken statues, his ships are moored in a harbor lost and vanished in the destruction of time, and only the wind drifts in the intervals of his meditation. The relationship of time past and time future to time present has been one of the most obsessive themes in Seféris' poetry in an attempt to break temporal barriers until we may be received "like time without break" in a suspension of time, as in the enmarbled vision in "Engomi," where the poet has a split vision of something transcendental, a motionless dance, an ache for the eternal, a glimpse of the assumption. This is as far as Seféris wishes to go toward a mystical apprehension of phenomena in a land where all "spend a long time dying."

Seféris' themes and preoccupations have remained stubbornly the same, but a progression may be traced in his style and method from the vague and obscure symbolism of his early poetry to the gradual development in the use of myth and symbols which, although still ambiguous, gradually proceed toward greater clarity and precision wherein both contemporary landscape and ancient ruins are sharply delineated, with coordination of message and metaphor, a directness that becomes more subtle than earlier indirect methods. In his mature poetry he is dramatic in style and structure, yet restrained, disdaining rhetoric always, and writing a poetry which, though simple and direct, reverberates with undertones and overtones of elusive meanings and becomes more and more lean in imagery. It is a low-keyed poetry which cannot be declaimed, as in the manner of Yeats or Sikelianós, but is to be whispered (a favorite word of Seféris') as music for the inner ear. In terms of diction and syntax, Seféris believes modern Greek poets have been mistaken in taking Caváfis and Kálvos as models and superimposing on the demotic tongue embellishments from all periods in the formation of the Greek language. In terms of vocabulary he has reacted to Caváfis as Hopkins did to Whitman: he admires, but does the opposite. He has used only those words in the living demotic tongue which have his own touch and weight and has honed them into what perhaps may be the purest and leanest of modern Greek idioms.

Nícolas Cálas

It was Nícolas Cálas, under the pseudonym Nikítas Rándos, who brought the first hints of surrealism to Greece, in *Poems* (1933) and more specifically in four *Notebooks*, broadsheets of single poems, which he published between 1933 and 1936, and a final *Notebook* in 1947. The poems in his book are more or less deliberately constructed, without much emotional depth, revealing a restless and acute imagination that is more intellectual than inspired. Some of the poems, such as "Santoríni," look forward to Elýtis' preoccupations with the Aegean. Perhaps a better indication of his orientation is revealed by the fact that he was among the first to translate Eliot into Greek, publishing, in the same year that saw the publication of his own book, his translation of "Ash Wednesday." Nevertheless, strains of surrealism erupt in his poems in strange and elusive echoes. A year after the publication of his book, Cálas went to Paris, where he lived until 1936, associating closely with André Breton and the surrealist group there. In 1938 he published in Paris, in French, *Foyers d'Incendie*, a Freudian and Marxist interpretation of surrealism. By this time he had become more critically than creatively interested in modern avant-garde movements, migrated to the United States in 1940, and in that same year edited an anthology of surrealist literature for a New Directions Press annual. Soon after, however, Cálas turned his attention primarily to painting, which he considers to be a form of writing, and became one of the foremost art critics in the United States.

Perhaps Cálas' true tendency and talent as poet lie in the conscious control of the subconscious, as evidenced in a series of poems he published in 1964. These are poems written with multi-level puns in a multilingual diction, both of which almost defy translation. In them he satirizes, with irony and sarcasm, with sharpness and acuteness of imagery, the foibles and pretensions of modern-day society as he knew it, curiously enough, as a young man in Athens. His figures take on the comic and exaggerated gestures of cartoons or pop-art caricatures. They are the only intellectual word games, a kind of witty scramble, to be written in Greek with a kind of Alexandrian and Byzantine artifice.

Ardréas Embirícos

Surrealism made its first orthodox appearance in Greece with the poems of Andréas Embirícos, who was born in Braila, Rumania, in 1901. Between 1925 and 1931, when surrealism was in full flower in France, Embirícos lived in Paris and associated closely with André Breton, with surrealist poets and painters, and was analyzed and trained in psychoanalysis by René Laforgue. It will be recalled that Breton published his first surrealist manifesto in 1925, and his second in 1929. When Embirícos returned to Greece in 1932, he lectured on surrealism, set up practice as the first psychoanalyst in Greece, and in 1935 published *Blast Furnace*, prose poems in automatic writing of the purest surrealist cast. Eleven years later he published *Hinterland*, surrealist poems in free verse, and has throughout his life remained true to the main tenets of an inspiration that wells up primarily from the subconscious.

Embirícos' poetry falls naturally into three groups: surrealist prose poems in automatic writing; surrealist poems in free verse; and poems both in prose and in free verse (published in various periodicals since 1962), which, although inspired by the free-flowing imagination of a surrealist mind, are direct in their clarity. Indeed, the line of demarcation between his last poems and the fantastic prose sketches published in his last book, *Amour Amour* (1960), is almost nonexistent. He has manifestly described his original poetic search and revelation in his prologue to *Amour Amour*, as translated by Níkos Stángos and Alan Ross:

"Once, many years ago, while on an excursion to Switzerland, I stopped to admire a huge waterfall which pounded over granite rocks among rich vegetation. During that period, which I could call a period of intense research, forced by an inner necessity that was almost organic, I was trying to find a more immediate and fuller expression in the poems which I then wrote. The sight of the waterfall gave me an idea. As I saw the water falling from high up to continue on its gurgling way, I thought how interesting it would be if I could use, in the sphere of poetic creation, the same process which makes the flowing of water such a rich, fascinating and indisputable reality, instead of describing this flowing or some other phenomenon, event, feeling, or idea on the basis of preconceived and predetermined plan or formula. I wanted, in other words, to weave in my poems all those elements which, whether we want this or not, are precluded from or evade us in traditional poetry. I wanted to include in my poems these elements in such a way that a poem would not merely consist of one or more subjective or objective themes, logically specified and developed within conscious limits, but of any element which would appear in the flux of its becoming regardless of any conventionalized or standardized aesthetic, ethical or logical construction. In this case, I thought, we would have a dynamic and total poem, a self-subsistent poem, a poem-event in place of consecutive presentations of static descriptions of certain events or sentiments, in this or that technique. . . . I would still be searching today if what was for me a shattering confrontation with surrealism had not opened my eyes. From that day on, I can say that almost at once I made out where the road lay and threw myself with enthusiasm and true exaltation in the stream of this historic movement. . . . And so a new world opened up for me, like a sudden bursting into bloom of inexhaustible miracles, a world around me and in me that was unending and immeasurable, a truly magic world to which surrealism has given us once and for all the right keys."

The titles of the prose poems in *Blast Furnace* seem never to announce the theme. Although image and thought follow one another syntactically but without any seeming coherence, some central object or theme, nevertheless, binds them together. "Light on a Whale" is delicately held together on the theme of what a woman is; "Winter Grapes" on that of a girl deprived of her toys and her lover; "Spindle of Nocturnal Repose" on that of the future; "Legendary Sofa" on the image of the river. George Thémelis has correctly pointed out that in each of the poems in

Hinterland lies a magnet around which the images cluster, and this holds true, though to a lesser degree, in these first, automatically written prose poems. This magnet Thémelis finds to be the goddess Libido, and although she may well be the fountainhead from which all of Embirícos' works spring, she undergoes many transformations. Such images as volcanoes, fuses, pyramids, sharks, metros, waterfalls, basins, rain, clefts, trees, lighthouses, canals and ships take on, in their content, a sexual significance and symbolism, yet all, without losing anything of their primitive and procreative power, are sublimated into an exalted praise of life and break down all barriers whether technical, ethical, or aesthetic. Perhaps because Embirícos is a lover and collector of avant-garde painting, his poems are often canvases of surrealist and symbolist worlds of landscape shattered by images that evoke subterranean sources, great cleavages as though a lightning bolt had penetrated into the mouth of a volcano. The poems are informed by a lyrical enthusiasm often of great purity, celebrating the ever-renewing daybreak of the world, the migration toward vast and magical horizons, a joy that surmounts tragedy and sings in a vigorous exaltation of renewal beyond death and decay, whether that of nature or that of man. With the single exception, perhaps, of Míltos Sahtoúris, the surrealist poets in Greece repudiate a Kariotákian pessimism and are heralds of joy and hope. Embirícos may well claim Walt Whitman as the first subconscious surrealist poet in the United States. Although tragically and sympathetically aware of Ginsberg's and Corso's screeching and howling over the degradation of the universe, as in "The Seasons," he trumpet-blasts Shelley's "If Winter comes can Spring be far behind?" and sees in the ram's and the lamb's bleating a sexual impetus in an instinctive urge to survive, an upsurging joy, a pagan-Christian polytheism in which Christ becomes equated with almighty Pan. In the appropriately named "In the Street of the Philhellenes," he juxtaposes a funeral procession with sexual groping in a passing bus and exults in "the glory of the Hellenes, who were the first in this world . . . to make out of the fear of death an erotic urge for life." Embirícos' last poems, although less automatic, less surrealist, are even more inspired by a frenetic, orgiastic, Dionysian ecstasy in an ultimate triumph of life, love, and a lust so cleansed of guilt and ethical distortions that it flows as from the pure source of creation.

Níkos Engonópoulos

Although Embirícos' poems were greeted with ridicule when they first appeared, they did not create as much uproar and satire as the surrealist poems and paintings of Níkos Engonópoulos. Born in Athens in 1910, he was to remain faithful to the tenets of surrealism by expressing in his poetry and painting as much a way of life as an aesthetic. Surrealism in the early Embirícos was almost clinical, liberating, didactic, whereas in Engonópoulos' two first books, *Do Not Speak to the Conductor* (1938) and *The Pianofortes of Silence* (1939), it was explosive, daring and revolutionary, outrageously yoking together the most disparate objects as in obedience to Lautréamont's notorious "beautiful as the chance encounter on a dissecting table of a sewing machine with an umbrella." A girl's hair is likened to cardboard, her mouth to civil war, her neck to red horses, her buttocks to fish glue, her knees to Agamemnon. Opposition to his poetry was intensified by the uncompromising, proud, egocentric and revolutionary stance of the poet himself against all that seemed traditional, an interpretation which Engonópoulos feels to be an almost willful misunderstanding of his purpose. He has a profound sense and love of tradition, but he believes that what was once revolutionary and fertile for one generation becomes reactionary and stifling for another, that traditions and institutions decay. He therefore believes in revolution in the name of tradition.

His surrealist paintings during the same period caused as much outrage as his poems. To his enemies who are poets, he is a better painter than a poet; to his enemies who are painters, he is a better poet than a painter. For Engonópoulos, painting and poetry are the media of a single expression. If he finds himself without colors, he will turn to words, if without words or color, to action. For him, surrealism liberates a man from the slave age, from decaying formal traditions, and makes way for a life and art based on truth and love as opposed to one based on reason and logic. His poems are basically erotic; love for him is a free-flowing, unhampered energy that breaks all bonds even if it must die in its search for fulfillment. His fanatic belief in himself, in the duty of all artists to keep the core of their integrity whole and alive, is uncompromising. He believes that the more personal a work of art, the more universal its significance, for the subconscious, which surrealism tries to reach, reveals the true man and therefore the subterranean man of all ages who is both uniquely himself and at the same time profoundly universal. The fundamental thing for Engonópoulos is the responsible presence of a man in a work of art, which is the expression of loneliness.

As the foremost surrealist painter of Greece, Engonópoulos has had many exhibitions in his country and other lands. He was the sole painter representing Greece, with seventy-four canvases, at the Biennale Exhibition of Fantastic Art, in Venice in 1954. In accord with his attitude, the poems of Engonópoulos are paintings, his paintings are poems. He likes to quote Mallarmé's admonition to Degas, when that painter complained he could not write poetry even though he had many good ideas: "But Degas, poems are not written with ideas, poems are written with words." A painter-poet does not *compose* or draw a structure of ideas. Composition is the shape that colors inadvertently form on a canvas, or that individual words make on a paper in order that they might contribute to the legitimate development of the plane surface of canvas or paper. Words and images are brush strokes of color. Engonópoulos will isolate a single word in a line, often not more important than an article, that its own peculiar mass might be felt. Yet in his early, thoroughly surrealist poems, all disparate images have a central harmony in that they create a coherent atmosphere of their own, and though they well up out of subconscious and subterranean sources, it is clear they flow into the control of a highly conscious will. The language of his bitter lyricism is always simple and immediate; his daring thought and imagery are lean and unadorned. The emotional directness of his basically demotic idiom is often interwoven with words and phrases taken from the purist, which lends to his tone a formality, an aristocratic, almost pedantic scholasticism that is also a part of his personality.

The Second World War, the invasion by Mussolini of Greece on the Albanian frontier, the German-Italian occupation of almost four years shattered the creative dream world of the surrealist poets, flung them into a deadly reality, and made it necessary for many of them to forget their personal concerns, to occupy themselves with communal matters, to speak out clearly in defense of liberty. Engonópoulos fought as a common soldier on the Greek-Albanian-Serbian front and was captured, but after five months of hard labor in road building, he escaped and made his way by foot to Thessaloníki, and then came on to Athens, where he was hidden by Embirícos during the tragic famine of 1941. In the winter of 1942–1943, he wrote *Bolívar*, wherein he abandoned the short brush strokes and dislocated imagery of his former poems, and wrote in long, sweeping, biblical cadences of great clarity, yet with no loss of fantasy. From now on his poetry was to take on a less irrational tone. Both his surrealist poems and *Bolívar*, it is evident, spring out of the same fanatic, fierce, egocentric source which bears many analogies, in temperament and style, to Walt Whitman and the universal egocentricity of *Song of Myself*. Bolívar is not only the liberator of South American democracies but also all Greek heroes of the Greek War of Independence and, in the final analysis, is Engonópoulos himself, for the poet declares with pride, "It is only known that I am your son." Basic to this conception is the poet's belief that the more national a poem the more international its scope. "Bolívar," the poet exclaims with national pride and universal application, "you are as beautiful as a Greek!" But at the center of this and all his other poems stands the poet-painter himself, a true human presence, whether as the red-haired bull in "Picasso" or the beleaguered creator of *Bolívar*.

All Engonópoulos' poems are stage settings in primary colors (he has designed sets and costumes for many plays) where, amid symbols, allegories and the landscapes of classical, Byzantine and contemporary Greece, he is the only protagonist, playing every role, donning many masks, some transparent, some secretive, through which his confessions are uttered, sometimes with the enigmatic riddles of a Sphinx, sometimes with the sure-sighted directness of a hawk falling on its prey. But at times he feels a need to tear off all masks from his face, to speak in his own person, to assure the audience that he and his roles are one and the same person. Art is a confession, a means of bridging the great loneliness of the artist with the outside world. It becomes clear that his constant reference to self, to his trials and tribulations, are all a formal ritual, a stage ceremony, a rich elaboration in which posture, stage acting, stance, dramatic utterance and lyrical effusion are all stylized devices of a universal Noh drama, a spontaneous outpouring that freezes into an elaborate artifice of almost religious intensity. But a shrewd irony prevents inflation; the heroic statue of all Bolívars, he is quite aware, will be torn down by those middle-class burghers for whom the noise of Freedom is too deafening to bear. Engonópoulos knows well that in our crippled times "it has become customary / to murder / the poets," that "art and poetry do not help us to live / art and poetry help us / to die," that poetry is written on the other side "of death / announcements."

Níkos Gátsos

When in 1943, in the darkest hour of the German-Italian occupation, Níkos Gátsos published *Amorghós*, it was violently attacked by the traditionalists as a joke, embraced by the young, and analyzed word by word in an attempt to reach the heart of its mysteries. Never reissued until twenty years later, in 1964, it had in the interim become legendary in the minds of the young, has since been translated four times into English and has become the subject of a doctoral dissertation at an American university. Gátsos, born in a small town of Arcadia in 1911, previously had published only two or three poems in periodicals and he has subsequently published as few. Although the images and meaning of this surrealist poem caused endless controversy, all were agreed that the language and rhythms showed a mastery of the demotic tongue at its purest, deeply rooted in the best tradition of folk song and legend. Of all Greek poets, Gátsos and Seféris are those who use the demotic tongue in its simplest, most uncompromising form, keeping a precarious balance, shifting neither to one extreme nor to the other. In Seféris, idioms, vocabulary and rhythms are more restrained, his emotions more contained, whereas in Gátsos the lyrical fountain wells up in words and images that often war with one another, at times tender, at times harsh. That such a richly endowed poet should forsake his gift has traumatically shocked those to whom the slightest spark of the divine fire is a gift from Prometheus to be nourished, fed and inflamed, and has fascinated all those to whom Rimbaud's renunciation has remained a tragic enigma. Many reasons for Gátsos' silence have been deduced: lack of volition, basic disbelief, a feeling of futility. Gátsos himself insists that the writing of poems comes easily to him, that he could daily grind out what passes for poetry by many of substantial reputation today, and he has often demonstrated his ability to do so on afternoons when he held court, for years, at first on the mezzanine of the pastry shop Piccadilly, or in later years at another confectionary shop, Flóca, surrounded by a bevy of admirers who came for advice or intelligent conversation, or to benefit from one of the best critical minds in Greece today.

Probably Gátsos is the classic example of what happens to the creative mind when it permits theory to supersede practice. He had for years been formulating in theory what a perfect poem should be, without undergoing the humble and humbling trials of advancing theory through constant purgations of experiments in imperfection. In such instances the gap between theory and practice becomes too wide later to be bridged. The untrammeled practice of surrealism permitted Gátsos to write *Amorghós* in one night (though with subsequent revisions) as a sleight-of-hand magical performance, a fanciful game, a labyrinthine interweaving of images, a free-flowing association in which, at one and the same time, he believed and disbelieved, writing the poem almost with insouciance, not permitting it to approach or touch him too closely. His attitude toward his poem has subsequently been as ambiguous, treating it as of little consequence at times, as a sport, and at other times, perhaps impressed by the attention and admiration it has received over the years, solicitous for its welfare and reception. Scorning, therefore, to write what passes for poetry today, he has perversely, some would say, squandered his considerable talent in writing, under commission and for pay, popular lyrics to fit the *bouzoúki* melodies of Mános Hadzidhákis, Míkis Theodhorákis, Stávros Xarhákos, and others. To the writing of these lyrics he has brought the same latent gifts that created *Amorghós*—that is, he has superimposed strange and unusual, almost surrealist images on metrics based on the demotic song. Only occasionally, as in Hadzidhákis's "Mythology" or Xarhákos' "One Noon" has he written the lyrics first, to be set later to music.

The title *Amorghós* has no reference to the Aegean island by that name, nor does its dedication, "To a Green Star," hide some cryptic meaning; both are evocations of unworldly, unattainable beauty. The motto, which states that the interpretation of the world depends relatively on him who observes it, is taken from the philosopher who has most influenced the poet, the Ionian

Heraclitos, whose further dictums—that everything flows and nothing abides, that one cannot step into the same stream twice, that strife is justice because all things come through the compulsions of strife—are the basic metaphysics of the poem. It is the poet's belief, consequently, that the essence of art, and therefore of life, is to be found in its eternal flux and not in its static forms. The poem itself, in its six parts, may be compared to chamber music, to a tender lament in which the traditions of Greek folk ballads and legends were combined for the first time in a strange, arresting and elegiac manner. The logical syntax of the poem, constructed out of relative and subordinate clauses, connected with conjunctions and prepositions, implies a similar logical interrelation of images, but the opposite is the case. The relation of one image to another, in logical and subordinate construction, is illogical in the extreme, fantastic, and at times bewildering. Yet throughout the poem one is teased by the possibility of sense or relevance where relations between seemingly unrelated parts seem gradually to be unraveled, like luminous plateaus slowly rising out of a mist-enshrouded mountain range. What is all-pervasive, on the other hand, is the tone, which is one of gentle melancholy and nostalgia, a reverie of quiet lamentation. Two worlds are juxtaposed and presented, one a world of horror and the other a world of distant dream. There are images of terror and distraction, often taken from the German-Italian occupation, but these are muted, as though battle and murder were being observed behind a thick and rather opaque glass pane. Brushing against this pane, closer and therefore more clearly in view, are symbols and images of hope and joy: the flowering branch of an almond tree, the light of the evening star, swans, cyclamens, the foam-flecked kiss of the sea.

The first and last parts of the poems are written in free verse. Part III, written in quatrains and the classical fifteen-syllable line of demotic song, is nonetheless the most surrealist section with delirious images much like those to be found in a canvas by Hieronymus Bosch: bats eat birds, foliage vomits tears, devils mount dogs. Part IV, in contrast, is written in prose but in cadences which are longer, more undulating than those in the free-verse sections. Part V, slow and ceremonious in movement, is written in the formal diction of the *katharévousa*. The dominant theme of the poem is the presence of evil and destruction in the world, counterpointed with a wistful, compassionate and tentative evocation of hope. The lost, the shipwrecked, will not return until good tokens appear in a devastated world where everything withers away, where the beloved is marked and condemned from childhood, where life will be everywhere the same, for there is no escaping Destiny. These sentiments come to their climax in images and symbols derived from the German-Italian occupation. But there are glimpses of a previous Golden Age, the memory we have of our forefathers, who have bequeathed to us tokens of our immortal origins. Symbols of hope predominate in the prose section, especially that of the water spring that will flow throughout all nature, reviving and refreshing, and that of the "song as yet unknown," inscribed by a human angel on a rock in a remote and legendary mountain and which will one day burst into the world until life will become more fabulous than anyone can possibly conceive. The poet holds in his fingers "the music for a better day," but the tragedy of this particular poet is that he has never written it. Instead, he offers an embroidered cloth for consolation, like that stitched by Greek peasant women, where colors often have no relation to the objects depicted, where orange trees are stitched in hyacinth and a blossoming quince is offered for solace. Like Engonópoulos, Gátsos feels that a tender consolation is the only thing art may offer man in an anguished world.

Odysseus Elýtis

If one were to draw a continuous line from Iráklion in Crete, where Odysseus Elýtis was born in 1911, to Lesbos, from which both his parents derived, then to Athens, where he has spent most of his life, a broad-based triangle would be formed enclosing the entire Aegean area and its luminous islands whose seascape gave him the basic imagery and ethos of his poetry. The young poet turned away from the poetry of the damned, the malaise of Ouránis and Kariotákis, the nostalgia of autumnal landscapes foreign to Greece, and embraced the tenets of surrealism as a liberating force, particularly in its discarding of traditional forms and meters, in its insistence that feeling and intuition have a logic of their own distinct from that of the conscious mind. The poems in his first two books, *Orientations* (1939) and *Sun the*

First (1943), are basically surrealist in inspiration. He never completely accepted, however, a purely uncontrolled onrush of associations, extravagant and far-fetched comparisons, such as may be found in his compatriot surrealists, for equally strong in him, though still latent, was a sense of composition which he admired, even then, in Pindar and the neoclassical constructions of Kálvos. He was immediately hailed as the foremost lyric poet of his generation in whom the deification of youth amid the legendary landscapes and sweet reveries of the Aegean received their apotheosis, the poet of whatever was lovely, carefree, and summery in burgeoning adolescence.

Early childhood receives its accolade in Elýtis' poetry, in his "Child with the skinned knee, / Close-cropped head, dream uncropped / Legs with crossed anchors / Arms of pine, tongue of fish / Small brother of the cloud," who carries the sun between his thighs. The natural destiny of these boys is the "grapehard girls" who are "slowly burning because of the hydrangeas," who are chiseled by the wind's experience. There is Marina of the Rocks, that "Heroine of Iambic," with a taste of storm on her lips, wandering all day long in the hard reverie of stone and sea, the epitome of whatever is untouched and desired. Elýtis created a "countryside of the open heart" and inhabited this dream landscape with metamorphosed boys and girls, mythical maidens with flowing hair and translucent bodies, "seablue to the bone," who held and brought in their hands an innocence as though from another world, making the invisible visible, reshaping objects according to the heart's desire, exposing the secret mystery of common things in an innocence of fused emotions from which the ideal cannot be separated from the real. He entitled his second book *Sun the First* to announce that in Greece the sun is an absolute monarch under whose refulgent gaze objects not only become cleared and cleansed but also dazzle away into a transillumination almost abstract, into an absolution of Justice, an ethical nudity, a physical metaphysics. In no other Greek poet, with the exception of Níkos Kazantzákis, has the sun and its light played such a central role. For Elýtis, the sun as the wellspring of light, not only found its true and absolute position in Greece, but also demands continual sacrifice in order that it may be maintained, the contributions of both the living and the dead. It is the magical sign with which he conjures away evil from the world and in whose purifying light Justice stands created and revealed. The Aegean for Elýtis is not only a geographical space, the triangle in which his own personal subconscious sank its racial roots, but is also a luminous, spiritual space, where the past and present of fragmented Greece promises to repossess an ethical unity. Two poems representative of his early manner are "Body of Summer," in which the abstract is personified by the concrete, and "The Mad Pomegranate Tree," the symbol of whatever with delirious recklessness battles all that is evil and suffocating in the world.

It is true that the over-all effect of Elýtis' early poems is one of hope and radiance, but there are nonetheless indications of dark clouds, inclement weather, wintry skies. Elýtis himself has never been the youths he so nostalgically hymns in his poems, except in wish-fulfillment and the transforming imagination. He felt impelled to describe not what life had deprived him of, but what he would have liked it to be, to transmute the "Melancholy of the Aegean" (the title of one of his poems) into joy out of an ethical need for Platonic idealization. Joy was for him not so much a reality as a vision of paradisiacal perfection. For Elýtis, the poet does not necessarily represent his times, but may heroically oppose them. Nor would it be correct to say that he is a poet of optimism as opposed to a Kariotákian pessimism, for hatred too is a falsification. "Hate is for me," he writes, "superfluous on the road of the sky."

When Mussolini invaded Greece in October of 1940, Elýtis, as a second lieutenant, was among the first to serve in the front-line trenches. Out of his own tragic involvement in the war, out of admiration for his people, who reacted with a beautiful rashness over self-calculation, and out of a desire to praise all Greeks, who throughout their long history have fought oppression and occupation, he wrote, in 1943, his "Heroic and Elegiac Song for the Lost Second Lieutenant of the Albanian Campaign." In this he turned to a poetry of clarity, out of a need to speak of the dreadful events in which he had participated, although with no loss of the fertile imagery surrealism had bequeathed him. The Second Lieutenant of this poem is the boy with the skinned knee now come of age. He is the same sturdy lad who, like Robert Frost's boy climbing birches, had once "defied the peach-tree leaves," or could have been found "scratching the sun on a saddle of two small branches," but who had been called upon, like so many heroes of Greek folk songs, to wrestle with Death on "the marble threshing floor." The brash "gamin of the white cloud" now lies on his scorched battle coat, a bullet hole between his eyebrows, "a small bitter well, fingerprint of fate." At his side, as though amputation were not so much an irrevocable severance of what had been as the promise of growth to come, lies his "half-finished" arm. Turning, as he was more and more to do, to symbols in the rituals of the Greek Orthodox Church, though without belief in its dogmas, Elýtis clothes his lieutenant in the blazing light of an Easter resurrection.

During the next ten years Elýtis said a long and lingering farewell to the enchanted dreams of his youth. Although he now wrote many poems and many essays on aesthetic matters, he discarded most of them, seeing that neither his poetry nor his theories were advancing much beyond his earlier work. In all this period he immersed himself in civic, cultural and critical affairs out of a renewed sense of racial consciousness and communal responsibility, and also traveled much abroad. Time no longer went by "like leaves like pebbles," but became a "frenzied sculptor of men." Then finally, in 1959, he published *Áxion Estí*, and in 1961 *Six and One Remorses for the Sky*. Although published two years later than the former book, the poems in *Remorses* were written between 1953 and 1958, like pendent jewels hung on the longer necklace of the matched precious stones of *Áxion Estí*, the light of the one reflecting and illuminating the light of the other.

All the poems in *Remorses* show the poet in his full maturity, come to terms at long last with the tragic element in the world. These poems are, nevertheless, regrets, pangs of conscience and guilt for the lost azure sky, for the *ouranós* (the word in Greek means "heaven" as well as "sky"), for an atmosphere no longer innocent or pellucid but overcast and polluted, the embattled regions where now not one soldier alone nor armies of men, but all mankind struggles on the field of the universe with eternal antagonists, for the stone gods have leaped out of the metope of the sky, brandishing their lightnings and thunderbolts. "Sleep of the Valiant" is written in two versions. The first thirteen lines of each poem are the same, but the first version has a coda of three, the second of six lines. In both versions the boy with the skinned knee of the Aegean islands, and the Second Lieutenant of the Albanian

Campaign have become the valiant symbols of mankind battling with the mysterious powers of the universe that are no longer oppositions of good and evil but agonizing and mystifying correlations of both. In the first version, the Valiants are depicted in their tragic courage. Vultures swoop down to savor their clay entrails and their blood, but their footfalls are not annulled, and like the earlier lad "drinking the Corinthian sun / Reading the marble ruins," they now "read the world insatiably with eyes forever open." In the coda of the second version, the Valiants wander in an ageless Time, restoring "to things their true names." In a world that had rotted out of ignorance, and where men "inexplicably have committed their dark iniquities," descends Arete, whom Elýtis identifies with excellence of every kind, with Greece, with the Virgin Mary, a girl with a lean, boyish body who performs miracles. She is the apotheosis of all of his Aegean girls, and now comes to the Vast Dark Places and labors to turn darkness into light.

In these poems Elýtis has finally embraced the tragic element in life, acknowledging evil as almost an equal element with good, but still reading the world insatiably with open eyes, with a nostalgia that rises as though from the "crevices in the sleep of the Valiant." And in one of the most moving poems he has written, "The Autopsy," the poet performs a dissection on himself, permitting the knife to penetrate there where "the intention sufficed for the Evil." Pricked by pangs of conscience, burdened with remorse and reconciliation, acknowledging the pollution of the azure sky and the heavens, Elýtis now asserts his lyricism with a grave and somber voice, rifted with strains of the tragic.

The single poems of *Remorses*, nevertheless, are finger exercises in comparison with the symphonic poem written concomitantly, *Áxion Estí* ("Worthy It Is"), a phrase that occurs often in the ritual of the Greek Orthodox Church. Elýtis had long been dreaming of an epico-lyrical poem which would combine within itself the consequences of the contemporary experiences he had undergone, the dangers and evils he had encountered (particularly in the Second World War and its aftermath) but which would, in composition, go beyond the loose structure of "Heroic and Elegiac Song." In the three parts of this book-length poem— "Genesis," "The Passions," and "Gloria"—all his earlier symbols derived from nature are named one by one, lovingly caressed as never before, placed in a sacred and profane hierarchy. "This then is I," he announces, "created for young girls and the islands of the Aegean / lover of the roebuck's leap / and neophyte of the olive trees; / sun-drinker and locust-killer." But also, he laments, "my girls are in mourning, my young men bear weapons." Now his images take on their deepest, their most ethical meaning, for they have become symbols derived from a transfiguration of nature into spiritual essence. In his early poems Elýtis sang of whitewashed courtyards, of whitewashed dawns, of a whitewash that bears all noons on its back, and even of casting whitewash into the horizons to whiten the four walls of his future. Finally, in *Áxion Estí*, he has abstracted lime into the transcendental realm of Ideas when he declares, "Now in whitewash I enclose and entrust / my true Laws." Here the cleansing and purifying essence of whitewash is transported to an ethical level of invisible Platonic *Laws*, to new Commandments by which to live, a new asceticism. "Light years in the sky," he has written in a poem as yet unpublished, "virtue-years in whitewash," as though there exists a measurement for ethical distances comparable to astronomical distances in the heavens. And in the "Gloria" all phenomena in Elýtis' personal mythology, whether good or evil, are embraced in an ecstasy of laudation, their ephemeral elements glorified in verses beginning with a "now," their eternal essences in those beginning with an "aye." As he marches toward a "distant and sinless land," the poet discovers that "it is the hand of Death / that bestows Life," and that, ultimately, although mankind must struggle ceaselessly for freedom and justice, for the triumph of good over evil, life must, nevertheless, be accepted in its total necessity, and he concludes, with sadness and resolution, in a phrase that sums up all his orientation: "WORTHY is the price paid."

I know of no other poem, in either English or Greek, with a comparable complexity of structure. Elýtis found it impossible to attempt a work of great length and spirit, one that would sum up his experience, his growth, his maturity, his awakened conscience, his national identification, without the firm foundation of an initial plan that would give him the assurance and grandeur an epico-lyrical work involves. He found a need to create new forms, new limitations which the poet would arbitrarily impose on himself that the struggle with structure, pattern, order, meter, stanza and thematic counterpointing might create a tension, as in Kálvos, as in Pindar, that would throw out sparks, fire the imagination, deepen thought, and achieve a new freedom in which density of symbol and sound, and a free-flowing association of images, are not caged in, but on the contrary are given greater wings and strength to fly to greater heights. Few better examples may be found of a poet's stubborn ability to grow and change, to reach in some regard a position almost diametrically opposite to that from which he began, and yet to retain integrally the basic component parts which from the beginning informed his personality and his temperament.

Áxion Estí is also a rich treasure house of the Greek language, for Elýtis is aware that he has been "given the Hellenic tongue," that his house, though a humble one, is built "on the sandy shores of Homer." He has kept to a strict demotic base with taste and discretion, but he has also added embellishments from all periods of Greek development, and even coined words of his own. In his entire career he has been primarily interested in the plastic use of language, manipulating words and images in the manner of a painter or a sculptor. Indeed, his own fine watercolors and collages are the mirror reflections of his poems. He has shaken off the tyranny of speech of the common man together with the purified diction of the pseudoeducated, for both, he feels, are strangleholds on the creative spirit. Of all Greek poets, Elýtis has shown a greater capacity for growth both thematically and technically, an ability to compose poems that are a distillation of each stage of his development, of his childhood, his adolescence, and his maturity.

VII | THE SOCIAL POETS

Yánnis Ritsos

The years 1934 and 1935 were significant ones for modern Greek letters. In 1934, Sarandáris published his second book of poems, *Celestial,* and Papatsónis his first, *Selections I.* In January of 1935, Karandónis launched his avant-garde periodical, *New Letters;* in February, Caváfis' *Poems* were published posthumously in Alexandria; in March, Seféris published his *Myth of Our History*, Embirícos his experiments in automatic writing, *Blast Furnace*, Sarandáris his third book, *Stars;* and in November, Elýtis' first poems, influenced by surrealism, appeared in *New Letters*. Amid all this ferment of avant-garde experimentation, Yánnis Rítsos published, in 1934, his first poems of social content in a book belligerently entitled *Tractor*. Although influenced by Palamás' interest in machines and written in traditional meter, stanza and rhyme, they retain some of the sarcastic pessimism of Kariotákis, are harsh, violent, almost barbaric in tone, with such revealing titles as "To Marx," "To the Soviet Union," "To Christ," and with individual portraits and caricatures such as "The Individualist," "The Intellectual," "The Undecided," "Revolutionaries." In the United States and England, during the middle and late thirties, poets also turned to poems of social protest, given intensity by their sympathy with the loyalist cause in the Spanish Civil War and the events that led to the Second World War.

In his early career, Rítsos may be considered to be the heir of Várnalis, whose proletarian books of poems, *The Burning Light* and *Slaves Besieged*, it will be recalled, had been published in 1922 and 1927, during and after the Asia Minor Disaster. Like Várnalis, and like Kazantzákis after him, Rítsos also places Christ among the revolutionary heroes of the world. Born in Monemvasía, the Peloponnesos, in 1909, his heritage was a tragic one, his future a time of trial. Suffering from tuberculosis, the same disease that carried away his mother and elder brother, he lingered for five years in various sanatoriums, and his sister spent several years in the mental hospital where his father died insane. At various periods, under different governments, he was incarcerated for seven years in various detention camps for his left-wing activities and his participation in the Resistance movement during the German-Italian occupation and the civil war that followed. Haunted by death, driven at times to the edge of madness and suicide, Rítsos throughout his life has been upheld by an obstinate faith in poetry as redemption, and in the revolutionary ideal. *Tractor* and his next two books comprise his first period during which his humanitarian poems of social concern and those of rhetorical inspiration ("Ode to Joy," "Ode to Love") were nonetheless written in strict meter and rhyme, most of them in quatrains, couplets, or in the traditional fifteen-syllable line. *Epitáphios,* published in July of 1936, written in the rhymed couplets of the folk *mirolói*, is a long revolutionary lament of a mother over the death of her son killed in a street riot during the breaking of a strike by army and police. When the Metaxás dictatorship came into power the following month, the book was confiscated and burned with others before the columns of the Temple of Olympian Zeus.

As though to announce and repeat the orientation of his second period, ushering in a dichotomy that was to follow him throughout his life, all the titles of Rítsos' next four books are firmly musical: *The Song of My Sister* (1937), *Spring Symphony* (1938), *The Ocean's Musical March* (1940), and *Old Mazurka to the Rhythm of Rain* (1943). In these poems he broke forever from the shackles of meter and rhyme, wrote in free verse of short, staccato lines and, in a riot of color, sound and imagery, turned to themes that express the pain and endeavor of man to overcome his fate, the nostalgia of adolescence, the durability of the Greek landscape. His titles in shorter poems during the same period express now some of the delicacy, nuance and impressionism of a Wallace Stevens or an Odysseus Elýtis: "Rhapsody of Naked Light," "A Glowworm Illuminates the Night," "Small Brother of the Sea Gulls," "Weekend in the Neighborhood of Summer," "Winds in the Western Suburbs." In the last of these books, his free verse took the form of long, undulating lines reminiscent of Walt Whitman's versification, a cadence he has used ever since in the writing of long poems. Although each of these four books consists of one long poem, the various parts are not arranged in a hierarchical or compositional order, for often one section may be interchanged with another without harm to the general structure. They are rather musical movements of various tonalities, speeds or colors in an over-all symphonic arrangement, a rise and fall from one mood to another rather than an arrangement of musical motifs such as may be found, for instance, in Eliot's *Four Quartets*. Perhaps a more fruitful analogy may be found in the poems of John Gould Fletcher.

At about the same time, however, between 1938 and 1941, Rítsos was also writing extremely short free-verse poems which are terse, hard, concrete, objective, imagistic and symbolistic, with laconic titles such as "Duty," "Punishment," "Myth" and "The Hill." All his subsequent poetry was to hover between the two extremes of long and brief poems; in the general total of his many works the poems of average length are few. To fulfill these dual aspects of his nature, Rítsos needs, on the one hand, the long discursive poem in which he can ramble almost to loquacious length, to ruminate, to amplify, to digress, to indulge in mood and musical movement; and, on the other hand, he needs equally the brief, almost epigrammatic poem that is sharp, cryptic and symbolistic, almost surrealistic, like the pebbles he likes to gather from the seashore and on which, following the natural curvature of grains and discolorations, he draws anthropomorphic or abstract designs in indelible ink and sends to friends or keeps on his mantle with his watercolors and oils. In the long poems, he orchestrates primarily with strings and woodwinds; in the short poems he raps out his Morse code with percussions. Trumpets and bugles are sparse or muted, for his general tone is low-keyed, tender in lamentation, lyrical in exultation, smoldering in anger.

The Second World War and the Occupation plunged Rítsos into his third period, wherein the lyrical element deepened into hardness to express the tragedy of those years, the civil war, the heroism of the Resistance. In various detention camps between 1948 and 1953, he wrote his poems on scraps of paper, stuffing them in bottles or tin cans and burying them in the earth, smuggling them out, although he was not to publish anything for seven years. His involvement in personal and communal suffering turned his proletarian poetry away from theoretical themes to those of a more concrete nature, to more humanitarian and less doctrinaire concerns. Like most poets of this nature, Rítsos is an idealist and romanticist, a man who identifies himself in empathy with the suffering of his fellow men, who espouses whatever movement promises best to alleviate mankind's slavery and injustice. He has taken Mayakovsky as example and hero. But the Occupation, the dread slaughter of brother by brother, defeat and detention lengthened his view into one of wider range, until he no longer believed in the limited gains and mirages of the immediate future. "To be without pain," he wrote, "and at the same time to see in its extension what this pain has to offer you for a more essential conquest of life, and, even more, to be able to observe your pain and you yourself." In the image of Chrýsa Papandhréou, Rítsos now has become a gardener who prunes and deforms a tree that it may bear fruit of finer maturity.

With the publication of *Moonlight Sonata* in 1956, Rítsos entered into his fourth period. His long poems become more structural in composition, the esoteric and thematic movements are better planned, the diction is stripped to more naked expression, the idioms are more colloquial, the themes shift from purely humanitarian concerns to existentialist problems of wider range expressed with clarity and precision as though the dark abysses of an inner world have been cleansed in the light of an ultimate certainty. Loneliness, death and decay are now among his basic themes, the dynasty of chance, the tyranny of necessity, the acceptance of the totality of life in all its incomprehensibility. The problem of loneliness, as in *Moonlight Sonata*, is seen in the larger context of decaying civilization, symbolized by the house in which the woman in black unravels her "terrible strength for resignation." This poem bears curious analogies to another Rítsos has never read, Eliot's "Portrait of a Lady," for both express the agonized loneliness, the sense of withering, the confession of an older woman to a younger man against a musical background, that of Chopin in the one and that of Beethoven in the other. Rítsos no longer draws conclusions from a priori standards, philosophical, political, or aesthetic. Although to reach heights of personal inner consciousness, or to lose oneself in larger humanitarian struggles may in some ways alleviate loneliness, these in themselves become a new, though more expansive, solitude. Nor is loneliness absolutely evil, for it may lead to self-inquiry and self-knowledge. Nothing is purely good or bad; serenity may be found in agony, goodness in bitterness, evil itself can discover motives for a better life, and even death becomes addition and not subtraction, for it heightens the sense and value of life. Nothing is lost.

In his later, longer poems, Rítsos perfected the technique of the dramatic monologue, somewhat as in Browning. The poems open with descriptive stage settings; usually two or three persons are involved, but there is no dialogue between them, only the dramatic projection of one mind restlessly exploring an obsession, monologues that strive in vain to become dialogues. These poems are small scenes of introspection from untheatrical plays that have no ending. In all these poems Rítsos hides behind the third person singular, not so much in an attempt to divert personal confession or preoccupation as to penetrate into the heart and mind of others, of existential problems seen from the outside, an endeavor to derive universal spiritual truth from some person, object or scene. This also holds true of his shorter poems, "Testimonies," as he now calls them, with their deep problematical and symbolic character, their esoteric theatricality, their reliance on objects, their sharp depiction of slices of life, their almost surrealistic overtones. Like the couple in "Honest Confrontation," the poet has now confronted the dual aspects of his nature, has stripped and offered himself—but always behind the veil of the third person singular—without proofs, justifications or guarantees, indulging in "the cruel pride of action." And yet, for Rítsos, no amount of whitewash—that healthy, new, classical simplicity of the modern Greeks—can wash away or dare cover up the black widow weeds of a peasant mother in her lamentation.

In his last period Rítsos has returned to classical myth, in such long poems as "Orestes" and "Philoctetes," in which ancient situations are seen to be problematically modern—the struggle of man with his fate, the clash of personal freedom with necessity, the themes of ancient tragedians given an existential projection into modern times. The Greek echo in Rítsos, as in "Ancient Amphitheater," does not imitate or repeat, but continues, to an immeasurable height, "the eternal cry of the dithyramb." Exiled, detained and persecuted once more by the present regime, Rítsos again is discovering new ways of adjusting personal to social tragedy.

Níkos Pappás

Later in his poetry, Níkos Pappás was to look back to the family affluence of his early childhood and youth amid the plains of Thessaly, where he was born, in Tríkala in 1906, as a dream world, a lost paradise, and to inform his descriptive images with the colors of his native region and a lost innocence. His early poetry in the thirties passed from a Kariotákian melancholy and obsession with death and suicide to a symbolistic and pure poetry influenced by Valéry. But whereas the German-Italian occupation and the civil war that followed soon left their mark on all Greek poets, in Pappás they wrought a complete and permanent change toward a poetic and social realism which he has passionately upheld in all his subsequent work. He castigates the disheartenment, the self-tormenting conscience, the confusion of decadence, all poetry that luxuriates in an individual anguish and existential agony in which poets narcissistically lament personal dilemmas at the expense of more humanitarian concerns. He attacks symbolism for its aestheticism and surrealism for its irrelevance.

Although deeply rooted in tradition and its forms, Pappás is impatient with technical dexterity in poetry when artifice and intellectualism make it unavailable to the common man. His poetry is written in the daily demotic tongue of the people, is deliberately unstudied in versification, disheveled and casual, and depends for its effect on passionate expression, original imagery, and social involvement in an attempt to express catholic emotions and give common ideals form. He discards a personal for a communal mythology that he may depict the epical magnitude of common events, the day-to-day tragedies of an Aghlaía Anthemiádhou or an Emmet Till. His mature poetry almost always springs out of actual events, external happenings, real persons and their problems, out of the strength of his daily experiences, until these become transformed by the warmth of his sentiment and concern into universal application. He wishes to write the kind of poetry that armies may carry in their duffel bags, high-school students on their excursions, a poetry that opposes the aloof tricks and elite sensibilities of an Eliot and that walks, lyrically, with Whitman and Mayakovsky (by whom he has been deeply influenced), that converses with the Jims and Murphys and Sergeis of the world, that keeps vigil with the Forrestals and Oppenheimers. Charged with anger at social injustices, his poetry is suffused with tenderness and kindness, with an artless simplicity, a credulity, a naïveté. He wears his heart on his sleeve and is fond of quoting Lautréamont's statement that "poetry is a consolation for mankind." The poet, for Pappás, encompasses all mankind and is a sensitive antenna that is daily receiving the desperate signals of suffering humanity. When a poet does not stand at the side of stumbling man or penetrate into his anguish, then art, for Pappás, has lost its primary function. Poetry must become an organ of absolute and heartfelt communication between men in times of crisis. Sentiment is its aim, sentimentality its precipice.

Ríta Boúmi-Pappás

Ríta Boúmi-Pappás, born on the Cycladic island of Sýros in 1906, shares with her husband, Níkos Pappás, the same beliefs and aesthetic. For her, art must be dedicated to a social purpose and not be degraded simply to psychological therapy for personal problems. Redemption means to lose oneself in mankind's struggle to free itself from suffering, poverty, ignorance, and oppression. Poets may assist by shaping the soul and character of man, by helping him in his intellectual aspirations, guiding him aesthetically on the road to truth, expressing what the common man feels but is unable to express for himself. Thus in one of her earliest poems, "The Oxcart," the monolithic and primitive vehicle becomes a symbol of the groaning peasant as it struggles "to conquer / the dread dynasty of mud," its century-old bones creaking, writing man's destiny for eons with its wheels. Her message and manner is much like that of Edwin Markham's "The Man with the Hoe," whose peasant was "stolid and stunned, a brother to the ox," the "slave of the wheel of labor." Like Markham, Boúmi-Pappás' passionate desire is to "make right the immemorial infamies / Perfidious wrongs, immedicable woes." And yet, as a young woman of twenty-five, she was hailed as a "moderrn Sappho," when her first book of poems appeared, *Songs to Love* (1930), love sonnets in the traditional manner.

At the age of fifteen she had been taken by her wealthy older brother, who had married an Italian, to live in Syracuse, Sicily. As her brother more and more upheld the fascist cause, the young girl found her thoughts turning obsessively to a concern for the poverty and oppression she saw about her, until she became more and more involved in socialism and the proletarian cause. The German-Italian occupation confirmed in her, as in her husband, a revulsion against dictatorship and exploitation. Like her husband, she wrote many poems stemming from events—the Germans' entrance into Athens, the slaughter of hostages in the village of Kalávitra, the torture and execution of martyrs. In "Data for an Identification Card," she calls herself "the enemy of weapons since childhood," and weeps "for the disharmony of world order."

Her poetry reveals an insatiable spirit, thirsty, restless, searching, passionate in its essence. In her book *A Thousand Murdered Girls*, from which "If I Go Out Walking with My Dead Friends" is taken, sixty-five girls, who had been condemned to death for participating in the Resistance during the Civil War of 1947–49, speak one by one of their tragic destiny, much as in monologues of Edgar Lee Masters' *Spoon River Anthology*. Perhaps a more adroit technician than her husband, Boúmi-Pappás nevertheless has the social realist's suspicion of technical devices when they seem to overwhelm content. In "The Juggler" she watches with apprehension a poet's propensity for performing "dangerous acrobatics on the silk rope," fearing that poetry may condescend to become "a game perhaps not quite honest," an exhibition of sleight-of-hand tricks, the metaphysical painting of a mournful charlatan.

Nikiphóros Vrettákos

Of all the poets in this anthology, Nikiphóros Vrettákos, born near Sparta in 1912, is the purest singing voice, Shelley's skylark in a joyous outburst of praise for nature, woman, the innate goodness in the heart of man. The world for him, as for Elýtis, is bathed and cleansed in sun and light. "My lips open," he declares, "and my soul utters light." He hangs a white carnation over his ear, gulps down "three cups of sun," flings the coat of joy over his shoulder as words well up, overflow, and become so entangled with light that he is metamorphosed into "one part voice, two parts light and love and water." Much like the early Edna St. Vincent Millay of "World, world, I cannot get thee close enough," in "God's World," Vrettákos also exclaims, "How beautiful life is, how beautiful the world," with a sincerity that dares to be simple, naïve, obvious. He trusts to the purity of his emotion, the lyrical lilt of his song to give his words an immediacy and quality that may turn them into sentiment and escape sentimentality.

"I am simple in my verses," he confesses, "and even more simple / in my tears." Tears that brim over with joy, or tears that flow because of man's cruelty to man are the two wellsprings of his poetry. As he plucks a flower to give in love, he knows, nevertheless, that there is "a trace of dust even on the white rose," and gazes with horror as that small stain becomes the bullet wound on a young soldier or in his own heart. Since he believes that "the perfect miracle may be found only in man," this great discrepancy between, on the one hand, the physical beauty of nature and the innate goodness in man and, on the other hand, man's inhumanity to man, becomes the battleground that motivates Vrettákos as poet and ethical being.

Vrettákos longs to sing in praise of life as he instinctively *feels* it is or could become, but he is often forced by realities about him to lament life as it is. Half of his poems, therefore, are in spontaneous praise of nature, goodness, woman, all the delicate nuances and ecstasies of simply breathing, walking, conversing, basking under the sun, gazing at dogwood blossoms, listening to the skylark, admiring the orange trees of his native Sparta, gazing on the lectern of the universe as God turns a page, learning to read the stars, becoming part of the "light that undulates / and overflows and rolls through the universe in one / unending ebb tide, uncontainable." The other half are lamentations on man's barbarism, the poisonous outburst of machine guns, the boy with the harmonica who must later become the young warrior, mount the pavement and learn how to play Man. As an involved social being, Vrettákos in his prose and poetry advocates a democratic socialism, a return to basic Christian ethics. As a poet, in line with all lyricists of tender heart and unfractured hope, he feels that "the cleanest thing / in creation, therefore, is not the twilight, / nor the sky reflected in the river, nor / the sun on apple blossoms. It is love." Love as redemption, as resurrection, as an innate force in man, is the power which ultimately will survive and make even evil immaculate. Art for Vrettákos, therefore, must become the expression of love and goodness, because these form the beauty of civilization as a higher ordering of human relations, a kind of divine law, a "brightness of man's soul" which is that radiant element called "the deathlessness of art."

VIII | RELIGIOUS AND EXISTENTIALIST MODES

Although all poets at all times have written of the mystery which is life and the annihilation or salvation which approaches us in death, the poets in this section have made such problems their overwhelming concern. All began initially from some dogmatic acceptance of the Church's teachings, but each has confronted Nietzsche's crushing announcement that God has died, and each has in his own way adapted dogmatic definitions of godhead, from Pendzíkis' full—although, it may be, heretical—affirmation, to Vafópoulos' nihilism and despair. Many poets and theologians in modern times, unable fully to accept the tenets of their Church, especially those pertaining to divinity, are nevertheless as unable to cast free from all dogma and are therefore impelled to write ambiguously in a limbo wherein faith does not rule and disbelief does not conquer or free. Few are those who have cast off all anchorage and tried to sail forth free into an unknown abyss, yet whose course, even though subconsciously, is not to a great degree directed by some impelling rudder of belief. Even the denial of such poets crackles with a tension fired by their need for affirmation inculcated into them since childhood. Unsure of their immortal souls, aware of the absurdity of their existence as a consciousness amid a universe of unconscious objects, condemned to freedom and choice, faced with the dread enigma of death, driven to discover or create their own essence amid loneliness, isolation and estrangement, such poets are forced to come to terms with their existence and to give metaphysical answers, if only to deny the validity of their ideologies. They are all wellsprings of existentialist agony and tension which, after the Second World War, have become the prevailing stance among the younger poets in Greece. Existentialism, in its many forms, has become a view by which to interpret life and death, but has not offered, as surrealism and symbolism did before it, any comparable technique with which to embody such disparate solutions.

Melissánthi

All but one of these poets were born or raised in Thessaloníki, the bastion of Greek Orthodoxy lying in the abstract shadow of Byzantium as Athens lies under the classical serenity of the Parthenon. The exception is Hébe Skandalákis, born in Athens in 1910, and who since her first book of poetry has been writing under the pseudonym of Melissánthi. A lifelong friend of her counterpart in Thessaloníki, Zoë Karélli, Melissánthi's development has progressed from a religious elevation and sense of sin to a metaphysical agony derived from the painful knowledge and consciousness of the self in its separation from reality, and finally to the dread realization that man is living through an existentialist nightmare in a waking dream. The exaltation of her early religious poetry, her hymnal disposition, her prayers and supplications to an Inscrutable God, whose physical presence and concern she desired, were rifted with the sense of sin and guilt, with a longing for and belief in expiation and forgiveness, as in "Atonement," where her soul becomes beautiful in the eyes of angels if not of men. During this period she believed that man could bring the Kingdom of Love to earth, for he carried it within himself, and she sang of love not so much in the relationship between man and woman as in the Great Promise, as in "the assured promise of eternity." Her early poetry, though subliminal, was often concrete, rich in texture, sensuous in images of nature, as in "Autumn," or "The Circle of Hours." Restless, wracked in her beliefs, she often oscillated in her poetry between a delight in the simple, physical presence of nature and a sense of inexhaustible sin, as in "Summer Hours," where she longs for a freshness and innocence wherein "all remain to be named from the Beginning." Words, at least, she felt, had the power to confer reality and existence, for "all that we thought were lost forever / return and in the song are named."

But Melissánthi has always responded, as a suffering being, with sensitive antennae to catastrophic changes in the social, spiritual and psychological world about her. In the middle thirties she suffered a religious crisis and began to realize, helped by a prolonged study of Jung, that her old religious images were in truth "archetypal images" of deep fundamental needs in all mankind, that poetry had become for her a progress in self-revelation, in identity, in an attempt to find integrity. Sin and guilt were transformed now from a religious plane to psychological and metaphysical planes where man is eternally condemned to pay a "ransom for the profane guilt / of *knowing* and *existing*." Anguish, loneliness and the dread presence of death now usurp the agonies of sin and guilt. Consummation, struggle for perfection, purification from error in the individual soul well up in her out of a knowledge of self and the dangerous disguises which the ego assumes to escape accusation. The position of man on earth becomes that of Kafka's accused, who must eternally appear before a court of justice in order to confirm his existence. Forced to defend himself, man must make his presence on earth a reality and not a series of illusions based on falsifications or disguises of reality. Man's fate, his freedom, the meaning of his existence, lie in his hands, and this is his metaphysical agony. Influenced by the Eliot of *Four Quartets,* by Rilke, by Sartre, Melissánthi tried now to understand the contradictions of an individual in his isolation, in his temporal condition in contrast to the timeless. In a late poem, "At the Registrar's," trying vainly to validate her existence in the Registrar's books, she realizes that everything is relative, that uncertainty and doubt are the general conditions of man, that perhaps the Registrar's clerk is right in proclaiming that "the greatest stupidity is trying to find / some sort of security in our world today" where an individual is crushed in the crosscurrents of those coming and those going up and down Jacob's or Saint John's ladder in his search for God or God's surrogate.

Melissánthi's growth in understanding herself and the universe has been punctuated by a series of annihilations as old certainties died within her, one after the other, and she began searching for that vantage point, in the interior space of death, where the world's truths are reversed and inverted, where suspicions and ambiguities pierce into the possibility, even, that we are alive. Looked at from the eyes of death, as in "Alibi," where the old self has died to others, life may take on other meanings, other values. Perhaps the most pervasive of her symbols, one which has undergone several metamorphoses in her poetry, is the barrier, or dam of Silence, which separates man's world of time from the timelessness of the universe. In her early poems, an inscrutable God might occasionally break down this dam to flood the world with His vengeance, but He would also always send the Ark of Hope to float on the inundation. In "The Circle of Hours," day represents the known order that gives us dominion over all things, but when its amber necklace breaks, sleep becomes the transitional ship on which we sail into a timeless world where the dead merge with the "sleepers of Sleep," where everything happens in the same space, where "all things could sometimes have been / or never have been," where we don't know whether we are waiting for our death or our birth. Dawn, and the gradual coming into conscious-ness, into the sense of our "existence," brings us back to the day world where, sensing "the chilling breaths of the Abyss," we build "Cyclopean walls / to shelter us from the Unknown." Death is no longer our companion, but the stranger who lies in ambush; and the Sun, so worshiped and adored by all Greek poets, becomes the Deceiver, luring us with its prism of colors, for "at any moment a chasm / may open in the uncracked expanse of the sky / . . . and from whatever point in the heavens, / the storm may come." Another early poem, "The Land of Silence," contains the germs of this theme, fully developed later in "The Dam of Silence." The poet has died and speaks to us from the other side of the barrier, where sound expires and silence reigns, where the dead scrutinize the living dead through a glass barrier of silence as in Plato's world of shadowy images. Death, from this point of view, is no longer the gateway to another world, but that which gives point, meaning, and ethical value to life.

Melissánthi has long passed from the religious, the mystical, the metaphysical, to the existentialist ambiguity of existence where man at every moment is "on approval" in the double nature of his existence between the real and the imaginary, between the "it is" and the "it is not," an ironic inversion of the real and the unreal, the meaningful and the absurd. Since the living dead do not understand how much the two worlds are intertwined, it becomes difficult for them to distinguish one from the other, what is object and what the mirroring in glass or water. It is in death that all become reflections of life, and not in life, which is a pale reflection of death. But her perspective becomes infinite, for she concludes that "Perhaps another position in space / would be sufficient for the images to become reversed," where the two worlds, faithful reflections of each other, can no longer be told apart. There is a constant flow of images, if not of sound, through the barrier until the black and white divisions of day and night of "The Circle of Hours" blend into an ambiguous light where differences between the two worlds are almost impossible to distinguish, where whether one is alive or dead does not matter.

The sharpening of her problem has given to Melissánthi in her late poetry a sharpening also of expression, a certain dryness of speech, a lessening of the lyrical note, a full use of colloquial speech, phrases, and images. It is as though the more expansive her sense of the ambiguous and the existential has become, the sharper her love of detail, of the homely, of the absurdly real.

Zoë Karélli

In her poem "The Poet," Zoë Karélli, born in Thessaloníki in 1901, invokes the "precious body, material vessel, state of the spirit." The body is for her the beginning and end of existence in space and time; but in seeking to understand her own unique position there, she does not deny the flesh, as mystics do, but delves more deeply into the flesh that she may surpass it. "I touch, therefore I am," she says; but again, "my material tongue speaks / my immaterial speech," because for her the entire universe is contained within her single voice. Her ever vigilant consciousness, therefore, keeps watch on the ambiguous borderland between the material and the immaterial, between the time world of Heraclitean flux and the space world of eternal silence, trying to spy out a realm where space and time are coequal and codeterminate. Unable, after her early years, to accept Christian dogma in relation to original sin, salvation, or a life after death, she felt her spirit stripped to a naked consciousness that struggled in anguish to relate the realm of eternal silence to the material world of speech, that tried to create and impose meaning on phenomena. Her themes became exclusively concerned with the split personality of the person of sensibility tormented to find his integrity and create ties of continuity in a world of spiritual disintegration.

Once the world beyond human existence had been stripped of the dramatis personae and valuations with which Christian Orthodoxy had overbrimmed it, Karélli was confronted, much as in

Melissánthi's "The Dam of Silence," by the "superb / immobility which possesses / perfect Love, and is possessed." Straining her ears to hear "Mysterious and dreadful meanings, whispers from thence," she struggles to make this silence, this feeling for the unheard and unspoken, comprehensible to others, that silence might speak prophetically. Poetry, for Karélli, becomes a tension between silence and speech, between secrecy and honesty. Like Persephone, she must descend to Hades, confront "Silence, unbesiegeable force," and during her brief yearly sojourn on earth invest man with "the justification of his presence," realizing that life is itself a longing for eternity. The poet, his life long, in the decaying flux wherein he temporarily resides, is tormented by his inadequacies, aware that heard melodies are sweet but that those unheard are far sweeter, and must try to bring across, from that almost impenetrable border, intimations of immortality.

A poem, a work of art, as described in "Worker in the Workshops of Time" and in "Adolescent from Anticythera," becomes for Karélli "erotic shapes for whatever exists / within time," the substance and round embracement of time where the materials used—words, paint, marble—are infused with the struggling spirit of the "maker" (the etymological root of "poet"), until one shapes the other. This becomes revealed to her as the presence and essence of being. Man is corrupted into life, but in the bronze adolescent from Anticythera, Karélli sees the "smiling face of incorruption," as in the Greek god in Caváfis' "One of Their Gods" who, taking the form of a youth to indulge in sensual pleasures on earth, wanders in the bystreets of Seleucia with "the joy of incorruption in his eyes." A work of art is reality and magic, the heightening of man's perishable position, a frugal meeting with the absolute, form snatched from eternity, "movement and immobility both / like the balancing of a regal bird."

The poet must now say, "Since I exist, I must speak," and, even more: "my speech is whatever has made me / . . . the cause of my existence." For poets, words become "actual visions," for they insist they can *see* words which, they tell us, "will give us names / and the meaning of our lives." Poetry, for Karélli, is not only an aesthetic receptacle of time, but also the best spiritual medium of modern times with which to understand contemporary man's struggle to give meaning to his existence in a time of the destruction of values. The poet becomes intensely aware of the uniqueness of her position. She feels, first of all, the great loneliness in which a creator must work in a world of silence which surrounds her and which she must strive to bring to speech through the medium of her own, personal, unique individuality. As in Rítsos, poetry for Karélli begins as monologue and strains to become dialogue. She is at once modest before the ineffable and at the same time exalted with a pride that becomes almost an arrogance when she considers the miracles creators can perform, the bronze adolescent which is the work of a sculptor who "loved his life / in a glory both arrogant and modest." The isolation of each self creates loneliness, and such loneliness intensifies the ego. In a time when each individual feels it almost impossible to communicate with another because a common faith, a common myth, is lacking, loneliness becomes intensified, and the poet is forced, both modestly and arrogantly, to usurp the role of prophet, philosopher and evaluator. He becomes one who, by naming conditions, gives them existence and worth.

But, for Karélli, the problem is further heightened by the fact that she is a woman in a world where values have been predominantly masculine. She broods on the semantic fact that the word which denotes our species is the masculine designation "man," and she writes a poem in which the Greek word for "man," *ánthropos*, which is of masculine gender, is preceded by a feminine article. This title can be translated into English, which generally lacks gender-signifying inflections, only as "Man, Feminine Gender." Although Eve may once have been taken out of the side of Adam and, like the feminine moon, may possess only a light reflected from the masculine sun, the violent separation becomes more painful the more a woman strives to form her own identity. Karélli longs to "know the world through myself, / that I may speak my own word," but this increases the sense of solitude and separation, and she realizes that "I must be alone, / I, 'man,' in the feminine gender." The tone of her poetry, in consequence, has neither the resilience of femininity nor the inflexibility of masculinity, but is rather hermaphroditic, combining the passionate turmoil of a feminine sensibility with the tough abstraction of masculine thought.

Karélli's poetry, though often concerned with objects, is almost devoid of imagery, metaphors and tropes, and for its effect depends mostly on the passionate expression of thought, on emotion analyzed. She has taken little from the pure lyric or the folk song or the manner of either, but has turned to the more abstract language of Byzantine hymnology, to a period which tried to make eternity comprehensible by an almost abstract arrangement of stylized tones and compositions. Her words are stripped bare of decoration and sentimentality, and are so often those of philosophical speculation that they take on a rationalistic tone, much as in the poetry of Laura Riding. Yet Karélli loves individual words themselves, as though they were made of flesh, and caresses them with a feminine eroticism. She plays with their sounds almost hypnotically, although not with the full assonantal and consonantal orchestration of a Milton or a Hopkins but limits her orchestral arrangement to a manipulation of like-sounding words, a device taken from Byzantine *tropária* and the artificed rituals of the Greek Orthodox Church. A chance similarity of prefix or suffix may cause her to shift her meaning to denote similarities or antitheses not only in sound but also in etymological and semantic meaning. She shifts the weight of her words, changes their expected place, breaks them in two to reveal contrary sources. This is almost impossible to reproduce in translation, although I have attempted something similar, as embellishment, in the least of her speculative poems, "Matutinal," where I have played throughout between *glittering, glittered, glides, glow, golden-edged, gilded, glorious,* and *gold-glittering.* The approximation would have been closer if this list contained words of similar sound but dissimilar meaning, such as *glacier, glare, glut* or *conglomerate.* Such play on words gives sensuous body to her thought, a feminine coloration to a mind of almost masculine strength.

From her first book on, Karélli has been remarkably consistent in her existentialist attitude. Whatever she has written has been a quest for a way out of man's impasse, for redemption from a feeling that the soul has been ravaged and devastated, that a promise for justice has been broken. For Karélli, a being is contained in the perfect movement of a moment in time until the poet is compelled to "perform" himself with a concentrated intensity and engrossment, seeking for an integrity he knows he will never find. The fate of modern man is to live in a constant but creative doubt—not a passive and enervating doubt, but one that, by indicating the duality of man's struggle, takes on existentialist value. The Greek word for *doubt—amfivolía—*means a "division in two," a "splitting apart," a "wavering between antitheses." Karélli is fond of quoting Unamuno's dictate that "faith which does not doubt is a dead faith." An energetic and creative doubt shakes the spirit but gives it glorious life and strength; it is a movement of the soul, the shock and pulse of spiritual life. It may become a negative strength that annihilates, but it may also create the strength of antithesis to surpass danger. It hovers on the borderline of the seen and the unseen, the concrete and the abstract, extends a life to the breaking point, corrodes it with the unknown, induces silence to speak. The body, by containing in the flux of time both the flesh and the spirit, becomes the well of doubt. The man of doubt lives in a double vision that helps him to illuminate the depths of his being, and this very split in his personality is that which imparts to him his creativity. Doubt is more the prerogative of woman than of man, for woman in giving birth to life also gives birth to death and knows that integrity is only a longed-for illusion, whereas the male longs for immortality, for perfection, and believes them to be attainable. Karélli may say, with Kazantzákis' Odysseus, "Blessed be that hour that gave me birth between two eras!" The absurdity of a life not conscious of itself disgusts Karélli to a point of horror. In "the moment of man's terrible trial," she exalts doubt as the only means by which man may keep alive and intense not only the sense of his existence but also that of his creativity. "All help me," she has written, "when they torment me, that I may be a witness within myself of the eternal." She has felt the burdensome love for an existence as it is tried and tested by the knowledge of death.

Nikos Ghavriíl Pendzíkis

Born in Thessaloníki in 1908, Níkos Ghavriíl Pendzíkis, the younger brother of Zoë Karélli, is a writer and painter of almost eccentric originality, whose creative roots reach deep into the Byzantine past of his Macedonian heritage. His creative works in both fields, like that of Engonópoulos, are two parallel aspects of one vision; furthermore, no clear line of demarcation can be drawn between his poetry and a prose that bears resemblance to that of Sir Thomas Browne or William Butler Yeats, neither of whom he has read. Indeed, perhaps his work in "prose" contains a higher "poetic" content and technique than his two books of poetry, *Images* (1944)—the Greek word *ikónes* also means "icons" and "paintings"—and *Transfer of Relics* (1961). *Images* consists of nine poems between 70 and 150 lines in length, in which the poet explores the problems a man must face in his relationship to other men; a tenth long poem, of 525 lines, concludes that where no personal relationship exists, a mythical one must flourish. By healing the trauma of a girl he loves, the protagonist of the poem discovers that their relationship has been transformed into a non-sexual one, that although they love one another, she will bear the child of another man. In a prereligious ecstasy he concludes that love must teach us to admit into our bodies and souls even the filth of others; that, in Yeats's merciless phrase, "love has pitched his mansion in the place of excrement."

The death of two beloved persons, that of his maternal grandmother in 1943 and his mother in 1958, served to deepen Pendzíkis' religious faith and impelled him, since he has accepted personal immortality and carnal resurrection, to find means by which the living may communicate with the dead. *Transfer of Relics* was written three years after his mother's burial when, according to the custom of the Greek Orthodox Church, the bones of the dead are disinterred and transferred to the family vault or chapel. In the cemetery, the poet apprehends the possibility of communicating with the dead, not through spiritism or the services of mediums, as in Yeats, but through symbols and rifts in the universe from which their presence may be felt; through slight fissures in the earth where a trickle of communication may reach us; through an automobile accident where the crash of the body in temporal time may reveal the land of the dead; through the blind or the crippled, whose disabilities may make them lethally sensitive; through some limited place or space in time—family, friends, groups, neighborhoods—where intimacy creates a phantom language; through the flow in the interchange of opposites, as between summer and winter; through the sea, at whose fluid bosom all earth has suckled, especially if we immerse ourselves into it in the magical or Christian form of the fish; through the graveyards of classical or Byzantine ruins, where we sense the present and the everlasting simultaneously coexisting. These twelve poems in free verse are preceded by a Prologue which declares that the dead are to be approached not through ideas or the mind but only through concrete objects, events, or relationships between men on earth, and are concluded by an Epilogue which states that in this manner the dead permeate all our lives consolingly and keep us "constant company."

Panoplied by a faith his sister lacks, Pendzíkis does not live in a tension of existentialist doubt, in a split of personality between the real and the unreal, but has turned absurdity and nihilism into an acceptance and justification of man's existence. He embraces death as one of the incidents that befall life and the body, and extends the life of man, without fear, beyond death itself. All phenomena, therefore, whether works of man or nature, are simply embodiments of eternity. Turning away from hierarchical or ideological systems which attempt to evaluate things or disembody them into abstract essences, Pendzíkis considers that the most despised, the most trivial, the most contradictory, the smallest particle has a value of its own as one of the countless sacred cells that compose the body of God and without which eternity cannot be evoked. With an obstinate, persistent, and monotonous zeal he places one object against another, taking care to preserve its individual shape, size, weight and tone, like individual grains of sand where "the gravity of the one encounters the gravity of the other." With these he creates the dome of his heavens, attaining thus an ecstasy not of tension nor of harmony but of rhythmic repetition, as in a dervish dance of a million veils that embellish the body of nonexistence. He cuts himself up into a thousand fragments, becomes every detail, that he may abolish loneliness to form the shape of the Other, that the vortex of his egocentricity may be dispersed and scattered like the limbs of Dionysos or Orpheus to become singing heads and resurrected bodies in the flow of time. God, for Pendzíkis, is present but fragmented into the infinite atoms and clusters of atoms (which we call things) that compose the universe. If he could heap enough of them, one on top of the other, he feels, perhaps a glimpse of the invisible might be discerned. Then, like his monk at the fountain, he might see "differently, within nothingness, within the cracked jug, another incontestable reality." Impelled by an almost heretical zeal to affirm (why such zeal, if not heretical?), he molds a life mask, which he knows is also a death mask.

Pendzíkis' "novels"—all are Notes Toward a Supreme Fiction —are crammed with detailed and loving descriptions of animals, flowers, plants, insects, clouds, rocks and all things created by God or man, sometimes depicted with scientific precision, especially in the realm of botany, of which he has a professional knowledge. In his earlier prose such descriptions are lush and extravagant, in his later prose they are more clinical and documentary. He hoards all the passing proofs of his existence—theater or bus tickets, menus, photographs, newspaper clippings, odds and ends—and out of this carton of his life, as in *Knowledge of Things*, picks up item after item at random and relives them in memory. By plucking them out and juxtaposing them by chance, he hopes that the permanent may be caught in the web of the fleeting. For Pendzíkis, chronological time does not exist; he lives only in memory, where time is a fluid continuity, where "the present is the past of memory." He struggles to include meaningless or conflicting details because only in this manner can he hope to discover that his existence, fragmented by daily contradictions, may take on integrity. By immersing himself in the present he hopes, through memory, to attain a sense of the infinite.

Pendzíkis' method is not that of automatic writing, but a concatenation of associations, much like that of Proust's, in which one object with all its penumbrae of outscape and inscape enfolds, as in overlapping circles, other objects and their own unique penumbrae. His is a dream world of delirium, wherein every individual thing, although sharply delineated, is nevertheless laden with the symbols and associations of the subconscious world of dream. "What is to prevent us from creating a dream life?" he asks, and so creates one. The title of another of his "novels" suggests his method—*Architecture of Scattered Life*—for all his writing is a Work in Progress, without plot, composition, logic, order, or any unifying myth. Like Joyce, part of whose *Ulysses* he has translated with the collaboration of others, he seeks to pile detail on detail, symbol over symbol, attributing at times some slight mythical correspondence to his figures. Although in *The Novel of Mrs. Érsi* he did attempt some sort of skeletal frame by superimposing the flux of his amorphousness on a commonplace novel by Yeóryios Dhrosínis, he lacks completely the architectural framework of myth, consistent symbolism, reference and parallelism that distinguish *Ulysses* and give it homogeneity. Unlike the Byzantine prototypes he admires, the scattered mosiacs of his works blur any clear outline of figures.

Like his writings, Pendzíkis' paintings are composed of in-
numerable small daubs of color in a pointillist technique, involving
sometimes fifteen layers of color and ten thousand clear and
separate brush strokes on a small canvas. Again, there is no sense
of organized composition, for the design is simply formed by the
outlines or shapes the colors happen to leave on the canvas, there
where they terminate. Bold and pure primary colors are often
placed side by side, as in the paintings of Seurat, so as to mix
illusorily in the eye. Often the borders around his paintings or
drawings, or within large areas such as those of sea or sky, are
crammed with crabbed writing taken from ecclesiastical texts,
or are simply banal commentaries on everyday occurrences which
may or may not be related to the paintings, traced in a crypto-
graphic script of his own devising in which every letter of the
alphabet may be represented by a dozen or more signs. It is as
though Pendzíkis wants to counter God's own cryptography in
nature with one of his own. Similarly, by far the strongest sense
represented in his "novels" is that of sight, comprising in some of
his books an analogy of seventy-five words to one, and including
references to color as bold and as primitive as those on his scripts
of canvas. The poet Dínos Christianópoulos has suggested that
his actual "poems" stand midway between his paintings and his
fiction.

It is to be expected, of course, that Pendzíkis should show the
same avid insatiability toward words and language as to objects.
Seemingly without regard for harmony or cohesion, his texts are
a dizzying depository of words that are demotic, purist, formal,
colloquial, archaic, modern, medieval, ecclesiastical, obsolete,
scientific—all strung together in an eccentric syntax of his own
devising, twisted into shapes that often go counter to the gram-
matical structure of the Greek language. He is often as deficient of
ear as he is penetrating of sight. By flying beyond convention and
good taste, by concentrating on things and not on rhythms or
cadences or composition, he has evolved an inner style of his own,
a nonstyle that is the man.

Although Pendzíkis embraces the dogmas of his Church, yet
in a delirium of detail he tries to evoke the face of God, to "set
up the mosaic of the universe," as though neither Holy Writ, the
Writings of the Fathers or the Saints, the Byzantine Chroniclers
(all of whom he emulates) have assuaged his loneliness in the

universe. He must erect his own Tower of Babel to reach God, much like the fantastic façade, the botanical frenzy and zoological exuberance of Gaudí's The Expiatory Temple of the Holy Family in Barcelona. Such eccentric worship may eventually be denounced as heresy, although Pendzíkis' deepest desire ultimately is to obtain the benediction of monks and theologians. Nor, with all his immersion in the multiform facets of existence, is he convinced, in his isolation, that he vibrantly exists in the present. The sense of being "absent" runs throughout Greek existentialist literature. His taste buds may tingle with the memory of a food which was almost tasteless when he first ate of it; the feel of the sun on his skin in retrospect might then begin to scorch him, whereas in reality it had simply warmed him; lust may overwhelm him more violently in reflection than the experience itself. For Pendzíkis, poetry is emotion recollected not in tranquillity but in an intensity which, strangely enough, evaporates the sense of being "present." What preoccupies him is the rebirth of the true self from the given self in time and on the road to Death in a cohesion granted only by memory. The ancient Greeks, he is aware, identified the goddess Memory with the goddess Lethe, or Oblivion.

Like Yeats, Pendzíkis has attempted to formulate an almost cabalistic or Pythagorean code of numbers with which he at times might appraise the living and communicate with the dead, assigning qualities, quantities, and various attributes to things. He may take the word 'Αγάπη ("Love"), for instance, and by adding up the numbers of each letter in their alphabetical order ($a = 1, \gamma = 3, a = 1, \pi = 16, \eta = 7$) derive the magical total of 28. The same total is derived from ῎Αννα ("Anna"), mother of the Virgin Mary; and the same total again from the four walls (to each of which he manages to attribute the number 7) of a chamber where the hero of one of his novels is confined. Also reminiscent of Yeats's Straight Path and the Winding Path of the Serpent is his geometrical abstraction from DNA (deoxyribonucleic acid) as the basic design of life: two interlocking spirals (like the revolving gyres and intertwining cones in Yeats's *A Vision*) which together form a straight highway to the heavens. Pendzíkis and Yeats have both evoked their own celestial geometry of the universe, Yeats systematically and Pendzíkis sporadically.

During the great famine and dreadful winter of the German-Italian occupation of 1941, Pendzíkis had a vision of Dante walking the earth in the heavenly mansions of his Lord, proceeding toward God, his destination, in the footsteps of Beatrice, his Revelation. But Pendzíkis also saw himself as the inverted shadow of Dante, the soles of his feet glued to those of Dante's, proceeding underground through earthen obstacles, having for guide a golden and glittering whore, who, he felt, might lead him to a shadowy revelation of God as both reality and shadow, good and evil, Virgin Mother and Holy Harlot. Pendzíkis' creations are like the first Byzantine dome of St. Sophia, built of hollowed-out stones in which the bones of the dead had been inserted that the heavens, which the dome and the Church symbolize, might become a heaven of relics: the Sun as Christ, the Moon as Virgin Mary, and the Stars the bones of the saints, a "primer-book of stars" (in Seféris' phrase) by which the heavens may be read by a mystagogue such as Pendzíkis, the visible text of an invisible author.

George Thémelis

George Thémelis was born on the island of Sámos in 1900, but has lived in Thessaloníki since 1930. Although he published poetry in various periodicals since he was twenty-two, he did not bring out his first book of poems, *Naked Window* (1945), until he was forty-five—that is, when Greece had not yet recovered from the German-Italian occupation and the civil war, and when questions raised by existentialism had fermented and brimmed over. As though to make up for lost time, he then published four books of poetry in about six years. Lyrical in tone, they showed the influence of the ancient Greek tragedians (he has translated Aeschylos and Sophocles), and the French, German and Greek surrealist and symbolist poets. Nevertheless, their lyricism was given density by a complexity of metaphysical thought, and for theme had primarily loneliness, the search for self-knowledge and integrity, the invocation of a lost innocence and paradise, a lost "face," and an inquiry into the meaning of death. He finds his "Hellenic Earth" a cemetery of everlasting ruins with memory of a great tradition that mercilessly exposes the decadence of modern times where the smiles of children are cracked mirrors of remembrance. He invokes in rhapsody the Aegean Sea—once immaculate, azure, pure and unmolested—which awakens every morning amid ancient Greek sculpture and Ionic columns. Now "by time and death made acrid," it nonetheless leans above us like a mother to cleanse the desolation in our veins.

But perhaps Thémelis' central image during this period is that of Odysseus, "The King of Voyages," "the captain with endless eyes," who discovers there is no return home to an era when men, touched by immortality, aspired to be gods; to a time when even death, as he strolled by, scattered his garlands. But now, in a land where, under the hammering sun, contemporary man frets in boredom and a peevish waste of time, "the sea has no ships for us." In "Orchard," the poet, a contemporary Odysseus, returns after an absence of many years to his ancestral home and verifies that he is not the person he once was; that he no longer knows who he is or where he is going; that in digging into the darkness of an existence to find himself, a man encounters a cemetery; that there is no possibility of return either to the innocent self of childhood or the glory of a golden age.

Thémelis now discovers that the true voyage is inward, toward the development of self-knowledge and self-consciousness, toward a discovery of one's true "face." The voyage is not one of return but of rebirth, of metamorphosis, even of the possibility of resurrection. The theme of "absence" begins to haunt the poet, a sense of unreality, a disjunction between self and soul, between man and God, between the individual and the phenomena about him in nature. The past becomes a burdensome memory of glories not to be revisited, the present is every moment of time that falls from the future like ripe fruit and decays until man feels absent from himself and from things. Man feels himself to be moving in a Platonic world of shadows and mirror reflections where nothing seems real, the poet himself a shadow struggling to find his body and soul, the reality of his substance and his essence. But in struggling to form his real self, his integrity, his singularity, his inner world, a man must first understand what "things" are and what relationship they have to the self, to mankind.

In "Flowers Do Not Question," florae exist for Thémelis in their integral entity, in the "province of the completed," where they have "no beginning and no end within the immobility of fulfillment." They are not burdened with consciousness—the one essence that distinguishes man from things—and therefore do not possess "the uncertainty of the probable, the bitterness of the irrevocable." Since they have no wounded recollections, they do not ask man's futile and eternal questions, are not scarred with the nostalgic ache for return, for they are not aware they have ever set out on a long journey. But Thémelis still has a far road to travel before he can believe that man can so truly understand his mysterious existence as to be able to say, "We shall not question: we shall be the answer." In "The Body," where this prophetic statement occurs, man is bored with being man, with his coursing blood, his growing hair, his own face that frightens him, and would rather be a nonconscious thing, like a worm or a root. And yet, with all his doubts and hesitations, his hovering between two worlds, Thémelis deeply knows that everything beyond man lies in a cosmic chaos, that "outside of us things die," that "animals die from anonymity and birds from silence," unless man names them and gives them meaning. "Things," he writes in one of his key essays, "lie outside of me, but they do not exist outside of me. They are elevated in existence according to how they are illuminated by my consciousness. My life is a continuous transaction of self with things. . . . Whatever does not have a relationship or reference to man, whatever is not mirrored in his consciousness, belongs in nature, but does not exist." Although crushed by the weight of things, Thémelis tries to develop a mode of discourse with them, engages with them in a spiritual marriage, embraces them and brings them into his soul, until the identity and relationship of things to self and soul become his overriding concern. Things do not have a fate other than man's fate. When a man dies, they remain motionless, struck by a perfect silence, much as in Book XVII of Kazantzákis' *Odyssey* where things and beings endure in existence only so long as Odysseus keeps playing the flute of his imagination. "Outside of us," Thémelis declares with stricken pride, "begins death's desolation." If amid the phenomena of nature Thémelis is overwhelmed by a feeling of "absence," Pendzíkis is equally overwhelmed by a feeling of "presence." If Thémelis seeks his true "face," Pendzíkis is assured in his egocentricity; Thémelis struggles to relate things to consciousness and an understanding of self; Pendzíkis accepts both himself and things as revelations of God.

In "De Rerum Natura" and "Spaciousness" Thémelis sums up in mysticism the final relationship he finds between self and soul to things or God. Although all things depend for their existence on man seeing and naming them, on caressing and loving them until they mirror man and take on his luminous countenance, Thémelis now realizes that man too is a thing; that things outside us also atavistically remember us and give us our existence; that we too are composed of material elements such as water, phosphorus, iron and iodine. But because our consciousness sets us apart and gives us our mysterious singularity, not only the things of this world, but also planets and stars, even Death, even God, ultimately depend for their existence on the individual or the collective soul of man. "And what sort of thing would God have been" without us? the poet asks. And he answers: "A thing without name and without splendor." "What would Death have been like without us?" Light came into being because man desired it and had need of it, sleep exists because man's eyes yearn for it. And in a final statement, where God and Death are identified as One, Thémelis says, "I desired Him, I had need of Him, and this is why / God exists . . . / I sought Him, and call Him, and Death comes." We are ultimately left with the speculation that from some other, perhaps metaphysical, place in the universe, and there from another point of view than any of those known to man, things may be reversed (as in Melissánthi's late poetry), there may be some other form of "reality" in time, in space or consciousness, other criteria, other measurements, or none at all. As a metaphor of reality, the world may be a single drop of water in which a trillion inhabitants teem in an ocean of Spaciousness.

The poetry of Thémelis, therefore, belongs to an inner space where the soul is the only reality, to a search for an exit toward redeeming heights, a quest for liberation, a way out, an evolution from agony to hope, from death to rebirth and even possibly resurrection, an inner ascent toward more and more self-knowledge, a tunneling from darkness into light. Poetry becomes an existentialist analysis of life and death, a spiritual exercise of things metamorphosed into inner symbols. In one of his essays (for Themélis is also one of the leading appraisers of poetry in Greece) he has written: "Poetry thus becomes a method of self-knowledge, a continuous elevation into the consciousness of the mystical seed of existence, an excavation of the soul, the experiencing of the self by the self, a *modus vivendi*. . . . Amid our inner contradictions, lambencies and confusions, we either find our self, and more clearly, or we lose it. Existence is hazarded in poetry. .. . Every new phase is a clearer expression of the same 'fact,' one step higher."

Themélis' style in the beginning echoed the surrealist and postsymbolist schools, depicting a metaphysical restlessness that resulted in obscurity and density. It was intellectual and fragmentary, with little architectural structure, and it revealed a tendency toward the abstract. His diction is demotic with a mixture of words taken from the purist tongue and Byzantine hymnology so that, as one critic has said, his demotic words take on a purist cast and his purist words a demotic lowering of tone, a mixture peculiarly his own. His later poetry is written in the tone of conversation, with greater simplicity and clarity, although with mystical penumbrae which are not so much contradictions, inconsistencies, or obscurities of conception as they are inherent ambiguities of speculations between the self, the soul, man, things, God and the universe. His lyricism turns inward, becomes subdued and depends not so much on what is heard as on what is overheard. What is impressive, on the whole, in his mature poetry, is the distillation of his thought in statements of simplicity, with few of the decorative aids of metaphor or trope, relying for poetic worth almost solely on the strength and clarity of his perceptions.

G. T. Vafópoulos

Born in 1903 on the Yugoslavian side of the Greek-Yugoslav border, George Vafópoulos was taken to Thessaloníki during the First World War and has lived there ever since. Brought up in childhood beyond Greek borders, struggling with adverse financial conditions in early youth, he discovered that an ingrained disposition for solitude and silence led him to a gradual withdrawal from the more communal aspects of life, and this has colored all his subsequent poetry. His few, deep, personal relationships, therefore, became for him so endearing that the death of his first wife, after a brief marriage of not quite three years, came as a traumatic shock that plunged him further into isolation and preoccupied him with a brooding contemplation of death as a living obsession. Before this time he had already published his first two books, *The Roses of Myrtale* (1931), and *Esther* (1934), a Biblical drama, both written in the traditional meters and imagery of his time, replete with Baudelairean and Kariotákian weariness, steeped in an adoration of classical times within an atmosphere of dream, of which "Return of the Satyrs" is a nostalgic example. Already amid the "shepherds' pipes in the forests of Arcady" a note of skepticism can be discerned and the first premonitions of death and dying.

After the death of his first wife, he published *The Offering* (1938), written in free verse on a demotic base mixed with words from the purist tongue and ecclesiastical ritual. But Vafópoulos was never to deny his love of stanzaic structure and underlying strong metrical beat, and although all his subsequent poetry has been written in free verse, it shows a basic strength of stanzaic composition and a line which never becomes unruly and never becomes sedate but hovers in a nice proportion of pattern and variation. In his wife's death he faced annihilation as an inexorable fact and attempted to resolve its relationship to life and faith. Then, after a silence of ten years, he republished the poem to his wife, with additions, as *The Offering and Songs of Resurrection* (1948), in which we follow the struggle he had undergone in an attempt to find a unity which, in a fatal necessity, might bind concepts of life and death together in some coherent whole. He found it in the very nature of man himself, who, through death, discovers that God dwells within him and not beyond him.

All the poems in *The Floor* (1948) are variations on the theme of death as a purely existentialist problem. In striving to discover which of all the masks of death might best suit him, the poet splits himself in two that he might scrutinize himself and others with as much objectivity as possible, and is the cause in Vafópoulos' poetry of a certain austerity, of a cool self-appraisal and irony. In the black-and-white tiled surface depicted in the title poem, he attempts to step on the white tiles only, with the compulsion of a child stepping only on the dividing cracks in a sidewalk pavement, but finds himself stumbling on black tiles also in a vertigo until distinctions between white and black blur and disappear, between good and evil, day and night, life and death. Faith darkens and vanishes. In his acrobatics on the obscenely "copulating colors," the poet understands that nothing in life is inseparably black and white, but a dizzying contamination of both; that man in vain attempts to construct hierarchical systems of value which may remain unchanged throughout the centuries;

that life is an ever-shifting seismic floor of uncertain design and duration.

Finally, in *The Vast Night and the Window* (1959), Vafópoulos comes to a final resolution wherein death is studied not as a personal loss but under the universal aspect of Time that binds, in an unbreakable unity, love, death, solitude and silence beneath the dome of the Vast Night that encloses the bottomless womb where the destiny of man was first conceived. In "The Mask" he becomes atavistically aware that he is but one in a long concatenation of ancestors. "Monster," he cries out to a forefather, "dragging about you the death of each of my deaths! / Reptile, tightly entwined about the root of time!" He broods now on death in its relationship to timelessness, symbolized by the statues that, in arrested motion, containing within their marble bulk the entire spirits of the artists who created them, have escaped "the swarming itch / of time" and know nothing of "time's crucifixion," for in their own pasts and those of the artists, "death holds time in a narcotic trance."

Vafópoulos now becomes so obsessed with the problem of time that he is impelled to mock himself and all other poets so preoccupied, for the study of time has become "too much the fashion," and indeed "to the accompaniment / of those famous *Four Quartets*." Self-scrutiny and self-irony are never absent from his poetry. An innate skepticism never permits him easy solutions or ready embracements. Men, in their element of air, unlike fish in their element of water where time for them does not exist, are ground to a pulp in the mangle of time. A fish for Vafópoulos is not the Christian symbol it is for Pendzíkis, and its immersion does not connote baptism. The window, both barrier and entry to the outer world, now becomes climactic in its suggestivity. It becomes the sentry box in which the poet, the desperate man of his age, seeks shelter and perspective, and from whose lookout he may study "the two faces on the coin of time," day and night, life and death. Primarily, as in "The Night," the window looks out on the specters of the vast night, on sin, love, duty and the eternal verities. What can there be, the poet is asked in "Dead Youth," beyond "the translucent song of joy?" He answers, "The vast night, silence, and all solitude." As in "The Frontier," only saints and rocks can pass borders "far beyond time / far beyond silence, far beyond all solitude."

But man is a living concatenation, like a growing tree, and not like a petrified forest. In his last book, *Death Songs and Satires* (1966), Vafópoulos deals with the same themes, but now his irony has turned to satire, as in "Admonitions" and "The Mikado and the Window." The Muses have sold out to the crass modern world. After the bombing of Hiroshima, the Emperor of Japan dons "a very smart suit of American cut," directs that the Samurai's gold-trimmed swords be placed in showcases as "best suited for works of art," and orders a haiku contest on the view from his window, which now faces toward the West. Thus, in the face of the dread problems of our age, Vafópoulos saves his sanity by an irony and a satire that are directed as much against himself as against others. Time, he concludes in a coda worthy of Wallace Stevens, "Time is a pretext for poems. Or / Time is a target to be shot down. Or / Time is a newspaper in Paris." Vafópoulos' attempt at synthesis, through a variety of personal myths, symbols and existentialist confrontations has come to a close in a kind of metaphysical anthropology.

IX | A FEW OBSERVATIONS

To sum up in depth, to make a comparative study of themes and variations, of similarities and differences amid modern Greek poets and their poetry is not within the scope of this introductory essay, but a few general observations that almost obtrude into attention when one has translated so many poets in the course of many years may serve as bell buoys in an as yet uncharted sea. Foreign readers of modern Greek poetry in translation, no matter in what language, are inevitably drawn to those poems that utilize classical myths and motifs and which they recognize as assuring guideposts familiar to them from similar adaptations in their own literatures. Yet these readers immediately sense a vast difference in the use of such myths and motifs by their own and Greek writers. Their authors have come into the Greek tradition by conscious education and application, by an attempt, in the Western world at least, to touch deep sources which have permeated their civilizations. Poets, of which Eliot and Pound are the most obvious examples for the English-speaking world, use classical myth with great sophistication and dexterity, but as elaborate attainments mixed with borrowings from many other traditions. Although their poems display a rich foliage of fruit and flowers in a many-branched tree, it seems in danger of toppling because the plant is not deeply rooted. The difference is that between tradition attained by application and education and that suckled through the bloodstream by racial memory in an indigenous environment of landscape and inscape.

Foreign writers, of course, have their own living heritage and roots by means of which they may speak with authenticity, but so pervasive have Greek myths and symbols become throughout the Western world that almost all writers have felt impelled, at some time or another, to adapt myths which have become a concrete and universal language not only for one nation but also for basic obsessions of the human race. Just as the dreams of an individual express in symbolic and transmuted form his latent desires, frustrations, fears or hopes, so are the myths of a nation an entire people's dreams in that they express similar motifs on a racial elevation. Such a distinction between the use of classical Greek myth by foreign and native writers would be meaningless if it were not universal in foreign lands, and if the Greek writer himself had no immediate and direct access to generative sources denied to other authors.

At a superficial glance, it might be expected that so many centuries of occupation and infiltration of foreign populations might have uprooted all continuous connection with the past and its heritage, but on closer view it might be argued that such seizure served the more effectively to shut off alien influences of a more penetrating and cultural kind and to isolate Greece and its common folk from political, cultural, religious and economic upheavals prevalent in the world outside. Greece was denied its Renaissance at a time when other European countries were flourishing with theirs, but on the other hand it preserved an integrity, though narrow, which made up in depth what it lacked in breadth. This emphasis was to some extent redressed by the infiltration of educated Greeks in the governmental and educational recesses of the conquering bodies. Unaffected, therefore, by the many distracting currents of a swiftly changing world beyond their boundaries, the Greek shepherd herded his sheep amid the

Cyclopean walls of Tiryns and Mycenae (worn to a smooth polish by the brushing of centuries of sheeps' wool); the Greek farmer casually placed on his mantle bits of pottery and fragments of statues he had plowed up in his field, or imbedded into the wall of his humble hut classical torsos or Byzantine inscriptions; the Greek fishermen, amid dolphins that once carried poets on their backs, caught in their nets fishes which peddlers in the streets of Piraeus hawked with their ancient and hallowed names. Although the common people of Greece had long lost almost all of their intellectual and conscious connections with the past, they sank deeper into their ancestral soil, sea and language, and in their isolation were subconsciously infused and pervaded by voices, roots, traditions, rituals, songs and ceremonies which had become the substance and essence of their blood and bones. They could not define or explain the relevance or significance of their emotions or their acts, but in dancing, singing, speaking, building, or in their almost mystical identification with rock, sea and sky, they *were* what they could not analyze. A poem must not mean, but be.

The architectural lines of ancient Greece are not to be found in the few (fortunately) imitative miniatures in Greece today, nor in the bastard Mediterranean buildings that make of Athens today a monotonous commonplace, but in the simple lines and proportions of peasant homes in such islands as Mýkonos, Khíos, or Skýros. The Pyrrhic dances are still to be seen in living transformation any evening in a Greek taverna when a worker rises to tread the intricate steps of the *zeïbékiko;* the Lydian and Doric modes are still to be heard in the modern strains to which he moves; pagan ritual and symbol are still worshiped in the liturgies of the Greek Orthodox Church; and the most genuine echoes of the ancient Greek language itself are not to be heard in the purist revival but in the vulgar tongue of goatherd and commoner whose mountain or city ballads continue Homeric traditions and motifs. The urban Greek poet, conscious of the fructifying nature of such demotic sources, makes periodic visits to his rural birthplace or ancestral village to keep in touch with the ground roots of his common heritage. Greek traditions flow like underground currents through Homeric, classical, Byzantine, medieval and modern times, sometimes murmuring and subdued, sometimes jetting to the surface, finding an outlet in folk ballads during the four hundred years of the Ottoman occupation, and branching into many fertilizing and irrigating streams after the Greek War of Independence.

Like the ancients, the modern Greeks do not consciously separate the self from the state, and if at times, influenced by a more extreme form of European individualism, they lose themselves in introspection and a preoccupation with self, the German-Italian occupation and its hardships of almost four years brought to most poets a sense of civic responsibility, a need to purify personal into national crises and to speak out, at first under a veiled symbolism, in order to circumvent censorship, and finally with clarity and courage. Among the best poems in this anthology are those written under the stress and purification of the occupation and after: Seféris' poems written in exile from his government, Sikelianós' Akritan poems circulated clandestinely by hand, Elýtis' "Heroic and Elegaic Song" and *Áxion Estí*, Engonópoulos' "Bolívar," Rítsos' "Romiosíni," Gátsos' "Amorghós," Panayotópoulos' "Eumenides."

It is indeed impressive to see how the racial Greek temperament has kept such an astonishing integrity throughout four thousand years of development and how it still shows qualities of clarity, precision and realism, although tempered with ideality and counterbalanced with romantic strains. Any overromantic manifestation may also be taken to be an indigenous expression of the race as the inevitable reaction to predominant Doric starkness, whether once found in Euripides' *The Bacchae*, the Orphic and Eleusinian mysteries, Sikelianós' rapturous "The Supreme Lesson," Kazantzákis' picaresque *Odyssey*, or in surrealist poets such as Embirícos and Engonópoulos. The Western world has made Greek myth part of its culture, but only the Greek himself, of whatever time, may use it with validity, not as the trappings of an outmoded religion, but as symbols still alive in the memory and emotions of the people. The Greek gods play a familiar role in modern Greek poetry, but it is the heroes and heroines of ancient days, taken from both history and literature, that still live on more vividly in the bloodstream of the Greek race. After Sikelianós had fainted at a gathering one evening, and remained unconscious for ten minutes, his anxious friends were astonished (and delighted) to hear him exclaim rapturously, on awakening, that he had spent an eternity of time conversing with Prometheus.

Although I have consciously tried, primarily with the aid of the poets themselves, to select their best or most representative work, I do not know myself how much I may have been subconsciously influenced by a predilection to choose poems based on classical mythology. I may have gone to the opposite extreme, for I do know that I have deliberately discarded an abundance of poems of this nature that might more critically, if not more poetically, have illustrated this theme. Nevertheless, although not selected with this purpose in mind, many poems remain to make the reader aware how pervasively and persuasively, either directly or indirectly, such myths and symbols are still part of the natural equipment of Greek poets.

Of all heroines, Helen of Sparta, and of all heroes, Odysseus, are by far the most prevalently living. A few poets, such as Papatsónis in "A Monday of the Year" or more specifically in "Beata Beatrix," may turn to Dante's Lady as the spiritual symbol of unattainable grace and beauty, but Helen is for most Greeks still the physical image of whatever has touched phenomena with ineffable desire, all beauty worth fighting for in a devastated world. Even in his "Helen," Seféris does not question whether she was worth the sacrifice of life and limb, but rather inquires ironically into the nature of illusion, of the deceit of men and gods. If Helen is the unattainable physical ideal, Odysseus is the hero with whom most Greeks identify, primarily because he is the most complex and contradictory of all heroes, containing within his temperament ample latitude for antithetical interpretations, a man of many masks as of many turns. He is the essence of *nóstos* for the often exiled Greek, of nostalgic return to his native land, although he may find, as in Caváfis' "Ithaca," or Kazantzákis' epic, that his voyages themselves have been his native land. As in Thémelis' "The Orchard," he may discover that a true return is impossible, for in the interim both place and persons have irrevocably altered. He may turn into a vague sensibility of refined emotions wandering amid the broken ruins of past and present civilization, seeking for meanings in the modern wasteland, as in Seféris' "Myth of Our History," or he can become the swashbuckling hero of Kazantzákis' *Odyssey* slowly metamorphosed into a prophet-saint and ascetic. At a time when it was agreed among critics of literature that no long narrative poem based on myth was possible, Kazantzákis summed up much that is still instinctively living of Odysseus in the Greek temperament and wrote his epic.

Symbols taken from the Renaissance literature of European nations have been few in modern Greek poetry. Chief among these have been borrowings from the figure and poetry of Dante, as Sikelianós' "The Mother of Dante," or throughout the poetry of Papatsónis. More pervading have been Near East, Oriental and African colorations, as in the poetry of Caváfis, Báras, Kazantzákis, Panayotópoulos, Antoníou and Kavadhías. If Engonópoulos turns to Bolívar as the symbol of the Liberator, it is to claim him for his own country and proclaim him as beautiful as a Greek. Such references are familiar to Western readers, but they may be surprised to note the prevalence of ritual, ceremony, image and ethos taken from a civilization vague in their minds: that of the Byzantine Empire and its still living heir, the Greek Orthodox Church. In some form or another, whether as belief, symbol, image, or artifice, the Byzantine Church has deeply influenced modern Greek literature and painting. Its hymnology and ecclesiastical texts can be traced in the poetry of Sikelianós, Caváfis, Thémelis, Pendzíkis, Karélli, Papatsónis, and particularly in the structure, diction, and rhythms of Elýtis' *Áxion Estí*. Caváfis probes into the clash between pagan and Christian cultures in "Myres: Alexandria, A.D. 340" and in "On the Outskirts of Antioch." The sense of sin or religious guilt in the Greek temperament is rare, as in Melissánthi's "Atonement," or Papatsónis' "Before the Advent," "To a Young Girl Brought Up in a Nunnery," or "The Stone." Less rare is a mysticism that has little relation to the frenzy of Saint Theresa or the psychological insight of Saint John of the Cross, but is a natural phenomenon, as in Mátsas' mysticism of the senses, an extension of the mystery that is nature, an identification with the rhythms of the physical universe, as we find it in the Dionysian ecstasy of Sikelianós' poems or the more harmonious numbers of Papatsónis. Sikelianós faces the abyss in rapture, in a surrender that is neither dogmatically religious or mystical, but is rather an identification that compensates for the loss of identity. For Thémelis the abyss is the masks we have been given to wear of life, death, or God, as man creates them out of his need for self-knowledge, with but a tenuous reference to another possible reality beyond man's consciousness. Melissánthi's and Karélli's abyss is an ultimate Silence, of which our world is a noisy and distorted reverberation, but whereas Melissánthi strives to awaken out of an existential nightmare, Karélli revels in a creative doubt that imparts to man's existence a desired intensity. Papatsónis, with sophisticated piety and devotion, prepares the soul to receive revelations of an ordered and harmonious universe, and in the hour of corruption says "Yes!" to an abyss which, although unfathomable, is neither obliterating nor cruel but the abode of an Unseen Wisdom reflected on earth in such symbolic divisions as the Canonical Hours or the rituals of the Orthodox and Catholic churches. For most Greek poets, the soul—or the spirit—has no distinct reality apart from the body but is rather a more refined aspect of the flesh, the flame of a burning candle that may, for an eternal moment, leap disembodied into the air. For Kazantzákis there is no consolation; the abyss is a devouring maw that annihilates all personal existence; man's glory is to affirm life in the teeth of death, to help nature or God attain in their evolution more and more refinement of spirit, to build and create as well as he can over a bottomless gulf which he knows will one day swallow up all his endeavors.

All these poets have to some degree revised, adapted or re-created what was for them a deeply moving religious experience in their early adolescence, and most often in the language, imagery and symbolism originally given them by their faith, even though, for some, these are utilized as implements of denial and not of affirmation. For other poets, such as Mátsas and Seféris, the abyss is not probed with Christian terminology but with the more primordial concepts of Fate and Necessity. For Seféris the abyss is simply the unfathomable void that remains after the face has disintegrated under the golden mask of life or art. The metaphysical agony of such a poet arises not from an attempt to come to terms with anything beyond life but from the effect of the void on transitory life and its futilities, on "the golden covering of our existence." Under the ancient deceit of the gods, under the bored and indifferent eyes of the Eumenides, man is driven round and round in a futile race that has no ending. For Melissánthi and Karélli, Silence is the Word beyond the veil of phenomena which must, though awkwardly, be translated into human speech; but for Seféris it is the pervading silence of snows, a silver cup into which moments fall, a skin that constricts the spirit, a language not to be decoded into human terms but a state of existence where all words end, a terminal of the spirit. Therefore Séféris is sparse and lean in his diction, striving for the purity of silence; therefore Kazantzákis is rhetorical and effusive in multiple modes of speech, erecting barriers he knows will one day topple into an unutterable stillness, the still center of the whirling wheel. The rest is silence.

For most Greek poets, the dead are not spirits of friends or relatives to be summoned (these, as in Ouránis, Vafópoulos and Pendzíkis, may be given a posthumous life only in the memory of the living), but the great ancestors of the race (and in Kazantzákis, of all races) who periodically must be visited in moments of crisis, as by Odysseus in the depths of Hades, that out of their accumulated wisdom and historical insight they might guide us in our "contemporary sorrow." For many Greek poets the dead are best symbolized by the ancient statues which in their immobility and eternal presence about us suggest something of the relative perfectibility of art and are a nostalgic evocation of eternity. In Greece, the poets walk not so much in a forest of trees as in one of statues, whose enigmatic smiles seem to hide from them an inscrutable knowledge of life once known and long forgotten, never again to be revealed. Amid this forest of statuary, the Greek poet is preoccupied with the sense of "absence" and of "presence," with the relationship between the living and the dead and the living dead. If the dead for the Greek poets are a living reality, Death himself, Charon, is not so much an abstract negation to be apprehended in metaphysical or existential nets as he is a physical enemy, only slightly more powerful than man, to be confronted on the marble threshing floor. The realistic Greek knows that he will eventually be conquered, but not ignominiously; what matters in life is not the goal reached but the voyage toward that goal, not freedom attained but the struggle for freedom. What matters is the quality of the battle, the trophies won, the loot plundered, the squandering of all energy and imagination in the battle until, when death finally conquers, he will find nothing to take but "trampled fires, embers, ash and fleshly dross." It is Death which forces us to evaluate life, that shocks us into an awareness of its fleeting worth and beauty. For Vafópoulos in "Taste of Death," as for Kazantzákis, Death is our own body, our twin image, our reflection in the mirror, our flesh and blood, our minds and our imaginations. Although the individual may vanish forever and his species may be annihilated, some find, if not consolation, at least an exaltation in the knowledge that life and death, beyond individual consciousness, beyond the survival of any species, lose their contrary identities as seen not from the vantage point of time as comprehended by the finite human mind, but by some other inhuman awareness where all things flow in an amoral and incomprehensible resolution.

Just as Hades and the Elysian fields were vague, ghostly realms for the Greeks—even, it seems, in their Orphic or Eleusinian mysteries—so Heaven and Hell for the modern Greeks are imprecise kingdoms for which Byzantine iconography has at times given concrete images less as revelation and more as a mosaic or mural façade that rivets the attention on artifice and ritual rather than on indications of salvation or punishment. Death and the dead for the Greeks are primarily continuous experiences in life rather than portals to immortality or damnation. But basically, it is life itself, the complicated, labyrinthine, and contradictory experience of struggling and creating that has most held the Greek poet's attention. Although he is therefore often impelled to depict whatever threatens the vibrancy of the living experience itself, and is rarely driven to suicide or despair, what characterizes him more profoundly is his intense embrace of all phenomena, physical or metaphysical. In this he is helped by the beauty of his physical surroundings, his endless mainland and island coastlines, the pure classical outline of bare rock silhouetted against a clarity of azure sky and sea, the lack of Gothic shadow, the absence of chiaroscuro, unless these are imported from more northerly regions. Azure is the predominant color by far to be encountered throughout Greek poetry, a dazzling dome of blue that encloses a limited repertoire of beloved natural objects: stone, rock, sea, olive or cypress trees, sea shells, sea gulls and nightingales. The Greek poet is as aware as any tourist of the pellucid quality of his sky. When in "I Sing the Wrath" Papatsónis seeks for an image of Greece that must be protected from the invasion of barbarian Italians during the occupation, he speaks of Athena's shield, which will protect "the Sun of Greece / that it may never alter or darken, never be deprived, / even in the slightest, of its ancient god-born Essence." Light and the sun are personified and glorified not only in Elýtis, Kazantzákis, Vrettákos, Mátsas, Sikelianós, but in almost all Greek poets, and ultimately become much more than physical and sovereign powers. They become a "god-born Es-

sence," symbol of all that through intensity of natural fire and
spiritual light impart an almost ethical meaning to the universe,
a whitewash of cleansing sublimity, a purification of absolute
noons. Many have felt that in the dazzling sun of Greece the
psychological dark labyrinths of the mind are penetrated and
flooded with light, that in this merciless exposure one is led not to
self-exploitation but to self-exploration under the glare of Neces-
sity, that to "Know Thyself" is for all Greeks, from ancient into
modern times, the only preoccupation worthy of an individual.
Beneath the blazing sun of Greece there is a sensuous acceptance
of the body without remorse or guilt. It is the rare poet, like
Caváfis, who prefers to draw the curtains, to confine himself in a
room of introspection only, to dissociate himself from nature, to
prefer artificial to real flowers. The window, most often un-
shuttered, is one of the predominant images in modern Greek
poetry, an aperture that looks out on courtyard and the world
and that permits the artist to adjust a frame, whether in the mind
or in the sight, around the disruption and chaos outside and to
arrange a composition of some depth and perspective. Rítsos' *The
Window*, Thémelis' *The Naked Window*, Vafópoulos' *The Vast
Night and the Window*, and Panayotópoulos' *The World's Win-
dow* are only a few book titles that indicate the modern Greek
poet's need for a lookout from which he might keep his vigilance
acute.

In a land which has produced so many masterpieces in archi-
tecture, sculpture and literature, the Greek creative temperament
has constantly to struggle against the crushing precedents set him
by his ancestors. For some, the Parthenon is not so much a symbol
of their glorious past as it is an overbearing weight that suffocates
inspiration and stunts expression. In comparison with Homer and
the ancient dramatic and lyric poets, what can the modern Greek
poet hope to attain? For some, such as Gátsos, the suffocation may
become entire and lead to abnegation and silence; for others,
such as Kazantzákis, the challenge must be confronted head on
with the reckless courage of daring to write a sequel—three times
the size of the original!—to one of the most prestigious master-
pieces of world literature. The invocation of the Muse in the
grand manner, as in Prevelákis or Sikelianós, is rare. For the
majority, the confrontations lead to a ceaseless inquiry into the
nature of art, its difficulties and occasional revelations. For Caváfis,

as in "The First Step," to have reached even the lowest level on the ascending staircase of poetry is sufficient attainment in itself; in "Darius" his poet frets for fear the disruptions of war may impede him from finishing a poem in which he must decide how another conqueror in a time past must have acted or felt. Seféris wishes for nothing more than to strip away all golden embellishment from the mask of poetry, to be granted the grace of speaking simply. Kazantzákis and Pendzíkis pile one adjective, image, or object on top of another as though by battery and assault they might breach the gates of silence. For Papatsónis the construction and polishing of a poem is a means of self-scrutiny, of self-discovery and self-improvement. Antoníou faces a terrifying blank paper under a "bruised necessity," until the cold imagination catches fire and the poem rises out of the flames that create it "unalterably serene in the triumph of our eternity." Rítsos knows of "the metal's endurance under the useful hammer," that from the formless we must pass toward form, that the poet is "Almost a Conjurer," a sleight-of-hand artisan. Even such a social-realist poet as Boúmi-Pappás admires the "dangerous acrobatics" with which the poet-juggler must contend. All modern Greek poets, whether consciously or subconsciously, in the formulation of their aesthetics, their views of self and the world, must sooner or later come to terms with their glorious but burdensome heritage in their struggle to create an identity in their own epoch without betraying their past.

None of these observations are to be accepted without a prudent balancing of opposite views, for the essence of the Greek character lies in its contradictions, its complexity, its extremities that strive for a moderation rarely attained, whether as harmony or tension. Ultimately, the balance must weigh in favor of clarity, simplicity and "classicism," but as qualities to be attained only as the distillation of great complexity, of warring opposites that threaten every moment to disrupt them. What is important in Greek literature is the vibrant clarity with which this battle is fought. Ancient and modern streams meet in the Greek poet as in a swirling vortex, casting up marble fragments of the past that are crushed into new molds by the pressures of modern life. The Greek poet struggles with a language unique in world development, so alive and changing, for all its venerable old age, that it slides like mercury in his hand, slipping from the grasp and transforming itself like Proteus, taking on myriad shapes but keeping the same recognizable identity, like the problem of self in philosophy. The symbols of Proteus, of metamorphosis, of Odysseus, of the eternally restless wanderer on the frontiers of the mind and spirit are still passionately alive in Greece today. Transformation, metamorphosis, and finally transubstantiation, wherein the old and the new are blended into a compound light and insight distilled from thousands of years' tradition, are keywords to the complex, constantly striving, ever-wandering Greek temperament which, like the self of an individual, changes momentarily but is basically the same.

Athens, December 1972   KIMON FRIAR

MODERN GREEK POETS

translations

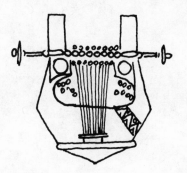

Constantine Caváfis

CANDLES

The days of all our future stand before us
like a long row of lighted candles—
warm, golden candles, full of life.

All our past days are left behind,
a mournful row of burnt-out candles;
the ones near by still curl with smoke,
cold candles now, stooped low, and melted.

I will not see them; their shapes make me grieve,
and I grow sad recalling their first light.
I gaze before me at the lighted candles.

I will not turn around to see with horror
how quickly the dark line is lengthening,
how quickly the burnt-out candles multiply.

THE PAWN

Quite often as I watched a game of chess
my eye would follow but a single Pawn
as he would slowly, slowly find his way
until at length he reached the final row.

As he advances toward the edge with such
good will, you'd think that there most certainly
his pleasures and rewards would soon begin.
Many the hardships on the road encountered.
Footsoldiers cast him lances slantingly;
castles attack him with broad battlelines;
swift horsemen try with guile and trickery
to trap him in the bounds of their two squares;
and here and there another lone pawn sent
from the enemy camp waylays with cornered threat.

But yet from all these dangers he escapes
and reaches at long last the final row.

With what great triumph he arrives at last
there to that final, that most dreadful row.
How eagerly he runs to embrace his death!

Because it's here the Pawn will die, and all
his trial and troubles only were for this.
Now for his Queen, she who shall save us all,
and for her resurrection from the tomb,
he comes to fall here in the chess's Hell.

THE CITY

You said, "I will go to another land, I will go to another sea.
Another city shall be found better than this.
Each one of my endeavors is condemned by fate;
my heart lies buried like a corpse.
How long in this disintegration can the mind remain.
Wherever I turn my eyes, wherever I gaze,
I see here only the black ruins of my life
where I have spent so many years, and ruined and wrecked myself."

New places you shall never find, you'll not find other seas.
The city still shall follow you. You'll wander still

in the same streets, you'll roam in the same neighborhoods,
in these same houses you'll turn gray.
You'll always arrive at this same city. Don't hope for somewhere
        else;
no ship for you exists, no road exists.
Just as you've ruined your life here, in this
small corner of earth, you've wrecked it now the whole world
        through.

THE FIRST STEP

One day the youthful poet Eumenes
complained thus to Theocritos:
"Two years have passed since I've been writing,
and I've composed one idyl only.
It's the one work that I've completed.
Alas, the stair of Poetry
is high, I see, most high. And here,
from this first step where now I stand,
I'll never mount much higher, alas."
Theocritos answered: "These words of yours
are most improper and blasphemous.
To find yourself on the first step
should make you proud and full of joy.
It's no small thing to have reached here;
what you've achieved is a great glory.
For even this first step, the lowest,
is far removed from the common world.
To set your foot on this one step
you must, in your own right, become
a citizen in the city of ideas.
And in that city it is rare
and difficult to be enfranchised.
You'll find Lawmakers in that conclave
whom no imposter can ever fool.
It's no small thing to have reached here;
what you've achieved is a great glory."

WAITING FOR THE BARBARIANS

What are we waiting for, all mustered in the forum?

    The barbarians are to arrive today.

Why is there so little activity within the Senate?
Why are the senators sitting there now, yet passing no laws?

    Because the barbarians will arrive today.
    What laws now can the senators possibly pass?
    When the barbarians come, they'll make the laws.

Why has our emperor arisen so early in the morning,
and why is he sitting there, at the city's greatest gate
in state upon his throne, why is he wearing his crown?

    Because the barbarians will arrive today,
    and the emperor is waiting there to receive
    their leader. Indeed, he has prepared to give him
    a parchment scroll. Therein he has granted him
    by writ a very great many names and titles.

Why have our two consuls and our praetors come out
today clad in their scarlet, their embroidered togas,
why are they wearing now their amethyst-studded bracelets
and all those splendid rings with their glistening emeralds,
why are they bearing today their precious staves of office
inlaid with gold and silver, so exquisitely wrought?

    Because the barbarians will arrive today,
    and things of this kind dazzle barbarians.

Why haven't our worthy orators come here as always
to spout their speeches at us, to say what they have to say?

    Because the barbarians will arrive today
    and they're bored by eloquence and public speeches.

Why suddenly should all this uneasiness begin,
and this confusion? (How grave now have all faces become!)
Why are all streets and squares so quickly emptying now,
and why is everyone returning home so lost in thought?

Because night has fallen, and the barbarians have not come.
And a few men who've returned from the frontiers
tell us that there are no barbarians any more.

And now, what's to become of us without barbarians?
These people were some sort of a solution.

ONE OF THEIR GODS

When one of Them, about the hour of nightfall,
passed by the agora of Seleucia,
in likeness of a tall ephebe of perfect beauty,
the joy of incorruption in his eyes,
and with his jet-black, perfumed hair,
the passersby would stare at him
and one would ask the other if he knew him,
and if he were a Greek from Syria, or a stranger.
But a few who might have observed with greater care
had understanding, and they stepped aside;
and though he vanished in the porticos
amid the shadows and the evening lights,
proceeding toward that quarter which comes alive
only at night with its debaucheries and orgies,
and all intoxications, every form of lust,
would wonder who among Those he might be,
and for what form of suspect pleasure he
had descended to the bystreets of Seleucia
from the Revered, Most Venerated Mansions.

INTERRUPTION

It's we who interrupt the work of the gods,
hurried and inexperienced creatures of an hour.

In the palaces of Phthia and Eleusis,
Thetis and Demeter begin their noble work
amid huge flames and dense smoke. But
always Metaneira from the royal chambers
comes rushing out, disheveled and terrified,
and always Peleus is struck with fear, and intervenes.

THERMOPYLAE

All honor to those who in their lives
have set themselves to guard Thermopylae.
Not swerving from their line of duty,
upright and just in all their actions,
yet filled with pity and compassion;
generous when they're rich, and when
they're poor, generous in little things;
still helping others all they can;
telling the truth always, and yet
holding no hatred against liars.

And greater honor still is due them
when they foresee (and many do foresee)
that Ephialtes finally will appear,
and that the Medes, at last, will get through.

ARTIFICIAL FLOWERS

I do not want the real narcissus—nor do
real lilies or real roses please me.
These but adorn the trite and common gardens. Their flesh
accords me bitterness, fatigue, and pain—
their perishable beauty bores me.

Give me but artificial flowers—glories of porcelain and metal—
that never wither and never rot, whose forms will never age.

Flowers of an exquisite garden in another land
where Rhythms, Theories, and Ideas dwell.

Flowers I love created out of gold and glass,
trustworthy gifts of a trustworthy art,
and dyed in hues more beautiful than nature's,
with mother-of-pearl and with enamel wrought,
with ideal stalks and leaves.

They draw their grace from wise and purest Taste;
nor did they sprout unclean from dirt and mire.
And if they lack aroma, we'll pour them fragrances,
we'll burn before them myrrh of our sentiments.

PERFIDY

During the wedding of Peleus and Thetis,
Apollo from the lustrous marriage table
arose and blessed the newly wedded pair
and the offspring, the issue of their union.
He said: Sickness shall never touch this child,
and he shall have long life. When he spoke thus,
Thetis was overjoyed, because these words
of Apollo, a god well versed in prophecy,
promised her child such firm security.
And when Achilles was growing up, and all
his beauty was bruited throughout Thessaly,
Thetis would often remember the god's words.
But one day old men came and brought her news
of how Achilles had been slain at Troy.
Then Thetis rent in grief her purple robes,
and from her arms and fingers tore away
bracelets and rings, and cast them to the ground.
And in her wailing she recalled the past
and asked to know: What was that wise Apollo doing,
where was that poet wandering who at feasts
spoke so divinely, where was that prophet roaming

when they were slaying her son in his first youth?
And then the old men answered her and said
that Apollo had himself come down to Troy
and with the Trojans there had slain Achilles.

HE SWEARS

He swears now and again to begin a better life.
But when night comes with its own suggestions,
with its own compromises and its promises;
but when night comes with its own strength
of the body that now craves and seeks, he goes
once more, foredoomed, to the same fatal joy.

PHILHELLENE

See to it that the engraving be artistic.
The expression serious and majestic.
The diadem had better be rather narrow;
I don't care for the broad Parthian kind.
The inscription, as usual, in Greek,
nothing hyperbolic, nothing ostentatious,
so as not to be misconstrued by the proconsul
who's always poking about and sending reports to Rome—
and yet, properly honorific, of course.
Something most eclectic on the other side,
some discus thrower, perhaps, young and good-looking.
Above all, I charge you, see to it
(in God's name, Sithaspes, don't let them forget)
that after *King* and *Savior* there should be
engraved, in elegant letters, *Philhellene*.
Now don't you start being facetious
with "What Greeks?" or "What Greek is there,
here behind Zagros, out there beyond Phraata?"

Since so many others, more barbarous than we,
inscribe it, we shall inscribe it too.
And finally, don't you forget that, now and then,
sophists *do* come to visit us from Syria,
and versifiers, and other pseudo scholars.
I trust we're not so unhellenic, after all.

ANTONY'S END

But when he heard the women weeping
for his sad plight, with all those lamentations,
the lady with her oriental gestures,
and the slaves, too, with their barbarious Greek,
pride rose within his soul
and his Italian blood felt nauseated,
and all he had so blindly worshiped once—
the frenzied life he'd lived in Alexandria—
seemed alien and indifferent to him now.
He told them not to weep. It was not fitting.
But rather they should praise him and extol him
because he had usurped such sovereign power
and had procured such riches and possessions.
Now that he'd fallen, he'd not fallen humbly,
but as a Roman by a Roman conquered.

ONE NIGHT

It was a cheap and vulgar room
hidden above a tavern of ill repute.
The window gave upon an alleyway
filthy and narrow. From down below
the voices of some workmen rose,
carousing as they played at cards.

And there upon that common, humble bed,
I had the erotic body and the lips,
the rose and amorous lips of intoxication,
rose lips of such intoxication that,
as now I write within my lonely house
after so many years, I become drunk again.

HIDDEN

From all I've said and all I've done
let no one seek to find out who I was.
An obstacle stood in my way, and this
transformed my acts, the manner of my life.
An obstacle stood in my way and stopped
me many times whenever I wanted to speak out.
From acts of mine that passed the most unheeded
and from my writings which I most obscured—
there only will you sense out what I was.
Perhaps, however, it's not worth your while
to try to know me with such toil and trouble.
Sometime—in a society more perfect,
some other person made as I was made
is certain to appear, and he will act freely.

ITHACA

When you set out on the voyage to Ithaca,
pray that your journey may be long,
full of adventures, full of knowledge.
Of the Laestrygones and the Cyclopes
and of furious Poseidon, do not be afraid,
for such on your journey you shall never meet
if your thought remain lofty, if a select
emotion imbue your spirit and your body.

The Laestrygones and the Cyclopes
and furious Poseidon you will never meet
unless you drag them with you in your soul,
unless your soul raises them up before you.

Pray that your journey may be long,
that many may those summer mornings be
when with what pleasure, what untold delight
you enter harbors you've not seen before;
that you stop at Phoenician market places
to procure the goodly merchandise,
mother of pearl and coral, amber and ebony,
and voluptuous perfumes of every kind,
as lavish an amount of voluptuous perfumes as you can;
that you venture on to many Egyptian cities
to learn and yet again to learn from the sages.

But you must always keep Ithaca in mind.
The arrival there *is* your predestination.
Yet do not by any means hasten your voyage.
Let it best endure for many years,
until grown old at length you anchor at your island
rich with all you have acquired on the way.
You never hoped that Ithaca would give you riches.

Ithaca has given you the lovely voyage.
Without her you would not have ventured on the way.
She has nothing more to give you now.

Poor though you may find her, Ithaca has not deceived you.
Now that you have become so wise, so full of experience,
you will have understood the meaning of an Ithaca.

THE GOD FORSAKES ANTONY

When suddenly at the midnight hour you hear
an invisible troupe of revelers passing by

with exquisite music and with voices,
do not then pointlessly lament your luck that now
at length runs out, your works that have failed,
your life's plans that have all turned out to be delusions.
Like one for a long time prepared, like a courageous man,
bid her farewell, the Alexandria that is leaving.
Above all, do not deceive yourself, do not say that this
was but a dream, that your hearing played you false;
do not condescend to such vain hopes as these.
Like one for long prepared, like a courageous man,
as befitting one once worthy of such a city,
approach the window with unflinching step
and listen deeply moved, not
with the faint-hearted man's entreaties and complaints,
but as a last enjoyment, to the sounds,
the exquisite instruments of that occult procession,
and bid her farewell, the Alexandria you are losing.

THE DANGERS

Said Myrtias (a student come from Syria
to Alexandria, during the single reign
of Augustus Constantius and Augustus Constans,
part pagan and but partly Christianized):
"Strengthened by theory and study, I
shall never fear my passions like a coward;
but I shall give my body up to pleasures,
to all voluptuousness longed-for in dream,
to the most daring and erotic urges,
to every lechery of my blood, without
a single fear, because when I shall will it
(and I *shall* will it, strengthened as I shall be
by theory and study) I shall but find
again, at any moment of crisis,
my soul to be, as once it was, ascetic.

ALEXANDRIAN KINGS

The Alexandrians came in swarms
to see Queen Cleopatra's children,
Caesarion and his younger brothers,
Alexander and Ptolemy, who for the first time
were being brought to the Gymnasium
to be proclaimed kings there
amid a glittering parade of soldiers.

Alexander—him they hailed as king
of Media, and Armenia, and of the Parthians.
Ptolemy—him they hailed as king
of Syria and Cilicia, and Phoenicia.
Caesarion stood a bit in front of the others,
robed in a pink-hued silk,
a hyacinthine garland on his breast,
his belt a double row of sapphires and amethysts,
his shoes bound with white ribbons
embroidered with rose-colored pearls.
Him they hailed oftener than his younger brothers,
him they hailed King of Kings.

The Alexandrians understood of course
that these were only theatrics and mere words.

But the day was poetical and warm,
the sky a limpid, azure blue,
the Alexandrian Gymnasium
a triumph of artistic execution,
the magnificence of the courtiers unprecedented,
Caesarion full of grace and beauty,
(Cleopatra's son, blood of the Lagidae).
And so the Alexandrians rushed to the festival
and waxed enthusiastic and began to cheer
in Greek, and in Egyptian, some in Hebrew,
enraptured by the beautiful spectacle—
although they knew exactly, of course, what this was worth,
what hollow words these kingships were.

ON THE STREET

His sympathetic features, somewhat pale;
his chestnut-colored, lacerated eyes;
age twenty-five, although he looks but twenty;
with something of the artist in his dress,
some color of the tie, cut of the collar—
he wanders aimlessly about the street
as if still mesmerized by the lawless lust,
the gross and lawless lust he has procured.

UNDERSTANDING

My years of youth, my life of lust—
how clearly I see their meaning now.

What futile, ah what needless repentances. . . .

I could not see their meaning then.

For in the dissipations of my youth
were shaped the volitions of my poetry,
was laid the groundwork of my art.

And therefore my regrets were never firm.
And resolutions to restrain myself, to change,
lasted but two weeks at the very most.

ITS BEGINNING

The consummations of unlawful pleasure done,
they got up from the mattress, dressed

themselves in silence, hurriedly,
then separately, in secret, left the house.
As they continue down the street disquietly
they seem uneasy with suspicion
that something upon them must betray
what sort of bed they had lain on recently.

And yet, how greatly was the artist's life enriched.
Tomorrow, the next day, or after many years,
the strong verse shall be writ that here had its beginning.

THEODOTOS

If you are truly one of the select few,
take care how you acquire your ascendancy.
No matter how much you are glorified, no matter how much
the cities acclaim your exploits
in Italy and in Thessaly,
no matter how many honorific edicts
your admirers in Rome proclaim for you,
neither your joy nor your triumph will endure,
nor will you feel yourself to be superior—superior, indeed!—
when, in Alexandria, Theodotos brings you,
on a blood-splattered tray,
the head of an unfortunate Pompey.

And don't repose on the fact that in your life
—restricted, well-ordered, and prosaic—
such terrifying and spectacular things do not happen.
Perhaps at this very moment in some neighbor's
well-regulated house, Theodotos
is entering—invisible, incorporeal—
carrying just such a frightful head.

IN A TOWN OF OSROENE

They brought us wounded from a tavern's brawl
toward midnight yesterday our friend Remon.

And through the windows which we left wide open,
the moon lit up his comely body on the bed.
We are a motley here: Greeks, Syrians, Armenians, Medes.
And such a one is Remon. But yesterday,
when on his amorous features shone the moon,
our minds turned toward that Platonic boy, Charmides.

THE TOMB OF LANES

The Lanes whom you loved so much   you will not find here,
  Marcus,
where by this tomb you come and weep   and stay for hour on
  hour.
The Lanes whom you loved so much   you keep much closer to
  you
at home where you enclose yourself   to gaze upon his picture,
that picture which somewhat preserves   all that was worthy of
  him,
that picture which somewhat preserves   whatever in him you
  loved.

Remember, Marcus, when you brought   from the proconsul's
  palace
that eminent, most celebrated   artisan from Cyrene,
and he, with all the cunning wiles   accruing to a craftsman,
no sooner saw your lovely friend   than he tried hard to
  persuade you
that in the role of Hyacinthos   he must, by all means, paint him
(for only in this manner would   his work win greater glory).

But your loved Lanes would not loan   his beauty in such
  manner,
and stanchly stood his ground and said   that he would be
  presented
not in the least like Hyacinthos,   nor any other person
than Lanes, son of Rhametichus,   who hails from Alexandria.

MORNING SEA

Let me pause here. Let me too look at nature awhile.
The luminous blue of the morning sea and cloudless
sky, the yellow shore—all
most beautifully and brilliantly lit.

Let me pause here. Let me delude myself that I see all these
(truly I saw them a moment when I first paused)
and not my fantasies here also,
my memories, the illusions of sensual pleasure.

DARIUS

The poet Phernazis is composing now
the important portion of his epic poem:
how Darius, son of Hystaspes,
took over the kingdom of the Persians. (From him
our own glorious monarch, Mithridates,
called Dionysos and Eupator, is descended.) But here
philosophy is called for; he must analyze
the emotions Darius must have felt:
probably arrogance and intoxication; but no—rather
something like an understanding of the vanity of grandeur.
The poet ponders deeply on the matter.

But he is interrupted by his servant who enters
running, and announces the gravest news.
War with the Romans has broken out.
The bulk of our army has crossed the frontiers.

The poet is stunned. What a calamity!
How could our glorious monarch,
our Mithridates, called Dionysos and Eupator,
be bothered now with poems written in Greek!
In the midst of war—imagine, poems in Greek.

Phernazis frets. What bad luck!
Just as he was positive that with his "Darius"
he would distinguish himself and strike dumb
his envious critics once and for all.
What a postponement, what a postponement to his plans.

If it were only a postponement, well and good.
But let's see first if we are at all safe
in Amisus. It's not a city exceptionally fortified.
The Romans are most frightful foes.
Can we, the Cappadocians, cope
with them? Is it ever possible?
Can we match ourselves with their legions now?
Great gods, defenders of Asia, help us.

And yet in all this evil and his agitation,
the poetic idea still insistently comes and goes—
the most probable, of course, is arrogance and intoxication;
arrogance and intoxication is what Darius must have felt.

THE AFTERNOON SUN

How well I know this very room.
Now this and the adjoining one are let
for business offices. The whole house has become
real estate, merchant offices, and companies.

Ah, how familiar is this very room.

Here by the door there stood the couch,
before it spread a Turkish rug;
near by, two yellow vases on a shelf.
To the right—no, opposite—a wardrobe with its mirror.
The table where he wrote stood in the center;
and then the three, large, wicker chairs.
Close by the window stood the bed
where we made love so many times.

These poor things now must somewhere still be found.

Close by the window stood the bed;
the sun in the afternoon would reach half way.

. . . At four o'clock one afternoon we parted
for one week only. . . . Alas,
that week became forever.

THE BANDAGED SHOULDER

He said he had bumped against a wall or fallen.
But in all likelihood his wounded
and bandaged shoulder was caused by something else.

With a small and abrupt movement he made
as from a shelf he tried to take down
some photographs he wanted to observe closely,
the bandages came loose and the blood flowed.

Then I rebound his shoulder, but in so doing
took my time, because it didn't hurt him,
and I liked seeing the blood. It was
but part and parcel of my love for him.

When he had gone I found beside the chair
a bloodstained piece of cloth from the bandages,
a rag that should have been cast out at once
among the rubbish, but which I brought to my lips
and kept as keepsake for a long time—
the blood of love upon my lips.

FROM THE SCHOOL
OF THE RENOWNED PHILOSOPHER

He remained a student of Ammonius Sakkas for two years,
but he became bored with philosophy and with Sakkas.

Afterwards he went into politics.
But dropped that too. The Eparch was a fool,
and his entourage solemn-faced, official blockheads;
their Greek was incredibly barbarous, the yokels.

The Church attracted his curiosity
a little: to be baptized
and pass for Christian. But quickly
he changed his mind. This might bring him on bad terms
with his parents, ostentatiously pagan;
and they would cut off at once—how dreadful—
their most generous allowance.

But he had to do something. He began to frequent
the corrupt houses of Alexandria,
every secret den of debauchery.

Fortune had been kind to him in this:
she had given him an extremely handsome figure.
And now he began to enjoy the divine gift.

His beauty would last for ten
more years at least. Afterwards—
perhaps he would once again go to Sakkas.
But if in the meantime the old man should die,
he could go to another philosopher or sophist;
somebody suitable can always be found.

In the end, it's possible he might even
take up politics again, laudably remembering
the traditions of his family,
his duty toward his country, and other such grandiloquence.

OF COLORED GLASS

I am deeply moved by one detail
at the coronation, in Blachernae, of John Cantacuzene
and Irene, daughter of Andronikus Asan.

Since they had only a few precious stones
(great was the poverty of our unfortunate nation)
they wore artificial ones. A heap of glass pieces
red, green, or blue. But for me
these small pieces of colored glass
have nothing about them that is undignified
or humble. They seem, on the contrary,
like a sorrowful protest
against the unjust misfortune of those crowned heads.
They are the symbols of what it was fitting they should have had,
of what certainly should have been the undisputed right,
at a coronation, of a Lord John Cantacuzene
and a Lady Irene, daughter of Andronikus Asan.

IN A TOWNSHIP OF ASIA MINOR

The news concerning the outcome of the naval battle at Actium
was certainly unexpected.
But it's not necessary to compose a new document.
Only the name need be changed. In the last lines there,
instead of "Having liberated the Romans
from the disastrous Octavius,
that parody, as it were, of Caesar,"
we will now insert "Having liberated the Romans
from the disastrous Antony."
The entire text fits in beautifully.

"To the conqueror, the most glorious,
to the incomparable in every military exploit,
the admirable in all political achievements,
for whom the township most fervently wished
the supremacy of Antony,"
here, as we said, the alteration: "of Caesar,
regarding it as the supreme gift of Zeus—
to the powerful protector of the Greeks,
to him who venerates our Greek customs benevolently,
dearly loved in every Greek domain,
exceedingly indicated for illustrious praise

and for the extensive recording of his deeds
in the Greek language, both in verse and prose,
in the Greek language, that is the messenger of fame,"
et cetera, et cetera. Everything fits in splendidly.

AMID THE TAVERNS

Amid the taverns and   the common brothels now
here in Beirut I wallow.   For I did not want
to stay in Alexandria   where Tamides left me
and with the Prefect's son   ran off that he might gain
a villa on the Nile,   a mansion in the city.
It would not do for me   to stay in Alexandria.
Amid the taverns and   the common brothels now
here in Beirut I wallow.   In cheap debauchery
I basely spend my life.   The only thing that saves me
like some enduring beauty,   like some faint perfume
that lingers on my flesh,   is that for two whole years
Tamides was all mine,   the most enchanting youth,
all mine, and not for a house   or a villa on the Nile.

SOPHIST LEAVING SYRIA

Distinguished sophist who are leaving Syria,
whenever, as you intend, you write of Antioch,
it's surely worth while in your work to mention Meves.
The celebrated Meves, who indisputably
is the most handsome youth, the one who is most loved
in all of Antioch. Not one of all the other
young men who lead here the same kind of life, not one
comes so expensively. That Meves might be had,
for two or three days only, many will often give
as much as a hundred staters. I said in Antioch—
yet even in Alexandria, and even still in Rome,
no young man can be found so amiable as Meves.

TWO YOUNG MEN,
23 TO 25 YEARS OF AGE

He had been in the coffeehouse since half
past ten, expecting him at every moment.
The hour of midnight struck—and still he waited.
One thirty came: the coffeehouse had almost emptied.
He was soon bored with reading newspapers
mechanically. Of his three solitary shillings
but one remained. He had so long been waiting
that he had spent the rest on coffee and cognac.
And he had smoked all of his cigarettes.
Such a long wait exhausted him. Because,
since he had been alone for hours, irksome thoughts
began to seize him of a life misled.

But when he saw his friend come in—at once
the thoughts, the weariness, the boredom fled.

His friend came bringing unexpected news.
He had just won at gambling sixty pounds.

Their handsome faces, their alluring youth,
all the aesthetic love they shared between them,
became refreshed, enlivened, invigorated
by the casino's sixty golden pounds.

Flushed in the bloom of youth, with joy and strength,
they went—not to the houses of their upright families
(and where, moreover, they were no longer welcome)
but to a house they knew, a rather special
house of corruption, where they asked for rooms,
expensive liquors, and then fell to drinking.

And when the expensive liquor was all gone,
and when by now the hour of four approached,
they gave themselves most happily to love.

KIMON, SON OF LEARCHOS, AGED 22, STUDENT OF GREEK LITERATURE (IN CYRENE)

"My end approached when I was very happy.
I was Hermoteles' inseparable friend.
In my last days, no matter how he feigned
not to be anxious, I could often discern
he had been crying. And when he thought that I
had fallen asleep, he'd fling himself in frenzy
beside my bed. But we were both quite young,
of the same age, but twenty-three years old.
Fate is a Traitress. Perhaps some other passion
might have in time snatched Hermoteles from me.
I ended well, within a love unshared."

This epitaph for Marylos Aristodemus,
who passed away last month in Alexandria,
did I, his cousin Kimon, receive in mourning.
Sent by the author, a poet of my acquaintance.
Sent by the author to me because he knew
that Marylos and I were blood relations;
but there was something else he didn't know.
My soul is filled with grief for Marylos.
We had grown up together like two brothers.
I am deeply melancholy. His untimely death
has wiped away all memory of wrong,
all memory of being wronged by Marylos,
although he had stolen the love of my Hermoteles
so that should now Hermoteles want me again
it would not be at all the same, for I
know well how sensitive my nature is.
The image of Marylos would come between us,
and I would think it said: Lo, Kimon, now
behold how you are finally contented;
behold how, as you wished, you've got him back;
behold now, you've no cause to slander me.

DAYS OF 1909, '10, AND '11

He was the son of a penurious, much-plagued mariner
(who dwelt amid the isles of the Aegean sea)
and worked as ironmonger. His clothes were old and grubby.
His working-shoes were torn and shabby.
His hands were soiled with rust and oil.

But when the shop closed down at night,
if there was something he'd delight
in having, a necktie somewhat dear,
tie that on Sundays he might wear,
or in some showcase saw and loved on sight
a lovely shirt of deepest blue,
he'd sell his body for a dollar or two.

I ask myself whether in ancient times
glorious Alexandria had a youth more ravishing,
a more perfect boy than this—who went lost.
No painting or statue, of course, was made of him;
cast in a dirty ironmonger's shop,
soon from the exhausting work
and vulgar, wretched debauchery, he wore away.

MYRES: ALEXANDRIA, A.D. 340

When I learned of the disaster, of Myres dead,
I went to his house, though usually I avoid
going into any Christian home—at times,
especially, of festival or mourning.

I stood in a corridor. I did not wish
to proceed much further, for I'd become aware
that relatives of the deceased were watching me
with evident astonishment and displeasure.

They had placed him in a large room
of which from the far end where now I stood
I saw but a small part: all filled with precious rugs
and vessels made of silver and of gold.

I stood and wept at the end of the corridor
and thought how our excursions and our gatherings
would have no meaning without Myres now;
and thought how I should never see him any more
amid our beautiful, our dissolute night revels,
rejoicing, laughing, and reciting verses
with his perfect feeling for Greek rhythm;
and thought how I had now forever lost
his beauty, how I had now forever lost
that youth whom I had passionately adored.

Then some old women near me began to speak
in a low voice of his last day of life—
how on his lips the name of Christ rose constantly,
how in his hands he held a cross.
Later, four Christian priests entered the room
and said their fervent prayers
and supplications to Jesus
or Mary (I don't know their religion well).

We had known, of course, that Myres was a Christian.
This we had known from the first hour when,
two years ago, he had joined our group.
But he had lived, then, like us precisely.
Of all of us, the one most profligate in pleasures;
squandering his money lavishly on amusements,
not for the world's regard concerned.
He'd fling himself into our night revels eagerly
when on the streets our group might chance
to meet sometimes with another hostile group.
He never spoke of his religion.
Indeed, one time we told him that
we'd take him with us to the Serapeum.
But then, as I recall,
he seemed offended with our little joke.

Ah, and two other times now come to mind:
once, as we were offering our libations to Poseidon,
he withdrew from our circle, and turned his eyes elsewhere;
and once, when one of us with much enthusiasm said,
"Now may our company always be
under the favor and protection of
the great, most beautiful Apollo"—Myres whispered
(the others did not hear), "Except for me."

The Christian priests, with their stentorian voices,
prayed for the soul of the young man.
And I observed with what great care,
with what intense attention to
the forms of their religion they prepared
every detail for such a Christian burial.
And suddenly I was overcome
by an odd impression. Vaguely, I felt
that Myres was receding from my side;
I felt that he, a Christian, had become
united with his own, and that I had become
a stranger, a total stranger; and also felt
a great doubt looming: perhaps out of my passion
I had deluded myself, had always been, for him, a stranger.
I flung myself out of that dreadful house
and quickly fled, before my memory of Myres
could be usurped and altered by their Christianizing.

THEY SHOULD HAVE PROVIDED

I've been reduced to a vagrant and a pauper.
This fatal city, this Antioch,
has eaten up all my money:
this fatal city with its costly way of life.

But I'm still young and in excellent health.
The possessor of an admirable knowledge of Greek

(Plato and Aristotle I know inside out,
and whatever orators, poets, or anything else you care to mention).
I've some notion of military matters,
and have struck up friendships among the mercenary leaders.
I've a certain inside track with the administration.
For six months last year I lived in Alexandria,
and I know a thing or two (this comes in handy) of what
        goes on there,
of that Evildoer's designs, and the villainies, and so forth.

In short, I believe I fit the bill,
fully qualified to serve this country,
my dearly beloved fatherland, Syria.

In whatever task they set me, I shall endeavor
to be useful to my country. That is my intention.
But if, on the other hand, they frustrate me with their systems—
we know these fine-feathered fools; need we talk about it now?—
if they frustrate me, how am I to blame?

I'll apply to Zabinas first,
and if that fool doesn't know my worth,
I'll go to his rival, Hooknose,
and if that idiot too won't take me on,
I'll go straight to Hyrcanos.

At any rate, one of the three will want me.

And as to the indifference of my choice,
I've a clear conscience.
The three of them are equally harmful for Syria.

But since I'm a ruined man, how am I to blame?
Poor devil, I'm only trying to improve my lot.
The almighty gods should have provided
by creating a fourth, an honest man.
I should have been delighted to work with him.

IN 200 B.C.

"Alexander, son of Philip, and the Greeks, except the
            Lacedaemonians . . ."

We can imagine perfectly well
how utterly indifferent they must have been in Sparta
to this inscription. "Except the Lacedaemonians,"
but of course. The Spartans were not made
to be ordered about and led by the nose
like invaluable servants. Besides,
a panhellenic expedition without
a Spartan king for leader
would not have seemed to them of much distinction.
Ah, most assuredly, "except the Lacedaemonians."

This, too, is an attitude. It's understandable.

And so, except the Lacedaemonians at the Granicus;
and afterwards at Issos; and at the final
battle where the dread army the Persians
had massed at Arbela was swept away:
which had set out for Arbela for victory, and was swept away.

And out of that remarkable panhellenic expedition,
so victorious and so illustrious,
so celebrated and so glorified
as no other before had ever been glorified,
and so incomparable, we were born:
a new world of Greeks, a great one.

We, the Alexandrians, the Antiocheans,
the Seleucians, and the innumerable
remaining Greeks of Egypt and of Syria,
and those in Persia, and in Media, and all the others.
With our far-reaching empire,
our various actions, the result of prudent adaptation,

and the Greek Common Language
which we brought far into Bactria, even to the Indians.

What's all this talk about the Lacedaemonians now!

ON THE OUTSKIRTS OF ANTIOCH

We in Antioch became bewildered when we heard
about Julian's latest antic.

Apollo had made it quite clear to him at Delphi.
He wouldn't utter a single oracle (we couldn't care less!),
and hadn't the slightest intention of speaking prophetically unless
his temple at Daphne were not purified first.
The neighboring dead, he signified, annoyed him.

There are many graves to be found at Daphne.
One of those buried there
was the illustrious, the saintly, the triumphant
martyr Babylas, glory of our church.

It was him the false god was hinting at, it was him he feared.
As long as the god felt him near, he didn't dare
utter his oracles; he became tongue-tied.
(The false gods are terrified of our martyrs.)

Then impious Julian rolled up his sleeves
and shouted, with irritation: "Raise him up, cart him away,
take this Babylas out immediately!
Do you hear there? Apollo is annoyed.
Raise him up, seize him at once.
Dig him out, carry him off wherever you like.
Take him away, throw him out. Are we playing games now?
Apollo has ordered his temple to be purified."

We took it, we carried away that holy relic, elsewhere;
we took it, we carried it, in love and in honor.

And that did the temple, really, a fine lot of good.
Without the slightest delay, a huge
fire broke out, a terrible fire,
and both the temple and Apollo burned down.

Ashes the idol; sweepings, with the rubbish.

Julian burst with rage and spread the rumor
—what else could he do—
that the fire was started
by us, the Christians; let him talk.
Nothing's been proved; let him talk.
What really matters is that he burst with rage.

Níkos Kazantzákis

---

from THE SAVIORS OF GOD:
SPIRITUAL EXERCISES

PROLOGUE

We come from a dark abyss, we end in a dark abyss, and we call
the luminous interval life.
As soon as we are born the return begins, at once the setting forth
and the coming back; we die in every moment.
Because of this, many have cried out: "The goal of life is death!"
But as soon as we are born we begin the struggle to create, to
compose, to turn matter into life; we are born in every
moment.
Because of this many have cried out: "The goal of ephemeral
life is immortality!"
In the temporary living organism these two streams collide: the
ascent toward composition, toward life, toward
immortality; the descent toward decomposition, toward
matter, toward death.
Both streams well up from the depths of primordial essence.
Life startles us at first; it seems somewhat beyond the law,
somewhat contrary to nature, somewhat like a transitory
counteraction to the dark eternal fountains; but deeper
down we feel that Life is itself without beginning, an
indestructible force of the Universe.
Otherwise, from where did that superhuman strength come which

hurls us from the unborn to the born and gives us—
    plants, animals, men—courage for the struggle?
But both opposing forces are holy.
It is our duty, therefore, to grasp that vision which can embrace
    and harmonize these two enormous, timeless, and
    indestructible forces, and with this vision to modulate
    our thinking and our action.

EPILOGUE: THE SILENCE

The soul of man is a flame, a bird of fire that leaps from bough to
    bough, from head to head, and that shouts: "I cannot
    stand still, I cannot be consumed, no one can quench me!"
All at once the Universe becomes a tree of fire. Amidst the smoke
    and the flames, reposing on the peak of conflagration,
    immaculate, cool, and serene, I hold that final fruit of
    fire, the Light.
From this lofty summit I look on the crimson line ascending—a
    tremulous, bloodstained, phosphorescence that drags
    itself like a lovesick insect through the rain-cool coils of
    my brain.
The ego, race, mankind, earth, theory and action, God—all these
    are phantasms made of loam and brain, good only for
    those simple hearts that live in fear, good only for those
    flatulent souls that imagine they are pregnant.
Where do we come from? Where are we going? What is the
    meaning of this life? That is what every heart is shouting,
    what every head is asking as it beats on chaos.
And a fire within me leaps up to answer: "Fire will surely come
    one day to purify the earth. Fire will surely come one
    day to obliterate the earth. This is the Second Coming.
"The soul is a flaming tongue that licks and struggles to set the
    black bulk of the world on fire. One day the entire
    Universe will become a single conflagration.
"Fire is the first and final mask of my God. We dance and weep
    between two enormous pyres."
Our thoughts and our bodies flash and glitter with reflected light.

Between the two pyres I stand serenely, my brain
unshaken amid the vertigo, and I say:

"Time is most short and space most narrow between these two
pyres, the rhythm of life is most sluggish, and I have no
time, nor a place to dance in. I cannot wait."

Then all at once the rhythm of earth becomes a vertigo, time
disappears, the moment whirls, becomes eternity, and
every point in space—insect or star or idea—turns into
dance.

It was a jail, and the jail was smashed, the dreadful powers within
it were freed, and that point of space no longer exists!

This ultimate stage of our spiritual exercises is called Silence.

Not because it is the ultimate inexpressible despair or the
ultimate inexpressible joy and hope. Nor because it is
the ultimate knowledge which does not condescend to
speak, or the ultimate ignorance which cannot.

Silence means: Every person, after completing his service in all
labors, reaches finally the highest summit of endeavor,
beyond every labor, where he no longer struggles or
shouts, where he ripens fully in silence, indestructibly,
eternally, with the entire Universe.

There he merges with the Abyss and nestles within it like the seed
of man in the womb of woman.

The Abyss is now his wife, he plows her, he opens and devours
her vitals, he transmutes her blood, he laughs and weeps,
he ascends and descends with her, and he never leaves her.

How can you reach the womb of the Abyss to make it fruitful?
This cannot be expressed, cannot be narrowed into
words, cannot be subjected to laws; every man is
completely free and has his own special liberation.

No form of instruction exists, no Savior exists to open up the road.
No road exists to be opened.

Every person, ascending above and beyond his own head, escapes
from his small brain, so crammed with perplexities.

Within profound Silence, erect, fearless, in pain and in play,
ascending ceaselessly from peak to peak, knowing that
the height has no ending, sing this proud and magical
incantation as you hang over the Abyss:

I BELIEVE IN ONE GOD, DEFENDER OF THE BORDERS,
OF DOUBLE DESCENT, MILITANT, SUFFERING,

OF MIGHTY BUT NOT OF OMNIPOTENT
POWER, A WARRIOR AT THE FARTHEST
FRONTIERS, COMMANDER IN CHIEF OF ALL
LUMINOUS POWERS, VISIBLE AND INVISIBLE.

I BELIEVE IN THE INNUMERABLE, THE EPHEMERAL
MASKS WHICH GOD HAS ASSUMED
THROUGHOUT THE CENTURIES, AND BEHIND
HIS CEASELESS FLUX I DISCERN AN
INDESTRUCTIBLE UNITY.

I BELIEVE IN HIS SLEEPLESS AND VIOLENT STRUGGLE
WHICH TAMES AND FRUCTIFIES THE EARTH
AS THE LIFE-GIVING FOUNTAIN OF PLANTS,
ANIMALS, AND MEN.

I BELIEVE IN MAN'S HEART, THAT EARTHEN
THRESHING-FLOOR WHERE NIGHT AND DAY
THE DEFENDER OF THE BORDERS FIGHTS
WITH DEATH.

O LORD, YOU SHOUT: "HELP ME! HELP ME!" YOU
SHOUT, O LORD, AND I HEAR.

WITHIN ME ALL FOREFATHERS AND ALL
DESCENDANTS, ALL RACES AND ALL EARTH
HEAR YOUR CRY WITH JOY AND TERROR.

BLESSED BE ALL THOSE WHO FREE YOU AND
BECOME UNITED WITH YOU, LORD, AND WHO
SAY: "YOU AND I ARE ONE."

AND THRICE BLESSED BE THOSE WHO BEAR ON
THEIR SHOULDERS AND DO NOT BUCKLE
UNDER THIS GREAT, SUBLIME, AND
TERRIFYING SECRET:

THAT EVEN THIS ONE
DOES NOT EXIST!

from THE ODYSSEY:
A MODERN SEQUEL

PROLOGUE

O Sun, great Oriental, my proud mind's golden cap,
I love to wear you cocked askew, to play and burst
in song throughout our lives, and so rejoice our hearts.
Good is this earth, it suits us! Like the global grape
it hangs, dear God, in the blue air and sways in the gale,
nibbled by all the birds and spirits of the four winds.
Come, let's start nibbling too and so refresh our minds!
Between two throbbing temples in the mind's great wine vats
I tread on the crisp grapes until the wild must boils
and my mind laughs and steams within the upright day.
Has the earth sprouted wings and sails, has my mind swayed
until black-eyed Necessity got drunk and burst in song?
Above me spreads the raging sky, below me swoops
my belly, a white gull that breasts the cooling waves;
my nostrils fill with salty spray, the billows burst
swiftly against my back, rush on, and I rush after.
Great Sun, who pass on high yet watch all things below,
I see the sun-drenched cap of the great castle wrecker:
let's kick and scuff it round to see where it will take us!
Learn, lads, that Time has cycles and that Fate has wheels
and that the mind of man sits high and twirls them round;
come quick, let's spin the world about and send it tumbling!
O Sun, my quick coquetting eye, my red-haired hound,
sniff out all quarries that I love, give them swift chase,
tell me all that you've seen on earth, all that you've heard,
and I shall pass them through my entrails' secret forge
till slowly, with profound caresses, play and laughter,
stones, water, fire, and earth shall be transformed to spirit,
and the mud-winged and heavy soul, freed of its flesh,
shall like a flame serene ascend and fade in sun.
You've drunk and eaten well, my lads, on festive shores,
until the feast within you turned to dance and laughter,

love-bites and idle chatter that dissolved in flesh;
but in myself the meat turned monstrous, the wine rose,
a sea-chant leapt within me, rushed to knock me down,
until I longed to sing this song—make way, my brothers!
Oho, the festival lasts long, the place is small;
make way, let me have air, give me a ring to stretch in,
a place to spread my shinbones, to kick up my heels,
so that my giddiness won't wound your wives and children.
As soon as I let loose my words along the shore
to hunt all mankind down, I know they'll choke my throat,
but when my full neck smothers and my pain grows vast
I shall rise up—make way!—to dance on raging shores.
Snatch prudence from me, God, burst my brows wide, fling far
the trap doors of my mind, let the world breathe a while.
Ho, workers, peasants, you ant-swarms, carters of grain,
I fling red poppies down, may the world burst in flames!
Maidens, with wild doves fluttering in your soothing breasts,
brave lads, with your black-hilted swords thrust in your belts,
no matter how you strive, earth's but a barren tree,
but I, ahoy, with my salt songs shall force the flower!
Fold up your aprons, craftsmen, cast your tools away,
fling off Necessity's firm yoke, for Freedom calls.
Freedom, my lads, is neither wine nor a sweet maid,
not goods stacked in vast cellars, no, nor sons in cradles;
it's but a scornful, lonely song the wind has taken . . .
Come, drink of Lethe's brackish spring to cleanse your minds,
forget your cares, your poisons, your ignoble profits,
and make your hearts as babes, unburdened, pure and light.
O brain, be flowers that nightingales may come to sing!
Old men, howl all you can to bring your white teeth back,
to make your hair crow-black, your youthful wits go wild,
for by our Lady Moon and our Lord Sun, I swear
old age is a false dream and Death but fantasy,
all playthings of the brain and the soul's affectations,
all but a mistral's blast that blows the temples wide;
the dream was lightly dreamt and thus the earth was made;
let's take possession of the world with song, my lads!
Aye, fellow craftsmen, seize your oars, the Captain comes;
and mothers, give your sweet babes suck to stop their wailing!
Ahoy, cast wretched sorrow out, prick up your ears—
I sing the sufferings and the torments of renowned Odysseus!

THE SEVEN HEADS OF GOD

He spoke, then from his bosom dragged an ivory god
with seven towering heads piled on each other, worn
by myriads of caressing hands and pilgrim lips.
Odysseus grabbed at the ivory wonder eagerly;
the seven heads all swayed, and seven-colored flames
rose in his mind as with his finger tips he stroked
and gently licked with slow caresses each strange head.
Time shut its wings for a brief moment and stood still
so that the lone mind could have ample time to climb
with skillful fingers all the rungs of mortal virtues.
Below, the most coarse head, a brutal base of flesh,
swelled like a bloated beast bristling with large boar-tusks,
and it was fortified with veins as thick as horns.
Above it, like a warrior's crest, the second head
clenched its sharp teeth and frowned with hesitating brows
like one who scans his danger, quakes before death's door,
but in his haughty pride still feels ashamed to flee.
The third head gleamed like honey with voluptuous eyes,
its pale cheeks hallowed by the flesh's candied kisses,
and a dark love-bite scarred its he-goat lips with blood.
The fourth head lightly rose, its mouth a whetted blade,
its neck grew slender and its brow rose tall as though
its roots had turned to flower, its meat to purest mind.
The fifth head's towering brow was crushed with bitter grief,
deep trenches grooved it, and its flaming cheeks were gripped
with torturous arms as by a savage octopus;
it bit its thin lips hopelessly to keep from howling.
Above it shone serenely the last head but one,
and steadfast weighed all things, beyond all joy or grief,
like an all-holy, peaceful, full-fed, buoyant spirit.
It gazed on Tartaros and the sky, a slight smile bloomed
like the sun's subtle afterglow on faded lips;
it sauntered on the highest creviced peaks of air
where all things seem but passing dream and dappled mist;
and from its balding crown, that shone like a smooth stone
battered by many flooding seas and licked by cares,

there leapt up like unmoving flame the final head,
as though it were a crimson thread that strung the heads
in rows like amber beads and hung them high in air.
The final head shone, crystal-clear, translucent, light,
and had no ears or eyes, no nostrils, mouth, or brow,
for all its flesh had turned to soul, and soul to air!
Odysseus fondled all the demon's seven souls
as he had never fondled woman, son, or native land.
"Ah, my dear God, if only my dark soul could mount
the seven stories step by step and fade in flame,
but I'm devoured by beasts and filled with mud and brain!"

DEATH DREAMS OF LIFE

Death came and stretched full length along the Archer's side;
weary from wandering all night long, his lids were heavy,
and he, too, longed to sit and sleep awhile beside
his old friend near the river, by a willow's shade.
Throwing his bony arms across the Archer's chest,
he and his boon companion slowly sank in sleep.
Death slept, and dreamt that man indeed, perhaps, existed,
that houses rose on earth, perhaps, kingdoms and castles,
that even gardens rose and that beneath their shade
court ladies strolled in languor and handmaidens sang.
He dreamt there was a sun that rose, a moon that shone,
a wheel of earth that turned and every season brought,
perhaps, all kinds of fruit and flowers, cooling rain and snow,
and that it turned once more, perhaps, till earth renewed.
But Death smiled secretly in sleep for he knew well
this was but dream, a dappled wind, toy of his weary mind,
and unperturbed, allowed this evil dream to goad him.
But slowly life took courage, and the wheel whirled round,
earth gaped with hunger, sun and rain sank in her bowels,
unnumbered eggs hatched birds, the world was filled with worms,
until a packed battalion of beasts, men, and thoughts
set out and pounced on sleeping Death to eat him whole.
A human pair crouched in his nostrils' heaving caves,

there lit and fed a fire, set up their house and cooked,
and from Death's upper lip hung down their new son's cradle.
Feeling his nostrils tingling and his pale lips tickled,
Death suddenly shook and tossed in sleep, and the dream vanished.
For a brief moment Death had fallen asleep and dreamt of life.

EGYPTIAN NIGHT

The sun, like a slain head, rolled slowly down the sands,
deep azure mists rose thickly by the river's edge,
and the light vanished sadly on the yellow banks.
The star-grains brimmed on the black fields, and the vast sky
like full-winged mills began to grind in the grim darkness.
Wild fawns slunk to their water-holes with quivering hearts,
the famished jackal dug among the poor men's tombs,
and night-gods calmly wrapped in fresh vine leaves all boys
who had just died, then crouched to eat them on the sands.
A beautiful Egyptian princess had died that day
then lightly walked along the riverbank at night
and stooped to hide her rotted face from her dear friends.
Night with her aromatic armpits drifted past,
an immature most tender light bloomed on the fields,
till dawn, an awkward calf, came stumbling down the banks.
The three friends followed the rose-lidded river's flow,
white birds that shed a lustrous light passed over them,
the fishes in the waters frisked, and on the sands
villages crackled, burned, and maidens tore their hair.
The Archer's brains breathed deeply the cool springtime breath
of Death with all its sweet and dizzying spells, unslaked,
as though he smelled night-jasmine in his gloaming garden.
His mind spun, all the boundaries of the world were lost
as though he'd gone amid his old acquaintances,
green fields and mountains, to hunt deer with his long bow
and all had suddenly changed, as in a drunken mist;
his murderous bow had budded like an oak-holm branch,
and deer approached it without fear and browsed on its green
        leaves.

THE RUTHLESS GOD

A peasant with his huge feet steeped in heavy mud,
day woke each dawn and went to work on the great town
as step by step it rose tall-columned in the light.
As ramparts rose with laws like high ferocious towers,
God talked, and gave his orders to the leader's mind,
and he strove slowly to distill the hid commands
deep in the black pit of his heart and make them song.
One day God sprang on earth with iron weapons armed
and struck Odysseus with his foot till he sprang up
and marshaled his loose wits, as cries of love and war
rang out and ruthless great commandments throbbed in light:
"I am your own dread God, your Chief of Staff in War!
You're not my slave, you're now no plaything in my hands,
nor yet a trusted friend, nor yet a favorite son,
but comrade and co-worker in the stubborn strife!
Manfully hold the pass entrusted you in war;
learn to obey—only that soul may be called free
who follows and takes joy in goals greater than he.
Learn to command, only that soul on earth who knows
how to give harsh commands can be my mouth or fist.
What is my road? A rough, rude, limitless ascent!
To say: No one but I can save the whole wide world!
Where are we going? Shall we win? Don't ask! Fight on!"
Thus did dread God command within the lone man's breast,
and the lawmaker's mind grew light, the air grew mute,
and he sped swiftly toward his city with great joy
to find smooth slabs of upright stones on which to carve
the great and difficult laws entrusted him by God.
As he walked on and thought how he might raise a troop
to aid that God who always mounted earth with groans,
he saw beside the town's south gate a monstrous stream
of blind black ants that swarmed with a devouring greed.
A baby camel had been caught in that fierce charge
and only its white bones now gleamed on the black ground;
the frightened people stopped their work and fled like leaves
but in the rush a baby fell from its mother's arms,

laughingly sank within that dread cascade of ants,
and in a flash only its bare thin bones remained.
The largest of the black ants, with thick solid jaws,
scurried like leaders up and down the frenzied troops,
bit, barked commands, and brought the stream to ordered flow.
The suffering man stooped low and watched the mystic powers,
greedy and blind, that welled from the ground's guts, and knew
that earth's crust at his feet was but a thin trap door.
When the dark plunderers suddenly swerved and disappeared,
the people turned to building with unruffled song,
and Death's grim raid became the cause of laughs and jokes.
Memory soon forgot all it had seen and feared
and covered horror with a colored cloak, as always;
when pots were set above the hearths that very night,
then Death, the Ant, became the fancy's glittering toy.
But the compassionate man's frenetic heart was wrung,
his black-robed memory stooped and loosed her matted hair,
held up the stream of ants for mirror, wept and wailed.
Silent, and sickened with all food, Odysseus lay
in the wild moonlight by the lake and called on sleep
till that old sunless codger came with all his brood.
The lone man dreamt that on his body blind ants swarmed
and ate him to the bone, that his flesh knit once more,
but that the ants swarmed once again and ate him whole.
All night his quivering flesh would fade and knit in waves
until in the dawn's light he felt these were not ants
but the dark stars that crawled above him silently and ate him.

ODYSSEUS BLESSES HIS LIFE

Then the mind-traveled man leant on the wild pear's trunk;
the pilgrims still lay, wearied, on the ground about him,
and in the shedding petals of dawn's rose he saw
his whole life like a legend walk toward the bright sun.
He spread his hands and blessed his mind and all his life:
"May you be blessed, my life, the bitter laurel's brief
and scented garland still upon your snow-white hair.

I kiss your slender ankles and your wounded feet;
how did you ever breach the pass or cross the great
main road, O most tormented life, one-breasted soul?
When I was young, I held the earth like a huge sphere
nor feared life's kiss nor quaked before the dreaded gods.
I scorned to feel compassion, my full powers seethed,
I brimmed with poison like the scorpion's stinging tail,
and like a scorpion I'd have writhed upon my mind's
hot coals had not a small maid come to touch my heart.
Ah, how she calmed my mind, made sweet my lips until
all earthquakes turned to flowers and you and I both fused
till in life's deep sea-lairs we two were merged in one.
Then my heart's double-bolted gates swung open wide
and a small boy with dappled wings led me through lanes
of colored flowers gently to cool garden plots
within that maiden's soul, and smiled on me. Dear God,
in just one night my heart had widened with a sweet kiss,
and my stern mind sailed long on strange seductive shores
in the deep body's frigate with a loot of women.
May you be blessed, my life, that passed the heaviest trial
of all, and with the light breath of a spring's cool breeze
knocked down the fortress of my own unpitying ego.
Then slowly as I grew more gentle, I longed to pass
even beyond sweet large-eyed Love and in my arms
clasp tight all of my native land like a maid's body.
O glittering harbors, sand-smooth beaches, tossing boats,
mountains with crystal waters and the pungent thyme,
old crones who spin their wool, maidens with fertile wombs,
brave gallant lads who fight the earth or foaming sea,
stones, bodies, souls, how could my mind contain you all?
Then pains for hurts not mine brimmed through my darkening
       heart
and all the joys of my luxuriant race poured out
as though a dam had burst and drenched my mind completely.
The soul's a thousand times more tasty than good meat,
and like a lion that once has tasted human flesh
and then disdains nor longer wants a humbler prey,
so I, too, wanted nothing less than human souls.
My native land seemed cribbed, for past its shores I felt
other bewitching lands and other lean-fleshed souls,

brothers and sisters, myriad forms of joys and sorrows,
that stood on their far shores and longed for me to come.
May you be blessed, my life, for you disdained to stay
faithful to but one marriage, like a silly girl;
the bread of travel is sweet, and foreign lands are honey;
for a brief moment you rejoiced in each new love,
but stifled soon and bade farewell to each fond lover.
My soul, your voyages have been your native land!
With tears and smiles you've climbed and followed faithfully
the world's most fruitful virtue—holy, false unfaithfulness!"

THE SIX WAVES OF WORMS

When the three messengers had left the golden tent
the ravished Prince then raised his tear-stained eyes and saw
his faithful slave alone in a far corner, weeping.
"O faithful slave, don't weep! Look in my eyes, reply:
What happens to a man's body when it stays a month,
what happens when it stays a full year in the grave?"
"O long-lived Master, I beseech you, don't, don't ask!"
"Slave, my request is my command! Answer at once!"
"O Prince, six kinds of fat worms, six invading troops,
six waves of famished worms rush swiftly toward the corpse;
each wave first towers high, swoops down, eats all it can
with leisure, then rolls off, makes way for other waves,
all in good order, Prince, and not one bickering quarrel!
Before the body well expires, the good news sweeps
the air and the dung-flies with their huge bellies swarm
from gardens, dung-heaps, stables, cow barns, filthy lanes,
and perch on the still-striving, dying man's pale lips,
on his blue nostrils, the deep pits of his dark eyes,
and quickly lay their eggs in clusters, heap on heap.
At once, when the man dies, the blowflies swoop down, Prince,
the savage meat flies, too, with their fat fuzzy bellies,
and heap on the warm corpse their white and welling eggs.
Then four pallbearers come, open and close the tomb,
and in the first nights slowly the corpse softens, swells,

the chest turns blue, the head becomes soft yellow wax,
the belly bloats up like a wineskin and turns green.
Then eggs hatch everywhere, on nostrils, eyes, and ears—
and all at once an army of blind silent worms
march, mount, possess the body, and begin to eat.
In time the fingernails drop off, the belly cracks,
the human corpse becomes a hogskin of fat lard,
O long-lived Prince, till finally a new white wave
of worms appears, like cheese grubs, and begins to eat.
The flesh becomes black broth and pours out in soft slush,
and then the third great wave leaps up and swells until
tall heaps of maggots sink into the broth, and eat.
Slowly the corpse becomes a tough dry hide, and then
a deep invisible host of larvae hatch and gnaw
what filaments still stick about the bones and skull.
Close on their heels the fifth most greedy wave mounts up
of strong-jawed worms and maggots that begin to saw
and munch away the nerves, the brains, the shroud, the nails.
At length, in three years' time the final wave mounts high,
the final table guests arrive deep from the earth
and squat about the corpse to eat what scraps remain.
Nothing at length is left of man's once mighty body
or his almighty soul, O scion of great kings,
but his white, naked bones strewn underground until
within his empty head, the bulwark once of God,
only a soft damp mold distills, a flabby dough.
But don't think, Prince, that this is man's once holy brain—
this is not brain, but dross, dregs, filth and sediment,
the myriad droppings of the waves of worms that passed!"

TO VIRTUE

O Virtue, precious and light-sleeping daughter of man,
how you rejoice when, all alone, biting your lips,
poor, persecuted, thrust into the desolate wastes,
you find no friend on whom to cling, no straw to clutch,
for there no souls crowd round to marvel at your grace,

no gods are there for whose dear sake you fling your lance;
yet upright, silent, you fight in the wild wastes and know
you'll never win, but battle only for your own sake.
Rise high, O Virtue, gaze now on that white-haired head
with its despairing brilliant brain that sails and plays
its gleaming tentacles like a frail nautilus.
Joy, sorrow, life and death blow through his tossing heart
like four swift winds and drive his flesh and mind down toward
the plunging cliff, two lovers clasped in tight embrace.
He's harvested the sea and all the joys of earth,
he's plucked their flower whose honeyed poisons choke the heart
and hung it on his ear, then sung and strolled toward Death.
If earth had mind, it would rejoice, if fate had eyes
it would embrace this old and mighty warrior, touch
with fear and admiration his deep wounds and clutch
him tight so that it, too, might not descend to Hades.
All stones would burst in threnody, all trees would wail,
all beasts would snarl and raise their paws to pounce on Death,
and the most lustrous maids would strip their bodies bare
to lure Death on so that upon the downy daze
of their sweet breasts he might forget that holy head.
But earth is stupid and fate purblind; both have sent
that mighty lighthouse, that great sleepless brain to die
unwept and unprotected in the frozen wastes.
The sun like a gold quoit sped down the heaven's road,
and the round silver moon rose like a dead man's mask
and covered the pale tranquil face of the brain-archer.
He sailed in his light coffin all day, all night long,
and the whole sky and sea stretched taut like a curved bow
against his hoary-haired swift-dying chest until
he felt his skiff between them speed like a swift arrow.
Above his white head seagulls slowly rowed and sailed
a day or two, but then grew tired and swerved back;
a lean sea-eagle wove him wreaths in air all day,
perched like a sleepless ship's boy on his mast all night,
but on the seventh day it, too, grew weary and flew away.
Two sharp-nosed frothing sharks followed like hungry dogs,
opened and closed their gleaming teeth with longing greed,
but when they lost all hope of food, they plunged away.
"Farewell! Turn to your prey, I'm not yet food for sharks,"

the boatman mocked, and cast off fish and birds like old
soiled clothes, and breathed the crystal solitude, stripped bare.
At times birds passed above him, smeared with sweetest scent,
and their sharp claw-tips dripped with musk and the air flashed
like a cock-pheasant's feathers, gold and crimson wings.
At times a feather fell upon his foam-washed deck,
but the quick-handed man flung it upon the waves:
"Farewell, O wings and fragrances, ideas, dreams,
farewell, O multicolored precious filigrees of air!"

EPITAPH FOR ODYSSEUS

Great Sun, O Father, Mother, Son, three-masted Good,
you sleep with our pure women on the fertile earth,
for if you do not thrust your seed deep in their flesh,
man's sperm is void and sterile, each drop lacks its son.
You are our mother, too, firm breast that brims with milk,
and all our open mouths await you, all lips gape
to grasp your light at break of day and suck it sweetly.
Great Sun, you cast your warm wings on the nested eggs,
peck with your golden beak upon their fragile shells
until the callow bills within peck in response
and the thin middle wall falls slowly, the shell cracks,
and fledglings drop into your lap and chirp for food.
You are our son, you splash in water, roll on grass,
cling to our breasts when hungry, turn blood into milk,
and when, my son, you wake at dawn and turn rose-red,
a thousand birds wake in our breasts, a thousand cradles.
O Sun, Great Son, profound joy of our earthen eyes,
hold us forever in your palm, hatch us, dear God,
turn all our feet to wings and all the earth to air.
Take the old Archer, Sun, in your caressing arms,
don't leave him here alone, for see, the worms have come,
their hidden jaws are munching at his entrails now!
Great Sun, flood down into his bowels, turn all the worms
to thousands of huge crimson-golden butterflies!
In a great blaze of wings and light, in salt embrace,

make Death come riding down astride a gallant thought!
Let Death come down to slavish souls and craven heads
with his sharp scythe and barren bones, but let him come
to this lone man like a great lord to knock with shame
on his five famous castle doors, and with great awe
plunder whatever dregs that in the ceaseless strife
of his stanch body have not found time as yet to turn
from flesh and bone into pure spirit, lightning, deeds, and joy.
The Archer has fooled you, Death, he's squandered all your goods,
melted down all the rusts and rots of his foul flesh
till they escaped you in pure spirit, and when you come,
you'll find but trampled fires, embers, ash, and fleshly dross.

THE DEATH OF ODYSSEUS

Erect by his mid-mast amid the clustered grapes,
the prodigal son now heard the song of all return
and his eyes cleansed and emptied, his full heart grew light,
for Life and Death were songs, his mind the singing bird.
He cast his eyes about him, slowly clenched his teeth,
then thrust his hands in pomegranates, figs, and grapes
until the twelve gods round his dark loins were refreshed.
All the great body of the world-roamer turned to mist,
and slowly his snow-ship, his memory, fruit, and friends
drifted like fog far down the sea, vanished like dew.
Then flesh dissolved, glances congealed, the heart's pulse stopped,
and the great mind leapt to the peak of its holy freedom,
fluttered with empty wings, then upright through the air
soared high and freed itself from its last cage, its freedom.
All things like frail mist scattered till but one brave cry
for a brief moment hung in the calm benighted waters:

"Forward, my lads, sail on, for Death's breeze blows in a fair wind!"

EPILOGUE

O Sun, great Eastern Prince, your eyes have brimmed with tears,
for all the world has darkened, all life swirls and spins,
and now you've plunged down to your mother's watery cellars.
She's yearned for you for a long time, stood by her door
with wine for you to drink, a lamp to light your way:
"Dear Son, the table's spread, eat and rejoice your heart;
here's forty loaves of bread and forty jugs of wine
and forty girls who drowned to light your way like lanterns;
your pillows are made of violets and your bed of roses,
night after night I've longed for you, my darling son!"
But her black son upset the tables in great wrath,
poured all the wine into the sea, cast bread on waves,
and all the green-haired girls sank in the weeds, and drowned.
Then the earth vanished, the sea dimmed, all flesh dissolved,
the body turned to fragile spirit and spirit to air,
till the air moved and sighed as in the hollow hush
was heard the ultimate and despairing cry of Earth,
the sun's lament, but with no throat or mouth or voice:
"Mother, enjoy the food you've cooked, the wine you hold,
Mother, if you've a rose-bed, rest your weary bones,
Mother, I don't want wine to drink or bread to eat—
today I've seen my loved one vanish like a dwindling thought."

NIETZSCHE

"O secret father and great-martyred mind,
I raise my hands in supplication, hear me!
You rush into the highest arenas of air,

into the head, the boiling pitch of battle,
lean scorpion with your tail raised high to strike.
Thick fires shake and tremble all about you,

and they are stirred by that black tigress, night;
O mind, and my great athlete, your bold gaze,
freed at the utmost rim of its despair,

disdains even death, and your sharp crimson tail,
filled full of freedom, uncurls and leaps on high
and bursts into your heart, fulfilled with joy.

The sun at last is setting, and that sweet
deceiving veil of earth is darkening now;
I grasp you in my hands with rage, O mind,

and prop you that you may not plunge in darkness.
Autumn is heavy, and the wet leaves about us
detach themselves and fall in Hades until

the holy light left in the darkening chill
leaps like a small and wounded bird from bough
to bough in the swift whirlwind of the night;

for a brief flash it clings with anguish there
on the highest peak of earth, then vanishes.
O holy fire, O stifled spirit of man,

who in the body's passions briefly live,
endure with courage, do not vanish yet."
I shout thus in the depths of deafened time,

and on the forehead, mouth, and heart of that
most holy Lone Man stir the smoldering ash.
O spark, most precious heir of all mankind,

and you, man's proud and bitter aspiration,
revere this ruined, desolate battlement.
Huge was the flag unfurled and flung on high,

and that divine enchantress, shy despair,
sang in the dark most sweetly as the heart
got drunk with too much hot and heady wine.

And now, behold, on the dark, roaring beach
of drunkenness the pirate has been smashed,
and in that insolent pursuit the mind,

that seagull, shatters both of its long wings
till that great coward, Death, crawls cunningly
in the mute dark and licks his holy skull.

Caught in the sharp claws of insanity,
he shudders mutely as the crows flock round,
until his brain, a frenzied mountain goat,

begins to butt its horns against the world,
and his pale fingers shape frail paper ships
that soar in streams of aery fantasy

—three-masted galleys!—whose enormous spars
have sprouted suddenly with clustered grapes;
there hairy daemons with thick, goatlike lips

and bushy beards leap high from shroud to shroud
as Bacchus the redeemer shares out full
emancipation to gods, men, and beasts.

The sea now rustles softly like smooth satin,
and as the freshening vision sails, it comes
to anchor in the lone man's turbid eyes.

It was as though he saw an azure harbor
filled with the clamor of unnumbered crowds,
and then from too much joy broke down and wept.

They all held palms, burnt myrrh and frankincense
and strewed his road with laurel as he passed
in dream and hailed his people regally,

a crown of thorns above his pallid head;
in his right hand he held the whole round earth,
a golden sphere, and gazed on it with pride.

But his mind slightly swayed, and all his joy
sank and was drowned completely as a harsh
and freezing North Wind rose on ruined gardens;

and suddenly a choked lament was heard
as there appeared among grapevines and thorns
the pale, nude body of Bacchus crucified.

The vision stood unmoving in the depths
of the lone soul's desolation as mute tears,
all the mind's sediment, ran down in streams

past the pale cheeks and down the gray mustache.
Father, I grasp your lean and wounded hands—
let's drink all poisons now to our good health!

The great wine press of earth ferments with must,
the mind grows drunk, flutters its new-fledged wings,
and chases away that scarecrow landlord now.

"We want no master over us here on earth!"
you shout. "Let every man shift for himself!"
On the far bounds of life and death you keep

your watch, O hunter, where the wild beast finds
his shelter, in the entrails' deepest folds,
and then rush headlong to the savage chase.

You subjugate God, kiss, and country—these
three sirens—roam earth like a vagabond,
and then push on beyond even joy or hope.

O Boarder Guard, God-Slayer gashed with wounds,
I hear you sigh and rush to hunt beside you
like a voracious bloodhound bred in Crete.

O rise, my Captain, for the time has come,
the night has fallen, the first stars are lit,
the heart grows hungry, I don't want to die,

and many-dugged Dame Fire appears, erect
in darkness, and beckons to us silently—
let every infamous castle turn to ash!

We don't want precious plunder here, my brother,
our minds do not search out great joys or glory,
no plump whore beats her tambourine for us

in the world's gaudy, shameless caravan;
we only want pure air—we stifle here
beneath the lowering ceiling of the earth.

Great peak of pride, my body's very breath,
O star-eyed joy of all my solitude,
in my first boyhood's crimson break of dawn,

and in my virgin and goat-savage youth
you rose, and all earth rose, a column of light,
and opened for me the earth's hidden roads.

Bare Cretan mountain ranges: there the fists
of all my flame-eyed youth creaked with their strength,
and passions, like dark beasts thrust deep in mud,

bellowed within my entrails to climb out
until I longed to burn the whole wide earth,
and you, O secret root, bloomed deep within me,

till my red fire was refined to light,
and solitude became my joyous country.
I saw you from afar—lone, desolate,

caught in the snares of life, breaking the bars
of the mad mind that you might breathe awhile.
Never before had I seen such proud joy,

for you had never deigned to tend a hearth,
or turn to shepherd, lamb, or dog, but stalked
each sheepfold like a lone and lawless wolf.

You broke through every scab of happiness
with your broad breast, your savage and wild wings,
your inner whirlpools swirling and unsated,

and in the desert as a rampart raised
tall stones, a stylite on the peaks of pride,
to keep a valiant watch on monstrous truth

who naked, all her body stained and blotched,
hung dangling down the dark abyss as round
her head entangled coils of serpents hissed.

What joy! No longer is the mind deceived,
for all the embellishments of earth and sky
are toys of the imagination, fear, or clay.

On the revolving wheel of life and death,
ideas, gods, and men whirl round and round
in a long endless sweep of destiny,

and you, the lyre of the ecstatic mind,
resound, till the earth hears and swiftly spins
in a proud dance around the blazing sun.

Amid the heavy banks of fog you hold
your heart, that wagtail weathervane, and point
it like a compass toward the empty sun.

Straight for the abyss, in a clear line before you,
you open roads of joy as all your troop
of barefoot and rebellious children, all

your pirates, lovers, your insurgents rush
on steeds of hopelessness to plunge far down
the cliffs of freedom, leader of all souls!

The spirit, my brothers, is a deep, dark wine;
come, let us drink now to our Captain's health.
It is a salty and bewitching blood;

let's open our veins that earth may be refreshed,
and may your shadow, that bold pirate, come,
O leader, to quench his thirst here in the light.

May Death die for a lightning moment's flash
that you, O gallant spirit, may soar above
the tall and flowering cypress trees where all

your ravenous and ragged troops may swarm
and cling in thick grape clusters round your form
like honeybees around their mother bee.

Behold, the struggle now begins! Rise up,
O soul, appoint each to his battle station;
your longing now intoxicates our hearts,

and in the onslaught of our drunkenness
your paper boats have swelled to galleys, all
our minds have sprouted leaves and fledgling wings.

Already the first bullets whistle past,
black Fate has bound her crimson sandals tight,
and those dark bearers of all evil news,

the fears of wretched man, knock on the door!
Time's sentient nostrils smell of sulphurous fumes,
your words like raging lions stalk about

the ripened earth, and the head's temples creak.
O bridegroom Nietzsche, the great nuptial march
begins, the tombs sprout curly lemon blooms,

and Victory finds you in your desolation.

BUDDHA

My brothers, playthings of our Father Mind
that mingles all winds well, O azure mists
of the tall head, the air's frail fantasies,

man, beasts, and gods, cobwebs of delicate dream
that you weave here in Death's palaces on this
bare earth, vapors of the imagination,

I blow now on your earthen eyes, I blow
now on your earthen ears that they might open.
At long last come and tear through Maya's nets

and let your bodies leap like fishes high
within the salt and open sea of death;
let the great portals of your brain resound

that earth may vanish and the mind empty, let
the Ganges pour its raging waters down
the deep abyss with all its pilgrim souls—

and let Necessity's great loom collapse.
The mountains are breasts wrapped round in mists, the mind,
a gray-white falcon, soars like a steep gorge,

and Death, a kindly grandfather, strolls past,
a pure white elephant with small sweet eyes;
stars molt and fall, the lighthouse of the mind

grows drowsy, all life's poisons have dried up,
until, their hunger sated, two by two,
fawns stroll with lions, hawks with nightingales.

Now in fraternity friend meets with foe,
there is great joy, cool mountain breezes blow,
and thousand-winged, emblazoned armies glide

in the honey-colored topaz of the sun.
All hasten with great speed at dusk to watch
victorious Buddha, after great carnage here

on the black crust of earth, the slaughter shed,
moor at long last like a triumphal king
at his old capital, the dark abyss!

The stitches of his cranium creak and strain,
and his five fearful elements once more
strive to pour back in Death the Savior's stream;

each element unsheaths itself from blood,
free at long last to fly and vanish in Chaos—
earth, water, fire, air, and breathing soul.

Forward, my brothers, open the way, put all
in order, build with aromatic woods
the chariot of his holy funeral pyre.

The Savior passes, and a shuddering shakes
the foliage of the stars until, erect,
the leaves of earth break into dance like wings.

Come all my brothers, come, gods, worms, and grass,
let's hover exultantly above our heads,
for the black doors of our divine escape

—his azure eyes—have opened, and we must dress
in freedom's earthen garb of coarse monk's cloth
to plunge and drown together in their blue waters!

A growling of wild beasts now shakes the woods,
the mind has risen like bread, and the old staves
on the immense wine barrel of earth have burst;

the inner lanes of men have sprung with flowers
and from the sun's bright skull, in varied hue,
the wings of tribal chiefs have leaped erect.

Then Buddha stretched his hand, and all the wheels
on the great Gate of Non-Existence creaked,
and all of Death's sweet wells and fountains flowed;

and Buddha, a white swan, bent over the flood
of all salvation, gazed with marveling pride
at Fate with silent and slow-moving eyes.

He grasped his bursting brow with reverence:
"I thank you, Mind, erect in your head's cave,
a fakir on his sacred threshing floor,

who all the dappled kingdom bring to birth
of earth and sky, and in the lowering storm
hold, like a frail-winged kite, the plunging sun!

For a brief hour upon the shores of time,
with clay and spirit, you shape your playthings well,
then blow upon them till they rush pellmell,

blue, twisting, swirling smoke-rings of the air;
you blow once more, O Mind, and they all vanish!
With sweetness once, and with both hands, I sowed

the imagination's treasures throughout earth,
and on all secret beasts I once let loose
that hound dog, the most headlong, fearless heart.

I've emptied at long last, my entrails hang
like carrion clusters in the bramble shrubs
until the mind blots out, with all its tricks.

O head, detach yourself, cut yourself off
from the slim neck, and like a crimson lamp
ascend serenely in the night to roads

of the wide desert lands that leave no trace.
The deep, dark pupils of my eyes rejoiced
one moonlit night to watch on a wild cliff

a heavy-laden honeycomb drip all
its honey, drop by drop, deep in the abyss.
O heart, O candlewick of sacred flame,

thunderous knocker on the Gate of Hades,
you beat on hopelessness with pride, then fall
into the lightless gulf, nor do you care!

You do not condescend to joy, nor yoke
yourself to love or hate—no matter now,
let the frail magic mirror of earth break!

With my pale hand I beckon to shy Death:
"O trusted, faithful friend, draw near, don't tremble!"
He spoke, and like a flame-winged, whirling reel,

savage, innumerable hands and feet
leapt round about him, an enormous wheel
that flashed and glittered in a swirling dance.

He lost control of all five elements,
all bolts were broken, all firm joints disjoined,
time and place ceased to be, the waterwheel

of earth strained, creaked, and burned as the full light
with lavish fistfuls scattered all its beams.
Then he snatched off and tore the deceiving masks,

and the earth filled with dwarfs, plague-ridden crones,
till in the dance's swirl, in the mind's rush,
ah, how all bodies shrank, how all girls turned

to puppets, and young men to gnomes and elves!
The constellations formed in drops of sweat
and fell in the black furrows of the earth.

The Savior turned his eyes, and the earth's odors
grew warm with life, and every dry branch bloomed;
he turned his eyes away and earth, dead now,

lay with crossed hands on the first savage snows.
Time had been vanquished, end and beginning both
met, joined, and fused, and for eternity

seed, fruit, and rot were tightly twined in one.
Between his eyebrows slowly the third eye
laughed, a deceiving star, and his brains rushed

to the high, towered embrasures of the head
like sated pillagers, replete with plunder.
Buddha is a tall tree with coral boughs

where pilgrims come with fear or cheerfulness
to bring in silence their rich offerings:
young men and girls the anguish of their youth,

old men the sluggish treasures of their minds,
children their only toys, and all the hot
and vehement, blazing sky the sun and moon.

Then a huge bull, a sacred votive beast,
with a red ribbon round its neck, stooped low
to the great Savior, though an arrogant God,

and humbly stretched out the bowl of beggary:
"Mercy, O Master, be compassionate
to your most ancient, your most faithful slave,

and take me with you now in your salvation.
I hungered, and you nourished me with psalms,
I thirsted, and you gave me—O recall—

the tears of the whole world in a clay jug.
You said, 'Brahma is a great god!' and I
at once grew greater; 'wise,' and the whole head's

round sphere rejoiced in brains to its far rim.
I want no more! Take pity on me, Master!
Life is a heavy sickness, and behold

that Archer, that great Master Worm, the Sun,
has struck my flesh with foul-lipped leprosy.
Deep in your eyes I see the earthen door

of no return! Ah, set me free and say:
'Brahma is empty,' that I too may empty!
We shout on earth, we suffer, we shed tears:

give me, O Lord, the black coarse cloth of health,
the loam itself, the mantle of your thoughts,
that I too may descend and rest forever

deep in your dark brain's bottomless abyss!"
Thus did the great god beg, but you, O Shepherd,
played sweetly to your flock on your reed flute

till in the luminous forests of your head
your great thoughts drifted past like vagabonds,
fawns, lions, and elephants composed of air.

In silence then the head's pale temples creaked,
and that dry tree, the Spirit, shook and cast
white flowers on the bare and earthless fields.

The nets of the fine flesh dissolved till rings
of blue smoke at the stroke of midnight swirled
through empty air, the ghost of gods and men.

Behold how Buddha encompassed the whole earth;
the soles of his pale feet hung down in chaos,
until the world's air-pregnant womb was emptied,

the violent flood of spirits ebbed away
and the nine Muses of our futile rage
lay in their graves, their heads enwreathed with laurel.

Behold then, from the blessed, worm-eaten wounds
gashed deeply in the putrid rind of flesh
virginal wings sprang suddenly and soared

of an enormous lunar butterfly;
thus Buddha hovered, gently balancing
in empty air, then vanished in the light,

an empty, azure thought composed of air.

Kóstas Várnalis

APHRODITE

The raucous laughter of the Immortal Gods
still rang and burned within her ears like flame!
And when her lame-legged husband's crafty net
was cut, golden-haired Aphrodite sprang

out of her bed, and speeding through blue skylanes,
reached Paphos' foam-flecked shores. There Eroses,
whose wings ordeals had never touched, played on
their lyres to cheer her mood. The Graces, too,

wiped off all trace of color or of shame
from her smooth snow-white skin and laved her flesh
with unguents incorruptible. Behold her now,

more chaste than ever, she leaps on the sea's calm;
and in the sun, that sets the sky afire,
not one drop clings to her not even one word.

THE CHOSEN ONE

When your three slaves have painted and perfumed
your lips, your hair, your fingernails, and loosed
about your temples all your wondrous locks,
then don your golden sandals and set out

to stroll the Market Place. Bastards and slaves
carouse in the Feast of Flowers. The new wine
now laughs and foams within the cup passed on
from mouth to mouth. Take it, and there where all

have drunk their fill, drink too. Then sink your teeth
deep in its wood. But your gentility
hold high, and even higher still your soul!

Do not once deign to talk with the gross crowd.
Like a chance passer-by respond with a nod
to a strange tongue you do not understand.

ORESTES

Celery your hair, as curly and as fragrant.
Unbind it, and reveal yourself to be
as indeed you are, most handsome. Cast from your mind
the onus of that fierce oracle, since there

is nothing else you can ever do. Smile now
to see how your destined road has brought you here
to the great gates of Argos where you must
soon extirpate the womb that gave you birth.

No one remembers you here. Like them, you too
must now forget just who you are, and go
to the dark crossroads of that golden city

and do your work, as though you were another.
No matter what you do, you'll be pursued
by your own mother's blood, or by your shame.

ALCIBIADES

With a girl's hand, a myrtle's grace,
you bring eternal summers with you,

and on your tongue lie fumes of wine,
honey and groans, O poisonous star
above Athena's citadel.

Always with swift and hissing lies
dyed deeply in your country's blood
you put to sleep both foes and friends;
in your profound and limpid soul
the Erinyes and the Muses bathe.

Your chariots lit seven flames
in sacred Olympia. Your steeds
with wings of Pegasos raised high
in the serene air your generation's
firm freedom and nobility.

And one night staggering from your revels
you smashed gods in the narrow lanes
like empty crystal cups of wine.
Then from the shattered marble quarries
of Sicily great wailing rose,

and as last solace, the choral odes
like Euripides' sweet nightingales.
You thought your hot heart, your cold views,
and your light chisel could defeat
even Fate, O Hermae-Mutilator.

And look! In the red light of dawn
the sails and the sweet flutes are singing.
Wreathed with the sacred laurel bough
you haul behind you like hetaerae,
like a bound herd, your enemies' ships.

Unconquered both on land and sea,
and only by your passions conquered,
your youth blooms always at twenty-two,
O Apollonian, myrrh-scented,
sweet lover and most sweet beloved.

MAGDALENE

In palaces where music echoed as in caves,
where clustered lights and burnished metals gleamed and glittered,
aromas glid like sweet narcosis on my cheeks,
that no sun ever saw, and bit them deep like vipers;
in my pellucid voice a husky, dim note slid.

In the four kingdoms of Judea, I was the Fountain:
the unwithering and musk-fragrant citrons of my breasts.
Earth never before had known such flames as in my body,
never had such ripe calm been found as in my arms,
my love games conquered even Rome the conqueror.

But darkness lay within me, stretches of vast, dry sand,
and on my dulcet lips my laughter would turn bitter.
Fears of the great unknown would suddenly shake my heart
and stop my breathing in my rich embroidered gowns.
There high on Triumph's peak I saw the world's destruction.

It was no sudden lightning bolt, for it came slowly . . .
You were not handsome or noteworthy in any way.
Your eyes cast down on pebbles, you talked slowly, calmly,
but on the third or the fourth time, my weak mind shuddered,
and when you raised your eyes, I could not bear their gaze.

I longed impetuously to cast myself at your feet,
and felt a still immaculate soul trembling within me.
I knew clean happiness in giving without fee,
freedom in slavery to a certain true ideal,
and noble knowledge, ultimate pleasure found in pain.

When I had given all my possessions to the poor,
my diamonds, silver, gardens, palaces, and silks,
I followed in your footsteps, and though the night wind always
erased them on the sand, they still remained forever
like sweet lights still on sand, on soul, in ears, in eyes.

You never said anything new, nor clad old things afresh.
All had been said by many men in times long past.
But yours the power to hear the silence of the heavens;
and men and all inanimate things, and even the heart
of God became for you—for me—transparent glass.

No one (not wise men, students, parents or multitudes)
could sense the agony behind your miracles;
and if you ever hoped to be saved from a death unjust,
then only I, who once was whore and mud, have felt
how mortal you were, Christ! And I shall resurrect you!

THE LEADER

I am not the spawn of Chance
nor the creator of a new life,
for I am the child of Necessity
and the mature offspring of Wrath.

Nor have I descended from clouds
because no Father has ever sent me
to be your only consolation,
O suffering and tormented slaves.

Heavenly powers and all the angels,
lilies and birds and psalmodies—
nothing of these! My support lies
within your own deep angry hearts.

I am your ship's figurehead
foremost on its upright prow.
There every savage hurricane
and the wild weather burst in rage.

Deep in my mind, deep in my heart
such everlasting shames have swollen

that these have armed my angry fists
with the flame-spitting lightning flash.

I am not one, but myriads!
Not only all brave living souls
but even the dead rise from their graves
and follow me dark row on row.

Thousands of all the uncreated
and all those still unborn have come
to bless me and to lean their swords
across my shoulder blades in trust.

Instead of warm, consoling words
I give sharp knives to those who come,
and when I thrust these deep in earth,
they become light, they become mind.

Now listen how the winds sweep up
the voices of all millenniums!
Within my own words you will find
the pain of all the human race.

O how the winds have swept them up
and how soon afterward we hear
black graves and black abysses howl,
and rivers clotted with thick blood.

Wherever it goes it topples down
like the North Wind, like the South Wind,
the murderous kingdoms of foul man
founded on fraudulence and lies.

One kingdom and but one alone
it hoists up high, the kingdom of Work,
(Peace to all men) the one kingdom
of Human Friendship throughout the world.

JUNGLE

Muslin stretched tight
on stiff upright breasts,
small, dark-skinned face
and Hawaiian lusts!

Raven-eyebrowed
and almond-eyed,
honeybee-downed,
if only I could sink

my steel-sharp nails
and iron teeth
in your firm nape
tanned by the sun,

as in a wild
and desolate gorge
a tigress rips
a gazelle to shreds

and throughout the thicket
savagely resounds
the joy of the one,
the Death of the other.

ONE-ALL

Whether with others or whether alone,
in the world's mire or the far skies,
on distant seas, on the high mountains,
beside my love, in day or darkness;

whether with nightingales in dales
whether with snows of the mad North Wind

whether with a poetic lyre
whether with logic or experience;

whether dead drunk or watered down
whether imprisoned or set free
whether I fight against great odds
whether I grope, blind with the blind

from my young years to my old age
(then when impetuous fire possessed me,
now when death's requisition takes me
and stoops me down to unsated earth)

in all the eternal elements,
in all the crumbs of daily life,
I ask, O joy, for the slightest joy.
Not found in my dreams, not even once!

I'd cast myself down a bottomless cliff,
I'd tie a stone around my neck
unless, goddess Idea, my sidereal flame,
you dared not look down! I shall look there too!

O what black darkness, what thick blood!
All of humanity weeps and groans.
"No salvation exists for you alone
(for One) unless these too are saved."

LAMENTATION OF THE ENSLAVED

THE FIRST SLAVE

A small face soft and smooth as silk,
small eyes that glitter like cold wells,
fourteen or sixteen years of age,
where are they now? In your depths, Earth!

THE SECOND SLAVE

A sea of roses below; on the fence
the honeysuckle hangs like a river.
Where are they now? Ashes and dust!
Above them all a burnt-out moon.

THE THIRD SLAVE

Without beginning, end, or middle,
but infinite: earth, sea, and sky!
An iron knot has bound them all.
An empty world inside and out.

ALL TOGETHER

All mute now in the muted air,
a blind sun looks and does not move.
Nor night nor day can be told apart.
Prophecy warns of the world's end.

Who now will save us? East or West?
What Greek or what barbarian god?
Will a new world march on ahead
or the old world always return?

MY SUN

Sun, with what longing now do I wait here
to see you leap up from behind Hymettos,
to see the whole world light up suddenly
and hold the miracle for a brief moment.

And afterwards? Green spreading fields. Walk down
and through these kingdoms, black and murderous.
Wisteria, honeysuckle, bougainvillaea,
are now all asphodels in dead men's meadows.

Flags everywhere! But of what king? Inquire,
but cast a glance now to your right and left.
Rejoice how under awnings, outside bars,
your foreign masters stretch their feet and yawn.

Read Shakespeare, Aeschylos, and Tolstoy too,
read Solomós' great "Hymn to Liberty,"
for in your vitals, wormwood conscience gnaws
and deep shame presses in your throat and chokes.

Sun, a great people wait for you with longing,
and all the people everywhere united!
But do not rise behind Hymettos as once
before, to drown at evening down the sea.

Like an unsetting source of light and joy,
honor and liberty, you shall be brought
and placed deep in the sky, on land and sea,
by the forerunner, the whole world's Pariah.

THE 4 MISTAKES
OF "THE UNKNOWN SOLDIER"

Your first mistake: a slave from the cradle on.
Your second: slave in a most slavish age.
Your third: you were not only flesh, but soul.
Your fourth: nor sold to strangers like a mule.

If you were a slave and rotten to the bone
you now would be a "someone" and not slain.
Nor would you have been the last "unknown" broke beggar,
but first and foremost, well known, even a sheik.

Nor would your own and foreign demagogues
have swindled you with a cheap tinsel wreath,
but as public hangmen, as black as all the others,
you would be swimming now in gold Grand Crosses.

CATECHISM

He has no mother, wife, friends, relatives,
brother or sister. One, and yet No One.
The wind that blows sweeps him away, nor can
he ever reach the middle of the road.

Bad to himself, but never to all other
bad men, those cannibals who eat their brothers.
All come in first. And they believe this! All
the best Traitors hold the high-jump records.

Why do you sit and smile? Get a move on!
Those who once tagged behind have passed you by.
The swiftest race in all this century
is the race run with mud up to the knees.

There is no greater power now in this dark
and dreary time of ours than mud and filth,
nor is there even a greater sacrifice
"for God and country" now than Treachery.

Ángelos Sikelianós

SPARTA

"As if from ambush now for a long time
I've held you in my eye, and from all others
have chosen you as if you were a star;
your countenance has gratified my heart.
Hearken; now let me tightly grasp your hand,
for youth is like a stallion thus subdued;
for one night only shall you lie upon
my bed, and be my own wife's counterpart.

Go; she is small in waist and as compact
in beauty as majestic Helen was;
and fill her generously with your seed.
For one night take her in your strong embrace,
and then uplift my desolate old age
before all Sparta with a worthy son."

THE VIRGIN OF SPARTA

Not of Pentelic marble nor of brass
shall I erect Thy deathless idol, but
from a tall column made of cypress wood
that my work may be fragrant throughout the ages.
And on that hill which wears like a tall crown

an old Venetian castle, I shall build
a massive church, and in it lock Thee fast
with mighty adamantine gates of iron!

Bells that shall bellow forth as if a shield
were struck by sword or sharp spearhead I'll raise
up high, and others higher, like a sistrum.
To shade Thee, from each window I shall match
crystals of many colors and deep tone,
and may each one of them be an embrasure!

PAN

Upon the rocks of barren shore and in the burning heat above the
   pebbled shingle,
high noon, like a bubbling well reclining beside an emerald wave,
   trembles and simmers . . .

An azure trireme far away amid the foam of early spring, rises
   Salamis;
the pines and rushes of Kinétas like a deep inspiring breath well
   up within me.

The sea bursts into trembling foam, and shaken in the passing
   winds breaks into silver
as stumbling now the countless herd of steel-gray goats from the
   hillsides come rumbling downward . . .

Placing his fingers under his tongue the goatherd takes a breath
   and blows two harsh shrill whistles,
then gathers all his scattered herd upon the shore, and even if they
   are five hundred!

And all the goats come crowding round and tightly crouch under
   the shrubs and the wild thyme,
and as they huddle, in a swift rush a numbing drowsiness sweeps
   up both man and beasts.

And then above the pebbled shore and on the burning heat above
   the steel-gray goats,
silence; and now between their horns like smoke above a bronze
   tripod the sun springs up . . .

And then behold the he-goat as, leader and chief, he rises slowly
   and in lone pride,
heavy in his stride and sure, from all the others cuts away, and
   where a rock

thrusts through the sea like a sharp wedge and is a glittering
   lookout there and promontory,
stands high upon its utmost edge where sprays the mist of the
   foaming sea, then stock-still turns

his head, and lifts his upper lip, his bright teeth shining in the sun,
   and there still stands
huge and erect upon the rock and sniffs, until the late twilight,
   the foaming sea.

PENTARKIS

Ὁ παῖς καλός

Deep was the mystic valley, and the wet woods
   of Kronion had donned
shadows both dim and clear from the mild wind
   that blew after the rain.

Along the gutters of the temples where
   rills sang like nightingales
the swallows there like dancers dressed in black
   soon gathered row on row.

Fragrance of honey struck the nostrils from
   old hollows of tree trunks,
and breathed from out the dry pine needles that
   from each forked bough hung low.

One quick wing-footed burst of wind roused up,
    another strewed perfumes,
and from the incomparable wealth of flowers
    unseen, the earth became

one fragrant mouth, for as the wind's heel swirled
    with unapparent grace
it spread out everywhere, luxuriously,
    an endless mystic feast.

The breast and throat of a young man whose teeth
    gleamed, as he deeply breathed,
like bitter orange bloom, glowed from the cold
    after the sudden rain;

he felt his teeth like unripe almonds set
    firm in his tightened gums
till his chaste mind rejoiced to its far depths
    to feel the freshened world . . .

Later, when cooling darknesses spread far
    and wide, a sudden flash
of silent lightning lit up everything
    like dry twigs blazoning,

and from the resin of the dampened trees
    a perfume breathed as if
with loving inclination toward the earth
    Zeus let his long locks fall.

And the dew-laden eyelids opened wide
    in meditation, sleep
would not draw near, so full refreshing were
    the feasts of fragrances;

and in the workshop on a tripod stood
    a lamp with triple flame
that lit the reflections of a man who leant
    his head on his open palm,

before whose calm Olympian eye a young
    pentathlete slowly paced
naked amid the various tools before
    the flickering triple flame.

But still the artisan remained serene,
    sublimely cool, alert,
long since accustomed how to eat at mystic
    banquets with all the gods.

And in the splendor of his mind, that flowed
    like Alpheos noiselessly,
the chryselephantine treasure stirred and glowed
    slowly before him. Then,

like the flax flower or pale sapphire stone
    of indigo, there shone
deep in his thoughts all gems with a cold light,
    mystic and myriad,

that for the indescribable nude stare
    of those Olympian eyes
confronting all of Nature, he might choose
    of diamonds the most blue.

And as the darknesses upon his closed
    eyelids now wove the myriad
and multicolored flowers, he fancied how
    the valanced ebony

upon the throne would glitter and how all
    the wealth of constellations,
that breathed a deep serenity, would close
    about it like the tail

turning about a peacock's legs. So did
    the God appear to him,
the Eternal Benefactor of all Youth,
    and in whose smile his mind

was laved as the Archer of Aegina who,
    kneeling, exults and grasps
the bow within his hands as though it were
    the bowstring of a lyre,

and life and death a double star. He raised
    his eyes and saw the youth,
and his soul filled with peace Olympian and
    the fading fragrant night.

Then, as an eagle swoops to lust, his eyes
    fell on the young man's breast,
shoulders, arms, thighs, and murmuring said:
    "Zeus, if I should erect

you in that high Olympian style, then let
    that grace be mine, to write
but on a corner of your foot: *Pentarkis*
    is a most beautiful youth."

ANADYOMENE

Ah, see how in the rose and blesséd light of dawn
    with hands upraised I rise;
the sublime calm calls of open seas to rise up thus
    toward azure upper skies.

But O the sudden blasts of earth that sweep my breasts
    and shake me to the bone!
O Zeus, the seas are heavy, and my unloosened locks
    sink me like stone.

Run breezes, run—O Wind-Swift, Seagreen, run—come seize,
    come lift me by mine arms;
I had not thought so quickly and at once to find myself
    surrendered to the Sun's arms . . .

THE MOTHER OF DANTE

"It seemed to her in sleep at break of dawn that bare
    and emptied Florence lay,
and that far from her women friends on roads alone
    she wandered aimlessly;

and roamed the crossroads dressed in silken bridal gown
    and veils of lily-white,
and every road she trod upon in dream seemed now
    both new and strange to her.

Then from the hillsides steeped in the pale dawn of spring,
    like a far swarm of bees,
the breathless belfries from small country chapels rang
    with sound profound and slow.

And suddenly it seemed as if she were within
    a garden of white air,
dressed in its bridal gown with bitter-orange bloom
    and apple blossom filled;

and as the fragrance led her on, it seemed as if
    a laurel tree drew near
toward whose tall top ascending, hopping step by step,
    rose a trim peacock

that bent its neck from one branch to another bough
    laden with laurel berries,
and some would eat and some pluck out to cast them
        quickly
    on the firm earth below;

and she, in the tree's shade entranced and unresisting
    raised her embroidered gown—
and lo, soon from the load of puckered laurel berries
    felt her full dress weighted down."

So from her labor at dawn she rested thus a moment
    as in a cooling cloud,
while gathered round the bed her women friends were waiting
    to welcome the coming child.

THALERO

Fiery, laughing and warm above the vineyards,
    the moon looked down—
but still the sun scorched every shrub, and set
    in a full calm;

on windless heights plants sweated heavily
    their seething milk,
and from the youthful vines that clambered up
    the terraced slope

vinekeepers waved and whistled, robins frisked
    by the river bank,
and over the moon's face a heat haze spread
    its gossamer veil.

Amid the crops three solitary oxen,
    one plodding straight
behind the other, cut through the mountain slope,
    their dewlaps dangling;

and a slim hound, bent low, sniffing the earth,
    bounded from rock
to rock with rapid feet to find my tracks
    in the twilight's hush;

as by a hill house under a grape arbor
    a laden table
awaited me where the light of the Evening Star
    hung like a lantern.

The master's daughter there, whose strength had grooved
  her stone-strong throat
like that of a dove's, brought me cold water, bread,
  and honeycomb;

her face, like the evening's glow, revealed full clear
  a virgin's flame,
and on her taut breasts through her tightened dress
  her nipples rose;

her hair was braided above her brow in two
  unswerving plaits
like a ship's ropes, nor could my fist have closed
  about them once.

Incensed by the steep mountain paths, the dog
  lay panting there,
on his front paws unmoving, and watched my eyes
  for a spare bone;

and there, as nightingales sang round and I
  from the tray ate fruit,
deep on my palate were merged the taste of honey,
  of wheat and song . . .

My soul within me churned in a glass hive,
  a joyous bee swarm
that secretly increased and hung on trees
  in thick grape swarms

until the earth turned crystal beneath my feet,
  the soil translucent,
and three-year plane trees round me rose up high
  with strong, calm bodies.

They opened their old wine for me, full-bodied
  in the sweating jug,
like mountain fragrances when the cold night dew
  weighs down the shrubs.

Fiery, laughing and warm, my heart consented
    to rest there a while
on sheets made fragrant with herbs, by bluing tinted
    an azure hue.

THE SACRED ROAD

Through the new wound that fate had opened within me
the setting sun, I thought, rushed through my heart
with swift tremendous force as when waves break
through widening cracks abruptly into a boat
that then sinks steadily.

            For at long length
that evening, like a man long sick who dares
to venture and to milk life from the outer world,
I found myself the one lone walker on that road
that starts from Athens and at Eleusis ends,
its sacred goal. This road had always been
for me the one road of the soul.

            And now
it seemed like a huge river that toward me rolled
rough carts by oxen slowly driven, with wood
or cornstalks filled, and other cars rolled by
whose men within seemed shades.

              But further on,
as though the world were lost and there remained
but nature only, hour by hour there reigned
a calm tranquillity. Then as I faced
a rock to one side rooted, it seemed that throne
which centuries now had destined for me alone.
I sat upon it then and clasped my knees
with both my hands, forgetting if I had set out
this very day or had taken this same road
long centuries ago.

           Soon in this calm,
out of a nearby turning in the road,
three shadows loomed: a Gypsy one of these,
and following close behind him, dragged by chains,
two lumbering bears.

           And then, a short while after,
before I had time enough to observe him well,
the Gypsy saw me, unhooked the tambourine from his back,
with one hand struck it hard while with the other
pulled forcefully on the chains. The two bears then
reared themselves heavily on their hind feet.

The large bear (clearly the mother), her brow adorned
with a white amulet above blue-plaited beads
used to ward off the evil eye, reared up
abruptly and majestically and seemed
like the primordial idol of the Great Goddess,
the Eternal Mother who in holy grief,
and as in time she took on human form,
was when she sorrowed for her daughter called
Demeter here, and later, grieving for her son,
was called Alkmene or the Virgin Mary.
By her side the small cub like a large toy,
a small and ignorant child, rose also now,
compliant, not guessing as yet the full extent
of his own pain, nor yet the bitterness
of slavery mirrored in his mother's burning eyes
that gazed upon him still.

           But when the she-bear
faltered from great fatigue and was slow to dance,
the Gypsy, with one sudden, dexterous pull
on the chain tied to the small bear's bleeding nostrils
—pierced, it was clear, but a few days ago,
with a brass ring—forced her to rise up high,
moaning with pain, and as she turned her head
in the direction of her child, to dance
a lively jig.

And I, as I looked on,
drew then far out of time, beyond time, freed
from forms enclosed in time, from painted forms
or marble forms, for I was out of time,
far out of time.

But there before me, drawn
erect by the ring's violence and the force
of mother love tormented, I could see
nothing but the majestic bear with blue
and plaited beads upon her shaggy head,
the martyred, monstrous symbol of all the world,
present and past, the martyred, monstrous symbol
of that primordial pain to which the tribute
owed by the soul itself has not as yet
been paid by all the mortal centuries.

For the soul still is, as it was, in Hell.

As I threw a coin in the tambourine, I kept
my head bowed low; I, too, all the world's slave.
But as the Gypsy dwindled far away,
dragging with him the lumbering two bears,
and vanished in the evening shades, my heart
bade me rise up to take that road again
that at Eleusis ends in the crumbling ruins
of the Spirit's Sanctuary. And in my heart
I groaned, as I walked on: "Shall that hour come,
shall that hour ever come when the bear's soul,
the Gypsy's soul and my own soul, which now
I name Initiate, shall one day be joined
in joyous festival?"

As I walked on and night
approached, I felt again great darkness brim
and break in my heart with swift, tremendous force
through that same wound which fate had opened within me,
as when waves rush abruptly through widening cracks
into a boat that then sinks steadily.

And yet, as if my heart had thirsted still
for such a flood, and sank as wholly drowned
in darkness, sank in darkness wholly drowned,
a murmuring sound took wing and spread above me,
a murmuring sound that seemed to say:

                                    "It shall come!"

THE SUICIDE OF ATZESIVANO

DISCIPLE OF BUDDHA

Though not dishonored, yet Atzesiváno
took up the sword. And at that very moment
his soul became a pure-white shining dove.
And as from out the inner sanctuary
of heaven upon the night a bright star glides,
or in a mild wind falls an apple blossom,
so from his breast did his calm spirit fly.

The great dead such as these do not go lost;
for only those who love life in its prime
and private worth may of themselves alone
and with divine tranquillity mow down
the tall wheat of a full life bowing down.

REHEARSAL FOR DEATH

Memory here has neither beginning nor end . . .

Fever was then a wreath of crimson roses
around my forehead, a tight wreath which I
could not tear off, and sacred the delirium
deep in me in that hour when from the holy
portal of shadow, through that mist wherein
I had sunk my lashes, you half-opened the door,

your hair unbound, and came—O not as comes
a bitter female mourner to lament
over my body that in early spring
lay like a corpse upon my bed,
                                    but like
Astarte, who for many days prepared
to bring her body wholly into Hades,
to bring the light of her body into Hades
that all of Hades might from her body glow;

and counted calmly the days of her great
godlike ordeal: three days of fast, three more
to cleanse herself complete in sacred springs,
to wash and comb her hair, refresh her head,
to paint her lips and then to clothe herself
in seven stoles which one above the other
around her holy nakedness revolved
like planets slowly; and thus descend to Darkness
step by step, and there before each gate
cast off a stole until in the profound,
the uttermost divine profound, she brought
her never-setting light deep into Hades
that her full nakedness might abolish Hades.

Thus in this way prepared did you descend
even to me, and here beside me lay,
and lay beside me mute and motionless,
and Hades was abolished from my heart,
Hades became victory and resurrection,
and in my fist I grasped the enormous pearl
and took spring in my heart, and swiftly felt
the crimson roses of fever to be a crown,
and my somber bed a ship, the ship of a god
unhindered, and the laboring of my mind
became a navigator amid the stars . . .

But ah, not even the Shunammite lay down
with David thus, to warm in his cold bed
the frozen limbs of David, prophet and king,

from whose soul psalms had fled and from whose heart
all holy manly warmth had blown away
that in him once awakened prophet and king,
dancer and warrior, foremost and first defender
before the Ark of the Lord;
                        not even the Shunammite
lay down by the side of David thus as you
beside me lay when my heart sank deep in Hades!

You came not by those paths where mortals walk,
to be among the treasures of my pain, but like
two stars that, wandering through countless aeons,
suddenly meet and revolve around each other
till heaven and earth are filled with their harmony;
so did you lay beside me, and I reached out
one hand to touch the sky, and with the other
most gently raised your head, till the whole earth
was filled with our embrace throughout, and the earth
was sailing in the midst of stars, and the earth
was chanting, and my bed rose like a prow
straight toward the pole, smashing the waves of time,
and the beginning, the voyage, and the end became
a single cataclysm of holy light before me!

Behold, then! from my very being's depth,
from that profundity where a god was hiding
deep in the shadowed regions of my mind,
the divine delirium sprang, now freed at last;
and from the dazzlement of my silences
great strophes quickly overbrimmed my brain,
swift sudden strophes that sang out:
                            "This bed
is not for you the bed of a sick man now
for it's become the mystic trireme of Dionysos
that there beyond the enormous waves of time,
beyond the confined, closed rhythms of Creation
is swiftly, forcefully flying like an arrow!

"Listen to the roar of your liberation! Although
you flamed with fever but a brief while ago,

and though your body burned like resinous pine,
this was to teach you how to burn! For now
you are approaching the flame that lies not in
the created but in the Creator's mind alone.
This star that glows beside you is that of Hebe,
it is the blazing star of eternal Youth,
the star that pierces through the light of day!

"You are no longer a part of what the sun
shines on. You are a soul that lives in fire
in the sun's depths, you are within the sun,
and those flames that light up the other stars
and all the world, are now outside, outside.
You see the stars, but they do not see you.
You see the world, but the world does not see you.
Deep in the sun of your passion where you are
you hide and shoot your flaming arrows toward
that place where the stubborn strifes of all creation
have not yet dawned. For you this passion here
is but a rehearsal, a noble rehearsal for death;
and practice for it now as the fire within you
deserves, and which you contain deep in your brain
not as created being but as the Creator himself.
This is a rehearsal for death, a great beginning,
where height and depth have finally become one;
your mind is on Olympos, and your heart
shines into Hades sweetly; a great beginning,
a giant bow has been given into your hands,
so do not shirk to bend it and to pass
beyond all obstacles with the swift dart
of your desire, until you reach the living god
who from one resurrection always toward
another resurrection rushes to create
the one and only flesh, deep from his flesh
another flesh; the living god who strives
forever, neither in marble nor in verse,
but in an immortal body to take on
both soul and stature worthy of his breath;
the unsleeping Artisan, who seeks from clay
to mold at last in fire the fiery statue
of man.

Listen to the roar of your liberation. . . .

"Death for you now becomes the Form of Desire,
so let it tower as high as its redemption,
trampling on death with death!

"I do not say: to go beyond all time
you must yourself become eternal. Look,
the world behind you burns like Troy, its wildfire
shines deep in the past like city windows that now
reflect the setting sun, blaze up, and then
are suddenly plunged in darkness.
      Far beyond,
like smoke and clouds of the same conflagration,
all things man dreams of for the future melt
slowly away and disappear. But you
are always freeing yourself from time. Leave here
the coarsely cut and ignorant generation
to its own thoughts, that are but ruins and lies,
and plunge complete into that infinite
cold chill that flows deep in your mind, where yet
the stubborn strifes of creation have not yet dawned,
that in your body and mind might glow the perfect
splendor of Thought and the perfect *Let there be!* . . ."

Thus did the god who deep within me hides
release in me the divine delirium
with sudden strophes in that hour when
like nude Astarte entering into Hades,
and as the Shunammite could never lie
in David's bed, you suddenly transformed
my blood and spirit, from that fever which then
burned in my brow, into that mystic fever,
into that perfect and noble practice for death
which now tears through into the day's illusion
that yesterday was locked within my heart—
lays waste and bare the barricades of time,
breaks down the barriers of the world and fate,

and then above time, fate, and the world enthroned,
in that place where creation's stubborn strifes
have not yet dawned, it suddenly lets loose—
(O star of Youth, star of eternal Hebe)
to mold one sacred reborn universe,

(Memory here has neither beginning nor end)

—the oceanic roar of my liberation! . . .

"HAUTE ACTUALITÉ"

"When the new King of Egypt, Farouk, ascended the throne,
he thought of transferring the mummies of the Pharaohs
from the museums to their original tombs with great official
pomp and splendor."
> —*Newspaper account of 1936*

Here where the final Lotus sprang for me,
in this desolate cape where I have turned
my face, that it may be hammered out,
at dawn, in the illimitable ocean and the sun,
and in the breaths of stellar wastes at night;

here where the wind blows without end
in the dry grasses round about me,
and a voice whispers, as if it were the very
language of my soul,

how was I suddenly turned,
so deeply immersed in listening,
to this distant message from the world?
> "The new

King of Egypt has decreed that the holy
corpses of the forty
dynasties of the Land of the Nile
shall from their crystal tombs be raised
where they have lain so many years enclosed,

gaped at by the irreverent multitude,
and with magnificent pomp
shall in their primal tombs once more be buried.

There shall precede, chosen amid all
the territories of Apis, the greatest female mourner,
who will from time to time burst out in great lament,
—as if Osiris for the second time endured
his death at Typhon's hands—

and there shall follow, behind the royal orchestras,
a Chorus of Youths and Maidens,
slowly,
upon their golden-woven pillows holding
the emblems of the Pharaohs;

and like a silver-swirling river,
a little behind,
the Egyptian priests, each with his white tiara,
and on his breast the multicolored jewels
inlaid with gold,
shall chant
funeral supplications from the Book of the Dead;

until the Desert is reached,
and there,
like an ostrich who thrusts her eggs in the sand
and waits for the Sun to hatch them,
they shall rethrust their holy dead
into the revolving centuries to await
from Osiris their glowing resurrection.

And then, with head unbared,
unarmed,
the King shall kneel upon the sand,
raising his hands amid the dead and living,
and call
upon the Spirit of his Ancestors
to descend like a blessing on the Land of the Nile,
on his own bent head,

and on all his people.
And with blood
and spirit thus renewed
from this great Ceremony,
all shall return to their homes and their work,
to continue with faith,
again, the toil of the forty
dynasties of the Land of the Nile."

This is what I heard
that for one moment swept me away
from the wind's whispering in the dry grasses,
from the illimitable ocean and the sun,
from drifts of wind in my face in the starry Desert,
and I said:
"In truth, it profits me to follow this funeral
of Pharaohs into the Desert,
and with denuded mind
to lean the Polar Star
of my Thought
on their magnificent and resurrectional expectation."

But for one moment only!

For behold, the wind's breath once more about me
scatters from the dry thistles
their star-shaped fluff into the distance,
and once more,
with my whole mind, now freed
from this greatly imagined Phantasm of Time,
that for a while had bewitched me,

like a snake
lately emerged out of its molting
with skin renewed,
I plunge
—a dragon now—
into the eternal coolnesses about me
of earth and of sea,
and with my entire being,

like a naked body
that for the first time leans
upon another naked and beloved body,
whose Touch redeems the infinite within me
and annihilates
all the horizons of the world around me,

I raise myself aloft,
holding within me deeply enclosed
my own Eternity,
while here where the final Lotus sprang for me,
and the dry grasses about me whisper in a tongue
which is the very language of my soul,
I feel on my mouth suddenly and again,
flaming and ready to hatch
my new Word with invincible pulse,
lip on lip glued,
flaming, burning,
the virginal kiss of the Abyss!

UNRECORDED

A little beyond the walls of Zion walking
one day somewhat before the set of sun,
Jesus and his disciples came by chance
to that place where for years the town had cast
its rubbish: burnt mattresses of the diseased,
rags, broken crockery, refuse, and filth.

And there upon the highest mound of all,
bloated, its legs turned upward toward the sky,
the carcass of a dog lay stretched, from which
at once, as vultures thickly piled on it
took fright at steps approaching, so foul a stench
broke forth, that the disciples as one man,
holding their breath within their hands, drew back . . .

But Jesus paced his way alone and paused
serenely awhile before that mound of filth,
and gazed upon that carcass, until one
of the disciples, unable to restrain himself,
spoke from afar: "Rabbi, can you not smell
that horrid stench and stand so closely by?"

And He, his eyes not swerving from that sign
on which he gazed, replied: "This horrid stench
does he whose breath is pure breathe even in that
same town from which we came . . . But now with all
my soul do I most marvel at that thing
which issues here from this decay . . . For see
how in the sun the teeth of this dog shine,
now like the hailstone, now like the lily, far
beyond the decay, like a tremendous vow,
reflection of the Eternal, but still more,
the hope and the sharp lightning bolt of Justice!"

Thus did He speak; and if they understood
these words or not, together the disciples
followed once more as He went on his silent way.

And now, my Lord, the last of all indeed,
how I do turn my mind on these Thy words,
and wholly in one thought consumed, do stand
before Thee. O grant, even to me, my Lord,
that when I walk beyond the walls of Zion,
and all, from the one end to the other end
of earth, are ruins, all are sweepings, all
unburied corpses that choke up the sacred spring
of breath, that in the city or beyond the city,
amid this horrible stench through which I pass,
grant me, my Lord, if only for a moment,
Thine own sublime serenity, that I may pause
unterrified within the midst of carrion
until I also may seize deep in my eyes
some white spot, like the hailstone, like the lily,
something that suddenly may glow deep within me
out of decay, beyond the world's decay,

as shone the teeth of that dog, O my Lord,
on which Thou gazed in the slow setting sun
and stood and marveled, a tremendous vow,
reflection of the Eternal, but still more,
the hope and the sharp lightning bolt of Justice!

GREEK SUPPER FOR THE DEAD

(O Dionysos-Hades, my divine protector!)

Because my friends had waited long to hear
flaming new songs rise to my lips, as once
they knew the artery of my speech would burst
and flood like a fiery stream, they had invited me
far out from the city here to dine in this
large room with all its windows opened wide
on deep-set gardens and all the stars above them.

On the linen cloth between the crystal cups
they had set scarlet roses, and had hung
green wreaths upon the walls from which
a fragrant and languid odor emanated;
in silver candelabra they had lit
candles whose flames, in a slight breeze flickering,
everywhere leant and lengthened, but burnt on.
Then of the frugal meal before us we ate
in a long silence, for all unwillingly
our minds were twisted around one single thought;
but when the black wine my belovéd friend
had brought for me was served, fragrant and brusque
as the blood of Dionysos spilled, he turned
toward me with his great glass filled to the brim,
and calling me by name, said: "Ángelos,
now if you wish, give voice unto the night."

But I replied: "And do you ask, O friend,
that I give voice even unto this night

which like that very glass you hold is filled
up to the brim, this night which may be said
to set a last circumference round our souls
and is the same circumference of our silence?
Tell me, who was it took such careful pains
over this meal, or like a hierophant
stood over it and so adorned it that
it now seems meant to be Pluto's sacred portion
or the entowered lonely Supper for the Dead
and where deep in the thoughts of each before it
the rites of their memorial service glow?
For as upon an ear of wheat a host
of winged ants falls, so have the souls of all
the dead who wake within our hearts enclosed
this feast, those souls of men whose steps and shapes
we and the eternal night still deeply hold
within us, as in silence once they climbed
above the rocks and beyond the high lookouts
of death to drink deep at the wells of courage.
But numberless other ancient spirits now,
numerous other souls that fill the night
are swarming still, I feel, from every corner,
drawn by the fervor of our silent hearts,
like moths attracted to the candle's flame,
until the dead by far outnumber the living.
O let them come here even to us, O friends,
to spread invisibly their open hands
over this feast of Pluto's, let them come
to this entowered Supper for the Dead,
even here among us, and with us be One.
And with this glass you gave me, friend,
filled to the brim, wherein now if I bend
I see my face as if reflected from out
another world, and with this wine you brought me,
fragrant and brusque as blood of Dionysos
spilled, let us like the Initiates of old
from the great goblet of Agathodemon
drink as from rites of holy sacrament,
and keep a silence profound until that time
(may it not be far off, my friends) when all

the powers of God shall suddenly begin
to groan within us deeply, when his roars,
louder than sound of earthquake, shall rouse up
living and dead together in full array
for the divine onslaught . . . And as for the new
and flaming songs that you now long to hear
rise to my lips, they too shall come, my friends,
in their own good time."

                         I spoke, and whether or not
they had well understood all I had sought,
they sipped of the wine, and I, the last of all,
drank to the last drop also, like the priest
who drains the holy chalice in the Inner Sanctum;
and then together as one we softly turned our steps
—the candles one by one had guttered out—
toward the wide-open windows, beyond which lay
the black enstarred vast ocean of the night
that on its pulse upheld us in our silence . . .

And if no one within that darkness spoke,
from deep within us the same thought and vow
rose upward toward the vast gloom and the stars:
"Hearken, divine protector, O Dionysos-Hades,
restrain our hearts now with the brusque black wine
of your deep pain, guard them and strengthen them
and keep them still untouched until that hour
when suddenly your cry, louder than roar
of earthquake, shall rouse up living and dead
together with us at once to the divine onslaught!"

ATTIC

On our two horses, brother,
the black-maned Orion,
and the blond Demogorgon, on the drop

of deathless noon,
we trotted on the road to Eleusis,
slowly conversing,
like two ancient priests of Athens, astride . . .

"Is this perhaps chimerical?
I see not from the measured light
but from a lightning prodigal
which has from all sides wrapped me round . . .

"And where is Time? From out my brain
the slightest breeze has taken it . . .
These pines are from eternity, this breeze
eternal that from the fresh thyme blows . . .

"And this same rhythm with which we trot
is as it were the same whose master mold
some ancient horses left faint traces of,
treading upon this holy ground . . ."

"Only that body which from death
can rise may gaze upon and face
such earth as this, in silence such as this,
victorious body that shall unloose

"even those final chains that wind it round
as from its thread the caterpillar that
shall bloom with wings, or from his mind
the thought of man that blooms with inner vision.

"No, it is not chimerical that we
on this divine day are astride a dream
where all, invisible, visible, our horses, the gods and we,
breathe in the same cool crystal sphere!"

"Would I might never waken from this dream . . .
Soon, as we reach the sea at that hour when

out of the heat we goad our horses on,
thrusting their flanks into the waves

"like prows, we shall awaken, it may be,
once more amid the impediments of time
to scatter once again the miracle amid
rejoicings mystical and the enormous strife . . ."

"Do you live still in the divisible tumult,
brother? and have you still from out
the thin soil of this earth not yet
redeemed the body mystically achieved,

"like the cicada which, emerging from its tomb,
enthroning itself upon the topmost bough,
stands sentry over earth and sun and gods
with its brief frugal hymn of resurrection?

"But we who have so often conquered death,
brother, and have the darknesses dissolved
of times like these, now for the indivisible push on,
and grow, the more we speed, younger than youth.

"And it may be that our horses now have here
divined all this which we as yet do not
perceive, for now behold them in the road's midst
how they begin to chew their bridles and to dance

"lightly, as if and suddenly they sought
to change their pace and, on this ancient lane—
hold fast to your bridle, brother, and push on—
to change their steady gallop and to take wing.

"No, it is not chimerical that we
on this divine day are astride a dream where all,
invisible, visible, our heroes, the gods and we,
rush in the same eternal sphere. . . ."

THE SUPREME LESSON

Ah, what commotion of the sea was heard upon the rocks
at early matin, black as the black shield
of God, with dreadful constellations written,
upon that hour when suddenly the veins swell up and sweep away
the Word within our brains,
like billows that uproot
the seaweed from the deep and cast them on the sand;
and thoughts, from the unutterable furor of the loins
bring up, dragged out of the abyss,
odor of their primordial procreative roots!

Ah what wild roaring of the sea was heard upon the rocks
as waves, from the night wind intoxicated,
increasingly got drunk, and strove with tongues of foam
to climb up and submerge the mountain on the desert isle,
and slowly bit by bit to eat away
its firm foundation and drag it with them to the deep! . . .

Meanwhile the Holy Men, locked in their cells
upon the Sacred Mountain, all night long with psalms
kept vigil, and in meditation sought
to learn how time might be subdued—the young
with neophyte ascetic rage, the old
still in their struggle seeking to forget
how their beards had grown white with the long years . . .

But this mad wind that blew tonight
was like no other wind, to say it had
the sea and earth and atmosphere for boundary,
it was no maniacal wind to blow
with malice on ships, nor was it the North Wind
nor the etesian winds of summer, nor the deep wind
of spring to summon flowers from the earth;
it was the great wind of full Intoxication
as if it sought in its embrace to take

back all once more, the heavens, sea and earth,
in its embrace, in its divine embrace forever . . .

And then these Holy Men, feeling that this
must be a message sent from Dionysos—
like swallows who as one first feel the breath of autumn
and thickly flock together for the great migration—
all rose together and convened to go
to the old hierophant, who had well past
a century yet still remained their leader,
(for still he seemed the youngest of them all,
and like a rod by generations smoothed
stood upright, and his hair from whiteness gleamed like gold)
that they might ask what is this wind that blows . . .

And he replied:
                    "The spirit poured out in everything,
spirit of the vast prenatal Drunkenness,
and on this night the sea is but one drop, one drop alone
on the masculine teat of that great God, our Giant . . .

"But you who are His mystic army, gather now
upon His summons, according to your seniority
and as the nature of each one dictates,
Satyrs, Sileni, Holy Men, and hierophants,
that we might go down to that shore which is
but symbol of our separation from the world,
(until the Vine shall bridge sea, earth, and stars,
till life and death are one), and say:

'We come before Thee virginal, my Lord, each with
his virtue bare, as it was planted from the seed,
we with the phallus, with our hearts,
and with our silence never cheapened with false words,
we who have here trained the black eye of theory
that it might pierce through the unfathomable ether . . .

'But this pith which in our bones remains tonight,
and this black lump of brain which now like bread
swells up on a dark night and strives to burst

the stitches of our skull, this sudden squall
of the cosmic pulse that swells gigantically
and drags us like sea monsters to the open seas of darkness—
can the Word satisfy all these, my Lord?
For Thy bare strength, at length, floods through us now,
and body, heart, and mind are all turned toward
Thy vast Abyss where Number chokes and calls on us
to measure up, once and for all, to Thy great Passion!

'O dreadful God, our God, great masculine joy
of ours, who far outstripst Olympos, and who makest
the lyres silent, for Thou speakest only with
the speechless eloquence of the black firmament,
give us to drink tonight from the great cup
of Thy omnipotence; and from its navel cord
cut off the earth and draw it in Thy immortal orbit,
unloosen it from the Sun's belt that it may, self-announced,
swing, free, in the Night!' "

Thus spoke the Holy Man, and taking up his staff
with ivy twined, went on before, and the others followed him . . .

But as they were descending to the shore
it seemed that—like a horseman bending down
close to his horse's ear to say a coaxing word,
until its unimpeded gallop turns at once
into a surging rhythm, while above them still
with pullulating pulse throb Hydra, Orion, Medusa,
Andromeda, Antares, Cepheus and Ophiucus,
so did God through the portal of the constellations
draw in the wind and bring it, deeply breathed,
into serenity, a new serenity; and like Io,
pursued by Argos and listening to the sounds
of her own exhaustion, or like one who hears
at night the double beat of his own footsteps
and fears that someone pounds behind him, so did the Spirit,
that once rushed headlong to escape her orbit,

sink suddenly in the vast flood of Ecstasy;
and lo, on the huge rock of the promontory

they could distinguish dimly as on a high
altar, emergent from the flood of night,
the outspread body of a woman clad in a shroud,
and over her with sword in hand and outstretched wing
a nude man bent his deathless head and thus lamented:

"Sleep, my belovèd. . . . Didst thou ever think
when thou didst lean thy head upon my breast,
upon that breast where throbs the whole world's heart,
that but a little more and thou wouldst sleep forever?

"Thou who hast sought the love of God thy whole life long,
behold now when today thy triumph rises!

"O simplicity, that knowest not thyself,
nor how from the abyss thou hast redeemed thy holy form!
But see how even the abyss her mantle leaves
for thee, and how thy own deification shines,
shines out of darkness, desire and satisfaction
both, and ah, behold how from the depths of the abyss
lightly arrives thy wreath for thee, Ariadne! . . .

"But men know only how to give a sepulchre
to thee, and know not the enormous bliss
of death, as thou hast known it here with me
upon this night, my Holy One, within creation . . .
Because for love of me thou hadst the storm
for cradle, and even Death for you was Life.
Now day breaks, and I take thy spirit behind
the light, but here let all the faithful bend
over thy holy corpse to face it for a moment,
who in their unrestrained desire to join
the Mystery now can no other peace possess
than this same miracle which is the Form
when She forever lies in calm repose!"

He spoke, and as an eagle of the sea
hearing a strange footfall takes silent wing
from off a desolate rock, so did the God
vanish beyond the waves, while the pomp with awe

drew near that place whereon the Holy Form
reclined in calm repose before the sea . . .

And lo, as they approached the Sleeping Form,
whatever the immeasurable commotion
had not swept from their hearts, trouble and toil
and the slavery of time, her Sovereign Matrix
now swept away, and in the early light of dawn
glowed softly; and on the veil that covered her, one hand
was placed with open palm upon her holy sex,
and from the shroud, alone, into the air
her big toe hung, as it were made of marble . . .

And as it slowly dawned they could no longer tell
whether the waves were those of sea or sky,
nor separate at length the heavens and earth,
but all the mountains seemed now without weight,
and all things in and round themselves lost heaviness,
and all in the profound depths of their hearts
were infinitely and eternally conjoined,
for everything converged in concord toward
the Immortal Matrix of the Heavenly Form
that now in her calm sleep reposed forever . . .

And then they formed a circle round about her
from far away, and did not speak, ecstatic,
because the spirit was not in conflict with the Word,
but as it sank within her radiant Form
they found nor start nor end to their vast silence . . .

But further on, the Holy Sage sat on a rock,
and lifting up his mantle, covered his white head
as though he sought to re-create the sacred vision
deep in himself with greater holiness,
with greater holiness and greater magnitude . . .

But suddenly—as if he were emerging whole
from out of silence, from the vision now reborn—
he rose again, and lo, it seemed as if his voice,
lightly commingling with the pulse of the heavens,
was like a rising sun that sprang from deep within him . . .

"Forward, go forward, raise the holy corpse,
as our great God ordained a while before . . .
For this is but one moment only that exalts
life above life, with the first touch of Death,
gigantic sculpture raised toward everything . . .
The noises of the world fade out before it,
and all creation is like incense round it,
and here before us dawns the peace of the abyss . . .
This moment is the greatest of all on earth
that God in His Intoxication has bestowed
on all the faithful who in unrestrained desire
to merge with the Mystery may no other peace possess
than this same miracle which is the Form
when she forever lies in calm repose . . .

"But yet I think, in truth, God tests us all
upon this moment, the most revered of all . . .
He casts the seed deep into us like bait,
but since He has with his own gifts equipped us,
He suddenly lights up our minds and goads us on,
if need be, to contend even with Him . . .
For soon the sun shall rise now, and the great
sculpture of our desire shall fall, as suddenly falls
the ashes of a tall fire that first lights all in gold . . .
Forward, go forward, raise the holy corpse,
and when we have entombed the splendid body,
let us erect a Gate above it which shall show
how all Eternity proceeds from Time alone . . .

"But not for us . . . Sufficient that thirst unto itself
that finds alone the wine for which it seeks
and casts off limitations for the highest Intoxication!
Such is our dreadful God who may one hour demand,
and suddenly, that we release ourselves from Him
in holy vertigo, until the cloud of the mad mind
itself shall burst, and all the torrents of new light
plunge at the expectations of our desires
in a sheer deluge, whether our minds can hold or not . . .
For we forever do contend with Death,
and if upon the utmost limit of our struggle

the Form, O Holy Seal, may for a moment grant us peace,
death, nonetheless, has set no limits to our God . . .

"But let us hold the Form up to the height of Death
always, wherever Form may dawn for us,
because this is for us the only limit worthy of her!"

Thus did he speak . . . And all together then
drew near to elevate the holy corpse devoutly . . .
But O, great miracle, the corpse could not be raised!
It had become united with the rock, it had become
enmarbled and united with all surrounding things . . .

Because whatever has with Dionysos once been merged,
and tasted deeply of the mystic Death, does not,
before it goes to face that other Death,
stop in the halfway road that leads to Eternity;
but since for that one gift it gave up all its breath,
and since its spirit was stripped bare by Love,
it shall be naked when it takes the wreath of the Abyss! . . .

Kóstas Ouránis

EDWARD VI

In damp Westminster Abbey's sunless vaults,
stretched taut at the feet of his great ancestors,
Edward the Sixth, a sixteen-year-old king,
sleeps his deep marble sleep, long, long forgotten.
He was a somber, sad, most noble youth
who in his ice-cold palace lived with books,
with bishops and stern sages for companions,
whose death became his only history.
Since love affairs he had none, nor made war,
on his cold marble tomb have not been carved
the triumphal escutcheons left him by his forebears,
but only these flowers for his royal crest:
the Galatian lily and the Tudor rose.

Fragrant his tomb, as though these flowers were real.

PRAYER TO GOD
FOR ALL WHO ARE UNHAPPY

Dear God, now on this mournful winter night, when all
your angels, from their countries of eternal peace,
lean down their lonely balconies to watch the earth
and slowly shower it with petals of white flowers,
the while it turns in silence in the infinite;

dear God, now on this night when every fierce wind howls
like low sin-laden souls rejected by the grave,
think of all those who lie here in their wretched beds
to sleep and muster their spent strength that they might bear
tomorrow also the same pains borne yesterday.

Dear God, take on a human heart and think tonight
of those old poets who've lived long in bitterness
because stern Glory never once knocked on their door;
of those whose destiny, like a malignant wind,
knocks down whatever they have raised with love and toil;
those who rebelled against their lives and would not await
tomorrows, different from others, but that never came;
think of all those at whom the whole world stares and laughs,
those innocent, half-looney fools that all men mock;
those who are chronically ill, who die their death each day;
those homely and shy girls who swoon away with love
though no one ever, ever comes to bring them love;
those who toil achingly that other men may rest,
the docile souls, the persecuted, and the good
who cannot shed a tear because they've wept so much;
dear God, think of all those who in this world are doomed
to stoop, to suffer, and to drag their heavy steps
yet in your tranquil churches find no consolation
because their wretched voices have long since been cracked
and your celestial throne looms far, far out of reach.

Dear God, think of all those most wrongfully unhappy,
but do not send them Happiness as recompense
—for this will not suffice them now for all their pain—
but when today they close their weary eyes in sleep
let Death come gently, softly to their wretched homes,
most gently and most softly that they may not waken,
and as a sister stooping low—not as a mother,
because a mother's embrace is strong, her clasp despairing—
kiss them most tenderly on their closed, bitter lips
and in that kissing take away their breath forever.

Dear God, now on this mournful winter night, when all
your angels, from their countries of eternal peace,
lean down their lonely balconies to watch the earth

and slowly shower it with petals of white flowers,
do not close by your side in Paradise among
the chosen place these dead, but let them still lie buried
deep in the bowels of earth so that the foul world's noise
might never reach their sleep. There let them lie forgotten.

FONTAINE DE MEDICIS

I know a far-off corner in an ancient park
where even loving couples never dare to go,
for darksome waters lurk there choked with rotted leaves,
and deep-green shadows lean low in their watery veils.
There stand stone benches by the twisted ivy twined,
and naked statues by pale moss and lichen dressed,
and a most deadly quiet where only ceaselessly
murmurs the lamentation of mysterious waters.

There have I always seen unknown and sallow women
that seeming without age, with no life in their eyes,
spread on their knees their old, eternal embroideries,
and pallid youths who in their hands hold ancient books:
yet those never embroidered, and these never read,
but in deep reverie gazed on the dark, stagnant waters.

I SHALL DIE ONE DAY ON A
MOURNFUL AUTUMN TWILIGHT

I shall die one day on a mournful autumn twilight
in my cold room where I have lived alone;
in my last anguish I shall hear the rain
and all the familiar noises the street scatters.

I shall die one day on a mournful autumn twilight
amid furniture not mine and scattered books;

the street police shall find me in my bed
and bury a man who had no history.

Among my friends who now and then play cards
someone will simply ask, "Has anyone seen
Ouránis? He hasn't been around for days."
Another, playing, will answer, "But he died!"

They'll stop their playing a moment, cards in hand,
shake their heads slowly, sorrowfully, and say,
"Ah, what is man! He was living but yesterday!"
And then renew their playing without a word.

Some friend will write in the "small notices"
that "poor Ouránis died abroad untimely,
a youth well known amid our set, whose book
of poems, just published, showed great promise."

And this will be my life's last epitaph.
Only my agéd parents, of course, will weep,
hold requiem with many, too many, priests,
with all my friends attending, even my foes.

I shall die one day on a mournful autumn twilight
in a room strange to me, in noisy Paris,
and some "Ketty," thinking I've jilted her for another,
will write to curse me. . . . But I shall be dead.

NEL MEZZO DEL CAMMIN . . .

Here am I, also, midway in my life's journey,
but no dark forest do I see before me,
not even Virgil's dim and darkling ghost
that might become my guardian and my guide.

Neither a forest nor a ghost, but only
a mournful wilderness in which I freeze;

the more I wander on the wider grows
the zone of silence that encircles me.

All of my long past life now seems to me
like an improbable and alien story
related in an old book long ago,
retained but dimly by my memory.

No news or message ever comes for me,
nor do I wait now for another spring;
I walk on down my naked, barren road:
I shall be dying until the day I die.

AQUARELLE

On the mole, half-asleep in the summer's heat,
scalding mists leap above the blazing sand,
and its small houses, whitewashed and stripped bare,
make white brush strokes on the unmoving sea.
There gold-green waters in translucency
reveal snake-twisted seaweed, silver pebbles,
red-rusting anchors, shadows of dark blue
cast round their rims by the becalmed caïques.

Not a single soul! A lone man fishing there
stretches his numb hands sluggishly and yawns,
then sprawls on the hot stones and falls asleep;
there only a ferocious, black-haired dog
squats by the prow of a large fishing boat
and squints on the dead seastrand drowsily.

THE LIVING DEAD

You have not died! Still in this quiet room
your fragrance lingers on as though you have just left me,

your still unfinished embroidery cast there on the couch,
the music you were playing still open on the piano.
There on my tabletop your portrait always lies
and gazes at me always with its tranquil eyes,
and it is not the wind, but you now at the door
which you half open to enter as the dark night falls.
You have not died. You are everywhere in all things:
in the fallen petals of the rose, in the wind's sigh,
in the cloud's golden glimmer when the day is dying,
and even at night I feel you lying by my side. . . .
You have not died. It does not matter if the months pass:

The dead die only when they've been forgotten.

PARK IN AUTUMN

How mournful seems the park in all this rain,
its pallid flowers wounded and bent low,
its statues washed and cleansed as round each base
in heaps rot withered leaves the wind has brought.
Under the dry horizon's ash-gray hue
the roads now seem deserted, endless, cold,
with their tall trees stripped to the bone as though
they led to the mute kingdoms of the dead.

And by the shadowed ponds the ancient urns
cast no reflections as in summertime
when the white pigeons flutter down to drink.
Only the fountain's musical lament
in the thin rain and the cold air in vain
is scattered through the nude and anguished day.

VITA NUOVA

I only want to live now like a tree
that rustles lightly on an April morning

in a calm field all filled with azure light,
red poppies and the pure white camomile.
I only want to live now like a rose
that in mild winter blossoms all alone
on a low parapet, sunbathed and poor,
whose whitewashed surface holds the earth in place.

Dear God, let me but live as only one
of myriad, useless insects drunk with light
who while away their life among the flowers,
far from the world, alone in a white hut:
within my soul the tranquil peace of the old,
and in my heart the poor's god-given goodness.

GIRL THIRTEEN YEARS OLD

Swift, lithe, and slippery, like a snake, whenever
I reached my hands to catch her, she slipped away,
provoking yet escaping me forever,
laughing and mocking in her happiness.
But as we played and I pursued, whenever
our bodies in the tussle touched and clung,
she laughed—but not as innocently as before,
and blood rushed to my forehead like a wave.

Thus for a moment, as I seized her waist
and held her in my arms with fierce desire,
enslaving her slim thighs between my knees,
I knew her sweet surrender in my grasp
as her eyes glazed and her thin lips trembled:
and felt the female within her awakening.

SUPPLICATION
TO MY GUARDIAN ANGEL

O angel, who once succored all my childhood years,
who like a shelter spread above me your vast wings,

on those wild nights when fleet rains beat the windowpanes
and frenzied winds shook all the house as I stared wide
awake, my poor heart trembling like a bird for fear
all gnomes and demons, creatures of the Lower World,
would smash the windows, rush into my room pellmell
and loom before me with their bellowing and guffaws;
O angel, with your herbs and all your myriad ways,
come, let's go wandering in untrodden, magic lands,
conquering all obstacles, outwitting every witch,
spearing gigantic dragons with their flaming tongues,
opening without a key old haunted palaces
till as we battle all alone his brave battalions
we force the aging King to beg and sue for peace,
to grant us half his kingdom, and his daughter too;
O angel, who grant life and speech to everything,
who turn my every day to a new miracle,
who when dark winter held me shut within my house
paraded all the world before my startled eyes,
who turned our house into a palace as I played,
our garden to thick woods, my stick to a swift steed,
who in my sickness hovered nigh, and for cool drink
gave me immortal water that I might never die—
I send you now my prayer like a dove to find you
that you might once more be the guardian of my life.

STARTING POINT

I give now a backward glance
and measure my life's sweep:
how great the swift rush forward,
how small the leap!

STOP SENDING NOW

Stop sending now these signals of alarm,
these shrill wails of the hysterical ship's siren,

and let the wheel run loose in the tempest's hands:
the most dread shipwreck surely is to be saved!

What then? Return to boring Ithaca,
to our cheap joys, our miserable concerns,
to our faithful spouse who weaves her smothering love
round, round our lives like a fine spider's web?

To know once more, beforehand, what tomorrow
will bring, nor feel a single yearning dawn,
until our dreams resemble the fruit once more
that withers away, then rots and falls to earth?

Since we lacked daring (and shall always lack it!)
let's rise alone from our smooth, narrow beds
and like free men at the world's early dawn
take to the great, the unfamiliar roads

with a light step like that of a bird on earth
as our souls shiver, leaves in a fine breeze;
let's not at least let this occasion slip
to become the playthings of the savage billows

no matter what the consequence! Grim waves
like tentacles can drag us down the dark depths
or in their sweeping onrush raise us high
aloft—until our foreheads touch the stars.

THE DARK WELL

Above myself, as over a well,
I stoop, and deep in its dark grounds
cast my voice like a small stone,
but not a single echo sounds.

Silence alone, and emptiness
roost there, as though the water's flow
in the vast darkness of the well
had dried up a long, long time ago.

Tákis Papatsónis

BEFORE THE ADVENT

I feel myself to be a man disgraced,
walking nightlong and daylong beyond the Paling
of a Garden lush with fountains and flowers,
waiting in vain for the Great Gate to open again, and to admit me.
And I am tired with the remembrance only
of the evil life I have lived to this day.
And I am downhearted because I am thwarted now
when I long to lie down under the foliage of the Shadow of Grace.
And the dumb beasts, the Hens and the Hares,
the Pigeons and the Bats, wander freely in the Bushes;
the Honeybees sing, and the Snails,
after the rain, proceed in their Easter Barouches.
Only I, by the Paling, like a Poacher or Beggar
expelled by the Gardeners and the Wicked Servants,
come near to dying in the oppressive dampness
of whole winter nights in the freezing North Winds.
Nor can I run off again into that City of Tumult
where I behold the embrace of Evil opening for me
with a warm welcome. For I am gripped
with nausea at the sight of her only.
I cry out, I cry out by the Threshold of the Outer Door,
I cry out like a False Prophet derided by all:
"Open the Church at least for me that I may go
there where you suffer the stray Tramps of the mountains."
But no mercy is heard for the entreating voice.
Punishment buffets me about like snow-beaten Winter,
like unbearable Cold, with no fire, no bed,

no roof, no food, nor pity, nor forgiveness,
and snowbound Christmas approaches.
The Shepherds take down their Flutes, dust off the Church
      Organs,
and the Magi watch the Heavens daylong and nightlong
to find the Star of the newly born Infant God.
A small Ray of life and warmth, like a glowworm
behind a Hedge in a dead Midnight of Vigilance,
reaches even to me. Can it be they will come for me also,
the Angels, the Village Visitors, with their joyful Caroling?

TO A YOUNG GIRL
BROUGHT UP IN A NUNNERY

SALVE, SANCTA VIRGO!

Storm, the first message of winter.
Black clouds only beshroud us now,
the freezing winds drive away our fervor
and cry out new messages in an uproar.
As in the year past and in a similar cycle
this tale, a reminder of old dreams,
flows from the lips like a blast
of delight and terror. And soon
a shivering in my body chills me by the Fireside:

"The Young Girl in the Nunnery has grown up
beside the Lilies, by the side of the meek Nuns;
she was the Heart and Gold of that Institution . . .
Moments of infinite beauty came to her
like those on Christmas Eve when she tied a small bow
on the neck of a toy Lamb and caressed it . . .
And the Snows were many. Ooo-ooo went the wind
and shook all the Trees, and bent the Firs.
And the Windowpanes permitted the Chill
of the day and its Terror to enter the cells . . .
Not a soul living, only the Sainted Women

moving about in the Holy Corridors:
only the Young Girl, their Blessed Toy,
giving passage of a sort to the Terror."

O Tranquillity, thou who art moved
by the mild mutations of nature only,
thou who dependest on the existence of God Himself,
abandon me not in the coming Winter
to be tossed about on the savage billows of the Sea:
throw me the end of a rope to haul me in.

BEATA BEATRIX

I saw my Beatrice on the road, and all at once the road became a
      road of dream.
I passed her by like a wayfarer, and all my soul blossomed like the
      spring.
We lost each other in the flux of the town, but the memory of
      each was enriched
by the vivid image of the other and the companionship of each
      other's luminous eyes.
At my side glances of love hover like Guardian Angels,
Singular Stars in the pitch-black Firmament of the void about me,
      the desert spaces.
We were tamed, each one, by the mystery that shrouds the soul of
      our neighbor.
We were confronted with each other in the chaos of worldly life,
      face to face.
The most common things of life became at once for us a wonder
      of dream,
and many ashes concealed a former and foolish illumination.
The flaming Sun of Midnight arose for us in splendor,
that held in its arms the myriad Star-Clusters of the Firmament
and never sought to destroy them in a blue annihilation.
We were suddenly veiled by the thick clouds of night.
We walked nightlong on wooded mountains, under cloudy skies,
      like gods,

and our conversation was lost amid the eternal spaces.
We provoked the interest of all creation, in love as we wandered
      by.
Nor purpose nor desire led us in these wanderings.
It was the indolence and ease of darkened worlds.
It was the joy of mystery that took us by the hand to guide us.
We were not disturbed by the encounter of streams or the flight
      of birds
nor by the blowing of winds or the vault of fog.
All was enchantment and gifts from heaven and a deep repose.
But Time, the terrestrial, came to peal out his metallic tunes
that like bullets unerringly traverse distances and reach
as far as we. The red clouds of dawn rose.
The sun rose. Rose out of the sea and shone.
The day came. And the seal to our wandering.
And the roads increased with movement, with much caution,
      with mundane preoccupations.
Only toward Memory now do I raise my hands in supplication
to grant me with all of its strength at some time the moments of
      dream,
now when these vast nights perhaps are being banished forever.

A MONDAY OF THE YEAR

(QUANDO REGINA SABA SALOMONI DATUR)

With this New Moon, which like a flaming sickle is now setting
over the distant fields, I saw a Pure White Lady approaching,
      robed like a princess.
A flowing radiance spread over her being, a dazzlement invisible
      in the encounter.
The spirit that blew with a sharp coolness from a fragrant grove
      of pine trees
stood powerless before her coolness and her dissolving jewels.
She possessed for me the grace of Daphne when she glows green
      in the flame-flickering darkness,
and the shadowy glory of a radiating star, of all-cooling,
      all-greening Vega

that flutters like a lonely heart when this midnight spirit appears.
The sweetest of nuptial dreams, the songs of birds hidden in
 golden cages,
gardens from which rich and summery fragrances exude, the
 burgeoning daisies,
and white Love shadowed over with the lunacies of a chaste night,
entwined the reason in that hour of cooling twilight;
and there were rejoicing birds that darted out of dense shrubs and
 the foliage
of tall trees. O these entreating marine eyes which, though gazing
 on mountains,
recall luminous depths in moments of tranquillity, the only blue
 ones, moreover,
in the celestial whiteness, and on waxen hands, and on the virile
 caresses
of her linen garment, and on the innumerable pearls around her
 neck,
and on the merciless gold of her ring that served to adorn
a finger on her moonlit hand. Such are Women,
in deren Süsse immer Bitternis ist, Spiel und Gefahr.

RAPE OF THE SABINES

Speak to me, riverine fountains, of the many Nereids, as noon
approached, who have come to bathe here under the shadowy
 foliage
of thick plane trees, behind the aromatic shrubs. And of their
 crystalline
voices that blended with the water's running current
and the warbling of birds hidden in the thick leaves, as two
by two and three by three they descended the slippery wooded
 slopes.
Speak to me of the riverine reaches so suddenly populated
by pure-white radiant bodies scattering their splendor,
like that of the most brilliant Full Moon at its zenith,
on the damp shadowy reaches that had never known the sun,
whose luxurious vegetation had turned into deep darknesses.
The maidens' laughter there reechoed with greater coolness

than the river's current, as one in astonishment gazed on the
      other's
Olympian nakedness and magnificent beauty of limb.
Every tree trunk, every leaf spray, every shrub quivered
with the embrace or the touch of the untouched virgins.
Speak to me how and what dark, manly ardor
sent pirate galleys sailing your waters, O river,
of that heroic savage race of men who by every riverbank,
as they cut upstream, dreamt their dreams
of bankside acacias smothered with flowers as though with snow!
Of how the rowers dropped their oars and gave themselves to the
      current,
of how the Warriors dropped their lances and their arrows,
completely abandoned to the ecstasy of their divine on-flowing.
Meanwhile their eyes glittered around the river bend,
on the dark, solitary side, where suddenly they were dazzled
by the rays of that moon-drenched noon until,
in a cry, in a heroic paean of triumph, they merged
with the nuptial procession of birds, with the smiles
of the light wind that blew and caressed them all,
were all merged in one warcry—both the Nymphs' astonishment
and the first dazzlement of those impetuous men.
Speak to me of how those early pirate Rafts,
laden with gifts of blossoming riverine plants,
became flower gardens sailing down the river's midst
to the rhythm of songs of supreme joy,
of Joy that was the gorgon figurehead of every Raft,
in that astonishing voyage that transported earthly men
from the nebulae of our ashy earth
to the purely azure Third Empyrean with its eternal
splendor in the very heart of the Supreme Sun.

THE UNLOOKED-FOR THEME

Today, after so many crooked byways,
so many detours, so many false leads,
there rises to the surface the great, the unlooked-for theme.

I do not want to maintain by this
that I have not hitherto encountered a violet,
or that a rosebush never blossomed before me—
with those all-crimson, those enormous, those flaming
and aromatic roses of May—but it is,
nevertheless, unexpected: it is the antithesis of the cataract
whose roaring tumult the melting snow enlivens;
it is, in the midst of our great wandering through life,
a plateau of pellucid air that bursts into view
up there in the mountains, at a great height,
with a panorama of all the lakes below,
untrembling silver disks with the mists
of spring and of forests that rise toward God . . . a plateau
of serenity, with Alpine flora, with the opulence
of gardens and even of hothouses
and that pierces the snows, a vegetation entirely
the colors of repose—those lavender tints
or those beautiful yellows—as they offer you
the absolute certainty that you have finally touched the heights,
that you are grazing the vast sky.
Something like the antithesis of the cataract. And yet—
how unclear the meanings, how ineffectual, how miserable the
            comparisons—
antithetical yet strangely similar to the essence of the cataract!
To the triumphal song of the cataract! And as for the onrush, as
            for the roaring tumult,
as for the strength of the primary element, as for the glittering
            brilliance
in the boiling sun, or as for the foaming spray—
the unlooked-for theme that welled up suddenly
is the theme of the cataract's essence.
It is the theme of *De Profundis*.

SUMMER TOURISTS GO TO MASS

On Ascension Day during morning Mass
a crowd of tourists rushed to the Cathedral,
from the ship *San Gervasi*. Burghers of Württemberg.

Summer tourists. It had been hot since morning.
They entered like a wave. They brought disorder.

Alone and unperturbed the Cathedral
held to its Hours. Proceeded with its Canons.
On the whole it governed like God Himself, and embraced
all the faithful together, wherever they were.
Within the Inner Sanctum all
was Apostolic Law and Moderation.
The discords of the moment touched
the Indivisible Order not at all.

THE STONE

As in summer that hour approaches when cool winds blow
to dissolve at once the dominion of the heavy sun,
arriving from the sea they suddenly ruffle until its motionless
mirror reveals the shudder of its vehemence, and glows with
        phosphorus,
—this huge flaming Disk does not cease to be, nevertheless,
the center of all the world around.
It is this that isolates every object in its stare.
It is this that grasps the scepter of the Day and the World.
It is this that troubles reason in the heat-haze of its scintillation.

And when Night falls, so silent and so mystical,
on the same but altered Seashore,
there where the sand is ceaselessly changing boundaries
with the line of the never-resting wave,
what but this same Sun colors the pallid
Moon with a proud and livid hue? And even though
but two or three hours ago it was preparing such a blazing
departure below and beyond the world, with trumpet blasts and
        crimson mantles,
and though hidden out of sight, it always knows how to send
something to remind us of its eternal presence.

Something secret during these hours is being weighed in the vitals
        of man,
and which, either as the Sun or the Moon, has enthroned itself
in the soul's midst, and grants him
the luminosity of a darkness that does not vary
from the mind of God or the contrition of the Church.
A disposition toward the good and the untroubled. A Love
and an embracing of all things round. Without distinction or
        preference,
without shading, without deterioration, without decomposition.

Without distinction, but for one exception, dear God: that of the
        heavy
and sharp Stone you have designated must weigh
on the chest of certain men at night so deeply and so oppressively,
so despairingly and so beautifully. And which, if ever it is cast
        aside,
may only be succeeded by the everlasting stone of the tomb.
So sovereignly, so tenaciously has it become implanted forever.

OUTLINE OF ERROR

Great shall his reward be who without hesitation admits
the likelihood of error in every day of his existence.
For if a man is directed by the given fact that all things
about him are fallacious and nothing in its nature errorless,
how can he deny that his every thought or deed
might not indeed be false? "What then is error?"
I know it to be none other than the sting of self-love,
the scourge of pride. And the admission of error?
Nothing more than our sting and our scourge.

Great-helmeted Hectors with the plume
of our Conceit waving are we all. Let us curb it,
let us bend its knee with all our will; let us be stung,
let us be scourged in the squares of the city, *in plateis oppidi*
behold the self-martyr. Out of this may the Great Reward be
        justified.

It is there, however, whenever we have rarely to do
with the superterrestrial, that error finds no place;
when a Descent of powers other than our humble ones intercedes
      for us:
in such matters as Death, Love, Faith, and the Attractions of
      Friendship,
like the Pope when he pronounces on the Articles of Faith.
Then in truth do I admit the great Infallibility,
for the contrary would be the denial of Life itself and of all things
      Divine.

THE SLUGGISH OF MIND

In passage here a flock of birds
brought us a message from the North, but we turned a deaf ear.

And the Quails in their color of ash reflected the icebergs,
but we were not only deaf—we set snares
and fired upon them and wanted to eat them.
And who? It was we—we who, having awaited
so impatiently the message from the North,
became blind, and not understanding it had come,
fired upon them, wounded them, chased them away.

I do not deny that the flocks were transient,
but we neither loved nor revered their weariness
or their exhaustion; and once they were gone
there fell upon us suddenly a compassion and weight of the spirit
for the ungracious act, the evil assault;
and behold, we remained the awkward ones,
the sluggish of mind to discern apparitions,
desolate, with no message from the North,
with our accustomed *mea culpa*
and our profitless self-accusation.

THE DEPENDENCE

In the realm of relativity, even Happiness
exists. But they err
who seek her in the Land of the Absolute.
In the realm of relativity, all is well;
an entire day may become satisfactory.
From early morning the Influences are enchanters.
Goodness hovers by with all her Feathers manifest.
How small a thing suffices to form such feeling!
Behold, two good coincidences, completely unexpected.
A philanthropic disposition that goes into action.
A change of the Wind. An inconceivable improvement
of a known Evil. And behold, the sum at once
of happy Hours, of a happy Total.
How easy the course prescribed for us.
Terce, Sext, None, Benedicite, Vespers,
Compline, and Tenebrae. Yet all are compounded
of wills not our own. Who is this that plays
with our innermost concerns? Who mocks us
with the fancy that we are the creators
of our own dispositions? Or perhaps this day
of Beautiful and that of Contrary Weather
comes from an Unseen Wisdom? In the realm of relativity
Good Hours exist. In the realm of relativity
Joyful Days exist. In the realm of relativity
a Full Life exists. But all depend on
and are placed in order by the attractions and repulsions
of a Mighty Element.

ADAGE

More wretched than the wretched Hour is to measure it.
Let it pass by unmeasured,
and, if you find this at all possible, without leaving its Traces.

Measure—if you consider it joyful and useful,
if it has become your habit to measure your life—
measure Delight, which the flight of the wretched Hour
and its dimness in memory most certainly offer you.
But never the wretched Hour.
Keep Trace of these rare Hours,
but not of those. Those are the dead
Moons of the West, on the opposite side
of the morning's Glow. They are false Contrivances,
cunning Combinations which, since ancient times,
were established to provoke the Divine Order.

ENCOUNTER

The morning dew drips from every Garden leaf.
And though it is damp, nevertheless the Joy,
of course, is great. The Passer-by strolls and lingers,
although at first he was going to Work. However,
if not in terms of time but only in mood,
his duty toward work is somewhat abridged. And yet,
he derives some benefit from the first tenderness of Day.
When it is least expected, beneficence descends upon him.
Coolness of Spirit, when it is least awaited. How blessed
are all the Hours that follow Morning! What an
immaterial impression they bear! Even when Twilight
comes with the dwindling of light and with stars,
it remains a light matutinal. It lasts until it is time
to sleep. And that Passer-by retires to bed, happy,
wrapped in the accustomed bedsheets of Quietude,
and does not feel alone; his soul is wrapped
in a Serene Light, not strange, not alien
to this coolness, which he encountered when he went out in the
        morning.

INVOCATION OF IMAGES

Reclining on a low divan, I celebrate today at dusk
the companionship of my daughter; she is called Maria.
Mountain summits, the tops of so many trees,
roofs, chimneys, farmhouse roof tiles, have all been hidden
from view by my low lying. Now only the east
window remains, revealing an azure atmosphere.
It is crossed now and then, momentarily, by a flock
of birds, artful embroideries on the frame of immensities,
as they go to roost, escaping from tomcats,
evil owls, and the perils of night.

The embroideries unravel, the azure loneliness returns.
A second flock throbs through the air, a second loneliness follows.
And this superb harmony proceeds in length.
I draw the window curtains that the memories of dusk
may remain with me, that I may collect myself, see what I am
          doing.
O beautiful images, I invoke you to descend from on high
to this enclosed space where I, a father,
have isolated myself with this gift, my child,
and the unknown future. Come and put in order
the arid thought that torments me,
so very arid without your cooperation,
the unflowering tree, the accursed fig tree,
the meters that limp on their wooden legs,
wingless and miserable, lacking in elevation.

In the accumulation of superfluous material, add
a small clod of earth, a useful bit of mosaic,
that I may enjoy, as is proper, the smile
of this young girl, who is my daughter.

MYTH

Tremors of dew—what am I saying?—almost a shivering,
has pierced the Poplar Tree of night; the same rustling
has been communicated to the depths of our souls;
together we sang the Hours of Meditation,
escaping the negations of sleep. The brimming dazzle
of the Full Moon in the mid-heavens has lit up
the Poplar Tree of night. Luminous
Forgiveness, that youthful bird of song,
flew toward us, came and roosted on the daedalian
foliage of man. Well then, O Night,
Night most serene, O most miraculous among
all other nights, for whom we waited, and you never came—
behold now, you are here! Continue now
through the long length of hours; do not disrupt
the created Equilibrium of the Elements,
for without it Chaos would come again.

THE INNS

Days, in the flow of the year, grow shorter, and nights
lengthen in despair; the wintry wind is harsh and freezing;
expectation seems endless, the streets slippery—
the time has come for the census of Caesar Augustus
to be taken once more, for the detailed registration of the
   inhabitants.
For such displacements, the time, of course, is inopportune.
Ordeal for the wayfarer, especially when traveling at night.
Here and there on the highways the night's darkness is broken
by the windowpane of an inn, dim in the oil lamp's light.
To what has the oil of the good Samaritan been reduced,
if I can judge by the noise of flutes played by the prostitutes!
Gold comes pouring in, for some, with this census taking.
Fatigue has exhausted the travelers now:

snow, slippery roads, freezing cold. The road forces them to turn
        aside
for a little warmth and fire, a bit of wine, a few caresses.

And so indifferent are they to what the night teaches,
to the whispering of date trees under the stars,
to the distant bleating of a lamb and the crowing of roosters
that these evil and debauched mortals, finding themselves
at odds with each other's views, their bodies
still clinging to fumes from places of ill repute,
begin to beat the shepherds they meet who, in a religious ecstasy,
are seeking with their musical instruments to find a God on this
        earth,
newly born, warmly wrapped, lying on the straw of a peasant's
        stable.

For what was this Caesar responsible with all his displacements?
He forced these mortals to such improper acts.
And now, guilty or innocent, they certainly will be punished
        forever in Hell.
Their weakness in committing these antics will be punished.
God's curse lies in this: man's lack of will.

THE OLD MAN'S LOG OF WOOD

Times locked up; locked, tightly locked,
far from a view of the sky, abandoned
to winds, storms, snow and gloomy skies.
Vainly do the cocks crow in the accustomed hour:
they cannot dissolve the darkness; light does not come,
bad news arrives. These a muffled-up Old Man
with a lighted oil lamp receives
toward noon. Behold the plight
of the wintry man, indifferent
to all, fearful only that his log
might burn down. The hours have proved to be fictitious,
fictitious the days of the month. Behold, January

the twenty-first: Agnes the Virginal Martyr (cast
at the age of thirteen into the Gehenna of martyrdom); January
the nineteenth, the second Sunday after Epiphany:
the wedding at Cana, Sebastian
and Fabian the Martyrs (they hurled at Sebastian
a shower of arrows, scales on the young man's body).
What's this to us? How can one day now
be distinguished from another? Each is equally locked,
since night no longer stands as a separation between them,
since day is ceaselessly being turned into night,
and the only concern we old men have is not the vision
of faith, not Martyrdom with its flames,
but that this log may not burn down once and for all.

THE ISLAND

Food is for eating,
Art is for arting,
Women are for . . .
　　　　—LAWRENCE DURRELL, *Justine*

Food is for eating, art
is for arting, women
for filling your life, islands
to anchor before them, we are told,
and so many other meanings for an equal number
of doubtful purposes. But islands,
with the curving line of their mountains,
with the slits of their ravines,
with their small valleys, with their coves
here and there, with the large banks
of wharves in the harbors, jutting out
to receive ships, with their long-drawn
piers on which generations
of fishermen swarm to mend their nets
—islands are by nature mystical.
They conceal hearts that do not offer themselves

to the first comer. And if you anchor
before them, you waste your time
in mooring. The seas
that surround the islands, the winds
that alternate in mood with clouds
for wind sleeves and weathervanes
(every variation of the wind
is a new legend), the stars
coming and going and swirling,
the leaden calm that spreads
toward dawn with resting gulls,
the morning mists and the delicate
half-lights that cannot obstruct
the awakening of the blood-splattered disk,
—all these are glimmerings and embellishments.
You do not have the island at all
if you do not thrust beyond the area of this integument;
the island has escaped you, no matter how much you study it
from your place of anchorage with your dream-taken,
your inexperienced sailor's eye.
Lower your dinghy at last, take up
the oars, abandon your ship,
place your feet on dry land, proceed and meditate.
You will learn strange things, a great happiness
awaits you, and if some abandoned
wilderness invites you, some little town
harmoniously composed, some closed
garden, the promise and substance of serenity,
then forget all nautical things, voyage and stormy seas,
forget your ship and hold
only the treasure hovering in mid-air.

I SING THE WRATH . . .

Now that the Dodonian will has vowed war,
and the Illyrian mountaineers with Western Hordes
battle the sharp-witted Achaeans in the gorges,

I sit here and reexamine the renewed oracle
that finds gradual fulfillment as the wheel turns.

In the innermost depths and the remotest part and far coves
of Ilium must the antithesis and enmity of ancestors be fished for.
All these sunwashed people with their marine
antics do not seem to be brothers at all.
Father Anchises, in leaving, mounted his son
and made off for distant lands, to colonize Latium.
Sea-Wanderings brought them, even then,
to Epiros and the mountains; and there Sybil
showed them Italy on the opposite shore, how to get there.
Well then, the pious took off with their holy images,
barbarians to a barbarian land, but in sailing were maimed
near Sicily's Drepanum, where Anchises gave up the ghost.
But if Anchises' bareback riding brought him to no good end,
nevertheless Aeneas tread on the West as a refugee
and bound himself in kinship with the sea-wolf's breasts,
from which, it seems, his descendants from that time on
have hauled up habits and antics to a bestial degree.
Scion of the Trojans, whose ambition was to sprout on western
        soil,
what else was he but a Trojan enemy, a descendant of Priam,
scion of those who sacrificed Hestia to the Cupids,
scion of those who kidnaped that beautiful Helen
whose equal in splendor may not be found anywhere else on earth.
Just as their abduction in ancient times did not bear fruit,
buffeted as they were by all the seas as derelicts,
thus today they resolved to carry off Wise Athena,
they, whom Zeus has turned into stupid dolts, now and forever.
For their Agamemnon and Achilles and Ajax they chose
the most barbarously named Visconti and Ubaldo
and Caballero; the elegant Galeazzo also arrived,
and the Middle Ages and the Albanians were blackened
with shameful deeds, of which the Illyrians would have blushed
        to hear.
The Archipelago was blackened with the infamies of the
        abductors,
and they begged iron loans from the Teutons with which
to burn down, to turn into ash, the land of their envy, Greece.

Even so, they were confronted with the spear of Pallas Athena
shining with serenity, glittering with sovereignty,
dazzling those eyes that debauchery had fed.
It was the orthodoxy of the Olympians that resolved
the outcome of the battle, as in ancient times, high
in the Olympian palaces. And the immortals scattered everywhere,
each with the instruments promised him by the High-Thundering
        God:
the bellows of Aeolos, the wings of Hermes, the trident
of Poseidon, the fire of Hephaestos, the thunderbolt of Zeus,
and, above all, the beloved form, the serene
and unperturbed understanding of pure Wisdom,
the panoplied, the flashing, the faultless, the beautiful,
more resplendent than Apollo, with her goatskin shield,
with her luminous and dazzling Spear of Majesty
that blazes in splendor, the Shield of the Virgin,
the Shield which so protects the Sun of Greece
that it may never alter or darken, may never be deprived,
even in the slightest, of its ancient god-born Essence.

THE BONFIRES OF SAINT JOHN

TATTOO

"Sentry, night sentry, what does the night bring
during your watch?" the terrified man asks
his soul as he comes out of his room's warmth past midnight
and runs frenziedly to his highest lookout.
"Sentry," he shouts, "what does the night bring?"—"The night
puts its magic worlds in motion. The night
is a dial that unravels enigmas.
The night puts gold to pasture. The night
directs the work of our days and tells no one.
The night, when birds perch on trees
and fall asleep, breathes life into myths,"
the sentry answers. What myths, since an instrument
of precision is sufficient to show how life

is interwoven with the stars. And life not in abstraction,
not as a naked knowledge, a more naked ignorance, but as the most
miserable endeavor, the most insignificant thought
of each of us, from the millions of mortals
and the armies, all lumped together, dead for centuries,
all pasturing on the night's dark formations
in the hours when birds are sleeping in the trees.
The night brings us these, and so many other things—
it is impossible for man's song to contain them all.
To some extent the vigilance of our sentry
grasps them here or there and proclaims them,
but for what purpose? We have not the power to deviate
from what the cauldron destines for us in its flames,
and once it writes them down, dear God, they cannot be effaced.
Made of blood and fire, its incandescent slate pen
sets its seal upon us while the tempest
of our terrestrial piracy endures. Scarred
with the stamp of fire, we burden ourselves
with the sacrificial fumes of our scorched flesh, memories
of our spitted pain that torments us insufferably,
—of that pain which the other night was supposedly extinguished,
as it sputtered, by the heartless act that revives it.

THIS CUP

At the point we reached, the only thing remaining
for us was to turn toward new orientations. The hour came,
entirely imperceptible, when whatever for us had been valid
now ceased to be valid. We had lain in wait
for a Canon of life where everything is foreseen
with exactitude, everything has its secure position:
the four seasons in succession are firm columns,
with whatever the long tradition and indestructible memory
of nature has set as their limits.
Among these we had placed with care
plans, values, stairways; we had developed
in study, imagination, struggle; we had deified

the ideas of our loves, the shape of our dreams,
the moments of our adoration, the expectations of our moments,
(perhaps it was only these expectations
that always showed themselves to be somewhat obscure;
but with certain acrobatic and trivial compromises,
contrasted to our austerity regarding other matters,
we cast, even on these, a beam of light,
unprotestingly, thus leaving them behind us as,
"white-garmented in our virtuous deeds,"
we proceeded down the road, untouched.) All things,
finally, were foreseen; all but one—
this unexpected change that in one night only
overturned our well-laid plans
and cast us into a foreign region
unknown to us until that time. Unsuspecting, we
embroidered diligently, entangling
threads of eternity with other smaller, more fragile
threads, a complete synthesis on which we gazed with pride.
And now we found the change confusing, found it
lusterless, faded, useless; where could we now derive the courage
to undertake a new occupation
with materials alien to our familiar craft,
and which, from this time on, would crumble away
to our touch, when we verified
that even the slightest attempt would be vain.

The only proper thing for us to do,
as soon as this change and all its consequences
enters our consciousness, is to assemble
and organize the Minutes of the Meeting,
the joyless, acrid, dry, impersonal Report,
that shriveled parchment dug out of a tomb,
showing, with its realistic gradation of tones,
that we have irrevocably settled our accounts
with the life we knew. And in the name of all,
I remain,
                your humble and obedient servant,
                                T. K. Papatsónis, Greek.

CROSSWAYS

Who said yes in the hour of corruption,
who whispered of wealth in a time of unspeakable poverty,
who draped himself with scarlet and gold,
with ceremonial grandeur in a time of grief?

Who directed the ideal eyes of night
to discover what we lack
and, discovering whatever we hoped for,
stood overjoyed to offer it,
exchanging his serenity for our agitation,
accepting war with all its weapons,
surrendering himself to our nightmares,
promising us companionship
in life and in death,
the oil of solicitude, vigilance in a time of pain,
identification with the joy of hours,
communion in the difficult distinction between Good and Evil,
generosity toward unformulated claims,
joint sharing in dread responsibility,
taste of the bitter drink from the same
chalice of sacrament, the wedding of lips,
the gift of imposition, the uprooting
and deposing of vain things
into the pyre of flaming constancy
that burns unceasingly with no other Vestal Virgin
than this hovering
this inconsumable
embellished Chrysalis,
this Armenian deacon who with peacock feathers
fans it and feeds it
with an Influence unexplainable.

That rocky island, black amid clouds,
has been embraced by dolphins in a ring
with arms of tenderness; from the ship
sailing in the open sea smoke swelled

in the windless calm and rose aloft
into the winter sky, a white Chrysanthemum,
a sacred Hymn, as the night deepened
and the Star in the West stood still
with no intention of setting,
crimson and superb,
proclaiming its thirst to see
what inscrutable thing was being perfected.

It happened that the Lord God saw it all,
like one utterly uninvolved,
and in commanding was Himself commanded:
such piety and devotion did this YES contain.

IN THE KEY OF RESURRECTION

The voice in Byzantine psalms has come true,
now that the transitory shadows have dissolved
in the inaccessible light of a certain Dawn.

Indeed, do You think the dead will praise You?
We the living will praise You now.
Or indeed the cold ones, whose blood has been depleted?
To us has it befallen to taste
the benevolence of the Omnipotent, the wish of the earth-born.
To us has it befallen to stress
in a loud, descanting voice,
"death has been seen to be futile,"
and who would have imagined it
a few hours earlier when the Veil
was rent in twain and the Cherubim frowned.
No, we shall not go away, one by one,
this world will not be wholly darkened,
we shall not retreat to the Cemeteries.

Holding his reed with its funnel
and sponge—exotic image

of an Unknown Spearman at Golgotha—
the Sacristan, after the end of the Service,
puts out the Altar candles, one by one.
There where you ministered and shone, my God,
darkness now reigns. In a hidden corner
only a wick illuminates the well
of Charity, the last trace of adoration,
and whatever still remains of aromatic incense.
The portals also close, the belfry left in solitude.

Not so for us: the dead will open
the new-dug graves for their own dead;
let the dead bury their dead, not we;
"all the Fellowship of the Apostles, as it theologizes,
buries deeply the dead voice of the Hellenes."
Let them do the burying, but not we.
And in a moment of arrogance
they even said, with narrow heart: "Peter orates,
Plato is silenced; Paul teaches,
Pythagoras sets like the sun." But not we,
we shall not say it. We proclaim both Peter
and Pythagoras with his triangles. And Paul of Tarsus
and soaring Plato, and all groups
timeless and spiritual, all in the name of Christ.
Hebrews and Hellenes, stumbling block and foolishness,
Jesus Christ and He Crucified,
Jesus Christ with a banner who was verily
resurrected, the true and living accusation
for drowsy and false witnesses
who scowl, and sentries
bribed and terrified.

THE THREAD

All roads converged, all pathways,
and have brought me to this least portion of earth.
I am not a Chaldean, nor an astrologer,

and yet it is the stars that show me the way.
I have never played the Magi, and yet
I loaded my tray with gifts and set out.

I cannot play the flute, nor was I appointed
a shepherd or shepherd's boy; I have not stooped
over a lamb or a wounded kid
to wash it; nor do I know how to guide
a flock. And yet, on the desolate slopes
of the mountains every winter, a song
pours from my ignorant mouth in a constant flow.
And as for visions of Angels dressed in white,
as they say, or in colors of rose,
with piercing looks, creations that hover in mid-air—
my nights have never encountered such; and yet,
dipped in the snows of a certain night,
under the sharp and glittering constellations,
how did I ever combine all phenomena until
their message emerged from the dark chestnut trees!

And I plunged down, insane, that I might find men,
as though I had something special to impart,
something swift and vast and matutinal of the brilliant day:
that I might offer it in time, though it had not
humanly matured within me yet, nor even begun to form.
As for the Nativity, all knowledge of it lies
in about six lines of the Gospel,
and from all paintings only in a few
steaming calves, a basin of water, the Babe,
a bundle of straw, the tears of Joseph,
and the smile of the Virgin, like sweet dawn breaking.

But I also know something else, the most important of all:
that the Public Registrar and the Tetrarch had opened
the large tomes and had dragged all the people out
to take the census according to tribes;
I know that the inns were crowded;
that the windows had sweated from the breathing
of such vast multitudes; that in the meantime
the night outside, cold and dark, was squandering her silence

as under the smoke of oil lamps
those driven from their homes emptied
earthen jugs of wine or lemonade, women
huddled in corners and fell asleep,
and children drooped with exhaustion;
and that to all, whether alert or whether
they lay surrendered to their indolence,
the Presence outside was persistently wandering,
the unsleeping essence of a life-bringing night
in which something was being conceived or had been born:
something not written down, something missing
from the huge pages of the Census Taker—something—a thread,
that delicately bound all things together into one body.

SELF-SCRUTINY

Feared neither death nor pain for this beauty;
if harm, harm to ourselves.
—EZRA POUND, *Canto XX*

Yes, these people, they are all right, they
can do everything, everything except act.
—EZRA POUND, *Canto XVI*

Each of our acts, to be made whole, needs a strong craftsman.
Nor is it at all perfected with the first attempt—much toil is
       needed,
many sleepless nights, a great many rough models, and much
       agony.
First in order comes the dream, still unwrought, and it traces,
somewhat dimly, what glory an act of ours may possibly enclose.
But the dream is shapeless and impalpable, it lacks sufficient
       material.
Both blessing and curse, inextricably bound, are the first real
       foundation.
Then the struggle begins with joy, but it is not as free as we
       thought,
for treacheries nestle beside it, a multitude of treacheries; inimical
powers fight it: negligence, terrors, doubts, escapes—

dark powers which, although we know they are not ours,
dominate every day a large portion of ourselves—
pushing us on to waste ourselves in an unforgivable squandering
for whatever is worthless and unfruitful, directing us at the same
      time
how to be thrifty with a stubborn miserliness
because this would help us keep the tree of life evergreen.
What don't they think of to poison that taste in us which
      distinguishes
good from evil! Thus each of them creates a discord of its own
in the direction toward which we should go. We fight them,
it's true, with all our strength, we hate them,
but does this hatred help us at all in the equilibrium
we shall need? It takes away our serenity, it uproots
the nature of tenderness, it makes us wild beasts until we become
      men
whose hearts have been so hardened that we no longer know
what blessedness means: a little before sleep comes, a good-night
spreads like the love of God from the pacifying hand that shapes
a caress from afar, predestined for our brow and our hair.

Because of this our acts are rough models with many errors
which we discern but do not use our full strength to avoid;
and we re-create the second one more perfectly, and again the
      third;
but because we are of little faith, something once more intervenes,
      and we find
we have not escaped from the vulture's claws, that it is necessary
to start all over again to attain some kind of perfection.

And yet, there is so much harmony, so many laws
in the spaces given us to perform our acts,
in hours set aside for us to depict the way!
It's a great thing how the twilight slowly, slowly falls.
And a little later falls the Night. With its enormous
Aphrodite. The one surrounded by all her handmaidens. The one
who despises the pale, silver-golden sickle of the newest Moon.
And she insists that her pulse measure the progress.
                         Nevertheless . . .
in these hours of the progress, that Scene Director of our lives,
      Satan,

interferes without revealing himself (how he always manages to
      slither away
and hide!) and rivets our eyes on the drought
of a dry, lumpy earth; and there where we thought
that petals of fresh-cut flowers would be strewn,
the Cunning One has sown his obstacles in shapes strangely
repulsive: bottles, packages, obstructions,
stumps of wood, and whatever else his weak remaining strength
could contrive. He knows well that victory
is not for him. But that Perfidious One wastes no time,
until those moments come (see, they're here already) that
      grind him to bits.
It is on these we live.

ATTIC SHAPES

> *O Attic shape! Fair attitude! with brede*
> *Of marble men and maidens overwrought* . . .
>   —JOHN KEATS, "Ode on a Grecian Urn"

Now the balance is shaken; now one of the scales
dips down toward the abyss, the other kicks high,
for the disk that holds the Night grows heavy
while the Day is as weightless as a bird.
If the inclination swerve much further down,
we shall see the balance standing straight
instead of finding its equilibrium, as we had expected,
pointing with its lever in a vertical line;
as when resistance has waned
and the counterweight vanishes in an assumption
—such an immaterial ascension, and so luminous!

Hail Day, in this your immaterial idea
of elevation that you shall touch the Moon.
Hail luminous Crescent; now you dismiss
the vapors of a morning torpor
and simultaneously display the Dawn of High Noon
the virginal caresses of the Graces

the azure awakening of Sea Nymphs
and the slow movements of wondrous nakedness.

A blesséd place in its blesséd hour
must have been spread before you because,
although the great instability and agitation of the balance
harshly brings the message of a heavy winter of darkness
and the tumescence of Night to dimensions
insupportable for the vast majority of men,
here the brief glittering of indolent Day
proffers the translucency of a Spring Morning
and the faint ripples a breeze of light distributes—
for all things find themselves converging on immobility.

Where every day the inexhaustible light
is drawn up and scattered in an Attic corner,
exquisite Hymettos at its ridges overbrims
with feathery clouds that linger on its slopes.
That is not the menacing Hood of the storm rising,
where the dainty-haired Demigoddess of the Sea reclines
and combs her hair, but the bucolic playfulness of the Sun.
A slow, surpassing flute, slowly and barely audible
in the surrounding regions, restrains all astonished creatures
to an absolute serenity—the near affinity of Harmony.

Fleeting and God-sent Blissful Weather stands by her side.
No matter how brief, this is a moment of eternity,
utter abolition of the tumescent Night,
triumphal Songs of Victory, but ready to flower
beyond the Law, gift of God, negation of Winter.

ODE TO AQUARIUS

Many waters cannot quench love,
neither can the floods drown it.

And how could it otherwise be, since this water
is the water of love.

A crevice of tranquillity, a crevice of meditation
is this segment of water that
from the beginning pours out with great impetus
from the Beloved's bucket, and is poured out
without cessation; and when the nights
come star-laden and weighted with gold,
and when the hermit,
vigilant in expectations and freed
from his tensions and his ecstasies,
feels the sweated blood of his agony
crowned at last with a certain approach
of his own to the clues of chaos, when
filings of gold shower down, during nights
when the mute, cruel element for one moment at least
is pierced, then the lone suppliant
with utter delight clearly hears
the buckets rattling in their joints,
the chains that rub and creak
as they glitter and drip with water,
the well as it bubbles and overbrims.
Then he sees the foam sparkling
and lives now in those lustral waters
where Zeus himself once delighted.

But behold, although there is such
clamor and such roaring in the dim expanse,
on the nebulae of his hearing, and a humming
froths everywhere, the onrush dwindles away
into deeper reaches, the Best Measure
comes to reign in farther depths.

Drop by drop
the rosary of prayer is formed
there, a little above,
where the commotion rages.
Drop by drop
the damp stillness turns stagnant,
proffering its childhood toys
to its god;
there the indolent Minor Waters create

small lakes of new worlds; phosphorescences
irradiate here and there, and two or three
small Fishes leap out now and then and twist
in that breathlessness where a drop
of water seldom measures
the immeasurable moment of eternity,
while with the whiteness of marble
and with adolescent arrogance
Ganymede does not move.

Kóstas Kariotákis

BALLADE TO THE
INGLORIOUS POETS OF THE AGES

Detested and abhorred by men and gods,
like noblemen who've fallen bitterly,
the Verlaines wither, but there still remains
for them a wealth of rich and silvery rhyme.
The Hugos with their sharp *Les Châtiments*
intoxicate the great Olympian gods'
most dreaded vengeance. But I still shall write
a mournful ballad for poets inglorious.

Though every Poe has lived unhappily,
though Baudelaires have lived a living death,
they've all been granted Immortality.
Yet a deep darkness covers heavily
and no one now can even recollect
those rhymsters who have rhymed unskillfully.
But on my part I'll make this offering
a sacred ballad for poets inglorious.

The world's contempt has weighed them heavily
but they passed on, still pale and obdurate,
surrendered to the tragic fraudulence
that somewhere Glory lies in wait for them,
a virgin merry with sagacity.
But knowing well how soon they'll be forgotten,

I weep for them now most nostalgically
in this sad ballad, these poets inglorious.

And in some far and distant time I want
it said of me, "What poet inglorious
once took his pen in hand to versify
this wretched ballad to poets inglorious?"

ATHENS

Sweet hour. Athens reclines and gives herself
to April like a beauteous courtesan.
Aromas are voluptuous in the air,
and there is nothing now the soul awaits.

Over the houses evening stoops and lowers
the silver of her eyelids' heavy weight,
and there beyond, the Acropolis like a Queen
wears all the sunset like a crimson robe.

A kiss of light, and the first star explodes.
By the Ilissós a light breeze falls in love
with rose-nymph laurels in their quivering.

Sweet hour of joy and love when the swift wind
of birds that chase each other through the air
beats on a column of the Olympian Zeus.

STROPHES

Gambling for twenty years
with books instead of cards,
gambling for twenty years,
I lost my life.

Penniless now I lie
and hear an easy wisdom
rustled into my ears
by an old plane tree.

ONLY

Ah, all things should have happened as they did!
The hopes and roses should have withered away,
years should have drifted off like little boats,
have drifted off and vanished.

And as at eventide we parted once,
many friends thus should have been lost forever.
The place where I grew up as a small child
I should have left one twilight.

The beautiful and simple girls—dear loves!—
life should have taken from me, a quick dance turn.
Even pain, that filled me once with fragrance, should
have weighed down my barren self.

All things should have happened thus. Only this night
should not have been as lovely as now it is,
nor should the bright stars sparkle there like eyes
that laugh at me and mock me.

I SAW THIS NIGHT

I saw this night
like a bouquet of roses.
A certain delicate
gold fragrance in the streets.
And in the heart

a sudden kindliness.
My overcoat over my arm,
the moon on my upturned face.
You'd say the atmosphere
had been electrified with kisses.
Poetry, thoughts,
were useless burdens.

Whatever wings I have are broken.
I haven't the slightest notion why
this summer has come.
For what unhoped-for joy,
for what loves,
for what voyage longed for in dream.

MERCENARY WORK . . .

Mercenary work, heaped papers, trifling cares,
small wretched sorrows—these awaited me today, as always. Only,
as in the morning I was leaving, I saw before my door
a globe of roses, and turning back cut off a spray.

WE ARE LIKE
CERTAIN RICKETY GUITARS

We are like certain rickety guitars.
Whenever the wind passes through it sets
astir our verses and their dissonant sounds
from the slack strings that dangle down like watch chains.

We are like certain incredible antennae
that with long fingers reach into the void
as on their tips the infinite resounds:
but quickly they shall snap and tumble down.

We are like certain senses scattered wide
that have no hope of ever reuniting.
All nature in our nerves falls in confusion.

We ache in both our body and recollection.
All things reject us, and all poetry
fills us with envy as our last asylum.

MARCH FUNEREAL
AND VERTICAL

I gaze at the ceiling plasterwork.
The meanders draw me in their dance.
My happiness, I think, would be
a matter of height.

Symbols of pre-eminent life,
roses transmuted and unchanging,
and white acanthi bordering round
a horn of plenty.

(O humble art that lacks pretension,
how much too late I admit your teaching!)
Bas-relief dream, I shall come close to you
in vertical fashion.

All the horizons will have choked me.
In every climate, all latitudes:
daily struggles for bread and salt,
love affairs, boredom.

Ah! it's now time for me to wear
that beautiful white wreath of plaster.
Thus, with the ceiling as frame around me,
all shall admire me.

IDEAL SUICIDES

They firmly lock their doors and take
their old, long-treasured letters out,
read quietly for a while and then
drag out their steps for the last time.

Their life, they say, was a tragedy.
Dear God, the frightful laughter of men,
the tears, the sweat, and the vast sky's
nostalgia, all the bleak waste lands.

They stand still by the window, gaze
at trees, at children, at nature there,
at marble cutters cutting marble,
at the sun setting now forever.

Everything's ended. And here's the note,
profound, brief, simple, as is most meet,
filled with forgiveness and unconcern
for whoever, reading it, will weep.

They gaze in the mirror, note the hour,
ask: is this madness, a great mistake?
"Everything's ended," they whisper, "now."
Deep down, of course, they know they'll postpone it.

OPTIMISM

Let us suppose that we have not yet reached
the dark blind alley and the mind's abyss.
Let us suppose now that the woods have come
with all the autocratic panoply

of the morning's triumph, with birds, with the sky's light,
and with the sun that here shall pierce them through.

Let us suppose that we are there beyond
in unknown lands far to the West, the North,
that while we toss our coats high in the air
strangers gape at us strangely, soberly,
and that she might receive us tenderly
a Lady has given her servants leave all day.

Let us suppose that our hat's slender brim
has suddenly grown wide the while our trousers
have narrowed and clung tight, that with our spurs'
command a thousand steeds move on their way.
We march on—banners flapping in the wind—
cross-bearing heroes, saviors of the Savior.

Let us suppose that we have not yet reached
frontiers of silence through a hundred roads,
and let us sing now—may the song resemble
a triumphal trumpet blast, a bursting cry—
that it may entertain the fiery demons
in the bowels of earth, and men in the heights above.

WHEN WE DESCEND THE STAIRS . . .

When we descend the stairs, what shall we say
to all those shadows waiting to receive us,
austere acquaintances, invisible friends
wearing a smile on lips that do not exist?

At least here where we are we're all alone,
the long day passes like the other dawns,
and in our eyes we have somewhat preserved
something that gives to things a certain color.

But what shall we say down there, where shall we go?
We'll need to look at one another then,

as motionless as faces in a painting,
our arms down from the elbow amputated.

If someone comes to knock on our tombstone,
he must imagine that we once had lived.
If he should take a rose or want to leave
one there on earth, it will be a desert rose.

And if we ever raise ourselves on tiptoe
we'll see the villas then of Posillipo,
Lord, Lord, and the terrain of Paradise
where all Thy followers will be playing cricket.

PREVEZA

Death is the buzzards that bicker and squawk
against black walls, on red roof tiles,
death is the women who make love
as easily as they peel onions.

Death is the filthy, commonplace streets
with all their great, splendiferous names,
the olive groves, the surrounding sea,
even the sun, death within deaths.

Death is the inspector who wraps up
a morsel to see if it's short-weighed,
death is the hyacinths placed on the porch,
the school teacher reading the day's news.

Army Base, Garrison, Troops at Préveza.
On Sundays we'll flock to hear the band.
I've opened now a bank account,
my first deposit: just one dollar.

As you stroll on the pier slowly, you say:
"Do I exist?" Then: "You don't exist!"

The steamship docks. Its flag hoisted high.
Perhaps the Prefect has just arrived.

If only among these men, at least
one, only one, but died of disgust,
with decorous manner, silent and sad,
we'd have high fun at his funeral.

George Seféris

from MYTH OF OUR HISTORY

> *Si j'ai du goût, ce n'est guères*
> *Que pour la terre et les pierres.*
> —ARTHUR RIMBAUD

I

We have awaited
the messenger intently for three years
scrutinizing closely
the pines the shore and the stars.
Merged with blade of plow or keel of ship
we sought to find the first seed once more
that the very ancient drama might again begin.

We returned to our homes, broken
our limbs ailing and our mouths ravaged
with taste of rust and salt of the sea.
When we awoke we sailed toward the North, strangers
sunken in mists by the immaculate wings of swans that wounded
        us.
On winter nights the strong East Wind would drive us mad
in summer we were lost in the agony of a day that could not
        expire.

We brought back
these carved reliefs of a humble art.

IV

The Argonauts

And if the soul
is ever to know itself
it must gaze
into the soul:
the stranger and the enemy, we have seen him in the mirror.

The companions were good lads, they did not grumble
either because of fatigue or of thirst or of the frost,
they had the bearing of trees and waves
that suffer the wind and the rain
that suffer the night and the sun
amid the change not changing.
They were good lads, for days on end
they sweated at the oars with downcast eyes
breathing in rhythm
and their blood would redden a skin submissive.
Sometimes they sang, with downcast eyes
as we passed the desolate island of Barbary figs
to the West, beyond the cape of dogs
that bark.
If it is ever to know itself, they would say,
it must gaze into the soul, they would say,
and their oars beat the gold of the sea
in the sunset.
We passed by many capes many islands the sea
that leads into the other sea, seagulls and seals.
Sometimes forlorn women in loud lamentation
wept for their lost children
and others raging sought for Alexander the Great
and for glories buried in the depths of Asia.
We anchored by beaches heavy with night aromas
with birdsong, waters that left on the hand
the memory of great happiness.
But the voyages never ended.
Their souls became one with the oars and the oarlocks
with the grave face of the prow

with the wake of the rudder
with the water that fractured their image.
The companions expired each in his turn,
with downcast eyes. Their oars
mark the place where they sleep on the shore.

No one remembers them. Justice.

V

We did not know them
                    it was hope deep within us that kept saying
we had known them since childhood.
We had seen them twice perhaps, and then they took to sea;
cargoes of coal, cargoes of grain, and our friends
lost beyond the ocean forever.
Dawn finds us by the weary lamp
drawing awkwardly and laboriously on paper
ships mermaids or shells;
at nightfall we go down to the river
because it shows us the way to the sea,
and we spend the night in cellars that smell of tar.

Our friends have left us
                    perhaps we had never seen them, perhaps
we met them when sleep still
would carry us close upon the breathing wave
perhaps we seek them because we seek the other life,
beyond the statues.

VIII

But what do our souls seek voyaging
on the decks of outworn vessels
crammed with sallow women and squalling babies
unable to distract themselves either with flying fishes
or with stars that the tips of the masts point out.
Ground thin by gramophone records
unwillingly bound to pilgrimages that do not exist
mumbling broken thoughts in foreign tongues.

But what do our souls seek voyaging
on rotted seacraft
from port to port?

Shifting broken stones, inhaling
the coolness of pine with greater difficulty day by day,
swimming in the waters of this sea
and of that sea,
without sense of touch
without human beings
in a country that is no longer ours
nor yours.

We knew that the islands were beautiful
round about here where we are groping
a little higher or a little lower
the slightest distance.

X

Our country is enclosed, all mountains
whose roof is the low sky night and day.
We have no rivers we have no wells we have no springs,
only a few cisterns, and these empty, that echo and that we
        worship.
A sound hollow and stagnant, the same as our solitude
the same as our love, the same as our bodies.
It seems strange to us that once we were able to build
our houses our huts and our sheepfolds.
And our weddings, the fresh marriage wreaths and the fingers
become inscrutable enigmas to our souls.
How were our children born, how did they grow strong?

Our country is enclosed. It is closed in
by the two black Symplegades. In the harbors
on Sundays where we go down for a breath of air
we see shining in the declining sun
broken timber of voyages that never ended
bodies that no longer know how to love.

XII

Bottle in the Sea

Three rocks a few scorched pines and a remote chapel
and farther above
the same recopied landscape begins again;
three rocks in the shape of a portal, rusted,
a few scorched pines, black and yellow
and a small square hut buried in whitewash;
and still farther above, over and over
the same landscape repeated tier upon tier
as far as the horizon, as far as the sunset sky.

We anchored our ship here to splice the broken oars,
to drink water and to sleep.
The sea that embittered us is deep and unexplored
and unfolds a vast serenity.
Here among the pebbles we found a coin
and diced for it.
The youngest won and disappeared.

We reëmbarked with our broken oars.

XV

Quid πλατανὼν *opacissimus?*

Sleep has enwrapped you with green leaves, like a tree,
you breathed, like a tree, in the quiet light
in the translucent spring I watched your face;
closed eyelids, and eyelashes cutting the water.
In the soft grass my fingers found your fingers
I held your pulse for a moment
and felt the pain in your heart was elsewhere.

Under the plane tree, beside the water, amid the laurels
sleep displaced you and dispersed you
about me, beside me, but I could not touch the whole of you,
inviolate in your silence;

watching your shadow grow and diminish,
losing itself amid other shadows, within the other
world that would release you and keep you.

The life that was given us to live, we have lived.
Pity those who wait with so much patience
amid the black laurel lost under the heavy plane trees,
and all those who speak alone to cisterns and to wells
and drown amid the circles of voices.
Pity the companion who shared our sweat and our privation
and plunged into the sun like a crow beyond marble ruins,
without hope of enjoying our reward.

Grant us a calm other than that of sleep.

XVI

ὄνομα δ' Ὀρέστης

On the race course, once more on the race course, on the race
       course,
how many rounds, how many laps of blood, how many dark
rows; the people who watch me,
who watched me when on my chariot
I raised my hand in splendor, and they thundered.

The froth of the horses smites me, when will the horses tire?
The axle grinds, the axle glows, when will the axle blaze?
When will the reins snap, when will the horse hooves
trample full-footed on the earth
on the soft grass, amid the poppies where
in springtime you plucked a daisy.
Your eyes were beautiful but you didn't know where to look
nor did I know where to look, without a country,
I who am struggling down here, how many rounds?
And I feel my knees buckling on the axle,
on the wheels, on the savage race course,
knees buckle easily if the gods so will it,
no one can escape, of what avail is strength, you cannot

escape the sea with reeds in autumn that sang in the Lydian mode
that cradled you and for which you seek here
in this hour of strife, amid the panting of horses,
that sea which you cannot find no matter how much you run
no matter how much you circle before the dark Eumenides who
      are bored
and unforgiving.

XVII

Astyanax

Now that you are going take with you the child
who first saw light under that plane tree,
on a day when trumpets resounded and weapons gleamed
and sweating horses bent down to touch
the green surface of water in the trough
with their moist nostrils.

The olive trees with the wrinkles of our fathers
the rocks with the knowledge of our fathers
and the blood of our brother alive on the earth
were a hardy joy a rich order
for souls who understood their prayer.

Now that you are going, now that the day of reckoning
dawns, now when nobody knows
whom he shall kill and how he shall end,
take with you the child who first saw light
under the leaves of that plane tree
and teach him to meditate on trees.

XIX

And though the wind blows it does not cool us
and the shadows are still slender under the cypress trees
and all about the steep slopes of the mountains;

they weigh on us
our friends who no longer know how to die.

XXI

We who set out on this pilgrimage
have looked on broken statues
forgot ourselves and said that life cannot so easily be lost
that death has its uncharted roads
and a justice of its own;

that when we die upright on our feet,
made one in the brotherhood of stone
united in hardness and weakness,
the ancient dead escape the circle and are resurrected
and smile in a strange stillness.

XXII

Because so very much has passed before our eyes
that even our eyes saw nothing, but far beyond
and behind us memory like a white cloth one night in a walled
         place
on which we saw strange visions, stranger than you,
drift and vanish into the motionless foliage of a pepper tree;

because we knew this fate of ours so well
wandering amid broken stones, three or six thousand years
searching amid ruined buildings that could have been, perhaps,
         our homes
trying to remember dates and heroic deeds;
shall we be able to?

because we were bound and scattered
and fought, as they said, with imaginary difficulties
lost, then finding again a road full of blind battalions
sinking in marshes and in the Lake of Marathon,
shall we be able to die in a normal way?

XXIII

And a little more
and we shall see the almond trees in blossom

the marbles shining in the sun
the sea breaking in waves

and a little more
let us rise a little higher.

XXIV

Here the deeds of the sea and the deeds of love have an ending.
If in the memory of those who shall in time to come live here
where we are ending, the blood should blacken and overflow,
may they not forget us, feeble souls among the asphodels,
may they turn the heads of the victims towards Erebus:

We who had nothing shall teach them serenity.

IN THE MANNER OF G. S.

No matter where I travel, Greece wounds me still.

On Mt. Pelion amid the chestnut trees the shirt of the Centaur
slid among leaves to wind about my body
as I mounted the slope and the sea followed me
mounting also like mercury in a thermometer
until we came on mountain waters.
In Santoríni as I touched the sinking islands
and heard a flute play somewhere on the pumice stone
an arrow suddenly flung
from the confines of a vanished youth
nailed my hand to the gunwale.
At Mycenae I lifted the huge stones and the treasures of the
        Atridae
and slept beside them at the inn of *The Beautiful Helen of
        Menelaus;*
they vanished only at dawn when Cassandra crowed
with a cock hanging down her black throat.

At Spétses at Póros at Mýkonos
the barcaroles nauseated me.
What do they want, all those who say
they may be found in Athens or the Piraeus?
One comes from Salamis and asks another whether he "hails from
          Concord Square."
"No, I hail from Constitution Square," replies the other,
          self-satisfied.
"I ran into Yánnis and he treated me to an ice cream."
In the meantime Greece voyages on
we don't know anything we don't know we're all seamen
          disembarked
we don't know the bitterness of harbors when ships have gone;
we mock those who feel this.

Strange people who say they are to be found in Attica and yet are
          nowhere;
they buy sugared almonds to get married
carry hair tonic get photographed;
the man I saw today sitting before a backdrop of doves and
          flowers
allowing the hand of the photographer to smooth out the wrinkles
left on his face by all the fowls of the heavens.

In the meantime Greece voyages on and keeps on voyaging
and if "we see the Aegean flowering with corpses"
they are of those who wanted to catch the great liner by
          swimming
those who wearied of waiting for ships that cannot set sail
the ELSIE the SAMOTHRACE the AMVRAKIKOS.
Now as night falls on the Piraeus the ships whistle
they whistle and keep on whistling but not a single capstan stirs
not a single wet chain glistens in the last declining light
the captain stands enmarbled in his white and gold.

No matter where I travel, Greece wounds me still;
screen of mountains archipelagoes bald granite.
The ship that voyages is named AG GONY 937.

A WORD FOR SUMMER

We have returned again to autumn; summer
like a notebook that has tired us with writing remains
full of erasures, absentminded scribblings
on the margins and question marks; we have returned
to the season of eyes that gaze
into a mirror under the electric light,
lips compressed and people strangers
in rooms on streets under the pepper trees
while the headlights of motorcars kill
thousands of pallid masks.
We have returned; we always set out to return
to solitude, a handful of earth in our empty palms.

And yet I have once loved Syngroú Avenue
the double undulation of the great road
that would leave us miraculously by the sea
the everlasting sea that it might cleanse us of our sins;
I have loved a few unknown persons
suddenly met at the day's ending,
talking to themselves like captains of a sunken armada,
a sign that the world is wide.
And yet I have loved their roads here, these columns;
though I was born on the other shore near
rushes and reeds, islands
where water welled up in the sand that a rower
might quench his thirst, though I was born
by the sea which I wind and unwind on my fingers
when I am weary—I no longer know where I was born.

There still remains the yellow distillate, summer,
and your hands touching medusae on the water,
your eyes suddenly unveiled, the first
eyes of the world, and caverns of the sea;
bare feet on the red earth.
There still remains the blond enmarbled youth, summer,

a little salt dried up in the hollow of a rock
a few pine needles after the rain
scattered and red like tattered fishing nets.

I do not understand these faces I do not understand them
sometimes they imitate death and then again
they shine with the lowly life of the glowworm
with an effort confined and hopeless
compressed between two wrinkles
between two coffeehouse tables covered with stains
they kill one another they decrease
they stick like postage stamps to the windowpanes
faces of the other tribe.

We walked together, shared bread and sleep
tasted the same bitterness of parting
built our houses with whatever stones we had
took to the ships, lived in foreign lands, returned
and found our women waiting
but they recognized us with difficulty, no one knows us.
And our comrades wore the statues wore the bare
and empty chairs of autumn, and our companions
slew their own faces; I do not understand them.
There still remains the yellow desert, summer,
waves of sand receding as far as the last circle
rhythm of a drum pitiless and endless
flaming eyes sinking in the sun
hands with the manner of birds cutting the sky
saluting the ranks of the dead that stand at attention
lost at a point I cannot control and that governs me;
your hands touching the untrammeled wave.

EPIPHANY, 1937

Mountains and the flowering open sea in the moon's waning
the huge rock near the Barbary-fig trees and the asphodels
the jug that did not want to dry up toward the close of day

and the shuttered bed near the cypress trees and your hair
golden; the stars of the Swan and that particular star, Aldebaran.

I have held on to my life, have held on to my life as I traveled
amid yellow trees toward the slanting rain
on hushed hillsides laden with leaves of the beach,
not a fire on their summits; the night comes on.
I have held on to my life; a line on your left hand
a cut on your knee, can it be they exist
on the sands of the previous summer, can it be
they remain there where the North Wind blew as I hear
a foreign voice about the frozen lake.
The faces I gaze on do not question, not even the woman
walking, bowed down, suckling her child.
I climb the mountains; blackened gorges, the snowfilled
field, everywhere the snowfilled field, they do not question—
neither time locked in mute and remote chapels nor
the hands stretched out to beg nor the roads.
I have held on to my life with whispers in the endless silence
I no longer know how to speak or how to think; whispers
like the breathing of the cypress tree that night
like the human voice of the nocturnal sea on the pebbles
like the memory of your voice saying "happiness."
I close my eyes seeking the secret meeting of waters
under the ice the smile of the sea the closed wells
fumbling with my own veins for those veins that elude me
there where the waterflowers end and this man
who paces blindly on the snows of silence.
I have held on to my life, with him, seeking the water that touches
          you
heavy drops on the green leaves, on your face
in the empty garden, drops on the still reservoir
finding amid its pure white feathers a dead swan,
trees alive and your eyes staring.

This road is unending is unchanging, as long as you try
to remember your childhood years, those who went away those
who were lost in sleep, the sea's sepulchers,
as long as you ask the bodies you loved to stoop
under the hard branches of plane trees there

302 MODERN GREEK POETRY

where a sun's ray stood, stripped naked,
and a dog frisked and your heart beat like a wing,
this road is unchanging; I have held on to my life.

                                                The snow
and the water frozen in the hoofprints of horses.

INTERLUDE OF JOY

We were happy all that morning
O God how happy.
First the stones the leaves and the flowers shone
and then the sun
a huge sun all thorns but so very high in the heavens.
A nymph was gathering our cares and hanging them on the trees
a forest of Judas trees.
Cupids and satyrs were singing and playing
and rosy limbs could be glimpsed amid black laurel
the flesh of young children.
We were happy all that morning;
the abyss was a closed well
on which the tender foot of a young faun tapped
do you remember its laughter: how happy we were!
And then clouds rain and the damp earth;
you stopped laughing when you lay down in the hut,
and opened your large eyes and gazed
on the archangel wielding a fiery sword.

"I can't explain it" you said "I can't explain it
I don't understand people
no matter how much they play with colors
they are all black."

OUR SUN

This sun was yours and mine: we shared it
who suffers behind the golden silk who dies?

A woman was shrieking, beating her dry breasts: "Cowards,
they have taken my children and torn them to pieces, you were
       the ones who killed them,
watching with strange expressions the glowworms at evening,
abstracted in a blind meditation."
The blood was drying on the hand dyed green by a tree
a warrior was sleeping clutching a lance that brightened his side.

The sun was ours, we could see nothing behind the golden
       embroideries
later messengers came breathless and dirty
stammering incomprehensible syllables
twenty days and nights across sterile lands and nothing but thorns
twenty days and nights feeling the bellies of the horses bleeding
stopping not even for a moment to drink rainwater.
You told them to rest first and speak afterwards, the light had
       dazzled you.
They expired saying: "There is no time," touching a few rays of
       the sun;
you kept forgetting that no one ever rests.

A woman was howling: "Cowards" like a dog in the night
she must have once been as beautiful as you
with a moist mouth, with veins alive under the skin,
with love.

This sun was ours; you kept all of it, you did not want to
       follow me
and it was then I learned about these things behind the gold and
       the silk;
there is no time. The messengers spoke truly.

THE KING OF ASINE

Ἀσίνην τε · · ·

All that morning we looked about the castle
beginning from the shadowy side where the sea
green and without brilliance, breast of a slain peacock,

received us like time without break.
Veins of rock descended from high above,
twisted vines, bare, many-branched, coming alive
at the touch of water, while the eye in following them
strove to escape the fatiguing undulation
and constantly weakened.

On the sunny side a long extended coastline
and the light grating diamonds on the great walls.
Not a single creature alive, the wild pigeons flown,
and the King of Asine, for whom we have sought two years now
unknown, forgotten by all, even by Homer
only one word in the *Iliad*, and that uncertain
flung here like a gold burial mask.
You touched it, remember the sound?—hollow in the light
like a dry jug in the dug earth—
and the same sound of our oars on the sea.
The King of Asine a void under the mask
everywhere with us, everywhere with us, under a name:
" 'Ασίνην τε . . . 'Ασίνην τε . . ."
                and his children statues
and his desires the fluttering of birds, and the wind
in the intervals of his meditations and his ships
moored in a vanished harbor;
a void under the mask.

Behind the large eyes the curved lips the curled hair
embossed on the golden covering of our existence
a spot of darkness that glides like a fish
in the dawning calm of the sea, and you watch it:
a void everywhere with us.
And the bird that in another winter flew away
with broken wing
the tabernacle of life,
and the young woman who went away to play
with the dogteeth of summer,
and the soul that sought the underworld screeching
and the country like a large plane tree leaf that the torrent of the
        sun sweeps away
with ancient monuments and contemporary sorrow.

And the poet looks at the stones and lingers, asking himself
are there I wonder
among these broken lines peaks edges hollows and curves
are there I wonder
here at the meeting place of wind rain and ruin
are there the movement of feature the form of the affection
of those who have so strangely dwindled in our lives
of those who have remained wave-shadows and thoughts
                boundless as the sea
or no, perhaps nothing remains but the weight only
nostalgia for the weight of a living existence
there where we live now without substance, bowed under
like the withes of the dreadful willow heaped up in a duration of
              despair
while the yellow current slowly bears away reeds uprooted from
              the mire,
image of a form turned to stone under the sentence of a bitterness
              everlasting,
the poet a void.

The shield-bearing sun rose fighting
and from the depths of a cavern a frightened bat
crashed on the light like an arrow on a shield:
" Ἀσίνην τε . . . Ἀσίνην τε . . ."
                     Was this the King of Asine
for whom we have sought so carefully on this acropolis
feeling at times with our fingers his touch upon the stones?

LAST STOP

Few are the moonlit nights I have cared for.
The primer-book of stars which you spell out
as much as your fatigue at the day's end allows
and from it gather other hopes and other meanings,
you may then read with greater clarity.
Now that I sit contemplative and idle
few are the moons that have remained in memory;

islands, color of a grieving Madonna, late in the waning,
the light of the moon in northern cities sometimes casting
on turbulent roads, rivers, and limbs of men
a heavy stupor.
Yet here last evening, in this our final landing,
where we wait for the hour of our return to dawn
like an old debt, money for years locked up
in a miser's chest, until at length
the moment of payment comes, and the coins
can be heard dropping on the table top;
in this Etruscan village behind the Sea of Salerno
behind the harbors of our return, at the edge
of an autumn squall, the moon
has outstripped the clouds, and the houses
on the opposite slopes have become enamel.
Amica silentia lunae.

This also is a train of thought one way
of beginning to speak of things you confess to
with difficulty, in moments when you cannot hold back, to a
                friend
who escaped secretly and brings
news from companions and from home
and you hasten to open up your heart
before exile forestalls you and changes him.
We come from Arabian lands, Egypt, Palestine, Syria;
the little kingdom
of Kommagene that flickered out like a small lamp
comes often to mind,
and great cities that throve for thousands of years
and later became the grazing lands of cattle
fields for sugarcane and corn.
We come from the sands of the desert from the seas of Proteus,
souls shriveled up by public sins,
and each holding office like a bird in its cage.
Rainy autumn in this depression of land
festers the wound in each of us
or as one might otherwise put it, nemesis fate
or simply bad habits, fraud and deceit,
or even selfishness that reaps profits from the blood of others.

Man crumbles away easily in the midst of wars;
man is soft, a tuft of grass;
fingers and lips that long for a white breast
eyes half-shut in the dazzle of day
feet that would run, no matter how tired
at the slightest whistle of gain.
Man is as soft and thirsty as grass,
as grass unslaked, his nerves are spreading roots;
when the time of harvest comes
he would rather hear the scythes whistling in some other field;
when the time of harvest comes
some shout to exorcise the demon
some become entangled in their possessions, some orate.
But when the living are far away of what use
are exorcisms, possessions, orations?
Is man ever anything else?
Is it not this that confers life?
A time to plant, and a time to pluck up that which is planted.

You will tell me, friend, it is the same old tale repeated.
But a refugee's thinking, a prisoner's thinking, a man's
thinking when he too has become a commodity
you cannot alter, no matter how much you try.
Perhaps he wants to remain king of the cannibals
squandering powers that nobody buys
strolling among the fields of agapanthi
listening to drums under the bamboo tree
while courtiers with their monstrous masks are dancing.
But the land they hack and burn like a pine tree, and which you
                envisage
in the dark train carriage, with broken windows, without water,
                night after night
or in the fiery ship that according to statistics is going to sink,
these have taken root in the mind and do not change
have planted images like those trees
that in the virgin forests cast down their branches
and take a firm grip in the earth and sprout again;
they cast their branches down and sprout again and go on striding
league after league;
our brain is a virgin forest of slain friends.

And if I speak to you in parables and fables
this is that you may listen with greater sweetness, and the horror
cannot be talked about because it is alive
because it is speechless and continues to advance;
pain of an anguished memory
drips by day drips in sleep.

To speak of heroes to speak of heroes: Michael
who left the hospital with open wounds
was speaking perhaps of heroes that night
when he dragged his foot through the city's blackout
and howled, groping the pain that is ours: "We walk
in darkness and in the dark proceed . . ."
Heroes proceed in darkness.

Few are the moonlit nights I care for.

HELEN

"The nightingales won't let you sleep in Platres."

Shy nightingale, amid the respiration of leaves,
you who bestow the forest's musical coolness
on bodies separated and on the souls
of those who know they will not return.
Blind voice, who in the night-glooming memory grope
for footsteps and gestures; I would not dare say kisses;
and the bitter turbulence of the slave-woman grown savage.

"The nightingales won't let you sleep in Platres."

What is Platres? Who knows this island?
I have lived my life hearing names for the first time heard:
new places, new insanities of men
or of the gods;
                    my fate that wavers
between the final sword of an Ajax

and another Salamis
had brought me here to this shore.
                            The moon
rose out of the sea like Aphrodite,
covered the stars of the Archer, now goes to find
the Heart of Scorpio, and changes everything.
Where is truth?
I too was an archer in the war;
my fate: that of a man who missed the target.

Nightingale, minstrel,
on such a night as this by the sea's rim of Proteus
the Spartan slave-girls heard you and dragged out their lament,
and among them—who would have thought it?—was Helen!
She whom we pursued for years by the Scamander.
She was there, at the desert's edge; I touched her, she spoke to me:
"It's not true, it's not true," she cried.
"I never boarded that blue-prowed vessel.
I never set foot on valiant Troy."

With full breast-band, sun on hair, and this stature of hers
shadows and smiles everywhere,
on shoulders on thighs on knees;
animated skin, and those eyes
with their large eyelids,
she was there, on the bank of a Delta.
                            And at Troy?
Nothing at Troy—a phantom.
That's how the gods willed it.
And Paris lay with a shadow as though it were solid flesh;
and we were slaughtered ten years for Helen.

Great suffering had fallen on Greece.
So many bodies cast
into the jaws of the sea, the jaws of the earth;
so many souls
given over to the millstones, like wheat.
And the rivers swelled with blood amid the mire
for a linen undulation for a cloud
for the fluttering of a butterfly, the down of a swan

for an empty garment, for a Helen.
And my brother?
                    Nightingale nightingale nightingale,
what is a god? what is not a god? and what between the two?

"The nightingales won't let you sleep in Platres."

Tearful bird,
                    on sea-kissed Cyprus
so ordained as to remind me of my country,
I anchored alone with this fable,
if it's true that this is a fable,
if it's true that men will not take up once more
the ancient deceit of the gods;
                                    if it's true
that some other Teucer, years afterwards,
or some Ajax or Priam or Hecuba
or someone quite unknown, anonymous, yet one
who saw a Scamander overbrimming with corpses
is not fated to hear
messengers who come to say
that so much suffering so much life
plunged into an abyss
for an empty garment for a Helen.

ENKOMI

The plain was wide and level: from a distance hands
could be seen turning as they dug.
In the sky, clouds with many contours, now and then
a trumpeting of god and rose; the afterglow.
In the sparse grass and thorns wandered
light gusts of air after the shower; it must have rained
beyond at the mountain rims that now took on color.

And I moved on toward those who were working,
men and women with picks in the ditches.

It was an ancient city; walls streets and houses
stood out like the petrified muscles of cyclopes,
the anatomy of a spent strength under the eye
of the archeologist the anesthetist the surgeon.
Phantoms and fabrics, lips and luxury, digested,
and the curtains of pain flung wide open
left the tomb exposed, naked and indifferent.

And I looked up toward the men who worked,
the straining shoulders and the arms that struck
this dead silence with a rhythm swift and heavy
as though the wheel of fate rolled over the ruins.

Suddenly I was walking and did not walk
I looked at the flying birds, and they were turned to stone
I looked at the air of the sky, and it was full of dazzling wonder
I looked at bodies that had been struggling, and they stood still
and among them a face ascending in the light.
The hair black, spilling over the collar, the eyebrows
fluttering like the wings of a swallow, the nostrils
arched over the lips, and the body
emerging naked from the laboring hands
with the unripe breasts of the Virgin,
a dance without movement.

And I lowered my eyes and looked about me:
girls were kneading dough, but not touching the dough
women were spinning, but the spindles were not turning
sheep were being watered, but their tongues hung
over green waters that seemed to be sleeping
and the plowman remained with his staff suspended in mid-air.
And I looked again at that body ascending;
many had gathered, an ant swarm,
and struck her with spears but did not wound her.
Now her belly shone like the moon
and I believed that the sky was the womb
which had begotten her and taken her back, mother and child.
Her feet remained marble still
and vanished; an Assumption.
                    The world

was becoming as it had been, ours,
the world of time and earth.
                            Fragrance of terebinth
began to stir along the old slopes of memory
breasts amid the leaves, moist lips;
and everything went dry at once on the field's expanse
in the stone's desperation in the corroded power
in the empty place with the sparse grass and the thorns
where a snake slid by placidly
where they spend a long time dying.

George Thémelis

THE KING OF VOYAGES

Quantum mutatus . . .

No, not Glory
Sung and resung a thousand times,
The wooden horse with the iron belly
The flames that danced at midnight

Nor the great adventures
The epic a heart wrote with a thousand keels on land and sea
On the ever-living stones of time with its eternal blood
More searing than the passion of fire
Stronger than the wind's longing

The seashores have sung it and sing it still
And shall sing it until the sun goes to sleep and lowers every light
The song of the captain with endless eyes

It is taken by the winds and given to the birds who scatter it in the
        sky together with light
And the fingers of the rain sow it on the bosom and rivers of
        earth that trees may bear fruit
That children may grow tall that statues may live
That masts may support the fate that strikes them from above
That men may rise in stature as far as the breasts of the gods
Who laugh from their high places and rejoice heartily in their
        good progeny

Daughters and sons, grandsons and great-grandsons, taken from
        between their broad knees
And who—look!—strain to resemble them, who clamber up to
        become admired images once again
The gods' sculptured shadows that deepen the earth and make it a
        mirror
Where women see gods and where goddesses see men
Where even death strolls by scattering garlands

Deep in their graves the dead hear the song and sigh

The north winds have taken the captain's voice
Storms study the sea and spell out his name
Lightning flashes scribble his stature with green pencils on the
        backdrop of mountains
And our soul rises and welcomes his imperishable presence like a
        long-awaited king of voyages
When his shadow appears and strides over the threshold of sleep
Then stoops to raise from the deep
Our sunken ships

No, not Glory . . .

Sing to us at last now of sorrow
Of the motionless noonday sun that hangs from above and drives
        nails into our faces
Of the ancient brine and the old winds that congeal in our hair
And of the bitter peevish waste of time that withers hands
Between a dead harbor and a tavern
Between half a cigarette and three harsh words
Of boredom
Of boredom

He is the one who smokes, spitting out tobacco and passion
Who spells out the messages of time, the history of the sea
And builds out of sand and nothing the most incredible dreams
Because he has nothing else to do
No space in which to breathe
No plank on which to stand, no place to spread
The endless skein of his hopes

Because he is stifled by becalmed weather, because time encircles
     him
And memory is a longing that digs into his lungs
Because his heart is heavy, his blood cannot endure it
Nor his ragged clothing endure the captain's towering shadow

Sing to us at last now of sorrow

The land has no balm nor the mountains air
The sea has no ships for us now.

HELLENIC EARTH

I poke amid the ashes of my ancestors.

I seek to find that hidden corner, those secret corridors
Amid collapsed nights and dawns with trees that stand
Supporting the grief of time, the age of the sun,
Preserving old rain, generations of motionless nightingales
In the niches of leaves, nor do the branches of birdsong stir
For they have turned into petrified sound.

Heavy ash, sacred ground, earth the nursling of the sky
Fermented with crimson springtimes, with modest folds, beautiful
     hair and trophies of death,
Bedsheet of unawakened erosion, of beauty's wound,
     water-cloven, cloud-thirsty,
Which free souls hold in their hands in order to plant sleep
Where the hidden bones of the dead awaken to feed their last
     smoke
When an evil North Wind blows and uproots the houses.

What night can blot out the names in the pits of the gods,
Can wither the rock flowers which death has opened.

If tombs sink, voices will remain,
Conversations of shadows that emerge at night to tread on earth,

To pick up a familiar stone and carry it about them
That it may weigh on their transparent forms and remind them
     of the body,
The beloved body made of mud and wind, of the sea's depth and
     the unknown day,
And with the light hull of a ship in its heart.

Earth, whom the cemeteries of time and the wind cleave,
With your everlasting autumn of ruins, your climate of
     incorruptibility,
Your children, your young children are filled with death,
With the shadow of death, and they can pick up its scent without
     trembling,
With a hollow sound that multiplies their footfall in endless
     crypts,
And their hearts are like sailing islands of lotuses and bitter laurels
     and birds of another time,
And their smiles are old cracked mirrors that remember.

Eternal children, light bodies with a thin flesh,
With transparent souls that blaze at the slightest provocation,
What relentless wing, what eye has struck you
That behind you follow a multitude of shadows, small houses,
     spacious tombs,
And all about you sea and time, time and sea and a distant sky.

RHAPSODY TO THE AEGEAN SEA

Here it awakens every morning
Amid Greek sculpture and Ionic columns,
On stones that deepen their wounds, ravaged by their passion for
     azure.

It rises and takes basil leaves and broom flowers,
Beating its hooves on high to kiss garlands of dead snow,
Then dismounts and walks with naked feet on marble basins,
Carving seashells and rosettes on the rocks of eagles.
Wrapping the frozen pigeons with seasalt and mist.

Immaculate
Blue-blooded
Gazed on from afar.

My windows are your crossed sails
My eyes your enclosed harbors full of white pebbles and the dead,
You who resound and shake the crypts of my sleep with the echo
      of a thousand birds,
Who with bedsheets of your secret dawn cover my walls
And my buried animals that guard my gardens like women sunk in
      sleep,
With what name shall I call you, with what sharp edge shall I
      strike you
That it may thicken your hair, that it may embroider your
      memory.
If I call you daybreak, the carnations will vanish,
If I draw you as pure and unmolested, the lilies will be pierced,
If I embrace you as mother, the birds will weep.
I write you down as the archer of tall smoke, the chorus of
      nightingales,
Ever-virginal gentle mother, who bleeds though never touched
By moon eagles, horsemen, dirty rivers
With mud, tattered rags, digested bones.

If only I were a seabird to count
The stairs of your diaphanous sleep one by one,
The twigs of the rose bush in the nights of the sea depths
Where your dead lie sleeping in luminous tombs
Of azure stone and oyster shell and seashell,
In gardens of sunken ships that have lost their souls,
Lost the captain of the seven keys who guards the winds,
The diamond portals that opened toward vast seas
And vanished because of withered sails and bitter tar.

It is there you suffer,
It is there you put out your lights and lick your heart.

Restless curve, cavern of roaring sound, by time and death made
      acrid,
Rise out of your hollow cry, drown the sun and roll your
      glittering wheel,

Lean like a mother over the torn earth and seal her blood,
Wash the clothing of children, the feet of birds
With cataracts of blue, with a clouddust of jasmine.
Then enter into the desolation of your veins and rig your
        morning ships.

FLOWERS DO NOT ASK QUESTIONS

Flowers do not ask questions. They await
Only the adventure of becoming the erotic book of birds,
Or of dying simple and unmourned under the glance of a girl.
They do not possess the uncertainty of the probable, the bitterness
        of the irrevocable.

They have no memory. They have forgotten their primeval
        beginnings and the nostalgic ache for return.
And like small children they give themselves candidly into the
        hands of the good day.
Their glory is to fall sleep on the bosom of the dead.

They ask no questions. Nor do they ask the wind from where it
        comes
Or where it goes. They do not dig in the snow to find the edge of
        whiteness, they do not seek
To learn about the fate of their shadows that vanish in the
        corridors of waters,
Nor why carriages roll, nor why clocks strike, wounding
        recollection,
Nor why men are born and die, die and are born,
Why the dead do not hear, do not speak, why they do not return
        from the other entrance,
Nor what happened to the bygone before every before so that it
        no longer exists and does not return,
What happened to the sun that it no longer returns, turning its
        horses, changing its horses.

Who knows, who can say in what direction and toward what goal
        the axles of the everlasting go . . .

Perhaps they drive on toward the point of the origin of origins to
     close the circumference,
To end the adventure of the long escape and to exclude
From the province of the completed all eventualities and all vain
     flights,
Casting themselves out, canceling themselves out,
Having no beginning and no end within the immobility of
     fulfillment,
Sealing the perfect movement in the fullest immobility,
Like a statue, like a ship in bas-relief that sails on and on . . .

Flowers will reach perfection by returning to their fullest reality
And their glory shall be to give themselves without hesitation to
     our fullest gaze.

DESOLATION

Outside of us things die.

No matter where you walk at night you hear
Something like a whisper coming out
Of streets you have never walked on
Of houses you have never visited
Of windows you have never opened
Of rivers over which you have never stooped to drink
Of ships on which you have never sailed.

Outside of us die trees we have never known.
The wind passes through vanished forests,
Animals die from anonymity and birds from silence.

Bodies die slowly, slowly, by being abandoned,
Together with our old clothes laid away in coffers.
Hands we have never touched die out of loneliness.
Dreams we have never seen, from lack of light.

Outside of us begins death's desolation.

TRAVERSING

Passing amid familiar walls, we hear the sound . . .

We don't know if it comes from our steps or those of another
Which at one time dragged behind us and now follow us . . .

We don't know if we are the musicians or the instruments.

If it is we who are walking, looking behind us
At our long shadow—or perhaps it transposes us
As though we were its hanged ones on some tree
(Or, it may be, in a cistern or an old mirror)
Falling from garden to garden, from corridor to corridor,
Like another face—other faces, one merging into the other,
Like the words of a poem which is continued
With interruptions, relapses, and a sequence of images . . .
Or reflections—shadowy lights on a blackboard.

Before every blackboard there is a child
Just as there is an ideal face before every gaze
Or a luminous meteor before every expectation . . .

(For this reason, when night falls we grow cold and are gripped
                with fears . . .
For this reason, when we meet we leave a trail of phosphorus,
One seeking the other, an encounter in the night . . .)

The blackboards open with a secret lock in back:
(All things have secret folds and places)
They present photograph frames, coffers, or empty boxes . . .

Within every frame there is a landscape.
Within every coffer there is a buried secret.
Within every empty box a probable doll
With glass eyes and crossed hands.

PLAYING AT CARDS

You must play in many gambling dens
And lay awake many nights
Before you can change your luck
The way one changes gloves.

Gloves are, in truth,
Among the most significant things in the world,
As are empty seashells, pebbles, keys.

Of all these, I love gloves
Most, because of their kinship
To real hands and to the Blind Goddess of Chance.

There is a profound affinity between hands, gloves, and luck,
Between sleep and daybreak,
Between birth and death.

Playing cards is like drawing a sword
To kill the puppets who are playing;
But your sword is made of wood, and you cannot;
You too become a puppet and gamble with your soul.

When you lose your soul, you have no one
To play with—you play with yourself,
Alone, in direct confrontation, *face to face*.

When you lose yourself, you have no one
To play with—then the unknown one comes,
Having tied his horse to your hitching post.
You draw your wooden sword, but he is like a cypress tree;
Your chest is naked, but he is sheathed in an armor of iron.

How many time have we set sail, how many
Times have we been shipwrecked: play, play,

Change the deck of cards: measure all things
With the joy that beautifies them: you may hope
That even tomorrow will dawn: you may exist,
The light falls on you: you may see
Your face in the faces of men.

Things are beautiful, beautiful even when they die,
(As in a deep mirror, more deceitful than dreams).
Because they die, because they will be resurrected
With us, because they die our own death,
They are beautiful: they narrate our glory.

They are our sky, our own sky,
Our clear, unsleeping mirror reflection.

God keeps vigil *in silence*—He sees man;
And man as *through a glass*—he sees God.

He gave us a face—We resemble Him.
He gave us love—We approach Him.
He has hidden from us His secret—We seek Him.

THE BODY

The body, you must say, is not your body.
We must adorn the dead with a rose on their chests,
With a wreath made of myrtle,
Let us love one another,
Let not the body of man fear
The body of woman, *in concord*, in silence,
Let us love one another,
The body of woman trembles and approaches.

Behind us the shadow protects us,
Love frightens us, sleep takes us on far voyages,
In concord, in silence,

In the end death takes us, *let us love one another*,
And puts us away in his cupboard.

(You must take good care of the body, and when it is spring
You must prepare its holiday, with a rose on its chest,
With a wreath made of myrtle.)

There lie the hands with their unmoving fingers
There lie the eyes and all that the eyes hide,
Stolen from the light, like empty seashells;
The cracked and firmly locked lips.

(We shall not ask for anything that cannot be given,
And we shall not question: we shall be the answer.)

Sometimes you are bored with being a man,
With walking and hoping,
Without hand or foot or face.
You would like to be a worm or a root
Thrust in your own mud, you would like to be a bird.
You are bored with the shoes you wear, the dust they raise,
The water basin, the filthy scum from your skin,
(Even God washes mud from his hands)
The hands that hang down and remind you
Of broken wings that drip with blood.
You are bored with your own coursing blood:
Your hair that keeps growing every night, your body that
          hungers.

Sometimes you are bored with your own face, it frightens you.

When I was small I liked to fetch water: I took joy
In the spouting fountain as it gurgled in the waterjug,
With the waterjug that grew as heavy as a good woman.
(The old tree cast its shadow above us and hid us.)
Once my mind wandered, as in a dream,
(That comes and winds time up like a ball of yarn)
And the waterjug slipped from my hands, the way
Your beloved slips from your fingers in play.

Earth drank the water as it drinks
Blood spilled to water the dead.
I stooped above the scattered limbs
Of a refreshing love, I stooped, weeping,
Then gathered them one by one to reshape my love.

(Who will gather our scattered limbs, who will compose them?)

from   DE RERUM NATURA

I move my body, and my soul moves,
I put it to sleep, it sleeps.
I love, and my soul loves,
It tastes my body and my blood.
I sniff the air, and my soul sniffs also.

It is I who hunger, it is I who thirst
In my soul, it is I who suffer.
It is I who wound my fingers.

Whatever my soul has heard
Within me, it hears.
Whatever my soul has seen, it sees,
It becomes, it reappears
In a clear sky.
Whatever it has touched, it transforms,
And makes it beast, fire, bird,
In an unceasing mirroring.

Whatever it has loved, it ignites and burns.

We shall never have enough, my soul,
Of bread and light, of sleep and love.
Light is insatiable, love is voracious.
We shall never satisfy our privation.
We shall eat and be hungry, we shall thirst.

Our trees shall be like lean
Bodies, skin and bone, half-lit,
Portioned out between darkness and light,
Between denial and assent,
As though they never had enough of sun and rain.

As though they seek another light in the light.

Our house shall be half dark
In an endless, motionless time.
As though it had not filled with sound and memory,
As though it had not had enough of sleep
Within that sleep in which we slept.

We shall never have enough, O my soul.

What would the earth have been without us?
Anonymous, insubstantial, desolate.

What would the sky have been without us?

Shapes without light and without one voice
To name them, without perpetuity.

And what sort of thing would God have been?
A thing without name and without splendor.
What flesh would he have taken to manifest himself
Without flesh on earth, what face
Without the human face,
Without human shape or clothing,
What blows and blood, what suffering
Without human suffering:
Behold the man, behold God.
Without human death, without
Burial and lamentation, without resurrection.

What would Death have been without us?

SPACIOUSNESS

I am no longer the one I was, I am being made over
From the beginning, I am preparing my birth.

I was lost and now am found,
I raised my body and continued on.

I learned to see and to move.
I learned to be and to exist.

Did I exist before, perhaps, and will I exist
Even afterwards, in motionless, endless time;
Am I not more than the shadow the body makes
And casts behind it in the darkness;
Am I not the light that falls and gives birth
To shadow and body and reflection?

Am I not more an image than a person,
And gaze in the mirror and recognize myself,
There where all things exist, are luminous,
And glitter in a profound consciousness?

I close my eyes, it becomes night,
I move, the earth moves.
I suspect that the star's light is my own.

The body is a small celestial body.

I compose the sound of rain,
I feel the drenched earth,
It is raining in my deep heart
And raining heavily in my soul.

The earth is odorous, the sky is odorous.

An odor of rotted leaves,
Of withered dreams, of closed houses,

Motionless and stagnant waters.
Like a woman in a room,
Crouching in a corner, unloved, barren.
An odor of flesh and fruit.

My memory is fragrant within, aromatic.

When I speak, an echo resounds.
Behind every word there are other words,
Behind every voice there are other voices.

As though many were speaking at once,
As though they were shouting from afar.

I hear the sounds, I can be seen from every direction,
I see the light and it sees me.
I have acquired a mirrorlike transparency.

I am a spectacle or an image.

Faces cross my face,
Look at one another, smile in their own smiling.

Their eyes glitter, a thousand eyes.

And other phenomena appear, other shadows,
Unborn shadows, invisible mirror-images
Who pursue their own selves
To emerge in light, to be born
From the other side, from within the night,
The unknown night, the one to come.

"Who are you, whom I do not know, yet
Whom I resemble as though I were one of you,
Created from the same shadow, taken out of the same night.

You have my face, my sorrow, my loneliness."

They have not yet arrived from afar
To take on flesh, to appear in the mirror,

Like half-lit gliding fishes
That the sun may play in light and shade on their faces,
That they might test the spectacle and pass
From the dark depths to the surface,
From the rattle and the noise into music.

I desired it, I needed it, and this is why
Light exists: I longed for it and I called it.

Sleep exists because my eyes yearned for it,
Love exists because my soul called it.

I desired Him, I had need of Him, and this is why
God exists: I called Him and sought Him.
I have need of Him, I call Him and seek Him.

I sought Him and call Him, and Death comes.

HYMENEAL

Perfect, dense, inescapable destiny of love
And of death; conquest first, and then resignation.
Ascent first, then descent,
Fall of the body and sorrow of the soul,
Like solitude when it opens and swallows
Bones heaped high, humiliated.

Love comes and mocks us,
A god or a demon,
Strips us without shame or fear,
Leaves us naked to shiver in the cold,
Leaves us fasting that we may hunger,
As in the Last Judgment.

We hunger his hunger, we shiver in the cold of his nakedness.

Love comes and changes us:

Shadow within a shadow,
Silence within the other silence.

Our lips smell of springtime
And of earth, our breasts of ripe apples.

From within the gardens of the dead, love comes.

Our limbs and our entrails tremble.
They are as fevered as a conflagration,
Frightened flights of birds, animals that run,
And the throbbing of the swollen sea,
Hollow and curving waves
And the deep swimming of fish at night.

Hair glitters on the pillow
Hands glow in the passion of love,
Fingers searching blindly on flesh.

From breast to breast love reaches
Souls, as on a ladder.

Souls cannot speak.
They have no tongue, they have only silence,
Speechless astonishment and sorrow,
Remembrance and dread of the void.

They can only reflect light,
Make fingers move,
Open and close eyes and lips.

Look at one another, as in a mirror.

Zoë Karélli

POET

I shall stand erect in the light to speak.
Since I exist, I must speak.
Since I have heard, I must speak.

Within the light that surrounds me,
the air, all colors, all forms
invest me with my own form.

I shall open my mouth to speak,
my speech is whatever has made me
and whatever I shall do in the future,
the cause of my existence.

The definition of life is an act of my own
which I define and which defines me,
I determine the attitude which upholds me.

May my own God help me raise Him high
that I may prove all he has lodged within me,
that I may retain my body's position.

Precious body, material vessel, state of the spirit,
my material tongue speaks
my immaterial speech.

What is the hue of the words I hear?
An intermingling of all in the smooth chord,
the entire universe within me in a single voice.

Hosannah to the magnificent Lord
who gives the dreams which untamed
reality surpasses.

Life in the embrace of death
carries and casts about her the gaze of rebirth,
and he who possesses the gift of speech
speaks of actual visions.

PRESENCES

You must remain very much alone,
—quietness of the fragile movement,
anxiety of perception—
that the presences may come.

Do not be afraid,
the dead never die;
even the most humble and forgotten
exist, and when you are very much alone
they come near you
invested with the mystic silence
of the ineradicable,
the incomparable presence of man.

WORKER
IN THE WORKSHOPS OF TIME

As he wrought the shape,
a worker, a blower of glass,
felt his love profoundly
for the material
into which he blew his breath.

At times crystal or like pearl,
mother-of-pearl, precious ivory
or opal with misty colors
drifting toward azure.
All these were materials that became shapes,
erotic shapes for whatever exists
within time.

The shape, receptacle of time,
enclosed it erotically,
an offering to time,
expectation and acceptance both,
that form which is an embrace of time,
the singular shape he wrought
out of his own essence,
his own imagination.

But as his material hand
caressed the final shape afterward,
he understood the materiality of time
as his own hand
together with the shape
and the precious, erotic material
were transformed into the diaphanous meaning of time.
All together,
but particularly he.

THE PROCESSION OF POETS

Look, this procession of poets
is made up of priests of the Word
who go singing, because these
know only how to sing, to speak
words, but from there on
expect nothing more from their hands.
Nor do they know some imposing
ceremony or any function

or ritual, but only how to recite,
how to proclaim words,
which they insist they can *see*.
Look at their eyes.
These men declare
they see angels,
that angels give them words
to rest lightly on their parched mouths.
In truth, they fast and seem
deprived. Look at their faces,
which are odd because of the very awkward
way they speak, because they want
to persuade us they are giving us
a gift of angels,
and miraculous angelic messages. They seek them
with prayers and great anguish,
they implore with much striving,
they accept them with contrition of spirit.
                                    In truth,
the expression of their eyes is another thing,
and the words these poets tragically sing
become altered
that we may understand their difference.
Of course they must be tormented
that we may believe,
that they may persuade us. We have
other concerns, and they
concern themselves with vain words only.
They want to preserve them, they say,
to present them to us,
that we may accept poets in the ceremony
of life. These men of words,
in order to win us over,
say they will give us names
and the meaning of our lives.

YOUTH IN A TIME OF DIFFICULTY

What shall the young men do, the beautiful ones,
with their tragic adolescence
cracked crystal of the soul,
battered flower, unripe rotten fruit,
melancholy yellow color of dawn?
The overclouded day begins
with an impassable sky, heavy, weighted
with evident storms, and treacherous.

What shall they do who have
the beautiful, the terrible eyes
of youth, clear and unpersuadable?

His closed eyelids, deeply shadowed,
sign of the lonely sin,
seemed like the wings of an enormous
night butterfly, lacking the lambent colors.
The almost savage yet oh so sweet
frank brown brilliant gaze of the other,
like that of a wild creature, brimmed
with purity and innocence and wonder, and then
a pretended indifference,
a painful pride.
                 What
can the young men do, who know
so much and cannot hope
even as their life begins?

They long for sky and a clear light,
to sail upon the azure open sea
freely, they seek to believe
in their own human strength entirely.
They were promised full freedom
that the sacrifice of blood might be paid.
Their task binds them the more heavily,

and the effort that grows fatiguing
prevents the blossoming of a good happiness.
Their purest desires are white pigeons
that thrash about enslaved, inhumanly wounded.
What do they know that they do not speak?
What cruelty have they learned?

Not Achilles, not even Odysseus
set forth to war believing
in the handsome gods, the guardians of men.
In the marble palaestrae of flawless beauty
not even one of the ephebes,
eager for the shining secret of life,
may speak with pride, may hymn the praises
of the inflexible sage of virtuous thought.

No one awaits—
the joy of waiting has lost its glory—
for the immaculate love of the maiden, the untouched dream,
to grant the message of another life.
What shall the young men do
when the deception of violence
does not become the incomparable vision?
When, before they begin
the tyrannous trial of life, they know
the terminal closed, the adventure dubious?
When they know so much, what hope
may they have in the splendid victory of virtue?

No angel appears
to proffer them the cup of bitterness.
The young man shall raise it himself
to his own mute, bitter lips
where no word of prayer or protection
blossoms, or calls on the father
in the moment of dreaded ordeal,
of unmerciful solitude, of unbelief,
in the moment of man's terrible trial.

DESIRES

Youthful desires,
like very beautiful youthful lovers,
with the irreproachable innocence of the impetuous,
with incomparable pride and nobility.

They have vanished.
As it is said of certain young men
that the gods loved them
and they died young.
Perhaps they have disappeared without any possibility of
            returning
on a lovely evening
with the full-flooded, honey-colored light of the moon.
Let us thrust aside the common notion,
the loathsome thought
that profane hands stifled them
on lawless beds
in rooms rented for cheap pleasure.

These restless ghosts of desire
that reappear,
tragic and very beautiful faces,
confess to some kind of crime,
nonetheless.

MATUTINAL

Hour of dawn, most beautiful, translucent,
glittered and glittering, cooled and cooling!
The light, a smooth-sounding music,
glides within and upon leaves
that glow from the kisses of nocturnal embraces.

Star-gleaming Eos comes,
golden-edged, flashing rosy light.
She walks on precious sandals, on alabaster feet,
leaving their golden traces on the azure
violet-covered mountains.
                              In your heart
do you not feel how their vast bodies leap!
She drops in ravines the opal mist
of her luminous veils.
                              In the valleys
she awakens the rustling trees, and is a little late in reaching
the green pastures of tranquil fields.
She approaches, dancing with hovering feet,
and zephyrs, without strength, whisper
delicate echoes, sweet-sounding conversations.
She strews gilded hyacinths
and rosy cyclamens on the crystalline
diaphanous and shivering waters of the sea.
And thus the glorious dawn proceeds,
gold-glittering, chryselephantine,
that she may cry out with all her echoes,
her lightning-flashing rays of light,
that her archon is coming, the most beautiful ephebe,
her flaming and sweet lover,
her great and wealthy magician,
that the omniscient Sun of Life is approaching!

KISS OF SILENCE

Kiss of silence, icy
pleasure in the well of warm conversation,
your seal is an indelible mark;
in the blossoming of another world, the voice of a whisper
that terrifies, mystic
fragrance that tears the living
entrails apart, promise
that no one knows,

and all the power of life
prepares your entire imagination.

You are not yet the expectation
of nonexistence. You are the integral,
the only difference, that superb
immobility which possesses
perfect Love, and is possessed.

MAN, FEMININE GENDER

I, woman, "man" in the feminine gender,
have always sought Thy face;
it was, until this moment, man's,
and I could not otherwise know it.
Who is more alone now,
and in what way,
intensely, despairingly alone,
he or I?
I believe I exist, shall exist,
but when did I exist without him,
and now, how do I stand, in what light,
what is my sorrow still?
O how I suffer doubly,
continuously lost,
when Thou are not my guide.
How shall I look upon my face
how shall I accept my spirit
when I struggle so
yet cannot find accord.
Because it is through Thee
that man and woman find their concord.
The tragedy of the impersonal
is not yet revealed, nor can I even
imagine it still, still.
What can I do since I know so well
so many things, and know better than to think

that Thou plucked me from out his side.
And I say that I am "man," completed
and alone. I could not have been formed without him
but now I *am* and am capable,
and we are a separated pair, he
and I, and I have my own light.
I was never the moon,
but I said I would not depend on the sun,
and I have such pride
that I am trying to reach his
and to surpass myself, I
and again I,
who now in learning about myself, learn
completely that I want to resist him,
that I want to accept
nothing from him, that I do not want to wait.
I neither weep nor chant a song,
but my own violent separation, which I am preparing,
is becoming more painful
that I may know the world through myself,
that I may speak my own word,
I, who until this moment existed
to marvel and to esteem and to love.
I no longer belong to him,
and I must be alone,
I, "man" in the feminine gender.

ADOLESCENT FROM ANTICYTHERA

I have come again for your sake.
As I walked on, I observed
the Corinthian vessels well;
they impressed me, of course,
with the grace of their shapes and their paintings.
I thought of the throbbing life
of that notorious city. Afterwards,
as though on purpose, I lingered in the halls

where the light seems almost watery.
I don't know whether this is due
to the color-tone of the walls,
the immobility of the exhibits,
or the glass of the showcases.
I lingered, therefore,
holding my anticipation of your presence
like a joy.

For a while Kroisos held my attention,
"Pause here and pity him . . . destroyed by belligerent Ares."
In the movement, in the placement of the hands,
a particular turn betrayed the spirit
that remains there still
and indicates the controlled desire
of the body as it leans forward.
Imagined rustling of the lives of statues
when the sculptor has been able to catch
the vital moment . . .

Wondrous youth,
unique moment, you are not only
the adolescent of perfect beauty,
of radiant youth,
that harmony in the form of the limbs' music
of him who keeps his posture and holds it
in natural strength and power,
like the stone or the plant
that exist both simple and perfect together;
hands spread out in ideal balance,
divine curvature,
indestructible innocence of caught time,
smiling face of incorruption,
heightening of our perishable position.

Reality and magic,
smooth surface of life,
convex and concave curves
from the impetuosity hidden within you,
guided and controlled.

Offering and acceptance of existence,
in movement and immobility both,
like the balancing of a regal bird.

You were born
before we were taught the meaning of sin.
You are the concession of the spirit
that quenches insatiable privation
and annihilates cupidity.
Though filled with longing, you remain ready to deprive yourself.
Every foreign disposition to your shape
glides away from you.
You seek the spirit's value,
yet it is you who proffer it, alive and serene body.

Frugal meeting with the absolute,
naked mystery,
form snatched from necessity,
you rise like the music of one sound,
divine sufficiency, created in human terms.

You were not tormented by that love
which is an uncertainty,
anguish and painful submission,
even though in your glance is held
the wondrous human melancholy,

for you are the work
of a man who loved his life
in a glory both arrogant and modest.

PERSEPHONE

At the height of sensitive adolescence,
just as I reached to touch the sweet-smelling narcissus,
the breach roared
and the level and firm earth opened at my feet,

a malevolent knowledge loomed like a ghost before me,
a gaping wound, chaos filled with darkness.

And you emerged, O dark spouse,
silence graven on your face
and fixed in your gaze,
silence as the expression and seal of that dreadful eruption
which brought you to the surface,
that you might seize and carry me off
to those untamed depths where luminous Phoebus
shall never visit.

Burning entrails of earth,
groans of birth that bear witness to death,
how fearfully I saw you before me
as I spread my hands, almost those of a child's still,
to those delicate, perfidious, those erotic flowers.

Glowering lover of my timid youth,
what great necessity brought you
to expose yourself to light,
afraid of it no longer,
and to rivet your features
on my terrified gaze?

Gods, not even you know
the meaning of the awe that seized me
so that I could not move
and remained riveted,
nor could I hear the wailing
or the dissuading cries of my mother,
for I could no longer hear.

Ah, what can anyone hear
of the charms of terrestial power
when earth is torn under his trembling footfall
as in great awe he sees the worlds of Erebos
and breathes and tastes on his tongue the Shadow's breath?

Then at once immobility becomes
the most astonishing power.

O light, which I adored like every mortal,
and you, O Sun, glory of the heavens,
why have you forsaken me? What made you
draw yourselves away from me,
take away your dazzling touch
and surrender me into the hands of darkness?

What change within me
made you deny me,
what power in the world ordered you to abandon me?
To what election did you submit me
so that I lacked the luminous voice of my youth
to invoke you?

And you came, O King of the Dead,
to apprehend me,
for your reception had already taken shape within me.
I was inexpert, my youth without experience,
nor did I know the end nor the beginning,
and my perception was rewarded
with the thick and rising vapor of the Kingdom of the Dead,
and numberless promises of the multitudes of the dead
apprehended me while I was still unprepared.

O freezing dread of my struggle!
Within me the glacial cold stopped me
in an unbelievable tension,
a dark and hovering arrow
that longed to encounter the motionless depths,
showing up the various vegetations of the world
as an ephemeral notion, a passing glory, and light
terminating into the unfragmented shape of nothingness.

Where can my mortal tongue find invocations,
O Hecaergos, Aleksikakos!
Syllables choked in my dry speech,
and only Silence, unbesiegeable force,
remained to carry me off
to the world there of the dead,
to the enchantment of darkness,
to the closed and unchanging essence.

II

Dreadful was my struggle
to snatch away from my face
the shadow's hue, knowledge
of the most mystical expression,

                              even though I emerge
from darkness once more.

O Cyprian, emerged
from the birth-giving swelling of the waters, translucent
and all-powerful beauty, help me
to surpass the thickness of matter
which has locked itself about me,
evident obstacle to the heaven's light.

What mortal, O Paphian, O rosy and white goddess,
can now have trust in me?
Who can ignore the thought that through my hair
the fingers of darkness have passed
with their dreadful caresses?
Who will not discern on my brow
the touch of their freezing kiss,
and in my gaze that knowledge
of which no one may ever speak?

Mysterious and dreadful meanings, whispers from thence,
how will you withdraw from my hearing
and will not stand between me
and the music of the mundane present?

Angels of Shadow, unspeaking sentinels,
withdraw and do not inhabit my gaze,
do not keep the limbs of my body
so inscrutably, O tenacious companions in the kingdom
of immobility.
Let the hour of speech approach
to unseal my lips of silence.
O Lethe, turn back in your course
and swerve the cup toward the light
that Phoebus may pour within it his golden vigor drop by drop.

Unconquered Aphrodite, send your maiden troops
of pleasure, with their melodic bodies and sweet-singing laughter,
bring them borne on the love of the winds,
their hands filled with imagination's flowers,
to conceal my pale forehead of thought,
and let them sing all the songs
devised by men, let them say
all the words to conquer our knowledge of death.

And you, O double-voiced Mother, come,
your hands filled with the earth's fruit,
come to show me your glory,
the double significance of fertility,
and the invincible essence, the endeavor
of man, the justification of his presence,
his resistance to unfruitful struggle
and unfruitful love.

Andréas Embirícos

LIGHT ON A WHALE

The original form of woman was the braiding of two
dinosaur necks. Times changed after that and woman also
changed shape. She became much smaller more fluid more
adapted to the two-masted (in some countries three-masted) ships
that sail above the calamities of life's struggles. Woman herself
sails on the fishscales of a cylinder-carrying dove of long
trajectory. Times change and in our time woman resembles the
chasm of a fuse.

WINTER GRAPES

They took away her toys and her lover. Well then she
bowed her head and almost died. But her thirteen destinies like
her fourteen years smote the fleeing calamities. No one spoke. No
one ran to protect her against the overseas sharks which had
already cast an evil shadow over her like a fly staring with
malice on a diamond or a land enchanted. And so this story was
heartlessly forgotten as always happens when a forest ranger
forgets his thunderbolt in the woods.

LEGENDARY SOFA

The continuity of the river was cut off. The coherence of the landscape was such that the river still continued to flow. From within the leaves of the field toward the bridge smitten by the sun the esparto grass the white breasts the flowers within the transparent shirts they placed on dawn girls stooped naked or almost naked to hug and generally to caress their bodies and the bodies of flowers. Its peripheral road became the road of an entire city and the river that divides it into six parts embraces the hour that captured the landscape in the fingers of the future.

SPINDLE OF NOCTURNAL REPOSE

We are all within our future. When we sing we sing before the expressive pictures of painters when we stoop before the straw of a burnt town when we render the drizzle of a shudder ours we are all within our future because no matter what we pursue it is not possible for us to say no to say yes without the future of our destiny just as a woman can do nothing without the fire she encloses in the ashes of her feet. All who have seen her have not stopped to stare either at the twisting garden plots or the feast of hair adored or the flutes of laboratory tranfusions from one land into the veins of a warm gulf of worldly things and the etesian winds of the blue reflections of lissome virgins. We are all in the future of a polysynthetic flag that holds the enemy's fleet before the lips of my heart safeguarding delusions vouching for intermediary beseeching reforms without the object of strife being understood. Snapshots have proved the correctness of our march toward the trainer of the same phantom of a dream's origin and of every inhabitant in the heart of a very ancient town. When our chronicles are exhausted we shall appear more naked than the arrival of the condemnation of similar tentacles and clean winches because we are all within the silence of pain plunging into the gurgling trickeries of our future.

CONCATENATION

The cocky boys! and yet they fall among the shrubs of the
        mountainside
At the very hour when pigeons blossom on the road
The cocky boys! and they prolong the silence
Of a limpid day which no pains will ever disturb
Smelling gardenias in the silence
Descending into the snowfilled valleys
The cocky boys! blooming in the dawn
And pouring libations with the sighs of the wind.

DAYBREAK

Frenziedly but certain
The colt of day charges into
The mouth of spring and the birds are singing
With the clear sky in their voices
Like flutes that echo and reecho in the flora
Of a handful of angels who remain in rapture
Like windflowers that arise
From the petals of pleasure.

THE EYELID

The waters rush pellmell always
The years fall into waterfalls
And a squall frightens the birds.

But the gardens will not be vexed
Bullets of bliss whistle in the leaves
The apples are red
And a passer-by cuts a few of them.

SPRING AS ALWAYS

Covering the waves of the spear-conquered town with her red
    dress
At first small and then large
She ascends to the top of the tower
And seizes the clouds and presses them to her bosom
Perhaps there was never a sorrow greater than hers
Perhaps no whisper ever fell more incandescent on the surface
    of a face
Perhaps there was never exposed to the comprehension of man
    an exhibition more extensive
Exhibition more varied more comprehensive than the story of this
    confession told by the clouds
Cut here and there by guillotines
Warm drops fall to the ground
The hillock formed on the principal spot of this fall
Swells and rises still
No tax can be so heavy as one such drop
No diamond more heavy
No suitor more passionate
Bright are the fringes of the hill and they gleam in the sun
On the summit a basin is waiting
It is full to the brim
And from its water a very small and very lovely girl emerges
Our hope for the morrow.

ORION

The indeterminate epoch with all its storks
Has remained afloat on the ice-floes and is drifting westward
Naked the crystals and naked the swallows in the sun
Who sing in the migration of the crossing
The surge of earth
The sheath of spring

Without hope of some sort the ice-floes cannot rush for long
The warmth of each voice contains the whole of its meaning
Keel of precipitation
In the migration of the omnipotent storks
There is a renaissance of polar iridescence among the clouds
And nets haul in the fishes from the shadows of yesterday
The heavens gape and the moths are fluttering
We have swallowed a mirage
The seagulls need not conceal themselves
The sailors are standing and searching the horizon
An ark appears on Ararat
An olive branch is proffered by a mermaid
She holds a ring between her teeth
Her fingers are eloquent
Her message comes from afar
We have waited for thirty years on the ice-floes to meet the siren
When the ship's whistle was heard
And the siren appeared amidst her smiling
She has been waiting no doubt for us since morning
When words are headlong the voice arrives
And the storks hover in the light of it
Sunrise sunrise
Keel of the sun on daybreak
Descent of the icebergs
Each of our domes fills with eiderdown of rose
Many of us smoke pipes of coral
And others pipes of seafoam
And the fluttering of our arrivals
Recalls the name of an ancient city
All of us rush to see if she has come to view
For the horizon shines
For it resembles her so.

MOMENT OF PORPHYRY

No cleft can be widened without desire
On the garden railing the birds open their wings
The neighborhood of the river attracts them

The passion of the vulture for a white pigeon
Is a mountain summit with snowy crest
When the ice melts we sing in the valleys
The waters intoxicate us
The pupils of our eyes wash their treasures
Some are blond and some brunette
They hold in their faces the reflection of our hopes
They hold in their breast the milk of our lives
And we stand about them
Eternal commands surround us
The mountain clots throb and dissolve
Their snows are songs of the coming of new years
These years are our life
In their hollows the birds rest at noon
No cleft can be widened without desire of widening
Sometimes we become hourglasses
And sponges throb to every single drop of ours.

THE CARYATIDS

O the breasts of youth
O the pallid waters of the fig-peckers
The pavements resound with the steps of the morning people
O vigorous groves with your trees of crimson
Youth knows of your meaning
Already dawning upon your fringes
Tassels of eiderdown frisk among the breasts of young girls
Who walk half-naked in your little bypaths
Their hair is more beautiful than that of Absalom
Among the locks the drops of amber fall
And the dark-skinned girls come carrying leaves of ebony
The squirrels sniff at their footprints
The woods are deeply moved
The woods are swarming with legions of brandishing lances
Here even the larks strip themselves of their shadows
The streetcars cannot be heard
And the day is sighing
For one of her very small daughters is fondling the day's nipples

And a spanking will do no good
Only a deer goes by holding in his mouth
The three cherries he had found between the breasts of youth
The evenings here are warm
The trees enwrap themselves in their silence
Rocks of silence drop now and then into the clearing
As the light does before it breaks into day.

THE RESPLENDENCE

The luminous wick becomes a lighthouse
Its crystals speak to us
Sometimes we seem to resemble its beams
Sometimes we seem to be its far-off voice
We stand erect in its resplendence
We are governed by its body
We are strengthened by its light
Our heart throbs with it
Its wheeling reflections are ships
And the sea is at our feet
Not one of us ever stands in his own footsteps
Each one of us proceeds and withdraws into the refuge of his
          dreams
In our entrails is the earth that covers us
Our desires herd together
Their locks are intermingled
Their mouths kiss each other
Their arms hug us
And the sphinx clasps us to her bosom
In the resplendent silence of the lighthouse.

THE ADVANTAGE OF A YOUNG GIRL
IS THE JOY OF HER HUSBAND

Before the anchor of the coast-guard cutter is cast into the sea
And the horses of the Carthaginians draw their longboats
The cool pharoses of the promontories
Accept foam and the cry of gulls
Accept gifts bestowed on the betrothed
Now that trumpets resound and trumpet blasts burst like
        pomegranates
For darkness has broken
And daybreak in the island's center
Recalls the winds that uplift
The veils of a bride in a tropical country
As gently as the mosquito-netting of a summer encampment
As gently as lips that break to dawn on white flesh
As gently as fingers dipped in milk
The bride at length unloosens her hair
And the lemon trees intoxicate the nightingales
Insects gather in their wings
And by the heat are cast upon the ground
The erupting shocks of a huge volcano
Traverse the canal's lips
No matter what the outcries of the two shepherds
For lava has now obliterated the mountain ridges
While the endurance of the one and the impatience of the other
Hug the wind before the uprearing head of a bear.

AUGMENTATION

It sometimes happens that one kisses
The hand of a morning reflection
In the silence of a landscape
Standing motionless with sealed mouth

Before the city awakens with a thousand fountains
And with the unfettered bathing voices
Suddenly released in the sudden sun
By the street-cleaners of the morning.

And so our pains have not gone for nothing
They lift their veils and reveal
Their mighty arms swelling
To reach into the heart of the city
Like the magi of the East, and to raise
The fingers of the sleepers one by one
Toward the row of boats that sail the streets
Laden with perfumes
With treasures and provision
From the remote lands, like the glance
Of a woman daydreaming.

CRANKSHAFT STROPHES

O great ocean liner you sing and sail on
White in your body and yellow in your funnels
For you have wearied of those filthy waters where you anchor
You who once loved the far-distant islands
You who have raised aloft the highest of banners
You who sail fearlessly through the most dangerous squalls
I hail you, for you abandoned yourself to the sirens' enchantments
I hail you, for never once did you fear the huge Symplegades.

O great ocean liner you sing and sail on
In the aurora borealis of the sea and its gulls
And I rest in one of your cabins the way you rest in my heart.

O great ocean liner you sing and sail on
The sea breezes have found us out and unloosen their hair
They also rush to embrace us with their fluttering folds
Some of them white and some of them crimson
Some folds of joy and some folds of heartbeats
Of the newly betrothed and of the newly wedded.

O great ocean liner you sing and sail on
Voices here and whales across your path as you proceed
From below your water line children haul up blessedness
And from your face haul up their similarity to you
And you resemble those whom both you and I know
Since you and I understand what *whale* means
And how fishermen track down their fish.

O great ocean liner you sing and sail on
They sneer at you secretly who run away from battle
All those who barter away your fishing nets and eat blubber
But you cut courageously through the sea prairies
Until you reach the harbors of eiderdown
And the jeweled adornments of that beautiful mermaid
Who in her bosom retains your kisses still.

O great ocean liner you sing and sail on
Your puffs of smoke are the traces of fate
That unravel in a clear sky and mount high
Like the black locks of a voluptuous and heavenly virgin
Like the melodious cry of the muezzin
When your prow glitters through the waves
Like the words of Allah on the lips of the Prophet
Like the gleaming, unerring sword in his hand.

O great ocean liner you sing and sail on
In the grooves of your deep-folded furrows
That shine in your wake like the tracks of triumph
Ditches of deflowering, traces of twitching lust
In the searing sun and the light or under the stars
When your crankshafts revolve more swiftly until you sow
Foam to the left and foam to the right in the shuddering waters.

O great ocean liner you sing and sail on
I think that our voyages coincide
I believe I resemble you, that you resemble me
Our widening circles belong to the universe
We are the progenitors of generations still to be hatched
We sail and keep advancing without remorse
We, textile mills and power plants
Flat plains and open seas and gathering places

Where the young bucks meet with their lady loves
And afterwards write on the heavens the words
Ármala Pórana and *Vélma*.

O great ocean liner you sing and sail on
Apple trees blossom forever in our hearts
With their sweet juices and their shade
Where all the maidens come at drop of noon
To taste with us together the flavor of love
And then to gaze at all the harbors
With their tall belfries and their towers
To dry out their hair in the sun.

O great ocean liner you sing and sail on
The lutes of our dazzling joy resound
With the wind's whistling from prow to stern
With birds on all the wires of the masts
With the echo of remembrance like binoculars
Which I hold up to my eyes and gaze
At the islands and all the seas approaching
The dolphins and the quails speeding away
Hunters, we, of the enchantment of dreams
Of that destination that flies and flies but never stops
Just as daybreak never stops
Just as shuddering never stops
Just as the waves never stop
Just as the churning foam of ships never stops
And not even our songs for the women we love.

THE EUPHRATES

It is true that complete solitude is difficult to bear and that
the desert is parched and tyrannical. But, but, and yet again but
(as in Islam's "Il Allah," or the Christian's "God will provide,"
or as in the lofty thoughts of the godless), no sweat, no thirst will
exhaust the secret Euphrates that even in the desert, even within
and beyond silence, within and beyond every solitude and every

complaint irrigates all things always, its source as invisible as the great unconstructed light (its own source invisible) that illuminates everything to eternity, everything, everything, even the most minute as well as the most ecstatic, the most imperishable, the never-setting, the great, foaming universe.

THE WORDS

When at times we return from Paris and inhale the breeze of the Saronic Gulf under its friendly light and the aromas of the pines, in the sobriety of myths—both today's and those of antediluvian times—then like a trumpeting of wind instruments or like a vibrating crash of drums there rise, like glittering geysers, certain words, oracular words, arched and summital words of unification, words of immeasurable meaning for the present and the future, the words "Eleleleu," "I love you," and "Glory in the highest," and then suddenly, as in the meeting of crossed swords or the clanging arrival of an onrushing train in the underground tunnels of Paris, these words also rise: "Chardon-Lagache," "Denfert-Rochereau," "Danton," "Vauban," and "Glory, glory in the highest."

IN THE STREET
OF THE PHILHELLENES

One day as I was walking down the Street of the Philhellenes, the asphalt softening under my feet, I could hear, from the trees that line Constitution Square, crickets chirping in the very heart of Athens, in the heart of summer.

Notwithstanding the high temperature, the traffic was brisk. Suddenly a funeral carriage rolled by followed by five or six cars filled with women dressed in black, and as my ears caught smothered bursts of lamentation, for a moment the traffic was halted. Then a few among us (unknown to one another in the crowd), looked into each other's eyes in anguish, trying to guess each other's thoughts. But all at once, like a charge of dense waves, the traffic continued.

It was July. In the streets, buses were lumbering past, crammed with sweating humanity, with people of all sorts—lean adolescents, stocky mustached males, fat or scrawny housewives, and many young ladies and schoolgirls on whose tight buttocks and palpitating breasts many in the jostling crowd, as was natural, (all flaming, all as bolt upright as the club-carrying Heracles), were attempting, with mouths half-open and eyes dream-taken, to make those contacts usual in such places, so profound in meaning and in ritual; all pretending that simply by chance, because of the dense crowding and the pressures of the crowd, these frictions, these pressures, these gropings were all simply happening on the spherical attractions of receptive schoolgirls and ladies, these intentional and ecstatic contacts in the vehicles, these pressures, these frictions, these rubbings.

Yes, it was July, and not only the Street of the Philhellenes, but the Fortifications of Missolóngi also, and Marathon, and the marble phalluses of Delos were all throbbing, vibrating in the light, as in Mexico's parched expanses throb the upright cactuses of the desert, or as in the mysterious silence that surrounds the pyramids of the Aztecs.

The thermometer had been constantly rising. It was not only warm but unbearably hot—that heat born of the vertical shafts of the sun. And yet, notwithstanding the burning heat and the rapid, gasping breath of all, notwithstanding the procession of funeral cars a short while before, not a single passer-by felt oppressed, nor did I, although the street was blazing. Something, like a lively cricket in my soul, compelled me to advance with a light step of high frequency. Everything around me was made manifest, tangible even to the sight, and yet, at the same time, everything was almost immaterialized in that great heat—men and buildings both—and to such a degree that even the sorrow of some of the bereaved seemed to evaporate almost completely in the equal light.

Then I, my heart fiercely beating, stopped for a moment, motionless amid the crowd, like a man who receives a sudden revelation, or like someone who sees a miracle taking place before his eyes, and I cried out, bathed in sweat:

"Oh God! This searing heat is necessary to produce such light. This light is necessary that one day it may become a common glory, a universal glory, the glory of the Hellenes, who were the first in this world, I think, to make out of the fear of death an erotic urge for life."

THE SEASONS

Raindrenched landscapes of autumn, with casualties of nepenthean flowers, with instantaneous downfall of leaves, and a gradual extinction of high summer voices, on seashores and beaches where the waves indulgently fall and cool all bodies with iridescent foam before each halcyoned sea subsides to the season, before the lofty harvester month sinks to oblivion.

Asphalt roads that lead into wintry cities, with avenues of groans and hideous murders, for a brother's honor, for spilled wine, for some nameless thing which Lethe is not able to cover, with white and black calamities that creak in the rafters like the ropes of hanged men when the wind sets the hovering corpses swinging—these blameless, these monstrous pendulums of the melancholic man's destiny.

Heavy winter bursts like a train under a low dome of heavy clouds—an express speeds where some believe there breaks in rose a radiant starting point, and others that the terminus throbs there like vaporous smoke.

And yet, a definitive terminus does not exist, as also no absolute law. Sometimes spring blossoms in the heart of winter, as at the height of harvesting one finds winter there.

Even so, that spring may return once more in heavy winter, a cloudless sky must be born at times in the heart of man, a sky as cloudless as a bridal poem sweet, nor must cumulus clouds be heaped high endlessly in the spirit, heavy and excluding cumuli as in Ginsberg's great poem *HOWL* or in Corso's *ALCATRAZ*.

And behold, although today I have read again these two poems, at the very end of September, here, in summery and sensuous Ghlifádha; now that summer has ended, now that the month of October arrives like an emperor dressed in purple, and

the rains of autumn begin to fall, and the billowing thunders of
airplanes reverberate above the rooftops, and I breathe in the
odors of rainsoaked earth, meditating, "But am I truly in Attica,
or in the mysterious, damp cosmopolis of London, in Highgate,
perhaps, or in Hampstead Heath?"; now, when in our garden a
few, last flowers have remained, and dusk falls early on our
veranda; here, where only a month ago the cicadas pulsed in their
flaming transport, as now lightning falls and at night in the
courtyards the chained dogs howl in heat; today, when once again
I read in the evening papers notices of disasters great and small
(a woman committed suicide by setting her clothes on fire,
Mr. K. P. put an end to his life with a stick of dynamite in his
mouth); yet, nothwithstanding all these things—or rather, exactly
because of all these things—behold, on this autumn night which
perhaps presages a heavy winter, although I read Ginsberg and
Corso again (for both move me profoundly), yet neither the
verses of the one nor of the other come to mind, but above the
screeching and wailing of *HOWL*'s winds, the lamentations of the
universe and the outcries of *ALCATRAZ*, there come to my lips,
I say, on this autumn night, not the verses of these other poets,
but of that archangel Percy Bysshe the swallow-winged verses:

> *Be through my lips to unawaken'd earth*
> *The trumpet of a Prophecy! O Wind,*
> *If Winter comes, can Spring be far behind?*

THE GREAT BLEATING
OR PAN–JESUS CHRIST

When the weight lifters of everyday life shoulder their
crushing burdens on piers, on station platforms, in courtyards and
roads, stepping in greasy shit, and thus render useless all the
Atlases of the world, then these unemployed Atlases, preferring
the punishment of Zeus to total inactivity, groan loudly and vomit
out their gigantic laments.

And yet, at the very hour when these burdens are heaved
high (straw bags and sacks crammed full of nameless things—

filled, that is, with crimes, with sins), the Universe still lives on,
rejoicing at times, but at other times (much more often) sighing
deeply under the weight of these burdens (nuclear weapons,
merchandise, mendacities of various kinds—all shit, all sins), at
that very hour one hears—and this always seems a miracle—one
always hears (although only a few hear) in fields and in cities,
under the midday sun and under the stars, one always hears a
great bleating (BAA-BAA) that drowns out the laments of the
Atlases, a most beautiful bleating, clearer than the voice of a
cock, much fuller, a bleating that pulses with light (BAA-BAA,
BAA-BAA) and spreads hope in the heart of those who hear it,
a great bleating like clear water falling from the cataracts of
heaven, the great bleating of a lovely lamb (baa-baa, baa-baa),
the bleating of a young ram (BAA-BAA, BAA-BAA); and
those whose ears drink it in become great cisterns of a never-
setting sound, those who clasp it to their bosoms are saved always,
a great bleating that ascends from on high like a procession of
perfumes, a great bleating as from the funnel of a gigantic
loudspeaker, the bleating of a lamb (a lamb that in Peru might
very well have been called a llama), the bleating of a young ram
with lovely large testicles, the bleating of an innocent lamb
(baa-baa, baa-baa)—O Glory, Glory Hallelujah!—of a beautiful
lamb-ram that lifts aloft all the sins of the world.

I. M. Panayotópoulos

EUMENIDES

My thoughts at night now cannot taste
Endymion's sweet Latmian sleep.
Clash of contending wills plows through them.
Around them brine and black solitude
of Cyclopean rock incite them
like schooners sailing out to sea.

The city, a voracious worm
crawls through the mud. A passer-by
leaves a trace of his light passing
amid the dark door swallowed whole
in its own shade, the tortured hearth,
the calling of nakedness and hunger,
and the barbarian's sleepless watch.

Man hunts man still in many ways,
some on illicit beds and some
on fraudulent scales, some with vain words
and some with deeds, with skills of war
and the imagination's lies
spawned by relentless strangers here.

My thoughts at night now cannot taste
Endymion's sweet Latmian sleep.
They see the empty cradle, the shut house,

the orphaned and unpracticed boy,
the idle plow, the poor man fallen
in snow, and hungry on empty streets,
duty forgotten and knowledge sunk
in stinking marshes stagnant still—
and dreams flash through his solitude.

Hecate sunk in a warm trance
weaves reveries of marble ruins.
Ships sail far off, grass sprouts in nude
bare fields; fruitful Demeter too
makes cheerful every household joy;
swans of Castalia ruffle all
their unbeclouded, luminous wings;
the reeds of fair Eurotas thrill,
the Argive reaps his golden crop,
and in tall Tegea, Artemis,
erect, breathes the Hellenic light.

But now it's time to hate! For see,
a faultless duty has ordained
our generation's steadfast fate.
The Eumenides' fierce croaking cries
surround our will with the wind's rage.

APOLOGY OF THE SMALL FAUN

The dawn is fragrant with the smell of thyme;
it was the small frolicsome Faun who awoke
and wore the broad-brimmed hat of the gold-glittering sun
and rode the wind down toward the sea.

This is the place where I was born.
I saw Dawn gleaming through the lyrical pines,
I saw her descending to the seashore of the gods
and fall like an ivy of crimson flame
on the shoulders of Ganymede.

This is the place where I was born.
I first breathed my longing in the shell of Aphrodite
who with her deathless contours rose amid the foam,
and her silver ankles bloomed on azure sand
till seas and land got drunk, like roses on the breast of love.
I first breathed my longing in the shell of Aphrodite
and felt there could be no other hour for me
beyond this hour of the Dawn
who opened her honey-gold palm
and on the roads of men scattered
longing and love.

On the roads of men, in the serene and ancient valley,
I encountered Helen of Sparta.
She was Aphrodite on her way to arouse the mighty war lord
and speak to him about the fate of Troy,
that unlucky fate, which was also mine.
The twin shields of her breasts,
with the flower of the pomegranate between them,
glittered in the sun of Laconia.
The undulation of her body became my destiny;
and I considered there could be no more fearful way
by which to mount Olympos.

On the roads of men, on Phaeacian shores,
I encountered the young girl Nausicaä.
Innocent her laughter, and her speech gentle.
I stood naked before her for I had no other garment
than the red garment of sin.
In her features glowed the desire of my homecoming:
a blue ribbon of smoke drifted in the distance.
And I felt this was the most serene of all destinies,
that it could be my destiny.

This is the place where I was born.
My spirit moans like a small frolicsome Faun
riding on the wind down toward the sea,
whipped by desire,
—imprisoned in a slight body
that shudders as it coils around the root of its longing.

from THE FROZEN MOON

IV

The trade winds ring their bells on the islands of the Cyclades.

The North Wind from the White Sea revives the night-shrouded
       country chapels
and the cathedrals of great name.
The North Wind from the White Sea sings on the fresh seashores,
and from mountain to mountain
from meadow to field
fills all deep solitudes with the ringing of evening bells.

The sea whitens under the white moon,
it whitens into hyacinths and jasmine.
The hiking Angels pass the night in the whitewashed belfries,
and demons in the heart of man.

The sea whitens under the white moon,
it whitens into hyacinths and jasmine.
And this is the supreme hour when churches sing and sigh,
when the crumbling country chapels sing and sigh,
and the divinely graced girl sings and sighs,
the Madonna of the seas, from Tinos,
that young Virgin who rejoices in the sea.

When they saw how the moon scaled the castle walls,
a thousand saints went to sleep in the Cyclades.
They put away their festive garlands and reclined
on a honey-golden seashell,
on a pebble the color of geraniums,
the ever-virgin daughters of the waters
and the fathers and martyrs of the spreading sea.

The heart of man sings and sighs,
—it is the sea with bells rung by the north winds.

"I laid me down and slept."
Now the martyrs on the islands have risen,
the weary fathers have risen
and descend to the orphaned shores
and fix their unsleeping eyes on the vast deep.

The trade winds ring their bells in the islands of the Cyclades.

Winds of night, winds of the white moon,
winds of that month which fills the grapes with wine,
take me on your spotless, angry wings
from island to island, from love to love,
—as far as unapproachable solitude, as far as the depths of death—
to an endless earth, an immaculate silence, an unfragmented sleep.

On this night the drunken gods dance
amid the islands of the Cyclades.

On this night the drunken demons dance
and plant desires in the heart of man.

On this night the angels dance,
the white-robed angels multiply,
drunk also under a drunken moon.

If I touched you, if I kissed you limb by limb,
I could teach you your body.
And then you would know at last that it's not right for you to die.

VIII

*"Do you consider that a man is happiest
when enslaved and restricted from doing
everything he desires?" "No, not I, by
Zeus," he said.*
                    —Plato, *Lysis*, 4

Day after day the roots multiply, the roots deepen
under my motionless feet.
After many years travelers will stop at this place
and point me out with an indifferent finger:
"See, this is the man who became a tree."

A sleeping, steadfast rain whips all the night.
It is turning dark now at the height of noon,
the nights have bound themselves to one another
until not a crack remains for the rejoicing summer.
Only a drunken sparrow hops close to the window grille
and begs for crumbs.

This drunken sparrow, it seems to me, must be some beloved
        person now dead,
hermit of the winter,
some beloved dead person who in his grave remembers me,
who remembers me in his dark loneliness.

But soon I shall even forget the dead, I shall merge with them.
I shall merge with the wind on the mountain slope,
the wind that uproots the stones.
All about me the stones multiply in despair,
without a suspicion of moss
without the drip-drop of water.

The seashores dwindle away.
At one time I tried to talk to men gently.
But I saw only their backs marking the distance.
At one time I wished to look men in the eye.
But they had no eyes.
At one time I thought that men could speak to me.
But it was as though I felt then that they lacked lips, that their
        mouths
emitted the pitch of Hell from their wasted entrails.

Here in this place man no longer exists.
A dog barks
achingly, barrenly, a Dog Bound.
If it stops barking,

—and it will fall silent at any moment now—
not a single living voice will be found amid the rotted dead.

A single living voice.
It was the clock that struck the hours.
Now it has grown bored.
It has allowed them to merge, one with the other,
even to die in an unfruitful time.

The nights merge, the hours merge, and the horizons merge and
        vanish
around the hollow spot.

Flame of song, ultimate hope and ultimate consolation,
may you at least be the one to wave your azure signal
to the unmoving tree,
in this high noon of endless night!

SUNDAY OF THE AEGEAN

Sunday, day of the sun,
walking like a dove on the washed stone wall,
falling into our hands
like the blossomed apple tree into a brook.

Green islands filled with flaming blackberry brambles
arrange themselves like anklets round your feet.

Azure islands, worn about your neck
as you sail on the billows,
O Sunday of the Aegean!

The seas are breathing citron and lemon,
—the maidens of Khios singing,
the masts singing,
the sails singing,
and all things round about them blazing

in the light of summer,
the sun sunk in their brains.

Soon the trireme of Paris will drift across our vision
—and it will mount high
toward the land of Troy.

With a reed pipe on their lips
let the unskilled shepherd boys stand
in the pasture lands of Mt. Ida
singing the hymeneal song.

It is thus in all its body, shivering in the midst of summer,
and when it turns into a drop of dew
that the Aegean remembers your passing feet,
that it remembers your beauty,
Helen!

HELEN

For me you are the mother, sister, and precious daughter
of that old man of the sea
whose name was Proteus;
I have lived you throughout a thousand nights
as you walked through my sleep like a dove,
singing to the morning star
like an industrious swarm of bees
about the drunken clematis,
the Aegean billows bringing you ashore,
laying you down gently
on a muskrose petal
and then, like the rosemary and the aroma,
planting you in my heart.

You are not one. You are bitter desire
with its myriad faces,
with its myriad names,

with that body which changes form like a garment,
a ghost of passion, that remains
forbidding and unfriendly;
nevertheless, in whatever skies and in whatever lands,
your never-setting light
envelops me, Helen!

Memory composed of numberless memories
and experience of the ultimate moment;
my fingertips think of you and shudder,
and like the pale waterlily
my thought descends into night amid the wind,
and like a waterdrop
of the hidden stream
hovers, quivering, at the cliff's edge.

White flower on the slender twig
of the green myrtle,
just as the frolicsome and wandering love
is about to touch you, you vanish.
You are not one. You are bitter desire
with myriad faces.
You are that northern love blossoming like snow
with a sea-blue star in your gaze.
You are love, the warm carnation of the South,
whose breathing leaps like a tall flame.
You are the precious love of the timid maiden,
and you are autumnal love walking slowly,
filled with affection.
You are the first love and the last
and the unkissed, the unwedded, the much-kissed,
but always the one and the unending and the unsleeping—

the Love that cannot learn
anything else, but only your name, Helen!

THE NIGHTMARE

I

This nightmare wears the conical straw hat of Tonkin.
It wears that country's pale face,
its slender fingers,
anklets on its feet.
And it has splattered its twig-slender body with silence.

In this room there is a ship with three sails,
a ship thirty centimeters long.
In summer, at the seashore, drunken crickets sail on ships like
        these.
As far as the first wave, as far as the second wave.
On the third wave the ship cannot be found.
Nor the cricket.

How can you go to Tonkin, to Malay, to the Marquesas Islands
with a ship thirty centimeters long
to meet the women of Maori, and Paul Gauguin ecstatically
sketching their backs?

How odd for Siamese elephants to be passing my threshold:
I cannot count;
it must be a herd, a vindictive herd destined to trample me.

And last night I wrote a letter to my lost friend,
the painter Gauguin:
"If there is a cocoanut tree on the Marquesas, near the sea,
among the women of Maori,
I shall set sail to die under its shade."
But I did not set sail.
Because I remembered that even Paul Gauguin is a person who
        does not exist.

He left only the "Noa-Noa."
And these questions:

"What are we?
Whence do we come?
Whither are we going?"

"Τάχα τί νἄμαστε;
Κι ἀπὸ ποῦ ξεκινοῦμε;
Καὶ ποῦ θὰ πᾶμε;"

"Que sommes-nous?
D' où venons-nous?
Où allons-nous?"

"Was sind wir?
Woher kommen wir?
Wohin gehen wir?"

"Che siamo?
Donde veniamo?
Dove andiamo?"

"¿Qué somos nostros?
¿De dónde venimos?
¿A dónde vamos?"

My friend Gauguin, this is something no one knows.
Not even in the Marquesas Islands.

II

Perhaps it is futile to ask.
Our essence is not an answer. It is a question only.
Despairing and irremediable.

At least let the indolent, drunken cricket exist!
On its light raft, a ship thirty centimeters long,
sailing on the first wave, on the second wave,
in the curving seashores of the White Sea!

If it were not for this nightmare with the conical straw hat of
        Tonkin,

I could reach out my hand
to pick up the severed ear of van Gogh.
The wind of Arles sang to this ear,
the indefatigable wind.

May the Most High be blessed, Vincent van Gogh, my brother,
because no one has ever sensed
how many nights the angry wind of Arles walked through my
        heart!

I wanted to tell you what a wonderful trophy
your severed ear was
in contrast to our prose futilities.

But how can you hear me? Your other ear has also died,
brother of the wind, van Gogh.

from THE WORLD'S WINDOW

13

Jerusalem, Jerusalem, the brutalizer of prophets!
Hiroshima, Hiroshima, the brutalizer of men!

Hiroshima is our fate in its youthful years.
Hiroshima abolishes History.
Heaps up civilizations as Sardanapalus his treasures.

Hiroshima is the new face, the fresh face, the face of the century.
Hiroshima is the presence.
Behind every smile lurks a Hiroshima.
Behind every kiss, behind every encounter, behind every spasm
        there lies a Hiroshima.
Behind the fire in the hearth, behind the ancient song, the
        ancestral legend, there lies a Hiroshima.

The new poetry is Hiroshima.
The new beauty is Hiroshima.
Hiroshima is our new skin, our new hide that renders all
          Argonauts futile.
Hiroshima is the new philosophy.
The chronology of the coming world.
Mankind has plodded for thousands of years to reach Hiroshima.
Mankind has pondered for thousands of years to find the theorem
          of Hiroshima.
Mankind researched, wandered, stayed up nights, crossed over
          many seas for thousands of years. Hiroshima is to be
          found at the edge of the waters, at the end of the street.

There man conversed with his ancestors.
There he reaffirmed his virtue.
There he decoded his compassion.
There he chanced upon his humanity.
Hiroshima is the crossroads,
the beginning and the end of the world,
the contrivance and the mask,
the face,
the real face,
the irrefutable.

      30

Space annuls my memory,
annuls my history,
annuls my heroism,
annuls my sorrow,
annuls my strength,
annuls my imagination.

Space creates new poetry,
creates new emotions,
creates new thoughts,
creates new faces.

Space is the monstrous "Elsewhere."
The new consciousness of time.
The new consciousness of the body.

We are going to spill out our entrails on the stars.
We shall fill the worlds with small futilities.

Our greatest glory is futility,
this Nothingness,
a lantern at the crossroads,
a lantern that glows for a brief moment.
Facing the wind.
The tree in the meadow,
solitary, despairing,
in the uproar of rain.

G. T. Vafópoulos

RETURN OF THE SATYRS

On the leaves, Lydia, where last night's rain dropped all her tears
there moves an inexpressible and grave tranquillity.
One might say that the spirit of an ancient pastoral god
has blessed and magnified the forest with his old glory.

Who says that the glory of ancient days has gone, that the flutes
and shepherds' pipes in the forests of Arcady are silent?
Lydia, my dear, come close—Pan still lives in these woods,
and the blood of his Satyrs threatens to burst in our veins.

THE FLOOR

Black and white tiles
in alternating order
suffer the touch of my footsteps.

On this, my prescribed arena,
I play like a child,
taking care to step
on the white surfaces only.

Difficult exercise.
Skillful acrobatics.

Sometimes I lose the body's
balance.
Sometimes I lose the spirit's
calculation.

And then the order of my steps
becomes confused,
and my erring sole
stumbles on the black tiles.

I must start the game
once more from the beginning.
I must train my spirit
to perfect
balance.

But my exhausted spirit
starts over and over again,
and swirls
in a whirling vertigo.

And now the motionless disk of the floor
spins swiftly round and round
and the alternating order of the colors
becomes confused.

Confusion of the senses!

Then like a child
whose game has been spoiled,
then like a child
whose patience has been exhausted,
I run spitefully
and trample
on the ordered system of the floor.
With the soles of my feet
I wipe out the lines that separate
the black and white tiles.

And then I sprawl on the floor,
with an overbrimming spirit,

and drench my broken faith
with tears.

Ah, how much this unrelenting
exercise has fatigued me!

But now at last I see clearly
what the whirling of the floor
signifies.

Now I understand the meaning
of the copulating colors.

APARTMENT HOUSE

In this apartment house of ours, our own dead
do not only snore. They have the privilege
of rising, of loving, and of dying once again.

At night they ascend in the elevator, the way the righteous
mount up to be judged in the presence of the Lord.
And in the morning they descend and go to be burned
in the crematory boilers of the central heating system.

This is why our apartment house smells so foul.
It is the stench of daily deaths that comes
from the kitchen. Not of that other death.
For that one emits a sweet odor.

THE MASK

You existed within me before I existed.
Protoplastic cell that voyaged in my forefathers,
changing your clothing after every death.

If I had not had the prudence to bolt
all doors and shut all windows
perhaps I would have lost the possibility of knowing you.

Now you can slip out of my skin with safety
the way a hand emerges from a glove,
and you can sit opposite me in an armchair.
But first I must light the lamp
that I may see my face
in this mirror you carry with you.

It would have been impossible to recognize you,
you old rascal, in this disguise you wear,
could I not guess at you: that stiff collar
is exactly like the one my father wore.
I think it's with this very watch chain I played
whenever I clambered up my grandfather's knees.
And this tailcoat of yours accompanied many a funeral.

I must pluck away your scales. I must unpeel you
to your deep marrow that I might find my roots
which are tightly twined about my own death.
Monster, dragging about you the death of each of my deaths!
Reptile, tightly entwined about the root of time!
I would open the door for you, if only I could bear
such emptiness. The empty sack
which now I am, I would bind up tightly
if only it could fill up with itself again.

Take off, at least, this fearful mask.
Wipe off the thick dust from your mirror.
In the safety of this solitude
I could even confront the head of Medusa.
But hush! I think someone is knocking on the door.
Hurry up, dress yourself and slip back into my skin.
Safety, it is clear, must be sought elsewhere.
Let's put it off, therefore, to another time.

—Yes, Dr. Wagner, you may come in now.

THE NIGHT

When midnight strikes, do not hasten
to open the window. At that hour
people are returning home from the theater,
and virgins make love in dark corners.

When midnight strikes, it is not night.
The uniforms of the generals dance with arrogance
and the frocks of the officials bow low
before flowering, empty muslins.

When midnight strikes, it is day.
And your own eyes cannot bear such light
nor even the lighted faces of men.

You must endure much. And when you have made certain
that all have entered the wardrobes, that the melodies
have curled up to sleep in the instruments,
then you may open the window with care and gaze
at the light of the stars: it is another light.
Or accept the slap of the hurricane: it is another slap.

And if suddenly your eyes discern
a certain shadow in the thick darkness
—a thief who has broken into the pavilion,
a mother who is waiting for her drunken son,
a doctor who is leaving a dead man's house—
do not hasten to close the window.

What you have seen is not man.
It is the specter of the vast night
and is called sin, love, or duty.
In that hour it was simply seeking shelter.

Lean into the darkness of this well
which is measured by the depth of your conscience

and give your hand to the night's specter.
Then quietly close your window once more
before men fling open their own windows.

THE STATUES

During the day even the statues have no expression.
If as it sometimes happens in a movie theater
the projecting machine should suddenly stop,
though the electric fan still keeps on running,
you will notice that on every fixed face immobility wears
an arrested mask caught in a frozen expression.
During the day statues wear a similar kind of mask.

But when night slowly begins to emerge from the thick
foliage, to creep softly with circumspection
and then stand with closed eyelids behind the back
of the park keeper, he shudders without knowing why.
He notices the hour, seizes the bell's tongue suddenly
and breaks open its enclosures of sound to the startled air.
Then the birds become small marble figures,
and the last cries of children hang frozen in mid-air.

Night binds time tightly to the locked iron gate.
But how can the statues feel time's crucifixion
since they hang about it, hovering in mid-air?
They seem to be like those stopped alarm clocks
that have lost their ancient, primordial memory.
Night winds them up one by one, and then withdraws.

Now the statues remember, feel the swarming itch
of time, and their naked bodies shiver.
Then they wear their masks inside out
and step down from their pedestals to stretch awhile.

But now they are not what they presented
to petrified time. This girl who cups

her naked breasts, like a white bird,
is not a girl. She is the spirit which has shaped her
and dwelt in her from the beginning. Now
she remembers, shivers, and falls in love with herself.

During the day the statues have no future. The museums,
into which they sometimes withdraw with weariness,
are the lost cemeteries of the past
wherein death holds time in a narcotic trance.

The statues possess only the past: but not that
eternally present in the marble quarries.
This is that decisive moment of the past when the spirit
has come to dwell in them forever.
But as soon as it became present, the alarm clock stopped
and cast away its key into the vast night.
And on their white faces time turned immovably to stone.

Night now holds their key; she winds them up
one by one, then transports them into the future,
that stretches out beyond time: because night
is beyond time and beyond death.

TIME AND THE FISH

*How long have I been locked up, I wonder
in this Tower of Solitude?
Have I lost, perhaps, the sense of time? . . .*
        —G. T. VAFÓPOULOS, "The Image"

In order to lose something, you must hold it in your hands.
Others would say: it must exist. It is prudent, however,
to avoid this word; it has become too much the fashion.
But since even the study of time has become fashionable,
how can one speak of the sense of time?
It has been so much sung, to the accompaniment
of those famous *Four Quartets.*

The fish does not have the sense of water.
It swims in the water, but the water is within it,
and blood travels in its secret channels
like a wayfarer who leaves no footprints.
Both water and blood exist when the fish
is suspended in air from a hook
when a dagger is planted in our hearts
and when on our breast a red rose blooms.

In this room, where we find ourselves with the windows
closed, with the lamp's unalterable light,
we swim within time like a fish
in a dark glass bowl filled with water.
If only at least there were a clock hanging
on the wall, its slow hands moving,
we might have, then, some sense of time.
But our beards take a long time growing.

You must open the window, regardless
of whether your eyes confront light or darkness.
Thus, with the touch of your hands, you may feel
the two faces on the coin of time.

As the train window is the mirror
on which the image of motion is reflected,
so through our own window, once it is opened,
the form of time shall be projected on our senses.

It is real to our touch. We can set it
on the table to have our tea.
But as it grows warm from the hot vapors,
it slowly melts, as though it were a figure of wax,
spreads over the tea set and dissolves,
and in dissolving loses all its unity.
Now from the teapot the future pours
and in the teacup becomes the past.
But in the strainer the dregs remain:
the bitter taste, the only taste the present has.

When you find yourself bound to a well-wheel
and the tug of the rope is pulling you to the other end,

it is as though you were traveling within time.
From the future you are drawn imperceptibly into the past.
But when you reach the drum of the mangle,
you will feel there your body breaking
and your crackling bones splintering.
This is because you have come now to the crucial point
where the future is already becoming the past,
where the only truth of the present exists.

Let us therefore take our tea. Its vapors
are an airy pool where the spirit
may in swimming take thought.
We have spoken of the only truth of the present.
And so, since our bones have become
a pulp mixed with flesh and blood,
we must accept this with sophistry:
the past does not exist because it has existed,
the future does not exist because it shall exist.

But if all your nerves have not taken part
in the mashed pulp of your body,
and if pain can still be weighed in one of these,
perhaps we may have to change our sophistry:
The present has existed as future, it will exist
as past. Conclusion: the present does not exist.
Since the parts do not exist, then the whole vanishes also.
Let us blot out, therefore, the existence of time.

But we should not hasten to close the window.
In a little while now from the neighborhood
we shall hear on the gramophone the Quartet of the Sirens:
"Time present and time past
are both perhaps present in time future,
and time future contained in time past."
This is as though we had said the past
may be found in the present and that
even the future may be found in the present. But then
we must conclude in the simultaneity
of time present and time past and time future.

Dear God,

let us close the window that we may hear nothing,
let us stuff all cracks that we may see nothing,
neither the day nor the night, those two
deceitful faces on the coin of time.
Light the lamp again. And never
hang a clock on the wall.
Let us once more become fishes in a fishbowl.

In the last analysis, what is time?

Time is a pretext for poems. Or
Time is a target to be shot down. Or
Time is a newspaper in Paris.

But Time can also be money.

THE FRONTIER

In order to pass through this frontier, you must
strip yourself of all memories; you must leave
fear on the threshold; you must lay down your love.
The saints, you see, travel without luggage,
stripped of harvests reaped by all their senses.

But as they pass, they pause a moment, turn their faces
back, as though remembering something: for it seems
they have forgotten to take off all their clothing.
They cast all off and then proceed: far beyond time,
far beyond silence, far beyond all solitude.

That forest you sense is not composed of trees.
It is made of rocks that have assumed the new
bodies of saints in which their spirits dwell.
They do not move, they do not speak, they do not feel.
For they communicate through underground
deep passages, and this is the reason why
they understand each other only.

These birds you see killed, as though they had fallen
with violence and struck the frontier wall,
are not birds: they are the small, empty bodies
they have discarded, for they had no other clothes.
The birds are now far, far away; they stand on those rocks,
but you cannot see them, cannot hear them, you cannot even
        feel them.
Yet they exist: far beyond love, far beyond time,
far beyond silence, far beyond all solitude.

You cannot pass over while you wear these clothes.
How can you take them off now, for they have grown on you!
And if you try to strip them off, you will remain
entirely within them; nothing will then be left
of what you were or shall be, that may pass over.

You are a foliage filled with memories; a chord
stretched taut between the children and the saints
that time has built with tree-rings round and round
like the slow growth of a primordial tree.
But how can you become a rock, for although
it understands, it does not feel. Your throbbing chord,
although built in, is still shot through with senses.

You are a tree. And thus you know that trees
do not travel; they only feel, and remember.

DEAD YOUTH

I: Within this grave a dead youth lies.

YOU: What, shall we still be talking of graves?
        Youths do not live in cemeteries now.
        They stand erect on rocks and stone the sun.
        They plunge in waves and wrap themselves with seaweed.
        Even when young men stroll amid these tombs
        they are still dreaming, singing, and pursuing love.
        How can a youth be found within a grave?

I: Within this grave a dead youth lies. He never
stood on rocks to measure himself with the sun.
He never wrapped his naked body with seaweed.
He only dreamt. Love never heard his song.
His voice within him dwindled and fell away.
And this is why he lies now in this grave.

YOU: How strange: this youth was killed by his own voice.
His voice was like a throbbing hand grenade
he held but threw when it was much too late . . .
Young men today have need of clever hands.

I: This youth, who now dreams here, did not have hands:
they had turned to heavy memories within him.

YOU: Youths have no past, and so do not have memories.
But they have hands with which to point at the sun.
But they have hair that may be tossed in the wind.
And voices, that they may quarrel with the loud sea.

I: This youth had traveled far beyond the sun.
This youth had passed beyond the spreading sea.

YOU: Beyond the sun? Beyond the spreading sea?
But we, who have discovered the first sun,
but we, who have sailed across the very first sea,
but we, whose voices sang in the first seashell,
saw nothing other than their simple joy.
And we can swear that no beyond exists.

I: The sun and sea can dim all watchful eyes.
They never let you see the first death too.

YOU: Beyond the spreading sea, beyond the sun,
how can one possibly see the first death too?

I: This young man always carried death within him.
It was for this he went beyond the sun,
beyond the spreading sea, beyond the song.

YOU: And even beyond the song? What can there be,
I wonder, beyond the translucent song of joy?

I: The vast night, silence, and all solitude.

YOU: Ah, ah! It is for this the young man died.

I: No. But because he could never go beyond love.

THE MIKADO AND THE WINDOW

*In Japan the annual poetry competition given by the
Emperor was a great success. The subject set was
"The Window." As many as 22,427 poems were submitted.*
—Newspaper item, 1959

When he was brought the news about Hiroshima
the Emperor received it without showing in the least
that the explosion had gone off inside himself.
He rose with dignity. And to his courtiers
said that a new duty now awaited him.
At once, with small steps, as though he feared
that the shaky columns within him would topple,
he proceeded alone to the chamber of his ancestors.
All profoundly brooded on hara-kiri.

He toppled into the first chair he found
without caring at all that he might wrinkle
his priceless kimono, regardless of habit.
And behind his myopic glasses, which now had blurred,
his eyelids closed most heavily over his eyes.

Outside, the courtiers waited in profound meditation
and brooded on who perhaps would first have the honor
of receiving in his hands the Emperor's entrails.

But he inside was brooding on other matters. Down deep,
he had never believed in his ancestral spirits.
What stupidity to say he was descended from the sun!
He was thinking that he was rather an artist: Poet

and Actor together. And the role of Emperor
suited him well during the palace presentations.
At rock bottom, he was not responsible for anything else.
His generals would have to account for the war.
And after all, the Japanese were not only warriors.
It was time to think a bit about poetry too.

Well then, let the curtain go down on Hiroshima,
and let a flowering garden take its place.
Even the Emperor now must change his role.
And as he opened his eyes and saw the window,
he felt he had awakened from a thousand-year-old dream.

Although in this chamber of his ancestors
all could be found in their original order,
the window showed him a new world outside.
And he thought: In this new role now
he must not forget this window, which had brought him
the great news of the greatest change of all.

And while all outside were waiting with patience and despair
to confront even the most bitter contingency, the one dressed
in the clothing of the most terrifying certainty,
they suddenly saw their Emperor approaching them,
wearing a very smart suit of American cut.

Pretending not to understand their astonishment
as he advanced, he said: "Gentlemen, I beg of you,
please close that window that looks out toward the East,
because the rising sun now hurts my eyes.
Let's open this one that looks out toward the West.
It's been a long time since we've seen such peaceful landscape.
Please have the Samurai's gold-trimmed swords
placed in showcases, as best suited for works of art.
And let all my followers, whose hearts sway
tenderly to the musical verses of the haiku,
arrange to buy fountain pens—Parkers, of course.
The High Desire of his Majesty is for the poets of Japan
to sing now of this window brought us by change."

(Twenty-two thousand and more poets of Japan
responded to that High Desire of his Majesty.
And while in the ears of the hanged generals
the wind whispered the song of eternal peace,
for the great imperial window of the Emperor
more than twenty-two cases of fountain pens sang.)

ADMONITIONS

Inspiration lived with us then. In summertime,
debilitated by the heat, we heard her voice,
or thought we heard it. Be that as it may,
we transcribed it conscientiously in verses.
Inspiration is not now alive. With other known dead
she sleeps under a tombstone of dictionaries.

In our remote village in the prefecture of Pieria
we made love with the girls of a Madam
who went by the name of Phrosyne or Mnemosyne or some such.
We were deprived of love when they left the countryside
and went to try their luck in the capital.

One entered the service of Mr. Papadhópoulos as a live-in maid.
One got a job as cleaning woman in a store
that sold musical instruments and gramophone records.
Melpomene went to sing with the *bouzoúkia*.
And the others got along somehow. One can't go wrong
in Athens. One will always find *something* to do.

It's only you that wander in the streets, as though lost.
Inspiration no longer exists for you to play with,
throwing you Ariadne's ball of yarn. All the girls
have found work and won't even turn to look at you.
Nor can you ever again load your dreams
on the proud back of that horse with wings.
Disguised now, painted red, it's been yoked
to pull the gasoline cans of Mobil Oil.

If at least those books with the "Letters"
of that society lady Rainer Maria Rilke
had not been made into small paper bags for peanuts,
you would at least have, in this labyrinthine solitude of yours,
some guide to orientate you, even though one-eyed.

Salvation doesn't exist then? But I believe you still
have your old flivver. Mount it on the run
and swiftly take your place in line with the other traffic.
You'll swirl in circles until the end of your days
on the track of a never-ending spiral.
                                        Fortunately
the gasoline stations of the world have plenty of gas.

TASTE OF DEATH

To study death in books
is an academic exercise in a seminar.
To count its blows on men's temples
can accomplish nothing more than a lesson in arithmetic.

Death does not exist either in wars
or in poison or in daggers.
Or in the night wards of hospitals.
It exists in the burning fuse
that only in your own secret channels
advances in a slow step from that first day.

And if you are able to sense this steady pace,
you will be granted the unique taste of death.
But you will not feel the explosion.
Because then you will have seen that which is called death
wearing your own face on its face.

Níkos Pappás

FOR A GROUP OF AMERICAN POETS

We have lost all our patience with sobriety.
If our hearts are to your liking,
flowers from the rapturous meadows of legends,
then hold them more tenderly in your hands.
And we in Athens and you in Michigan
have simply come out for a walk
and have no intention of leaving, not even with our funeral,
in company with butterflies
in company with the Christians of Murdock
when his verses stripped them naked in church.

I have lived in two rooms for a long time now,
sheltered against history,
I live high up and greet the sun as soon as it bursts into flower.
I am inaccessible to the crowded pedestrians;
on Sunday afternoons young poets seek me out
clutching their manuscript verses;
on Sunday nights I gaze into my dreams of thick darkness,
I speak with pale adolescents about the temperature of verse.

I live in a neighborhood whose streets are legends;
at midnight the girls return barefooted to their homes
but they cannot open their courtyard gates
because sleep has taken away their keys.

A convoy of seafaring verses
would betray nothing of our hearts.
We shall load our youthful years on huge waves
on vessels newly painted by small cabin boys
and then in dreams rolled up like sheets of paper
you will read our lives.
I am a man of property, my beloved friends,
the Atlantic sprouts a grass of marine poison
the islands light their lamps from the Pole Star,
I have plunged my plow into the heart of strangers.
But I too am a man of property
I own a large portion of the Gardens of Babylon
I own verses of large plots of land and voices of metal
and on the moon I own two hundred acres inherited from my
        ancestors,
I shall plant them with dreams when the first spring comes . . .

In a Baltimore hospital a man of the same blood as I
in the desolation of a thousand rooms
broods all alone on his funeral,
separated from his Thessalian village
by a hemisphere of earth and water.
To avenge ourselves on nature we have refused to give her
        descendants,
to strip ourselves bare of every reputation
we whisper the same words with the first created on earth
and recite the same verse cut into a leaf
by the first man there in the depths of Asia.

The legends of the sleepwalker tread on our hours
their hovering footsteps awaken you
the clash of their bronze verses is heard from afar
the sighs of genuine men are heard close by.
O you are right, Mr. Mark Van Doren,
our horses gallop in snow and summer
we plunge our hands into crude reality
we hear all those voices which at night call out our names
we are afraid of no one and nothing

we confess to everything by hauling poetry fearlessly drop by
      drop
out of the muddy bog!

A Storm Trooper's bullet in Haushofer's back
when he was scrutinizing his last sonnets
when he was gazing on Berlin for the last time
plunged him with blood-soaked hair into the ages.
This is why you listen to us in such an hour, Mark Van Doren,
this is why our emotions are without reins
and why we always leave behind us a double sigh:
one for ourselves and one for mankind . . .
The color of my blood is of a deep dye
I am flooded by a life made of your own hours also,
I plunder the forests of legends
I pillage the voices of alien agonies
my days are great and successive storms
I hear orphans crying behind the official reports of war
I hear the delicate breathing of maidens asleep in old poems
I see tiny dawns in the sleep of children
and I hear small and sudden names
in the lightning's color.
Mr. T. S. Eliot, do you hear me?
I am Níkos Pappás from Tríkala!
I cry from a great distance and behind heavy rain
I cry out of pages grooved by fingernails
and out of most solemn tomes.
Tomorrow with the skeleton of your history, Mr. Eliot,
I shall speak in my own language from Thessaly
I shall be discolored by vowels
nor shall I sleep or sweat,
I shall also speak of your death!
How vast are the town squares of oblivion . . .
All the statues of those poets who never overtook us
are made of ice and sorrow.
What's the use of tiring myself? What more can I do for you?
I lean my head crammed with mad ideas
on your books as though I leant on your hearts
on soft stones in the place of pillows
and on megatons of roses made of lead.

I have mislaid my life amid dreams,
have you found it perhaps amid your footsteps?
Streets unfolding in ribbons from my march
will end in the avenue
on a sign inscribed with the street number of your dwelling.
The American postoffices send us your verses,
cool palms on our foreheads,
your faces unknown
your words heavy with timeliness,
a bridge that unites us over the seas.
You know us better than our old neighbors
we know you like our own secrets;
O that skyscraper on your Eighth Avenue
that holds two drops of sweat from my forehead,
the quiet sleep on the shores of life
that holds a little of the soldier's vigil.
There are a few verses made of sugar and Holy Script
that take all prizes and thousands of dollars for eulogy,
there are a few slight details
that stop in the last chamber of shame.
You know this . . . you know this as though it happened in
        New York. . . .

Until they understand our own poetry
until they recover from the terror of our voices
until their nakedness catches fire in our warmth
until charity falls into the outstretched hand
until you go out walking with Walt Whitman
and hear Lincoln speaking with a Negro
all will have become a drop of nothingness
bits and scraps cast by a hand
into a billion firmaments. . . .

BECAUSE OF THIS POETRY

Because of this poetry which like the Gospel
opens its pages and our hearts,

which impels us to walk with open shirt
a little before the firing squads execute us;
because of this poetry which makes us brothers
with the Americans, the Slavs, and the Yellow Race
in that hour when the merchants howl
because they have not sold their cargoes of death
and the newspapers shriek with murderous headlines;
because of this poetry, sister, that with a tender hand
covers the sailor, the exile, the emigrant, the imprisoned,
and without our asking opens
a door toward green landscapes
without coffins or invalids or wars;
because of this poetry which in one embrace
unites Hell and Paradise together
and cools all sorrows and sighs in passing
and knocks on the most incompassionate doors
in that hour when we thought everything had been lost;
because of this poetry which, fragrant and feathery,
sits by the bitter sea of separation
and lurches on the ship's deck
dressed in the colors of woman and of home;
because of this poetry which the soldier holds in his heart
as he reclines on a rock in Korea
murmuring one of Tsitsánis' popular ballads
with 20 degrees below zero in his soul,
which the student in despair bites like bread
tonight when he has neither a date nor a dollar;
because of this poetry which Mayakovsky
and Whitman crunch in their teeth,
which armies carry in duffel bags on their campaigns
and high-school students on their excursions,
with which we sleep every night arm in arm
blissfully happy in our poor attic
with a distant "goodnight"
from unknown girls over the radio;
because of this poetry which does not fit into fixed patterns
and refuses to deal in rhymes and quatrains,
which with its typhoons uproots
the Bastilles and the hard hearts of rulers,
which fondles the hair of nations

with a hand of motherly tenderness
and has a voice more powerful than the roar of explosions
eyes more luminous than promises
and hands as clean as the deeds of apostles;
because of this poetry which bears
the wings of sparrows, of doves, of condors,
and in its beak carries its message
to pottery workers, to fishermen, to shepherds, to coal miners
either with twitterings or with iron wings;
because of this poetry which whistles like a great wind
in the funnels of battleships
and in the windows of palaces,
and like a breeze refreshes all sweating brows
and is like a huge bridge uniting
this blackest of all lives
with that other one now dawning;
because of this poetry which in our blood
leaps like a fawn or like madness
and talks with you, O village lad,
who for three dollars war with your brother;
because of this poetry which caresses and converses
with Jim and with Mustapha and with Sergei,
which will not permit poets to beg
and scatters drops of coolness
above the wastelands left by explosions;
because of this poetry which keeps awake
the Forrestals and the Oppenheimers and me
that I may erect bayonets for them with my verses
among my manuscripts under my lamp;
because of this poetry which separates us
even from those who have given us birth
and has nailed a red flower on our breast
like a knife-thrust;
because of this poetry for which boys and girls
filled with dreams took up their guns
and over our planet spread a thick shadow of kindness
we keep our heads held high
and men recognize us because of our clean glances
amid this menacing darkness spread
by progress and the Middle Ages

by your poetry and the multiple dollar
until all legends lose their color
until all men in the meadows devastated
by great mathematicians and the great scientists
bleat and moo, bleat and moo like sheep and cows . . .

OF WHAT USE TO ME
ARE YOUR VERSES?

Of what use to me are your verses?
Your songs have been born in restful apartments
Or on low shrubs scorned by the sun
Nourished with safety in days of dread
By the side of prisons where condemned
Poets sigh because they breathed freely.

Of what use to me are your verses?
Your anxiety does not deceive me
Nor your apprenticeship in existentialism
The way you smile at divine hope does not delude me
When your Sunday microphones slice it for delivery
Your panic confronted with your own death
Your indifference before the death of others.

Of what use to me are your verses?
I can no longer play with your fragile toys
Or adorn myself with your paper flowers
I hate your sugary colors and I open
My arms wide to greet the multitudes
That with shouts take the pre-eternal roads
Dressed in blouses the color of dawn.

Of what use to me are your verses?
I am waiting to see the moon falling into bottomless pits
The crippled masses arming themselves with sunrays
I am waiting for your epoch to change its garment

I am waiting for a cataclysm that I may quench my thirst
The trumpet blasts your hearing cannot endure.

Of what use to me are your verses?
I wear white slaughter like a collar and it chokes me
I hold in my heart the explosion in Hiroshima
I hold in my eyes the deserts of Nevada
I feel the cold of millions of roofless people
I hold the pride of children who preferred to be martyred
And the knife of your calumny in my back.

Of what use to me are your verses?

EMMET TILL

All this age belongs to them,
Emmet Till:
the bankers, the dowry dollars,
the elections in West Germany
the sailor lads of the Sixth Fleet, Rock and Roll
all the colors of our era.
You too, my dear Negro Till,
at Kalamáki, at Záppion, at Kastélla
crammed with weekends and romantic moons
can seat yourself with a girl from Fáliron
in sports cars that terrorize the seacoast.

All this age belongs to them:
Sikelianós and *The Visionary* are memories only,
the poems and the names have been covered with an enormous
                movie screen
by Madam Melína Mercoúri!

Everything is theirs, Emmet Till,
the radio, the newspapers,
the assured careers of the young who drive
hot rods crammed with corruption,

theirs the countryside sun
and the marine moon
the love of the young girl you don't dare look at sideways,
and even the Ark which might have rescued our dreams
is their own private property.

The hours are like faded stars
our hours contain small wounds
wear narrow white bandages
and are murdered night and day
in darkness or May afternoons
by the same ones who lie in ambush even for you
along some riverbank
in the same spring.
Toughs with silk shirts
and high-school diplomas encircle us
beat up their mothers
smoke hashish and gulp gin
while we write verses,
our thirst still unquenched by the cataracts of silence.
When these become enraged, Emmit Till,
because a young man blackened by the sun
(who keeps his youth as fresh
as a bouquet of flowers on a fine May day)
takes delight in a white girl passing by
and emits vowels like a bird
in admiration of her beauty,
then these men with their white faces
tear the bird to shreds, my young Negro lad,
tear it to shreds. . . .

AGHLAIA ANTHEMIADHOU

Aghlaía the young girl from Corinth
leapt from the balcony of her house
and killed herself.
This news item, this suicide

took place only because
a Corinthian girl had to make the world
take notice of a particular presence
with ribbons in her hair and a broad coiffure,
of love letters to strangers
which she wrote on September afternoons
when the Corinthian Gulf colored with bluing
the face of Roúmeli, the feet of the Moréa;
but wounded Aghlaía
had not a single love or a single reminiscence
to color the void in her soul
a little before she crushed her delicate bones
by leaping down from a balcony
where she had now become bored with simply looking.

DEMOLITION

All the dusty buildings have been torn down
the multicolored dreams have been torn down
all that belongs to the past has been torn down
without pity, without distinction,
the tender nooks have been torn down
wherever hands once represented the soul
joined together lightly in two bonds.

The neighborhood mansions have been torn down
balconies and sentimental terraces
from the moon to the small window
the small rose bushes have been torn down
new houses laden with imperfections
the palaces of the Atridae have been torn down
the renown of beautiful Helen
the tender afternoons have been torn down
on the deck of the ship's bridge
the boundaries of age have been torn down
the schoolyards with their songs
our youth has been torn down

unprepared, ancient material
loaded on large mythical carriages
and now it fills the city with midnight.

The tender masterpieces have been torn down
which we bred in our souls
statues strewn on the ground
without hands, without feet, without torsos
with only the soul hovering beyond the matrix
in a lofty firmament
wherein men, masses, and ideas are confounded,
the tiny cages have been torn down
with their colored and babbling occupants
the solitary groves
the small cool winds that hide in their own foliage,
the rooms of students have been torn down
the rooftiles where kittens lick themselves in the sun
the springtime breezes which are the only fingers
that linger on our foreheads.
The serenades have been torn down
that from the crazy honeysuckle mounted to the roof,
the wooden balconies heavy with romance
the bedrooms have been torn down
which have founded families and forefathers,
all that belongs to the past, all the nostalgias
the countryside coffeehouses with Papadhiamándis and
                    Melahrinós.

The horizons that gaze toward poetry have been torn down
governments have been torn down
when they tended toward democracy
the rhymes
and the poets who drag their verses like chains,
the social orders have been torn down by old age,
when they are raised high with oppressive stones
and piled on innocent breasts,
the symphonies of all who have come before us have been torn
                    down
inaccessible paradises of white ecstasy
all lofty heights have been torn down

by insignificant, vulgar hands
pride has been torn down
entire blocks of jails
erected by history and terror
the romantic ocean liners have been torn down
the carriages in all the small railroad stations,
our friends and our domestic animals have been torn down
our lofty ancestors
the escutcheons celebrating a thousandth anniversary
the music stands with all their scores
all, all have been torn down. . . .

Attention! We are waiting. What new landscape
will our eyes uncover?
Attention, the coming day must possess color
it must assemble many birds
it must ask us why we have torn down
so many great things, so much that seemed useless. . . .

Ríta Boúmi-Pappás

THE OXCART

Chariot of sanctity
and the virginal old age of our parents,
brought from the earth Canaan
to the Thessalian plains with their wheat,
as huge and as mute as a patient church
under the flames of the sun.

You move sluggishly like a biblical turtle
bearing the fate of mankind on earth,
sadder still than the bucket-well and the snail,
your dark wheels without spokes;
slices of an old oak tree chopped by an ancestor,
you roll over a field without roads
that is an arched disk with East and West
and God between them of enormous size
covering all our fields.

In the month of harvesting you carry a blond mountain of hay
gliding on a huge straw mat scissored out
by the moonfaced harvesters, my sisters,
and you plod on alone under the blazing sun
because your master, wounded by great heat
and sunken in his treasure,
even more yellow than his hay
more naked than stone,
dreams perhaps of a partridge
bathing itself in a mountain spring.

Your monolithic roughhewn sides
joined together with primitive seams
guarded the noon sleep of Abraham
and Rebecca's heartbeat
measured by camel bells
in a flaming desert without wells.

Your powerful oxen, descendants of the Achaean herds,
are like two monuments of kindness,
as tranquil as twilight on the prairies.
In the morass of their eyes
our spirit is baptized,
their voice is a rich wellspring
when it sluggishly flows in the valley
where Peace lies asleep on her back,
her hair spread out over the grass
and over her fresh white garment.

We bind red ribbons
on their stalwart and guileless necks
that the thread might remind us of their fate,
and with coarse beads trim their twisted horns
where butterflies are not afraid to perch
and where the night angel out of the Old Testament,
hangs his halo
before he falls asleep by the moss of the seven-mouthed fountain.

First-created, overclouded cart,
on small days with the great rains
when at times the despairing plain has lost its borders,
you are blindly bound to a yellow sea
with the rain's thundering bridges,
sinking as far as your callused knees
in an autumn as bitter as your life,
groaning as you struggle to conquer
the dread dynasty of mud.

Always the struggle of your oxen conquers
as from their nostrils flows a stream of mist
and your century-old bones creak
with a tenderness

much like the sobbing of a child
who has been crying for hours.

And you plod on slowly, stumbling,
wounded by clay
where Esau with his enormous hands
guides you every day;
you have been writing his destiny with your wheels for centuries
in mud, in snow, on grassland,
who has always been cheated without knowing it
and dearly beloved only by his oxen
who are frightened by shadows.

Like a Lydian chariot on a day of joyous sunshine
with tambourines and girls whose breasts are adorned with golden
        coins
you plod on toward town where the pigeons lie thickly
and the gunfire of azure joy resounds,
that grandfather may empty flasks of wine
as he holds your reins with a childlike hand,
that the minds of boys might take flight
in an arc of ancient dance
with their white shirts and their striped stockings,
where the folds fall from the girls' hips like cataracts
and thick pomegranates are tightly clasped
in their breasts with silver buckles, and do not burst.

I saw you taking the bride's girl friends to the river,
where they sang as though lamenting,
that the wild-eyed, blond-haired maiden
might bathe near the thick laurels
for she had been promised in marriage without her consent.
There she will wash her embroidered dowry
hidden away so long in musk
and then spread out its glory on the grass,
for on Sunday you will be loaded again with her dowry
dyed with Scythian wood and walnut leaves,
and thus in splendor, as never before,
hung with silver bells and crosshatched blankets
like a loom fully equipped out of Homer

you will plod on to the village hidden in clouds
while a girl who has never laughed in her life
will cry with great sobs because she is going to be married.

Ah if only once in a thousand times
as you were pulling a tower of hay
to the round threshing floor of noon
all your patience would suddenly burst into flame
pierced by the enraged lance of the Thessalian sun
until the pain of many prairies melted in your blaze,
until all the joints in your sides snapped loose
and the nails of your slavery leapt toward the sky!

And as your smoke struggled with the wind
and your ashes sprinkled the entire world
would that the wings of eagles had glued themselves to your
         wheels
until you had become the carriage of the King of Air,
and as your stud bulls discern red banners afar
would they might rush enraged onto the fields . . .

IF I GO OUT WALKING
WITH MY DEAD FRIENDS

If I go out walking with my dead friends
    the city will be flooded with mute girls
    the air with an acrid smell of death
    the fortresses will send up white flags
    and vehicles of all sorts will stop—
if I go out walking with my dead friends.

If I go out walking with my dead friends
    you will see a thousand girls with bare
    pierced breasts, and they will call out to you:
    "why have you sent us away to sleep so early
    with so much snow, uncombed, weeping?"
if I go out walking with my dead friends.

If I go out walking with my dead friends
    the crowd will watch with astonishment
    how no other battalion ever stepped on earth so lightly
    how a more holy litany never passed in procession
    nor a more glorious or blood-splattered resurrection—
if I go out walking with my dead friends.

If I go out walking with my dead friends
    the full moon will rise to adorn them like a wedding flower
    within their hollow eyes orchestras will weep
    their locks, their bandages will flutter in the wind;
    O many then will die out of regret and remorse—
if I go out walking with my dead friends.

THANK YOU, FATHER

Thank you, father, because you planted me like a tree:

Like a tree I was filled with birds and tender nests
I felt storms on my face
lightning bolts clove me deeply
and I reached heights, just as you wished.

I bore on my branches the weapons and the lyre of my
            forefathers
which you taught me by your knees on winter nights
when you spoke to me of liberty;
heavy rains cleansed me
and snows made of me a Holy Altar.

I plunged my roots as deep into earth as I could,
spread them wide that I might prevail,
offered fruit and shade
to the hungry, the wayfarer, the fugitive,
and proffered green wreaths and arches to heroes.

I dressed myself with flowers once every year,
honeybees harvested my pollen
and I tasted the great joy of giving without receiving.

I shared the happiness of children
who hung swings from my branches
and sang carefree with the nightingales;
I saw that an immobile life is not captivity
but a foundation for many generations.

They carved dates and names on my body,
hearts in love
that had no trust in others,
and was told secrets never given to a confessor.

Twelve-year-old boys plundered me
in the fruit-bearing month,
and when they shook down all my olives
—for I was an olive tree—I did not complain
and became the light in their candles, their lanterns,
food in the callused fists of workmen,
and a message in times of peril
in a dove's beak.

I gave my warm hair to the wind
and let the breeze make love to me,
—for I desired it—
as he came freshly washed at night to meet me,
and in the silence of the countryside
my rustling betrayed his visitation.

At night the moon dressed me in diamonds,
angels descended to my topmost leaves,
the lance of the Evening Star pierced me.

An old shepherd wrapped in his fog clung to me for support,
that the maniacal wind might not sweep him away;
and a young Christ with downy cheek,
an outlaw, hunted by the police,

leant against my trunk
to calm his fright.

And the woodcutter,
when the time comes for me to turn into smoke
and unite forever with the sky,
seeks my forgiveness with tears
before his heavy ax cuts me down

and I become a bright blond flame in his rustic fireplace,
and begin an insane dance
before the enchanted eyes of his children

Thank you, Father, because you planted me like a tree.

DATA FOR AN IDENTIFICATION CARD

I was not born on a stone bed
and became thus the enemy of weapons since childhood
and joined alliance with the singing birds.
How sensitive I was
only the fishermen of Sýros knew
when in their nets I cast
out of unbearable longing
the silver fish of my heart.
I never betrayed my seafaring heart
with a farm,
nor my first thirst
with a chance fountain;
I studied the sea that never speaks
but ponders and becomes as enraged as I,
I borrowed its strength in time of danger.
If I hid myself early amid the foliage of verses
I did so that I might weep unseen
for the disharmony of world order
the unhappiness of the good and the innocent.
I studied by observing the seasons with care
the highways of the heavens at night

computing the distances with common-day measures
even though mother would say
that Jacob's ladder could not be raised with calculations.
I interpreted the murmuring of the forest
penetrating into its hinterland
bore on my shoulders delicate green shadows
conversed with stones
and among many anonymous scattered bones
carefully examined the dimensions of time.
I spent many hours gazing at ants:
their black and thoroughly prudent heads
their weak legs, their industry,
taught me much.
All I observed to this moment, I discovered
and tried to save from oblivion
because even the most trivial things
give me material for my craft
when the poem descends in an onrush like a hawk
and leaves only after it has grazed on my entrails,
at a time when I become a tender, persistent drop of water
and transform rocks into statues.
Pain fought me without conquering me
I swallowed all my tears
and was burned body and soul in that fire
which fate had entrusted to me,
alone,
my burns still uncooled.
One further detail
regarding my fingerprints:
my hands are light
because they have never grasped gold.

THE CROW

To Stalin

You cannot from the open window invade
the country of my reveries
or my inviolate asylum,

trying to make me believe you are the white dove
for whom I wait and sing.
You cannot take my creations by surprise
to scatter them terrified in the night
to tear our sleep to tatters, our only good,
to spread your black wings and cover my house
to enter my still wet words as in a net
to control their arrangement
to measure their weight grimly
to examine their substratum with suspicion
the aroma I succeeded in finding after so many blendings
to approve
to disapprove
to laugh sneeringly when you catch me weeping
to dictate to me your stupid croakings
to direct me
to perch on my shoulders with your grasping claws
for fear I might escape you
to nest in my conscience
to force your way into my clothing
into my bed
under my skin
seeking to persuade me that you are sage
that your loathsome eyes drip with paternal kindness
that your savage beak cannot possibly commit an injustice
that it has never plunged into human flesh.
Do not touch me!
You cannot count on my own blood also,
it is an undrinkable wine.
You cannot choke me
or steal my soul like a bandit.
I shall resist,
I shall shout for help!

THE JUGGLER

I am a juggler in a garden and I play
with my dream. I exhibit it,

and though I roll it on the points of swords
it never bleeds
among the many-colored flames,
like a butterfly flirting with death.

Recollection, do not besiege me with love's touch
do not distract my attention with music and such,
I know the dream has begun and where it shall have an ending;
let the world applaud me that sees nothing beyond
the brilliantly lit stage
the trickery of trained fingers
the dangerous acrobatics on the silk rope.
It's no small attainment to make them believe
in all I show them,
in the roses, the luminescent woods,
in the jets of water that glow with phosphor,
in the phantasmagoria of the ages,
watching me light fuses in the ice
watching the seed sprout in my fists
and bear fruit beyond place and season.
I know of course that all these
are not real
not even the eyes that watch them
nor the voice that narrates them so alluringly.
But as well as I can, I try not to let them see
that I am only a mirage
a dance of photons in a magnetic field
a metaphysical painting that has for hero
a mournful charlatan.
How to explain to them without peril
that the world of my images is an optical illusion
that a refraction of light gives birth to the crowd of colors
that all, everything, is a game perhaps not quite honest
a skillful trick that costs, however,
much patient exercise and long night vigils?
They see the dwarfs
that assist me in the game
like supernatural beings,
gigantic Nibelungs,
my magic as splendid instruments
though these are nothing more than a tall hat

with the bird that dwells on my head
and which I release at times to astonish
though it seeks for nothing more in the wilderness
than a tree to inhabit,
a bird they machine-gun with applause
until it writhes.
How to tell them
that the broadsword I expose in its velvet sheath,
folded into seven equal parts,
broke in assaulting my gristly heart;
that I exhibit my handkerchiefs,
the red, the green, and the blue,
only that I may better hide the one
stained with tears.

O the dogs, my faithful friends,
who on their backs support the sorrows of the world
and love me as much as I need
because with great toil I taught them
to stand erect on their hind legs
to write with chalk on a blackboard
the Alpha and the Omega,
devoted with me, and faithful,
to the dream of brotherhood.
"But who will undertake this task?"
the dogs ask
with as much joy as you, applauding, never feel
as you sit with your beer, your ice cream,
as you queue up with your ten-cent tickets
that I may place even the moon into your hands . . .

I beg of you, do not look at me thus
now that the end is approaching
and I shall be stripped bare,
do not penetrate into my sensitive instruments with your glances
that arrive from the auditorium full of disbelief
to search me down to the bone. I insist.
My veins are rivers that irrigate
fields of rapture,
your theater boxes are galleries of prehistory;

beyond the bridge of silence
the large blue butterflies rest
and you never thought it was for them perhaps
that the open windows ask in the night.

Take care, however, no matter how much I perform
in a land that symbolizes the end,
I am a magician who can revenge himself
by falling silent
by crossing his hands forever
casting away his name into the lake like a copper coin,
drowning the dogs in a deep river
chasing far away into the jungles
the white bird that flies out of his hat
in the seasons of its intoxication to enchant you.
I can before your very eyes swallow all my firework display
put out my multicolored flames with a rain of tears
and fall silent
following an early morning troupe of actors
before your alarm clock rings.

D. I. Antoníou

O TELL ME IF YOU
NO LONGER BELIEVE IN PHANTOMS

O tell me if you no longer believe in phantoms!
Those winged horses that fly toward legendary lands,
those witches with herbs for death and for love
and that human, that simple being, bequeathed us by the ages;
her hair was the sun of our dark tower.
But what am I saying! You are not blond, and now,
I may speak to you this evening
as I look at you, for you are my night:
"Here I am since you wished it,
all of me, that I may exist with you;
look, this hand in its struggle
holds fate
displaces mountains
and places stars as toys in your hands . . ."

WHY SHOULD WE DENY IT?

Why should we deny it?
Let's speak the words that rise to our lips—
it's not routine!
Man's emotions are extremely old

416

in a young heart—what does this mean?
The magnets have become a magnet,
the roses a rose.
—Say everything just as you want to.
No matter how much you lack simplicity, my heart,
no matter with what difficulty you express yourself,
no matter how many thousands of miles weigh you down,
shout it out;
do not be ashamed; the voice that kneels
will remain alien to profane ears, confessing
the emotions that is the experience of all your emotions;
make the sacrifice
before her human feet . . .

LET'S STILL SAIL ON LIKE THIS

Let's still sail on like this, tacking to the wind! . . .
On New Year's Eve, six times distant from home:
—There are new harbors still where they can send us,
chasing for freight worth less than twelve shillings a ton;
you will never finish sailing upriver through the Continent.
On New Year's Eve, six times distant from home,
letters piled high in a drawer
bore me now; do not ever write me again.

Let's still sail on like this, tacking to the wind . . .
Are there still new harbors to allure us?
A bed on land with eight hours' sleep,
a book to read quietly at night
in a corner: how can these exist, my friend?
Let's still sail on like this, tacking to the wind . . .

TONIGHT
YOU REMEMBERED THE BEGINNING

Tonight you remembered the beginning,
that rainy evening when you decided
to turn into experience the nostalgia for distant lands
that left us useless
for life.

We asked you to pity us Lord,
seed of a gaudy flowering
in the sterile earth.
Crushed to silent supplication,
ravaged to desperation,
we longed for the destiny of simple men,
the astonishment of the ignorant.
Empty us of all we know,
give us—we wept within ourselves—
weariness
after the honest struggle.

Condescension;
the decision to take the road we took
to the end; to rise
from where we fell.
Do not give us practical dreams,
do not awaken the magnets of inheritance:
prows lost and found at sea.
In our anonymous endeavors, deliver us;
that we may rise from where we fell
victorious over victory
body to body.

TO THE COLD IMAGINATION

The walls of my room fell down and left me in the garden,
disclosing its interior to space like an opening flower;
so many centuries embalmed, the light of the moon
leapt; and with forces restrained for so many years
flooded the interior, dark but a while before.
But it stayed in a corner no longer a corner,
there where I stood not yet comprehending,
clinging to silence like a bulwark to change.
Amid arcs and broken lines and this rain
of forms in a shifting wind I stood,
half in shadow and more and more mastered with light,
and heard less and divined more my unrhythmical heart
then knew myself for the first time to be without rhythm
lacking that rhythm which had always tyrannically ruled my
              heart,
and for the first time felt the music of Bach to be without
              meaning;
only ruins wept over the redemption within me.

Dazzling is a work of art
rising out of the flames that create it,
unalterably serene in the triumph of our eternity.

TO CONQUER THIS BLANK PAPER!

But my heart, alas, freed finally from all things, finds
the ancient torment more cruel than that upon the first day.
          —GOETHE, *Wilhelm Meister*

To conquer this blank paper! now
securing in words that fill it this bruised
necessity, in half-feelings and in the mirror

of resolution that becomes an immovable mountain in our
        way . . .
What do you long for?
The star will no longer rise nor turn to sleep
as your road is ending, there where you
shall say: and a little more and day will break . . .
The simple daisy in the green meadow does not stay you,
nor shall you weep ever again
over the nameless small flowers of the field.
Thus drunk with melancholy
we murmured until yesterday, strolling in the countryside:
we recall all of this today and pass it by
as we might consent to the course of the wind in a blossomed
        almond tree,
your ring turning to rust on the finger of another.
Your pleading voice brings our years to their knees,
those years I spent in an open sea blossomed by sails of return.

THE BAD MERCHANTS

Lord, we were simple men,
we sold merchandise
(and our souls were the material
no one could buy).
We did not fix prices according to the selvage
measurements were exact by yard and inch
we never sold remnants at half price.
This was our sin.

We dealt only in merchandise of quality
a small corner in life was all we wanted
the precious things in life take little room.
Now with the same rule by which we measured,
measure Thou us. We have not enlarged our premises.
Lord, we remained bad merchants.

THIS NIGHT
ABOVE THE FRAGMENTED SURFACE

This night above the fragmented surface
matches with our silent craft—
Thus did we rise to heights, winning the abyss,
finding the cry and giving it existence
with a simple and quiet narration.

Far away in the desolation of his hearing
who waits for our craft in order to win all this?
Who gathers the fragments of the worlds,
of the tormented skin of earth?
Who shall ascend to measure the depths,
knowing he is leaving a flower of simplicity lost in the abyss?

We paid by constricting our hearts
until we could not contain the kindness of a fatherland,
whenever we opened sail on leaving the harbor,
whenever we decided to stay on land.
We said, making easy conversation and difficult literature:
The harbors that exist much more in the sea's midst,
the towers and tower ladies in romantic years,
the mermaids and their craft, forerunners of our craft,
are passions fallen silent and jasmines long past,
touch of silk and velvet, nonexistent
for our hands callused from pulling into coves of departure
from all those cities we knew and you did not.

Tonight: what did we do so many years,
tearing up this map not meant for tearing,
making our hearts bleed on every quest,
sharing out our sensitivity
in various harbors?

Who waits tonight?
Is there anyone perhaps?

And who, like us, won
with such expectation?
Hearing all we said:
wandering
from this square table
in an Athenian tavern
with three friends who met every Monday night.

LIBATION AT SEA

And he said:
this wood begot the first spark
in our brain and for the craft of fire:
that we might know of distant shores.
We wanted the natives there to be different and nature different,
we believed that whatever we had of value was there an
          inexhaustible treasure
and that today in the heart of the well-known lies the well of the
          unknown;
but no matter what we possess, an unquenchable thirst
          remains . . .
And may you who have mastered our mind and are mastered and
          become a ship
become a blesséd wood: our reverence to your genesis,
O holy floating legacy, Ark!
And thus did all of nature voyage on the back of the waters,
and sweet was the greeting at last when Wrath got weary;
the pair of doves we released
was our first attempt to placate the Lord.

Ships of iron today with souls of fire
plow the anger of the sea and are cradled in her laughter;
some among us in our voyaging are careful and others are careless
spending their blood on this watery road
and others concerned once more for distant shores . . .
What is a pair of doves here among us?
Only the hunting seagulls

wheel about freely, seeking their own satisfactions.
In our day, on our voyages, the iron machinery grinds;
and our cares are always human cares that serve
the release of oppressed man.

On the island where I brooded over this one morning,
listening to the old priest giving his blessing on deck,
the winches were laboring, two or three among the crew crossed
        themselves,
and the others strolled by the priest indifferently
and the white sure motion of a seagull spotted the sky.

I remembered and I remember all this;
the origin of the Idea of a ship
and the deductions that give us this life, on this day,
on a skyblue silken sea, our ship an image,
and we on board her in thought, deep in the thought of further
        and farther places,
filled with thought of that wood which received the first spark
        of our hearts.

from   THE INDIES

. . . .
All things now have become one, I thought,
present things and past,
as I gazed at the empty place about me,
. . . the coolies have at last fallen asleep—
and I write you still, sinking
deep into lost roots;
the rhythm, an opiate, brings to bitterness,
to the flow of life, to veins,
the heavy fruit of my silence,
merging with ancestral voices:
I hear them this evening, swaying
together and ascending,
contesting

with storms in their intoxication;
then I too remember how I won out
in the struggle, body with body.
Finding the thread where it had broken,
rising from where I had fallen, victorious;
this is how our loading ended
on this roadstead;
we greet past things at their roots,
feeling the smile of a certain springtime.

. . . .

Then we dragged our lumbering
footsteps farther on
into the spreading field;
there the first houses began
built of mud and bamboo . . .

The small houses of their village
were lost among the trees.
In the beginning a variety of palm trees,
the areca betel and coco palm.
The custard apple or Anona, and mangoes
as luxuriant as laurel.
As we went on
the papayas seemed to resemble
the molted tops of palm trees,
but they possess a soul divided
in two separate trees,
like that of mankind's
into man and woman.
And last of all
the flowers of my heart!
The arrogant white and red of love,
the temple and pagoda tree of flowers,
in that strange and inimitable
solitude of theirs.
Proceeding with these,
we entered their village;
around us there the thirsty stares
of foreign eyes
and the voices of children tinkling

the silver for which they begged.
The older natives,
men and women,
gathered around us
and their silence shouted,
deafening us;
afterwards they began to speak first,
in their own tongue,
lilting and choked, flowing,
and the children with them
—a gathering of birds in the trees.
And the women—
what invitation of dark roots
in their glances;
they moved their bodies slowly
in the beginnings of dance like the undulation
of a tropical breeze . . .

. . . .

How long I remained I do not know,
I remember only that I rose
as though I wanted to stretch my limbs;
but now I say that I felt my footsteps
had led me to this blind alley;
and in the midst a structure
as though built by children.
The altar of a god, where shadow and light
played mistily about me.
Its small idol
wore an expression of boredom,
withered flowers at its feet,
chips of sandalwood incense.
Can it be that the other timelessness
is here, which I never knew,
the thirst for which brings serenity . . .
Where is truth, where falsehood?
Around you the world was split in two;
what piece have you chosen?
The filters—
the one and only timelessness
would simply have changed one into the other.

Time and timelessness,
each the space of the other;
in the unlimited, undivided *it is*.

Who was it?
Another moment pulled me out of all this;
I felt someone retreating from my side,
and saw him dwindling away in a cloud of dust . . .
Who was it?
And the moment was shattered; in this chasm,
what was I still seeking?
The truth would have been like this now:
if it did not divide into its two aspects,
you would remain beside me there where you found me;
without my being the other, and you disappearing.
You!
Later I felt your eyes
like arrows
when I entered your village.
Sita, it was you!
Striding through timelessness with her
there in its flowing . . .

I found my companions sleeping still
and went straight to the fourth engineer;
he was closer to my footsteps
and closer in the world's separation.
I thought: these consider their small world
to be the large world . . .
I wanted to say: it is the pit
in a fruit that will not ripen,
will not even mature . . .
They may have believed this only in the fruit's flowering . . .
Even though he to whom I spoke
would always tell the others to spread out their hands
to the professional fruit
of paradise,
beyond fear and necessity . . .
It was to him now I spoke
because in evaluating all things he thought

everything profitable lies in the stomach, everything wasteful in
          the heart . . .
Finally, I prodded them, and they half awoke.
Then in another tongue, that of their awakening,
I began to speak to them of what had happened a while before,
and they, in the truth of their sleep, only
half understood;
in the falsehood of their awakening now,
in listening, did not understand
time that had rolled on the old and new together,
perhaps only half felt it . . .
—Voices thirsty by the dry river beds
of time; only tentacles rose and fell,
forgetting, you might say, they once had wings
and that most sweetly
most cunningly they took the lead.
Their mouths were still drinking in this other life . . .
Memory is like the legend of an entire life:
they were consoled;
to hear such voices is a consolation.

. . . .

Night had fallen,
and when I found the captain
I told him all about the land and what I had seen;
he listened to me beside the Indians as they were loading,
and then, pointing to them, said:
"I wonder if there is anyone among them who remembers
we are of those, so many years ago,
who reached their country?
Close by here is Tinnevelly
with its pearls.
Greeks had all their business then,
as the old books say."
I listened to him together with the first mate, Yańnis Katramádhos.
And he added, as though teasing me:
"Will you write all this down?
But you must find some other way
—that we may remember all this once more,
like the day that each time becomes new again;
even though it is the same,

if this sameness is not false, it is always new . . ."
The next day, Tuesday evening, the ninth of January 1934,
we left India dwindling in our wake.

.   .   .   .

WHAT DID YOU WANT, I WONDER

Debussy: Prelude in A Minor

What did you want I wonder
that you have once more descended from the sky
this night, for only as long as this night lasts,
on the wings of dream and imagination
amid pale roses and golden and azure light?
All this prepares us and we wait for you
without life's weight on us to receive you
as we gaze on this night's stars
and sink into the flowering field of the sky . . .
Descend; the stars have descended into my hands
—small toys of a desire that has vanished
into a magical light that now guides my thought.

I wait, endlessly wait
seeing the sea in your eyes changing
from a shuddering into serenity again
and the clarity of the sky and its gloom once more.
And I become their mirror to express you
to speak of you since I will then have forgotten you . . .

THE SLEEP OF SOLITUDE
IS A HALF DEATH

The sleep of solitude is a half death;
it revolves images, like thirsty dreams,
their depths are colors . . .

It returns to life with strange music
and so is not death;
shifts of a cyclical wind
give me time to meditate
when you, O awakening, seduce
dreams, and I dress the branches
of a wintry nightmare, like a bridal gown,
with the magical flowers of spring.
You hold the two-edged dagger of life.

HE STOOD BEFORE THE MIRROR

He stood before the mirror
in the hour of reckoning;
and the corner beside him was being retold—
the forgotten edge of the sea
by a precipitous wilderness;
at times it smiled at him, at times dimmed with tears.
Two birds there rejoiced in their own beauty,
and in a flash he saw himself
once more smiling:
did he command the past imperturbably?
But the mirror could not bear it,
and blurred;
a clouded crossing
over the water
erased the image . . .
But in vain,
because he
has finally under his control the danger of a passion,
and sips the unquenchable liquor of memory.

A HUNTED MOON WAS CAUGHT

A hunted moon was caught
in the desolate, naked branches of winter.
Don't you remember the sunset,
the purple that flared in the black of your hair?
Your kingdom, the night reclining in its dreams,
ruled over the same moon . . .
You don't remember . . .
nor does it remember now,
it forgets,
remembering voyages only and drownings in the night,
dream-deceitful and nightmarish,
dawning days that brought it round to a moribund bed;
entangled now in the storm
when clouds led it along, hunted,
and you rejoiced in its confusion;
this that now I do not forget remembers you again,
pursued shepherdess,
without words, the salvation of your solitude;
words of poets, heavy shield
in the battle of a dream's bitter immortality . . .

THIS MEAGER GRASS

This meager grass
amid the church rubble . . .
I stop, gazing at the stones,
I can't recall the flowers any longer.
With a tune, an old heartbeat,
I return to my first love:
"Your beauty was a fire that wasted away . . ."
—sang the cicadas—
"Now in the earth you grow cold . . ."

Once it happens
it doesn't matter how it's forgotten;
it is as though, without growing old,
you see her beauty committed to the worms.
In these times
only remembrance remains unwithered,
the spells of an illusion
are the means of life.
Eyes remain tearless
and the heart keeps chronometric time;
what is needed for your art is this:
to burn coldly
that you may exist . . .

The garden cleared up
under the rain
and the sun flashed;
you chose it in winter
in which to speak,
for in that season no colors exist,
only a design
in black and white—in gray . . .
(A sudden fire
will erase the image . . .)

Forget what forced us to part,
we haven't time—
trees of a wintry nightmare
embrace the dark windows.
Don't you remember any more?
How can a voice stop
time that passes? . . .
From within the windows of pain
they embroidered the darkness
in spring with wheatstalks and poppies . . .
Buzzing beehives
intoxicated birds
tear apart the heavy, unpersuaded silence.

Do not forget;
exist only in a different manner:

first as idea
then as deed.
This the mind and the heart vindicate.

. . . .
. . . .

Peace in the house
understanding under necessity
a strong hand at the helm
a great heart in the sharing . . .
the wind and the rain
with sun in the garden.

Alexander Báras

THE *CLEOPATRA*, THE *SEMIRAMIS*, AND THE *THEODORA*

Once every week,
on a specified day,
and always at the same hour,
three beautiful ships,
the *Cleopatra*, the *Semiramis*, and the *Theodora*,
set sail from the wharves
at nine o'clock,
for the Piraeus always,
for Brindisi and for Trieste
always.

Without maneuvers and meanderings
or hesitation
or fruitless shrieking of sirens
they turn their prows toward open waters,
the *Cleopatra*, the *Semiramis*, and the *Theodora*,
like certain well-bred persons
who leave a salon
without insipid and unnecessary
handshaking.

They set sail from the wharves
at nine o'clock,

433

for the Piraeus always,
for Brindisi and for Trieste
always—whether it's cold or whether it's hot.

They go
to soil the azure waters
of the Aegean and the Mediterranean
with their smoke.
They go to scatter their lights
like topazes on the waters
at night.
They go
always with people and with luggage . . .

The *Cleopatra*, the *Semiramis*, and the *Theodora*
for years now
make the same voyage
arrive on the same day
leave at the same hour.

They resemble white-collar workers
who have become such time machines
that an office door
might crash down
if one day
it does not see them passing below.

(When the road is the same always
what does it matter if it crosses an entire Mediterranean
or goes from one house to another neighborhood?)
The *Cleopatra*, the *Semiramis*, and the *Theodora*
for a long time now and for many years
have felt the tyranny of boredom,
pacing always on the same road,
tied up always in the same harbors.

If I were a shipmaster,
yes—*si j'étais roi!*—
if I were a shipmaster
on the *Cleopatra*, the *Semiramis*, the *Theodora*,

if I were a shipmaster
with four golden stripes,
abandoned on this same line
for so many, many years,
I would climb to the fourth deck
in the middle of the sea
on a night of full moon,
and with my official uniform,
with my golden stripes
and my golden decorations,
—although I could hear music
playing from the salons of the first class—
I would describe a most harmonious curve
in the water
from the fourth deck
thus dressed in all my gold,
like a shooting star,
like a hero of unaccountable death.

THE ASIATICS PASS

In the night yesterday
long rows of white elephants
passed in a procession
through the narrow, hushed streets of the city.
These holy pachyderms
were somewhat disturbed.
All their magnificence
plodded slowly in a striking antithesis
to the poverty-stricken surroundings of the city.

Mounted on their backs,
the Grandees of Asia,
wondrously dressed
in luxurious materials
from Burma,
kept in balance their sunburnt,

their voluptuous, indolent
and handsome bodies.

The sky was crowded with stars,
the moon wore her sweetest gold,
their slaves burnt aromas
profusely,
and the voluptuous and sluggish smoke
rose toward the starry swarm.
Emeralds and rubies cast
green and vermilion reflections
and the adamantines glittered swiftly
like momentary desires,
vehement desires.

The slaves,
a multitude of retainers,
each one with his own slave,
and the Grandees from the safe backs
of the elephants,
cast curious glances about them:
"Why must there be such great crises,
such crises? . . ."

Thus did they all proceed,
Knights of Nirvana
and Kings of Tranquillity,
thus did they merge indolently
with the beautiful summer night.

SOUTH AMERICAN DEMOCRACIES

In some extremely central neighborhoods
with their aristocratic quietudes
reside in luxurious mansions
in Consulates and in Embassies
the Dons from breeds that represent

South American democracies
peculiar and remote.
Every Sunday
when the church bells are ringing
gold-decked janitors
raise various flags
of fantastic coloring
which only in *Larousse*
may be encountered,
and perhaps not even there.

And those who do not go to church
because now it can no longer assuage them,
nor even their cities, their homes, their times,
those who saunter every Sunday
as on other days
pause and thoughtfully watch
the mansions, the unknown flags,
filled with craving curiosity
and a tension adventurous and narcotic
which uneasily awakens:
. . . Venezuela . . . Honduras . . . Paraguay . . .
—Asunción is the capital—
(they have remembered now
the name of the capital, learned at school).

The soul thirsts for something new.
Dreadful is the repetition
always of familiar things,
and the circle of life grows narrower still
from the repeated blows
of separations and of deaths.
. . . Unlucky love affairs,
secret sins,
great failures
one after the other . . .
Ah, they should decidedly have come
on a more appropriate day.
Their souls thirst for new things.
If it were only possible to begin

life from the beginning!
How careful they would be,
how cautious they would be now
if they could begin again in a new country,
if they could begin there
how much they would learn from old lessons.

South America . . .
The equator and the tropics . . .
Perhaps the world's evils
have not as yet reached that far,
and perhaps the transoceanic companies
take passengers
who are tired of living
always the same despairing life
in the same city always . . .
If they could only begin again from the beginning
in some tropical country!

So. Now see, the churches in the meantime
have emptied,
people pass
and the taxi horns
awaken them from their reveries,

and—there they go again—
the neurasthenics,
walking amid the crowd,
their tedium following faithfully after . . .

CENTAUR

At the height of his youth and beauty,
naked, mounted on his horse,
he walked it in the shallow waters
on the shores, there, of the sea.

Young and beautiful:
his supple body glowed
from the sun, from the water,
from his overbrimming health.
His hair glittered black,
full light on his forehead,
lightning in his eyes,
stubbornness and desire on his lips,
the cords of his neck
stretched taut, holding his head high,
his chest open and broad
that his strong heart might resound,
that it might hold many loves,
his muscles tight and well-knit
on his shoulderblades and his arms,
on the hands that seized the mane,
tense curve of a bow
shaped by his back,
exquisite folds of his ribs,
his sex not deliberately hidden,
his sleek thighs
squeezing the wet body of the horse,
his knees smoothly shaped,
his calves perfectly cast
down to his delicate ankles,
the small curve of his heels,
and his soles circumflexed.

And the horse!
Its unmanageable movements in abrupt rhythms!
At times, ready to rush toward the sea,
it sucked in the azure open expanses with its eyes,
at times it turned toward the shallow waters,
toward the land in order to emerge,
but again, longing for the waters,
it churned them until they glowed
in dust and foam about it!

BACK COUNTRY

For days and days I tread the long
long road toward my inner self.
I plod on and on and wonder
at the great expanses and the distances . . .

White and unending wasteland,
snow.
Everywhere spreads the virginal
and immaculate snow, and does not melt,
field of a dead ocean,
surface of eternity,
and above it the expressionless and merciless sky
of the First Day,
black, hopeless, morose.

In this my spiritual landscape
my hours have turned to crystal,
the chilling light has shaped
its stable tension
and fixed its attention
somewhere afar like the eye of a dead man
as its pulsation gradually quieted.

I plod on and on and wonder
at the great expanses and the distances
—when did the last bird of creation
fly away from here?—

For days and days I plod the long
long road toward my inner self,
I reach remote inns
whose doors are covered with snow
and find deep imprints beginning there,
the footsteps of Another who has now gone,
footsteps I follow forever
as always before me the field opens unexplored . . .

I MAKE THE "FIRST" MOON RISE

I make it rise according to my desire—
an immense moon
like a bronze shield
which the greatest and most ugly
anthropoid hand of the universe
raises high
amid prehistoric murky forests,
raises it high and hangs it
on their gigantic boughs
that by striking it with stones
—gong for the assembly of the marching worlds—
it might awaken, out of chaos and the deep profound,
slumbering life
and the first rhythms of History . . .

MAGNOLIAS

The magnolias were an orgy and a miracle
in the summer of 1950
on the Asiatic shore
of the Bosporus.

August had gone crazy
—and I also long since—
and in the moonlight
of the heavily scented midnight
I lost all my clothing,
I lost my body
and abandoned my soul to sail free
in that aromatic insanity.
But one thing is certain:
in that curve of the road
the vestibules of Paradise begin.

This is why I encounter
more and even more
barefoot children
who walk on the sands of tenderness.
The soles of their feet,
made of magnolia petals,
their small footsteps thoughtlessly
going nowhere,
they saunter only here
by the large vestibules
of Paradise,
and their voices reecho
like chandeliers tinkling
in the zephyr of felicity
that enters through the open window . . .

I think we are going
to the golden ever-flowing waters
that gush out from the diversity of the marbles.

ETHIOPIANS IN VIEW

The boats of the Ethiopians
with their straw sails
are silhouetted against the torrid
and cherry-colored sunset
and struggle with the doldrums
that do not want to bring them here . . .

We have never depended
on a fickle alliance with the winds.
And the Ethiopians are not in a hurry.
In sight of the temperate earth,
they can now wait a bit longer.
They are not concerned.

Dipping their hands
in gourds filled with oil,

they smear their lean limbs,
glitter cherry-colored
for a moment in the setting sun,
and afterwards recline
in their boats
and call on sleep . . .

(The straw sails creak
and smell of the day's sun,
forgotten rays
freeze in the matted strands.)

Vanguards of the South
—a fifth column—
the phoenix trees wait motionless
in long rows
beyond the sands of the seashore.

We never paid them any attention,
we never thought of them as strangers,
nor did we ever ask ourselves
what they were waiting to hear,
leaning for centuries,
or toward where they strained their hearing.

They grew up together with our marble columns,
and when those fell
the phoenix trees remained standing,
silently observing their agony.

THE UNATTAINABLE

And one day the great desire pulses
to turn back
to resettle once more
in that first happy country:
our youth.

Hastily we leave unfinished
the variegated works of maturity
and seek to flee however we can
from the closed valley of Jehoshaphat.
In circles around us, one within the other,
the mountains of the hinterland await us.

Only one thought prevails:
the voyage of Return.
(Some descend rapidly
from scaffolds of endeavor
raised with great toil,
and others roll down from hilltops of gold,
stumble to their feet, bruised,
and follow the first ones.
A few pallid faces
emerge out of the low-rolling
vapors of chimeras;
termites seek
a hurried exit
out of labyrinths of designs;
and from dry wells
of toil and research
eyes emerge which had forgotten the light.)

We all seek that narrow pass, that narrow pass
which opens out beyond the mountains
toward the meadow of the pastoral idyll
with its small flowers
with its small sounds
with its vast peace
with its endless sky
that leans down lovingly . . .

We run, a confused flock,
thunderclaps roll behind us,
already thick drops of rain have begun to fall,
it has darkened fearfully,
and finally we file through a narrow pass,
we have found it at last and are filing through . . .

But what is this uproar
heard at the exit?
What can this clamor, what can this commotion be?
What shudder runs through us?
What are those in the vanguard saying,
what presents itself like a lightning flash
to the entire retinue?

The pass opens toward a sea
black, endless,
without sun, without birds, without fishes,
without shores, and bottomless.

George Sarandáris

BRIDE

Joy comes to us as a bride
The first rains burst into bloom
Nightingales strike up a dance in our neighborhood
Elegant water nymphs bring songs
Thoughts turn into gold
And gold all conversation
Poets and girls
Learn kisses by heart
Someone arrives at the festival out of breath
It is Time with his flute

WHAT LIES?

The road roller of sleep passed over me
And now I am young. I no longer remember
I am young. I know nothing of lies
What lies? Have I perhaps forgotten you
O love, vigor, justice
Beautiful statues of my republic?

WE ARE NOT POETS

We are not poets means we are leaving
Means we abandon the struggle
Abandon joy to the ignorant
Women to the kisses of the wind
And the dust of time
Means we are afraid
That life has become a stranger
And death a nightmare

I WRITE YOU VERSES

I write you verses
And I no longer know
What holds me back
From kissing you.

It is not the beautiful lively sea
It is not the sky
It is not the elements
There is nothing that holds me back
I do not kiss you and so I do not know
If I love you.

IN MUSIC

There is enough space in music
For the wind to sleep
And for us to travel with the wind

In music they planted a strange
Desire

A flower is our life a flower
It passes from mouth to mouth
Our knees buckle under
When we mount horses
And gallop headless into battle
The clouds won't permit us
To raise up something from the earth
To bring some remembrance with us

Somewhere the danger is great
But we drive ahead impetuously
We no longer advance in music
But in death

And the road has no ending

THREE POEMS OF THE SEA

We are always reading the waves.
And time takes us
And leaves us on other seas
And brings us to other seas.

La danse dans la danse
On devient l'enfant.

I

Has our life left or have birds left the palm of God?

They shot at them to kill them
Our life became so much more beautiful
That it resembles a star
And I cannot take it down to the beach
And turn it into a ship

O dove of the soul may you fare well
Go now with the etesian wind

And kiss for me whatever pearls you meet
If you cannot see me do not fear I shall keep holiday with you
On our voyage we shall raise waters from the sea
To bless whatever we have loved
And whatever we no longer forget

The dove moored in a garden
My soul moored in a garden
Well, I remember now the summer of my life
As though you were the earth's only springtime
I confront you O day of my birth

II

Lilies are in a mood for eyes
Beautiful noblewomen
Go hunting on the sea

Will whoever harvests the sea
Gather white grass
To nourish our youth
Not with foam
But with salt wheat?

The lucky sea waves to us
As though the birds above it were guiding it
As though they were taking it into their arms
The ether is a straight road
Everyone walks within it
As though within his shadow
Or within his sleep

Whoever takes the sea into his arms
Seems not to suffer from weight
Seems not ashamed of going with the wind
Seems as though he holds all the earth in his glance
As though he sings in the night
And behold night becomes a mother for him
That he may sing in the sun
And love a woman

Who seems an infant to him
That he may sing in the wind
And thus keep on losing and winning his voice

III

The sea shatters into numberless crystals
We scoop them up and mounted on air go voyaging
We scatter them wherever we see women lamenting
As though deprived of their children
Then the seas are created again
And an unsurpassable innocence discerns them
Then men fly higher in the sky
To take in all they can of light from far away
While women dressed in black eternally narrate
The birth of seas

AGAIN THE SKY
HERE OPENS ITS GATE

Again the sky here opens its gate
Again raises its flag
We enter fearlessly
And with us enter eyes and birds
The city glitters our minds glitter
Fantasy floods the gardens
That are children idling around fountains
Skylarks lean on daybreak
On lemon trees satiated angels
Are nightingales that awaken everywhere
Flutes are playing, insects buzzing
The dust of the dead are songs
And the dead are somewhere born again
God gathers us from every corner
We have clean hands and we go.

SPRING WILL COMMIT MURDER

They say that spring will
First commit murder again

Will first commit murder
And then will die

They say that spring has
Kissed everyone again

The gallant lads have gone
The girls have remained

And nothing will return again
If spring does not return

They say that our warm
That our warmest day has come

WITH BRUTAL HANDS

With brutal hands I covered the face of the lake
That would no longer answer me

Beggars and birds had scratched its skin

Hidden in its fires the tears of our companions swam

Above it swam the clouds
Now and again our hearts sang
With a voice like a last shadow

Around us spread mountains
That had only just come out into the light

The wind became angry with their forests
The children played
As they came out of school into the arms of the wind

I HAVE SEEN ETERNITY
IN THE FOREST

I have seen eternity in the forest
Come toward me trampling on corpses
But when all were raised from the dead the moment glowed
The stars smiled
And the sea rose like the pulse of our hearts

Then eternity appeared wearing a fustanella.

O FLOWERS—MIRRORS OF GIRLS

O flowers
Mirrors of girls
Whom we loved
When the seasons of the year
Like children
Odd and generous
Like unsuspected victories
Of the sun
And like statues
That for a holiday only
Cast stones
Have given meadows away
To our frenzied spring!

O flowers—mirrors
O mouths—flowers!
The time has passed when lovers

Burst into tears
When they brooded on youth
That withered away
Even more quickly than unripe fruit
Now kisses cool us
Before and after a swim
In wild green woods
Or in calm blue waters
In scarlet fires of air
Or ashy returning to the past
With winds of sleep

O girls—queens!
Queens of the awakening
Of boys!
O violets
The sudden shower has spread
To the four corners of the world!
Untried feluccas
Have brought us to your side
To measure the pulse of the dreams
In your eyes
And with your voices to cover
Our voices
Before the heart locks us up in the hold
Of some beautiful harbor

O girls—queens!
Youthful years in the Mediterranean!
O two-voiced daisies
A white sound for happiness
Another for the wind
Of voyages.
O empresses of the world
When the universe was ours
And the whole world a field
Through which the horses
Of our own desires gallop
Enchanted close by
An overbrimming fountain!

THE FLOWERS PASSED BEYOND SLEEP

The flowers passed beyond sleep
With open arms
And their hearts beat on the sand

In the ear of a windflower
Light turned into a seashell
Men did not sing
Nor awaken
Spring was lips
Clouds were thunder
That leant on men

And earth was honey
That babbled
And senses were the wind
That blew
Nature was numbering her beauties
Her green beauties

AS IT LAY DYING

As it lay dying the sea thirsted
For the sun
But the wind
And the smoke of the sea
Had flung the sun on the mountains

So much wind passed
That we measured the sea
And found she was the true mother
Of our desires

But
The life of the sea

Was not
A candle that melts
Our wishes were not
Rabid dogs

The days sang beautifully

I HAVE A NEED

I have a need to be buried
Only by nightingales
Only by fountains
Sing to them tell them to stop
And listen
To my own pain!
Sing to them tell them to whiten
Like courtyards cast
To the honeysuckle!
There are days
When the nightingales have gone
And the fountains
Have told their secret
To passers-by
I would not want to catch
Such hours
Such ugly virgins
Nor the flower and the soil
The flower and the earth

TIME TODAY FLIES QUICKLY

Time has taken to his heels
Today and flies quickly

I will speak to it and it will pause

That the ice might break

And summer come with its peacocks
The fountain with its honeybees
The sand mountain
And teardrops in the eyes of girls
Holding the moon
In the laughter of boys
That waves might break

The sky enters the ship
And suddenly the sea has had enough
Its memory enfolds man
Who at once sings with a shepherd's flute

THE BEAUTIFUL MISTRESS OF ROCKS

Today the bird
Sprinkled the snow
And from our window swans entered
The swans
Even more voracious

In the meadow people ate violets
Wolves roamed docilely
Vipers in spring knitted
Worldly baskets
In which we placed the year's grapes
In which whole vineyards could be contained
With holes toward the sky

Memory dressed early
And peacocks appeared on balconies
Infants with blood-shot eyes
Climbed up the tree of their age
And if you could see at a great distance
You would feel all of creation

Gazing backwards
With such bodily laughter
With such haste
That flowers
Or something else
Leap out of calyxes
When they learn of it
Fearlessly the star of music
Presses on alone

Pearls here
Pearls there
Pearls behind us
O the needles of the sun adorn us
Women who have just given birth greet us
With air with wine
Fir trees
Become entangled in our imagination
That suddenly becomes
The beautiful Mistress of Rocks

THE HOUR WAS AN IMAGE

The hour was an image
Our mind on the contrary was a lever
Cypress trees ascended the slope
Gold ascended the streams
Mist intended to grasp
The chiton of winter
As a noise neighed clearly
As though dawns had not died
On a single meadow
Bronze idols burst
Into tears and spasms
Nepenthes passed by haughtily
With violins over their shoulders
And the song was a circle again

And the song was a wave again
And the song was a sleep again
That grazes on air as soon as the chords of pain
Turn cowardly as soon as they slacken
And all remained in winter a long time

And we a flock of sheep
Were intoxicated by the star-strewn sky

Nicolas Cálas

WARMTH

The sea fondles the loneliness of the ruined windmill blindly
that for years now on a nonexistent wheel has been turning
the sorrows of those who broke their wings on the siroccos of
      their love life.
They are like me, I imagine, when they come to this hollow
      windmill,
without axle or sail, to listen to the North Wind's song;
they eat away the hours with ears glued to the lashed stone
seeking from the wind, rather frivolously, the gambler who toyed
      with their pain,
but he is heartless and gazes impotently into blurred mirrors
where the narcissi of a cultivated happiness have sprouted.
Unyoked loneliness listens to the naked walls crying out its
      questions.
But the windmill does not answer, presses its lips proudly on
      marine lips
and finds it sufficient at night, in the morning, in sun and in moon
to double at times its lovely stature
by rooting it in the numbed expanse of crystalline waters.

COLUMNS OF THE TEMPLE
OF OLYMPIAN ZEUS

At night the azure columns of the temple turn pale
but lift their wounded stature to unreachable skies in vain
no one understands the wordless supplication of an old adoration
directed to Zeus by the suggestive lines of chiseled stone
the acanthi have rusted and the fearless capitals are blown bodily
by erotic winds that seek refuge there
these marbles have been reduced to being liturgists of the hymen
any other meaning they had has vanished
archeologists strive in vain to find a coherence
in fragments that history has cast far away from itself
the muted members lie on the ground
not even one footfall of a faithful follower disturbs them
not a single shadow reechoes amid the ruins
and these have betrayed my walk
its purpose has vanished in a night far distant from its starless roof
and the coherence of history has vanished, cannot be found.

I become envious of these cold stone masses
that have been standing here wordless for centuries now
listening to the sweet echo of past emotions.

SANTORINI IV

With its nocturnal scream the lighthouse terrifies the tall rocks
forces them to play gigantic games
that spread their revels from the sky to the polyphonic caves
for hours the monstrous cries of despairing shadows echo afar
only heroic words can tame this substance into rhythms
but the pleasures that Santoríni offers a person
transform passions quickly, shatter every cyclopean blast
on the mountain's porcelain that whitens its black beauty.

From here the island gazes dramatically at the volcano that
      created it
and follows its work with the perfectionism of mesmerized
      superiority.
Intoxicated then by so many contradictory humors
I give way, and for a moment unwillingly become the spectator
      of the play in which I am acting.

Only beauty remains and underlines the difference between us.

ATHENS 1933

Now that the silence of orators and sophists tramples on the
      children of other townsmen,
Teutons—fallen patricians, heroes of many deaths in Venice—
English poets with Wildean features and Byronic scandals,
and Egyptian and foreign victories, are transferred to her areas
      and her playfields.
Regular habitués of her life are those children of modern Greece
who, from countries where Ephesius Maximus performed his
      miracles,
from places of other faiths,
daily arrive in Athens on ships of bankrupt firms.
The time has come for us to abandon the weed-covered ground
      of her toppled walls.
Alone now in the middle of summer months, let her follow
the sun as it hides behind rusted columns,
as for the last time it plays with the watery images of the Ilissos.
They have been constructed so in order to water the ends of the
      earth
with the glory of a city that bathes itself in a waterless river,
with whatever remains of this glory.
And there's no hope at all that their compositions will ever change,
that the river bed will be covered with more water.
For the Athenians to drown now, they must seek a sepulchral
      bath elsewhere.

WITH KISSES

Irma with her peppermint, but whiskey for the customers.
"Forgive me, my precious, it was the porter at the Cairo City
        Hotel.
An American wants me—no I can't today—
That's what I told him, for your sake; don't you forget it.
Dear boy, you didn't give me your name."
"And you, when you're not called Irma?"
"My dear, you want to know everything!"
"All for a single night, from mouth to mouth to all your body.
You were Aspasia, and I met you on Perikles Street
with your permanganate. She sent me a postcard from Port Said.
On the following day the Italians entered Addis Ababa.
Permanganate! I see it still. Peculiar smell."
"Whiskey is more expensive."
"Irma, you are like a rime turned round about."
"You want everything, my precious.
Is this the way Perikles' Aspasia behaved?
Come, I'm in a hurry; the customer from the Cairo City Hotel
        will arrive any moment now."

PARADISE

"May you rise and shine, my dashing young man!" said
        Papa-Adam.
"Come on, get up! Did your side pain you a little?
Get up, look at the girl I've brought you for spouse.
She's from Cyprus, and she's called Zoë. So long, kids.
But on one condition: *Never on Sunday*."
Two days passed, and three and four.
The couple spent the weekend at the Elysian Bar.
It was sheer fate that found Sophia there.
They stayed up all night at her house while
she took movies of them as they played *The Banquet of the Apple*.

LIRACISM

In the garden of tears
Helen P walks.
Will Margó steal off with Helen's Kóstas?
Neither the one nor the other comes from a good family,
but of course it's not M who has the money.
Count Kóstas abandoned them both
now that he has had gold lires for three months
and five days exactly after his stroll
in the Garden of Sighs with his new friend
P, Helen's father.

DHIYENIS

Mrs. Peacock (originally Pagoni) from Miami and Pharsalia
is celebrating "Christ Is Risen" this year by dancing
Rock and Roll with an evzone guard.
Meanwhile, in the Pláka, an Englishman with a faultless Erasmian
          pronunciation
recites Cafávis. Mr. Stevenson,
Stefanákos by origin, is spending the summer at Hýdra
in an ancient pirate's house, with leather furniture
of genuine linoleum.
At the Aphrodisiac-Cyprus, formerly the Angleterre,
a group of existentialists are holding a convention, socially
          nonexistent.
Tomorrow *Hecuba* is playing, as she dances
to the strains of "The Volga Boatman."
We've adulterated the honey of Hymettos, it's become floor wax
for Greeks to tango on. After receiving our passports,
we lost count of Easter.
Fortunately Beer is good for the character.
Fortunately we still have Tsitsánis and King David and Orpheus.

SWEET-KISSING ASPASIA

Above the Pláka, in the Taverna of Perikles
the "Son et lumière" will flood
with light and sound three erotic scenes.
With "Musica pro Boúzika"
Miss Hellas and Michel Micheline will collaborate.
They will smile with smiles.

The Akropolis was overcrowded:
Potter, who discovered the poetic worth of hot water,
recites today "Baclavas is sweeter than death,"
unless the market inspection police have any objections.
The film "From Hill to Hilton" also will be shown
inspired by the uphill march
of a regular woman reader of the *Azvestía*.
That moment is very moving when Xénia
shouts: "Monné Dié, Monné Dié, Elpís, le téléphon!"

Masterless priests and spiritless pussycats
rush out of remote chapels
and the neighborhood meatstands
singing the "Aman, aman, amen, amen, meou-meou."
And an innovation: in the blind alleys
the chauffeurs with their swift taxis
will transport by means of Collisions Avenue
everything crushed, in order to toast them with general
         exasperation.

HAPPY CITY

They go to Rotten Gardens to enjoy
the splendor of their failures.
Old Man Courtier patriotically
chews on a Copenhagen pastry
while at the adjacent table

a Gypsy woman reminds her son
that in Denmark the statue of a siren had been beheaded.

But the theme has no poetic sharpness.
Will Mrs. Courtier give or not give
her annual garden party
since Mrs. Honirable is no longer with the Ministry of Scrambling
and the Director of International Tourtourism has been fired?
Will Dora not make her pool available to the left wing?
Far better not to open her newly built cistern!
Far better to drown! But then, what would be the use?
At the palace they heap contempt on theatricals.
She will adapt herself to the new situation to a certain degree,
and every night before going to the Tennis Club
she will stroll in the lower-class Záppion Gardens
frequented, as they say, by studs.
In the meantime
the Gypsy woman reminds the left-wingers of the saying
"Beware of Greeks bearing gifts!"

A HERO'S MAUSOLEUM

Whoever for a little or a long time sips poison
forestalls the priest.
He has Mithridates for hero.
Knock on wood! Whoever receives Holy Communion heals
salvation without medicine, crawls into History
and into its hangouts, a troupe of actors and heroin.
In the assembly the satiated spectators of love attend mass.

XENO DOCHIUM

Said Mr. Fix to Callirrhoë: "I am the Ilissos River."
Said Hilton to the Parthenon: "I am the Akropolis."
Said Edison to the Owl: "I am the light."

Said little Helen to Belefonte: "You are my Homer."
Honoris causa the Admiral will be named "Néarhos"
and his pontoon "Tosítsas."
The Unknown God becomes a crossword puzzle
Glory be to the Word because the Areopagos remains a rock
And the G. B. "Grande Bretagne" and not "Cyprus"!

Nikos Ghavriil Pendzikis

THE MONK AT THE FOUNTAIN

When he went out before dawn, he had already learned of the death of his kin. At daybreak, he found himself by the fountain.

Darkness had been banished. Colors ascended lightly in the air. The curved heavens were pure dream. Sentiment took wing with a grace that charmed the heart. The soul fluttered like a flag. A heavy wind sprang out of the folds of radiant clouds. Moored royal ships, loaded with Homeric myths, the daedal clouds danced, brimming with light, reflecting roads beyond the heavens, the unending highway toward the stars, precious stones of the mind that vanish before Phaeton's actual brilliance, in the depths of the heavens where the glittering creator embraces all terrestrial things.

He pauses to marvel. Raises his hand that resembles a wing, a butterfly palpitating in a celestial lake. The sky becomes idea once more, a world of virginal reflections forever deflowered, with all its hovering silver clouds, toward Arcturus at all points. Clouds above the promontory, a brilliant wreath, like a dragon's beard, like beasts and monsters. From within the soul, like buildings or men, the clouds dwindle in the distance, navigating their fearless way, white slanting sails and rigging of all shapes. One moors at the summit. It turns from ash-gray into rose, crimson and gold. And then all the sky shines again with a clear azure light.

The breeze is fresh and cool; mythical youthfulness and poetry pervade the atmosphere. Brimming with enthusiasm, the soul breathes in the nostalgia of another life, more just than ours. You remain suspended between heaven and earth, like the Stylites on their heights, slaking your thirst with wind, receiving ambrosia for nourishment in a serene longing, in a profusion of light that illuminates all life. The heart, together with birds, joyfully conquers the sky.

Amid the warbling of birds, day breaks. Sounds in the ear are filled with mystery. Hairy ears hide themselves in waves. Like the fishes of the sea, he too hears the fisherman's conch.

Past meandering coastlines of gulfs, harbors, and promontories, he rows with his small boat. Rich treasures spread out on shore: stones of precious lamentation, pearls of tears, shells from the sea depths, embellishments on the beach, bracelets on the sand, whispers of the infinite.

Leaping on shore, the wave scatters its brine over innumerable grains of sand, porous material where the gravity of the one encounters the gravity of the other, where a new vessel is launched for distant lands, leaving behind a rusted anchor, an old boat turned upside down, exposing its rotted bones.

Without a single futile anxiety, the monk gazes at the world. A breeze widens his thoughts. On his hair and eyes, his hand voyages far into destiny. He gazes into his innermost being, and is astounded. Within the folds of his vestments, his stature towers. A skiff cuts away from his arm, his palms turn into a raft.

White wing on the horizon, beyond the blue promontories, the vessel cuts through the sea. Essence which cannot be caught within or outside ourselves, spilled milk, a plaster cast—the sea, a bluing, unsuspectedly imprints all characters. It glows silverly with myriad, light-toned, golden and brown signs, multiform, a first life. Every current of emotion wrinkles its features variously. At times as tranquil as oil, lightly ruffled by a gust of wind; at times bellowing ferociously. A pellucid, deep-colored glass mirrors the sky. There where the thoughts of wild pigeons fly.

He had gone out alone to walk in the Virgin's Garden, in a lovely meadow thick with shadows. Mountains everywhere about him, and ridges, waves, ornaments of the terrain; steep slopes ascending one after the other to the summit, intricate architecture

of masses heaped on the Titans. Gullies, hollows, stooped
shoulders, rocks and boulders as far as the shore. Mountains,
dark-azure and rose, where even the clouds spread their shadows.

He leans his elbows on a rock and supports his head. The
stone protrudes out of the ground, the garment in which it dies.
Red and yellow soils conceal springs of abundance; configurations
like men, recent and older formations of various kinds with veins
and scales of rock strata where life suckles, sprouting odors and
touch from out the insensate rock, ruins amid whatever is called
life.

In the middle of the field, he sets his foot down unobtrusively
on the rich carpet. His feet vanish in the moist grass. He no
longer knows whose limbs they are. He depends no longer on his
senses. Amid the nuances of the morning, his features forget
themselves in the humble flowers of earth.

Greenery of all tones; leaves of all shapes; stems shaggy and
hairy, with thorns; leaves with hidden spores; stalks that ooze
with milk; flowers of crimson, white, violet and gold, like funnels;
stars and tassels; thimbles; geraniums, like old women wearing
headkerchiefs, like other faces; crowfeet; broom rape;
snapdragons; small flowers bunched together like globules;
clusters; grape hyacinths (the bread of birds); a diffused scattering
of glory, many-branched embroidery, delicate needlework.

His hand, which reaps whatever is innermost, like that of an
angel's touches a flower, wing-petaled, and the fingers are
stigmata, wide strips of the pistil, and ripen the pollen of
knowledge that passes from the hand into the heart, resurrecting
the world of miracles.

Behind the tree's back, the buckthorns exhale. With
lofty-headed trunk, it lifts its long hair in its hands like a regal
train. Its branches raise terrestrial things to the highest physical
elevation, to the foliage on which the sky descends. Leaves rustle
in the sun, squint, casting a blond shadow. A fairy tale is the
forest, like a thick comb. Trees secretly confess. All the
vegetation does not blossom at the same time. Other branches
have not as yet sprouted leaves. The new foliage is in its
springtime, wherein nightingales flutter, birds of many-colored
feathers, a secret life that hides in marine, green shadows. Small
animals, tame and wild. Master Hare, the householder, with his

mustaches. In the undergrowth a night butterfly spreads its wings like a peacock. Ants and small flies with red spots scurry up and down the slender stalks. Goldfinches find sustenance on heavy-scented, beneficial herbs.

A branch breaking by chance teaches him the fragrance of the other world. Beyond any material limit, as though he were not himself. He does not know where he is, like a cavalier who has lost his horse. Unmoved, he gazes further on. Olive trees in their old age gleam silverly in the clearing. Light glitters on the footpath. The footfall of a wayfarer is heard, bells from animals on the mountain slope.

Amid flower-filled banks, a rainbow in the vegetation, the ripe apples of the Hesperides, fruit that leave their seed behind them, stripping bare of soil all roots linked with the bowels of the earth, sprawling like a body in its bed, as far as wild ducks wander in the shallows of its estuary, the river, murmuring, flows.

The monk hears the song. More poetic is the susurration on high. In the stony and infertile glen it descends like a torrent, indifferent to any watery shape, an alternating exaltation of passion, a rush of atoms in chaos.

Over the stream beside him, where a fresh sun has spread serenity, he suspends his hand which measures the vortex of all things ephemeral. Like a mass of tentacles, the water devours his fingers. A multiformed spectacle waters the weeping willows of Babylon.

"O waters in which I baptize my hands," he prays, "cleanse me of the filth of sin, of all personal vicissitudes the flesh has sheltered, that I may become pure and free of care in the midst of deceitful life, according to the example of the Fathers who returned clean to their Creator.

"From out my eye, a well as yet undug, their memory is drawn up, bones that emit fragrance, holy and reverent relics, human flowers.

"You descend from all sources, O water, to irrigate the desert. Flow coolly from this fountain also, with its ivy, its ancient marble. Pour precious stones, gold, and diamonds to enrich, to widen the sea."

From his eyes, a purifying source of man's pain, tears flow profusely and alter his vision. He sees differently, within nothingness, within the cracked jug, another incontestable reality.

DOES IT FLY? DOES IT FLY?

In the arms of his robust mother
the fingers of the blind child browsed
a beautiful woman strolled along the seashore
her body brimming with the desire of existence
the child goes to cleanse its eyes
a city is outlined by the dark marble chips of the mosaic tiles
precise cartography of four hundred thousand
the road descending from the hillslopes
continues toward the city in name only
beyond the houses to the crossroads and the grocer's
grandfather's face is a savage wind
the glasses of the girl brewing coffee are patient
uncombed window shutters, patched windows
with a mountain on his forehead he knocks on the door at night
everywhere fences, obstacles of apartment buildings
the great empress refuses to open
unsuitable hour, locked iron door-shutters, bolted doors
you cannot find a single blanket to buy or clothing
the firemen keep watch that blood may not be spilled
the roof gutter deeply mourns its mother
he doesn't see where he's going to right or left and is imperiled
he stoops over the downpour's soup with its corpses
"I can't come" she kept saying "the pebbles hurt my feet"
with his money bags the enemy spoils our appetite
the bread, the dough, a beautiful child
the butcher slaughtered and the place filled with wounded
with the gashed the lashed those directly through the heart slashed
cardiology is knowledge of the heart's anguish
the aorta is a romantic street with wild rose trees
and coronary arteries are small plazas bordered with rich houses
pursued by his imagination how comically he ran
a Karagiózis program for all the world to laugh
the school bell rings out "forward"
"is this the place please where the newlyweds have settled?"
how very much more has the lawyer to say

the doctor or the astrophysical discoverer
obstacles to right and left "where are we going?"
she was so very beautiful, a mole on her cheek
"no I can't complain that my husband's been unfaithful"
the blind child dreams of gardens
beyond at the other end of the road a gazelle comes out of the
        house
the house is red but not the red of blood or fire
it is a cloud of love that bridges East and West
behind Mt. Hortiátis the full moon rose
there is a green meadow beyond the obstacle of houses
as it browses the finger asks "what is it that flies?"
it is the bird that flies that flies it is the moon that flies
see all the houses and shops and streets are flying
the family finds itself where the road continues
the moon and the bird bring eyes to the blind child
they eat by the seashore and then go rowing.

SCATTERED LEAVES

Scattered leaves of autumn
the farmers waited for rain to begin their sowing
the wind whirled and opened the celestial heavens
"what road is taken by the yellow leaves that fall?"
the Apostle of Nations taking a contrary road
from Neápolis now Kavála
reading in the First Epistle to the Thessalonians
but I would not have you to be ignorant, brethren,
concerning them which are asleep, that ye sorrow not,
even as others which have no hope
the belfry as tall as a farseeing lighthouse
with arched openings toward all the points of the horizon
what is and is not a series of coincidences
in the garden are graves with crosses
just opposite a fire was consuming a ship
his dearly beloved mother died
outside the wooden door the girl sat and waited

like a butterfly resting on a flower
a beautiful butterfly and an empty letterbox
though the doors were closed
she would come at night to find him
at the gulf's mouth through which the hinterland flows
into the open sea that swallowed his father
when he could not understand his son's actions
or that bereavement means victory and a great joy
the ship comes to load up wheat from the wharf
at which prudent interpreters of the living dream
commenting on the scene point their fingers
behind them the village is a tombstone with eyes
which an abundant vegetation of lofty stature shadows
amid the towering roofs of the foliage
and the low-lying shrubs, the ivy—a memory
a devotion and a warm faith—crawls
exactly as you were and it used to be
when he dove under the surface of the sea
where Mardonios' fleet was shipwrecked
but we know of course that the treasure was saved
in seacaverns where seals wail
on the crystalloid rocks of the Mountain of Holy Name
a succor to whoever has contrived many things and great
the sun that plunges into the basin of his mother
mourned by all who had faith in him because he vanishes
offering another possibility out of the water depths
       take us to strange lands
       take us to lands beyond
       blow O wide wide sea
       blow O fair wind blow

SEASIDE THOUGHTS

Our thoughts are living fishes
silvered glimmering fish on wet searoads
the maternal waters of the universal sea
on the claws of the deep water-precipices the fishes

gather, silent expressions of horizontal position
newly wed mothers are accustomed to saunter
on the pier with their baby carriages
along its entire length with its benches and its lanterns
a folksy image with vendors of dried fruit and nuts
"don't go too far away" mummy and daddy shout
the child with its tricycle spins in circles
young girls like flowers and young men in love
after an absence of many years the professor
finds it difficult to adjust to daily routine
cannot justify the interruption of his thoughts
almost fears that his return may mean death
"it's turned cold, it's time to return home"
the householders say, well armored in their overcoats
they fear the children may catch cold
but an orphan strips and for a few coins
dives from the ladder's head at the boat landing
and then sprawls out on the pier once more
his immature pecker like a fountain of truth gazing at the sky
"heavenly father give him the strength to dive
again and again for the few pennies of his daily bread"
without doubt the weather will turn rainy
clouds have gathered above the red buildings of the harbor
like ashes hiding the solid appearance of matter
for the embodiment of the soul demands moisture
as when the prince impatiently cracked open the walnut shell
and the beautiful maiden who leapt out and begged for water
died because they found themselves far from any fountain
the adversary wind will present things in another light
hiding the sun under goatskins of water
and bringing it back to dry the sailing boats
the world will come to a fierce boiling point
"hello, wife! what good food have you prepared today?"
amid today's and tomorrow's episodes
the sun that stretches its big legs and tears the clouds to tatters
the waves of the sea that turn as green as the fresh leaves of an
          almond tree
the troubled cares of the householders and the orphan
the thoughts of the professor continue deep within him
"now I understand that in maritime navigation

the horizontal position is not the only one that exists
medusae like flowers rising vertically
break off from the zoophytes of deep waters
and the seahorse proceeds unpredictably
suddenly a fish leaps out of the water
all are woven like the rich embroideries of the Word
for the skirt of the Most Blessed Madonna"
the bell of a ship weighing anchor is a yearning
Well then all sins flow from woman I remember
But the best also has its source in woman I repeat
into many sins have I fallen.

CONSTANT COMPANY

We keep constant company with the dead
the wind from the open horizons ruffled his hair
he stood outside with his tie knotted tightly
the youngster was waiting for Aurora to appear
"mother" he kept saying "where are you? father, how are you?
grandmother, friends, relatives, I call you"
when the ship was endangered he remembered them
he could not see before him, darkness
night the great sea
night the rivers and mountains
night the fields and villages
night the dreams of the fruit-bearing trees
"tell me where am I, where am I going?"
a herd of cattle passed by
the bell of the leading ram clanged loudly
they exit from houses built partly of ancient marbles
escorts of the hidden treasure
they smite the damp earth with iron rods
"read to see what the inscriptions say"
we keep constant company with the dead
"empty the tombs here and empty those further down
to whom has the snake given up what was hidden?
into what hole has the guardian slithered now?

does some sin perhaps weight us down?"
they walked for hours without end
an old man kept saying they were nearing the sky
stooping, the young man picked up his father's skull
many of his small bones had been scattered and lost
the young man could understand nothing of the world
"see how much lighter the dead man has become though not
        decomposed"
he hears them saying "I think I'll raise him up by the armpits"
but with all the pulling the right upper extremity
came away from the rest of the body
from the corpse that so disjointedly was harrowed
the face of the Moon leant down sadly
further on a bend of the river was lighted up
grief-stricken reflections of loss
"where shall I find you, mother, where shall I meet you?"
we keep constant company with the dead
his hand searches amid the ashes to find her beauty
his fist believes it grasps her rich hair
his heart shakes with fright and a flock of birds scatters
the hunted stars hang down from the heavens
the young man finds himself in a city of myriad men
gazing down from on high, he thinks "doubtless
the living and the dead walk here arm in arm"
"welcome" he hears someone saying
as he goes to shut the glass door behind him
a fellow student who had died while still in high school
welcomes him, wearing a dentist's uniform
"have some coffee, Kósta" he says "sit down"
"I am now" he adds "in Rodholívos, sleeping"
winter is blowing and from the slightly open window
the snow in a wide avenue
spreads out on the worn bed covers
in a constant companionship with the dead.

DOCUMENTARY

Maria lay on the cart with another woman who had died during an operation. After Maria's funeral, the same cart was loaded with seven infants, three together in a sheet apiece, and one wrapped up alone. The driver of the municipal cart went over the facts pertaining to the indigent dead. Death from emaciation caused by a malignant tumor. Sarcomatous and cancerous emaciation. Features rotted and earth colored. Skeletal. Dugs like those of a man. Tits flattened to the bone. "She died knowing she was dying," the doctor said. "Dreadful pain. The cancer had filtered through branches of nerves and ganglia underlying and compressed. Morphine was a small consolation." An old woman dressed the corpses in the hospital, washing them like plates in a sink. "Not you, sonny boy," she would say, preventing anyone from helping her. She would place the soap on the top of her downturned hand that the doctor might take it from there. The wine used in washing the corpse had been brought too late, so when it was all over, she drank it herself. The dead woman had been spread out on a marble bench. Wrapped in an old dressing gown. Her comb near her head, together with a notification from the Board of Health. She could come to apply as a nurse of the second category. There was a position open. Also, letters of recommendation would be necessary for the job. Empty envelope from the Clinic. Document from the General Administration, with its protocol number. Three or four of the painkilling powders she used to take. On the floor, an empty brown handbag. Her overcoat. A pair of unwashed stockings. The head nurse kept the overcoat to send her mother: Argos, district of the Virgin Mary. Her husband had divorced the dead woman, and then remarried. Her child had not been informed of her death. She was still breathing when she took off her wedding ring from her finger and gave it to the nurse who had been taking care of her. Then she turned her head on a pillowcase spotted with dwarf mallows. The small flowers on the cart (snapdragons and road-flax) had been especially gathered by a few children. The only characteristics that could still remind one of Maria were her brow and hair. Before she breathed her last, her voice seemed to come only from her lips, without any help from her lungs. When he saw her, Níkos wept. Whenever she grieved, she used to weep silently, without a single wet tear. Her eyes would flutter, her face would pucker up, her breathing would come in gasps, but the same unchanging color in her face always. The aged Director of the Hospital looked on with dry eyes, although his nose dripped. The doorkeeper and others passed by in single file. Fanny kept telling me: "Do you know who else died? Nína, Kerdhelákis' married daughter. She left behind a small child."

Pandelís Prevelákis

TWILIGHT ENTERED MY ROOM

Twilight entered my room
like a red lion.
Its reflected light fell in the mirror
and I felt its soft paws
touching my naked feet.
I stooped under the table
which the day's work had blessed
and saw the sun kissing my feet
with its red tongue.

WHEN UNDER THE LAST VERSE

When under the last verse
of my first epic poem
I signed my first and last name,
the wind lying in wait
behind the open door
entered my room and embraced me.
The May night had begun to brighten,
and the early-awakened waters to run
on the naked shingle.
I wrapped myself in my overcoat and fell asleep.

And in my sleep that dream came
which I had never achieved seeing in my waking hours:
I was like an archangel who had fallen asleep,
holding his sword in his hands.

AS IN AN HOUR OF DROUGHT
THE BUFFALOES

As in an hour of drought the buffaloes
beat with their hooves on barren earth
because they feel those wellsprings buried
that without warbling drench all roots,
thus with the hooves of a Pegasos unmounted
and inflamed with the thirst of eternal time
I struck you, I struck you, O desolate land.
And like a bell that in its ringing
contains a crystalline, silvery vein,
you replied to the hammer stroke of impatience,
O voice, rich as the song of angels.
And your deep wellsprings that watered
roots and foundations, warbled
in a new bed whose banks had turned to stone
in the necessity of verse, that master-mason.
As long as the winged horse measured
your desolation, O land, and blew
on your body with its flaming breath,
the unspent voices matched their tune
with its beating hooves, as the weaver
weds her song to the shuttle.
And unmounted Pegasos, who browsed
on Helicon's green pastures only,
got drunk on your sand and your dust,
O desolate land, grassless as a grave,
resounding like a bell with a vein
of silver in its heart!

WITH THE CONSCIOUSNESS

With the consciousness that fruit
shall have as it ripens
we sunned our bodies yesterday
in the noon of winter.
For us the warm earth,
for us the green horizons,
the immaculate light
and the sun's numberless hands.
Within us like a white rose
kindness and valor opened
and we shared our joy like bread.
And as the years tighten
the rings of age around a tree
thus round our youthful bodies
the sun-drenched afternoon
wrapped an all-golden bark.

I FEEL LOVE TO BE A GREEN

I feel love to be a green
wild olive wreath on the curly temples
where the victorious blood throbs.
And in the hour of triumph
when crimson lusters surround me
and the body soars by itself
like a hawk from the fist of the falconer,
I rushed toward you as toward a cliff
with my unwounded youth.
And swiftly the shield of my chest, the spear
of my erect body cover you
as an `eyelid covers an eye
startled or imperiled.

I am the sentinel of your youth!
If you turn toward my eyes
you will see unsheathed swords,
tall lilies planted upright like scimitars,
and behind them, like a flowing curtain,
the fearful conflagration of poetry.

IN THIS UPPER JERUSALEM

In this upper Jerusalem
supported by clouds like buttresses
gilded and engarlanded by the sun
my thought is a golden morning,
large, immaculate, indivisible.
I climbed here treading on my senses,
five stairs, one above the other,
planted in the soil and watered
as plane trees are watered.
And with my body inflamed, flushed red,
like an open wound that knits into flesh,
I fought the winds and the wings of night,
the fears and the longings of conscience.

The man killed the boy, and that man
was killed by the man grown older . . .
And as the reed leaps joint
by joint, as flame mounts flame,
as the fir tree hoists
to its topmost peak a two-forked tongue,
thus mounting and ascending,
mounting on the heights of poetry,
mounting on the fullness of humility,
treading on the purity of my virtue,
I set my foot and hung my wings
on these air-tossed crossroads.

Human things no longer frighten me,
and I feel my soul turned

like an enormous mirror toward the sun,
and stretched out like an azure sea
on which are written clouds, birds of passage,
air-channeled roads of migration,
falling stars, comets, their glittering trains,
and the dust of burning systems.

I KNEW WITH YOU
THOSE QUIET HOURS

I knew with you those quiet hours
sweet as the clouds that dissolve
in a slow shower on springtime meadows;
I knew with you those hours of struggle
that turn the firmament black and crimson.
We loved each other in serenity, and the hours
passed among us with a light
step, the way shadows pass
between mirrors placed on opposite walls,
gazing into each other in the half-light.
We loved each the other in the darkness of nights
that prepares youth for love,
and the hours shone, black-eyed,
their cheeks flushed red.

Today, now that I have lost you,
I feel my soul is like the snow
that thaws on a sunless day,
—bitter, unspeaking, ungoverned.
And sometimes I feel it with the desire
of pain that does not restrain its voice,
a mourner of those departed, dust upon her head,
like Priam wailing for his son.

SACRIFICE

To our union I bring for dowry
those worlds my thoughts revived:
continents, constellations, comets.
Sometimes I feel this head of mine
that bends toward yours to be a great nobleman
who over my worldly body holds dominion,
and sometimes a sphere of fire wherein
my invisible stature takes root.
As in Christian icons the Immaculate Virgin
ascends on a silvery sickle
and the heavens about her roar like cataracts,
so do I feel my thoughts, virginal and theogonic,
rushing upwards from the top of my crown
like a just sacrifice for your sake alone!

PRAYER FOR A YOUNG POET

God of wakefulness and passion,
source and spirit of poetry;
You who dilate my heart
and inflame my blood,
who in the darkness of my desolation
make the lands, the skies and the seas
flow as in a magic crystal;
You who immerse my life
in the abyss of fire
and cool it with ocean breezes,
fuser of rhythm and word,
crossroad of inspiration,
cataract of light;
You who shoot with the eager word for arrow,
hunter of beasts and ideas,

masculine and feminine will,
life, purgatory and resurrection,
palpable hope of immortality;
You, my God, if I have served you well,
lower your eyes
and loosen your azure locks
on this small and flaming creature
who sings in the bloodstained brambles;
cast the seed in his heart,
that seed which conceals
the roaring and many-leaved plane tree of poetry,
increase his power within him,
unloosen his tongue,
awaken words within his spirit,
and rhythm in his hearing,
and make him Your mouth,
make him the trumpet of Your throne,
make him the voice of the winds and the seas
and the sigh of lands
and the cry of fire
and the silence of starry regions.

BARCAROLE

The waves rock me as in a cradle,
the Dionysian festival of flowers
is being celebrated in the heavens,
and the stars are falling.
The mind no longer inquires, it dances
enwreathed with night as with ivy.
I am free at last, and I am alone
like a saint bound naked to the wheel
who in his nostrils feels
the myrrh of Paradise.
The planks of my boat creak
and by its side the constellations sparkle.
If you are not worthy, you will die.

Keep vigil! The celestial system is crumbling,
its harmony was unbearable.
Keep vigil! The land has let loose
her dogs upon me.

THE FRONTIER

Here is the frontier.
Night greets the day
and detains her still.
But I am Greece,
do not hurt me.
I want to say it,
I want to name it,
then let me be lost!
Let my bones be scattered,
I want to baptize all things
in the Jordan of language.
Thousands of years ago,
with her eyes to the ground,
even Cassandra
was able to speak.
Let the frontier be,
I want to name it,
then let me be lost.

LOST INCORRUPTIBILITY

Before you existed you lay sleeping in darkness,
but since you were enfleshed in my spirit
you have become the large-eyed idea
that gave birth to heavens and to continents.
Now that you have set at last,
you have been left only with your mundane body,

your shoulders, your curves, your breasts,
and the Africa of your loins.
When they greet you good day, my beautiful one,
the Wind stands with its scythe
and threshes their words.
The sun of Greece no longer bakes
on my lips the bread of poetry—
the words wither.
The Unsleeping Worm
lies for us in ambush.

Yánnis Rítsos

from   ROMIOSINI

I

These trees cannot adjust to lesser sky,
these stones cannot adjust beneath the tread of strangers,
these faces cannot adjust unless they feel the sun,
these hearts cannot adjust unless they live in justice.

This landscape is as harsh as silence,
it hugs to its breast the scorching stones,
clasps in its light the orphaned olive trees and vineyards,
clenches its teeth. There is no water. Light only.
Roads vanish in light and the shadow of the sheepfold is made
      of iron.

Trees, rivers, and voices have turned to stone in the sun's
            quicklime.
Roots trip on marble. Dust-covered lentisk shrubs.
Mules and rocks. All panting. There is no water.
All are parched. For years now. All chew a morsel of sky to
            choke down their bitterness.

Their eyes are bloodshot for lack of sleep,
a deep furrow is wedged between their eyebrows
like a cypress tree between two mountains at sunset.

Their hands are welded to their rifles
their rifles are extensions of their hands
their hands are extensions of their souls—
anger lies upon their lips
and anguish deep within their eyes
like a star in a salt-pit.

When they clasp hands, the sun becomes certain of the world,
when they smile, a small swallow flies out of their savage beards,
when they sleep, twelve stars fall out of their empty pockets,
when they are killed, life sweeps up the ascent with kettledrums
        and flags flying.

For so many years all have starved, all have thirsted, all were
        slaughtered,
besieged by land and sea;
drought has consumed their fields, brine has drenched their houses,
the wind has knocked down their doors and the few lilac shrubs in
        the village square,
death comes and goes through the holes in their overcoats,
their tongues have become as acrid as cypress cones,
their dogs have perished, wrapped up in their own shadows,
the rain beats down on their bones.

Transfixed on their outposts they smoke cow-dung and the night,
scanning the frenzied sea where the broken
mast of the moon has sunk.

They have run out of bread, exhausted their ammunition,
now they load their cannons with their hearts only.

So many years besieged by land and sea,
they are all starved, are all killed, yet no one has perished—
there on their outposts their eyes glow,
a huge flag, a great crimson conflagration,
and every dawn a thousand doves soar out of their hands
toward the four gates of the horizon.

IV

They pushed on straight into dawn with the disdain of hungry
     men,
a star had thickened in their motionless eyes,
they carried on their shoulders the stricken summer.

The armies passed through here with banners clinging to their
     bodies,
with stubbornness clenched between their teeth like an acrid pear,
with the moon's sand in their heavy army boots,
with the coaldust of night sticking in their ears and nostrils.

Tree by tree, stone by stone, they passed through the world,
passed through sleep with thorns for pillow.
They brought life like a river cupped in their parched hands.

At every step they won a league of sky—to give it away.
At their outposts they turned to stone like scorched trees,
and when they danced in the village squares the ceilings in the
     houses shook
and the glassware clattered on the shelves.

Ah, what songs shook the mountain summits!
Between their knees they held the platter of the moon and ate,
and squashed an Ah in the depths of their hearts
as they would squash a louse between their coarse fingernails.

Who will bring you now a warm loaf of bread in the night that
     you may feed your dreams?
Who will stand in the shade of an olive tree to keep the cicada
     company lest the cicada fall silent,
now that the whitewash of noon paints the low stone wall of the
     horizon all around,
obliterating their great and virile names?

This earth that smelled so fragrantly at daybreak,
the earth that was theirs and ours—their blood—how fragrant that
     earth—

and now how is it that our vineyards have locked us out,
how has the light thinned out on roofs and trees,
who can bear to say that half are now under the earth
and the other half in chains?

Though the sun waves you good-morning with so many leaves
and the sky glitters with so many banners,
these lie in chains and those under the earth.

Be silent, the bells will ring out at any moment.
This earth is theirs, this earth is ours.
Under the earth, in their crossed hands
they hold the bell rope, waiting for the hour, they do not sleep,
        they never die,
waiting to ring in the resurrection. This earth
is theirs and ours—no one can take it from us.

from V

They sat under the olive trees in the early afternoon
sifting the ashy light through their coarse fingers,
they unbuckled their cartridge belts, estimating how much toil
        could be crammed into the path of night,
how much bitterness in the knots of the wild mallow,
how much courage in the eyes of the barefoot boy who holds the
        flag aloft.

In the field the last swallow had lingered late,
balancing in the air like a black ribbon on the sleeve of autumn.
Nothing else remained. Only the gutted houses smoldering still.

The others left us some time ago to lie under the stones,
their torn shirts and their vows scratched on the fallen door.
No one wept. We had no time. Only the silence grew deeper still,
and the light down by the beach was as tidy as the housekeeping
        of the murdered woman.

What will happen to them now when the rain seeps into the earth
        with its rotted plane tree leaves?

What will happen to them when the sun dries out in the woolen
        blanket of clouds
like a squashed bedbug on a peasant's bed,
when the stork of snows stands embalmed on the chimney stack
        of the previous night?

Old mothers scatter salt into the fire, scatter earth over their hair,
uproot the vines of Monevasiá lest even one grape sweeten the
        mouth of a foe;
they have put the bones of their grandfathers in a sack together
        with their knives and forks
and wander outside the walls of their homelands searching for a
        place in which to take root in the night.

It would be hard for us to find a language
less powerful less stony than that of the cherry tree—
those hands that remained in the fields
or up the mountains or down under the sea
do not forget, they never forget—
it will be hard for us to forget their hands,
it will be hard for hands that grew callous on a trigger to ask
        questions of a daisy,
to give thanks, resting on a knee or a book
or on the breast of starlight.
It will take time. And we must speak up.
Until they find their bread and their rights.

Two oars nailed in the sand in the storming dawn. Where is the
        fishing boat?
A plow thrust into earth and the wind blowing.
The earth scorched. Where is the plowman?

Ashes the olive tree, the vineyard, and the house.
Niggardly night with its stars in a peasant's sock.
Dry bayleaves and oregano in the middle cupboard on the wall.
        The fire has not touched them.
Blackened kettle in the hearth—and the water boiling by itself
in the bolted house. They had no time to eat.

   . . . .

On the threshing floor where one night the gallant young men
        took their supper

the olive pits and the moon's dried blood remain
with the folk meter of their guns.
The cypress trees and laurel groves remain.

Next day the sparrows ate the crumbs of army bread,
children fashioned toys out of the matches
with which the soldiers lit their cigarettes and the thorns of the
        stars.

And the stone, on which they sat under the olive trees in early
        afternoon by the sea
will be turned into whitewash in the kiln tomorrow,
the day after tomorrow we shall whitewash our houses and the
        low stone wall of Saint Savior,
and the day after that we shall sow seed there where they slept
and a pomegranate bud shall burst like a babe's first laughter
        on the sunlight's breast.

Afterwards we shall sit on the ground to read all their hearts
as though we were reading the history of the world for the first
        time.

from VII

Every night the moon in the fields turns the magnificent dead over
        on their backs,
searching their faces with savage, frozen fingers to find her son
by the cut of his chin and his stony eyebrows,
searching their pockets. She will always find something. There is
        always something to find.
A locket with a splinter of the Cross. A stubbed-out cigarette.
A key, a letter, a watch stopped at seven.
We wind up the watch again. The hours plod on.

When tomorrow their clothing rots away
and they remain amid their army buttons
like pieces of sky between summer stars,
like the river between laurel shrubs,

like the footpath meandering between lemon trees in early spring,
we may then find their names and shout: I love.

Then. But again these things are perhaps a little too remote,
perhaps a little too close, as when you clasp a hand in the darkness
        and say good evening
with the bitter civility of the exile who returns to his ancestral
        home
and not even his own kinfolk recognize him
because he has known death,
because he has known the life that comes before life and beyond
        death,
but he recognizes them. He is not embittered. Tomorrow, he says.
        And he is certain
that the longest road is the shortest road into the heart of God.

And now the hour has come when the moon kisses him below the
        ear with some distress;
the seaweed, the flowerpot, the footstool, and the stone staircase
        bid him good evening,
and the mountains and the seas and the cities and the skies
        bid him good evening,
and then at last, flicking his cigarette ash through the balcony
        railing,
he may weep in his assurance,
he may weep in the assurance of the trees and the stars
        and his brothers.

REFORMATION

This which you term serenity or discipline, kindness or apathy,
this which you call a closed mouth with clenched teeth,
showing the sweet silence of the mouth, hiding the clenched teeth,
is only the metal's endurance under the useful hammer,
under the dreadful hammer—it is what you know:
that from the formless you pass toward form.

UNDERSTANDING

Sunday. Buttons glitter on every coat
like small laughter. The bus has gone.
A few cheerful voices—it is strange
how you can hear and reply. Under the pine trees
a worker is learning to play the harmonica. A woman
says good morning to someone—such a simple and natural good-
        morning
that you too want to learn how to play the harmonica under the
        plane trees.

Neither division nor subtraction. To be able to gaze
outside yourself—warmth and quiet. Not to be
"only yourself," but "you too." A small addition,
a small deed of practical mathematics, easily understood,
in which even a child can succeed, playing with his fingers in the
        light
or playing this harmonica that the woman might hear.

INTERCHANGES

They took the plow to the field,
they brought the field into the house—
an endless interchange shaped
the meaning of things.

The woman changed places with the swallow,
she sat in the swallow's nest on the roof and warbled.
The swallow sat by the woman's loom
and wove stars, fishing boats, fish.

If only you knew how beautiful your mouth is
you would kiss me on the eyes that I might not see.

NECESSARY EXPLANATION

There are certain stanzas—sometimes entire poems—
whose meaning not even I know. It is what I do not know
that holds me still. You were right to ask me. But do not ask me.
I do not know, I tell you.
                              Two parallel lights
from the same center. The sound of water
falling in winter from an overbrimming drain pipe,
or the sound of a waterdrop as it falls
from a rose in a watered garden
slowly, slowly on a spring evening
like a bird's sobbing. I do not know
what this sound means; even so, I accept it.
Whatever I do know, I've clarified for you. I've not been
              neglectful.
But these, too, add to our lives.
                              I would notice,
as she slept, how her knees formed an angle on the bedsheet—
It was not only a matter of love. This corner
was a ridge of tenderness, and the fragrance
of the bedsheet, of cleanliness, and of spring supplemented
that inexplicable thing I sought—in vain again—to explain to you.

MOONLIGHT SONATA

*A spring night. A large room of an old house. A middle-aged
woman, dressed in black, is speaking to a young man. They have
not put on any lights. Through the two windows of the room a
merciless light enters. I've neglected to say that the Woman in
Black has published two or three interesting collections of poetry
of a religious nature. Well, the Woman in Black is speaking to the
Young Man:*

Let me come with you. What a moon tonight!
The moon is good to me—you can't tell
my hair has turned white. The moon
will make my hair golden again. You won't be able to tell the
         difference.
Let me come with you.

When there's a moon, the shadows in the house grow long,
invisible hands draw the curtains,
a ghostly finger writes in the dust on the piano—
forgotten words—I don't want to hear them. Be still.

Let me come with you
a little ways down, as far as the brick factory's low wall,
there where the road turns and you can see, suddenly,
the cement yet airy city, whitewashed with moonlight,
so indifferent and immaterial,
as positive as metaphysics,
that at last you can believe you exist and do not exist,
that you have never existed, that neither time nor its ravaging
         ever existed.
Let me come with you.

We shall sit for a while on the low wall, there on that height,
and as the spring wind blows about us
we may even imagine we shall fly
because many times, even now, I hear my dress rustling
like the flapping of two strong wings beating the air;
and when you enclose yourself within that sound of flying
you feel that your throat, your ribs, your flesh have grown firm;
and thus tightly wedged within the muscles of blue air,
within the vigorous nerves of the elevation,
it doesn't matter whether you go or come back,
nor does it matter that my hair has turned white,
(This is not my sorrow—my sorrow is
that my heart, also, has not turned white).
Let me come with you.

I know that every human being goes his way alone toward love,
alone toward glory and toward death.

I know this. I've tried it. It doesn't help.
Let me come with you.

This house has become haunted, it repels me—
I mean to say—it's grown very old, its nails are falling out,
its picture frames tumble down as easily as though plunging
        through a void,
its plaster falls as noiselessly
as the hat of a dead man from its peg in a dark corridor,
as the worn woolen glove from the knees of silence
or as a strip of moonlight on the old, gutted armchair.

Even it was new once—no, not the photograph you're looking at
        so incredulously—
I'm speaking of the armchair, very restful, where you could sit for
        hours on end
and with closed eyes dream of anything
—of smooth, sandy beaches, wet, polished by the moon,
even more highly polished than the old patent-leather shoes I send
        every month to the corner shoestand,
or the sail of a fishing boat that vanishes at sea, rocked by its own
        breathing,
a triangular sail like a handkerchief folded diagonally in two only,
as though it had nothing to cover up or hold,
a handkerchief to flutter wide in farewell. I was always crazy
        about handkerchiefs—
not to keep anything tied within them,
like flower seed or camomile plucked in the fields at sunset,
nor to knot in each of their four corners like those worn by the
        workers of the half-built house opposite,
nor to wipe my eyes with—I've taken good care of my eyes,
and I've never worn glasses. A mere whim, those handkerchiefs.
Now I fold them in four, in eight, in sixteen,
simply to keep my fingers busy. And now I remember
that's how I kept beat to the music when I was going to the
        Conservatory
in a blue frock with white collar, with two blond braids
—8, 16, 32, 64—
clinging to the hand of a small friend of mine who was a peach
        tree, all sunshine and rose-colored flowers,

(forgive these words of mine—it's a bad habit)—32, 64—and my
       folks cherished
great hopes for my musical talent. Well, I was telling you about
       the armchair—
disemboweled—its rusty springs are showing, the stuffing—
I was thinking of taking it to the furniture man next door,
but where's the time or the money or the mood—what's one to fix
       first?—
I thought of throwing a sheet over it—but I was afraid
of a white sheet in such moonlight. Here sat
men who dreamt great dreams, even like you or me, that is to say,
and now they're resting under the earth where neither rain nor
       moon can trouble them.
Let me come with you.

We shall pause for a while on the top of the marble staircase of
       Saint Nikólaos
and then you shall walk down and I shall turn back,
retaining on my left side the warmth of your coat as it touched
       me by chance,
and even some square lights from small windows in the poorer
       neighborhoods,
and this pure white mist of the moon like a long retinue of
       silvery swans—
I'm not afraid of using such an expression because
on many a spring night, formerly, I have talked with God when
       He appeared to me
dressed in the haze and glory of such moonlight;
and many a young man, even more handsome than you, have I
       sacrificed to Him
as thus, white and unapproachable, I turned to mist in my white
       flame, in the moon's whiteness,
inflamed by the voracious eyes of men, by the hesitant ecstasy of
       youths,
besieged by splendid, sunburnt bodies,
vigorous limbs exercised in swimming, rowing, track, and soccer
       (though I pretended not to notice),
brows, lips, and throat, knees, fingers, and eyes,
chest and arms and thighs (as in truth I didn't notice)

—you know, at times, in admiring, you forget what you're
          admiring, your admiration is enough—
Dear God, what starry eyes, and I was lifted high to an apotheosis
          of stars denied
because, thus besieged from within and without,
No other road was left me but to go upward or downward.—
          No, it's not enough.
Let me come with you.

I know it's very late now. Let me come,
because for so many years, days and nights and crimson noons,
          I've remained alone,
unyielding, alone and immaculate,
even in my marriage bed, alone and immaculate,
writing glorious verses on the knees of God,
verses that will survive, I assure you—as though carved on
          faultless marble—
beyond your life or mine, much beyond. It's not enough.
Let me come with you.

I can't bear this house much longer.
I can't bear to keep carrying it on my back.
You must always be careful, very careful
to support the wall with the large buffet
to support the buffet with the carved antique table
to support the table with the chairs
to support the chairs with your hands
to place your shoulder under the dangling beams.
And the piano like a black coffin closed. You don't dare open it.
You must always be careful, very careful, for fear they'll fall, for
          fear you'll fall. I can't bear it.
Let me come with you.

This house, despite all its dead, does not intend to die.
It insists on living with its dead
on living on its dead
on living on the certainty of its own death
and even on accommodating its dead on dilapidated beds and
          shelves.
Let me come with you.

Here no matter how softly I walk in the evening's haze,
either in my slippers or my bare feet,
something or other will creak—a windowpane cracks, or a mirror,
certain footsteps are heard—they're not mine.
Outside in the street it's possible these steps cannot be heard—
repentance, they say, wears wooden clogs—
and if you try to look into this or that mirror,
behind the dust and the cracks,
you'll discern your face even more dim and more fragmented,
your face, though you asked nothing more from life than to keep
       it clear and undivided.

The rim of the water glass glitters in the moonlight
like a circular razor—how can I bring it to my lips?
No matter how thirsty I get, how can I bring it? Do you see?
I'm still in the mood for metaphor—this is still left me,
this assures me that I'm still here.
Let me come with you.

At times, as night is falling, I have the feeling
that outside the window the Gypsy is passing by with his old
       lumbering she-bear,
her fur covered with thorns and thistles,
raising a cloud of dust in the neighboring street,
a desolate cloud of dust that rises like incense in the twilight;
and the children have gone home for supper and are not allowed to
       go out again
though behind their walls they guess at the plodding steps of the
       old bear,
and the bear proceeds wearily in the wisdom of her loneliness, not
       knowing where or why—
for she has grown heavy, she can't dance on her hind legs any
       more,
she can't wear her lace bonnet to amuse the children, the idlers,
       or those who make demands on her—
she only wants to lie on the ground,
letting them step on her belly, thus playing her last game,
showing her terrible strength for resignation,
her disobedience to the interests of others,
to the rings in her snout, to the needs of her teeth,

her disobedience to pain and to life
with an assured alliance with death—even though with a slow
     death—
her supreme disobedience to death with the continuation and
     knowledge of life
that ascends with knowledge and action above her slavery.

But who can play this game to its end?
And the bear once more rises and plods on,
obedient to her leash, to her rings, to her teeth,
smiling with her torn lips at the nickels and dimes thrown her by
     the beautiful and unsuspecting children
(beautiful precisely because they are unsuspecting)
and saying: thank you. Because the only thing
that bears grown old have learned to say is: thank you, thank you.
Let me come with you.

This house stifles me. The kitchen in particular
is like the bottom of the sea. The hanging kettles glitter
like the large, round eyes of improbable fishes,
the plates move sluggishly like jellyfish,
shells and seaweed catch in my hair—I can't pull them out
     afterwards,
I can't rise to the surface again,
the tray falls noiselessly from my fingers—I collapse
and watch the bubbles from my breath rising and rising
and I try to divert myself by watching them,
and ask myself what would someone from above say if he saw
     those bubbles—
that somebody was dreaming, perhaps, or that a diver was
     searching the sea's depths?
And in truth there in the depths of drowning I discovered, and
     not a few times only,
corals and pearls and treasures of shipwrecked vessels,
unexpected encounters, things of today and yesterday and of the
     future,
a verification, almost, of eternity,
a certain breathing spell, a certain smile of immortality, as they say,
a happiness and intoxication—an enthusiasm even,
corals and pearls and sapphires—

only, I don't know how to present them—and yet I do present
        them—
only, I don't know if the world is capable of receiving them—
        nevertheless, I present them.
Let me come with you.

One moment till I get my jacket.
In this unsettled weather, however, we should take care of
        ourselves.
The evenings are damp, and the moon—
well, don't you think it intensifies the chill?
Let me button your shirt—how strong your chest is!—
what a strong moon . . . the armchair, I say . . . and when I lift
        the cup from the table
a hole of silence remains under it, and immediately I cover it
        with my hand
that I may not gaze inside—I put the cup in its place again,
and the moon is a hole in the world's skull—don't look inside,
it's a magnetic power which attracts you—don't look, don't let
        anyone look,
listen to what I'm saying—you'll all fall inside. This dizziness
is beautiful and weightless—you'll fall—
the moon is a marble well,
shadows and wings are moving, mysterious voices—don't you
        hear them?
Deep, deep is the falling,
deep, deep is the rising,
the airy statue is firmly knit amid its outspread wings,
deep, deep is the implacable beneficence of silence,
tremulous illuminations on the other bank as you sway in your
        own wave,
the breathing of the ocean. This vertigo
is beautiful and weightless—be careful, you'll fall. Don't look at
        me,
for my role is to waver—the exquisite vertigo. Thus every day
        toward evening
I have a slight headache, a few dizzy spells.

Often I run to the drugstore opposite for a few more aspirins,
then at times I can't be bothered going, and remain with my
        headache

and listen to the hollow noise made by the waterpipes in the walls,
or I brew some coffee and, absent-minded as always,
forget and make enough for two—who will drink the other cup?
It's really amusing; I let it get cold on the windowsill,
or sometimes I drink the second cup too, gazing from my window
        at the green electric light of the drugstore,
like the green light of a noiseless train coming to take me,
with my handkerchiefs, my lopsided shoes, my black bag, my
        poems,
and with no luggage at all—of what use would it be?
Let me come with you.

Ah, you're going? Good night. No, I'm not coming. Good night.
I'll go out myself in a little while. Thank you. Because, really,
        I must get out
of this exhausted house.
I must see a bit of the city—no, no,
not the moon—
the city with her calloused hands, the city of the wage-earner,
the city that swears on her bread and her fist,
the city that can bear all of us on her back
with our trivialities, our vices, our hates
with our ambitions, our ignorance, our old age—
I hear the large strides of the city
that I may no longer hear your own footsteps
nor the footsteps of God, not even my own footsteps. Good night.

    *(The room grows dark. It seems that a cloud must have
hidden the moon. Suddenly, as though someone had
turned up the radio in the neighboring bar, an extremely
familiar phrase is heard. I understand then that this entire
scene has been accompanied softly by the* Moonlight
Sonata, *by the first part only. The Young Man now must
be descending the slope with an ironical and perhaps
compassionate smile on his beautifully chiseled lips, and
with a feeling of being freed at last. Just as he reaches
St. Nikólaos—before he descends the marble stairs—he
will laugh, a loud uncontrollable laugh. His laughter will
not sound at all discordant beneath the moon. Perhaps the
only discordant thing about it may be that it is not at all*

*discordant. In a little while the Young Man will fall
silent, he will turn sober and say: "The decadence of an
age." Thus, thoroughly calm once more, he will
unbutton his shirt again and continue on his way. As for
the Woman in Black, I don't know whether or not she
finally went out of the house. The moonlight glitters
once more. And in the corners of the room the shadows
stiffen and grow tense out of an unbearable repentance,
out of rage almost, not so much against life as against a
confession that was quite futile. Do you hear? The
radio continues:)*

BUILDERS

Have you seen those who build out of instinct
and those who build professionally
and the third who build to revenge themselves against death
and those who build consciously, with resolution?

Both these and the others stop from time to time,
wipe their plastered hands on their blue jeans,
wipe away their sweat, and weep.
They do not wipe their eyes.

In this way, moreover, the mortar knits better.
And this proceeds much *beyond* their purpose.
Because of this, all the builders dream at night
of that unknown, that invisible "beyond,"
and every morning they build the "here" a bit better.

ABSTRACTED PAINTER

A painter one afternoon drew a train.
The last carriage cut away from the paper
and returned to the carbarn all by itself.

In precisely that carriage sat the artist.

THERAPY

A historic weariness spread over the afternoon
like the hide of an animal spread out in a sick man's room.
The sick man always remained in bed. His fever had fallen.
A smell of sweat-drenched undershirt and alcohol. This hide
was taken from an animal skinned alive—this is what he maintained.
The fur, obedient, neutral, dead; but from the other, the naked
          side,
the dehydrated pain still remained, flattened out. He insisted on
          this:
the animal had been alive when it was skinned. And when at last
he placed his naked feet there, its hair stood on end,
the hide curved up and shaped a back, and the sick man
tore through the corridor astride the animal's back, whizzed
through the kitchen, dashed out into the yard, into the street,
and the pots boomed like metal drums.

MOMENT

A downtrodden sailor's quarter. The light globes sleepy.
Shabby beer pubs strung out in a row like poverty-stricken women
waiting without hope in front of the County Hospital.

The street is dark. Everyone planned to sleep early.

But suddenly
the beer pubs lit up to their very last chairs
from the pure white laughter of a young man. And immediately
        afterwards
was heard the endless, uniform, unconquerable sea.

CONFORMITY

This bronze statue had a position of its own in the midst of winter;
this horse's heroic stride as though it were leaping over
all-powerful, contrary winds; even the somewhat pompous
and haughty air of the horseman matched well enough
with the downpours, the bolting clouds and the storms
when lightning flashes changed the reins into two steadfast,
        narrow flames
until you couldn't tell whether the howling rose out of the
        wind along the naked avenues
or out of the statue's open mouth. But now
with this spring, relaxed, facilitated, acquiescent,
with this forgetful, this good-tempered light (perhaps out of
        timidity already,
or exhausted from the heat) with which available sunrays
bind up one leaf with another,
one tree with another or with houses,
one glance with another or with mouths—the attitude
of the statue had now become unbearable, provocative, almost
        improper,
so much so that the bronze horseman himself dismounted,
called three unemployed who were waiting in the park with
        pickaxes,
and began, perspiring and satisfied, to tear his statue down.

HONEST CONFRONTATION

All night long they talked, raged, wrangled,
strove with passion and sincerity to find some compromise, a
        separation,
humbled and were humbled; regretted
the lost year—foolish people; at last they cast off their clothes
and stood beautiful, naked, humiliated, and unprotected. Dawn
        was breaking.
From the roof opposite, a flock of birds took wing
as though some gambler had finally cast into the air a marked
        pack of cards.
Thus, without proof, justification, or guarantee,
day ascended from the hills with the cruel pride of action.

FOR GREATER ACCURACY

He would always return to the same theme. One and one—he kept
        repeating,
simply in order to convince himself—make two. Two and two:
        four. But then,
before he could make this addition, the slightest interval
would intervene, a slight breath, and then he felt the need
to add even this, for greater accuracy—a breath—
and behind its vapor the same number could be discerned
as though written on a door or on the sides of a ship,
or like a star behind a light veil of mist at that quivering hour,
so very beautiful, between the twilight and the night.

THE BUCKET

You've seen a bucket drawn from the depths and emptied
ever so many times, filling water jugs, watering flowers.
Now, upside down, beside the well, it turns its back to the sun—
a circular void, a half kettledrum (if you struck it,
it would give out a rhythm only, without song),
a perfect glossy zero; while in its cavity,
still damp and cool, several naked, prehistoric reptiles
take shelter, sluggish, meaningful, sticky.

MISCONSTRUCTIONS

The first drops of rain struck the sea. Being young, they didn't
    mind.
Though their hair and clothes became drenched, they laughed. At
    last
they opened their umbrellas—a whole forest of umbrellas,
blue, yellow, violet, but above all black,
the sea for background, and a boat in the distance
lightly leaping from umbrella to umbrella. This he liked much
    better,
as though the umbrellas were not made for the rain
but the rain for the umbrellas. Many years ago—how many?—
and could he simply be an onlooker and yet be young,
always an onlooker, observing himself, and always young?—
without an umbrella, in the rain, a few feet away,
changing his distance under the necessity for perspective,
his physical distance, alone in this distant happiness of his.

ANCIENT AMPHITHEATER

When toward noon the Greek youth found himself in the center
of an ancient amphitheater, and yet as handsome as They had been,
he let out a shout (not of astonishment, for astonishment
he felt not at all and, even if he had,
would certainly not have shown it), a simple shout,
perhaps out of the untamed joy of his youth
or simply to try out the acoustics of the place. Opposite,
from the precipitous mountain, the echo answered—
the Greek echo, which does not imitate or repeat
but simply continues to a height immeasurable
the eternal cry of the dithyramb.

A TREE

This tree had taken root in the far side of the garden,
tall, slender, solitary—perhaps its height
betrayed a clandestine idea of intrusion. It never produced
either fruit or flower, only a long shadow that split the garden
      in two,
and a measurement at variance with the stooped, laden trees.
Every evening, when the glorious sunset had vanished,
a strange, orange-colored bird roosted silently amidst its foliage
like its only fruit—a small golden bell
in a green, enormous belfry. When the tree was cut down,
this bird flew about it with small, savage cries,
describing circles in the air, describing in the sunset
the inexhaustible shape of the tree, and this small bell
rang invisibly on high, and even higher than the tree's original
      height.

STONES

The days come and go without haste, without surprises.
The waters become drenched with light and memory.
One sets a stone for pillow.
Another, before swimming, leaves his clothes under a stone
so that the wind won't take them. Another keeps a stone for stool
or as a boundary mark on his farm, the cemetery, the sheepfold,
      the forest.

Late, after sunset, when you've returned home,
whatever stone from the seashore you placed on your table
is a statuette—a small Nike or the hound of Artemis,
and this stone, on which a young man at noon leaned his wet feet,
is a Patroclos, with shadowy, closed eyelashes.

MOMENT OF REVERENCE

They sieved the beach sand and loaded the wagons,
dripping with sweat in the burning heat. Past noon,
they undressed, mounted their horses, and plunged into the sea,
blackened by the hair on their bodies, gold in the searing sun.
    A handsome youth
uttered a cry and dropped his hand on his groin. The others
sped to him, lifted him on their arms, laid him on the sand,
and looked at him silently, gaping, until one of them
with reverence took away the hand from the groin,
and then all in a circle around him made the sign of the cross.
The horses, drenched, all-golden, sniffed at the far horizon.

PLASTER MODEL

When he closed his eyes he could remember nothing of the
     summer,
only a golden haze and his ring warm on his finger,
but still more the naked, broad, sunburnt shoulders of a young
     farmer
whom he managed partly to see behind the willows—at two in the
     afternoon—
as he was returning from the sea—an odor of burnt grass
     everywhere.
At that very moment the crickets shrilled, and a ship's siren blew.

Statues, of course, are made much later.

ALMOST A CONJUROR

From a great distance, he lowers the lamps, moves chairs
without touching them. Tired, he takes off his hat and fans
     himself.
Then, with a sweeping movement, he takes three playing cards
from the side of his ear. He dissolves a green, painkilling star
in a glass of water, stirring it with a silver teaspoon.
He drinks the water and the spoon, becomes transparent.
A goldfish can be seen swimming around in his chest.
Then exhausted, he lies down on the couch and closes his eyes.
"I have a bird in my head," he says. "I can't get it to come out."
The shadows of two vast wings fill the room.

ASCENT

He sat for days in a stranger's field, always planning
to climb up the stripped fig tree secretly one day and gaze
at the world from on high, with a leaf's sensation
or that of a bird, but always someone would pass by,
and so always he kept putting it off.
                                    One twilight
he looked carefully about him—not a soul—and clambered up
to the highest branch. It was then
voices were heard among the bushes: "What are you doing up
        there?"
Loud voices, and he answered: "A fig,
there was a last fig here." The branch broke.
They raised him up. His right hand was tightly clenched.
When they forced open his fingers, they found nothing.

THE FIRST SENSUAL DELIGHT

Proud mountains, Kallidromon, Oeta, Othrys,
dominating rocks, vineyards, wheat fields and olive groves;
here they have dug quarries, the sea has withdrawn;
the heavy fragrance of bulrushes burnt by the sun,
and resin dripping in thick clots. A large
descending evening. There by the bank, Achilles,
not yet an adolescent, as he held his heel
in tying his sandal, felt that singular sensual delight. For a while
he paused and gazed abstractedly at the water's reflections. Then
he went to the ironmonger's and ordered his shield—
he knew precisely its shape now, its scenes, its size.

REVERSE SIDE

He said: "Even solitude is an answer."
He paused. Considered: "To what?"
Moon, beautiful loss, exhaustion,
ancient coin, I shall turn you on your other side
to see the sculptured profile of a youth
shaded by a horse's tail and a helmet.

THE PEACOCKS OF PYRILAMPES

Why in the world did Pyrilampes, that man of taste, want to
      carry off
those peacocks from the court of the Persian king?
Inappropriate on Hellenic soil, swaggering
with their vulgar coat of many colors on Periktione's
pure-white marble staircase. Of course the crowd
admired them extravagantly. And perhaps Pyrilampes
brought them to Athens not for their feathers
but for their one unique croak. Plato, it is certain,
knew why. Moreover, even then, did not the ancients paint
their words and water jugs and faces and statues?
Even though all these today seem dazzlingly white?

AFTER THE RITUAL

With the voices, the noise, the beautiful multicolored garments,
we forgot ourselves completely, nor did we raise our eyes
toward the high temple pediment cleansed only a month ago
by workers on erected scaffolds. However, when night fell
and the tumult had quieted down, the youngest of our company

cut away, ascended the marble stairs again and stood
alone in that empty space where the morning's ceremonies were
       held.
As he stood there (and we a bit behind him, so as not to be
       left out)
with his beautiful head raised lightly, absorbed, drenched
in the June moonlight, he gave us the impression
of being part of the pediment. We approached him, therefore,
clasped one another by the shoulders, and once more descended
the many steps. Nevertheless, it was as though
he had remained there, naked, enmarbled, withdrawn,
amid the youthful gods and the horses.

DISPLACEMENT

No matter how much he called them "harmless," there was always
       a danger
lurking in a color, a movement, when opening
a door in or out, when emptying
the glass ashtray out the window, for sometimes the wind
would blow the cigarette butts into the room, and the dust into
       his eyes,
and then he was obliged to kneel and pick up the butts one by one.
It was in precisely this position we found him, as though he were
       praying,
and perhaps in truth he was. "No, no," he said,
and spread out his palm for proof, the cigarette butts
arranged in rows like those lead soldiers who, it is safe to say,
never took part in any battle. Nevertheless, we could see in his
       face
the extremely cunning triumph of the totally defeated.

GRADATIONS

Euryalo's improper words wrongfully enraged Odysseus.
Improper he wanted them, and so spoke them. A merchant, he
      said,
who cares only for his merchandise and lawless profits,
and not for noble contests. Thus did he speak, and Odysseus
and the other succeeded in lifting up the large discus
and flinging it beyond all the other marks, with such a whistling
that the long-oared Phaeacians cowered (even though we do
      not take into account
how the invisible Goddess grooved the mark a good bit
      beyond).
Even so, how many other improprieties have there not been,
and these without the noble intentions of an Euryalos,
plain improprieties that have never succeeded in arousing
our strength? One should feel sorry for all
this sleeping power, and not at all for such improprieties.
And the worst of it is that one feels sorry *only* for these.

MEMORIAL SERVICES

The youthful stone hand on the chair;
the headless torso before the mirror;
a solitary foot in its marble sandal
going elsewhere (not unsuspectingly) among
objects rendered useless: paper roses,
fresh asphodels.
            "These, at least"—he said—
"these have not been lost; not everything is lost, you know."
"Nothing is lost," he added (the constraint
was evident in his hands).
              "Nothing is lost,"
the old women repeated, cleaning grains of wheat

in large white platters, boiling the wheat
in a wide copper kettle. "Nothing. Nothing,"
they repeated, and wept, leaning their heads
on the shoulders of the steadfast steam in the kitchen.

Aunt Lahó brought in the tray and sugar,
set them on the table, stepped aside,
turned toward the wall, and licked her fingers.

WHITEWASH

With the years, purely by chance, they replaced
the white of marble with the whiteness of slaked lime—a
            whiteness, of course
much more blinding, more on the outside—it simply was needed:
there were too many scrawls and sketches on the walls. Now,
one after the other, they whitewash the courtyards, the
            flowerpots, the stones,
and even trees, up to the middle—a kind of clarity, a cleanliness.
It smells of health, so that now the sidewalks and churches glitter
with a new classical simplicity—something entirely ours. At dusk,
they place a pot of geraniums on the low whitewashed wall
and gaze out at sea. On her threshold across the way, Madam
            Pelayía
seems to be furious—her black widow weeds are splattered
with drops of whitewash, as though flowering with small daisies.

THE STAIRS

Up and down the stairs he went. Little by little
the going up and the coming down became confused in his
            weariness,
took on the same meaning—no meaning at all. The same spot
on a revolving wheel; and he, unproceeding,
bound to the wheel, with the illusion that he was traveling,

feeling the wind combing his hair back,
observing his companions, successfully disguised
as bustling sailors, pulling on nonexistent oars,
plugging up their ears with wax, although the Sirens
had died at least three thousand years ago.

Níkos Kavadhías

MAL DU DÉPART

I'll always be the ideal, the unfit lover
of distant voyages and azure seas,
and I shall die one night, a night like the others,
and not have pierced the horizon's misty line.

And though ships always proudly set their sails
For Sfax, Madras, Algiers and Singapore,
still in some office I'll stoop over sailing charts
or add up sums in thick accounting books.

I'll soon stop talking of far voyages;
my friends will think they've faded from my mind,
and mother in joy will tell all those who ask:
"It was a youthful whim, but now it's past."

But my own self one night shall rise before me
and like a dry judge ask me to give cause,
until this unworthy, trembling hand of mine
shall take aim fearlessly and shoot the offender.

And I, who have longed to find my grave one day
in some sea deep in the far distant Indies,
shall have a very common, wretched death,
and a funeral like that of all the others.

A KNIFE

Thrust in my belt, I always carry with me
a small steel knife made deep in Africa,
like those which the Arabians like to wield,
bought from some secondhand dealer in Algiers.

I remember as though it were today how that
old merchant looked, like some old Goya oil,
erect by long swords and tattered uniforms,
telling me this strange story in a hoarse voice:

"This knife here, which you say you want to buy,
legend has wrapped with most peculiar tales,
for all here know that everyone who once
has worn it has soon killed some man of his.

"With this knife Don Bazilio killed his Julia,
his lovely wife, because she played him false;
with this knife Count Antonio one dark night
killed his unfortunate brother secretly,

"an Arab his young mistress jealously,
and some Italian sailor a Greek coxswain.
From hand to hand it fell into my hands.
I've seen much, but this makes my blood run cold.

"Look closely, here's an anchor, a coat of arms.
Hold it. It's light. It weighs no more than a quarter.
But I'd advise you to buy something else."
"How much?" "Seven francs. Then take it, since you want it."

Thrust through my belt, I wear a small stiletto.
Some strange quirk made me make it mine, but since
there's no one I hate enough in the world to kill,
I'm afraid I'll turn it on myself one day.

A NEGRO STOKER FROM DJIBOUTI

When they relieved him of his all-night shift,
Willy the Negro stoker from Djibouti
would come to find me in my cabin, laughing,
and talk to me for hours of strange things.

He told me how in Algiers they all smoke pot,
in Aden how they dance and take white powder,
of how they shout and babble afterwards
when dizzy spells enfold them in strange dreams.

Of how one night, well potted, he'd seen himself
galloping on white steeds on the sea's back
as full-winged mermaids followed in pursuit.
When we reach Aden, he said, you'll try yourself.

I always gave him sweets and razor blades
and warned him that hashish can kill a man,
but he would laugh uproariously, and with
one hand he'd raise me high up toward the ceiling.

In his huge body beat an innocent heart.
One night in the Regina Bar, in Marseilles,
he was trying to guard me from some Spanish lout
when an empty bottle crashed down on his head.

One day in the Far East we left him parched
with fever, his body in flames, wasting away.
God of all blacks, forgive good Willy now.
Wherever he is, give him some white powder.

WILLIAM GEORGE ALUM

Once working on a foreign ship, I knew
a curious Englishman, a stoker there
who rarely spoke, had not a single friend,
but always smoked a carved pipe by himself.

All said that his was a heartrending story,
and those who worked with him in the furnace room
told us that long ago in distant ports
he'd had himself tattooed from neck to toe.

His arms were stippled full of swords and crosses,
a naked ballet girl danced on his belly,
and on his side above the heart, a girl
of savage beauty was indelibly tattooed.

They said he once had loved this girl with a love
most savage, unrestrained, profound, and true,
but she had been a common, callous girl
and had betrayed him with an Arab sailor.

He tried to blot out of his mind completely
the exotic beauty he once adored so deeply,
and threw away all that recalled her, but
the tattoo persisted where his heart had been.

The stokers often saw him, deep in the night,
rubbing his chest with herbs of various kinds.
But all in vain. He knew—as we all knew—
that the stigmata of Annam would never vanish.

One night as we steamed out of the Bay of Biscay
we found him with a knife thrust in his chest.
Our skipper said: "He tried to erase the stain,"
and ordered him buried in the freezing sea.

A MIDSHIPMAN ON THE BRIDGE
IN AN HOUR OF PERIL

In the ship's log we wrote: "Cyclones and hurricanes."
We've sent our S O S far off to other ships,
and as I gaze, gone pale, on the wild Indian Ocean,
I doubt that we shall reach Batavia one day.

But I don't give a stinking damn. They say that we,
who roam the seas, have sold our grim souls to the devil.
I'm thinking only of a mother, worn and sad,
who through long years has waited for her son's return.

I know we find ourselves in imminent peril now.
The sea has overwhelmed the bridge with pounding waves,
but my one sorrow is that now I shall never tell
a living soul some things that rack me dreadfully.

Dear God, although I'm only nineteen years of age,
I've roamed time after time to far-off distant shores.
Dear God, although I've still the pure heart of a child,
I've wandered much in error and have sinned so much.

Forgive me, God . . . Once in Algiers, after I'd had
too much to drink and didn't know what I was doing,
I flung my knife deep in some stranger's chest, and all
for a young Arab girl who was dancing in the nude.

Forgive me, God . . . On a dark night in Sante Fe,
as some whore held me tightly clasped within her arms,
I slipped out of her stocking-top a roll of bills
that she had toiled all day to earn in her crude trade.

And still more, Lord . . . I blush with shame to think of it,
(ah but his lovely lips were so rose-red and moist,
and somewhere a Spanish guitar raised its lone wailing cry)
I slept with a young Jewish boy one night in Seville.

O Lord . . . my body, burdened with so many sins,
will soon fall dead and drown in these deep watery jails,
and I keep thinking always of four golden stripes
and a sad midshipman who never shall wear them now.

MARABOU

All sailors I have bunked with say of me
that I'm a thick-skinned roughneck, and depraved,
that I despise all women treacherously,
that never once have I shacked up with them.

They even say I take hashish, cocaine,
that some vile, loathsome passion grips my soul,
that my whole body is deeply stigmatized
with lewd tattoos, disgusting and perverse.

They also speak of still more dreadful crimes
that are crude myths and fabricated lies;
but that which cost me my deepest lethal wound
not one man knows: I've told no living soul!

For when at twilight tropic nights have fallen
and flocks of marabou fly toward the West,
something persistent goads me to write down
what has become my endless, secret wound.

I was midshipman once on postal ships
that sailed the Egyptian line to southern France,
and knew her then—a white Alpine flower—
until close filial ties bound us together.

The aristocratic, frail and melancholy
child of a rich Egyptian who had killed
himself, she sailed her sorrow to far lands,
hoping to drown her deep grief somewhere there.

She almost always read Bashkirtsev's *Journal*
and madly adored the Saint of Avila,
she'd often read to me French mournful verses
and gaze for hours on the sea's expanse.

And I, who'd only known the flesh of whores
and had a spineless and sea-battered soul,
found by her side my long-lost childhood joys
and listened as to a sibyl, ecstatically.

Around her throat I hung a small gold cross
and she in turn gave me a handsome wallet;
on earth there was no sadder man than I
that day we reached her port of debarkation.

Sailing the freighters, I called constantly
to mind my patroness, my guardian angel,
until her photograph by the prow became
a green oasis in the desert's heart.

I think that I should stop my story here,
for my hand trembles, the torrid wind inflames me.
Here gorgeous riverine tropic flowers stink,
a stupid marabou shrills in the distance.

But I'll write on . . . One night in a strange port
I soon got drunk on whiskey, gin, and beer,
until toward midnight, staggering heavily,
I took the road toward houses lewd and lost.

There where coarse women lure their sailor friends,
some whore in laughter suddenly snatched my hat
(an old French habit of street prostitutes)
and I tagged after, almost against my will.

Her room was small and filthy, like all the rest,
plaster hung down in shreds along the walls,
and she but human rags with a hoarse voice,
yet with strange, brooding, demon-driven eyes.

She dowsed the lights, and we flopped down together,
My fingers could quite clearly count her bones.
She stank of absinthe. I woke, as the poets say,
"as soon as dawn had strewn her rose-red petals."

When in the pallid morning light I saw
her plain, she seemed so sad and cursed a creature
that with an awe most odd, as though with fear,
I hurriedly took my wallet out to pay her.

Twelve sad French francs . . . But she screamed frantically
and stared with frightened eyes once on my purse,
once on my face, with horror. Then I, too, froze,
for round her throat I saw a small gold cross.

I rushed out like a madman, without my hat,
like one insane who lolls and staggers on,
but bearing in my blood a dread disease
that in great torment racks my body still.

All sailors I have bunked with say of me
that it's been years since I've shacked up with girls,
that I'm a roughneck, that I take cocaine.
If the poor wretches only knew, they'd all forgive me . . .

My hand shakes . . . fever . . . I've lost count and stare
at a still marabou by the riverbank
that stubbornly stares at me. We're both alike,
I think, in loneliness and stupidity.

FOG

Since last night the fog has fallen,
vanished now the lone ship's lantern,
and you've come unlooked, unhoped for,
staring in my steering cabin.

Your white dress is drenched with spray;
I plait gaskets in your hair.
Down in far Port Pegasos
in this season rains are falling.

There in ambush lies the stoker;
both his feet are bound in chains.
Never look at mainyards when
storms are raging; you'll grow dizzy.

Coxswain curses the vile weather,
Tocopilla lies far distant.
Better periscopes, torpedos
than to wait and sweat in fear.

Go! Firm land is your abode.
You've not seen me, though you've come.
Long past midnight I've lain drowned
miles beyond the Hebrides.

ARMADA

Captain Jimmy's pirate ship
on which you too will soon embark
is laden with hashish and pot
and keeps its lantern on the stern.

It's months now since we set our sails,
and with the assistance of the weather
until we land in far Peru
we'll have smoked up all our cargo.

We sail on seas that are crammed full
with all sorts of exotic plants,
an ancient sun stares down at us
and now and then gives us a wink.

The hatches are all empty, dark.
How have thousands of tons vanished?
In Chile every empty pipe
and custom guard awaits our coming.

And the North Star has been forgotten,
all anchors have been lost at sea.
On the rope ladders row on row
twelve sirens hang and dangle down.

The Gorgon on the prow one night
leapt down into the sea, dead drunk,
and by her side as convoy glid
five of Columbus' cursed crew.

Then on the reefs of Akora
the savage waves will spew us out,
monsters painted a deep crimson
with wings of gulls stuck on our heads.

Andréas Karandónis

OLD HOROSCOPES

You may be certain Mr. Silvester that my shop is one of the best.
I do not want to say *the* best because everyone that exalteth
        himself shall be abased
and no one can ever know the kind and moment of his
        punishment.
When I was born a thousand beings were born with me
with specified time limits prescribed to each
for works, learning, love, pilgrimages to monasteries,
for vacations by the sea or in the mountains
and for the highest offices of the State.
I, of course, was born a male. As you can see, Mr. Silvester.
My parents rejoiced and my father celebrated my birth
by shooting three times at the roof tiles opposite
while trees glittered in the snow, for a heavy winter had encircled
        the earth.
Men shouted with joy and my father
opened the window and fixed his eye on the first star there
—and it so happened that only a single star had remained in the
        sky that night,
the one we call Hesperos.
My father thought that by beseeching the star
they would come to an agreement between them regarding my
        destiny.
What father doesn't want his son to become king?
But as you see Mr. Silvester I have not become king
or anything like it.

529

I've made a name for myself of course in the community as a good
        businessman.
I've one of the best shops in our city.
If this star we call Hesperos
could descend low on the horizon and set a date for our meeting
there behind that last clump of trees,
I would go with pleasure, leaving my work for a little while—at a
        loss of course—
And I would ask it
Why it hadn't taken into account my father's glance,
The beseeching glance of my poor father. . . .

A MAN

There are no personal stars in my firmament
but only the familiar stars of night
strewn with the indifferent hands of the Maker—
since then, O Creator, your hands have remained
motionless in the shape of a cross, and we bow to your grace.

(The lady with the silver fingernails goes traveling
but I cannot follow her,
she's accompanied by a man who's indifferent to her
and unaware of my own passion—
if he knew, perhaps he might have given her to me
but I couldn't have accepted because I'm a cavalier.)

And now, rapping on your door
with three discreet knocks
or telephoning you round about midnight
I can introduce myself:

Propagandist of efficient apparatus for disinfecting
harbors of epidemics
municipal offices of flies
and hearts of false hopes;

untiring customs official of ancient ideas
and connoisseur of food recipes and quack nostrums
an approximately good prophet of election results
gay deceiver of women of the third or fourth category
amateur writer of feature articles only during fund drives
or when churches are built for the melancholy fits
of peasants with their shabby clothes;
thus, with uncertain annotation, I speak to you of the misconduct
       of others
—my own is no small matter—
and I'm indifferent to the unending parade of my fellow men
before their own objectives:
how boring are all our neighbors' objectives!
With a flower in mind
or even in hand or nowhere at all,
with a permanent an overclouded tie
I forget my daily bread for the sake of my daily bread
and love for the sake of love,
I squander time for fear of growing old
cut in half every gold coin proffered me
throwing half to the old and half to the new
but snarling up both old and new,
and the lady with the silver fingernails goes traveling
she may even have arrived at her objective
and is now standing completely naked before her mirror
not for him beside her but for the bitterness
of the No One she has never met or whom she thinks
she once encountered during a swim
though fate did not desire them to become One. . . .

As the stars proceed uninterruptedly in the night
—and I must sleep since I'm a working man—
they force me to finish and to conclude that
whether others remove me or place me somewhere
my sensations are always:
a little hunger, a little thirst, a little sensuality
and a good mood when I look on grass.

Perikles Crookshade or John Doe
from the village of Lakkiá near Lake Veghorítis.

A LADY

Perhaps one day you too will meet her
this woman so well known to all of us, Mrs. Básta.

She's not tableware—she's a low hill
of dreams,
a timetable,
a brooding meditation long after the encounter.

No one expected her when she first appeared
with a gold pin tied to her dress—
since then she's been identified with miles and miles of sea
with tempestuous rain outside an empty tavern
and I'm constantly pushing her hair
out of my eyes;
it keeps falling into my eyes as though it were my own
and makes it difficult for me to see her again and again;
besides, I don't even know where she lives
even though we dwell in the same neighborhood,
nor could I find her name in the telephone book;
of course she probably doesn't frequent our harbors
nor does she think on trees,
the poor thing.
I know what occupies her:
pins, rubber bands, perfumes, hair nets
colors, glassware, pastry, learning French, fresh vegetables
and a body like a candle in flames;
but I, poor wretch,
have no place in her memory.

Poor Mrs. Básta.

Even so I like knowing she exists,
like the frontiers of nations we shall never cross,
but they do symbolize something

for we may plant dream flags there
and appoint customs officials dressed in gold embroidery.

We may encounter her sometimes
about the harbor with its fruit-bearing trees
and its cobwebbed clouds which are the only things sailing
in its mercurial waters
in those waters that took her and drowned her,
this woman unknown to all of us, Mrs. Básta
this woman so well known to all of us, Mrs. Básta.

AT GALVARNA

I too was at Gálvarna. Don't forget me,
I beg of you. Reporters, journalists, historians,
editors of almanacs, investigators of orgies,
spies, wireless operators, informers,
representatives of dream syndicates,
do not forget,
I too was at Gálvarna. Under what circumstances?
Oh, I don't remember. It's you who'll have to tell me.
It might have been in the morning, it might have been at night,
I may have been young or old—what does it matter?
I held a flag or a spear, cornstalks or flames,
perhaps. I might also have been a roofless prophet
like those our neighbors chase from their doors
at noon with stones.
But what's important
is that I too was at Gálvarna.
I'm afraid of talking about such tall tales.
Ask the postman or some old witch.
What I was doing at Gálvarna or who had sent me
I don't know, and now I wouldn't want you to know.
Something good must have happened to me down there,
or something bad—who can be so choosy?
I'd known a certain carriage driver named Boozy,
though I'm not sure he ever lived,
or perhaps only the rhyme popped him out of death

together with ruins and running water.
At Gálvarna I met Ólafo. He was a god,
he became President, and then he too grew old
with many others, together with thousands of things.
What's to be done with "worn-out slippers
and the consumptive moon,"
or, to put it another way, what's to be done with men?
The technique of one differs from that of another
but for all of us at times a lady appears
who'll throw down her rope ladder from the high battlements,
one we never expected to find as we read philosophy
at Gálvarna. Where once I was. I remember:
two rusted lampposts right and left of the stairs in the harbor
that went up into the fishing village. And she'd taken
one of them in her arms, as we were leaving,
and waved to us with her handkerchief
in the sun. A green sea
awaited us. The village dwindled away
in the distance. We could still see the lampposts
and the harbor stairs, and further still
a single cypress tree—the only one they had
at Gálvarna, watered with their tears.
Once I too had sat under its shade
and now the wind was taking me
far out into the new sea,
alone, without companions,
with a straw hat for the sun, and dark glasses;
within these glasses, at the height of noon,
the rusted lampposts vanished.

A SEA

When her hair covered the telephone
the whole world resounded with love.

Hands passed before her eyes
but she brushed them away as though they were clouds,
keeping a room in mind.

The plebeian paused before her bitterly,
measured her stature and went off

to sea—and others waited
their turn to telephone

those who accept calls incorporeally,
take notes, and die.

Tell her not to leave, to remain there still
until I may be reborn that we might meet.

The first time Roughneck saw her
his eyes filled with knives.

"Cynthia," shouted the mute beggars
against the walls—and were forgotten.

I plead with Hierarch Time
to locate me in her current.

I shall melt down all
my gold heirlooms to sing of her.

I saw her once in Thessaloníki
and died with her—but now

she's taken another face, mixed in with the crowd,
vanished in the shops of night

and is always telephoning, her hair
cornstalks in the telephone, her feet

planted in black earth, her hand
with its green fingers suspended in air.

AVAILABILITY

Green leaf being born, you exist before your birth;
you appear somewhere and someone sees you from his window
who has himself not as yet been born,
and the white leaf where the poem has not yet sprouted
exists for the poem that has not been born and shall be born,
(amid all these you are offered available positions
and you may select the place where you shall sing)
and the green leaf observed in a far country
falling one evening from its branch into a deep canal
of antediluvian tears and drowsy boats,
capped houses, vertical stairs, polite housewives,
things we collect by chance as they swirl
before our open window with this day's sudden wind.
To live is a double row of columns that fall to ruin
to sing is a harmony of dancing leaves
to remember is a litany of girls disappearing
behind a preparatory school on a hill
to think is a barn of harvested hay
to look is a girl standing
by a wall close to the sea as from the waterwheel,
remote and ruined, the flowing stream sweetens the salty water
and the girl gazing into the distance seeks the company of
                    strangers
and you watch her and drink of the mill water.
Not to see is to see the same girl again
in the same position the same waning moon the same distance
in the same summer—only that now she turns
a bit in this direction and whispers something;
to add is to place a pebble beside another pebble
to move is to know more land and water
to see the starry skies is a revelation
as though an eagle had clutched you by the chest
and taken you to Upper Chambers—but you fall once more on
                    grass;
to cry out is nothing more than to hear your voice

returning from somewhere near by as though it can't find a
      shelter,
to want or not to want is as though you are wanted or not
and all these and many other similar things
that you may have discussed by chance
are wonderful to carry about with you
from country to country and from person to person
say even from sea to sea
from the English Channel with its heavy ships and its gray
      grumbling
up to the brilliant beaches of our sunny seas with our third-class
      hotels
to small decrepit harbors
to our much-beloved small harbors
and to our available garden benches where night has fallen.

PHOTOGENIC STREETS

It's high time we believed with the priests of Apollo
we've been photogenic from the beginning of the world
and that the spiders of time, weaving us into periods of time
and a complex history of the darknesses of men
people and religions,
have not killed off, have not dimmed our photogenic qualities.
Our streets overbrim with sun night and day,
and following the voyage of Odysseus to Hades
over seas and lands but in particular
amid cities, they seek the sun like old wide swords.
On these photogenic streets
we walk, carefree beings,
and vanish in the light—or rather
we flicker on and off, and stroll on.
One by one I pass the morning houses, reading
on luminous plaques the names of landlords or tenants,
of doctors or lawyers, professional men or serious
scholars, but also of men
whom only a name symbolizes,

yet most luminous
with black letters on a bronze plaque
glittering in our photogenic flowering streets.
Thus in the light every morning, in the light every evening,
in the light of companions and secret sorrow,
with the small steps of an awkward pedestrian, I come and go
looking at doors and windows, balconies, faces of passersby,
all emerging from the light
into these our photogenic streets.
Sometimes you can't tell one thing from another. Sometimes
you'd think you were a saint with a halo around your head
and, frightened or proud, put up a hand to caress your glowing
wreath or your dream in the Apollonian winter.
Suddenly a woman turns into light and walks on.
A large-bodied woman on a ship. She has awakened
long before dawn
and dressed in front of you that she might tower over the waters
and see the sun as the first thing to explode in her eyes
and redden her breasts
which you still hold as though they were lights.
All the large streets of the sun opened out into the sea.
How photogenic our world is! And the island
on the other side of us slowly taking form
is light in the shape of a woman voyaging.

HORSE BREEDERS

What foul weather, unceasing rain, the cities filled with umbrellas
green, red, and sea-blue undulating beautifully on the sidewalks,
but the countryside is deadly, and the mountain slopes in the rain
and the curves on the highways with wretched inns
where horse breeders scurry out of the storm
in present or bygone times—it doesn't matter which.

It was then
the horse breeders went crazy
because their horses escaped,

those animals sleeping in stables and by trees
while the horse breeders lingered awhile in the bar
under the great church of the Virgin Mary,
chattering away among themselves about their affairs
cursing each other as they drank
and rubbing their hands because of the cold.
Many had left their horses tied to leafless trees
and a few in an unprotected stable,
and there they were, gabbing away about the secrets of their
            trade,
getting flushed with drink, banging on the table
for more wine, scowling at the stout girl
who kept running up and down the one stair at the inn.
They'd forgotten their horses and their horses' special problems,
and these, in an insane fit that had neither rhyme nor reason,
burst from their harnesses, rushed out of the stable,
uprooted five or six trees and two or three stakes,
and as the night groaned with anxieties and rain
the horses became metaphysics
and vanished into thin air.

Melissánthi

AUTUMN

Hour of dusk;
the skirt of the sky is wrung
and hung out to dry by autumn clouds;
and in the recess after rain
the snails come out to stroll
under the fading parasol
of the sun . . . Now earth,
that lamia, suns her wet wool blankets
adorned with the embellishments of meadows;
and from the grasses
and from the high pastures
waterdrops glide—beads
and pearls
of heavenly rings
that are gathered by Nereids, who weave
in their underground sunless grottoes and seraglios;
candelabra and silvery night lamps
are hung in hollows
and in nets of crystal spheres
by that old sorceress, the spider;
and one by one
insects of every kind
come crawling out of the earth
and from beneath the bark of trees
in a drunken carousal.
An ant clambers onto a blossoming thorn
and gazes at all the world from such a sunny lookout—

there, a furrow of water!—
and loiters lazily.
Over the straw raft, wherever it moors,
the frogs play leapfrog.
An entire cosmos of minute animals
sail in canoes of husks and walnut shells.
A cold shivering falls on the waters,
and now the siphon will strip
the dry leaves from the trees
like a swarm of butterflies.
The wind-shepherd blows his pipe
amid the reeds, and as he goes, goes, goes,
he shoos his flock of summers
to other haunts
and other winter pastures.

ATONEMENT

Every time I sinned a door half opened, and the Angels
who in my virtue had never found me beautiful,
tipped over the full amphora of their flower souls;
every time I sinned, it was as though a door had opened,
and tears of sweet compassion dripped among the grasses.
But if the sword of my remorse chased me from heaven,
every time I sinned a door half opened, and though men
thought me ugly, the angels thought me beautiful.

SUMMER HOURS

We have turned to marble in the bluing . . .
—ANDRÉAS KARANDÓNIS

Summer hours grow luminous in the mornings;
how many new faces, new footsteps, new voices,
beckonings from everywhere, radiances, messages,

which come and go with the light etesian wind
that drives the loosened hair of children wild
as they run barefoot on the sands.
And then it runs off to push our sailing vessels
in the midst of the sapphire sea.
We are crossed by so many birds of passage,
by so many banner-bedecked ships! . . .
They come and go laden with greetings,
watered with salt
and a sea nostalgia.
Together with the dawn, large schooners weigh anchor
and set out like birds,
taking from our tears the brine on their sails,
our greetings on the wings of seagulls.

The hours of summer blaze in midday,
scorch the earth, set the heart of rock vibrating,
pulse with the agitation of flame,
water with sun the roots of rock
where tamarisk bushes have sprouted,
the cool gulfs of the sea
who abandons herself to the play of dolphins
and complies with our daring adventures,
smiles like a mother,
holding our freshly painted boats
on her open palm,
dripping phosphorescent sparks from our oars.

Every hour of summer
throbs like a holiday bell
full of beckoning echoes and voices
in whose reverberations the skies deepen.
Every hour of summer
is a glance of the gods cast down to earth.

All things arrive from everywhere, they set out
to bring us the message of their presence;
converging from all points of time,
they consent in the flame of the moment,
burning in a great conflagration,

and the eternal present is created.
The hours of summer blaze,
scorch the earth, set the heart of stone vibrating,
and all test their existence
on the heartbeat of Time.
The new moment leaps, flame after flame,
in each of its pulses the miracle is completed,
and we exist, the world exists—we are encircled
by its evident secret—
with the clarity of the Sun
with the clarity of waves
with the clarity of rocks vibrating
in the blaze of noon.

The hours of summer grow luminous at evening,
the sea sings
like a happy mother
murmuring lullabies with sleep or with death,
and the eye, careless of the beckoning gestures
all things send us,
returns from wakefulness to sleep.
The lips, tired
after so many smiles and so much radiance,
turn back the wave of speech.

Behold, how all remain to be sung once more,
to glow once more in the lightning flash of the new moment!
Behold, how all remain to be named from the Beginning!

THE LAND OF SILENCE

The land of silence is made of crystal,
of blue crystal, like that of ice.
All things dance there noiselessly
and all images are refracted in eternity;
tears and the complaints of children
leave but the slight echo of a guitar.

Smiles of all silent creatures
raise to mid-heavens a rosy reflection,
and the deep eyes of love
blaze up with the blue flames of a conflagration.
In the land of silence whatever is genuine
is heard like a holiday bell
that opens up resounding domes in the heavens.
In the land of silence I often listened
to the silvery tintinabulations
raised by a certain flock of cranes.
I was present at mystic marriages,
at litanies, at celestial ceremonies
in the land of Silence, which is made of crystal,
of blue crystal, like that of ice.

ANCIENT SHIPWRECKED CITIES

Ancient shipwrecked cities
tell us of the omnipotence of Silence,
of her sudden overwhelming floods within their walls;
the snows of time are heaped on her breast;
in a slow movement voyaging,
the icebergs of millenniums proceed . . .
All set out from the primordial space of Silence
and return to her once more;
all are weighed on her bronze shield,
our words, our footsteps,
and our most deeply hidden thoughts.
Nothing can be lost,
not a secret tear, not the leaf of a tree,
not a single raindrop on the grass.

Her holy Night fills up with sacrilegious
ears and eyes.
The slaughter of the innocent steams in the meadows
—where the mirror of the moon has been misted over—
ransom for the profane guilt
of *knowing* and *existing*.

THE CIRCLE OF HOURS

I

The gray cock crowed at dusk.

The swirling rings of light softly settle
like ashes on dry leaves,
and slowly on the mountain ridges the day dissolves
like spring snow sweetly lingering
as from the primeval cold
of the untrodden woods
the sovereign night ascends.
Walls the light had raised in its open view
crack and crumble like dams
till the flood of darkness mounts,
and as the earth tosses on its waves,
it covers the mountains and drowns our homes.
It takes our voices and scatters them.
The Galaxies pour into the firmament
from the dugs of night
and in her gulfs are lit the seeds of suns.
All of creation clings to her breasts,
sucks without sound and slowly sighs.
The tresses of Night
have become entangled with the tresses of the sea.
Her stars wink in the waves
amid starfish and floating medusae.

We glide into the sea of sleep
and our memory sinks in moist moss.
Sea flora entwines us,
seaweed covers our eyelids,
entangles our feet, our hands,
and drags us down into the half-light of azure deeps.
We are tossed in a forest of sea vegetation,
in landscapes that heave
with the breathing of the sea.
Our body stops resisting the current

our breasts cease fighting the ebb tide
our hands stop battling with fate
in order to shape the hard metal of life.
The iron collar of law breaks
the known order of day vanishes
the amber necklace of names breaks
that gave us dominion over all things.
The image of the World is shattered into fragments,
—our memory is filled
with splinters of sky,
pallid moons, ghostly suns—
we ramble in green labyrinths,
we stumble in byways, we twist and turn in circles
in the enclosed space of sleep.

II

The black cock crowed: Midnight!

In this hour, time leaps up like a wave,
the flood drags the dead out of their graves.
Without footsteps, they proceed beyond all things
—the vision of the World has been enfolded within them—
and they advance amid the abysses
of the Former and the Now.
Not a single obstacle impedes them
and when the sleepers of Death reach
the third depth of Midnight, they merge
with the sleepers of Sleep.
Newborn stars cross the path
of extinguished suns.
Everything *happens* in the same space.
What has been and what is becoming
do not have special characteristics here
for they are all of the same age.

That which is becoming or has become
loses its irrevocable meaning;
all things could sometime have been
or never have been.
All things may come into being again in another way.

No one knows in what waters we are sailing
not even if we are making for the Open Sea
or whether we have anchored in the immobility
of a closed eternity.
We do not know if we are advancing or turning back
if we are waiting for our Death or our Birth.

The season of sleep weighs heavily on our breast
like an iron chopper.
Someone walked on her waves
someone made the miracle possible.
If we wished, we also could walk
on her breast
as on the breast of a mother.

III

The white cock crowed: Daybreak!

Four angels, sentinels of the day,
guard the four gates of the horizons
and with their wings cover
the open view of the world.
We return once more to the known day,
to the quiet light, to familiar faces and forms,
to known shapes.
We build cities of sand
we raise Cyclopean walls
to shelter us from the Unknown
from the chilling breaths of the Abyss.
The sun rains Lethe on our bodies
deceives us with colors
waters our memory with opium
with wine made of light,
blinds our eyes with radiance
so as not to see the evil eye of Night
that sometimes tears the sevenfold mantle of day.

Heedless of secret voices,
wise with the corners of our lips only,
we withdraw our hand from the companionable hand of Death,

our gaze from his brotherly gaze.
Again he becomes for us the silent stranger
who lies in ambush at every crossroads
like an assassin.
Beneath his mantle
he smiles with condescension,
hearing us calling him
by names to which he has no claim
with a voice that does not resemble ours
while in our fists we squeeze
our heartbeat like a bird.

IV

The red cock crowed: The Blaze of Noon!

—The shadows have gone to roost under the stones—
The sun turns on its eight-winged wheel
and inflames the firmament from end to end.
We remain locked within the circle of light
surrounded by familiar faces and forms
while Night besieges us invisibly,
and yet at any moment a chasm
may open in the uncracked expanse of the sky
and from any of its corners the Unforeseen may swoop
like a grasping hawk.
At any moment now,
and from whatever point in the heavens,
the storm may come.

ALIBI

When I died—a long time ago—they buried me
in a fictitious time. Afterwards
they hung on the wall an enlarged photograph
taken in my childhood years.
I was always thinking of slipping back, of returning

to put my things in some kind of order,
to tear up certain of my papers, and in particular
to hang up all my scattered clothing.
This mania for order is a trial indeed—
what a mess they must have found my room in after the funeral!

Once I returned on the sly.
My memorandum pad was still there on the table
with two columns of urgent things to be done,
written down on the night previous. "New soles
for my summer shoes." Really,
where has the time flown! We're already
in the middle of autumn. "Buy
a few nails." I can't possibly remember
what it was I wanted so badly to brace then.
"Telephone B. Not to wait for me
at the meeting." Did I wish to avoid a quarrel?
Perhaps it would've been better had I gone.
And yet I didn't. They came to the funeral.
I had a perfect "alibi."
And if any of them did not come
they would hear about it from the others.
"Tell the plumber to fix the faucet." It's still dripping.
Who knows how much the leak has added to my water bill
           by now!
And yet, this sound—plop . . . plop . . . plop . . .
is the only sound that can be heard within me still.
You'd think it continues me somehow as though
it were counting my absence since then.
And yet no one has noticed
that I've gone—perhaps only
my next-door neighbors—they came
and brought me some very lovely carnations.
They spoke with their eyes riveted
to the photograph on the wall. (Well then,
they still hadn't understood a thing!)
After all, there were many photographs
and everyone chooses the one he likes best.
I slipped away out of their sight
(for I was always afraid of frightening them).

"Isn't that you in there?"
I heard them saying from the kitchen
as they kept addressing the photograph.
They stressed their words in a strange manner
as though hinting at something or other
(or so it seemed to me). But as I returned
with a tray full of coffee, I replied without really wanting to,
"Yes, as you see, I went away a long time ago."
And again, no one looked at me. (Who is it
that's written about slips of the tongue? I don't recall.
As for being accident-prone, it'd be strange indeed
to break your backbone just to avoid making a decision.)
They all got up to go. Perhaps they'd been startled
by the door's banging when a chilly draft had blown in.
And as they left:
"Really, if you're going to the country this year
don't forget to leave us your address.
Let's not lose touch!"

AT THE REGISTRAR'S

—What's your name? —My name's M.
—Just M? —Yes, just plain M.
—No, we've had no instructions concerning you.
—That's not possible. Have you looked well?
—There's nothing, I tell you.
—Perhaps there's been some mistake?
—Impossible. See for yourself.
Here's the index of the Registration
Books. You don't exist.
You're not written down anywhere.
—I've told you, I've been written down in Archive A
for some thirty years now.
—We're consulting only the recent issues at the moment,
the letter H, for instance, or the letter K.
—Wait a moment. Did you say K?
Well then, I'm recorded
on page 34. Do you doubt it?

—I don't, but you've not been briefed
in the General Catalogue of names
and so your position's remained ambiguous.
Our new Registrar hasn't been able to find you.
—Your new Registrar? What's happened to Diogenes?
—He's aged terribly and grown myopic.
We've had to put his lantern on the auction block
and pension him off many years ago.

Well, as I was saying, we confine ourselves
to the General Indexes (it's a matter of saving time).
We live in the era of the speed of sound
and we'll soon attain the speed of light.
However, if you want to wait for Mr. Klamm,
you may sit down somewhere in the corridor.
Perhaps you'll be lucky enough to get a hearing.
—I've caught pneumonia five times
in your damned drafty corridors.
I've not much time left.
—I understand you very well,
but believe me, you're not the only one,
there are thousands in your position. You see,
in our times everyone wants to be insured
in the Registrar Books.
What can I tell you? When you consider that everything's
relative in the perspective of time,
you'll see that uncertainty
and doubt are something much more general.
Most of the time the orders cancel each other out.
An unheard-of confusion prevails.
How can you expect our new clerks
to take on such responsibilities?
Believe me, even here there's nothing that's certain.
A conflagration of carelessness, an atomic
war! If you want my opinion,
the greatest stupidity is trying to find
some sort of security in our world today.

As I was going toward the exit, the crowd
thickened in the corridors, in the offices.
Voices jammed to the point of suffocation,

an endless tramping up and down the stairs
(the entire building shook and reverberated)
as they descended and ascended without stop.
And all those who couldn't manage to stand back
were caught and crushed
between the two opposing currents—between
those who were leaving and those
who were swiftly arriving.

THE DAM OF SILENCE

Our world is here and their world is there
with not the slightest difference at all between them.
They both have the same dimensions. There is only
a dam made of glass, almost invisible,
which separates them. Many
do not know this, and visit us.
If no one tells them, they do not understand
and do not suspect anything—in the beginning.

We too have our houses here, trees,
streets, bars, restaurants,
assembly halls, corporations,
theaters, movie houses, cemeteries.
The only difference is that there the names
are inscribed not, as here, on sand,
but on hard granite or metal.

We still have social security
for those who arrive in great multitudes every day
from the other side of the dam.
Numberless are those badly injured
in automobile accidents, those secretly
murdered with the new atomic weapons of speech:
the microphones or the megaphones. These
we place for some time in solitary confinement
until they become habituated.

We cover up all mirrors
that they may learn nothing prematurely.

Thus we too are forced to deal with the problem of space,
with the anguish of overcrowding in centers of traffic congestion.
Meanwhile the parks remain almost desolate,
besieged by a great variety of noises
in the very center
of our silent city's roaring sea.
Nevertheless, we give them special care
in "Forest Lawn" that all who understand
may stroll about and then fall silent
by the side of those who do not know
and perhaps will never learn.

As for those who will not admit
they have come here permanently, and are always shouting
and troubling the common peace—
they become ridiculous to all.
Much more sympathetic are those who escape
with tranquilizers. Crises recur at regular intervals,
in cycles that slowly spread out
as on the serene surface of water.
As time goes by the sick learn
to take long walks by the sea
that invites us and waits for us always.
Of course there are those incurable ones
who keep everyone in a constant uproar
with untimely protestations, hoping
their words will be heard beyond the dam.

Many times they slip away secretly
but return quickly with head hung low
and relive the agony of their last moments from the beginning.
We always pretend we saw nothing, know nothing,
and fall silent out of sheer humanity.
And even we, who find ourselves still in the same space,
have difficulty in hearing
those who shout under water. We see only
the movement of their lips, their distorted mouths,

and if we didn't know better, perhaps we might have thought
they were smiling.

Our few visitors
finally begin to suspect something
and fly in panic in the opposite direction,
and even our most beloved cannot endure it
and forsake us—They do not understand
how much our two worlds are intertwined,
how much one extends into the other—
so much so that finally you cannot distinguish
which is the faithful reflection of the other:
the mirroring in the glass or in the water.

Only that among us the way up is the way down.
In order to ascend, we descend.
In order to approach, we retreat.

Behind the dam of silence, however,
the same jumble of voices,
the same contests in the dusty race courses.
Speed tracks, world records,
deadly embraces in wrestling rings,
celebrations, recitations, theatrical productions faultless
in the technique of acting (each one
of their actions a faithful portrayal,
secret or manifest)
faithful reflections in the glass
of their most unconfessed gestures.
With only this imperceptible difference—that there
their murderous weapons are as real as they
—but are they truly real?—
while here all things and all persons
are but a pale reflection of themselves.
Our masks and our murderous weapons are made of shadow,
our poison is imaginary, and everything else that happens here.
It is as though we kill, as though they die, as though everything
is an imaginary production
in an imaginary stage setting.
He who falls only seems to fall, seems to drown,

his blood only seems to be blood
(cheap makeup for the performance, nothing more)
and our only justification
is that whatever is done here—can it be undone?—is a game
of shadows, the mirroring of that
which is happening elsewhere in reality.

Perhaps another position in space
would be sufficient for the images to become reversed.
And our two worlds, since they seem exactly the same,
faithful reflections of one another, can no longer be told apart
to see which is real and which imaginary,
in this ambiguous light of the day and the night.

Alexander Mátsas

OF SLEEP

I

Sleep came and lay between us
like a rival. He took your eyes
and closed them; he took your lips
and swept away your smile and your kiss.

Your pale hair was combed by the tranquil
waters of Lethe that bore your beloved body
away to the world of stars and shadows.

Filters of silence are forcing your sealed lips,
sleep-living voices your ears, and in your veins
I hear the deep rumor of the voyage.

II

You have emerged from the depths of sleep
with stars and seashells in your hands
and in your eyes the dark coolness
        of seas.

When you open them, I want to be the first to receive
their glance, that I may capture before it fades
the meaning of that world which has kept you away
        the night long.

MIDDAY CONTEMPLATION AT DELOS

No shadow remains on column and rock
in the purification of absolute noon;
the divine axle nails Time down.
Light totally carves the dimensions;
    shine, O moment!

You also have stripped shadows away, O my torch,
body quietly burning toward death. Joy
and security of dust: let it be good
for other vessels more deep, more prodigal
    in echo and ecstasy.

Stop movement and stop decay, and cease
O loom of thought! Suspend
your vain thread, a flaw
in the mighty diamond, a worm
    in the all-radiant fruit.

O felicity of the column, cypress
of the Numbers! To the desperate imploration
the vein on my hand already replies,
little river of death, without oblivion,
    without escape.

Behold the cicada gone blind on the marble
column and suddenly silenced. You surge
everywhere and advance, O vanguard of darkness!
The divine vertical is shaken. Archer Apollo,
you bring back to me the bittersweet realm
    of imperfection.

SLEEP AT DELOS

You slept, your head shaded by a water jug
from the lamp's light. I was alone.
Your eyes were closed to me
and our kisses had been swept away
from your lips by the black milk of night.

Outside were stars and living columns,
islands and marble dolphins
on the sacred sea of the Cyclades,
a sea familiar to your body, the most graceful
of all that have swum in it. Your body
that vanishes now, a diver of Time.

Divine head, urn of serenity,
marmoreal in sleep, with your luminous eyes sealed,
what secret gods have snatched you away
to be their festive consort crowned
with the poppies of Lethe? Who holds now
this shell so splendidly filled
with sustenance of light and sea?

Only the rhythmical beat of your heart
measures your night-blooming footfall now.

AUBADE

A cistern of night, with coolness
and lethargy resisting the golden siege
of day, and of a dove
that on the rooftop blazons light,
and furnished with symbols of joy,
this room still keeps the beautiful body
a captive of sleep.

The night still nests in your hair,
in the conch of your ears, in the dark
breath that shakes the constellations
of your sealed eyelids. Dew
in your armpits and on your breast distills
the springtime of your body and the labor
of your secret immersion.

In these dark grape-clusters of your hair
from which the drunkenness of night wells up,
in this sealed amphora filled
with the quintessence of your hours
there ripens in starred fermentation
the all-radiant, the imminent day.

This body is to sun and wave
an offering acquainted with the play
of sunbeam on the eye and on laughter,
of the lightning feathers of foam:
worthy of column and tree,
vulnerable and richly corruptible
in the delicate equilibrium
of the Hermetic Numbers.

An infant, the soul rises to lips
bitter with the salt of the deep waters
of sleep. She shivers, numbed
in the forgetful eye that recounts
the dimensions of her dwelling, the hand
wise in the labors of life, the skin
experienced with the shudder of caress
and of death. A timid sibyl
forgetful of herself, she surrenders
to assimilation with the delightful tomb
of flesh that now begins to awaken.

O blissful dove, radiant
plume on our rooftop,
as light on the seabreeze
as foam that sprays the air,

awaken—O flutist of dawn—
movement within this divine statue
that night now delivers to me.

THE SEDUCTION

You turned your head toward darkness
as though you thirsted for silence and escape
beyond the equator which the lamp's light
traced on your nape and hair.

Your shoulders narrated tales
of seas and caryatids in the sun
and supported a golden burden of noons.
Adolescent nights nested in your hair,
in the dark wild vines and the olives
of a myth you did not understand.

O steps on the sand with heels
swift-winged and foaming, and without trace;
fulgurant dives in the waves amidst
a thousand broken plumes and arrows!
Engraved memory of your body on a bed,
images in eyes and in water,
are the witnesses of your existence,
the boundaries of your legend.

Fragment of beauty, warm statue
carved on the pediment of night
beyond identity and Time;
anonymous like a tree and detached
like a marble—what sibyl seeks
your gaze turned toward darkness?

What murmur of a deeper sea
you have never swum whispers
in the shells of your ears?—Desire,

bring back to me, O desire, the body
that with insoluble riddles
the Dark Rival is luring away.

AWAKENING

A shudder, a deep tide from the depths
that brings the soul trembling like a naked child
to the inarticulate lips. A shudder, O Detachment,
on the morning numbness of branches
that casts the olive to the ground; control center
on the boundaries of sleep and time.

Amid the cold twilight of dawn,
dampness on foliage and hair,
with vague reflections in mirrors
and echoes timid as the dryad—speak,
O lethargic Sibylla, soul!

As light falls in the drizzling rain
and every raindrop brightens every leaf
and kindles a small lamp in the hidden
cyclamen—explore now
with a gaze devoid of memory
the dimensions of your habitation:

this hand that still feels
some thread from the labyrinth of sleep
and completes some movement begun
on the other shore: this ingenuous lever
cramped in the perspective of Time,
its palm open to expectation,
its elbow numbed by forgotten actions;
and the pulse
like a small watch of death wound up
on the white coral of the bone.

Warm and lovely glove of the skeleton,
this hand will stretch out to explore
its boundaries—the mold of the cheeks,
some curl in the hair, the eyelid's
arch drained of memory: narrow limits
of the infinite solitude of flesh,
perishable monuments of its history.

What figure of all those buried
in Time will oblivion return
like a statue lost at sea?
What images will rise in memory
while time resumes once more
the varied gears of the engine?
Ghosts from sunken territories
of the past, dazzling dawn
of daily creation formed
by the reassembling of the imperfect!

As the sea murmurs in the shell,
teach, O crucible of genesis, Head,
all that flesh and nature ignore,
locked within the moment of no memory.
From the ivy at the window
engender trees and forests, conjure
springs out of the sound of rain,
some city of porticoes and fountains,
and perhaps that gold-wheeled day
when two lovers bathed at noon
naked under the mountain waterfall.

Awake, stern phantoms of lust,
gods of the body! Stretch the nerves
on the impassivity of bone.
And you, our disinherited, awaken
—O tearful faces of tenderness—
echoes of voices long since silenced.
Body, remember the radiant yoke
of some caress in the golden reflection

of a night. O my eyes, give now
the glance you had perhaps refused
to the tranquil shadow you now lament.
Honor and glory of the immortal body,
the captive prince of imperfection!
Admire once more, hostage of Time,
the funereal ornaments of the dust
which you so richly embalm for oblivion.

THE TREE

Around this tree memory coils and lurks,
golden viper poised to strike
a slowly pacing passer-by
        who had forgotten.

From the rough trunk and the brawny
armpits of its branches will rise again
the mythical moment hidden like a dryad
        in the fragrant grave.

Silver of moonlight on the leaves,
sighs on bodies hastily bared,
and impatient hands and lips
        on lips and limbs
        on secret fruit and grasses,

all untouched forever beyond Time,
beyond the aging of the flesh,
safe from the soul's weariness
        in the green corpse

of the sacred olive tree that proceeds
with experienced roots and silvery plumes within Time,
every bough a Spring
        every branch a century,

and that for a moment will turn again
into a vibrant body under the hand
that on the bark blindly seeks a golden fleece
                    and the uneven struggle.

THE REUNION

Between our two bodies
Time crumpled up and shrank,
its dimensions and perspectives
                    broken.

Touch and fragrance and taste and lust
had leveled out, in the darkness,
presence and remembrance, past
                    and present.

Your body once more became a potent crater
of inexhaustible intoxication, and a crucible
for the twin poisons of memory
                    and oblivion.

Every caress revived landscapes
and hours engraved on the senses,
like old gramophone records that have found
                    their needles again.

And cruel youth surged out
from the grave of our own flesh,
embalmed in the precious cinders
                    of days.

And there rose, under our closed eyelids,
lights and images and those incongruous things
that always without reason seem to float
                    on the flood waters.

Thus did darkness protect us for a while
from mirrors and our own glances,
like an ark on the tranquil deluge
        of Time.

LANDSCAPE

Here, in this mineral landscape
of rock and sea, sapphire and diamond,
which to the wheel of Time offers nothing
        that's perishable;

here in the great victorious light
whose only stain is your own shadow,
and where only your body carries
        a germ of death;

here perhaps for a moment the false idols
will vanish; perhaps once again
in a dazzling flash you may stare
        at your true self;

that self hidden by so many masks,
distorted by necessities and yokes,
that you betray; and everyone robs you
        with violence and seduction.

Thus cleansed like an earthen jar
or bones stripped bare, your clay shall escape
for a brief moment the implacable weights
        of life and of death.

ANTHROPOS

No matter how far you advance, the mystery
recedes; and you must always remain
at the same distance from the mirrors that block
    the mortal vision.

Nailed to the moving escalator of Time
like a hurried buyer in some huge supermarket,
you speed on, motionless, laden
    with useless purchases:

with food and drink that will not deceive
your hunger or your thirst; with clothing
that cannot cover your nakedness, and cosmetics
    that will not convince.

And you always fear you have lost some
of your packages, those fraudulent wares
once more expensively purchased with Time,
    that priceless coin.

Thus you proceed toward the fatal solution
in a dimension that chokes and scorns
the one you had sometimes felt unfolding
    within you,

elusive and most fulgurant
sole diamond that could ever tear
the transparent and deceptive walls
    of your prison.

THE HOMECOMING

With a thousand signals of their silver hands,
with fluttering ceremonial plumes,

the familiar olive trees, nourishers and companions,
welcomed you at the entrance of the estate.
And the oleanders, with courtly curtsies,
spreading their rose-engarlanded fans,
greeted you before the house.

Yet a fig tree, but three years old, like a childish
hand of Time, prevented the wrought-iron gate
from opening wide; and the honeysuckle had sealed,
with fragrant wire, a window shutter
in sign of some secret inventory.

Leave the years on the clothes rack in the hall
like useless garments, near the straw hat
that still creaks with the sands and suns
of bygone summers. Enter that space where every piece
of furniture keeps guard like a boundary stone
and as a bulwark against Time.

Cisterns of Time, the closed rooms offer
dimensions in which your various forms
now merge conciliated: child, boy, and youth,
disarmed ghosts of your multitudinous dead.

Silence, rustle of pine trees, sistrums of cicadas.
Creaking of a door, of a staircase. All
gramophone needles for the forgotten records
of memory. And the burning pyre of noon,
the essential element of the spell, in order to distill
the philter of the pardon given by shadows and things.

PSYCHE'S ADVENTURE

While her beautiful vestments decline
with the rich ecstasy of the flesh,
the Soul pursues tirelessly her great adventure,
hidden behind a thousand illusions,

hidden behind hours, days, years,
    hidden behind yourself.

Like the gleaner who timidly follows the harvesters,
she gathers much that on your way you despised,
behind actions, behind words, behind thoughts,
    behind labor and sleep.

With these fragments she shapes the powerful figures
that rule the inexorable firmament of Myth,
always uncapturable, but ever so close
that you feel their breathing and their command
    behind the scenery.

Thus you may sometimes recapture the outcast
Soul, in some abyss of silence or some tear;
when the body unexpectedly shivers under a breath
    of life, from the lips of death.

DIVER

The trap door of myth has suddenly opened again;
the ground, that seemed so solid, has abruptly subsided like a
    marsh,
and now you sink, a diver holding for weight
this head you had buried and that had turned to marble
in the shallow graves of oblivion.

You will find no mercy on the lips or glance
of the stone head with its hundred faces
that go on changing, uncapturable, in the depths;
and that sometimes take on the relentless visage
of repudiated selves.

Do not hope for absolution, do not await mercy
from the statues that claim life,
from the idols that do not forgive apostasy,

from the ghosts demanding justice
in the starry depths of the soul.

However artful you might have been in your negotiations,
whatever security you think you might have acquired,
they will lay ambush to your vigil and your sleep:
behind the mirrors of creation, behind Time,
you will find the stone face of reproach.

Níkos Engonópoulos

ELEONORA

for hands she hath non, nor
eyes, nor feot, nor golden
Treasure of hair.

(f r o n t   v i e w)

her hair is like cardboard
and like a fish
her two eyes are
like a dove
her mouth
is like civil war
(in Spain)
her neck is a red
horse
her hands
are
like the voice
of dense
woods
her two breasts are
like my own paintings
her belly is
the romance
of Vélthandros and Hrisándza
the story
of Tobias

the fable
of the ass
the wolf and the fox
her sex
is
sharp whistlings
in the tranquillity
of noon
her thighs are
the last
glimmerings
of the modest joys
of road rollers
her two knees
are Agamemnon
her two adored
small
feet
are the green
tele-
phone with the red
eyes

(back view)

her hair
is
a kerosene lamp
still burning
in the morning
her shoulders
are
the hammer
of my
desires
her back
is the
eyeglasses
of the sea
the plow

of misleading
ideograms
it whistles
mournfully
on her waist
her buttocks
are
fish glue
her calves
are
like
lightning bolts
her small heels
illuminate
the
evil
morning
dreams

and finally
she is
a woman
half
seahorse
and half
necklace
perhaps she is
even
part pine tree
and part
elevator

TEN AND FOUR THEMES
FOR A PAINTING

    1. Three men. Two of them sitting. The third is standing, his beautiful gaze wandering in the infinite, his back turned toward the window. He holds his right hand extended, as though

he were saying something, as though there was something he wanted to say.

2. Three men. Two of them standing. The third is sitting in the center of a richly furnished room on an ancient marble capital in the Doric style, his elbows leaning on his knees with his face in his hands. The two standing men have approached one another and converse between themselves either with gestures or in a low voice.

3. Three men. Two are frantically gesturing as though to a frenzied mob. The third approaches the window and, leaning out, tries to discern something, tranquilly, in the narrow street hidden from the beholder.

4. Three men sitting.

5. Three men sitting. One of them wears a beard and has a very beautiful gaze.

6. Three men. Two of them, standing, exchange greetings in the position of "The Two Friends." The third is wearing a military uniform.

7. Three women, of great and rare beauty, with something lofty and extraordinarily noble in their bearing, dressed in heavy garments of vivid colors. Two are sitting on gold-trimmed stools, leaning their beautiful arms on marble columns in the ancient style. The third, standing, wears a velvet garment of a vivid crimson, with a large ribbon of costly silk tied behind her waist. She is called Maria.

8. Three men in the room on horseback. Dark walking habits, spurs, whips, helmets.

9. Three men silently examining a globe of the earth. Near them a table, and on it a hammer and sickle, an open book, a compass, and other symbols of freemasonry. An epigraph with the word "travelers."

10. A garden, a palace in the center, a jet of water with cypress trees on either side, a clock tower. And Saint Nikólaos, dressed in a chasuble and in the attitude of Liturgy, holds the Gospels in his left hand and in his right a cartoon on which is written "Hovering over the flowering gardens of the Church." Behind him a crowd of soldiers and in their midst Saint George, a beardless youth, and Saints Dhimítrios, a curly-haired youth, and Várvaros, wearing chains. At the left of the painting a ship is imperiled, and at the right a ship sails on.

11. Three men, two of them sitting and looking full face toward the audience. The third, standing, is lost in shadow in the far depths of the room.

12. Three men. Two of them standing, the third sitting. In the attitude of anxiety.

13. Three men. Two standing and looking at the third who stands erect, reading.

14. Three men. Two sitting, the third standing.

THE HYDRA OF BIRDS

Far-distant concerts and opaline sparks of our first home in the
      burning heat of summer,
In Tierra del Fuego the endless hunting, in the fields,
      in the woods, in the heavens,
I shall softly kiss the lips of icons, I shall give away
      hopes to seashells and castles
That mutely support all those whom Destiny touches,
      and when skylights of idols set among the pine trees
They plow with horses of wood the caresses of low-lying cedars,
The grave speculations of mystical dinosaurs, intrigues of water
      that swans encircle,
Black swans, sky-blue, all idea, and a passion which, as one says,
      is on the verge of vanishing and suddenly seeks
To mount higher, to hurl down, to smash, to fling open windows,
      that I may cry out, that it may weep,
That I may destroy, that it may anchor, that it may be torn,
      that I may engrave on copper deeper and deeper still
Pigeons, lions, the night of her hair, the weapons of soldiers,
      the earth of Albania,
And wherever it reaches, if it reaches, the metal of imagination,
      words that I, the Pythoness, said in waterless expanses,
It shall traverse tropics and wells until the dawn, that seductress,
      shines with orgies of incorporeal Kurds,
To purchase guitars that drown my eyes, until I drag down the
      veils the moon keeps,
That it may bind on my face the mask of birds.

BOLÍVAR

A GREEK POEM

ΦΑΣΜΑ ΘΗΣΕΩΣ ΕΝ ΟΠΛΟΙΣ ΚΑΘΟΡΑΝ, ΠΡΟ
ΑΥΤΩΝ ΕΠΙ ΤΟΥΣ ΒΑΡΒΑΡΟΥΣ ΦΕΡΟΜΕΝΟΝ

Le cuer d'un home vaut tout l'or d'un païs.

For the great, the free, the brave, the strong only
Belong the great words, the free, the brave, and the strong,
For them the complete submission of all elements, the silence, for
      them the tears, the lighthouses, the branches of the olive
      tree, and the lanterns
That bob up and down with the boat's rocking and scribble on the
      dark horizons of the harbor,
For them the empty barrels piled high in the most narrow street,
      again, of the harbor,
For them the coils of white rope, and the chains, the anchors, and
      the other monometers
Amid the enervating fumes of petroleum,
That they might arm their ships and set sail and leave
Like the streetcar that passes, empty and flooded with light,
      between the nocturnal calm of vegetable gardens,
To the one goal of the voyage: toward the stars.

For them will I speak these words of beauty which Inspiration
      dictated to me
As it nestled in the depths of my brain, filled with emotion
For the figures, austere and illustrious, of Odysseus Androútsos
      and Simón Bolívar.

But now I shall sing a psalm of Simón only, parting with the
      other for a more suitable time,
Parting with him now that I may dedicate to him, when the time
      comes, the most beautiful song perhaps that I have ever
      sung,

Perhaps the most beautiful song that has ever been sung in the
      whole world.
And this not for what they have both been for country and for
      nation, for all the people, and for other similar items,
      which do not inspire,
But because they stood amid the ages, both of them, always alone,
      and great, and free, and brave, and strong.

And shall I now despair because until this day no one understood
      me, no one wanted to, no one could remember what I
      say?
Indeed, shall the same fate befall that which I now say of Bolívar
      and which tomorrow I shall say of Androútsos?
After all, it is not easy for such lofty figures as Androútsos and
      Bolívar to be understood so soon,
Symbols such as these.
But let us proceed quickly: in the name of God, let there be no
      emotion, no exaggeration, no despair.
It doesn't matter, my voice was destined for the centuries only.
(In the future: the near, the far; in the years: the many, the
      few; perhaps from the day after tomorrow or the day
      after the day after tomorrow,
Until that hour when the Earth shall begin to roll empty and
      useless and dead in the firmament,
When youth will awaken with mathematical precision in the wild
      nights, on their beds,
To water their pillows with tears, wondering who I was, thinking
That I once existed, what words I said, what hymns I sang.
And the sky-reaching waves that burst every evening against the
      seven shores of Hýdra,
And the wild rocks, and the high mountain that brings down the
      storms
Shall endlessly and without tiring thunder my name.)

Let us return, however, to Simón Bolívar.

BOLIVAR! Name of metal and wood, you were a flower amid
      the gardens of South America.
All the nobility of flowers lay in your heart, in your hair, in your
      glance.

Your hand was as large as your heart, and it scattered good and
      evil.
You would rush upon the mountains and the stars would tremble,
      you would descend into the fields with your gold
      ornaments, your epaulets, all the insignia of your rank,
With your gun slung from your shoulder, your chest bare, your
      body full of wounds,
You would sit wholly naked on a low rock by the edge of the sea,
And they would come and paint you in the tradition of Indian
      warriors
With lime, half white and half blue, that you might resemble a
      remote chapel on the coast of Attica,
Like a cathedral in the district of Tatávla, like a palace in a
      deserted town of Macedonia.

BOLIVAR! You were reality, and are, at this very moment—you
      are not a dream.
When the savage hunters nail the wild eagles and the other wild
      birds and beasts
Above the wooden doors in the wild woods,
You live again, and cry out, and thrash about
And are yourself the hammer, the nail, and the eagle.

When on coral atolls the winds blow and overturn the empty
      fishing boats,
And the parrots squawk in an orgy of cries as the day falls, and
      the gardens are at peace, drowned in dew,
And ravens roost on the high treetops,
Then consider how near waves in the darkness the moisture eats
      into the iron tables of the coffee houses,
And in the distance how the light goes on, goes out, goes on again,
      shifts here and there,
And dawn breaks—what terrible agony—after a sleepless night,
And the water reveals nothing of its mysteries. Such is life.
And the sun rises, the jetty houses with their island arches
Painted rose and green, with white cornices (of Náxos, perhaps, or
      of Chíos).
How they live! How they shine like diaphanous Nereids! Such is
      BOLIVAR!

BOLIVAR! I call out your name as I lie sprawling here on the
        peak of Mt. Ére,
The highest peak of the island Hýdra.
From here the view spreads out enchantingly as far as the islands
        of the Saronic Gulf, as far as Thebes,
And beyond Monevasiá far below to renowned Egypt,
Even as far as Panama, Guatemala, Nicaragua, Honduras, Costa
        Rica, Haiti, San Domingo, Bolivia, Colombia, Peru,
        Venezuela, Chile, Argentina, Brazil, Uruguay, Paraguay,
        Ecuador,
And farther still to Mexico.
I engrave your name with a hard stone on rock that later on men
        may come to worship here.
The sparks shower as I engrave—such, they say, was Bolívar—and
        I follow
My hand as it writes, brilliant in the sun.

You saw light for the first time in Caracas. It was your own light,
Bolívar, for until you came South America was wholly steeped in
        bitter darknesses.
Your name is now a blazing firebrand that lights up the Americas,
        both North and South, and all the universe!
The rivers Orinoco and Amazon spring from your eyes,
The tall mountains are rooted in your chest,
The ranges of the Andes are your spinal column.
On the crown of your head—O gallant youth—run the wild horses
        and the wild oxen,
The wealth of Argentina.
And the endless coffee plantations spread across your loins.

When you speak, terrifying earthquakes demolish everything,
From the imposing deserts of Patagonia to the multicolored
        islands,
Volcanoes erupt in Peru and vomit their wrath to the skies,
The ground everywhere trembles and the holy icons of Kastoriá
        creak,
That silent city by the lake.
Bolívar, you are as beautiful as a Greek!

I first met you, when I was a child, on a steep cobbled lane of
        Phanár,

A candle from the church of Mouhlió lit up your noble face.
Are you perhaps one of the many forms which Constantine
   Paleológos took up and abandoned one by one?

Boyacá, Ayacúcho. Brilliant and eternal symbols. I was there.
We had long since passed the old frontiers: back, in the far
   distance, in Liskovíki, bonfires were blazing,
And the army was ascending in the night toward the battle,
   already we could hear the familiar sounds.
At one side of the road, a dark convoy, the unending cars of the
   wounded, were descending.

Keep calm. Down there—see—the lake.
They will pass by there, behind the reeds.
The roads are mined, the work and glory of the man from
   Hórmovo, famous and unparalleled in these matters. All
   in your places. There goes the whistle!
Cavalry gunners, unharness! Set up the cannons, clean their
   mouths with mops, the fuses lit in your hands,
The cannon-balls to the right. VRASS!
VRASS! Albanian for FIRE, for BOLIVAR!

Every grenade thrown and exploded
Was also a rose for the glory of the great general
As he stood unshaken and stern amid the dust and the tumult,
Gazing with steadfast eyes at the heights, his forehead in the
   clouds,
And the sight of him was dreadful: a fountain of awe, the road of
   Justice, the gate of Liberty.

Yet how many have plotted against you, Bolívar,
How many snares have not been set for you to fall into and be
   lost?
One man above all, that villain, that worm, that man from
   Philippoúpolis.
But nothing touched you: unshakable as a tower you stood
   upright before the dread of the Aconcagua,
You grasped a terrible cudgel and brandished it above your head.
The bald-headed condors were terrified, whom neither the smoke
   nor the tumult of battle had frightened, and flew about in
   ferocious flocks,

And the llamas avalanched over the mountain sides, trailing, as
       they fell, clouds of earth and stone.
And your enemies in black Tartaros were speechless, lost.
(When the marble shall come, the very best, from Alabanda, I
       shall anoint my head with lustral water from the Holy
       Church of Blachérnes,
I shall dedicate all my craft to sculpt you in this pose, to erect the
       statue of a young Kouros on the mountains of Síkinos,
Not forgetting, indeed, to carve on the pedestal that famous
       "Hail, passer-by.")

And here we must insist in particular that Bolívar never feared,
       never "trembled" as they say,
Neither in the most deadly hour of battle, nor at treasons, the
       unavoidable, the bitter darknesses.
It is said that he knew from the very first, with unimaginable
       precision, the day, the hour, even the second: the
       moment
Of the Great Battle fated for him alone.
Where he would himself become the army and the enemy, the
       vanquished and the victorious both, the triumphant hero
       and the sacrificial victim.
(And a magnificent spirit arose within him like that of Cyril
       Loúkaris
As he calmly confounded the sinister plots of the Jesuits and of
       that wretched man from Philippoúpolis!)

And if he were ever lost, if ever a Bolívar is lost, who like
       Appollonios ascended into the heavens,
He had set like the sun, amid unbelievable glory, behind the noble
       mountains of Attica and the Moréa.

invocation

Bolívar! You are the son of Rígas Ferréos,
Of Andónios Ikonómos who was murdered so unjustly, and you
       are the brother of Pasvandsóghlou,
The dream of the great Maximilien de Robespierre lives again on
       your brow.

You are the liberator of South America.
I do not know how you are related to that other great American,
      the one from Montevideo, whether he is your descendant
      or not,
It is only known that I am your son.

CHORUS

strophe

                                    (*entrée des guitares*)

If the night as it lingers in passing
Should send us old moons for a sweet consolation,
If the darkness of phantasms roam the wide prairies
To weigh down with chains every virgin unbraided,
Then the hour of victory, of triumph has come,
And the tricornered hats that are soaked now with blood
Shall be placed on the skeletons of high-ranking generals
And their pre-sacrificial, old color of crimson
Shall cover with sunrays the brilliance of banners.

antistrophe

                            (*the love of liberty brought us here*)

the plows at the roots of the palm trees
and the sun
that in splendor arises
amid trophies
and the birds
and the spears
shall announce—as far as a teardrop
rolls
and is carried by the wind to the
depths
of the sea—
the most terrible oath
the more terrible darkness

the terrible story:
Libertad

epode

(*dance of free masons*)

Go far from us now, maledictions, approach us no more, *corazón*,
From the cradle to the stars, from the womb to the eyes, *corazón*,
Where precipitous rocks hang down, volcanoes and seals, *corazón*,
Where dark faces loom, and broad lips, and gleaming white teeth,
    corazón,
Let the phallus be raised, the fiesta begin, human sacrifice start
      with the dance, *corazón*,
With carousal of flesh to our forefathers' glorious fame, *corazón*,
That the seed of a new generation be sown, *corazón*.

CONCLUSION

    After the South American revolution was established, a
bronze statue of Bolívar was erected in Náfplion and in
Monemvasía on a deserted hill dominating the town. But during
the nights the storming winds would blow and flap the frock coat
of the hero, and the resulting noise was so great, so deafening, that
no one could sleep, it was impossible even to think of sleeping. So
the good burghers of the town asked the proper authorities with
the proper petitions (and they were successful) that the monument
be torn down.

HYMN OF FAREWELL TO BOLIVAR

(*Distant music of great melancholy is heard, the
nostalgic folk songs and dances of South America,
preferably in the rhythm of the sardana.*)

general

what were you seeking

in Lárissa

you

a

native of Hýdra?

THE APPRENTICE OF SORROW

this statue
arose and left in the morning
—at daybreak—
that it might steal
the stars
it arose and left
in the night
and killed
all the dreams

—and its bare feet
as it walked
became entangled
in the brambles
and bled among the thorns—

and its noble consecrated hands,
the very birds of spring, caressed
the geranium it named in a night of love
and the secret clasps
of her virginal dreambook

and of her breasts { the cries
of crimson
and the hidden
fringes

SOUVENIR OF CONSTANTINOPLE

on the marmoreal piers of the palace
are placed at intervals approximately regular
tall piles of wood
brought by boats from the far
forest beaches

and other woodpiles are of tall
slender trunks like the bodies of young girls
and other piles are of
huge and monstrous
trees

and it rains unceasingly and the persistent rain drenches
the dreary wood
and the marble of the flagstones glistens
as the water washes and rewashes them endlessly

and the heavens both heavy and black
—I wonder who knows what time of the day it is?—
are not disposed to grant us hope

(the opposite shore has vanished
you might say it never existed)

and the sea is dark and savage
as if thick drops of rain that thrash her
have awakened within her a monstrous fury
which she restrains but with
what effort

no one else seems to be on this desolate seascape
save I alone—I only—
standing erect with my red hair drenched
and glued to my forehead

it is the torments of love have brought me to this noble shore
and all my thought is on one superb

impervious magnolia
that in these regions
grows and flourishes

THE LAST APPEARANCE
OF JUDAS ISCARIOT

The small American city, the one lost in the endless expanses
of the Áïrton prairies, was deprived of the deep serenity to which
it had become accustomed since the rather recent days—round
about 1867—of its foundation. Regularly about midnight a man,
strange and somber, crept even into the most well-bolted houses,
terrified the dreams of the sleepers, upset all easy consciences,
mortally embittered all hearts, and with a metallic flute, which he
played to perfection, awoke in everyone an intense, tyrannous, and
at the same time vague and nostalgic mood. It is unnecessary to
add that, when day broke, no one remembered anything of that
dreadful nightmare. But during the day you would have said that
a heavy weight seemed to crush all spirits. A walker of the night
solved this tormenting mystery. One night as, completely by
chance, his uncertain footsteps brought him to a hill in the
country, dominating the city, he discovered that the bronze statue
of Abraham Lincoln, which had been erected there, was gone, for
the marble base was revealed to be deserted and forsaken under
the floodlights. The "President," this bronze Abraham Lincoln,
was therefore the strange and somber night visitor! The informer
was rewarded with a certain sum of dollars. He answered to the
name of Judas. His surname: Iscariot.

THE GOLDEN PLATEAUS

in Gabon
on the banks of the Ogooue
they fashioned a mug

and all who wear it
represent
the moon and the sun
in the moment of dance

for eyes they gave it a dove
for eyelashes they gave it the dove's complaint
for mouth they gave it the name of Bolívar
and the beard
is a pit of flaming coal
and tears
and holy relics of Christian martyrs
and the river Ogooue is the comb and the love

our boat is now softly sailing on the river
trees wave to us and greet us from the banks
and I hold on my breast the
mask
I say the prayers of Bithynia
I dip my hands gently into the lukewarm water

on the estuaries of the river
sharks gaze on us slantwise
and then withdraw
—caresses are not suitable for sharks—
flying fish
dart about us
at our command

the phoenix trees
according to their shapes
are sometimes the fan
and at other times the parasol of Friday
in the moment of dance

my bird
is
my
bird
and always
Euthalía   Athanasía   Tamar   Calliope
I love you

POETRY 1948

this age
of civil strife
is not an age
for poetry
or similar things:
when something
is
to be written
it is
as if
it were written
on the other side
of death
announcements

this is why
my poems
are so bitter
(and when, indeed, were they not?)
and why they are
—above all—
so
few

MERCURIUS BOUAS

He kneels and opens the chest, and as with one hand he holds
    the cover, with the other he rummages and searches within.
—What do you have there? I ask him.
He turns:
—*Lettere d'amore*, he replies.
And then:
—Don't they interest you?

—But of course . . . if they're about love affairs, I answer.

Then very slowly, with extremely careful movements, he begins to take out different things, one by one, and to show them to me.

First he draws out and shows me various velvet materials, piles of disheveled bolts, some embellished and others in monotone colors. Then a rotted mattress, and finally he lets go of the cover and brings out the body well preserved, of a dead man, and lays it down on the floor. That which was particularly interesting about this corpse, however, was the glossy and dazzling whiteness of its skin, as well as its unruly hair and its long martial mustache.

NEWS ABOUT THE DEATH OF THE SPANISH POET FEDERICO GARCIA LORCA ON THE NINETEENTH OF AUGUST 1936 IN THE DITCH OF THE CAMINO DE LA FUENTE

"... *una acción vil y disgraciada.*"

art and poetry do not help us to live
art and poetry help us
to die

an absolute contempt
is fitting
for all these clamors
the investigations
the commentary on commentary
which ever so often come fresh from the oven
of otherwise unoccupied and conceited scribblers
concerning the vile and mysterious circumstances
of ill-fated Lorca's execution
by the fascists
but at last! now everyone knows

that
for some time now
—and in particular in our crippled times—
it has become customary
to murder
the poets

ON BOEOTIAN ROADS

beware: this swellfoot
we are about to encounter
on the forks of Boeotian roads
no: he is not the Oedipus of mythology

in spite of all the—so to speak—elephantism
of gout—the enlargement of extremities—
from which he suffers
this has no relation at all, I tell you, to the Oedipus of old

neither had he killed his father
nor—go, get there in time to tell Jocasta—
nor is he going to marry his mother

let him continue on ahead for a while
and then—in a little while again—he will vanish forever

but that black dog
that lies in the middle of the sun-washed road
"sun-washed" by the sun that is about to set
asleep or dead among the horse manure
eh! well, that one
that one is something

learn this: that one is the legendary Sphinx
who fell from her pedestal
when she saw
that "enigmas"
no longer exist

Odysseus Elýtis

AGE OF BLUE MEMORY

Olive groves and vineyards as far as to the sea
Red fishing boats farther still to memory
Golden cricket husks of August in a midday sleep
With shells or seaweed. And that boat's hull
Newly built, green, that in the water's peaceful embrace still reads:
The Lord Will Provide

Like leaves like pebbles the years went by
I remember the young men, the sailors, leaving
And painting the sails in their heart's image
They sang of the four corners of the horizon
They wore the north winds tattooed on their chests

What was I looking for when you came painted with the sunrise
The age of the sea within your eyes
And on your body the sun's vigor—what was I looking for
Deep within sea-caverns amid spacious dreams
Where the emotions foamed of a wind
Anonymous and blue, engraving on my chest its sea emblem

With sand on my fingers, I would close my fingers
With sand in my eyes, I would clench my fingers
This was torment—
It was April, I remember, when I felt for the first time your
    human weight
Your human body of clay and corruption

590

As on our first day on earth
It was the fête of the amaryllis—But you suffered, I remember,
The wound on the bitten lip was deep
And deep the nailmark on the skin where Time is forever
   engraved

I left you then

And a thundering wind swept up the white houses
The white emotions freshly washed
On a sky that illumined all with a smile

Now I shall keep beside me a jug of immortal water
A form of freedom's ravaging wind
And those hands of yours where Love shall be tormented
And that shell of yours where shall echo the Aegean.

MARINA OF THE ROCKS

On your lips there is a taste of storm—But where have you
   wandered
All day long with the hard reveries of stone and sea
An eagle-bearing wind stripped the hills bare
Stripped your desire to the bone
And the pupils of your eyes seized the relay-rod of the Chimera
And lined memory with traceries of foam!
Where has it gone, the familiar slope of childhood's September
Where on red earth you played, gazing below
On the deep thickets of other girls
On corners where your friends left armfuls of rosemary

—But where have you wandered
All night long with the hard reverie of stone and sea
I would tell you to keep trace in the unclothed water of all its
   luminous days
To lie on your back rejoicing in the dawn of all things
Or to wander again in fields of yellow
With a clover of light on your breast, O Heroine of Iambic

On your lips there is a taste of storm
And a dress crimson as blood
Deep within the summer's gold
And the hyacinth's aroma—But where have you wandered

Descending toward the shore, the pebbled bay
Where you found a cold salty seagrass
But deeper still a human emotion that bled
And opened your arms in surprise, calling its name
Lightly ascending to the limpidity of the underseas
Where your own starfish gleamed

Listen, the Word is the prudence of the aged
And Time a frenzied sculptor of men
And the sun stands above it, a beast of hope
And you, much closer, embrace a love
With a bitter taste of storm on your lips

You may no longer count on another summer, O seablue to the
          bone
That rivers might turn in their courses
To carry you back to their mothers
That you might kiss other cherry trees again
Or ride the horses of the Northwest Wind

Pillared on rock without yesterday or tomorrow,
On the dangers of rock, wearing the headdress of the storm
You shall say farewell to the enigma that is yours.

THE MAD POMEGRANATE TREE

an early-morning question mood of high spirits à perdre haleine

In these whitewashed courtyards where the South Wind blows
Whistling through vaulted arcades, tell me is it the mad
          pomegranate tree
That leaps in the light scattering her fruit-laden laughter

With a wind's caprice and murmuring, tell me is it the mad
      pomegranate tree
That frisks with newborn foliage at early dawn
Unfolding all her colors on high with a triumphant tremor?

When in the meadows the naked girls awaken
To harvest with blond hands the green clover,
Roaming on the borders of sleep, tell me is it the mad
      pomegranate tree
That unsuspecting places lights in their fresh-woven baskets
That overbrims their names with birdsong, tell me
Is it the mad pomgranate tree that skirmishes with the world's
      cloudy skies?

On the day that enviously adorns itself with seven varied feathers
Encircling the eternal sun with a thousand blinding prisms
Tell me is it the mad pomegranate tree
That seizes on the run a horse's mane of a hundred lashes,
Never sad and never complaining, tell me is it the mad
      pomegranate tree
That shouts aloud the newborn hope now dawning?

Tell me is it the mad pomegranate tree that greets us afar
Tossing a leafy handkerchief of cool fire
A sea about to give birth to a thousand and one ships
To waves that arise a thousand and one times and go
To untrodden shores, tell me is it the made pomegranate tree
That creaks the rigging aloft in the translucent air?

High up aloft with the blue grapeclusters that glow and revel
Arrogantly, filled with peril, tell me is it the mad pomegranate tree
That in the world's midst shatters with light the demon's
      inclement weather,
That spreads from end to end the crocus collar of day
Richly embroidered with sown songs, tell me is it the mad
      pomegranate tree
That hastily unravels the silks of day?

Amid the petticoats of April first and the cicadas of mid-August
Tell me, she who frolics, she who rages, she who allures,

Shaking out of all menace its black and evil shadows
Pouring out upon the sun's bosom the giddy birds
Tell me, she who unfolds her wings on the breasts of all things
On the breast of our deepest dreams, is it the mad pomegranate
      tree?

MELANCHOLY OF THE AEGEAN

What coherence of soul amid the halcyons of the afternoon!
What windcalm amid the cries of distant shores!
The cuckoo-bird amid the handkerchief of trees
And the mystic moment of the fishermen's supper
And the sea that on its accordion plays
The distant longing of a woman
The beautiful woman who bared her breasts
When memory entered the nests
And lilacs showered the sunset with fire!

With a caïque with sails of the *Madonna*
They left, and with the good wishes of the winds
All those who loved the lilies' sojourn in foreign fields
But see how night here has poured out warbling sleep
Like gurgling hair on the gleaming necks
Of vast white seashores
And how the dust of maiden dreams
Fragrant with spearmint and basil
Was scattered and brimmed on high
By the golden sword of Orion!

On three crossroads where the ancient sorceress stood
Setting the winds aflame with dry thyme
Lightly stepped the slender shadows
Each holding a jug immured with muted water
Easily as though they were going into Paradise
And from the crickets' prayers that foamed on all the fields
The beautiful ones emerged with the moon's skin
To dance upon the midnight threshing floor . . .

O signs drifting in the depths
Of a pool that holds up a mirror
O seven small lilies that glitter

When the sword of Orion wheels round again
It will find the bread of poverty under the lamp
But a soul on the glowing embers of the stars
It will find huge hands branching into the infinite
Desolate seaweed, the lastborn children of the seashore
And years, green precious stones

O green stone—what storm-diviner saw you
Halting the light at the birth of day
Light at the birth of the world's two eyes!

SHAPE OF BOEOTIA

Here where a desolate glance blows on the stones and the
      deathless cacti
Here where the footsteps of time resound in the deep
Were the enormous clouds open into golden six-winged
      cherubim
Above the metope of the sky
Tell me from where has eternity arisen
Tell me what is the bruise that hurts you
And what the destiny of the humble tapeworm

O earth of Boeotia brightened by the wind

What has become of the orchestra of nude hands below the
      palaces
The mercy that rose like the smoke of holiness
Where are the gates with archaic birds that sang
And the clang of metal that daybroke the terror of the people
When the sun entered like a triumph
When fate writhed on the lance of the heart
And the civil strife of birdsong raged

What has become of the immortal March libations
Of Greek traceries on the watery grass

Brows and elbows both were wounded
Time from too much sun rolled crimson
Men advanced
Laden with lament and dream

Acrid shape! ennobled by the wind
Of a summer storm that leaves its flame-gold traces
On the lines of hills and eagles
On the lined palms of your destiny

What can you face and what can you wear
Dressed in the music of grass and how do you proceed
Amid the sage and the heather
Toward the final reach of the arrow

On this red earth of Boeotia
Amid the desolate musical march of rock
You shall ignite the golden sheaves of fire
You shall uproot the evil crop of memory
You shall leave a bitter soul in the wild mint!

BODY OF SUMMER

A long time has passed since the last rainfall was heard
Above the ants and the lizards
Now the sun burns endlessly
The fruit-trees paint their mouths
The pores of the earth very slowly open
And beside the trickling and syllabic waters
A huge plant stares into the sun's eye.

Who is this who sprawls on the far beaches
Stretched on his back, smoking the smokesilver olive leaves
Crickets warn themselves in his ears

Ants scurry to work on his chest
Lizards glide in the long grasses of his armpits
And through the seaweed of his feet a wave lightly passes
Sent by that small siren who sang:

"O naked body of summer, burnt
And eaten away by oil and salt
Body of rock and the heart's tremor
Great fluttering in the willow's hair
Breath of basil on the curly groin
Filled with starlets and pine needles
Profound body, vessel of day!"

The slow rains come, the pelting hail,
The shores pass by, flogged by the claws of the wintry wind
That with savage billows lowers in the sea-depths
The hills plunge into thick cloud udders
But behind all this you smile unconcernedly
And find again your deathless hour
As once more you are found on the beaches by the sun
And amid your naked vigor by the sky.

DRINKING THE CORINTHIAN SUN

Drinking the Corinthian sun
Reading the marble ruins
Striding over vineyard seas
Aiming with my harpoon
At votive fish that elude me
I found those leaves that the psalm of the sun memorizes
The living land that desire rejoices
To open

I drink water, cut fruit
Plunge my hands through the wind's foliage
Lemon trees quicken the pollen of summer days
Green birds cut through my dreams
And I leave, my eyes filled

With a boundless gaze where the world becomes
Beautiful again from the beginning according to the heart's
    measure.

HALF-SUNKEN BOATS

Half-sunken boats
Wood that swells with pleasure
Winds barefoot winds
On the deafened cobblestone streets
Stony downhill slopes
The mute one, the crazy one
The hope left still half-built

Great news, bells
White washlines of clothing in the courtyards
Skeletons on the seashores
Paints, tar, turpentine
Preparations for the Virgin Mary
Who to celebrate her fiesta hopes
For white sails and small blue flags

And you in the upper gardens
Beast of the wild pear tree
Slender unripe boy
The sun between your thighs
Sniffing the scent
And the young girl on the opposite strand
Slowly burning because of the hydrangeas.

THIS WIND THAT LOITERS

This wind that loiters and gapes in the quince trees
This insect that sucks the grapevines
This stone that the scorpion wears next to its skin

And these wheat-stacks on the threshing floor
That play the giant to small barefoot children

Images of the Resurrection
On the wall that the pine trees scratched with their fingers
This whitewash that bears all noons on its back
And the cicadas the cicadas in the ears of the trees

Huge summer of chalk
Huge summer of cork
Red sails slanting in the squalls
Bleach-blond creatures on the sea-bottom, sponges
Accordions of the rocks
Sea-perch fresh from the fingermarks of the awkward fisherman
Proud reefs on the fishing lines of the sun

One, two: no one shall tell us our fate
Three, four: we shall tell the sun's fate ourselves.

CHILD WITH THE SKINNED KNEE

Child with the skinned knee
Close-cropped head, dream uncropped
Legs with crossed anchors
Arms of pine, tongue of fish
Small brother of the cloud!

You saw a wet pebble whitening beside you
You heard a reed whistling
The most naked landscapes of which you knew
The most colorful
Deep oh deep the funny walk of the gilthead
High oh high the cap of the small church
And far oh far a ship with red smokestacks

You saw the wave of plants where the hoarfrost
Took its morning bath, the leaf of the prickly pear
The bridge at the turn of the road

But also the savage smile
On the huge buffeting of trees
On the huge solstices of marriage
Where tears drip from the hyacinths
Where the sea-urchin unravels the riddles of water
Where stars forecast the tempest

Child with the skinned knee
Crazy amulet, stubborn jaw
Airy shorts
Breast of the rock, lily of the water
Gamin of the white cloud!

from HEROIC AND ELEGIAC SONG FOR
THE LOST SECOND LIEUTENANT
OF THE ALBANIAN CAMPAIGN

IV

He lies down on the scorched battle-coat
With a halted breeze on his quiet hair
With a twig of forgetfulness on his left ear
He resembles a garden from which the birds have suddenly flown
He resembles a song muzzled in the darkness
He resembles a clock of an angel stopped
Just when the eyelashes said: "So long, boys"
And amazement turned into stone . . .

He lies down on the scorched battle-coat.
The black centuries around him
Bark with the skeletons of dogs at the dreadful silence
And the houses that have become stone pigeons again
Listen with attention;
But laughter was burned, but the earth was deafened,
But no one heard the very last shriek
All the world was emptied with the last shriek.

Under five cedar trees
With no other candles
He lies on the scorched battle-coat;
The helmet empty, the blood muddy,
At his side the half-finished arm
And between his eyebrows—
A small bitter well, fingerprint of fate
A small bitter black-red well
Well where memory grows cold.

Oh do not see oh do not see from where his
From where his life has fled. Do not say how
Do not say how the smoke of the dream rose high
In this way then the one moment   In this way then the one
In this way then the one moment abandoned the other
And the eternal sun in this way suddenly left the world.

VI

He was a handsome lad. On the first day of his birth
The mountains of Thrace bent down to show
The cheerful wheat on the shoulders of firm earth;
The mountains of Thrace bent down and spat on him
Once on the head, once on the chest, and once amid his crying;
Greeks came with terrible arms
And raised him up in the swaddling clothes of the North
          Wind . . .
Then the days ran, to see who could cast the farthest stone
They leapt and bucked as they rode
Then morning Strymon rivers rolled
Until the gypsy windflowers rang everywhere
And from the ends of the earth
The shepherds of the sea came to take the flocks of jib-sails
To where a sea-cavern breathed deeply
To where a great stone sighed.

He was a sturdy lad;
In the arms of the bitter-orange girls at night
He would soil the large garments of the stars,
Love was so huge within him

That in wine he drank the flavors of all earth
Joining in dance later with the white-popular brides
Until dawn heard him and spilled light into his hair
Dawn who with open arms would find him
Scratching the sun on a saddle of two small branches,
Painting the flowers,
Or again with love singing a slow lullaby
To the small owls that lay awake all night . . .
Ah what a strong thyme was his breath
What a map of pride his naked chest
Where seas and freedom burst . . .

He was a valiant lad;
With his dull gold buttons and his pistol
With a manly air in his stride
And with his helmet, a glittering target
(They pierced so easily into his brain
He who had never known evil)
With his soldiers to left and right
And revenge for injustice done before him
—Flame on lawless flame!—
With blood above the eyebrows.
The Albanian mountains thundered
Then they melted snow to wash
His body, silent shipwreck of dawn
And his mouth, small songless bird
And his hands, wide plains of desolation.
The Albanian mountains thundered
They did not weep
Why should they weep
He was a valiant lad.

XII

With a morning stride on the growing grass
He ascends alone and blazing with light . . .

Flower tomboys wave to him secretly
And speak to him in a high voice that turns to mist on the air
Even the trees bend toward him lovingly

With their nests thrust into their armpits
With their branches dipped into the oil of the sun
Miracle—what a miracle, low on the earth
White races with azure plowshares cut the fields
Mountain ranges flash like lightning far away
And farther away the inaccessible dreams of springtime mountains!

He ascends alone and blazing with light
So drunk with light that his heart shows through
And the true Olympos can be seen amid the clouds
And the hosannahs of his comrades in the air around . . .
The dream now beats more quickly than blood
On the sides of footpaths the animals gather
They rasp like crickets and seem to be speaking
All the world is in truth enormous
A giant who fondles his children

Bells of crystal are ringing far away
Tomorrow, tomorrow they say: the Easter of the Sky!

SLEEP OF THE VALIANT, I

They smell of frankincense, and their features are scorched from
their passage through the Vast Dark Places.

There where the Immovable suddenly hurled them

Prone, on a land where even its smallest anemones were enough to
embitter the air of Hell

(One hand outstretched, as though it were striving to grasp the
future, the other under the desolate head turned
sideways,

As though it were seeing for the last time, deep in the eyes of a
disemboweled horse, the heaped ruins smoking.)

There Time released them. One wing, the most red, covered the
world, while the other was already tenderly moving in
the distance,

And not a single wrinkle or pang of remorse, but at a great depth

The ancient immemorial blood beginning laboriously to dawn in
the inky darkness of the sky,

A new Sun, still unripe,

Not strong enough to dissolve the hoarfrost of lambs on the living
clover, yet dispelling, before a thorn could sprout, the
oracle-making powers of Darkness . . .

And from the beginning, Valleys, Mountains, Trees, Rivers,

A creation of avenged emotions, glowed, identical yet reversed,
through which the Valiant now might pass, the
Executioner slain within them,

Peasants of the infinite azure!

Neither the hour striking twelve in the abyss, nor the Polar voice
falling vertically annulled their footfall.

They read the world insatiably with eyes forever open, there
where the Immovable had suddenly hurled them

Prone, where vultures swooped down to savor their clay entrails
and their blood.

SLEEP OF THE VALIANT, II

They smell of frankincense, and their features are scorched from
their passage through the Vast Dark Places.

There where the Immovable suddenly hurled them

Prone, on a land where even its smallest anemones were
       enough to embitter the air of Hell

(One hand outstretched, as though it were striving to grasp the
       future, the other under the desolate head turned
       sideways,

As though it were seeing for the last time, deep in the eyes of a
       disemboweled horse, the heaped ruins smoking.)

There Time released them. One wing, the most red, covered the
       world, while the other was already tenderly moving in
       the distance,

And not a single wrinkle or pang of remorse, but at a great depth

The ancient immemorial blood beginning laboriously to dawn in
       the inky blackness of the sky,

A new Sun, still unripe,

Not strong enough to dissolve the hoarfrost of lambs on the living
       clover, yet dispelling, before a thorn could sprout, the
       oracle-making powers of Darkness . . .

And from the beginning, Valleys, Mountains, Trees, Rivers,

A creation of avenged emotions glowed, identical yet reversed,
       through which the Valiant now might pass, the
       Executioner slain within them,

Peasants of the infinite azure!

Without months or years to turn their beards white, they
       wandered through the seasons to restore to things their
       true names.

And for every infant that opened its hands, not even an echo, only
       the fervor of innocence that continually strengthens
       the cataracts . . .

All day now young Arete descends and labors hard in those places
    where the earth has rotted out of ignorance, and where
    men inexplicably have committed their dark iniquities,

But at night she would fly always for refuge there high in the
    embrace of the Mountain as on a Man's hairy chest.

And the mist that ascends from the valley, they say, is not smoke,
    but the nostalgia that evaporates from the crevices in
    the sleep of the Valiant.

LACONIC

Ardor for death so enflamed me that my radiance returned to
    the sun,

And it sends me back into the perfect syntax of stone and air.

Well then, he whom I sought *I am*.

O flaxen summer, prudent autumn,

Slightest winter,

Life pays the obol of an olive leaf

And in a night of fools once again confirms with a small cricket
    the lawfulness of the Unhoped-for.

THE AUTOPSY

Well, it was found that the gold of the olive root had dripped
    into the leaves of his heart.

And because of the many times he had kept vigil close by a
candlestick, waiting for dawn to break, a strange ardor
had gripped him to the marrow.

A little below the skin, the cerulean line of the horizon in a hue
intense, and ample traces of azure in the blood.

It seems that the cries of birds, which in hours of great loneliness
he had learned by heart, had all burst out together, so
· that it had not been possible for the knife to penetrate
to any great depth.

Probably the intention sufficed for the Evil

Which he confronted—it is evident—in the terrifying posture of
the innocent. His eyes open and proud, the whole
forest still moving on his unblemished retina.

In his brain nothing but a shattered echo of the sky.

And only in the conch of his left ear, a few grains of delicate,
extremely fine sand, as in seashells. Which indicates that
many times he had plodded by the sea, utterly alone, with
the withering grief of love and the roar of the wind.

And as for those flakes of fire on his groin, they showed that in
truth he had moved time many hours ahead whenever
he had merged with a woman.

We shall have early fruit this year.

from AXION ESTI

GENESIS III

But before hearing wind or music
as I set out to find a clearing
(ascending an endless tract of sand
and erasing History with my heel)
I struggled with my bedsheets What I was looking for
was as innocent and tremulous as a vineyard
as deep and unmarked as the sky's other face
And a bit of soul within the clay
Then he spoke and the sea was born
And I saw and marveled
And in its midst he sowed small worlds in my image and likeness:
Steeds of stone with manes erect
and amphorae serene
and the slanting backs of dolphins
Íos   Síkinos   Sériphos   Mýlos
"Every word a swallow
to fetch you spring in the midst of summer," he said
And ample the olive trees
to sift the light through your hands
as it spreads softly over your sleep
and ample the cicadas
that you may not feel them
as you do not feel the pulse in your hand
but sparse the water
that you may hold it a God
and understand the meaning of its speech
and alone the tree
without a flock of its own
that you may take it for friend
and know its precious name

sparse the earth beneath your feet
    that you may have nowhere to spread root
    but must reach for depth continually
and broad the sky above
    that you may read the infinite yourself

     THIS
     small, this great world!

GENESIS V

Then I came to understand the sea-murmur
and the long endless whispering of trees
    I saw red jugs lined up on the mole
    and closer by the wooden window-shutter
    where I lay sleeping on my side
       the North Wind spoke in a louder tone
       And I saw
girls as beautiful and naked and smooth as pebbles
    with a bit of black in the nook of their thighs
    and that abundant and luxurious spread of it along the
        shoulder blades
     some erect blowing the Conch Shell
     and others writing with chalk
     words strange and enigmatic:
ROES, ESA, ARIMNA
NUS, MORIMLATITY, YLETIS
     small cries of birds and hyacinths
     or other words of July
At the stroke of eleven
    five fathoms deep
    perch gudgeon sea-bream
    with enormous gills and short tails astern
       Rising higher I found sponges
       and starfish
       and slender silent anemones

and higher still at the water's lips
pink limpets
and half-open wing-shells and saltweed
"Precious words," he said, "ancient oaths
preserved by Time and the sure hearing of distant winds"
And close by the wooden window-shutters
where I lay sleeping on my side
I pressed the pillow tight against my chest
and my eyes filled with tears
I was in the sixth month of my loves
and in my entrails stirred a precious seed

THIS
small, this great world!

PSALM I

This then is I
created for young girls and the islands of the Aegean;
lover of the roebuck's leap
and neophyte of the olive trees;
sun-drinker and locust-killer.
This is I face to face
with the black shirts of the resolute
and the empty womb of the years that aborted
its children, the erotic cries!
Air unleashes the elements and thunder attacks the mountains.
Fate of the innocent, you are here, alone again at the Pass!
At the Pass I opened my hands
at the Pass I emptied my hands
and saw no other riches, and heard no other riches
but cold fountains pouring out
Pomegranates or Zephyrs or Kisses.
Each with his own weapons, I said:
At the Pass I'll deploy my pomegranates
at the Pass I'll post my zephyrs guard
I'll set the old kisses loose, made holy by my longing!

Air unleashes the elements and thunder attacks the mountains.
Fate of the innocent, you are my own fate!

PSALM II

I was given the Hellenic tongue
my house a humble one on the sandy shores of Homer.
My only care my tongue on the sandy shores of Homer.
There sea-bream and perch
windbeaten words
green currents within the cerulean
all those I saw blazing in my entrails
sponges, medusae
with the first words of the Sirens
pink shells with the first dark tremors.
My only care my tongue with the first dark tremors.
There pomegranates, quinces
sunburnt gods, uncles and cousins
pouring oil into enormous jars;
the exhalations rising out of ravines, perfuming
osier and mastic
broom and pepper root
with the first chirping of the goldfinch,
sweet psalmodies with the very first Glory to Thee.
My only care my tongue, with the very first Glory to Thee!
There laurel and palm branches
the incense burner and the incensing
the blessing of battles and flintlocks.
On the ground spread with the vineyard cloth
fumes of roasting meat, the cracking of eggs
and Christ is Risen
with the first gunfiring of the Greeks.
Secret loves with the first words of the Hymn.
My only care my tongue, with the first words of the Hymn!

ODE 5

With the lamp of the star · I went out to the skies
In the meadow's chill air · on the earth's only shore
Where I might find my soul · that four-leaf teardrop!

Myrtles in their sorrow · silvered over with sleep
Have sanctified my face · I blow hard, prod alone
Where I might find my soul · that four-leaf teardrop!

O guide of all light rays · Magician of bedrooms
Soothsayer who knows what · the future brings, tell me
Where I might find my soul · that four-leaf teardrop!

My girls are in mourning · for century on century
My young men bear weapons · but not one of them knows
Where I might find my soul · that four-leaf teardrop!

Nights with a hundred arms · in the vast firmament
Set my entrails astir · This agony burns me
Where I might find my soul · that four-leaf teardrop!

With the lamp of the star · I went out to the skies
In the meadow's chill air · on the earth's only shore
Where I might find my soul · that four-leaf teardrop!

ODE 7

This oh this world · is the same world
Of many suns and dustclouds · of uproars and vespers
The weaver of constellations · the silverer of seamoss
In memory's waning · in the dreamworld's departure
This same world · this world is
A cymbol a cymbol · and distant futile laughter!

This oh this world • is the same world
The plunderer of pleasures • the ravager of fountains
High above Cataclysms • far below all Hurricanes
The crooked, the hump-backed • the hairy, the sanguine
Piping at nighttime • fluting in daytime
The platycephalic • the macrocephalic
On the asphalt of cities • on the jib-sails of prairies
The involuntary • and the voluntary
King Solomon • and Haggith's son.

This oh this world • is the same world
Of ebb-tides and orgasms • of remorse and storm clouds
The inventor of zodiacs • the daredevil of skydomes
At the ecliptic's edge • to the Creation's far end
This same world • this world is
A trumpet a trumpet • and a distant futile cloud!

ODE 11

I shall be tonsured as a monk • of all verdant things
And modestly I shall serve • the order of all birds
To the matin of each Fig Tree • I shall come from nights
Refreshed • bringing in my lap
Cerulean • rose and violet
And I shall light up • all the valiant
Waterdrops • I, more valiant than all.

For my icons I shall have im • maculate maidens
Dressed in the linen only • of the wide spreading sea
I shall pray that my purity • take on the myrtle's
Instinct • the muscles of beasts
That in my vig • orous entrails I
May choke the pallid • the vile the perverse
Forever • I, more vigorous than all.

Sins of various kinds shall come • and go in all times
Of profiting of honor • of flogging of remorse

Then the Bucephalos of blood	•	will charge enraged to
Lash out	•	against my yearnings:
Manliness and	•	love and light. Then sniff-
Ing them out to be	•	the more powerful
He whinnied	•	I, more powerful than he.

But when the sixth hour of all the	•	erect lilies strikes
At that hour when my judgment	•	shall make a breach in Time
Then the eleventh commandment	•	will leap from my eyes:
This world	•	will or will not be
Birth-Pains the Aye	•	Deification
Which I in my soul's	•	justice will have pro-
Claimed to all	•	I, the most just man of all.

VI PROPHETIC

Many years after the Sin they called Arete in the churches,
and blessed. Relics of old stars and cobwebbed corners of the
sky swept by the storm to be born out of the mind of man. And
Creation, paying now for the works of the ancient Governors,
shall shudder with horror. Confusion will fall upon Hades and its
planking will give way under the great pressure of the sun,
which at first will hold back its rays, sign that the time has come
for dreams to be avenged. And afterwards it will speak, to say:
Exiled Poet, tell me, what do you see in your century?
—I see nations, once arrogant, given over to the wasp and the
sourgrass.
—I see axes in the air splitting busts of Emperors and Generals.
—I see merchants stooping to collect profit from their own corpses.
—I see a sequence of hidden meanings.

Many years after the Sin they called Arete in the churches,
and blessed. But before this, lo, many handsome Philips and
many Roberts will be created to fall in love with themselves at
the triple crossroads. They will wear their rings backwards, they
will comb their hair with a nail, they will adorn their chests with
skulls to allure the prostitutes. And the prostitutes will be

astounded and they will consent. In order that the saying may
come true: that near is the day when beauty shall be surrendered
to the flies of the Market Place. And the body of the whore shall
rage with indignation, not having anything else to crave. And the
whore will become the accuser of wise men and mighty, bringing
as witness on her behalf the seed she had served so faithfully.
And she will cast off curses from upon her, stretching out her
hand toward the East and shouting: Exiled Poet, speak, what do
you see in your century?
—I see the colors of Hymettos at the sacred base of our New Civil
Code.
—I see young Myrtó, the whore from Síkinos, raised as a stone
statue in the square of the Market Place with its Fountains and
its Rampant Lions.
—I see young men, I see girls in the annual Drawing by Lot of
the Couples.
—And high in the ether I see the Erectheum of Birds.

Relics of old stars and cobwebbed corners of the sky swept by
the storm to be born out of the mind of man. But before this, lo,
generations will guide their plows over the barren earth. And the
Governors will secretly count their human merchandise, declaring
wars. Whereupon the Policeman and the Military Judge will be
sated, leaving gold to the insignificant that they may themselves
collect the wages of insult and martyrdom. And large ships will
hoist flags, martial music will take to the streets, balconies will
shower the Victor with flowers—who shall be living in the stench
of corpses. And next to him, unfolding to his measure, darkness
will gape open like a pit, crying: Exiled Poet, speak, what do you
see in your century?
—I see Military Judges burning like candles on the great table of
the Resurrection.
—I see Policemen offering their blood as sacrifice to the purity of
the skies. I see the unending revolution of plants and flowers.
—I see the gunboats of Love.

And Creation, paying for the works of the ancient Governors,
will shudder with horror. Confusion will fall upon Hades, and the
planking will give way under the great pressure of the sun. But
before this, lo, young men will sigh, and their blood for no reason

at all will grow old. Shorn convicts will beat their platters on
their iron bars. All factories will fall empty, but after the
requisition they will be filled again to produce dreams conserved
in myriads of tin cans and a thousand varieties of bottled nature.
And lean years will come and pale, wrapped in bandages. And
each man will have his few grains of happiness. And all
things within him already will have turned to beautiful ruins.
Then, having no other exile to lament, and emptying the storm's
health out of his open chest, the Poet will return to stand amid the
beautiful ruins. And the first word this last of men shall say will
be for the grass to grow tall and for women to emerge at his side
like a sunray. And once more he will worship woman and lay her
on the grass, as commanded. And dreams will be avenged, and
together they will sow generations unto the ages of ages!

PSALM XVIII

Now I'm marching on to a distant and unwrinkled land.
Now azure girls follow me
    and stone ponies
with the sun's wheel on their wide brows.
    Generations of myrtles recognize me
from that time when I trembled on the iconostasis of water,
    crying out to me, holy, holy.
He that defeated Hell, he that liberated Love
    he is the Prince of Lilies.
And for a moment I was once more painted
    by those same zephyrs of Crete,
that crocus yellow might receive justice from the empyrean.
    Now in whitewash I enclose and entrust
my true Laws.
    Blessed, I say, are the strong who decode the Immaculate,
For their teeth alone is the grape-nipple that intoxicates
    on the breasts of volcanoes and the vineshoots of virgins.
Behold, let them follow in my footsteps!
    Now I'm marching on to a distant and unwrinkled land.

Now it is the hand of Death
    that bestows Life,
and sleep does not exist.
    The churchbells of midday are ringing
and slowly on sunhot rocks are engraved these words:
    NOW and AYE and WORTHY IT IS
Aye aye and now now warble the birds.
    WORTHY is the price paid.

from *GLORIA*

    PRAISED BE the mountain pass that opens
through clouds an endless azure pathway
    a voice somewhat mislaid in the valley
an echo the day drank up like balsam

    The effort and strain of oxen hauling
a heavy grove of olive trees westward
    the unruffled smoke that is always trying
to disperse the works man has created

    PRAISED BE the oil lamp as it passes
filled full of ruin and black shadows
    the page that under the ground was written
the song the Slender Girl sang in Hades

    The wood-carved beasts on the iconostasis
and the fish-bearing the ancient poplars
    the girls with stone hands, the enchanting Korae
and Helen's neck so like a shoreline.

    THE STAR-STUDDED trees with their benevolence
the musical notation of another cosmos
    the ancient belief there exists forever
what is very close by and yet invisible

    The shadow that leans them on their side earthward
some nuance of yellow in their remembrance

their ancient dancing above the gravestones
and far beyond all price their wisdom

The Olive, the Pomegranate, the Peach
the Pine, the Poplar, the Plane
the Oak, the Beech, the Cypress

PRAISED BE the teardrop that falls without reason
that slowly dawns in the lovely glances
of children who hand in hand go walking
and gaze at each other without ever speaking

The lovers who on rocks go stammering
a lighthouse discharging the sorrow of centuries
the cricket insistent as stings of conscience
and the woolen sweater alone on the hoarfrost

The oath-breaking mint that on teeth is stringent
two lips that cannot consent—however
the "goodbye" that shines awhile on lashes
and then the world grown dim forever

The heavy slow church-organ of hurricanes
Heraclitos' voice destroyed of its utterance
the other the invisible side of murderers
and the small "why" that remains unanswerable

EVER BE PRAISED the hand returning
from a heinous murder and is now enlightened
of what in truth is the world that's superior
what is the "now" and the "aye" of the cosmos:

Now to the wild beast of the myrtle *Now* to the cry of May
AYE to full consciousness and *Aye* to the full moon's ray

Now now to hallucination and the mimicry of sleep
Aye aye to the word itself and *Aye* to the astral's Keel

Now to the lepidoptera's swift undulating cloud
Aye to the lofty hovering light the Mysteries enshroud

Now to the husk of Earth and *now* to Dominance
Aye to the spirit's nutriment and *aye* to quintessence

Now to the still incurable melanosis of the moon
Aye to the Galaxy's gold-glittering azure sheen

Now to the amalgam of peoples and the Black Number
Aye to the statue of Justice and the Great Staring Eye

Now to the humiliation of the gods *Now* to the ashes of Man
Now Now to Nothingness
                    and *Aye* to the small world, the Great!

Níkos Gátsos

DEATH AND THE KNIGHT (1513)

Dürer zum Gedächtnis

As I behold you motionless
Traveling through the ages with the steed of Akrítas and the
          lance of Saint George,
I would place at your side
These dark forms that shall attend you eternally
Until one day you too will vanish with them forever
Until you become a fire again in the great Chance that gave you
          birth,
I would place at your side
A bitter-orange tree from the snowcovered meadows of the moon
And would unfold before you the veil of an evening
With the red Heart of Scorpio singing of youth
With the River of the Heavens pouring into August
And with the North Star weeping and growing cold;
I would place pasture lands,
Streams that once watered the lilies of Germany,
And I would deck this iron you wear
With a sprig of basil and a spray of rosemary
With the weapons of Plapoútas and the sabers of Nikitarás.
But I who saw your descendants tearing
The sky of my country like birds, one dawn in spring,
And saw the cypresses of the Moréa grow silent
There on the plain of Náfplion

620

Before the ready embrace of the wounded sea
Where the centuries battled with the crosses of gallantry
Shall now place at your side
The embittered eyes of a child
And the closed eyelids
In the mud and blood of Holland.

This black land
Shall one day grow green again.
The iron hand of Götz will overturn the carts
It will load them with sheaves of barley and rye
And in the dark forests with their dead loves
There where time has turned a virginal leaf to stone
On breasts where a rosetree trembled, hung with tears,
A silent star shall shine like a spring daisy.

But you shall remain motionless
Traveling through the ages with the steed of Akrítas and the
            lance of Saint George
A restless hunter from the generation of heroes
With these dark forms that shall attend you eternally
Until one day you too will vanish with them forever
Until you become a fire again in the great Chance that gave you
            birth
Until in river caverns shall resound again
The heavy hammers of patience
Not for rings and swords
But for shears and plows.

AMORGHOS

To a Green Star

Κακοὶ μάρτυρες ἀνθρώποισιν ὀφθαλμοὶ
καὶ ὦτα βαρβάρους ψυχὰς ἐχόντων

I

With their country tied to their sails and their oars hung on the
wind
The shipwrecked slept tamely like dead beasts on a bedding of
sponges
But the eyes of seaweed are turned toward the sea
Hoping the South Wind will bring them back with their lateen
sails newly painted
For one lost elephant is always worth much more than the two
quivering breasts of a girl
Only if the roofs of deserted chapels should light up with the
caprice of the Evening Star
Only if birds should ripple amid the masts of the lemon trees
With the firm white flurry of lively footsteps
Will the winds come, the bodies of swans that remained
immaculate, unmoving and tender
Amid the streamrollers of shops and the cyclones of vegetable
gardens
When the eyes of women turned to coal and the hearts of the
chestnut hawkers were broken
When the harvest was done and the hopes of crickets began.

And indeed this is why, my brave young men, with kisses, wine,
and leaves on your mouths
I would want you to stride naked along the riversides
To sing of the Barbary Coast like a woodsman hunting the mastic
shrubs
Like a viper slithering through gardens of barley
With the spirited eyes of pride
Like a lightning bolt as it threshes youth.

And do not laugh and do not weep and do not rejoice
And do not tighten your shoes in vain as though you were
      planting plane trees
Do not become D E S T I N Y
For the imperial eagle is not a closed drawer
It is not a tear of the plum tree nor a smile of the water lily
Nor the undershirt of a dove nor a Sultan's mandolin
Nor a silken garment for the head of a whale
It is a saw of the sea that rips the seagulls apart
It is a carpenter's pillow a beggar's watch
It is a fire in a blacksmith's shop mocking the wives of the priests
      and lulling the lilies
It is a wedding procession of Turks, a festival of Australians
It is a hideaway of Hungarian Gypsies
Where the hazel trees in autumn secretly congregate
They watch the sensible storks dyeing their eggs black
And then they also weep
They burn their nightgowns and dress themselves in the duck's
      petticoat
They strew stars on the ground for kings to walk upon
With their silver amulets, with their crowns and their purple
      mantles
They strew rosemary in garden plots
That mice may cross on their way to other cellars
To enter other churches and to eat of the Holy Altars,
And the owls, my lads,
The owls are howling
And dead nuns rise up to dance
With tambourines and drums and violins, with bagpipes and lutes
With bannerets and censors, with simples and magic veils
With the pantaloons of bears in the frozen valley.
They eat the mushrooms of martens
They play heads or tails with the ring of Saint John and the gold
      florins of the Blackamoor
They mock the witches
They cut off the beard of a priest with the yataghan of
      Kolokotrónis
They bathe themselves in vapors of incense
And afterwards, slowly chanting, enter the earth again and fall
      silent

As waves fall silent, as the cuckoo bird at dawn, as the oil lamp
    at evening.

And thus in a deep jar the grape shrivels and in the belfry of a fig
    tree the apple turns yellow
And thus flaunting a gay-colored necktie
Under a grapevine bower the summer suspires
And thus naked among white cherry trees a tender love of mine
    lies sleeping
A girl as unwithering as the branch of a flowering almond tree
Her head resting on her elbow and her palm on her golden treasure
On its early morning warmth while slowly and softly like a thief
From the window of spring the Morning Star comes to awake her.

II

It is told of the mountains how they tremble and of the fir tree's
    fury
When night gnaws at the nails of roof-tiles that the gnomes might
    enter
When Hell sucks in the foaming turbulence of torrents
When the hairline of the pepper tree becomes the North Wind's
    kick-about.

Only the oxen of the Achaeans browse, vigorous and strong
Amid the fat meadows of Thessaly, under the eternal sun that
    stares upon them
They eat green grass, celery, leaves of the poplar tree, they drink
    the pure water of furrows
They smell the sweat of the earth and then fall heavily under the
    shade of willow trees to sleep.

Cast off the dead said Heraclitos and saw the heavens grow pale
And saw two small cyclamen kissing each other in the mire
And himself fell down on the hospitable earth to kiss his own
    dead body
Like the wolf that comes down from the woods to look on the
    dead dog and to weep.
What good is the raindrop to me that glitters on your forehead?
I know that on your lips the thunderbolt has written its name

I know that in your eyes an eagle has built its nest
But here on the sodden bank there is one path only
One deceiving path only, and you must pass through it
You must steep yourself in blood before time overtakes you
And cross over to find your companions again
Flowers birds deer
To find another sea another tenderness
To seize the horses of Achilles by the reins
Instead of sitting there silent, scolding the river
Pelting the river with stones like the mother of Kítso.
For even you will be lost and your beauty shall wither.
Among the branches of an osier I see the innocent shirt of your
       childhood drying
Take it, a flag of life, to make a shroud for death
And may your heart yield not
May your tears fall not on this implacable earth
As once on the icy wastes rolled the tear of a penguin
To complain is useless
Life will be everywhere the same, with a flute of serpents in a
       land of phantoms
With a song of thieves in a forest of fragrance
With the knife-blade of sorrow in the cheeks of hope
With the yearning of spring in the innermost heart of an owlet
If only a plow may be found and a keen-edged scythe in a joyful
       hand
If only there blossom
A bit of grain for the holidays, a little wine for remembrance, a
       little water for the dust.

III

In courtyards of the sorrow-stricken no sun rises
And only worms emerge to mock at the stars
And only horses sprout amid the ant heaps
And all the bats eat birds and piss their sperm.

In courtyards of the sorrow-stricken no night falls
Only the foliage vomits a river of tears
When the devil passes by to mount the dogs
And ravens swim in a deep well of blood.

In courtyards of the sorrow-stricken the eye has dried
The brain has frozen, the heart has turned to stone
The flesh of frogs hangs down from the teeth of spiders
And starving locusts scream at the feet of vampires.

In courtyards of the sorrow-stricken the grass grows black
On a May evening now, a breeze drifts by
A footfall as light as a faint prairie tremor
A kiss of the sea adorned and decked with foam.

And if you thirst for water we shall wring a cloud
And if you hunger for bread we shall slay a nightingale
Wait but a moment only for the rue to unravel
For the black sky to blaze, the mullein to flower.

It was only a breeze and is gone, a lark and is lost
It was only the face of May, the moon's cold whiteness
A footfall as light as a faint prairie tremor
A kiss of the sea adorned and decked with foam.

IV

Awake purling water from the pine tree's root to find the eyes
of sparrows and to revive them, refreshing the earth with the
fragrance of basil and the spluttering of lizards. I know you
are a vein laid bare under the dreadful gaze of the wind, a mute
spark amid the bright throng of stars. No one attends you, no
one pauses to hear you breathe, but you with your sure tread amid
arrogant nature will reach one day to the topmost leaves of the
apricot, you will climb the slender bodies of small broom shrubs,
you will glide from the eyes of the beloved like an adolescent
moon. Somewhere an immortal rock exists where a human angel
once passing inscribed his name and a song as yet unknown by
anyone, not by the most delirious children nor the profoundest
nightingales. It is locked now in a cave of Mt. Dévi in the remote
valleys and the ravines of my forefathers' land, but when this
angelic song bursts out one day and flings itself against time and
corruption, the rains will suddenly cease and the mud will dry, the
snows will melt on the mountains, the wind will sing like a bird,
the swallows will come to life, the osiers will quiver, and men with

cold eyes and pale faces, hearing the bells in the cracked belfries
ringing by themselves, will find holiday caps to wear and
gay-colored ribbons to tie on their shoes. For then no one will
ever joke again, the blood of brooks will overflow, the animals will
burst from their bridles in the mangers, the hay will turn green
in the stables, on the roof-tiles fresh poppies and mayflowers will
sprout, and suddenly on all the crossroads at midnight red bonfires
will blaze. And then the timid girls will come slowly and quietly
to cast their last garments into the flames and to dance about them
nakedly, exactly as when we too were young and a window
would open at dawn that in their breasts might sprout a flaming
carnation. Ah lads, it may be that the memory we have of our
forefathers is a deeper consolation and a more precious companion
than a handful of rose water, that the intoxication of beauty is no
different from the sleeping rose tree of Eurotas. Goodnight, then:
I see a multitude of falling stars rocking your dreams, but I hold
in my fingers the music for a better day. The travelers returned
from the Indies have much more to tell you than all the Byzantine
chroniclers.

V

Man during the course of his Mysterious Existence
Has bequeathed to his Descendants tokens, diverse and worthy,
     of his Immortal Origin
As indeed he has also bequeathed traces of the ruins of early dawn,
     snowfalls of celestial reptiles, kites, diamonds, and the
     glances of hyacinths
Amid sighs, tears, hungers, lamentations, and the ashes of
     subterranean wells.

VI

How much I loved you only I know
I who once touched you with the eyes of the Pleiades
And embraced you with the mane of the moon and danced with
     you on the summery plains
On the hewn stubble and ate cut clover together
O dark vast sea with so many pebbles around your neck so many
     colored stones in your hair.

A vessel sails into the bay, a rusty well-wheel groaning
A tuft of blue smoke within the rose of the horizon
Exactly like the wing of a crane throbbing;
Armies of swallows await brave men to offer them welcome
Arms rise up naked with anchors engraved near the armpits
The cries of children mingle with the birdsongs of the West Wind
Honeybees buzz in and out of a cow's nostrils
The kerchiefs of Kalamáta are waving
And a distant bell dabbles the sky with bluing
Like the sound of a small gong traveling amid the constellations
So many centuries fled
From the souls of Goths and the domes of Baltimore
And from lost St. Sophia, the renowned cathedral.

But who are those who watch with unwavering eyes and serene
    faces from the top of the highest mountains?
This dust-storm in the air is the echo of what conflagration?
Can it be Kalívas fighting or is it Levendoyánnis?
Is it a clash perhaps between the Germans and the people of Máni?
No, it is neither Kalívas fighting nor Levendoyánnis
Nor is it a clash between the Germans and the people of Máni.
Towers are guarding in silence a princess turned phantom
The tops of cypress trees companion a dead windflower
Shepherds with reeds of linden serenely sing their morning songs
A foolish hunter fires on turtle-doves
And an old windmill, forgotten by all
Mends by itself its rotting sails with a needle of dolphin bone
And descends from the hillsides with a favorable northeaster
As Adonis descended the paths of Mt. Hélmos to say good evening
    to Gólfo.

Year after year have I struggled with hammer and ink, O my
    tormented heart
With gold and fire to stitch you an embroidery
The hyacinth of an orange tree
A blossoming quince to console you
I who once touched you with the eyes of the Pleiades
And embraced you with the mane of the moon and danced with
    you on the summery plains

On the hewn stubble and ate cut clover together
O dark vast solitude with so many pebbles around your neck so
        many colored precious stones in your hair.

OLD-FASHIONED BALLAD

To George Seféris

Time flows into time and year on year
till the world's river dulls and dims
but on dream's balcony I walk
to watch you stooped over your clay
embroidering your ships and swallows.

The sea is bitter our earth but little
and precious is water in the clouds
nakedness wraps each cypress tree
grass burns its ashes silently
and the sun's hunt goes on forever.

Then you came by and carved a fountain
for the old shipwrecked sailing man
who vanished though his memory stays
a brilliant shell on the Aegean
and a salt pebble in Santoríni.

From waterdrops that swayed on fern
I've taken a pomegranate's tear
that I too in this ledger may
spell out the heart's deep anguish there
with the first star of every fable.

But now that Holy Tuesday's here
and Resurrection is long in coming
set forth for Máni and for Crete
take there for everlasting friend
the wolf the eagle and the asp.

But if on your forehead you should see
a fallen star of old times shining
with a gentle glittering secretly
rise up and once more bring to life
the spring that lurks in your own rock.

Time flows into time and year on year
till the world's river dulls and dims
but on dream's balcony I walk
to watch you stooped over your clay
embroidering your ships and swallows.

Nikiphóros Vrettákos

ELEGY OF FLOWERING FIRE

Like the dead who are taken away to be burned
in a place preordained for this holy practice,
so in a velvet coffin my destiny now
carries me on its shoulders under black clouds.
And though it rains on my white shroud, the hooded
nights of my life follow me, stumbling.

The funereal pomp takes to the hills and descends
into the mist. Among the trees. Toward the far depths
where an enormous fire is waiting for me, made
from all the colored fires of this world,
from those of the sunset, of the ocean, of the stars,
from the fires of many moons on snow, from the dazzle
of atmospheres and the night colors of Taíyetos.

Azure, green, white, scarlet and silver
flames, as in a dance a group of nymphs and angels
who as they sing hymns peacefully gaze on the lectern
of the universe. And while Christ with a dog cuts
through the field, and my mother gathers crocuses
in her apron, the kingdom of flowers with all
her shepherds dance around the fire, illuminated,
as on the opposite slope they carry me through the noisy rain.

Beloved friends! O my beloved friends!
I am simple in my verses and even more simple

in my tears. Our century has darkened. Snowflakes
are thickly falling in all my blood, and I am naked
to the core, like an indifferent shepherd awake all night
on a thunder-lit, savage, and cloud-covered
mountain. Now gather my wretched sheep and kneel
before God for whatever is the most sorrowful,
most dark, most unbearable, most fallen thing
in the world today.
                  With heavy hammers they are nailing down
the windows of night. An evil wind is blowing;
it is growing dark. What rain! What frost! And this lone moon!
My coffin has filled with water. I grow cold, my brothers . . .

Whirled in the fury of the evil wind,
azure, green, white, scarlet and silver,
far in the distance, the fires shed their petals in the mist.

ELEGY ON THE TOMB
OF A YOUNG WARRIOR

On this your ground we say our name.
On this your ground we draw the plans for our gardens and our
        cities.
On this your ground We Are. We have a country.

I have kept your bullet-shot within me.
Within me wanders the poisonous burst of the machine gun.
When I remember your opening heart,
certain hundred-petaled roses rise in my brain
and resemble the conversation of the infinite with man.
Thus did your heart speak to us.
And we saw that the world is greater
and has become greater that it might contain love.

Your first toy: You.
Your first pony: You.

You played fire. You played Christ.
You played Saint George and the bold Border Guard.
You played the clock hands that descend from midnight down.
You played the voice of hope when no voice existed.

The square was deserted. Our country had gone.

It was time! Your heart could no longer endure
to hear under your roof the human thunderbolts of Europe.
Under your coat you lit the first thief's lantern.
Heart of hearts! You thought of the sun, and advanced . . .

You mounted the pavement and played Man.

BOY WITH HARMONICA

No longer shall the machine gun pass judgment on liberty.
No longer shall the torturers waste us away.
No longer will they come out to confront you,
boy of the wind with the harmonica!
Statue of the sidewalks whom the northwest wind blows
as you stand on one foot, whistling the ordeals of your country,
with a voice like that of the brook that warbles in your heart
—small heart of freedom that quivers like the Pleiades—
boy of the wind with the harmonica!

Your blood embraced the pepper trees of the avenue.
Your blood became a bird and it soared to sing for us
above the cypress trees of Constitution Square.
"*Titív, titsíou*, don't be afraid! *Titív, titsíou*, don't be afraid!"
You became the bird and the almond tree, the star and the window.

Limned by the lightning flashes against our door
that death embraced at night to force it open,
you shoved away the darkness by yourself—and we, what can we
        tell you?
Such intoxication of deathlessness our hearts cannot contain,
boy of the wind with the harmonica!

And we, O poet of poets, how shall we sing of you?
Companion of our hopes, tell us what to call you.
Tell us, because our lips suffer.
We don't want our words to fall useless to the ground,
to fail in a task like this.
Otherwise it would be better to go out and get killed in battle.
Otherwise it would be better to escape with ships in the oceans,
rather than steal the bread crumbs of the despairing
while you alone guard the narrow passes of night,
boy of the wind with the harmonica!

I shall go out to the fields to gather the fallen lights of the sun
and to mold its lightrays—this very summer,
to mold its lightrays into leaves, that I may write
of the sky and of your song, child of Greece,
because the soil is not enough for me! My blood is not enough
          for me!
Because my tears are not enough with which to mold my clay.
Of what use is my house? Outdoors they sing of you,
outdoors they talk of you. My voice is not enough.
I shall run where I heard you say "No" to death,
I shall run there where you walked and whistled against
the thunderbolt, against the command and the sweet bread of
          earth, against
your azure eyes made for love.

And I shall shake off your sorrows from the pepper trees.
And I shall gather all your tiny voices. And I shall cover
the Holy Altar of my poetry with your common workshirt.
And I shall gather wildflowers as though I were raising your flag
that I may plant it at dawn on the threshold of our country,
on the threshold of time and of ships. As though I were raising
the Host of Greece from the asphalt,
pierced with the bullets of the enemy. To raise you
and to place you on a bronze pedestal that you may whistle
standing on one foot, leaning your head jauntily on your shoulder
under the cloudlets of time
in Constitution Square.

How shall I see you? What shall I call you? How shall I draw you,
boy of the wind with the harmonica!

THE MORNING SKYLARK

My spirit bursts in an azure torrent,
all the veins of my blood run in my voice,
my blood gurgles in the silence like crickets in the bushes,
like the river that never considers the number of its drops,
descending like a splendor or like a drunken kiss toward the sea.
Above me the worlds buzz on festive crossroads,
violet, rose, white, and azure rivers
rolling among stringed instruments, and the atmosphere shines.

Wheatstalks quiver with the silvery echoes of the universe.

Struck dumb, I listen to the friendly message of God
who asks me from the heart of light with all the mouths
of His angels to answer Him whether I am happy,
who asks me with the golden flutes of the sunbeams,
and I answer Him with His own light, which overbrimming
makes blue the larklike stream of my spirit.
Like a star between the light of the sun and of love,
fluttering in the high tree of His window,
I peck at the morning light and answer Him by whistling like the
            birds, without words.

WITHOUT YOU THE PIGEONS

Without you the pigeons
would not have found water

Without you God would not have lit
His light at His wellsprings

An apple tree strews her flowers
in the wind; in your apron

you bring water from the sky,
the light of wheatstalks, and on you

a moon made of sparrows.

SUNSET

What sapphire changes, what festivities of the Omnipotent!
a music of colors in watery hues,
and whoever counts the colors loses count of his fingers
and begins from the beginning, and weeps in the miracle;

and my lips open and my soul utters light.

THE ORANGE TREES OF SPARTA

The orange trees of Sparta, snow, flowers of love,
grew white with your words, bent their boughs,
I filled my lap, and went to my mother.

She was sitting under the moon, brooding over me,
she was sitting under the moon, scolding me:

"Yesterday I washed your hair, yesterday I changed your dress.
Where have you been roaming,
who filled your clothes with tears
and bitter-orange blossoms?"

SLEEP

For you I spread pine needles on the hilltop
and over them cast the rays of the sun, and above these
spread a smile that your body might not tire.

And I told time not to awaken you.
Or, better still, to awaken you as late as possible,
because very often things happen but once only
though the days are all alike and the sun eternal.

THE FLOWERING DOGWOOD

We could see since morning there would be an excess of light
        that day.
It was then spring. And the dogwood trees in flower.
Their blossoms seemed like wellsprings filled to overflowing.
Appearing on the high slopes, they descended and foamed white
under the sun like thrashing river waters.
The light their blossoms emitted had such force
you stood beside them speechless, hesitating to approach them.
And when I stretched out my hand, broke a branch
and offered it to you, God then illuminated
his most beautiful day in the world. The foliage dripped gold.
All creation above shook wholly and lost its rhythm.
The houses took small steps in the light,
and as the zephyr blew, flowers from your cheeks
and your garments fell to the ground.
Looking about you, speechless, you asked me
if the world, if beauty, if colors, if love had any limits.
And I did not answer—everything around me gestured no.
Because on your breast you had placed the small branch
of the dogwood and it glittered endlessly. Because the sun
had cut off the shadows of the trees, and the stone
had become light, the wind light, time light. Because
all the world about us had turned to Easter and to love.

RETURN FROM DELPHI

Mounted beside me on the float, the Charioteer drove on.
The Phaedriades followed close behind us.
Strange echoes drifted through the night,

a night which seemed so unlike all other nights
of the world, that even the kingly nights
of my childhood years gave way before it.
All things were so translucent, the mountains
so sharply limned in light, it seemed as though
some universal torchbearer, running along the heights,
had been sent by Pythian Apollo to escort us,
lighting the horizon with his flaming torch above us.

Beyond the mountain firs, the gold and glittering
sickle of the moon ran lightly beside us
like a slim fawn, until it set and the world changed,
as though God had turned a page. The sky
seemed like a flowering bough, as though
a strange Spring had bloomed above us. Always erect at our side,
the charioteer now and again loosened his reins,
gazed at the universe above him, and smiled.

We looked at one another in amazement, nor knew
if it was night on earth or daylight
somewhere in another world. Clasping each other's hands,
we gazed above us and about us, nor understood
why all things around us had become so beautiful.
Not knowing what had happened, we felt as though
our souls had become treasured music. We drove on,
and our hearts rang like bells at dawn. Will it end?
One fear we harbored only. Can it be that soon
this journey will end? Dear God, will it end?
And what will become of all this light that undulates
and overflows and rolls through the universe in one
unending ebb tide, uncontainable? All things shone as though
the Springs of all the ages had come out in the firmament
to saunter slowly throughout the heavens in single file,
holding stars and flowers in their hands.

                                                 For the first time
we felt there were moments in this world
that exist beyond time. Unknown, the length
of their duration. Months? Years? Centuries?
Moments that counterbalance all our lives.

                                                     Let it not end!

Without speech, without a whisper, as though all words
had been exhausted, as though we knew no language, as though
no language would do, like the stars and fir trees of Parnassos,
we fell silent. When beneath the holy firmament you return
from Delphi, your weeping barely restrained, a single tear
becomes a language myriad-tongued. It seemed to us that something
could be dimly heard, as though from somewhere beyond her star
Sappho was playing her lyre. Meanwhile all were silent,
we and the stars and the poets of the ages and the wind
asleep in the olive trees, and nothing could be heard
but the echoes of the Phaedriades, humming and resounding
all night long, that night the most beautiful in all our lives,
and which shall never come again; echoes which seemed as though
an arch-herald, erect within the silence, kept repeating:

"In the name of Zeus! Of what use are words when one's in love?"

Like lilies fell the shooting stars. Echoes swayed
the jasmine of the skies. All doors were left unlocked.
No flower was left unblossomed. No star unlit.
And Omnipotence, dressed in all her graces,
descended from above us! As we traveled on,
we felt there was no road or earth beneath our feet,
as though a maddened river rocked us on its crest and swept us on.

O overbrimming ocean, Heart, take us where you will!

SAYING FAREWELL

I believe it was the month of July, on an afternoon when I
        saw you
ascending the road with the eucalyptus trees,
a little above the sea. I recognized you
because you had a soul as fragile as the lemon tree's first blossom,
and on your crimson skirt you carried a fawn's tremor.
The sun had taken you by both hands, and was bringing you.

The sea had turned your back into azure hues. All things were
       bringing you.
The road to Delphi was bringing you, and the half moon.
The sparrows were bringing you, fluttering with joy.
The leaves of the vineyards were bringing you, the honeybees,
       the glittering
of grapes, the creaking of the well winch,
the white gulls, the almond trees.
                    My Pleiades, farewell.

The light wandered softly above the hilltops
and the sunset over them seemed like a triumphal arch
made of carnations, wild rose shrubs, and anemones.
We set out hurriedly and climbed to come in time.
Whenever you threw a stone, it would flower in the air.
We said the word "eternity" and we had said nothing.
We said the word "joy" and we had said nothing.
We walked under forest trees, we stopped at springs,
and you slept at the side of love, innocent, without a care,
in a cradle of reflections which the sky had taken
by its sides and was rocking.
                    My Pleiades, farewell.

Now you have become entangled in your footsteps, you strive.
But come now, tell me: Where are you going? Wait a moment,
your dress has been hooked by the sun,
and no matter what you do, you shall not escape. Wait till I speak
       to you.
Sometimes the roads take us and bring us somewhere else.
We leave, in truth, we change, we study the sky,
searching unceasingly for the stars of happiness.
But I, who know these horizons well,
who know what lies beyond the mountains, know these roads.
I have stopped up your passageways with flowering trees,
I have gathered whatever good still remains in my heart,
whatever beauty still exists in the heavens,
to prevent your passing. Do not leave, no.
I would have suffered if you were cold there,
in the depths of anonymity, a stranger and alone; in the darkness

that levels out all faces, that unites
pebbles with lemon blossoms.

My Pleiades, farewell.

If you wish, I will say goodbye. If you wish, I will see you out.
But whatever you had that was good, whatever was sun,
whatever was color, will not come with you. If you wish, go.
But you can no longer leave. You will remain here.
Like the Castalian waters, you will flow in my verses forever.
You will sway in my book like the olive groves of Delphi.
Do not look: the sycamore trees will wither
and the years will fly over you like migratory birds,
but you will remain to keep the Charioteer company.
And since I will not, perhaps, see you another time,
keep your mind sharp when the zephyr blows. Be careful
of spring when you stride over its flowers, when you gaze
into the waters of the stream, when the morning star
goes by with its white ponies, because you are as frail as light.
I have woven you a halo made of a slender moon.
I have dressed you in May and starlight. I have written you
on the elements which revive the life of the world, that you may
        remain.
That daybreak may always find you. That the sun
may run at your side when it rises and when it sets.
And every year the two of you together would enter the
        firmament,
springtime before you, and you following after, wearing in your
        hair
a garland of dogwood blossoms.

My Pleiades, farewell.

THE CLEANEST THING IN CREATION

I'm not sure, but a smudge of darkness has remained.
The sun has poured into me through a thousand wounds.
And this whiteness with which I surround you now
you will not find even in the Alps, because this wind

swirls to that great height and dirties the snow.
You will find a trace of dust even on the white rose.
The perfect miracle may be found only in man:
vast stretches of whiteness that radiate truthfully
throughout the universe and are superior. The cleanest thing
in creation, therefore, is not the twilight,
nor the sky reflected in the river, nor
the sun on apple blossoms. It is love.

DRUNKEN MAN WITH CARNATION

Now and then from on high the starry night showered
our faces with white light. And as we walked on,
you staggered for a moment and, leaning on my shoulder,
a wheatstalk blinded with light, you told me to write that
"we two shall die together."

                    Now I have become
a golden skylark that darts up and down
in the light; but the sky has many folds
and is filled with many clouds of the sun, and you will lose
the lark in the beehives of light. But you must always
have a bit of blond grain ready in your hand,
a bit of God's water in the dimples of your laughter,
because your small hands, my love, are even more tender
than poetry. Because your friendship
is even more azure than the sky—and you know
that if death existed, we would die together.

                    See where again
I come toward you, staggering under the firmament,
with the coat of joy flung over my shoulder.

                    But look!
How beautiful this life is! How beautiful this world!
As I was coming, what should I see? Around me the grasses were
        kissing,
the zephers embracing, the birds crazily darting,
and over my ear I had hung a white carnation;
but as I was coming to find you, when dawn was turning

velvet in the sky, the light blew, and my carnation fell.
As I tried to find it, now here, now there, everything blazed up—
        and it was spring!
Everything had flowered! And all wellsprings, and my heart
and my tongue were unloosed, and my lips are now a rose-red cleft
in the air. My words well up and overflow,
and as I speak them, my love, they become entangled with light.
One part voice, two parts light and love and water
and color and springtime breezes blowing and—
        they become all entangled!
As I was coming to find you—forgive me—
I stopped by our old and familiar tavérna,
there where the shooting stars would meet—messages
from the present, from the future, from eternity!
And there I was welcomed by friends and friends and other
friends and hands and voices and laughter—
        I overdid it!
I gulped down three cups of sun, my sweet lemon flower,
and I overdrank with angels for company—
        I blazed up!
and now I stagger drunkenly; and you know, my love,
that death is a star that enwreathes our hair.

TO A FRIEND

The sun is setting. Its rays hang across from me like a harp.
I see your hands growing longer, ready to play me
a song. Your hands, which you forgot in that place where
we had been sitting by the sea. Your hands which you forgot
amid the wildflowers one morning as we sat on the grass.
Which you left on my table, and though I ran after you,
I could not find you. You had vanished on the crossroads of the
        world.

Your hands which you forgot on my forehead,
as preoccupied God forgets his streams. Your hands
which you forgot on my verses

as you listened to them breathing like the small
breasts of Mangalís, that night when above her she had placed
the icon of Saint Mary to watch over her,
at her side the nurse with the white blouse.
Your hands which you forgot on my life,
tied with a sea-blue ribbon, and which now
I keep in my traveling bag where
there is nothing more than my father's
blessing and a few crumbs, more than enough for me
as I cut my way through my eternal rain, bareheaded,
halfway through our century, to create
a smile for those to come.

Your hands, which you forgot
I shall never give back to you. I shall never return them to you
throughout the unending century. At this time
I am thinking of leaving for my village. There is
a church there. As you enter, to the right,
you will find an angel without hands, painted
about two hundred years ago. I shall give him your hands.

THE OTHER MORNING

When I got up the other morning,
Jenny had thrown the window shutters wide open
to the blue horizon. She was wearing her new
rose-colored dress that glittered
like the emerald sea at daybreak. Her hair tumbled down
over her shoulders like a small
golden waterfall.
                 Dante was playing
his harmonica, and one would say his fingers
dripped with music and water into his
mother's soul. Helen also came
to the house in the afternoon and brought three flowerpots,
our roses for tomorrow. I wandered about, I looked,
I found the papers on my table sympathetic,

the idea of war improbable.
No sort of coffin could possibly fit into the universe.
Indeed, I wanted to write to the world:
If ever I talk to you about
such things, know this: I will refer to a coffin
filled with sun.

ON TRANSLATION

I. General Observations

It is vain to insist, like Robert Frost, that poetry is that which is lost in translation. The hyperbole of this statement simply draws attention to the difficulty of a task which confronts both original poet and his interpreter, for both are translators. The poet is possessed by a vision, an inspiration, a complexity of thought and emotion, which he must then try to embody in words, sounds, cadences, images, rhythms. He must wrestle in the labyrinth of grammar and syntax with all the wealth of his language, and in Greek with a language which is also schizophrenic, split as it is between demotic and purist, and with the variety between these two in the long history of its development. The poet cannot hope to present his vision intact, just as a translator cannot hope to present the poet's work unaltered. Such a hope is an illogical absurdity and is tantamount to saying—if I may be permitted another hyperbole—that Homer must be translated back into Homer, Shakespeare into Shakespeare, Rilke into Rilke. The ideal translator, in this sense, is he who insists on reading the poem in the original only; but even then, he must "translate" the work in terms of his own imagination, abilities, age and culture. All the original poet can hope to do is to present, both to himself and to others, not the vision itself, but an approximation of that vision. We must set aside, in this essay, the more difficult task of ascertaining whether the vision is possible or even exists without the words in which it is apprehended, and in what way language itself creates or alters the vision. The poet is inevitably a betrayer of his own vision, and the translator of the poet's embodiment into words.

Even the poem itself, from the moment it is created, never exists as an unchanging integrity. If it is read and interpreted

649

differently by the poet himself, his friends, his contemporaries, consider what metamorphoses it undergoes when read after the intervening centuries, and even millenniums, of an astounding variety of cultures in ceaseless evolution and revolution. The *Oedipus the King* we read or see or hear or understand today, whether in the original or in translation, is not the same play Sophocles and his contemporaries heard or interpreted, for our minds are laden with all the accumulated detail of historical knowledge that has intervened since then, and with minds, in this particular instance, oriented by Freudian and more modern psychology. The music of Beethoven played today by Karajan under the shadow of the Akropolis, or at the New York City Center by Bernstein, is not that which Beethoven or his contemporaries heard in Vienna in the early nineteenth century. The St. Francis that El Greco painted in Spain in the early seventeenth century is not the same painting that we gaze on today at the Chicago Art Institute. The poem itself does not exist. It is simply a series of marks printed on paper, or sounds audible to the ear, to be variously "translated" by varied readers or listeners at various stages in history and the development of national or world cultures. The marks on the piece of paper do not change, but the poem itself is constantly being reinterpreted and retranslated in the minds and imaginations of its readers. The work of the translator is only one aspect of this general and protean metamorphosis.

We must not lament, therefore, that translations are betrayals of the original poem. The original vision may never be regained; yet this situation is not tragic, but simply irrevocable, and even magnificently exhilarating. A fine translation not only reshapes the body of a work, striving to attain to a reasonable and recognizable likeness. It does much more. It infuses new life into this body by injecting into it the warm, living blood of its own time, place, and language. It brings it back into life, gives the phantom shape in such a way that it becomes meaningful again for our own time and place, and continues to contribute to the ever-shifting multiformity of life and its evolution. Great translations help to break down the barriers of time, place and language, of unique customs and traditions. One has only to consider what gaps of knowledge, sensitivity and national growth would have existed in countries throughout the world had they not known one another's culture through translations. The original work is often a depository or a summation or a blossoming of an entire culture—like the *Iliad* and the *Odyssey* of Homer, like the Bible of the Hebrews—and in which modes and manners of life are extremely different from those of nations into whose languages it has been translated. If a translation manages to live on in another language as a literary masterpiece in its own right, or even as a fleeting contemporary likeness, then one nation, one way of life, has enriched another by injecting into its life stream one of the myriad sources in the astonishing multiformity of life. Good translations are thus blood transfusions, often giving life to what was on the point of dying; but these transfusions must be given repeatedly as languages and cultures change from generation to generation. The work itself remains beyond time or place, like a Himalayan peak, rising serenely in abstract embodiment above the stormy waves of history, enshrouded in its own particular place and time, monolithic and enigmatic, a cryptogram to be solved into different values and meanings at different times and places. It can never be carried across integrally as it once was, but as it has been reinterpreted by new eyes, new spirits, new insights.

To *translate* means literally "to carry across," and implies all other forms with which the prefix of this word is laden. It means not only transportation or transmission or transposition or transplantation; it is not only transformation and transmutation and transcendence and transillumination, but ultimately it is transubstantiation: "The changing of one substance into another, a removal or conveyance to another realm, without death." It is certainly not transgression. It is not only metathesis or metastasis or metabasis or metaphrase; it is not only metaphor and metagenesis and metaphysics, but finally it is metamorphosis and, ultimately, metabiosis: "A form of relationship between two organisms when one of the two can flourish only after the other has preceded it and prepared the environment for it." Translation is the urge to go beyond and over, beyond lands and nations and times and languages, proceeding under a million guises and disguises toward that ideal realm, that Ithaca, that universal language longed for but never attained, a spiritual if not a physical communication. Translation may become obsolete only when man develops an instantaneous sense of communication, like that of telepathy; but even then, the imperfect embodiment of a work in translation imparts a meaning and a manner, transfuses something of its own cellular structure to the essence and becomes something else again, gains something of the wounded, the imperfect, the human, and thus becomes lovingly mortal and fills us with an enriched compassion. Everything in this world, as we know it, is an approximation, whether from God to Adam, from vision to poet, from poem to reader or translator. Even in our approach to understanding we must read between the lines to discern the spirit and not simply to transliterate the letter.

The questions to be asked and the problems confronted, therefore, should not have to do with the possibility or value of translations, but with the various kinds possible and their intent, from the most literal to the most free. There is no one form of translation which is valid or "better" than another, for this depends on intention. Once the translator has stated clearly what he set out to accomplish, and for what purpose, his work then should be judged according to the integrity of his accomplishment and not be condemned for what it never meant to be. All forms of translation are valid and should be judged on their own terms.

One of two extremities is the interlinear trot, or pony, wherein the translation is printed exactly under each line of the original text, word by word, distorting syntax and grammar in order to remain faithful to the original and thus point out similarities and differences in the structure of both languages. This, accompanied by notes, is extremely helpful for the beginning student of a language (as recommended long ago by Milton) and for those readers whose desire is more to read and learn the original poem than to enjoy an approximation. Notes are mandatory because such a literary rendering, contrary to popular opinion, often distorts the sense of the original, and is more an aid to the vocabulary and structure of the language than to the total impact of the poem. For instance, an American reading a colloquial Greek poem with interlinear aid may be startled to be told that it was raining "table and chair legs," and may well conclude he was reading a surrealist and not a folk poem. A Greek reader, on the other hand, would be similarly bemused to read in his interlinear text of an American poem that it was raining "cats and dogs." A Greek would say "He took out his larynx," instead of "He shouted his head off," or "It makes cold" instead of "It's cold."

A further step would be a literal rendering which would be

faithful to the original text in terms of meaning, where every word would be accounted for in the general sense of the phrase or the clause, but which would be reformed into the syntactical and grammatical structure of the language into which it was being translated. This also, as in Stanley Burnshaw's *The Poem Itself*, should be accompanied by the original text and supplied with notes. It may be the place here to point out, however, that even the simplest word can never be rendered with its exact equivalent into another language. The word "bread" in a Greek poem would have different connotation to a Greek reader, depending on what part of the country he came from, what the kind and quality of the bread baked there, whether he was living abroad and in what land. The Yiddish, the Polish, the African, the French, the American reader would visualize the word according to his local experience and so feel it on his imaginary taste buds. The famous azure "sky" and the clear blue Aegean "sea" can be evoked only approximately by an Alaskan on the Bering Straits or by an inhabitant of Tierra del Fuego. The transliteration of physical objects, therefore, must always of necessity be inexact, and this is multiplied a thousand times when equivalents are sought for such cultural abstractions as "justice," "love," "sex," "truth," "happiness" and "honor." There is nothing exactly synonymous between languages or, for that matter, within a language itself.

Every translator is filled with envy to find words, concepts and views of life for which there are not even equivalent words in his language. The word παλικάρι, translated "palikar" (as found in unabridged English dictionaries) cannot possibly contain the historical or folk connotations it holds for a native Greek, and must be paraphrased in various ways to denote a brave, dashing, reckless and gallant young man or warrior. This is true of a similar Greek word, λεβέντης, and of παλικαριά and λεβεντιά, the essence of such youths. And how to translate φιλότιμο, a quality of personal and family honor peculiar to the Greek alone, saturated in the ethos of his national character? For that matter, even though a Greek should phonetically translate the word "cowboy" (or "drugstore cowboy"!) and retain something of its indigenous use from the many Westerns he has seen, it still cannot mean for him what it means to a Texas ranger. What is one to do with γιορτόπιασμα, a contemptuous expression used to denote a child conceived during the lax gaieties of a fiesta? Or with λιόκρουσι, used to describe that moment when the full moon, rising in the east, is struck by the rays of the sun descending in the west? What cannot be translated, as Saint Jerome has noted, is the indigenous quality of a language. It has often been said that a thought or idea, if fully paraphrased, cannot be lost in another language, but this is not altogether true, for often the quality of a racial concept, or cultural experience, or mode of living cannot be separated from the sounds, words and intonations into which it has been incarnated.

All this a conscientious translator knows better than his readers, but ultimately he should be less discouraged than exhilarated to see what astonishing common ground of understanding and communication can, nevertheless, exist on such ambiguous and ever-shifting terrain. If we grant that in their nature all translations of any kind are basically absurd, we can then be stimulated by the myriad possibilities of simulacra, by the tension of challenge, by the act of re-creation itself and its occasional accomplishments. A good literal translation is what a black-and-white photograph is to the original painting: form, proportion, content, whatever is compositional and structural, can adequately be reproduced, but the original colors, tones, nuances, intensities and suggestivities must irrevocably be lost and be replaced by "synonymous" qualities peculiar to one language alone. It is not the translator's business, said Sir John Denham, "to translate Language into Language, but Poesie into Poesie."

The extreme opposite to interlinear transliteration is free adaptation or paraphrase where a poet may use the original work of another simply as a springboard, as a source of inspiration, and adapt it with extremely deviant degrees of "faithfulness" as he sees fit, limited only by the creative powers of his own free-flying imagination. I have in mind, to name a few, such imitations as Lowell's Baudelaire, FitzGerald's *Rubáiyát*, Pound's *Propertius* or *Women of Trachis*, Jeffers' *Medea*, or Yeats's *King Oedipus* and *Oedipus at Colonus*. Such adapters should never claim to have presented the original work authentically, nor should critics attack such works for what they were never intended to be. They are what they are, depending on the degree of faithfulness or free adaptation intended. They are never faithful equivalents of the original work, nor completely free creations without obligations to the original. Many such adaptations have taken their place among the authentic treasures of English literature. Pound's *Women of Trachis* is by no means Sophocles, but it can be enjoyed as an adroit, eccentric and slangy creation that has its own integrity and rationale. Yeats's choral poem from *Oedipus at Colonus*, "Come praise Colonus' horses, and come praise / The wine-dark of the wood's intricacies" is, to my mind, one of the great glories of *English* poetry. Such adaptations, if created by true poets, may be enjoyed as original creations, and a comparison with the text from which they have departed can only serve to heighten our delight and appreciation of both. Often they add an essence or image to the original which ever after subtly prevents us from reading that poem again in the same way. It is in this sense that translations can become a form of criticism. Walter Pater's description of Mona Lisa's smile has forever made it impossible to gauge da Vinci's intent without taking that notorious remark into consideration. Such adaptations have become a legitimate genre of literature, a form in which a poet may find a new kind of freedom, variations as legitimate in their field as Beethoven's on a theme by Mozart or Diabelli, or Bach's organ adaptations of Vivaldi's concertos. Everything depends on the talent of the adapter. Fifty composers were invited to write one variation each on a waltz by Diabelli, and Beethoven wrote thirty-three uninvited. Who remembers the others? Where is the slush of yesteryear? Good adaptations may be likened to a graft on the main trunk of an original poem, branching off to produce a related but different fruit or flower of the same species, or even a sport or mutation.

But "variation," by its very nature, implies an original pattern from which it has departed, and a reader, fully to appreciate the extent of originality or faithfulness, should also have available on the market a reasonably literal translation of the original. There is nothing to prevent a poet, of course, from being inspired and freely adapting contemporary works which are little known or still unknown in translation, but he should then clearly make known his procedure that readers may not confuse his mutation with the original work, or scholars quote from it as proof or example of the original poet's thought or style. On the whole, such free adaptations are more legitimate and may more thoroughly be enjoyed when they are re-creations of famous works already available in several more or less literal translations. It is then that the work of the original poet can best be gauged, as well as that of his adapter, and the languages and literatures of both cultures appreciated and enriched. If a poem has a value in its own right and is worthy of being translated, an adaptation of it by another poet of talent will enlarge the possibilities of its overtones and suggestivities. If, however, it is freely adapted by a poet of little talent, twisted and distorted to meet an inferior style and insight, the results can be appalling. Such adaptation is not for all. A true translator-poet feels impelled to create such mutations, I imagine, because he can work in a medium and style not native to him in his own language, but which fascinates and challenges him. In his own poetry he plays himself, but in his adaptations he can take on many masks of which he is enamored and play many roles. A poet of some talent can find in another's poem in another language an already given, completed vision and composition which may help him round out his own dexterity and extend the range of his imagination. A poet of little talent can only create a disaster; such a translator, impelled by an ambition beyond his reach, and under cover of recent toleration for free adaptation, invariably impoverishes the original work. I have often noticed, in such cases, that a good literal translation of a fine poem preserves more daring, imaginative, and true innovations than a poor adapter's mediocrities.

Between interlinear transliteration and free adaptation a translator may adjust according to the demands of the situation, the poem, the differences of time, culture and language, and the permissiveness of the poet himself if he is still living. All combinations are permissible, provided that the translator is talented and responsible, and makes his intention clear. In my own translations from the modern Greek, because all the poets have been my near contemporaries and most of them are still living, my intention has been that which Carne-Ross calls "transposition." It occurs when "the language of the matter to be translated stands close enough to the language of the translator—in age, in idiom, in cultural habits, and so on—for him to be able to follow the letter with a fair hope of keeping faith with the spirit." This has been my method on the whole, but I have permitted myself a wide latitude according to the problems and the exigencies presented by each poet or poem. Although one must have a more or less clear idea of how he wishes to proceed, he should never permit himself to be bound rigidly by any one set of rules but should allow himself the freedom or luxury of breaking them whenever his intuition or the circumstances demand. This should be kept in mind as a corollary to whatever rules I may propound in this essay.

II. On Translating from the Modern Greek

Perhaps some description of how I have worked may be of aid to readers and translators both. But first I must account for my boldness in undertaking to translate so many different and even antithetical poets in this anthology, and a number as large and as varied in a companion volume, *Contemporary Greek Poetry*. I began meeting and translating these poets when I first went to Greece in 1946, and have worked on these translations on and off during these intervening twenty-six years, interrupted by a span of some four years during which I translated Kazantzákis' *Odyssey, Saviors of God,* and two of his plays. About eighteen years ago I could have published a volume of about fifteen poets, but came to the conclusion that these represented only those in the surrealist and symbolist traditions, and would not adequately represent the richness, variety, and value of a literature which, in my opinion, can compare favorably with that of any other modern country, and which is not put to shame by its illustrious progenitors. Had I known that these anthologies would have grown to such proportion, I might have solicited the aid of other translators and have been content to remain the general editor, but my love and admiration for these poets and their work led me on, imperceptibly. Of course, in most cases a translator should attempt to re-create only those poets for whom he has a natural affinity, or who may excite or challenge him in some aspect of insight or technique.

I have been aided in the variety of my response, I believe, by several factors. Born on an island in the Sea of Marmara, I spoke Greek as a child of immigrant parents in the United States, and returned to Greece primarily to explore my roots and heritage, although whatever mastery I may have of the Greek language was attained later primarily by working on these translations with the aid of the poets, and by setting up residence in Greece. As a professor of English and American literature, I discovered in myself a proclivity for the appreciation and understanding of many contradictory schools of poetry, even though, as one who has written some poetry himself, I have my own predilections. I am impatient with poets and translators who blindly believe that poetry should be written or translated according to this or that theory only—although I do understand that a poet, in order to write with total belief, must become so passionately steeped in his own vision and its expression as almost of necessity to consider it the one and only mode of expression. A teacher or translator, however, need not necessarily be limited by such allegiances. Indeed, to a person such as myself who, regardless of his predilections, is loathe to surrender himself to any one mode of thought or expression, translating a wide diversity of poets permits him, like an actor, to assume many roles without entirely surrendering to any or even blurring his own personality and predispositions. Such a translator, I imagine, must by nature be sympathetic to an aesthetic which holds that poems are infinite resolutions between opposites, from the most harmonious to the most intense, and that what is valid is not any one manifestation of this interrelationship but a series of organic resolutions unique and peculiar to each. I first became aware of this inclusiveness in my own temperament when at the University of Wisconsin, at the age of twenty, I wrote metaphysical poetry in imitation of Eliot, but at the same time translated, designed, and directed *The Bacchae* of Euripides.

Such temperamental delight in the heterogeneity of life in all forms has permitted me to respond, with engrossed attention in each case, to extremely different and antithetical modes of expression, and I have attempted to reproduce these divergences in my translations. Seféris, for instance, must be translated with an almost literal exactitude by choosing words that are simple, discrete, neither colloquial nor formal, and in rhythms that are muted, restrained, whispered, to be heard in the inner ear. Kazantzákis, at the other extreme, must be translated with much greater freedom, in a language that is robust, unrestrained, adjectival, rhetorical, and in rhythms and orchestrations that may be vigorously declaimed. Correspondingly, Seféris himself will not brook much latitude in his translations, whereas Kazantzákis often urged me to take more liberties than I felt were necessary. Each poet, in his use of language and rhythms, offers new challenges and exciting problems to the technician and man of vision both: in Papatsónis, the language and rhythms of deduction and prose statement; in Karélli, abstract yet passionate thought almost devoid of metaphor; in Mátsas, a languid sensuality and an elegant diction; in Antoníou, a gnarled terseness and a lyrical notation; in Cálas, a pyrotechnic of multiple puns and connotations; in Elýtis, a plasticity of imagery and patterns; in Rítsos, an indirection of symbolic statement on the one hand and a loose loquaciousness of monologue on the other; in Sikelianós, an aura of mystical exaltation in highly subordinated cadences; in Caváfis, a dryness of wit and an expert manipulation of traditional and free rhythms.

The first duty of a translator with a protean sense of empathy, therefore, is to surrender himself as much as possible to the singular vision and aesthetics of the poet and poem he is translating. Nevertheless, true protean strength can arise only in a constant play (as all good actors know) between the singularity of the original author and an almost equal singularity of the translator-poet himself. Although we may be astonished by the extraordinary changes in voice, tone, dialect, makeup, tricks of mannerism and style of a Laurence Olivier—from Sophocles to Sheridan to Beckett—there is no mistaking the total stamp of his personality on each of his multiple roles which distinguishes them as re-creations of Laurence Olivier, and no one else's. Nothing truly creative can arise out of an amorphous personality, whether that of an actor, a poet, or a translator. In the work of a good translator who essays a wide variety of forms, styles, and points of view, his own personality, his own tone of voice not only *is* but *should* be overheard as that one quality which gives unity and cohesion to his anthology, just as we understand immediately that it is Toscanini's or Mitropoulos' or Szell's interpretation we are hearing, say, of Beethoven's Great Fugue, Opus 135. The translator's voice should be there, but overheard, not heard, subordinated to the primary strength of the original creator.

A reader of this anthology has by now become aware of the language problem faced by all Greek poets, and the extent to which each has utilized the full resources of his heritage. Although most poets have based their structure and morphology on the demotic, each has taken his vocabulary and phraseology from all periods according to his own peculiar temperament and tastes, as in the limpid demoticism of Seféris or the extreme form of the purist of Embirícos in his early period. This admixture cannot possibly be reproduced in English, which is a language that will not permit similar amalgamations of its historical evolution, even though the time span of its development is much shorter than that of the Greek. All the translator can do is to impose, on a basic English, colorations taken from colloquial, literary, and formal usages. A note of the purist may occasionally be indicated by the use of rather stilted words or expressions derived from the Latin or Greek and which, against a general Teutonic structure and diction, may sometimes take on a formal and even exotic note. Indeed, in order to impart the impression that these poems may originally have been written in English, I have often deliberately not availed myself of a word in English derived from its counterpart in the Greek, but have preferred a word of Anglo-Saxon cast. When I do use a word ostentatiously derived from Greek or Latin, I am in hopes that it may have an effect somewhat analogous to that of a purist word in a demotic Greek text.

My task was made pleasanter and easier because only four of the poets in this anthology—Caváfis, Ouránis, Kariotákis, Sarandáris—were not available when I began these translations. With all the other poets I have collaborated in various degrees, meeting with them in my cottage, The Medusa, on the island of Póros, in my apartment or theirs in Athens or Thessaloníki, sojourning with them on several Greek islands, discussing fine points of interpretation in tavérnas or confectionery shops where all Greeks prefer to congregate. My method was first to choose, together with each poet, a large group of poems which he and I thought were among his best or most representative. Often, however, a poet would inform me that a certain poem was among his very best, but so *very* Greek that its quality could not possibly be transferred into another language. It has been my experience, however, that often it is exactly such poems which, although they offer the greatest resistance (or perhaps because of this), provoke imaginative daring and may, eventually, be translated best of all. They are of special interest to a foreign reader because they offer something unfamiliar and enrich his language and his understanding. With the aid of each poet, then, I would set down a first, literal, almost interlinear rough draft, taking notes, meanwhile, on meaning, nuances, ambiguities, sources or references, trying to understand the poem in detail and as a totality. Only a portion of the poems thus transcribed were finally chosen for this anthology and polished to final shape. Often I would make the first literal translation myself and later check with the poet directly or by correspondence. When I felt assured that I had grasped, as much as I could, the totality of his insight and had verified details of interpretation, I would try to mold the poem into definitive form, having as final goal a poem that would read as though it were originally written in English, with nothing of the "translationese" about it. I would ask myself how the poet would have expressed himself in a particular word, phrase, clause, or entire sentence had he, at the moment of composition, the entire resources of the English language at his disposal, with its own traditions, its own syntactical and grammatical laws, and how this might have induced him to shift his language or image in English into what would not have been native to his Greek. At times, of course, it became more honest to ask not how the poet might have expressed his thought in English but how *I* might have expressed it, for the personal factor cannot ever—and should not—be completely ignored, but should simply be subordinated. Any evident departures in my translations from the original texts have always been made after I had discussed these with the poet and obtained his approval and permission.

During this period, and again after my final draft, I would check for total effect, for tone of voice and individuality of rhythm, by checking my translations as I listened to available records of the poets reading from their work, or to the many tapes they were kind enough to make for me in my apartment in Athens over the years. Even though a poet may read his own work badly in a physical or a professional sense, only he can indicate his pauses, his cadences, his colorations, his shifts of emphasis from meaning to meaning, the tone of his suggestivity. I was extremely fortunate to have had such full collaboration and confidence of the poets with whom I worked; in many cases where their English was admirable, or when they supplied me with their own literal first version, my translations must be considered to be as much their work as mine.

After reworking a poem to the best of my ability, until I could no longer respond to it, I would set it aside for many months, often for years, taking it up again with a refreshed interest and imagination, discovering that in the interval many solutions had come unsought for as they germinated in the subconscious. Often I would try to impart to a phrase which, translated more or less literally, seemed adequate enough in English, that slight nuance, rhythm, or change of structure that might dissipate any faint suggestivity of a foreign source incompatible with transference into another language. But on the other hand, I would often dare in English what I may for a long time have thought impossible. Basically, my effort has been to translate in such a way that the reader may be beguiled into thinking the poem was originally written in English; but because the English language is extremely resilient (and for this reason a superb instrument for poetry), and has throughout its development assimilated idioms, vocabulary, forms and color from many other tongues, it often can, and should, be stretched to the breaking point—up to the brim and even beyond the brim, as Frost would have it—so as to incorporate within it new extensions, new words, new rhythms, new horizons, new constructions without violating its essential integrity.

A translator from the inflected Greek tongue into the relatively uninflected English must keep in mind basic differences in syntax and grammar. A simple sentence in Greek can be rearranged in about nine different ways in contrast to a possible three in English, and for this reason offers more variety in word order and consequently in pitch and intonation than is possible in English. Nor, because of the lack of case endings, can English use as much inversion of noun and adjective combinations as the Greek. On the other hand, by depending greatly on its inflections, modern Greek is poor in prepositions and conjunctions. For this reason, a wider range of subordination in long and complex sentences can be achieved in English, especially by variously interpreting the overused conjunction καὶ ("and") and the overextended connective ποὺ ("where," "somewhere," "who," "which," "because," "for," "about," "since," "as long as," "that") which does duty as adverb, conjunction, pronoun, preposition and exclamation. Care must also be taken in the translation of tenses because the exact counterpart in English is often misleading—the Greek, for instance, will use an imperfect tense where an American or Englishman would use a past tense. Again, a Greek writer can shift with impunity from present to past and back again to present tense in a way which is chronologically illogical in English syntax.

The polysyllabic character of Greek permits the easy formulation of many compound words where two or sometimes three adjectival roots are fused into one word. An exact translation into English, however, although sometimes effective and enriching, would most likely be cumbersome. Such compressed compounds as Hopkins' "dapple-dawn-drawn falcon" or Yeats's "haystack-and-roof-leveling wind" cannot long be sustained in English. It is wise to break down such compounds into their component parts, and even then, more often than not, to choose the more striking or precise adjective and to delete the second or third. Nevertheless, one should try first to reproduce compound by compound whenever possible, adding thus at times a legitimately exotic color, to which the experiments of a Hopkins or a Dylan Thomas have again made us attuned. One should not hesitate to enrich our language with such inventions as Kazantzákis' "rotten-thighed Hope," or Thémelis' "water-cloven" or "cloud-thirsty." But what is one to do with the three following compounds used by Kazantzákis to describe Helen of Troy: μυγδαλογελάστρα, "she whose laugh is like the almond tree," ροδοστάλαχτη, "she on whom roses fall," and ποθογλίστρες πλάτες, "shoulders on which desire glides"?

Care should also be used in the transference of a poet's use of capitalization and punctuation. Whenever a poet uses what seems excessive or Germanic capitalization, such as that in Papatsónis' earlier poems, a translator should follow suit in order to retain the rhetorical emphasis or formal tone such capitalization supplies. The same holds true for the use or lack of capitalization at the beginning of each verse line, even when a poet may differ in his practice during various periods of his development. Punctuation in Greek is not exactly analogous to that in English, and should be altered accordingly to meet the demands of English usage, although discretion should be exercised when a poet uses his punctuation not for syntactical purposes but more as musical notation to indicate breath groupings or melodic phrasing, as in Antoníou. Many modern Greek poets use a sparse punctuation, as in Seféris, or none at all, as in Pendzíkis. By and large, a translator should reproduce such notations as carefully as possible, but he should also feel free to ignore these, to add or subtract proportionally where it best suits his over-all purpose.

A translator learns not only how far he can extend his own language but also what experiments taken from foreign sources he might find possible or enriching in the writing of his own poetry. Such orientation should also make him sensitive to the

influences his poet may himself have admitted from foreign lan-
guages—words, rhythms, expressions—and should impel him to
indicate, as best he can, such translation within translation. But
most of all, he should be as finely attuned as possible to the extent
to which the poet has tried to stretch his own language to the
breaking point, noticing where he has used words, phrases or con-
structions which, even to readers of his own race, seem strange or
daring innovations, and he should try to reproduce something
analogous in his own translation. This is where a full bilingual
command of both languages is imperative, although the free
adapter—we have only to consider Pound, Yeats, or Baudelaire—
need not be so constricted. Often the translator will be tempted
to consider such innovation or wrenching as crudities and try to
smooth them out in his versions, but this would be to erase exactly
that slight difference of tone that may be a distinguishing stylistic
characteristic. Many translators of Kazantzákis, for instance, have
a tendency to smooth out in English what is crude, roughhewn
and ungainly in his original. On the other hand, if he freely adapts
and has an original talent of his own, a fine translator may try
occasionally to "better" a passage where he believes his poet has
been careless or technically inadequate, particularly if he is deal-
ing with ancient texts. In the "transposition" I have attempted
in this anthology, however, I have often deliberately preserved
what I thought might be blemishes because I felt that even these
were part and parcel of the poet's unique individuality. What
would Walt Whitman be like in translation without his "barbaric
yawp"? In a person we love, often it is the blemishes in particular
that arouse us to tenderness and empathy. I am content to leave
such "improvement" to better translators and more assured minds
than mine when I am dealing with a modern text presented to the
public for the first time.

When my first translations, twenty years ago, were read by
educated Greeks with a good command of English, I was told, as
a form of praise, that although they found it difficult to under-
stand the original poems they could grasp them much more easily
in my translations. I suddenly realized into what error I had fallen.
A poet begins with the amorphous vision rising out of an emotion,
then works from a penumbra of feelings, thoughts and intuitions,
struggling to give them concrete embodiment in rhythms and
images. The total poem, even the simplest, reverberates with many

ambiguities of overtone without which it is a corpse and not a living and breathing body with its own protean spirit. The translator, however, works in exactly the opposite manner. He must approach the form itself on a sheet of paper and then try to resurrect it and give it the breath of life in his own language. He must start from the concrete, the details, the grammar and structure, the images and cadences, and try to make the poem explode for him into the vision which must have originally inspired the poet. The poet, on the whole, begins with the spirit and works toward the letter; the translator, on the whole, begins from the letter and works toward the spirit. Before he begins his translation, of course, he must have tried to attain such total participation, but when he works technically and microscopically to *understand*, that he may make no error, he often clarifies in translation what was creatively suggestive in the original. His version gains in clarity but loses exactly those overtones that are the essential spirit of a poem, echoes that keep a poem vibrant and alive. He has been tempted to incorporate into the body of his text notes that were meant simply to aid him in his approach to the poem. He must not perform such drastic plastic surgery, for it will produce a malformation and not an improvement of the true face or its expression. For this reason I reworked these first translations, trying to bring back into the phrases some of the ambiguity of meaning or emotion that they might have had in the original.

A phrase in its particular place in the original may have several meanings or overtones, many of which are necessarily lost in transference. A translator is often forced to choose one of these, or, if he is fortunate in his manipulations, suggest more, although often not of the same kind or quality as those in the original. In this regard, my close collaboration with the poets was of the utmost importance in trying to obtain the best possible approximation of the poet's over-all intention. If a translator notes that a particular poet is especially rich in ambiguities, and he cannot reproduce an analogous correspondence in the same place, he may try to reproduce a similar effect in another place or in general throughout the poem—in orchestrations, puns, plays on words— provided that nothing is falsified and that everything is in harmony with the general style of the poem. In other words, even when he transposes and does not freely adapt, he must be careful not to lose sight of the entire tone and meaning of larger units within the poem—sentences, paragraphs, stanzas—or sacrifice them for the exact rendering of a word or phrase. He neither freely adapts nor literally renders but hopes that he may remain basically faithful and at the same time retain the intensity of the original vision in a poem that reads as though it were first written in English. I have in mind such a transposition as that of Saint-John Perse's *Anabasis* by T. S. Eliot.

Unless the translator of modern poetry tries, preferably with the aid of the poet himself, to apprehend as fully as possible the multiple extensions of a poem, he may, in bland overconfidence, and often in arrogance, fall into another parallel error: that of being smugly content to present a version of the poem as he alone interprets it, without troubling to ascertain whether he is falsifying or perverting the original and may therefore be concocting a monstrosity which may have its own fascination but may effectively cripple the original and malform any true understanding of the poet. Partly because modern poets as a whole lack common sources of reference or belief, and partly because of the multiple proliferations of modern life, poetry has become notoriously difficult and obscure. The modern poet leaps from image to image, from emotion to emotion, from thought to thought, with few syntactical bridges of logical connectives. The poem often must be comprehended not with the logic of the mind but with leaps of intuition or imagination and must first be experienced by the translator as an entity before he can hope to begin unpeeling it phrase by phrase or sentence by sentence. Some irresponsible persons hope that by translating literally phrase by phrase they may mechanically capture the spirit by being faithful to the letter. Or in self-assurance they may completely misunderstand a phrase or an entire poem, feeling no need to verify their version with the poet or others. Thus, because much modern poetry offers ground for several interpretations if read with sensitivity and care, many careless translators have conveniently embraced the concept of "imitation" or free adaptation, thus effectively shielding their incompetence or incomprehension. Even when translating from an ancient or familiar text, a free adapter should first understand fully the original intention of the poet before he takes whatever liberties he pleases. His freedom has value only in reference to his responsible understanding and not to his willful ignorance. No translator can hope to be free of error, and those academic critics who gleefully pounce on occasional errors in a translation which in its totality is a fine and responsible piece of work are only revealing their own narrow understanding and their own insecurities. But when a translator has obviously made error after error due to ignorance of the language or insensitive reading—and this is easily discerned—no castigation can be severe enough, for such translators place their own ambitions and egos above their love of the poem or the poet they so irresponsibly misrepresent. If a translator wishes to depart from the original text, the flight of his imagination and his own creativity is enhanced, and not hampered, by his true and exact knowledge of the original.

III. On Craft

I doubt whether poetry can be well translated by one who is not himself a poet, has not written some poetry, has not been a student of poetry his life long, or who has not given a great deal of attention to the craft itself. I have been immeasurably helped in my translations not only by writing some verse myself, but particularly by conscious methods I have had to apply in teaching the writing of poetry to individuals, at the Poetry Center in New York City and at various universities. Two types of students would usually be admitted to my classes: those whose submitted manuscripts persuaded me they were already poets who wished to acquire a more conscious control of their craft, and those who wished to attain a technical knowledge that they might read poetry with greater depth and aesthetic appreciation. There is no better method of understanding poetry, or of translating it, than trying to write it.

The approach of the teacher of poetry to poets in a classroom has analogies to that of a translator toward a poem he wishes to re-create, for both must have a rather conscious knowledge of craft, the first that he may impart it to his students, the second that he may more proficiently embody another's vision. Translators and poets are like each other in reverse, the translator being a mirror image of the poet. The general public does not question the need of a painter, a sculptor, a musician, a dancer or a theatrical worker to attend schools and workshops where he may be taught the techniques of a profession, yet it sentimentally sets the poet aside in a unique isolation in which he is thought to be seized sporadically by a wayward and divine inspiration and to set down oracular utterances as best he may. It is misconceived that the poet needs nothing more than himself, his pencil, and a medium—language—which is the common and daily tool in all professions, whereas other artists must work with special materials or in an ensemble. Even the younger or amateur poet, in the pride of his imaginative independence, considers that a poet is not made but born, and often enfeebles the freshness of his vision by an inadequate technique. The answer is too simple to be labored: although the poet—the writer in general—is more independent in his medium than other artists, and although he, like other artists, and indeed like men in other professions, attains stature by self-teaching and self-development, it is nevertheless true that in general he is engaged in what Yeats has called a "sedentary trade," demanding as great an exactitude in the use of tools and as dexterous a handling of them as in any other profession. By inducing a young poet to write exercises with conscious deliberation involving a wide variety of meters, rhythms, free verse, cadences, stanzaic structures and tropes, by experimenting in the styles of many schools, the teacher hopes that these will in time become part of the poet's subconscious equipment, like those of a pianist practicing his scales or a novice learning to ice-skate, that they may come unbidden and with transmuted ease in the moment of spontaneous creation. No one can be made into a better poet who is not already a poet, but all can improve in their profession when they are young, and under the guidance of a compatible group, a sensitive teacher, or a friend.

One of the basic equipments of teacher, poet, or translator is a firm mastery of traditional meters and their variations. Ancient Greek meter was based, as in Homer, on a quantitative measure; that is, syllables were counted long or short according to the length of time, or duration, they took to be pronounced. This distinction has long since disappeared from the Greek language, and syllables are now counted long or short according to whether or not they receive a primary or secondary stress in pronunciation, exactly as in English. There is, however, one basic and most important difference between all inflected languages, such as the Greek, and an analytical language, such as English. An inflected language, because nouns, verbs and adjectives must show case or

tense by the addition of extra syllables to root stems, has almost
no monosyllables of any importance. The metrical accent, there-
fore (keeping the beat with secondary as well as with primary
accents), almost always coincides with the rhetorical stress when
the line is read to indicate not its meter but its meaning. I shall
take all my examples from my translation of Kazantzákis' *Odys-
sey* into iambic hexameter.

The opening of Book I reads: Σαν πιά ποθέρισε τους γάβρους νιούς
μες στις φαρδιές αυλές του. The marks below the line indicate the
metrical accents; the marks above the line indicate how the lines
would be stressed by most people to indicate the meaning. It will
be noticed that there is coincidence of metrical accent and rhetori-
cal stress on every syllable except the last syllable of ποθέρισε and
the monosyllable στις. This is the only kind of variety possible, in
so far as beat is concerned, in an inflected language such as modern
Greek; that is, it is possible *not* to stress in recitation a syllable
which receives a *strong* or *long* metrical accent. This is what I
call a *light* syncopation or counterpoint (the term preferred by
Hopkins), and I use these terms to indicate a variance, a disagree-
ment, between metrical accent and rhetorical stress. But it is almost
never possible to stress emphatically in recitation a syllable which
receives a *weak* or *short* accent in meter. This is because there are
very few monosyllables in the inflected Greek language. In every
line of the *Odyssey* in the Greek, the metrical count will be eight
metrical accents (a rare metrical form), but the rhetorical stresses
may vary from a hypothetical one (in actual practice, four) to a
possible eight when there is exact coincidence between metrically
accented and rhetorically stressed syllables.

The sixth line of Book I reads: και μαύρα στάζαν αίματα πηχτά
κι απο τις δυό του φούχτες. Again, it will be noticed that there is
here exact coincidence between metrical accent and rhetorical
stress on every syllable except the last syllable of αιματα and the last
syllable of απο. I have translated this line thus: and thick black
blood dripped down from both his murderous palms. It will be
noted that although every metrically accented syllable has a cor-
responding rhetorical stress, the unaccented monosyllables "black"
and "dripped" are also stressed and thus receive what I call a *strong*
syncopation or counterpoint, for here the meter is wrenched
from its position and an opposing cross current is set up. There is
more than enough coincidence between metrical accent and

rhetorical stress on "thick," "blood," "down," "both," "murderous" and "palms" to keep the prevailing beat which the strong rhetorical stresses on "black" and "dripped" attempt to vary or destroy. Such strong syncopation is possible *only* with monosyllables, for their pronunciation remains always correct whether they are stressed or unstressed. All other words can only receive a longer *duration* if rhetorically stressed on a secondary accent, and cannot be placed metrically in the line where the unaccented syllables receive a metrical accent. For instance, if I wish to preserve, say, the iambic pattern of my line, I must fit in the word "syncopation" in such a way that the metrical accent will fall properly, as in "syncopation" and not improperly, as in "syncopation." The English language is singularly rich in monosyllables, and in the strong syncopations which these make possible in our metrical system resides much of the true beauty and orchestration of traditional English verse. Some poets, such as Pope, use little strong syncopation, and others, such as Donne, have used so much that for a long time it was thought his verse was unmetrical, whereas, on the contrary, it is structured on severely patterned metrical accents with so many strong syncopations as to bring his lines often to the breaking point. A good reader of traditional English poetry must hold these two counterpointing measures in balanced harmony or tension, keeping the steady underlying beat, as a pianist keeps his, but varying it with inflections of pitch and the free-flowing cadences of rhetorical or interpretive stresses. It seems to me that a comparable counterpointing must have occurred in ancient Greek verse between the quantitative accentual beat of long and short syllables and the rhetorical stresses of words as they were pronounced regardless of quantity in a modulation of pitch.

In every line of my iambic hexameter, the metrical count will always be six (with the exceptions of heptameters with which I often conclude long sections in a book), but the rhetorical stresses can vary from a hypothetical one (in actual practice four) to a possible twelve. Let us take a few examples to show possibilities.

Line 947 of Book VI reads: the hón ey of ob lív ion on the shín gled shóre. This has only four rhetorical stresses, all of which coincide with the metrical accents, and only weak syncopation on the unimportant syllables "of" and "on."

Line 446 of Book VI also has four rhetorical stresses: like a cléar foún tain on a láwn com plaín ing ly; but although it, too, contains a weak syncopation on the syllables "a," "on", and on the last syllable of "complainingly," it contains a strong syncopation on the syllable "clear."

An example of a line that contains five rhetorical stresses (with strong syncopations on "God" and "deep") is line 414 of Book XX: Gód is a lab y rín thine quést deép in our heárts."

Line 511 of Book XVIII contains six rhetorical stresses which coincide exactly with its six metrical accents: e réct on freé dom's hígh est súm mit, Laúgh ter leáps.

Although line 904 of Book XVIII also has as many rhetorical stresses as it has metrical accents (that is, six of each), the relationship between the two is syncopated or counterpointed: But Í hold Deáth like a bláck bán ner and márch ón!

Line 425 of Book XIV shows seven rhetorical stresses: the fí nal lá bor stíll re maíns—kneél, aím, and shoót!

I have rarely gone beyond the eight rhetorical stresses shown in line 6 of Book I, which I have already quoted, or in line 925 of Book XXIII: Soúl, coún try, mén and eárth, góds, sór rows, jóys and thoúghts, for this is possible only when a catalogue of monosyllables are predominant in a line.

A reader may recite line 795 of Book XXII with nine stresses if he chooses to stress the adjectives as well as the nouns, for although the metrical accent is always rigidly the same in number, a wide flexibility is permitted among rhetorical stresses according to the interpretation of each reader, as well as a wide variation in duration and tones of pitch: Níght-prowl ing án cient ghósts, deáf eárs, glázed eýes, múte moúths.

Theoretically and practically, it is possible to have as many as twelve rhetorical stresses in a hexameter, for instance, which contains a packed catalogue of objects, all monosyllables: cát, dóg, óx, lámb, goát, búll, hórse, beár, fóx, lýnx, rám, eẃe.

The metrical accents in all my hexameter lines must, of course, always be six, although often a certain unit, a foot, of a line may be inverted for the sake of variety, or augmented by occasional extra syllables. The rhetorical stresses, on the contrary, are always free, varying from a theoretical one to a possible twelve; their placement and their number depend on how an individual reader may wish to stress the meaning or emotion of the line, according to his interpretation. Although all metrical accents are of the same theoretical weight and emphasis, the rhetorical stresses are of different weights and intensities, and they can range considerably in pitch and intonation. Oftentimes a syllable is not so much stressed as held on a level tone, either because it carries less emphasis in meaning than the one preceding or following, or because there is a great phonetic difference between syllables as, in the last line quoted, between the four sounds in "prowl" and the two sounds in "ing," or the two or three sounds in "eyes" and the five or six sounds in "glazed." In line 1209 of Book XII: Gód is the món strous shá dow of deáth-grap pling mán, the first syllable of "grappling" would be stressed by some but only held by others. It will be noted that the semantic meaning, in a qualitative sense, and the prevalence of consonants and vowels or diphthongs, in a quantitative sense, in a word or syllable determine to a great degree the long or short duration with which it is pronounced.

This by no means exhausts the prosodic complications of a traditional metrical line, but I have thought it necessary to make clear the relationship between metrical accent and rhetorical stress because the two are still often confused in academic and creative circles. Metrists have often been led astray by the metrical systems of inflected polysyllabic languages such as Greek, and have tried to impose these systems on English, unaware of the great role Anglo-Saxon monosyllables play in the English metric system, not only giving English poetry its peculiar beauty but also forcing on the language a meter indigenous to it alone. The various groupings into which the rhetorical stresses or the unstressed syllables may fall, whether iamb, trochee, amphibrach, dactyl, et cetera, should not be confused with the metrical scansion. If a regular pattern is set up among the rhetorical stresses and is then repeated from line to line, another measurement is then involved, that of sprung rhythm. An unjustly neglected book, which contains the best analysis I know of the relationship between metrical accent and rhetorical stress (although it is inadequate in a consideration of modern measures), and from which I have taken some of my terminology, is *Pattern and Variation in Poetry* by Chard Powers Smith (Scribners, 1932).

Because of the analytic and monosyllabic character of the English language, the majority of verses written in that language end on a strong or "masculine" accent, and the lines are therefore counted in *even* numbers; but because the Greek language, in common with all inflected tongues, is polysyllabic, and because the accent frequently falls on the syllable before the last, the lines are counted in *uneven* syllables and are predominantly weak or "feminine" in their endings. Typical English lines are of six, eight, ten, or twelve syllables; typical Greek lines are of seven, nine, eleven, thirteen, or fifteen syllables. I have discovered that because of these syllabic differences in the two languages, a Greek line may be constricted by a foot in English (and sometimes by more), a Greek hexameter becoming thus an English pentameter, a Greek pentameter an English tetrameter, et cetera. On the whole, it has been my practice to translate in an analogous meter poems written originally in meter, and to keep to the stanza pattern, because in such cases the rhythms and structures impart to the poems a formal tone related to the meaning. The content of a poem shaped by stanzaic form, meter, or rhyme has a different intensity than that which is not limited by such formalities. The wealth of adjectives and images, and the rhetorical nature of Kazantzákis' *Odyssey*, for instance, would have sunk under the slacker rhythms of a prose or free-verse rendering and demanded instead the regular beat of a metrical unit and line, like the surging waves of a sea about to burst into storm, in order to keep its epic vessel afloat. This holds true for such poems as Caváfis' "The City," "Waiting for the Barbarians," "The Tomb of Lanes," and "Amid the Taverns" (where, in the last two, the caesural pause has also been kept); in sonnets by Sikelianós, Várnalis, Ouránis, Kariotákis, and in other formal patterns such as Kariotákis' "Ballade to the Inglorious Poets of the Ages" or the looser structures of some of Mátsas' poems. I have also tried to reproduce the variety of rhythms which are possible between the strict use of traditional meter and the loosening of rhythms and line lengths without the over-all pattern being entirely broken, as in most of the longer later poems by Sikelianós, from "The Sacred Road" on, many poems by Caváfis such as "Ithaca," "Two Young Men, 23 to 25 Years of Age" and in some later poems by Vafópoulos. A phenomenon in modern poetry not too often noted by critics is the tendency of many poets who, wishing often to write neither in free verse nor in strict traditional patterns, have taken forms beyond the breaking point, keeping an *approximate* pattern, permitting themselves more variations than were formerly admitted, keeping to a general *appearance* of structure, as we know it, for example, in some poems by Emily Dickinson, Hart Crane, or John Crowe Ransom.

The majority of the poets in this anthology write in free

verse, although, again, a great variety is possible, extending from poems written in uneven line lengths but with a more or less regular iambic beat (as in many poems by Caváfis in his middle period) to the extremely loose prose rhythms used by Rítsos in "Moonlight Sonata," to the vague hinterland between poetry and prose rhythms in works by Embirícos, Engonópoulos, Elýtis, Kazantzákis, Pendzíkis and Gátsos. Here a translator must have a sensitive ear for the phrasal units peculiar to each poet's breath groups (as once measured by Amy Lowell with stop watch in hand) and which, like small but irregular waves breaking on the shore, serve to measure the more undulating billows of sentences or paragraphs. He must also be sensitive to the degree with which each poet uses enjambment, either to separate or unite his lines with one another. His ear must be attuned to differences of cadence and pitch, as in the low-keyed whispered asides of Seféris, the Whitmanesque bravado of Engonópoulos in his "Bolívar," or the short, staccato rhythms of his early poetry, the melancholy ebb and flow of Gátsos' "Amorghós," the plasticity of Elýtis, the deductive conversational tone of Papatsónis.

The majority of modern poets write in this vast region between strict traditional forms and the rhythms of "prose poems," but few in Greece have attempted sprung-rhythm patterns as we know them in Anglo-Saxon poetry, in the complex harmonies of Hopkins, or the looser compositions of MacLeish. I proposed this system to Elýtis when he was writing *Áxion Estí*, and also that of syllabic versification as we know it in the poetry of Marianne Moore, where no regularity of metrical accent or rhetorical stress is set up, but where a strict stanzaic pattern is organized, composed of lines differing in syllable count and then exactly repeated throughout the poem. These are two measures, I believe, which may have some future in Greek versification. Elýtis wrote the "Gloria" of *Áxion Estí* in a form of sprung rhythm, and his "Odes" in the same poem in an extremely elaborate variation of syllabic patterns. In my transpositions of these poems, I have attempted analogous patterns.

One who undertakes, therefore, to translate a variety of poets should understand and have at his command the metrical and stanzaic structures I have outlined. But perhaps more basic to his equipment is a mastery of the orchestral possibilities of the English language. Images and tropes, thoughts when they are not indigenous to one language alone, and metrical and stanzaic structures can best be carried over into another language with little loss. The poems which, I have found, are too difficult to translate, or sustain too much loss, are those written in dialect, in the pellucid and clear strains of song, or in a complex orchestration of sounds such as we know it in the poetry of Milton, Hopkins, Dylan Thomas or, say, in Sir Thomas Browne's *Urn Burial*, Djuna Barnes's *Nightwood*, or James Joyce's *Finnegans Wake*. No modern Greek poet has used comparable orchestral effects, but a translator into English may well utilize a fuller orchestral arrangement than that found in Greek poems, taking this liberty, of course, with much tact and discretion. Modern Greek has only five vowels (no true diphthongs) and about twenty-one consonants, or a total of some twenty-six sounds, whereas English has approximately about eighteen vowels (including true diphthongs) and twenty-four consonants, or a total of some forty-two sounds. Greek therefore has a greater limpidity of orchestration, as in chamber music, whereas English has one of the richest symphonic orchestrations of any language. An English poet may, with zest and infinite elaboration, compose his poems with alliteration, assonance, consonance, harmony, cacophony, onomatopoeia, full or approximate rhyme, pitch or duration, much as a musician may compose with a full range of woodwinds, violins, percussions, horns, or electronic vibrations. Consider, for instance, the blurred *r* sounds, as of a low underlying buzzing of violins, and the play of back and middle vowels, in the opening of Milton's "Lycidas" (one of the most magnificently orchestrated of all English poems):

> Yet once m*ore*, O ye l*aur*els, and once m*ore*
> Ye m*yr*tles b*row*n, with ivy nev*er* s*ere*,
> I come to pluck y*our* b*err*ies h*ar*sh and c*ru*de,
> And with f*or*ced fing*ers ru*de,
> Shatt*er* y*our* leaves bef*ore* the mellowing y*ear*.

The back vowels in the entire first paragraph of this poem soon give way to middle and front vowels, but the *r* sounds in the lines that follow, only gradually fade away—in bitt*er*, constr*aint*, d*ear*, dist*ur*b, *ere*, pr*ime*, p*eer*, rh*y*me, b*ier*, welt*er*, t*ear*—accompanied, from the very beginning, by their sister side consonant *l* which, assisted by the two stops *p* and *k*, suddenly combine and rise to a sharp pizzicato in "pluck" above the blurred *r* sounds, as of a plucked violin string.

A good translator should have a full technical and conscious command of the intricate possibilities of sound combinations in English and utilize not only the simplest of its forms, that of initial repetition of the same sound, whether vowel or consonant, in simple alliteration. He should know when to use back vowels, as in Meredith's line from "Lucifer in Twilight": "The army of unalterable law"; or middle vowels, as in the passage I have quoted from "Lycidas"; or front vowels, as in Swinburne's line from "Mater Triumphalis": "And chirp of linnets on the wrists of kings"; or an adroit play of back, middle, and front vowels, assisted by a family of the stops *d*, *k*, *b* and *p* in Milton's description of Satan being cast down from Heaven into Hell:

> Hurl'd headlong flaming from th' Ethereal Sky
> With hideous ruin and combustion down
> To bottomless perdition . . .

The dexterous translator (and poet) will play more with consonance than with assonance, more with approximation than with agreement of sound. He will not simply alliterate, for instance, the unvoiced labial *p* with another *p*, nor only with its fellow consonant, the voiced labial *b*, but also with other pairs in the family of stops to which it belongs, with *k* and *g*, with *t* and *d*. The sides *l* and *r* may be alliterated with the other sides *sh* and *zh*, and these, as part of the dental group also, may be alliterated with *s*, *z*, *th*, or *dh*, and further with dentals that are also labials, *f* and *v*, and which again in turn may be combined with the labial *w*, the labial and breath *wh* and the breath *h*. All these sounds may further be orchestrated together, since they belong to the family of fricatives, as opposed to stops or nasals. Again, the dental fricatives *s*, *z*, *th* and *dh* may be orchestrated with the dental stops *t* and *d* and the dental nasal *n*. Such complex orchestration is one of the great aesthetic delights of English poetry, and can produce an effect which the modern Greek cannot hope to emulate.

A translator from the modern Greek should, I believe, make effective use of such orchestration for several reasons, playing more often with sounds than the original poet or poem. In this way he can, on one plane, add aesthetic elements of color and

tone which he necessarily must lose on another, taking care, never-
theless, to keep a tacit proportion of orchestration to some degree
analogous to that used by the poet he is translating—less in Seféris
and Papatsónis, for instance, more in Kazantzákis and Karélli.
When a reader recites a translated work that plays masterfully
with orchestration, with elements of sound that seem native to
his language alone, he will—sometimes consciously, but more often
subconsciously—be impelled to the illusion that the poem may,
perhaps, have been originally written in his own tongue, for we
look to find such dexterity, such wedding of sound and meaning,
only in an original poem and not in a translation. On the other
hand, I have rarely translated a rhymed poem back into rhyme
again (a condensed form of consonance or assonance). Because
my aim was to transpose and not to paraphrase, I was reluctant
to pad or alter the contents of a poem in order to meet the
exigencies of rhyme. A fuller range of orchestration throughout
the poem permits the translator, in such cases, to compensate in
total texture for what is lost in terminal orchestration. Similarly,
if a poet is fond of puns or plays on words, and a translator finds
it impossible to reproduce the effect in context, he can then play
similarly elsewhere in the same poem if the opportunity offers
itself in English, or in some other poem if he finds this to be a
general stylistic device of the poet, as in my "we'd have high *fun*
at his *fun*eral" (a sight pun) in Kariotákis' "Préveza," or "a
cymbol a cymbol" in Elýtis' "Ode 7," or "my erring sole
stumbles" in Vafópoulos' "The Floor," or in the later poems of
Cálas.

A note of warning: a too zealous use of orchestration may
cause a severance of sound from meaning so that they will seem
unrelated to one another; the sounds may be too full for the
delicacy of the thought, or not full enough for the dramatic im-
pact of the meaning. Also, it is false to believe that any single
sound in itself may denote some particular quality. The lateral *l*
has often been thought to be a "lovely" sound, but it may also be
found in "louse" or "leper" or "listless." The sibilant sounds are
often thought of as ominously hissing and lecherous, as indeed
they are when they serve to embody such thought, as in Hamlet's
condemnation of his mother's haste—"To *post* with *such* de*xterity
to* in*cestuous* s*heets!*"—aided and abetted by the explosive sides *p*,
t, *d*, and the repeated combination of *s* and *t* in the four main
words. But in the opening of Shakespeare's Sonnet XXX

> When to the *sessions* of *sweet* *silent* thought
> I *summon* up remembran*ce* of thing*s* pa*st*,

the sibilants, aided by the dental *th* and the nasals *m* and *n*, and accompanied by a thought that induces to such interpretation, combine to form a mellifluous euphony. The effectiveness and quality of any orchestral arrangement depend on the reciprocal total meaning which these sounds try to embody.

In this essay I have been able to make only a few remarks about translation in general, about particular problems in translating from the modern Greek, and about craft in an original poem or a translation. My aim has been to equip the reader with guideposts that may help him understand my approach when the translation of so many and varied poets is involved, and to aid him toward a better reading of these poems. Perhaps these translations may spur him to learn a language which is the natural heir of classical Greek and offers a poetry as rich as any in our time.

Athens, December 1972

BIOGRAPHIES
BIBLIOGRAPHIES
NOTES

A Brief Note

Modern Greek words and proper names throughout this anthology have been transliterated as phonetically as possible to approach modern Greek pronunciation, although no consistency has been possible. Some poets or persons have already Anglo-Saxonized their names; some prefer to preserve the Greek form "Yánnis," for instance, but others prefer "John," some "Eléni" and others "Helen." Some spellings of well-known words, ancient and modern, accepted by long usage, have been retained: "Athens" instead of "Athína," "Euripides" instead of "Evripídhis," "Kazant-zákis" instead of "Kazandzákis." The more modern and unfamiliar the word, the more phonetically exact the transliteration. With some ancient words an attempt has been made, wherever feasible, to retain the Greek instead of the Latin spelling: "Dionysos" instead of "Dionysus," and to use *k* instead of *c*, as in "Akropolis" or "Sokrates."

It seems a pity, since the sound does exist in English, not to utilize *dh* for the open dental sound as in "*th*en." Before palatal vowels (ε, ι) the Greek gamma, γ, has the sound of *y* in "yes"; before guttural vowels (α, ο, ου) and before consonants, it is pronounced somewhat like the *g* in *ich sage* of some German dialects, here represented by *gh;* those unable to pronounce this sound may substitute the hard *g*: "Glifádha," for instance, instead of "*Gh*li-fádha," an Athenian suburb. The formal pronunciation of "George" in Greek should be transliterated "Yóryios" in English, and the informal "Yórghos." Before consonants and guttural vowels, χ has been transliterated *h* as being approximate enough in sound, as in *ého* ("I have") or *hrónos* ("time"), but before ε, αι and the iota sounds, I have used *kh* to denote the sound as in the German i*ch* or ste*ch*en: *makhéri* ("knife") or *Khíos* (an Aegean island). If χ is preceded by an *s*, I have used *kh* to avoid mispro-

681

nouncing the combination in English as *sh*: "Par*áskh*os" instead
of "Par*ásh*os."

All dates of birth have been given according to the New
Style (Gregorian) Calendar, instead of the Old Style (Julian)
Calendar, to avoid confusion in English-speaking countries and to
conform with practice in these countries. Greece did not adopt
the New Style until February 16, 1923, which then became March
1, New Style. Before that date, twelve days must be added to
those born between 1800 and 1900, and thirteen days to those born
on or after 1900. Kazantzákis, for instance, was born on February
18, 1883, according to the Old Style, but on March 2 according to
the New.

The poets and their poems are presented in chronological
order. Dedications are placed after the title in the table of contents
with dates of composition or publication. A date standing alone
indicates the date of composition, whether first or final draft;
c (*circa*) stands for an approximate date, and *p* for the date of
first publication in book form. Most of the dates were supplied by
the poets, but their memories, especially if they have not kept
records, are not to be relied on fully. Nevertheless, a reader may
thus follow the historical progress of modern Greek poetry, and
also the poet's development, and obtain some understanding of
what was being written in Greece during parallel periods in his
own and other countries.

All books of poetry and poetic drama have been listed, with
some dates indicating reissues where often poems have been added
or revised. Whenever a poet has written a book of prose that
might be of some interest to the reader, or throw light on his
character or preoccupations, it has been listed in the biographical
note itself. Listed also are all books, whether poetry or prose,
published by a poet in English; books or articles about him or by
him in book form, in English; books about him or his poetry in a
major foreign tongue.

At the end of the Notes is A Select General Bibliography
of book anthologies of modern Greek poetry available in English
or in a major foreign tongue; a bibliography of American and
English periodicals which contain a substantial selection of modern
Greek poetry; a list of recordings of modern Greek poetry in
Greek, and tape recordings in the Lamont Poetry Room at Har-
vard University. Most Greek books are privately printed, so no
publisher or printer has been listed; inquiries should be directed to

BIOGRAPHY: D. I. ANTONÍOU | 683

the poet himself or to the main bookstores. When no place of publication is listed, this means the book was published in Athens.

State Prizes in poetry were given by the Department of Letters and Fine Arts of the Ministry of Education from 1938 to 1941. Interrupted by the German-Italian occupation, these were resumed in 1956, then stopped again after the military coup of April 21, 1967. Usually a first and second prize were given, but sometimes prizes were awarded jointly and evenly divided between two candidates. The first prize was 20,000 drachmas ($666) and the second 10,000 drachmas ($333); if joint awards were given, each poet received 7,500 drachmas ($250). Prizes were given also in fiction, essay, and drama, although the award in drama for a printed book was replaced in 1961 by giving the best manuscript submitted a production by the National Theater in Athens. The Group of Twelve awards were given with private funds since 1956, in fiction, poetry, travel and theater, but only when the panel of twelve judges decided a deserving book had been published; these too were discontinued in 1967. The award in poetry, 15,000 drachmas ($500), was given by the shipowner Hadzinéstoras in memory of his father. The Athens Academy, occasionally, gives Honorable Mentions, and also the Palamás Prize for a book of poetry or a study of the poet Palamás.

D. I. Antoníou

D. (Dhimítrios) I. (Ioánnis) Antoníou was born on April 10, 1906, in Beira, Mozambique, then Portuguese Southeast Africa. After spending three years of infancy in Suez, and after some travel with his mother in Egypt and Europe, he was brought to Athens, about 1912, where he completed his early education. He enrolled for a short time at the University of Athens, but left to serve as an apprentice and later as navigation officer on various Greek cargo vessels in trips throughout the world. He then served on board the passenger vessel *Akropolis*. During the Second World War he was appointed second commander of a torpedo ship, which was sunk by the Germans a few days before they occupied Greece. Since the war he has served as staff captain and then as captain of the *Achilles* and the *Agamemnon* in cruises throughout the Mediterranean, the Canary Islands, and down the West Coast of Africa.

POETRY. *Poems*, 1936. "Twelve Poems 'Of Music,' " *The New Letters*, July, 1944. *Poems*, 1954. *The Indies* (Second State Prize), 1967.

NOTES

THIS NIGHT ABOVE THE FRAGMENTED SURFACE. THREE FRIENDS: George Seféris, George Katsímbalis, Lawrence Durrell.
THE INDIES. These are lines 208–229, 485–530, 619–698, and 793–814 of this poem of 1040 lines. Antoníou began it as a second officer during the visit of his ship the *Peleus* to the villages of Masoulipatam and Kalingapatam in the Bay of Bengal in January of 1934.

Alexander Báras

Alexander Báras (Menélaos Anaghnostópoulos) was born on May 27, 1906, in Istanbul, Turkey, where he completed his early education. After the Asia Minor defeat of Greece by Turkey in 1922, he spent three years in Cairo, but in 1925 returned to Istanbul, where he served in the Royal Greek Ministry of Foreign Affairs from 1925 until his retirement in 1966, when he settled in Athens. During 1947–49, however, he served in the Ministry in Athens in the capacity of secretary. His vacation periods were spent traveling over most of Asia Minor, the Middle East and Europe. He married in 1939, divorced in 1947, and has a daughter. He has translated from contemporary Turkish and French poetry, particularly Rimbaud, Baudelaire, and Aragon.

POETRY. *Compositions*, 1933. *Compositions, II*, 1938. *Compositions, III*, 1953. *Poems, 1933–53*, 1954.

NOTE

THE *CLEOPATRA*, THE *SEMIRAMIS*, AND THE *THEODORA*. SI J'ÉTAIS ROI: "If I were king."

Ríta Boúmi-Pappás

Ríta (Margaríta) Boúmi-Pappás was born on December 29, 1906, on the Cycladic island of Sýros. There she completed her grade-school and almost all of her high-school education, and spent a year in a French boarding school. Between 1920 and 1929 she lived with an older brother and his Italian wife in Syracuse, Italy, where she took a two-year correspondence course in infant education under the famous Montessori method. After a quarrel with her brother, she returned to Sýros in 1929, directed the periodical *Iónios Anthology* for a year, tried her hand in journalism in Athens briefly, but returned to Sýros, where between 1930 and 1936 she reorganized and directed the Protection of Babes and Infants, an institution founded by an Englishwoman in 1912. Her work in that field was acknowledged by the Greek government and led to several reforms in infant upbringing. During 1930–32 she edited the magazine *Cyclades*. In 1936 she married the poet Níkos Pappás and lived with him in Tríkala, Thessaly, until they moved to Athens in 1939. In 1950 she served on the committee of the magazine *New Rhythms*, and during 1956–58 edited the magazine *The Poets' Newspaper*. For seventeen years she has written on international political themes for many progressive Greek newspapers. With her husband she visited East Germany on the invitation of the East German Academy, and on the invitation of writers' societies has visited Czechoslovakia, Bulgaria and Rumania. She attended a conference for children in Vienna in 1952, and one on behalf of women in Copenhagen in 1954. Her translations of many plays, primarily Italian, have been produced in various Greek theaters. She has published book translations of the poems of Mihaï Eminesku and Tudor Arghesi and, in collaboration with her husband, has compiled and translated a *World Anthology of Poetry* in two volumes. She has translated several novels, and has undertaken to translate those works in Italian which have won the Nobel Prize, a project sponsored by the Swedish Academy.

POETRY. *Songs to Love*, 1930. *The Pulses of My Silence* (First Honorable Mention by the Athens Academy), 1935. *The Passion of the Sirens*, Tríkala, 1938. *Athens* (Prize by the Greek Resistance Movement), 1945. *New Grass*, 1949. *Ritorno in Ortitzia* (First Golden Laurel, the third prize in an International Poetry Contest, Syracuse, Italy), 1949. *The Illegal Oil Lamp*, 1952. *The Rose of Candlemas*, 1960. *Brilliant Autumn*, 1961. *Flowers Blooming in the Desert*, 1962. *A Thousand Murdered Girls*, 1963. *There Is No Other Glory*, Bucharest, 1964. *The Inflexible Amazon*, 1964. *The Magic Flute* (poems for children; prize by the Woman's Literary Society), 1965. *Foam*, 1965. *Cheerful Light*, 1966.

Nícolas Cálas

Nícolas Cálas (Kalamáris) was born in May, 1907, in Lausanne, Switzerland. He was brought up in Athens, where he completed his early education, then took his degree in law from the University of Athens in 1930. During 1934–36 he lived mostly in France. He migrated to the United States in 1940, married there, worked in the Office of War Information during the Second World War, and became a citizen in 1945. Increasingly concerned with aesthetic matters from a surrealist point of view, he published *Confound the Wise* (Arrows Editions, 1942), a series of essays on poetry, Portuguese baroque, portrait painting and modern architecture. In 1948 he became associated with Research in Contemporary Cultures, a Columbia University project headed by Margaret Mead, and in collaboration with her edited *Primitive Heritage* (Random House, 1953), an anthology of texts of primitive customs and ethics. Turning almost exclusively to art in its relation to aesthetics and culture, he published many articles in *Art News*, *Arts Magazine*, *Art International*, *The Village Voice;* collaborated with his wife, Elena Cálas, on *The Peggy Guggenheim Collection of Modern Art* (Harry A. Abrams, 1967) and *Icons and Images of the Sixties* (Dutton, 1971); published *Art in the Age of Risk* (Dutton, 1968), primarily a collection of his articles on art; and has completed a still unpublished book on Hieronymus Bosch. At present he is professor of art at Fairleigh Dickinson University, Teaneck, New Jersey. He has translated Eliot, Poe, Masters, and Benjamin Péret.

POETRY. *Poems* (under the pseudonym of Nikítas Rándos), 1933. *Notebook I*, 1933. *Notebook II*, 1933. *Notebook III*, 1934. *Notebook IV*, 1936. *Notebook V*, 1947. Ten poems appeared in the Athenian periodical *Páli* (*Again*), No. 1, 1964, and four poems in the same periodical, No. 2, 1964.

NOTES

COLUMNS OF THE TEMPLE OF OLYMPIAN ZEUS. The Olympieion, or Sanctuary of the Olympian Zeus, is a colossal temple, of which only fifteen columns are still standing. It was built on the same site as another sanctuary, dedicated to the same deity, dating back to the Pisistratids, around 515 B.C. The surviving colonnade is from the sanctuary which was begun under the Seleucid king of Syria, Antiochos IV Epiphanes, between 175 and 164 B.C., and completed by the Emperor Hadrian, who consecrated the temple in A.D. 131–132.

SANTORÍNI, IV. Part IV of an eight-part poem with the same title. Santoríni is one of the Cyclades, the ancient Tyra, composed primarily of volcanic rock, pumice stone and china clay.

ATHENS 1933. EPHESIUS MAXIMUS: A miracle worker, like the Nazarene, from the most famous city of ancient Ionia, Ephesos. The poet associates his name with Greek refugees from Asia Minor.

WITH KISSES. CAIRO CITY HOTEL: In Athens. ASPASIA, PERIKLES STREET: The Milesian consort of Perikles. The word derives from "welcome," but the poet is also punning with ἀσπασμός ("kiss," "embrace") and σπασμός ("spasm"). PERMANGANATE: An antiseptic once used by prostitutes. IRMA . . . RIME: Anagrams in the original.

PARADISE. PAPA-ADAM: Priest or father of Adam; God. ZOË: "Life." "Eve" also means "Life." SOPHIA: "Wisdom."

LIRACISM. Pun on λίρα ("pound sterling") and λύρα ("lyre"). GARDEN OF SIGHS: Klathmónos Square, in Athens.

DHIYENÍS. VASÍLIOS DHIYENÍS AKRÍTAS: A tenth-century Byzantine hero; *Dhiyenís* means "of double birth," for his father was a Moslem and his mother a Christian Greek, much like Mr. and Mrs. Peacock, "from Miami and Pharsalia." *Akrítas* means "border guard" of the Byzantine Empire. PHARSALIA: City in Thessaly where Caesar defeated Pompey in 48 B.C. CHRIST IS RISEN: Refrain sung in the Greek Orthodox Church on Easter. EVZONE: The full-skirted soldier of the royal guard. PLÁKA: The old city of Athens around the base of the Akropolis. ERASMIAN PRONUNCIATION: A system of pronouncing ancient Greek devised by Erasmus, and still in use in all but Greek universities where modern Greek pronunciation is used. HÝDRA . . . PIRATE'S HOUSE: During the eighteenth century, when more refugees poured into Hýdra than the island could support, many Hydriots became pirates, and great fortunes were begun in this way. Some brought architects from Venice and built palatial houses. ANGLETERRE: Hotel in Athens. BEER . . . CHARACTER: The slogan for Fix's beer in Greece is "It's good for you." TSITSÁNIS: Popular song writer and *bouzoúki* player.

SWEET-KISSING ASPASIA. See note to "With Kisses," above. PLÁKA: See note to "Dhiyenís," above. SON ET LUMIÈRE: Tourists seated on Philopáppos Hill, opposite the Akropolis, may now see the temples illuminated with various colored lights to the accompaniment of orchestral sound and pompous rhetoric. MISS HELLAS: In the Greek poem, the word used is Ἑλλαντό, a bad pronunciation for "come here," and a reference to Ἑλλάδα (Hellas, or Greece). MICHELINE: In the Greek the word used is Μισελίν (Miselín); if the accent is shifted to Misélin, it becomes "Miss" applied to Ἕλλην, a male Greek, or, in combination, a male whore. AKROPOLODEION: The poet's neologism, meaning "The Odeion of the Akropolis"—i.e., the Odeion of Herodes Atticus, where concerts and plays are performed. HOT WATER: Reference to an untitled couplet by George Seféris—"Hot water reminds me every morning / that I have nothing else alive near me." BACLAVAS: Cakes made of honey and nuts. AZVESTÍA: 'Ασβεστία, a compound word made up from *Izvestia,* the Soviet newspaper, and *Estía,* a Greek newspaper; also reminiscent in sound to ἀσβέστι ("whitewash"). XÉNIA: With a shift in emphasis, *xenía* means "hospitality," the common name of tourist hotels in Greece. MONNÉ DIÉ: Corrupt French for *"Mon Dieu"* ("My God"). ELPÍS: Feminine name meaning "Hope." AMAN: A Turkish lamentation or melancholy love song. CHAUFFEURS: The Greek word here is σεφέριδες, a pun on Seféris, the Nobel Prize winner for literature in 1963. COLLISIONS AVENUE: A pun on Συγγροῦ (a main highway in Athens, named after a philanthropist) and σύγκρουσις ("collision").

HAPPY CITY. In Greek, the title "Εὐτυχούπολις" is a pun on "Glücksbourg," the Danish royal family from which the present King Constantine derives. ROTTEN GARDENS: In Greek, Σάπιο ("rotten"), a pun on Ζάππειον (Zappion), a park adjacent to the National Gardens in the heart of Athens, with an exhibition hall, confectionery shops, etc. COPENHAGEN PASTRY: A pastry so named, and a reference to King Constantine. THAT . . . BEHEADED: A recent vandalism. MRS. HONIRABLE: In Greek, ἐρέτιμος, mispronunciation of ἐρίτιμος ("honorable"). TOURTOURISM: Pun on τουρισμός ("tourism") and τουρτούρισμα ("shivering with cold"). DORA: Etymologically the word means "gifts." See last line of this poem. POOL: The Greek word is πισινίσει, a verb form of the noun πισίνα ("pool"), but evoking, phonetically, πισινός ("the behind"). TENNIS CLUB . . . STUDS: The Tennis Club is situated in the Zappion Gardens, prowled at night by prostitutes and hustlers. BEWARE . . . GIFTS: A Latin proverb, apparently derived from Virgil, referring to the Wooden Horse at Troy.

XENO DOCHIUM. Separately, the words in Greek mean "receptacle for strangers," or "alien receptacle"; spelled as one word, today it means "hotel." FIX: Cárolos Fix, Greek industrialist, maker of beers and wines. CALLIRRHOË: An ocean nymph. HONORIS CAUSA: "For the sake of honor." NÉARHOS: A triple pun. Νῆαρχος from νῆα, a Homeric word meaning "ship," and ἀρχός meaning "leader"; the two words combined are equivalent to "admiral"; Νέαρχος was a Macedonian general and admiral under Alexander the Great; Νίαρχος is Stávros Níarhos, the modern-day shipowner and shipbuilder. TOSÍTSAS: From the renowned Avérof-Tosítsas family, great benefactors who have given Greece prisons, battleships, etc. GRANDE BRETAGNE: Famous old hotel on the main square in Athens, known familiarly as "The G. B." During demonstrations against the English at the time of the Cyprus crisis, many establishments with English names were hurriedly renamed, for a time, "Cyprus."

Constantine Caváfis

Constantine Caváfis was born on April 29, 1863, in Alexandria, Egypt, the last of nine children, all but one of them male. Both parents came from Constantinople, where his father traced his ancestry to about 1701, and his mother to long before 1680 from the aristocratic section of Phanar. His father inherited a firm which he and his brothers later built into the biggest and richest export-import firm in Alexandria, dealing primarily with the exporting of seed and cotton, and the importing of woven materials. The young Constantine was brought up in luxury with many servants: a French tutor, an English nurse, and an Italian valet who doubled as carriage driver. His father's death in 1870 left the family in straitened circumstances, so that in 1872 his mother took her family to live in Liverpool, where she derived a small income from a branch of the firm there. The boy was probably sent to school in Liverpool, and may have received some private tutoring, for his command of English became almost perfect; he even spoke Greek with a slight English accent. After the firm was dissolved in the economic crisis of 1876, his mother took her family to London, early in 1878, for about a year, then returned to Alexandria early in 1879, visiting for a while in Marseilles, where the firm had another branch. In Alexandria, Caváfis studied for about a year in a Greek commercial high school until the family once more left Alexandria to stay with his maternal grandfather in Constantinople for over two years. In October of 1885 they returned to Alexandria, where Caváfis was almost exclusively to live from now on, except for brief stays in London and Paris in 1897, and four brief trips to Athens in 1901, 1903, 1905 and 1932, lasting all told less than a year.

In 1892, at the age of twenty-eight, he was engaged as a temporary clerk (he could never hope for permanent status because of his Greek citizenship) in the Department of Irrigation of the Ministry of Public Works, and remained there until he left in 1922 at the age of fifty-eight, with the rank of Assistant to the Bureau Chief. His immediate superiors were English, and records exist indicating the high regard they set on his services; at times he also taught English to the Egyptian employees. He had some knowledge of Italian, and a superb command of French, and for about four years he wrote unsigned journalistic articles in French, primarily about political conditions in Turkey. From 1894 to 1902 he also worked as a broker on the Alexandria Stock Exchange.

Caváfis published his first poem in 1886 at the age of twenty-three in a Leipzig Greek periodical, *Hesperos*, then published others in periodicals in Constantinople, Athens, but most often in

Alexandria. He also wrote articles in Greek, primarily on Greek and English literature, and an article in English entitled "Give Back the Elgin Marbles." It was not until 1904, however, that he published a small volume of fourteen poems, which was reissued in 1910 with the addition of only seven poems. All the rest of his poetry he published privately in reprints and broadsheets from 1911 to 1932. In 1914 he made the acquaintance of the English novelist E. M. Forster, who wrote the first article in English about him for the *Athenaeum*, London, in 1919. Lawrence Durrell was later to fictionize him in *The Alexandria Quartet*. In 1926 Caváfis was awarded the Order of the Phoenix by the Greek government. When he discovered, in 1932, that he had cancer of the throat, he went to Athens for about three months for medical consultation. By this time he was forced to speak little or in whispers, and after a throat operation in Athens, he could communicate only by writing. He returned to Alexandria in October, was later taken to the Greek Hospital there, where he died on his seventieth birthday, April 29, 1933.

POETRY. *Poems*, Alexandria, 1904. *Poems*, Alexandria, 1910. Broadsheets, pamphlets, and printed offsheets, some sewn into booklets and folders, privately distributed between 1891 and 1932. *Poems*, edited by Ríta Sengópoulos, illustrated by Tákis Kalmoúhos, Alexandria, 1935. *Poems*, 1948. *Poems, 1896–1918* and *Poems, 1919–1935*, edited by G. P. Savídhis, 1966. *Poems, 1896–1933*, with 45 illustrations by Ghíka, edited by G. P. Savídhis, 1966. *Unpublished Poems, 1882–1923*, edited by G. P. Savídhis, 1968.

IN ENGLISH. *The Poems of C. P. Cavafy*, translated into English with a few notes by John Mavrogordato, with an Introduction by Rex Warner (London: Hogarth Press, 1951; distributed in the United States by Grove Press). *The Complete Poems of Cavafy*, translated by Rae Delvan, with an Introduction by W. H. Auden (New York: Harcourt, Brace & World, 1961). *Passions and Ancient Days*, new poems translated and introduced by Edmund Keeley and G. P. Savídhis (New York: The Dial Press, 1971).

NOTES

THE FIRST STEP. The poet Theokritos of Syracuse, who lived in the first half of the third century B.C., was the creator of pastoral poetry.

ONE OF THEIR GODS. SELEUCIA: A capital, with Antioch, of the Seleucid Empire (*c.* 312–65 B.C.) which, at the height of its power, ruled over Bactria, Persia, Babylon, Syria, and parts of Asia Minor. It was founded about 312 by Seleucus Nicator, one of the generals of Alexander the Great. Seleucia was built near the aged Babylon and the future Baghdad.

INTERRUPTION. In her wanderings, the fertility goddess, Demeter, came in disguise to Eleusis and became the wet nurse to Demophoön, the newborn child of King Keleos and his wife Metaneira. Wishing to make the child immortal, Demeter held it in the fire to burn away its mortality, but was interrupted by the terrified Metaneira. In another myth, the goddess and Nereid, Thetis, married to a mortal, King Peleus of Phthia, burned away the mortality of six of her sons, but Peleus interrupted just as she had burned away all mortality from Achilles but for his heel, which remained mortal and, consequently, vulnerable.

THERMOPYLAE. In 480 B.C. the Spartan general Leonidas defended the pass of Thermopylae against Xerxes, with a band of only three hundred Spartans. Ephialtes of Trachis is said to have shown Xerxes the route by which the Persians, or Medes, outflanked the Spartans and killed them almost to a man.

PERFIDY. Under the title of this poem Caváfis placed the following motto: "Then though there are many other things that we praise in Homer, this we will not applaud . . . nor shall we approve of Aeschylos when his Thetis avers that Apollo, singing at her wedding, 'foretold the happy fortunes of her issue'—

> Their days prolonged, from pain and sickness free,
> And rounding out their tale of heaven's blessings,
> Raised the proud paean, making glad my heart.
> And I believed that Phoebus' mouth divine,
> Filled with the breath of prophecy, could not lie,
> But he himself the singer . . .
> Is now himself the slayer of my son."
>
> —PLATO, *Republic, end of Book II*
> (translation by Paul Shorey, Loeb
> Classics)

PHILHELLENE. "To what extent Hellenism had penetrated the Parthian court at the time we do not know, but it is obvious that the Arsacids were fain to present themselves to their Greek subjects as sympathetic protectors. The money of the kingdom was stamped exclusively with Greek legends, and from the time of Mithridates I, they commonly added to their other surnames that of 'Philhellene.' But they were unable to make the Greek overlook the difference between a barbarian and a western dynasty." (Edwyn Bevan, *House of Seleucus*, London, 1902, Vol. II, p. 159.) ZAGROS: Mountain on the borders of Media and Babylonia. PHRAATA: City of northwest Media, winter residence of the Parthian kings.

ITHACA. After the sack of Troy, and early in his voyage to his island kingdom of Ithaca, Odysseus killed the one-eyed Cyclops, Polyphemos, son of Poseidon, and thus incurred the sea god's wrath. Later, the Laestrygones, giant cannibals, destroyed eleven of Odysseus' twelve ships. Almost twenty years after he had left to fight at Troy, and after almost ten years of adventures on the way, Odysseus finally reached Ithaca.

THE GOD FORSAKES ANTONY. Plutarch, in his "Life of Antony," relates that before the fall of Alexandria and his own death, Antony heard "the sound of all sorts of instruments, and voices singing in tune, and the cry of a crowd of people shouting and dancing, like a troop of bacchanals on its way. This tumultuous procession seemed to take its course right through the middle of the city to the gate nearest the enemy; here it became the loudest, and suddenly passed out. People who reflected considered this to signify that Bacchus, the god whom Antony had always made it his study to copy and imitate, had now forsaken him." (Plutarch, *The Lives of the Noble Grecians and Romans*, translated by John Dryden, revised by Arthur Hugh Clough, The Modern Library, p. 1147. All subsequent references to Plutarch are to this edition.)

THE DANGERS. Constans and Constantius, together with their brother Constantine II, jointly succeeded their father, Constantine the Great, to the throne of the Byzantine Empire, on his death in 337. After the death of his two brothers in 351, Constantius reigned alone until 361.

ALEXANDRIAN KINGS. Though Cleopatra and Antony proclaimed that Caesarion's father was Caesar, there is some doubt about his paternity. Alexander and Ptolemy were Antony's children by Cleopatra. The title King of Kings was conferred by Antony himself in 34 B.C. "Nor was the division among his sons at Alexandria less unpopular; it seemed a theatrical piece of insolence and contempt to his country. For assembling the people in the exercise ground, and causing two golden thrones to be placed on a platform of silver, the one for him and the other for Cleopatra, and at their feet lower thrones for their children, he proclaimed Cleopatra Queen of Egypt, Cyprus, Libya, and Coele-Syria, and with her conjointly Caesarion, the reputed son of the former Caesar, who left Cleopatra with child. His own sons by Cleopatra were to have the style of king of kings: to Alexander he gave Armenia and Media, with Parthia, so soon as it should be overcome; to Ptolemy, Phoenicia, Syria, and Cilicia. Alexander was brought out before the people in Median costume, the tiara and upright peak, and Ptolemy, in boots and mantle and Macedonian cap done about with the diadem; for this was the habit of the successors of Alexander, as the other was of the Medes and Armenians." (Plutarch, "Life of Antony," p. 1135.) The three children were all later killed by Octavian. See also Shakespeare's *Antony and Cleopatra*, III, vi. LAGIDAE: The descendants of Lagos, father of one of Alexander's generals, Ptolemy, who later became King of Egypt (306–285 B.C.) and founded the Greco-Egyptian dynasty.

THEODOTOS. In A.D. 48, after the battle at Pharsalus, where he was defeated by Caesar, Pompey fled to Egypt, but was murdered when he landed—"It was indeed a miserable thing that the fate of the great

Pompey should be left to the determinations of Pothinus the Eunuch,
Theodotos of Chios, the paid rhetoric master, and Achilles the Egyptian.
. . . It seems they were so far different in their opinions that some were
for sending Pompey away, and others, again, for inviting and receiving
him; but Theodotos, to show his cleverness and the cogency of his
rhetoric, undertook to demonstrate that neither the one nor the other
was safe in that juncture of affairs. For if they entertained him, they
would be sure to make Caesar their enemy and Pompey their master;
or if they dismissed him, they might render themselves hereafter
obnoxious to Pompey, for that inhospitable expulsion, and to Caesar, for
the escape; so that the most expedient course would be to send for him
and take away his life, for by that means they would ingratiate them-
selves with the one, and have no reason to fear the other; adding, it is
related, with a smile, that 'a dead man cannot bite.' . . . Not long after,
Caesar arrived in the country that was polluted with this foul act, and
when one of the Egyptians was sent to present him with Pompey's
head, he turned away from him with abhorrence as from a murderer
. . . Achilles and Pothinus he put to death. . . . Theodotos, the
rhetorician, flying out of Egypt, escaped the hands of Caesar's justice,
but lived a vagabond in banishment, wandering up and down, despised
and hated of all men, till at last Marcus Brutus, after he had killed
Caesar, finding him in his province of Asia, put him to death with every
kind of ignominy." (Plutarch, "Life of Pompey," pp. 795–97.) It will be
noticed that it was an unnamed Egyptian, and not Theodotos, who pre-
sented Pompey's head to Caesar.

IN A TOWN OF OSROËNE. Kingdom in northwest Mesopotamia. In
the second century B.C. it broke away from Seleucid control and
formed a separate kingdom with Edessa as its capital. The population
was mainly Armenian, with an admixture of Greeks and Parthians.
CHARMIDES: In Plato's dialogue of that name, Socrates watches a group
of young men, Charmides among them. "When I saw him," he says, "I
confess I was quite astonished at his beauty and stature. All the company
seemed to be enamoured of him. Amazement and confusion reigned
when he entered, and a second troupe of lovers followed behind him.
That grown-up men like ourselves should have been affected in this
way was not surprising, but I observed the boys and saw that all of them,
down to the very smallest, turned and looked at him, as if he had been
a statue." (154 C. Jowett's translation.)

THE TOMB OF LANES. CYRENE: Capital of Cyrenaica, ancient Greek
colony in North Africa, west of Egypt. HYACINTHOS: A beautiful boy
loved by Apollo, who killed him accidentally with a discus. Apollo
caused the hyacinth, a kind of iris, to spring up from the boy's blood.

DARIUS. PHERNAZIS: An imaginary poet. MITHRIDATES: Mithridates IV, the
Great, also called Dionysos and Eupator ("born of a noble sire"), was
King of Pontos, 120–63 B.C. AMISUS: A sixth-century colony of Phocaea
or Miletus, situated at the head of the one easy road from the Euxine
coast into the interior of Pontos, and which by 250 B.C. belonged to the
Pontic kings.

FROM THE SCHOOL OF THE RENOWNED PHILOSOPHER. AMMONIUS SAKKAS: Philosopher who taught at Alexandria, died in A.D. 243, and is said to have been the teacher of Origen and Plotinos. Sakkas was a nickname given him because of his former occupation, that of a cornsack carrier.

OF COLORED GLASS. Although the poem describes only the coronation of John Cantacuzene and Irene in 1347, there was actually a dual ceremony: the crowning of John Cantacuzene as joint emperor with John Palaeologos, only eleven years old, and the wedding of Cantacuzene's daughter Helena to him. "Two emperors and three empresses [Anne of Savoy, Irene Asan, and the thirteen-year-old Helena] were seated on the Byzantine throne. . . . The festival of the coronation and the nuptials was celebrated with the appearance of concord and magnificence, and both were equally fallacious. During the late troubles, the treasuries of the state, and even the palace, had been alienated or embezzled; the royal banquet was served in pewter or earthenware; and such was the proud poverty of the times that the absence of gold and jewels was supplied by the paltry artifices of glass and gilt leather." (Gibbon, *Decline and Fall of the Roman Empire* [Bury ed.], Vol. III, Ch. lxiii, p. 503; see also John Finley, *History of Greece*, Vol. III, p. 446. Both passages are based on the description of the Byzantine historian Nikephoros Gregoras [Bonn, Vol. II, pp. 788–89].) BLACHERNAE: A Byzantine palace on the seashore at the end of the Golden Horn. ANDRONIKUS ASAN: A feudal lord who lived in Byzantium and held the honorary titles "King of the Bulgarians" and "Despot of Rumania."

IN A TOWNSHIP OF ASIA MINOR. In the battle of Actium in 31 B.C., off the west coast of Greece, Antony and Cleopatra were disastrously defeated by Octavius. Caváfis wrote about this poem: "It is a poem representing the changing mentalities of the (small) Greek towns, during the struggles for power of the Roman dictators, struggles which could have no beneficial effect on these towns—towns, in fact, for which it was completely indifferent whether the ruler of the world was called Antony or Octavius."

SOPHIST LEAVING SYRIA. ANTIOCH: The capital of Seleucid Syria, on the left bank of the Orontes, was founded in 300 B.C. by Seleucus I and became one of the greatest cities of the East, disputing primacy with Alexandria. STATER: Principal gold coin of various ancient Greek states.

KIMON, SON OF LEARCHOS. CYRENE: See note to "The Tomb of Lanes," p. 693.

MYRES: ALEXANDRIA, A.D. 340. "According to the tradition of the Egyptian Church, Christianity was introduced into Alexandria by Saint Mark, who in 62 was martyred for protesting against the worship of Serapis. . . . The Egyptian Church . . . dates its chronology not from the birth of Christ but from the 'Era of Martyrs' (A.D. 284). A few years later Emperor Constantine made Christianity official . . . and this gave the monks the opportunity of attacking the worship of Serapis. The Serapis temple at Canopus (Aboukir) fell in 389, the parent temple at Alexandria two years later." (E. M. Forster, *Alexandria*, Garden City, N.Y., Anchor Books, 1961, pp. 49, 51, 55.)

THEY SHOULD HAVE PROVIDED. ANTIOCH: See note to "Sophist Leaving Syria," above. EVILDOER: Or "Kakeryetis," nickname of Ptolemy Euergetes ("Benefactor") II, commonly known as Ptolemy Physcon ("Bladder"), King of Egypt, 146–117 B.C. ZABINAS: "Bought and Sold Slave," nickname given by his people to Alexander II, who seized the throne of Syria in 128 B.C. HOOKNOSE: "Grypos," nickname given to Antiochos VIII, who defeated and killed Zabinas, and reigned at Antioch from 125 to 96 B.C. HYRCANOS: Son of Simon Maccabaeus, founder of the Judaean monarchy which culminated in Herod, reigned from 135 to 106 B.C.

IN 200 B.C. An unnamed Greek is supposed to be reading this inscription in 200 B.C., a hundred and thirty years after Alexander the Great's victories and his Hellenization of Asia. The Spartans (the Lacedaemonians) had refused to take part in the expedition. Plutarch, in his "Life of Alexander," writes: "And that the Grecians might participate in the honor of his victory he sent a portion of the spoils home to them, particularly to the Athenians three hundred bucklers, and upon all the rest he ordered this inscription to be set: 'Alexander the son of Philip, and the Grecians, except the Lacedaemonians, won these from the barbarians who inhabit Asia.'" (P. 812.) The three great battles in which Alexander overthrew the Persians were fought at the River Granicus (344 B.C.), at Issus (333 B.C.), and near Arbela (331 B.C.).

ON THE OUTSKIRTS OF ANTIOCH. See note to "Sophist Leaving Syria," p. 694. The Christians of Antioch had buried the body of their martyred bishop Babylas in the grove of Apollo at Daphní on the outskirts of the city, and had built a church above his grave. This forced the priests of Apollo at the temple there to stop uttering oracles, and to depart, for since ancient times the Olympian gods could not bear the presence of the dead in their precincts. When Julian came to Antioch, about A.D. 362, he tore down the church, had the temple rebuilt, and the body removed to Antioch. On the night of October 22, A.D. 362, the temple was destroyed by fire. See Julian's *Misipogona*, Loeb Classics, Vol. II, p. 484.

Odysseus Elýtis

Odysseus Elýtis (Odhiséas Alepoudhéllis) was born on November 2, 1911, in Iráklion, Crete, to an old industrial family originating in Lesbos. He completed his grade school education in Iráklion, his high-school education in Athens, where his family moved in 1914, and spent the summers on various islands in the Aegean. In 1923 he made his first trip abroad, to Italy, Switzerland and Germany. During 1930–35 he attended the School of Law at the University of Athens, and during 1948–51 studied literature at the Sorbonne, not taking a degree from either school. During

1940–41 he served as a second lieutenant on the Albanian frontier. During 1948–52 he set up residence in Paris, making trips also to England, Switzerland, Italy and Spain, associating closely with the poets and painters of the Parisian school (Breton, Éluard, Tzara, Char, Jouve, Michaux, Ungaretti, Matisse, Picasso, Giacometti, de Chirico, and others), and writing articles in French for the magazine *Verve*. At this time he began his career as an art critic and also wrote literary criticism for the Athenian newspaper *Kathimerini* (*Daily News*). After the war he translated many plays for the Greek theater, served during 1945–46 and 1953–54 as Director of Broadcasting and Programing for the National Broadcasting System in Athens. He was President of the governing board of the Greek Ballet, 1956–58; on the governing board of Károlos Koun's Greek Art Theater, 1955–56; and a member of the Group of Twelve. In 1950 he represented Greece in the Second International Meeting of Modern Art Critics in Paris, of which he was elected a member. Elýtis is an accomplished painter himself, working in watercolor, guache, and collage. He is a member of the European Society of Culture. In 1961 he visited the United States for three months on the invitation of the State Department, and the Soviet Union on the invitation of its government in 1962. The Greek government has made him a Commander of the Order of the Phoenix. Among those he has translated are Éluard, Jouve, Lautréamont, Lorca, Ungaretti, Rimbaud, and Mayakovsky.

POETRY. *Orientations*, 1939, 1961. *Sun the First Together with Variations on a Sunbeam*, 1943. *Heroic and Elegiac Song for the Lost Second Lieutenant of the Albanian Campaign*, 1945, 1967. *Áxion Estí* (First State Prize), 1959. *Six and One Remorses for the Sky*, 1961. *The Tree of Light and the Fourteenth Beauty*, 1971. *The Sovereign Sun*, 1971. *The Monogram*. Photographed in the poet's own hand. (Published by Adam of Brussels, Éditions L'Oiseau, Famagusta, Cyprus, 1971.) *The Death and Resurrection of Constantine Palaeologos*. Designed by Cóstas Colentianós in Chavannes-sur-Reyssouze. 111 copies, No. 1–11 not for sale, on *vélin d'arches* paper, signed by artist and poet. (Geneva: Duo d'Art, S. A., 1971, silk screen.)

TRANSLATIONS OF ELYTIS IN BOOK FORM. Robert Levesque, *Poèmes* (Athens: "Estia," 1945). Mario S. Vitti, *Poesie:*

Precedute dal Canto Eroico e Funebre per il sottotenente caduta in Albania (Roma: Il Presente, 1952). Antigone Kasolea übertragen von Barbara Schlörb, *Körper des Sommers* (St. Gallen, Switzerland: Tschudy-Verlag, 1960). Vincenzo Rotolo, *Elitis, 21 Poesie* (Palermo: Istituto Siciliano di Studi Bizantini e Neoellenici, 1968).

NOTES

AGE OF BLUE MEMORY. THE LORD WILL PROVIDE: Greek boats are often named after saints or Biblical phrases such as this. IMMORTAL WATER: A legend dating from antiquity relates that if anyone bathed in or drank from the waters of the River Styx on Mt. Hélmos near Patras, he would become immortal. This phrase is often used in Greek folk songs and legends.

THE MAD POMEGRANATE TREE. À PERDRE HALEINE: French for "out of breath."

MELANCHOLY OF THE AEGEAN. MADONNA: See first note to "Age of Blue Memory." MUTED WATER: Literally, "speechless water." On June 24, John the Baptist's birthday, a boy or girl fetches water in a jug from a well or fountain. The one who carries the water must not talk to anyone on the way. It is taken to a house where the congregated boys and girls of the village throw some personal article into the jug, a ring, an earring, an apple. The jug is then covered with a red cloth and exposed to the stars all night. In the morning, as the articles are taken out one by one, divinatory, satirical, or laudatory couplets about the owners are recited, often predicting whom they are to marry.

SHAPE OF BOEOTIA. See note to Engonópoulos' "On Boeotian Roads," p. 706.

HALF-SUNKEN BOATS. VIRGIN MARY . . . FIESTA: August 15, the Dormition of the Virgin, marks the end of a fifteen-day fast in her honor. Pilgrimages are made to the two great shrines of Greek Orthodoxy, to the Church of a Hundred Gates in Páros, and particularly to the miracle-working icon of the Virgin in her church in another Cycladic island, Tínos.

HEROIC AND ELEGIAC SONG . . . ALBANIAN CAMPAIGN, VI. SPAT ON HIM: In the Greek baptismal ceremony, the infant is spat on to indicate the eviction of the devil through the mouth, according to medieval belief and practice. ANDROÚTSOS: See note to Engonópoulos' "Bolívar," p. 703.

SLEEP OF THE VALIANT, II. ARETE: See Introduction, p. 86.

AXION ESTI. This phrase "Worthy it is" often occurs in the Divine liturgy of the Greek Orthodox Church: "Worthy it is to glorify Thee, verily the Mother of God," and is the name of a holy icon of the Virgin Mary in a monastery on Mt. Athos. It also occurs in several hymns, particularly in a long funeral hymn sung on Good Friday, and which begins, "Worthy it is to glorify Thee, the Giver of Life, Thou who didst extend Thy hand upon the Cross, and shatter the power of the enemy. Worthy it is to magnify Thee, the Creator of all; for by Thy suffering we are freed from suffering and delivered from corruption."

The poem is divided into three parts. In Part I, "Genesis," the poet autobiographically depicts his life, but symbolically that of all poets, from the day when he first saw light to manhood, when he first came face to face with the dangers of this world. On another plane, together with the poet is born "this small, this great world"—the small world, according to the poet's or an individual's apprehension and the limitations of his senses, the small world that is Greece, but which is also representative of the great world of the universe, microcosm and macrocosm, not one within the other but each interchangeably the other, a new cosmology. Every time a child is born, the world is born within him. Like the Biblical Genesis, this part is divided into seven sections depicting the creation of land, sea, plants, flowers and animals, and also the development of the Greek language from Homer to the present day. The poet speaks twice, in the first person singular, and then in the third person, for he also represents the Platonic eternal Self, the one that exists before birth, that knows everything, that guides the poet toward God, talking, advising, explaining the mysteries of the world, a technique reminiscent of some Picasso figures where one sees the same head from different points of view simultaneously. Each of these seven sections ends with the same refrain, "this small, this great world," and shows a development also from dawn to sudden dusk, from childhood to manhood, from innocence to a knowledge of an Evil often equated with war, all interwoven in a pattern parallel to the poet's own thematic autobiography. There is no reference to afternoon in this part, for night falls abruptly after midday, as war fell suddenly on the poet in the middle journey of his life. All of Part I is written in free verse.

Part II, "The Passions," is composed of three categories—Psalms, Odes, and Readings—which are mathematically grouped in three sections. Each of the three sections is arranged thus: two Psalms, an Ode, a Reading, an Ode, two Psalms, an Ode, a Reading, an Ode, two Psalms—that is, PPOROPPOROPP. Each section, in other words, contains six Psalms, four Odes, and two Readings. Entire Part II, therefore, contains eighteen Psalms, twelve Odes, and six Readings. The first section has as its theme the development of consciousness within tradition, the second the development of consciousness within danger, and the third the development of consciousness in the overcoming of danger. The Psalms, of which Byzantine *tropária* and the Psalms of David are the models, are written in free verse and grouped in pairs. The Odes, one on either side of the Readings, are written in a highly elaborated version of syllabic versification familiar to American and English readers in the poetry of Marianne Moore, with many additional complications.

The stanzas of each Ode are composed not of lines containing a set number of metrical accents, but of lines identical in syllabic count only, exactly paralleled and repeated from stanza to stanza. Furthermore, on either side of an ornamental black circle that divides each line, the number of syllables often varies, but is repeated with exactitude in each stanza. That is, a single line there may have three syllables in the first half before the circle, and seven after it. This pattern is then exactly repeated in other, parallel stanzas. No two odes are alike, and each introduces some new form of variation. The stresses at the end of each half line are repeated in a pattern from stanza to stanza, whether iambic ($\cup-$), or trochaic ($-\cup$) or dactylic ($-\cup\cup$). For instance, Ode 5 in the original is composed of six triplets; each half line of all the triplets has seven syllables, and each half line ends with a trochee. Ode 7 is composed of three stanzas, the first and last of which are identical sestets, and in which the half lines end with varied stresses arranged in a repeated pattern; the last two lines, furthermore, are variations of a refrain. The middle stanza, since it is not repeated, repeats instead a similar count of syllables in the half lines on either side of the circle; in addition, the stresses at the end of each half line of the first three lines are dissimilarly placed, but similarly placed in each half line of the remaining six lines. Ode 11 is composed of four stanzas which are all identical both in patterns of syllable count and in stress endings. Some words in this ode are separated in relevant places by the circle. In my translations of these Odes I have kept to a syllable count, although not that of the originals, but have not kept terminal stress patterns.

The Readings, which constitute the spine of this middle part, are written in an extremely simple form of demotic prose modeled on the style of General Yánnis Makriyánnis and on those excerpts read from the Bible in the liturgy of the Greek Orthodox Church as Gospel Readings. The subject matter, however, is entirely contemporary, and in particular is a realistic and graphic description, yet exalted and transcended, of the poet's experience, now given its final form, as a Second Lieutenant in the Albanian War. The titles of the first three Readings give some indication of the contents: "The March to the Front," "The Mule Drivers," "The Great Retreat." I have represented the Readings with the sixth and last "Prophetic," which, although not typical of the description of war and its terrors, nevertheless sums up the poet's ethical stance on these events.

Part III, the "Gloria," is a doxology, a laudation of the phenomena in Elýtis' personal mythology. All phenomena here, whether good or evil, are embraced in an ecstasy of praise, their ephemeral elements glorified in the verses that begin with a *now*, their eternal essence in those that begin with an *aye*. Like a triple gateway in which the central arch is larger than those flanking, Part III is composed of three sections of similar structure, the middle being longer than the other two. The first and third sections are ordered as following: six quatrains, a triplet, six quatrains, a triplet, five quatrains, seven couplets. All quatrains contain four beats to a line, whether counting the metrical accent or, much more often, the rhetorical stress (something like sprung rhythm); and all, though unrhymed, have feminine endings, excepting for the quatrain before the last in each section, which has a dactylic ending. The lines contain an uneven syllable count, are primarily iambic-anapestic in meter, with additional weak syllables here and there. The couplets are rhymed, but, with a few exceptions, they differ in rhetorical stress from section to section and keep approximate patterns in each section; in addition, each couplet of the first section begins with a "Hail," of the second section with a "He" (the Poet), and of the third section with an "Aye." I have translated here all but the first six quatrains and the first triplet of the first section, keeping to an analogous structure. In the triplets, each line contains three beats (with the exception of one line) and names of things separately: sea winds, islands, flowers, girls, ships, mountains and trees.

GENESIS III. íos . . . MÝLOS: Cycladic islands.

GENESIS V. ROES . . . YELTIS: Anagrams for Eros, Sea, Marína, Immortality, Elýtis.

PSALM II. CRACKING OF EGGS: The red Easter "eggs of Resurrection," as they are called, are believed to have miraculous qualities. In some places in Greece they are placed beneath the tabernacle at Easter so that the joyful "Christ is risen" can be uttered over them. It is a common Easter custom to tap the end of one egg against another. Whoever succeeds in cracking someone else's egg may claim the cracked egg as his own. HYMN: "Hymn to Liberty" by Dionýsios Solomós. See Introduction, p. 17. The first words are: "I know you by the cutting edge / Of your dread sword, / I know you by the visage / That strides the earth with violence. / Drawn out of the sacred / Bones of the Greeks, / And as valorous as at first, / Hail, hail oh Liberty!"

ODE 7. HAGGITH'S SON: Adonijah, David's son by Haggith, who tried to usurp the throne while David was dying, but David named his younger son, Solomon, heir to the throne. See II Samuel, 1.

VI PROPHETIC. ARETE: See Introduction, p. 86.

PSALM XVIII. PRINCE OF LILIES: Reference to a Minoan mural at Knossos of a young man holding lilies, and so named. LAWS: Oblique reference also to Plato's Laws.

GLORIA. SLENDER GIRL: Or "Liyerí," the representative type of lovely girl found in many Greek folk tales and songs. KORES: Specific reference to the "maidens" of archaic stone and marble statues of the sixth century B.C.; some of the most beautiful are in the Akropolis Museum. NOW, AYE: From the most common refrain in the liturgy of the Greek Orthodox Church—"Glory to the Father, and to the Son, and to the Holy Spirit, now and aye, and to the Ages of Ages, Amen."

Andréas Embirícos

Andréas Embirícos, whose family of international shipbuilders and shipowners comes from the island of Ándros, was born on September 2, 1901, in Braila, Rumania, where his father happened to be on business. Brought to Athens in his infancy, he completed his primary and secondary education there and studied for about two years in the School of Philosophy at the University of Athens. From 1922 to 1925 he worked for the Byron Steamship Company in London, a firm owned by his family, and attended courses at King's College at the University of London. He then joined his father, who had established a permanent summer home in Paris and a winter home on the French Riviera between Nice and Monte Carlo. From 1925 to 1931, he lived in France. Returning to Greece in 1932, he became a member of the council of the Vassiliádhis Shipyard, owned by his father. After two years, he resigned and set up practice as the first psychoanalyst in Greece, but retired in 1951 to devote himself to writing and photography. He has completed but not yet published a long erotic novel, *The Great Eastern*, concerned with the lives of the passengers on what was the first crossing of the Atlantic by a steamship, from Liverpool to New York in 1867.

POETRY. *Blast Furnace*, 1935. *Hinterland*, 1945. *Poems* (consisting of the previous two books), 1962.

IN ENGLISH. *Amour Amour, Writings or Personal Mythology*, translated by Nikos Stángos and Alan Ross, with drawings by Mínos Aryirákis (London: Alan Ross, 1966). "Argo, or the Voyage of a Balloon," in *Two Stories*, translated by Nikos Stángos and David Plante (London: Magazine Editions, 1967).

NOTES

THE WORDS. ELELELEU: An exclamation of enthusiasm, and a war cry, dating from ancient days. CHARDON-LAGACHE . . . VAUBAN: Stops along the Parisian metro.

IN THE STREET OF THE PHILHELLENES. MISSOLÓNGI: Town on the Gulf of Pátras, remembered for one of the most glorious exploits in the history of Greece, the heroic resistance of the Greek insurgents besieged by the Turks in 1825–26. Byron died there in 1824, where he had gone to fight for Greece's independence. MARBLE PHALLUSES OF DELOS: Huge fertility symbols, still standing on the island of Delos, the heart of the Cyclades.

THE SEASONS. GHLIFÁDHA: An Athenian suburb on the sea. BE THROUGH . . . FAR BEHIND: The ending of Shelley's "Ode to the West Wind."

Níkos Engonópoulos

Níkos Engonópoulos was born on October 21, 1910, in Athens. His father derives from Constantinople, and his mother from an Athenian family originating in Hýdra; these two strands have played an important role in the formation of his character. Just before the outbreak of the war in 1914, he was taken to Constantinople, where he attended a private school. He returned to Athens for a year in 1918, then spent the years 1919–27 in a high school in Paris, where he was well grounded in classical Greek and at the same time became immersed in the surrealist revolution. On his return to Athens he completed his military service, then enrolled in the School of Fine Arts in Athens, where he studied with the painter Parthénis, and from which he was graduated in 1938. In the meantime he studied engraving and woodcutting with Kefalinós and served for several years as apprentice to the painter of Byzantine murals Kóndoghlou. Engonópoulos is now Professor of Art in the School of Architecture of the Technical Institute of Athens, where he has been teaching since 1943. He has exhibited his surrealist paintings in the Panhellenic exhibits of 1949, 1952, 1957, 1960, 1963; with the group "Armos" in 1949, 1950, 1953; in New York City in 1939, Oslo in 1951, Rome and Ottawa in 1953, Edmonton, Montreal and Vancouver in 1954, São Paulo in 1955, Thessaloníki in 1957, and Brussels in 1964. He was the sole painter representing Greece, with seventy-four canvases, in the Biennale Exhibition in Venice in 1954. He gave two architectural exhibitions in 1951 and 1954, and a one-man show in 1965 at the Athens Technical Institute. He has designed costumes and stage settings for many Greek theaters, in particular for works by Aeschylos, Sophocles, Euripides, Molière, Goldoni, Shaw, and Brecht. He is a member of the European Society of Culture, and of the Greek Section of the International Institute of Theater. His marriage of 1950, from which he had a son, ended in divorce in 1954. From his second marriage in 1960 he has a daughter. In 1966, in recognition of his painting, the Greek government awarded him the Golden Cross of the Order of George I, and in 1971 made him Commander of the Order of the Phoenix.

POETRY. *Do Not Speak to the Conductor*, 1938. *The Pianofortes of Silence*, 1939; reprinted in 1966 together with *Do Not Speak to the Conductor*, with four paintings in color and one in black and white by the author. *Seven Poems*, 1944. *Bolívar: A Greek Poem*, 1944; reprinted in 1962 with eight paintings in color by the author. *Return of the Birds*, 1946. *Eleusis*, 1948. *The Atlantic*, 1954. *In the Blossoming Greek Tongue* (First State Prize), 1957.

NOTES

ELEONORA. FOR HANDS . . . OF HAIR: The poet believes he may have taken these lines from a Petrarchan sonnet by the Elizabethan poet Giles Fletcher the Elder. VÉLTHANDROS AND HRISÁNDZA: The hero and heroine of a Byzantine narrative poem. TOBIAS: In the Apocryphal Book of Tobit, it is related how Tobias, by the help of God through the archangel Raphael, safely marries a wife under discouraging circumstances, recovers some money owed to his father, and cures his blindness: the whole illustrating the need and the reward of trust in God's goodness. FABLE . . . FOX: Greek folk tale of the twelfth century in which a wolf and a fox inveigle an ass to go out to sea with them in a boat. When a great storm rises, the wolf and the fox declare that this must be because someone among them must have committed a great sin, and they both begin to confess how many lambs they've eaten, etc. The ass says he cannot think of any sin he may have committed unless it was a head of lettuce he ate when his master had burdened him with vegetables. "What!" exclaim the wolf and the fox. "You ate it without oil and vinegar? That is the greatest sin of all!" And they rush upon him to eat him. But the ass farts loudly several times, then kicks them overboard into the sea. Goethe used this fable in his own "Reynard the Fox."
TEN AND FOUR THEMES FOR A PAINTING. The poet notes: "I take this opportunity to say I was never an admirer of abstract art."
THE HYDRA OF BIRDS. PYTHONESS: See "Pythian Apollo" in Vrettákos' poem "Return from Delphi," pp. 758–59.
BOLIVAR. Written during the German-Italian occupation of Greece, in the winter of 1942–43, circulated in manuscript copies and read in many meetings of the Resistance movement. ΦΑΣΜΑ . . . ΦΕΡΟΜΕΝΟΝ: "The armed specter of Theseus was seen stalking before those who were marching against the barbarians" (Plutarch, *Theseus*). LE CUER . . . PAÏS: "The heart of a man is equal to all the gold of a nation." From Gabriele D'Annunzio, *Le Dit du sourd et muet qui fut miraculé en l'an de grâce 1266*; the line, however, is printed in brackets, and there is some doubt whether it is D'Annunzio's own, though no other source is indicated. ODYSSEUS ANDROÚTSOS: One of the greatest and most violent of the generals during the Greek War of Independence. Because of his generosity and high-spirited character, he made many impetuous errors of policy and action. By order of the Revolutionary Council he was killed by being hurled down the rock of the Akropolis in Athens. THEY STOOD . . . ALWAYS ALONE: See *"Se tu sarai solo, sara tutto tuo"* ("If you remain alone, you will be completely yourself")—from the

Notebooks of Leonardo da Vinci. HÝDRA: The town on the island of that name, all desolate rock, in the Saronic Sea; formerly a haunt of pirates and revolutionary leaders, who donated many ships and sailors to the cause of Greek independence. HIGH MOUNTAIN: Mt. Ére, in Hýdra. HALF WHITE AND HALF BLUE: During important religious holidays it is customary throughout many parts of Greece to paint the exterior of the church, or its courtyard, with whitewash and bluing, colors of the Greek flag. TATÁVLA: A crowded district of Constantinople in what was originally the Byzantine *Tabula* (Plateau), first settled by people from Máni (in the southernmost tip of the Peloponnesos) as workers at the Turkish Imperial Naval Base. To the Greek visitor, Tatávla evoked feelings similar to, yet stronger than, those evoked by the Rio dei Greci in Venice or the Griechengasse in Vienna. With its dense population it was a vigorous remnant of Turkish-occupied Greece, full of the subtle charm of Orthodoxy and the widespread elegance and pride of Hellenism. Its heroic youth opposed the Turkish oppressors in frequent bloody clashes. Between the two world wars the Turks finally managed to uproot and exterminate the community, renaming the district "Redemption" or "Good Riddance." DESERTED TOWN OF MACEDONIA: Many great and beautiful towns during the years of oppression after the fall of Constantinople in 1453 were built far from the main roads to avoid the soldiers and the Turks. This, which made for their prosperity, has been the cause of their desertion and ruin today. NÁXOS, KHÍOS: The joyous and luminous appearance of such Aegean islands as these are contrasted with the drab and dark towns of northern Greece. MONEVASIÁ: The demotic pronunciation of what is Monemvasía in the purist Greek tongue (so used later on in the poem by the poet). Now an empty town on a Gibraltar-like tip of the southern Peloponnesos, but famous in medieval times and during the Turkish occupation as an almost impregnable fortress. KASTORIÁ: A noble town on a romantic lake in Macedonia. According to folk tradition, the creaking of the holy icons, which adorn every Greek home, is the harbinger of evil. YOU ARE AS BEAUTIFUL AS A GREEK: One should recall the Socratic definition that to be a Greek is not a question of origin but one of upbringing. PHANÁR: A rich section of Constantinople. The inhabitants were all Greek, learned and brave men who held important posts in the Ottoman Empire. Many of them were princes of Moldavia and Transylvania. They were patrons of the arts and fond of Ancient Greek. The first stirring of Greek Emancipation arose from within their ranks. MOUHLIÓ: A portion of Phanár which contains a small church built by a Mongolian ambassador. CONSTANTINE PALEOLÓGOS: The last Greek emperor who died fighting against the Turks in the fall of Byzantium in 1453. According to folk tradition, he was said to have disappeared in a wall of St. Sophia and will return one day to lead Greece to greater glory. BOYACÁ, AYACÚCHO: Territories of Colombia and Peru respectively, where the decisive battles of the Emancipation were fought by Bolívar and his lieutenant de Sucre. I WAS THERE: The poet's vivid remembrance of his participation in the 1940–41 war against Italian and German forces on the Albanian frontier. LISKOVÍKI: The first town of northern Epiros beyond the Greek frontier in Albania, many times in Greek hands, first in 1940 when the poet fought there and was among the first to enter after the Italians had set it on fire. HÓRMOVO: Chrístos Lagoumdzís (or Lagoumidzís) from Hórmovo in North Epiros. Famous during the Greek War of Independence for the tunnels he dug under enemy camps in order to set up explosive charges. PHILIPPOÚPOLIS: A Greek town of Romelia, Bulgaria, since destroyed and now named Plovdiv. The man was a scoundrel against whom the poet here takes private revenge. ACONCAGUA: Highest peak of the Andes. ALÁBANDA: Ancient town of Ionia, famous in antiquity for its marble quarries. BLACHÉRNES: Magnificent monastery of Byzantium, previously the chapel of an Emperor's palace by the same name. It is built over an underground spring used for miraculous healing. KOUROS: Archaic Greek statue of a young man, representing Apollo. LOÚKARIS: Famous humanist and ecclesiastical patriarch of Constantinople. He fought the Turks and Jesuits to save the Greek nation from slavery. A progressive man, he insisted on the Scriptures being translated into the demotic tongue. In order to help the Greek people, he asked for the aid and friendship of great Protestant leaders of Europe, and was then accused of turning Protestant by jealous Greeks, Turks, and especially Jesuits. APOLLONIOS: Famous neo-Platonic philosopher from Tyána in Cappadocia during the time of the Apostles. He was an enemy of Christianity because he said it was a Hebraic and anti-Greek religion. He was said to have disappeared into the temple of Zeus Serapis in Alexandria and to have mounted into the heavens. His pupils declared he would descend when Hebraism and Christianity would finally disappear from the world and Hellenism reappear. RÍGAS FERRÉOS: Pseudonym of Andónios Kiriazís, poet and revolutionary from Velestínon in Thessaly, site of the ancient Pherae. He was a preceptor of Phanár, learned in French revolutionary doctrine, and became the enflamed apostle of freedom for a Greater Greece, declaring that in the coming Greek Empire all men, all races, all creeds would be equal, and that Greek culture would be the synthesizing agent. ANDÓNIOS IKONÓMOS: A revolutionary from Hýdra who at the time of the Greek War of Independence urged the hesitating people of Hýdra to cast in their lot with the revolution. He was killed by them, and is a symbol for the poet of impetuous youth. PASVANDSÓGHLOU: A Moslem brigand who took the town of Vidín from the Sultan and declared his freedom. A friend of Ferréos. MAXIMILIEN DE ROBESPIERRE: The poet notes that this great democratic leader of France was very different from the person about whom he was taught at school. Robespierre was not a bloodthirsty tyrant but, on the contrary, a pure ideologist, an upright politician of lofty stature who never succeeded in neutralizing the infernal intrigues of the enemies of law and morality. THAT OTHER GREAT AMERICAN: Isidore Ducasse, born in Montevideo, known as Count de Lautréamont, author of "Les Chants de Maldoror" in which he wrote "C'est le Montevidéen qui passe" ("He is a man of Montevideo who passes"). CORAZÓN: Spanish for "heart." THE LOVE OF

LIBERTY BROUGHT US HERE: Motto on the coat of arms of the Liberian Republic. The shield shows a hot broiling sun over a stony land on which a plow rests. NÁFPLION: City of Argolis in the Peloponnesos, the first capital of the Greek nation. SARDANA: Catalonian dance and song rhythm much admired by the poet. GENERAL: "General Engonópoulos—the grandfather of the poet—did you desert your native Hýdra to be blown up with the powder stores in Lárissa?"—Robert Levesque, in the introduction to his French translation of "Bolívar" in *Domaine Grec* (Paris: Éditions des Trois Collines, 1947).

THE LAST APPEARANCE OF JUDAS ISCARIOT. AÏRTON: A name invented by the poet, but which later he found in Jules Verne's *The Mysterious Island*.

THE GOLDEN PLATEAUS. OGOOUE: River in Gabon. BITHYNIA: Ancient Greek colony in northwest Asia Minor.

POETRY 1948. DEATH ANNOUNCEMENTS: Black-bordered announcements posted up in the village squares or on church doors telling of a death and funeral services.

MERCURIUS BOUAS. When the Turks invaded Albania, toward the end of the fifteenth century, Greek-Albanian chieftains such as Mercurius Bouas migrated into Greece and founded various villages in Attica and the Peloponnesos.

NEWS . . . DE LA FUENTE. CAMINO DE LA FUENTE: "Path of Fountains." UNA . . . DISGRACIADA: "A vile and disgraceful act," from a Spanish newspaper report.

ON BOEOTIAN ROADS. Boeotia is the myth-laden province of Thebes, where Oedipus unriddled the enigma of the Sphinx and unknowingly married his mother. The Sphinx had asked: "What is that which walks on all four in the morning, on two feet at noon, and on three at night?" The answer was "man"—on all fours as a baby, on two feet when old enough to walk, on two feet plus a cane when an old man. "Oedipus," in Greek, means "swollen-footed."

Níkos Gátsos

Níkos Gátsos was born on November 25, 1911, in the village of Aséa, Arcadia, where he completed his grade-school education. He attended three years of high school in Trípolis, then at the age of sixteen moved with his family to Athens, where he finished high school and then majored in classics, philosophy and history, at the University of Athens, 1932–36, though he did not take his degree until many years later. During 1935–36 he spent some eight months in Paris and southern France. He supplemented a small income by working for the National Broadcasting System in Athens, by translating plays produced in various Greek theaters, and by writing lyrics, primarily to the music of popular composers like Mános Hadzidhákis, Míkis Theodhorákis, and Stávros Xarhákos—in particular the *Blood Wedding* (1962) and *Mythology* (1964) of Hadzidhákis, and the *One Noon* (1966) of Xarhákos, all brought out by Columbia Records of Greece. He has translated Tennessee Williams' *A Street Car Named Desire*, the one-act plays *27 Wagons Full of Cotton, Portrait of a Madonna, Hello from Bertha, This Property Is Condemned, Talk to Me like the Rain*, and, among other plays, MacLeish's *J. B.*, O'Neill's *Long Day's Journey into Night*, Strindberg's *The Father*, Lope de Vega's *The Sheep Well*, Genet's *Haute Surveillance*, Lorca's *Blood Wedding* and *Don Perlimplín with Berlisa in His Garden*.

POETRY. *Amorghós*, 1943; reprinted with four illustrations by Ghíka, 1963.

NOTES

DEATH AND THE KNIGHT. Written during the German-Italian occupation and inspired by the famous Dürer engraving *The Knight, Death and the Devil*. DÜRER ZUM GEDÄCHTNIS: "To the memory of Dürer." AKRÍTAS: See first note to Cálas' "Dhiyenís," p. 687. PLAPOÚTAS AND NIKITARÁS: Heroes of the Greek War of Independence. GÖTZ: Götz von Berlichingen (1480–1562), otherwise known as "The Iron Hand" and immortalized by Goethe in his drama by that name. He was one of the most celebrated representatives of the feudal spirit, lost a hand in the siege of Landshut, and replaced it with one of iron. RINGS AND SWORDS: Allusion to the Nibelungs who made rings and swords in their caverns along the Rhine. SHEARS AND PLOWS: See Isaiah 2:4.

AMORGHOS. An island in the Aegean Sea, which Gátsos has never visited. The island is not the subject of the poem, for the name was chosen only as a symbol of evocative beauty. Since Gátsos was translating Lorca at the time, he may have been influenced subconsciously by the word *amargo*, meaning "bitter." Κακοὶ . . . ἐχόντων: "The eyes and ears of men are bad witnesses when the soul is barbaric." (Heraclitos, Diels, *Fragm. der Vorsokr.* B. 107.) EGGS BLACK: That is, in the color of mourning, instead of the resurrectional red with which eggs are dyed at Easter. KOLOKOTRÓNIS: Theódhoros Kolokotrónis, 1770–1843, a chieftain of the klephts or brigands, and one of the principal heroes of the Greek War of Independence. KÍTSOS: Hero of a Greek folk song. A guerrilla fighter during the Turkish occupation, he is about to be hanged by the Turks. His mother tries to join him, and stones an impassable river, pleading for it to turn back in its course that she may join her son. IN COURTYARDS . . . SPERM: One version of this folk ballad, a lamentation, is: "In the courtyards of the embittered man the sun does not rise, / there it is always cloudy, and turbulence reigns, / there the rue grows and the dead eat of it, / the mothers eat of it in order to weep, the men to fight, / and the small children to forget their mothers." MT. DÉVI: A mythical name invented by the author. EUROTAS: River near Sparta. KALAMÁTA: Town on the coast of the southern Peloponnesos, famous throughout Greece for its hand-woven, many-colored kerchiefs. There is a saying: "If you go to Kalamáta and come in good weather, bring me a kerchief to tie about my neck." ST. SOPHIA: From a folk ballad that begins: "God rings out, the earth rings, the universe rings, / and St. Sophia, the renowned monastery, also rings out / with its four hundred small bells and its sixty-two large bells; / for every bell there is a priest, and for every priest a deacon." KALÍVAS, LEVEN-DOYÁNNIS: Two famous klephts before and during the Greek War of Independence. From a folk ballad, part of which goes, "What is this sound and what is this tumult? / Can it be Kalívas fighting, or is it Levendoyánnis? / No, it is Dhéspo fighting with thirteen thousand enemies." Dhéspo was a famous Greek heroine from Épiros who fought the Turks before the War of Independence broke out. MANI: A mountainous region of southern Peloponnesos, which the Turks never managed to subdue completely. GÓLFO: The heroine of a mediocre yet popular play of the nineteenth century by Spíros Peresiádhis. The scene is on Mt. Hélmos, near Pátras. Gólfo, a shepherdess, goes insane when her lover leaves her.

OLD-FASHIONED BALLAD. SANTORÍNI: See note to Cálas' poem "Santoríni," p. 687. MÁNI: See above.

Andréas Karandónis

Andréas Karandónis was born on February 25, 1910, in Ándros, capital of the island of Ándros, where he completed his grade-school and began his high-school education. His family moved to Athens in 1923, where he finished his high-school education. In 1927 he enrolled in the School of Law at the University of Athens, but left after two years. He then worked in the construction company Láskos, 1927–35; in the insurance company National Life, 1935–42; and in the managerial department of the Greek State Railroad System, 1942–45. Since 1945 he has worked for the National Broadcasting System in Athens in various capacities, including that of director, and since 1948 has been its permanent weekly literary critic, during which time he has given about two thousand programs on literary and theater themes. From 1935 to 1940 and 1944 to 1945 he edited the influential periodical *The New Letters*. During 1940–41 he fought in the Albanian campaign against the Italians and, in his capacity as reserve officer, second lieutenant, fought against the Communist forces during the Civil War of 1947–50.

During 1945–67 he was a regular contributor to the newspaper *Daily News,* and is now a regular contributor to the newspaper *Free World* and the periodical *New Hearth.* He is a member of the Group of Twelve, of the committee awarding the State Prizes in Literature, and of the state committee awarding pensions to men of letters. In 1951 he toured the United States at the invitation of the State Department, and West Germany at the invitation of the West German government. He also has visited France, Italy, Yugoslavia, Switzerland, England, Belgium and Holland.

He has written three travel books, one of which is *I Remember America* (1963), and thirteen books of essays and literary criticism, among the most influential in modern Greek literature, particularly *The Poet George Seféris* (1957), *Introduction to the Newer Poetry* (1958), *Physiognomies I* (1959), *Physiognomies II* (1960), *Round About Contemporary Greek Poetry* (1962). He has translated the poetry of Jules Supervielle, Gide's *The Prodigal's Return* and, from the French, Henry Miller's *The Colossus of Maroússi.*

POETRY. *Horoscope* (Municipality of Athens Award), 1957. *Life and Pediment,* 1959. *The Third Firmament,* 1961. *Hermine's Rug,* 1962. *Episodes,* 1964. *Indicators,* 1966.

NOTES

OLD HOROSCOPES. EVERYONE . . . ABASED. Christ tells the parable of the Pharisee and the publican. In praying to God, the Pharisee praised himself, whereas the publican prayed with humility. Christ concludes, referring to the publican: "I tell you, this man went down to his house justified rather than the other; for everyone that exalteth himself shall be abased; and he that humbleth himself shall be exalted." (Luke 18:14)

A MAN. LAKKIÁ, LAKE VEGHORÍTIS: Both in Macedonia near the Yugoslav border.

AT GALVARNA. This name, and "Ólafo" farther down, are both inventions of the poet. WORN-OUT SLIPPERS AND THE CONSUMPTIVE MOON: Sentimental symbols of romance.

Zoë Karélli

Zoë Karélli (née Hrisoúla Pendzíkis) was born in Thessaloníki on August 4, 1901, and received the education of a girl of good family according to her class and period. That is, she was tutored at home in English, German, French and Italian, was taught piano and singing (she has a fine contralto voice), drawing and recitation. After her marriage in 1918, at the age of seventeen, she audited courses at the University of Thessaloníki, where her husband directed the Experimental Farm. She was widowed in 1953; in 1960 she began a year-and-a-half visit to one of her two sons in Australia. In periodicals, she has published translations of William Carlos Williams, Djuna Barnes, Eliot's *Family Reunion* (with an essay and explanatory notes). Parts of her translation of Eliot's *The Cocktail Party* were given over the Athens Radio. In book form she has published translations of Benjamin Franklin's *Autobiography*, Kimon Friar's *Introduction and Synopsis to Níkos Kazantzákis' The Odyssey: A Modern Sequel*. In periodicals she has also published her studies of Caváfis, Joyce, Dostoyevski, Pirandello, Kafka, and Beckett. In 1959 she was given the Palmes Acadèmique by France's Ministry of Education.

POETRY. *The March*, 1940. *Season of Death*, Thessaloníki, 1948. *Fantasy of Time*, Thessaloníki, 1949. *Of Solitude and Arrogance*, Thessaloníki, 1951. *Etchings and Ikons*, Thessaloníki, 1952. *The Ship*, 1955. *Cassandra and Other Poems* (Joint Second State Prize), 1955. *Garden Legends*, 1955. *Antithesis*, 1957. *The Mirror of Midnight*, 1958.

POETIC DRAMA. *The Devil and the 7th Commandment* and *Suppliants*, 1959 (both plays given over the Athens Radio). *Simonís, Princess of Byzantium*, 1965 (produced by the State Theater of Northern Greece). *Orestes*, Thessaloníki, 1971.

NOTES

YOUTH IN A TIME OF DIFFICULTY. CUP OF BITTERNESS: See note to Papatsónis' poem "This Cup," p. 729.

MAN, FEMININE GENDER. BECAUSE . . . CONCORD: From the marriage ceremony of the Greek Orthodox Church.

ADOLESCENT FROM ANTICYTHERA. Bronze statue of a youth, *c*. 350–330 B.C., found in 1900 in the sea near the island of Anticýthera, off the tip of the southern Peloponnesos, and now in the National Museum in Athens. He is probably an athlete, or Paris giving the apple to Aphrodite, for his right hand is extended and his fingers cupped as though they once held a round object. He may be the Paris of the sculptor Euphranor. KROISOS: The Kouros from Anavysos, *c*. 540–515 B.C., in the National Museum, Athens. Marble statue of a youth on a stepped base. On the middle step is carved the inscription: "Pause here at the tomb of the dead Kroisos destroyed by belligerent Ares, as he was fighting among the very first."

PERSEPHONE. Demeter, goddess of the fertile and cultivated earth, had an only daughter, Kore. One day, as Kore was gathering flowers in the fields of Nysa, she suddenly noticed a narcissus of striking beauty. As she bent down to pick it, the earth gaped open and Hades, the god of the underworld, leaped out with his chariot and dragged her with him into the depths of the earth. On Demeter's intervention, Zeus ruled that Persephone, as Kore was now called, should stay with Hades for one third of the year, when vegetation and crops died with her, and with Demeter two thirds of the year, when plants sprang to life again and animals become fertile. HECAERGOS: Epithet of Artemis, meaning "She who manages to achieve something from afar." ALEKSIKAKOS: Epithet of Apollo, meaning "He who wards off evil or mishap." Apollo and Artemis were twins. CYPRIAN: According to one version, Kronos castrated his father, Ouranos, and cast the severed genitals into the sea. They floated on the surface of the waters, producing a white foam, out of which rose Aphrodite ("foam-born"). Carried across the sea by Zephyros, the West Wind, the goddess was borne along the coast to Cythera, but was eventually carried to the shores of Cyprus. PAPHIAN: Paphos was an ancient city of Cyprus which had one of the oldest and most powerful shrines to Aphrodite. DOUBLE-VOICED MOTHER: Demeter is double-voiced because she represents both the seed that sprouts and the seed that dies.

Kóstas Kariotákis

Kóstas Kariotákis was born on November 11, 1896, in Trípolis, the Peloponnesos, where he lived until 1909. His father's occupation as mechanical engineer took his family to many parts of Greece. During 1910–11, they lived in Lefkádha, Arghostóli, Lárissa, Pátras, Kalamáta, Athens, and finally Haniá, Crete, where, in 1913, he completed his high-school education and had already begun to acquire a masterly command of French. As a child he was fearful, sickly, timid, prone to melancholy and solitude. In the fall of 1913 he went to Athens, enrolled in the School of Law at the university there, and felt betrayed to learn that the girl he had cared for in Haniá had married. He took his degree in 1917, but never pursued a career as lawyer. For a while, by studying in the School of Philosophy at the University of Athens, he was deferred from military service, but in 1920, after spending some time in the army, he was given a medical discharge. In 1919 he founded and edited, with a friend, a satirical review, *Ghámba* (meaning both "calf" and "leg"), but after six issues, it was closed by the police. In that same year he became a government clerk in the Ministry of the Interior, and was sent to Thessaloníki, Sýros and Árta. Every departure from Athens caused him great anguish; he could not bear the life of routine, of provincial dullness and uprooted solitude in what he considered to be virtual exile. He was returned to Athens in 1921, wrote a musical revue, *Pell-Mell*, in collaboration with a friend, and in 1923 transferred to the Ministry of Public Welfare in hopes that his chances of remaining in Athens would be improved. In 1922 a romance sprang up with him and the poetess María Polidhoúri, but inexplicably unraveled in the next few years. A poem he published in 1923, "Song of Madness," has given rise to the speculation that he may have been suffering from syphilis. During his vacation periods he visited Italy and Germany in 1925, and Rumania in 1926. His efforts to remain in Athens, however, proved to be futile, for in February of 1928 he was sent to Pátras, although soon afterward he spent a month in Paris on leave. His family offered to support him for an indefinite stay in Paris, but he refused, knowing what a monetary sacrifice this would entail for them. After his return to Pátras, he was transferred to Préveza, where he committed suicide on July 22, 1928.

POETRY. *The Pain of Men and Things,* 1919. *Nepenthe,* 1921. *Elegies and Satires,* 1927. *Collected Works* (published and unpublished), edited by G. P. Savídhis, 2 volumes, 1965, 1966.

NOTES

BALLADE TO THE INGLORIOUS POETS OF THE AGES. LES CHÂTIMENTS: "The Punishments," a series of satirical poems against Napoleon II which Victor Hugo wrote in 1835 in exile on the island of Jersey.

ATHENS. ILISSÓS: A stream in Athens near which Aristotle founded his Peripatetic School. THE OLYMPIAN ZEUS: See note to Cálas' "Columns of the Temple of Olympian Zeus," p. 686.

WHEN WE DESCEND THE STAIRS. POSILLIPO: Suburb of Naples named after an ancient Roman villa there. Kariotákis visited Naples in 1924. He wrote the word in Latin letters; but the word in Greek, Παυσίλυπον, as he no doubt intended his readers to surmise, means something that causes sorrow to cease.

Níkos Kavadhías

Níkos Kavadhías was born on January 24, 1910, in Harbin, Manchuria, where his father, who had been living in Russia and was engaged in selling supplies to the army, had gone after the Russian Revolution to carry on his business. When Níkos was seven, his family moved to the Ionian island of Kefaloniá, where he completed his grade-school education. They then moved to Piraeus, where he completed his high-school education in 1928. In 1929 he joined the merchant marine as a ship's boy and subsequently served in many capacities aboard many ships, traveling to all parts of the world with the exception of the United States. Since 1939 he has served as wireless operator and third officer. In addition to his own poetry, he has translated a few poems by Ford Madox Ford and written a novel, *Night Watch*. He has a smattering of languages—enough, he says, to get along with in various ports.

POETRY. *Marabou*, 1933. *Fog*, 1947. *Marabou and Fog*, 1961.

NOTES

MAL DU DÉPART. French for "anguish of departure." SFAX: A port of Tunisia on the Gulf of Gabes.

A KNIFE. DON BAZILIO, JULIA, COUNT ANTONIO: Fictitious names.

A NEGRO STOKER FROM DJIBOUTI. Djibouti is a port of French Somaliland on the Gulf of Tadjoura.

WILLIAM GEORGE ALUM. ANNAM: When this poem was written, the French protectorate of Indochina, now Vietnam. BAY OF BISCAY: Between the northern coast of Spain and the western coast of France.

A MIDSHIPMAN ON THE BRIDGE IN AN HOUR OF PERIL. BATAVIA: An island of west Java. SANTA FE: Province of east-central Argentina.

MARABOU. A large stork, African species. BASHKIRTSEV'S JOURNAL: Marie Bashkirtsev, 1860–84, Russian painter. Her fame rests on her *Journal*, published posthumously in Paris in 1887, and known for its Rousseau-like candor. SAINT OF AVILA: St. Teresa, Spanish Carmelite nun and mystic, 1515–82.

FOG. PORT PEGASOS: In Pegasos Bay, East South Island, New Zealand. TOCOPILLA: Seaport of northern Chile, Antofagasta province. ARMADA. GORGON ON THE PROW: Many Greek ships had the figure of a gorgon or mermaid carved on the prow. COLUMBUS' CURSED CREW: Five of Columbus' sailors, who brought syphilis to the Indians. AKORA: A reef off Samoa.

Níkos Kazantzákis

Níkos Kazantzákis was born in Iráklion, Crete, on March 2, 1883, during the Turkish occupation. Except for two years spent in a Catholic school in Náxos, he completed his early education in Iráklion, then took his degree in law from the University of Athens in 1906. In that same year he wrote a play, *Dawn Breaks* (which won a dramatic contest in 1907), published an essay and a novel, and thus launched himself on his career as the most versatile man of letters modern Greece has produced. In 1907 he went to Paris to continue his studies in the School of Law at the Sorbonne and also attended the lectures of Henri Bergson at the Collège de France. Thus began the first of his many peregrinations and long residence abroad: France, Germany, Austria, Spain, Switzerland, Palestine, Egypt, Cyprus, England, Yugoslavia, Czechoslovakia, Japan, China, and the Soviet Union. All told, he spent about a third of his life abroad, often as journalist to cover some expenses, writing for Greek newspapers a series of articles that were later gathered and expanded into travel books. In 1910 he began another distinguished career as translator, publishing, through 1915, Nietzche's *Thus Spake Zarathustra* and *The Birth of Tragedy*, Bergson's *On Laughter*, William James's *Theory of Emotion*, Plato's *Alcibiades* and *Ion*, Eckermann's *Conversations with Goethe*, and Darwin's *The Origin of Species*. Later in life he was to translate, into meter, Homer's *Iliad* and *Odyssey*, Dante's *Divine Comedy*, and the first part of Goethe's *Faust*. Although a complete bibliography is not yet available, it may be said that Kazantzákis wrote about eleven novels, about twenty-one plays in verse form, about five travel books, a history of Russian literature, about nine scenarios for film, three philosophical essays of book length, many books for children on the grade-school level, and many articles for newspapers, periodicals, and encyclopedias. Much material has not yet been collected or published. He knew

French, German, Italian and Spanish well, and some Russian, and had a working knowledge of Ancient Greek and English.

In 1911 he married Galátea Alexíou from his native town of Iráklion, but four years of marriage and ten of separation ended in divorce in 1926. In 1924 he had met and lived with Helen Samíou, from Athens, but their marriage was not legalized until 1945. During the Balkan War of 1912–13, he served as a volunteer in the office of the Prime Minister, and in 1919 was appointed by Venizélos General Director of the Ministry of Public Welfare, where he served for about a year and a half, occupied primarily with repatriating about 150,000 refugee Greeks from the Caucasus into Thrace and Macedonia. As one of his assistants, he chose Yióryis Zorbás, whom he had met in 1917, and about whom later he was to write one of his best-known novels. Most of 1922–24 he spent in Austria and Germany, where he completed the first draft of *The Saviors of God*, first published in a periodical in 1927, but not given its final form until published as a book in 1945. In 1930 he was accused by the civil courts of espousing atheism in *Saviors of God*, but though his trial date was set, he was never summoned. In 1924, in a suburb of Iráklion, he had begun his long epic poem, *The Odyssey*, which he wrote in seven drafts during a four-year period spread over a duration of fourteen years. It was first published in Athens in a deluxe edition of 300 copies. Much of it he wrote on the island of Aegina, where in 1935 he had built a home, and during two separate periods of almost two years altogether in Gottesgab, Czechoslovakia. During 1932–37 he wrote *Terza Rimas*, poems to those who had influenced him most in life. Between 1941 and 1944, during the German-Italian occupation, he and his wife barely managed to survive in Aegina, and in 1945, after serving briefly, for a month and a half, as minister without portfolio in the cabinet of Premier Sofoúlis, he resigned. In September of 1946 he settled in France, serving as Adviser on Literature to UNESCO for less than a year in 1947, then from 1951 on lived in Antibes and never again returned to Greece. In 1953 the Greek Orthodox Church sought to persecute him for several pages of *Freedom or Death* and for all of *The Last Temptation of Christ*, but he was never excommunicated. In 1956 he was given the State Prize for drama, and in 1957 the International Peace Prize.

In June, 1957, on the invitation of the Chinese government,

he paid another visit to China, after an absence of over thirty years. For some years he had been suffering from allergic infections, a swelling of his lower lip, and after an injection in his right eye for an infection there, he suffered the loss of sight in that eye. When he was hospitalized in Paris for these ailments and for Asiatic flu, it was discovered that he had been suffering from leukemia, analyzed at the University Clinic in Freiburg, in 1954, as "benign lymphoid leukemia." In Canton, on his way to Tokyo, he was given smallpox and cholera injections, but because of his blood ailment, these poisoned his right arm. After a short stay in Japan, he was flown over the North Pole route to a hospital in Copenhagen. The wound had turned to gangrene, and on August 29 he was taken to the clinic in Freiburg, where he made a miraculous recovery and was there visited by Albert Schweitzer. However, he had caught Asiatic flu. His exhausted body, unable to withstand the ravages of this disease, succumbed, and he died in the clinic on October 26, 1957. The Archbishop of Athens refused permission for his body to lie in state in Athens, but he was given a hero's funeral in Iráklion by the autonomous and autocephalous Greek Orthodox Church in Crete, and was buried on the Martinego Bastion, part of the old Venetian wall that still surrounds part of his home town. The following words are engraved on his tombstone: "I do not hope for anything, I do not fear anything, I am free."

His plays *Dawn Breaks, Julian the Apostate, Kapodhístrias, Mélissa,* and *The Master Craftsman* (as an opera by Manólis Kalomíris) were produced in Athens. *Sodom and Gomorrah* was produced in Germany, at the University of Los Angeles, in New York, off Broadway (as *Burn Me to Ashes,* translated by Kimon Friar), and at Columbia and other universities (in a translation by Angelo James Skalafúris). His novel *The Greek Passion* was staged in Athens as a play, by Manólis Katrákis, and was produced in Norway, at the Yale Graduate School of the Drama; it was made into a French film by Jules Dassin (with Melína Mercoúri), *He Who Must Die;* and into an opera by the Czech composer Bohuslav Martinu, and produced in Czechoslovakia and Switzerland. His novel *Freedom or Death* too was mounted as a play in Athens by Manólis Katrákis, with music by Mános Hadzidhákis, available as a disk brought out by Columbia of Greece. His novel *Zorba the Greek* was made into a film by Mihális Cacoyánnis, starring Anthony Quinn, Alan Bates and Lila Kedrova, with music by Míkis Theodhorákis, available in disk form. It was also mounted as a musical on Broadway with Herschel Bernardi, John Cunningham and Maria Katnilova. Portions of *The Odyssey* in Kimon Friar's translation have been set to music, for tenor by William Jay Bottje and for baritone by Thomas Beveridge, and sung in Athens and the United States. The first four books of *The Odyssey* were mounted as stage productions by the University of Michigan Players in 1970 and by The University Theater of Wisconsin State University in 1971. Kazantzákis' works have been translated into some twenty languages. He was sponsored for the Nobel Prize in literature by Albert Schweitzer and Thomas Mann.

POETRY. *The Saviors of God: Spiritual Exercises,* 1927, 1945. *The Odyssey,* 1938, 1957, 1960. *Terza Rimas,* 1960.

POETIC DRAMA. *The Master Craftsman,* 1910. *Nikiphóros Phocás,* 1927. *Christ,* 1928. *Odysseus,* 1928. *Mélissa,* 1939. *Julian the Apostate,* 1945. *Kapodhístrias,* 1946. *Theater,* Vol. I (*Prometheus* [a trilogy], *Koúros, Odysseus, Mélissa*), 1955. *Theater,* Vol. II (*Christ, Julian the Apostate, Nikiphóros Phocás, Constantine Palaeologos*), 1956 (State Prize). *Theater,* Vol. III (*Kapodhístrias, Christopher Columbus, Sodom and Gomorrah, Buddha*), 1956. *Othello Returns,* 1962.

IN ENGLISH
In the United States all of Kazantzákis' books have been published by Simon and Schuster. In England some have been published by Faber and Faber, and one, *The Odyssey,* was published by Secker and Warburg. Dates given are those of the first editions; titles marked by an asterisk are available in paperback.

POETRY. *The Odyssey, A Modern Sequel,** translated into English verse, with Introduction, Synopsis and Notes, by Kimon Friar, illustrations by Ghíka, 1958. *The Saviors of God: Spiritual Exercises,** translated, with Introduction and Notes, by Kimon Friar, 1960.

FICTIONAL AUTOBIOGRAPHY. *Report to Greco,* translated by Peter Bien, 1965.

FICTION. *Zorba the Greek,** translated by Carl Wildman, 1953. *The Greek Passion,** translated by Jonathan Griffin, 1954. *Freedom or Death,** translated by Jonathan Griffin, 1956. *The Last Temptation of Christ,** translated by Peter Bien, 1960. *Saint Francis,** translated by Peter Bien, 1962. *The Rock Garden,* translated by Richard Howard and Kimon Friar, 1963. *Toda Raba,* translated by Amy Mims, 1964. *The Fratricides,* translated by Athena Dallas, 1964.

TRAVEL. *Japan-China,* translated by George Pappagéotes, 1963. *Spain,* translated by Amy Mims, 1963. *Journey to the Morea,* translated by F. A. Reed, 1963. *England,* 1966.

DRAMA. *Three Plays: Mélissa, Kouros, Christopher Columbus,* translated by Athena Dallas, 1969.

ABOUT KAZANTZÁKIS. "The Re-integrated Hero," in W. B. Stanford, *The Ulysses Theme* (Oxford: Basil Blackwell, 1954; rev. ed., 1963). Pandelís Prevelákis, *Níkos Kazantzákis and His Odyssey, A Study of the Poet and the Poem,* translated by Philip Sherrard (New York: Simon and Schuster, 1961). Helen Kazantzákis, *Níkos Kazantzákis: A Biography Based on His Letters* (New York: Simon and Schuster, 1968). *Journal of Modern Literature* [Kazantzákis issue], Vol. II, No. 2, 1972.

IN FRENCH. "Ascese," ce texte, traduit et preface par M. Octave Merlier (Athènes: l'Institut Français, 1951). *L'Odyssée.* Traduction de Jacqueline Moatti. 2 vols. Preface par Alan Decaux. Lithographies originales de André Cottavoz, Paul Giuramand, André Minaux, Walter Spitzer. (Paris: Éditions Richelieu, 1968.) Colette Janiard, *Níkos Kazantzákis* (Paris: Éditeur Maspero, 1970). *L'Odyssée.* Traduction de Jacqueline Moatti. Introduction par Nikos Athanassíou. (Paris: Plon, 1971.)

NOTES

THE SAVIORS OF GOD. DEFENDER OF THE BORDERS, OF DOUBLE DESCENT: See note to Cálas' poem "Dhiyenís," p. 687.
THE ODYSSEY: A MODERN SEQUEL. The subtitle of the book, and all titles to the selections from the poem have been added by the translator.
PROLOGUE. CASTLE WRECKER, CAPTAIN: Odysseus.

THE SEVEN HEADS OF GOD. Book V, pp. 588–634. In Knossos, Odysseus buys from a peddler an ivory god with seven heads. For the first time, he finds himself moved by the prescience of the gradual purification that his vision of God must undergo, from pure beast to pure spirit. See also lines 23–30 of Prologue.

DEATH DREAMS OF LIFE. Book VI, 1265–92. After the bull rituals in Knossos, Odysseus lies down by a riverbank and falls asleep.

EGYPTIAN NIGHT. Book X, 1375–1402. Odysseus with Kentaur and Orpheus, two of his crew.

THE RUTHLESS GOD. Book XV, 801–63. An incident during the building of the Ideal City on the lake source of the Nile.

ODYSSEUS BLESSES HIS LIFE. Book XVI, 906–61. After his Ideal City has been swallowed up by the earth, Odysseus sits on the edge of the chasm and falls into contemplation. This section is part of his meditation.

THE SIX WAVES OF WORMS. Book XVIII, 750–802. The Prince is Mothérth, the representative type of Buddha.

TO VIRTUE. Book XXII, 1–54. Odysseus has just pushed off in his small skiff, his "light coffin," to sail and row toward the South Pole.

EPITAPH FOR ODYSSEUS. Book XXIII, 1–37. Invocation to the sun as Odysseus nears his death toward the South Pole. The last eleven lines would make a true and admirable epitaph for Kazantzákis himself. The play on words *sun* and *son* is lightly suggested by the Greek words ἥλιος and γιός.

THE DEATH OF ODYSSEUS. Book XXIV, 1380–96. Clinging to an iceberg in the last moments before death, Odysseus summons his three Fates—Tantalos, Heracles, Prometheus—who come and plant themselves on the deck of his snowship like three towering masts. Women he has summoned in his imagination deck these masts with the fruits of Greece.

NIETZSCHE. For Kazantzákis' identification with Nietzsche, and Nietzsche's relationship with Dionysos, see *Report to Greco,* Chapter 23, "Paris. Nietzsche the Great Martyr." SPARS . . . BEASTS: See note to "mystic trireme" of Dionysos in Sikelianós' poem "Rehearsal for Death," p. 751. THORNS . . . CRUCIFIED: As a god of vegetation who is slain every winter and resurrected every spring, Dionysos prefigures Christ.

BUDDHA. For Kazantzákis' identification with Buddha see *Report to Greco,* Chapter 34, "Vienna. My Illness." MAYA: In the theology of Hinduism, Maya is illusion or deception, the physical and sensuous universe conceived as a tissue of deceit, or as mere appearance, having no true reality, sometimes personified as a female goddess. THE THIRD EYE: See Kimon Friar's Introduction to Kazantzákis' *The Odyssey: A Modern Sequel,* pp. xvi–xx. Buddha says that we must look upon the world as if we were seeing it for the first and last time; this he calls the "elephant's eye." RED RIBBON: In ancient Greek ritual, a red ribbon was tied around the necks of sacrificial animals. SOLES OF HIS PALE FEET: There is a Buddhistic belief that the thirty-two signs of the perfect man, of the savior of the world, were schematized on Buddha's foot.

Alexander Mátsas

Alexander Mátsas was born on May 3, 1910, in Athens, and died in London, where he had gone for medical treatment, on February 5, 1969. He completed his early education in Athens, took his degree in political science from the University of Athens in 1931, studied Ancient Greats at Christ Church College, Oxford, for two years, and in 1934 joined the Greek diplomatic service. He held the post of vice-consul in Mansurah, Egypt, 1938, and that of consul in Alexandria, Egypt, 1939–40. He followed the Greek government-in-exile to London and later to Cairo during the German-Italian occupation, 1940–45. He was First Secretary at the Greek Embassy, Paris, 1947–50; chargé d'affaires at The Hague, 1949; Director of Economic Affairs at the Ministry of Foreign Affairs, Athens, 1951–53; counselor at the Greek Embassy in Rome, 1953–57; director of the First Political Division at the Ministry of Foreign Affairs, Athens, 1957–59; Minister Plenipotentiary, Athens, 1958; Ambassador to Turkey, Iran and Pakistan, 1959–62; Ambassador to the United States, 1962–67. He married in 1948 and has a daughter. Decorations: Commander of the Phoenix, Greece; Golden Cross of George I, Greece; Supreme Commander, Italy, Yugoslavia, Spain; Commander of the Legion of Honor, France; the Polar Star, Sweden; Great Ribbon of the Lion and the Sun, Iran; Knight of the Order of Merit, Austria. He was granted an Honorary Degree by the University of Michigan. His poetic dramas *Clytemnestra* and *Croesus* were produced by the National Theater in Athens in 1955 and 1963 respectively.

POETRY. *Le Vieux Jardin* (written in French), with a Foreword by Kostís Palamás, 1925. *Poems*, 1946. *Poems*, 1964.

POETIC DRAMA. *Clytemnestra*, 1936. *Jocasta*, 1950. *Croesus* (State Prize), 1959.

NOTES

MIDDAY CONTEMPLATION AT DELOS. Delos, regarded as the center of the Cyclades, is a small island in the Aegean. When Apollo was born there, the island, hitherto a floating island, became immovably fixed in the sea, and was from earliest times sacred to that god, who was honored there by song, dance and games. The entire island at present offers, perhaps, the most varied ruins in all of Greece. CICADA GONE BLIND: When a shadow falls on a cicada, it suddenly stops singing.

AUBADE. HERMETIC NUMBERS: Reference to the teachings of Hermes Trismegistos ("thrice greatest"), a late name for the god Hermes, as identified with the Egyptian god Thoth. He was the fabled author of a large number of works embodying Neo-Platonic, Judaic, and cabalistic ideas, as well as magical, astrological and alchemical doctrines. Certain of these, called "Hermetic books," were preserved and studied as sacred by the ancient Egyptian priests.

PSYCHE'S ADVENTURE. Psyche ("Soul"), a princess of remarkable beauty, was loved by Eros, the son of Aphrodite, and the youngest of the gods. After she had endured many tribulations, Zeus conferred immortality upon her.

Melissánthi

Melissánthi (née Hébe Koúyia) was born on April 8, 1910, in Athens, where she completed her early education. She also studied music and drawing, and for some time ballet and classical dance, with the intention of becoming a professional dancer. A serious illness, tuberculosis, forced her to spend a year and a half in 1923–24 in various sanatoriums in Switzerland; on her way back to Greece she visited Italy. She is proficient in English, has obtained diplomas in French from the French Institute and in German from the German Academy in Athens, and has translated Frost, Dickinson, Longfellow's "Hiawatha," Verlaine, and Pierre Garnier. During various times she taught French in public and private high schools in Athens, and worked as a journalist, writing many articles on Greek and foreign poets and on philosophical questions. In 1932 she married the statesman and writer Yánnis Skandalákis. Her play for children, *The Small Brother*, won the Sikiarídhion Award of the Children's Theater, and in 1965 she was decorated with the Royal Order of the Golden Cross.

POETRY. *Insect Voices*, 1930. *Prophecies*, 1931, 1940. *Flaming Bush*, 1935. *Return of the Prodigal*, 1936; 2d ed. with added poems (Athens Academy Award), 1938. *Hosanna*, 1939. *Lyrical Confession* (Palamás Honorable Mention), 1945. *The Season of Sleep and Forgetfulness*, 1950. *Human Shape*, 1961. *The Dam of Silence* (Second State Prize), 1965. *Selected Poems*, 1965.

NOTE

AT THE REGISTRAR'S. DID YOU SAY K?: Melissánthi's maiden name was Koúyia. MR. KLAMM: The person whom, in Kafka's *The Tower*, the hero tries in vain to find.

Kóstas Ouránis

Kóstas Ouránis (Níarhos) was born of Greek parentage on October 27, 1890, in Constantinople; his father was a wine merchant there and, later, a wheat merchant in Bulgaria. As an infant Ouránis was taken by his mother to her native village in Leonídhion, in the southern Peloponnesos, where he completed his grade-school education. For a while he attended high school in Náfplion, was dismissed because of his unruly nature, attended Roberts College for two years, an American high school in a suburb of Constantinople, but was again dismissed because of an indiscreet love affair, taking his diploma eventually from a private high school in Constantinople. He refused to take part in his father's business and in 1908 went instead to Athens, where he worked successfully as a journalist, using the pseudonym Ouránis for the first time. In 1910 he persuaded his parents to send him to Geneva to study business and agriculture, but used the money, instead, to travel throughout Belgium, Holland and France. Ouránis spent the rest of his life in traveling and in newspaper writing, publishing many books and articles on Spain, Italy, France, Greece, Portugal, Palestine and Mt. Sinai. He also wrote short stories, sketches, and a biography of Baudelaire, and translated into Greek several books from English and French. For a while during the Balkan War he was a war correspondent in Épiros. He had suffered from asthma since childhood, and in 1916 was stricken with tuberculosis and spent almost two years, 1917–18, in the Davos Sanatorium in Switzerland. There he met and married, in 1929, a rich Portuguese girl, Manuela Santiago, by whom he had a daughter. During 1920–24 he served as the Greek consul in Lisbon. After a period of about ten years, he was divorced, and in 1930 married Eléni Negropónti, better known as Álkis Thrílos, one of the foremost literary critics in Greece. He became editor of the Athenian newspaper *Free Speech* for one year, and for twenty years served as Greek correspondent for the *National Herald,* a Greek newspaper published in New York. He died of tuberculosis in Athens on July 13, 1953.

POETRY. *Like a Dream,* 1909. *Spleen,* 1912. *Nostalgias,* 1920. *Poems,* 1953.

NOTES

EDWARD VI. The title is in English in the original text, followed by this motto: "That godly and royal child, King Edward the Sixth, the flower of the Tudor name, that was untimely cropped as it began to fill our land with its early odours . . ." (Charles Lamb).

FONTAINE DE MEDICIS. In the Luxembourg Gardens, Paris.

NEL MEZZO DEL CAMMIN. The opening lines of Dante's *Divine Comedy:* "Midway in our life's journey, I went astray / from the straight road and woke to find myself / alone in a dark wood. How shall I say / what wood it was! I never saw so drear, so rank, so arduous a wilderness! / Its very memory gives a shape to fear." (Translation by John Ciardi, *New American Library,* 1954.)

VITA NUOVA. Reference to Dante's first book of poetry and commentary, *Incipit Vita Nuova,* "The New Life Begins."

SUPPLICATION TO MY GUARDIAN ANGEL. IMMORTAL WATER: See "immortal water" in Elýtis' poem "Age of Blue Memory," p. 697.

STARTING POINT. The last quatrain of a ten-quatrain poem bearing this title.

THE DARK WELL. A posthumous fragment. The title is the editor's.

I. M. Panayotópoulos

I. (Ioánnis) M. (Mihaíl) Panayotópoulos was born on October 23, 1901, in Etolikón, an island town near Missolóngi. He completed half of his grade-school education there, then finished the rest of his grade- and his high-school education in Athens, where his family moved in 1910. In 1923 he took his degree from the School of Philosophy at the University of Athens and then immediately after began an extremely varied career as educator, lecturer, traveler, poet, novelist, critic. During 1923–38 he taught language and literature at one of the best private secondary schools in Greece, the Hellenic School in Athens, which he then took over with a partner and has directed ever since 1938. From 1947 to 1957 he was also professor of modern Greek literature at a normal school in Athens. He edited the literary periodical *Muse*, 1920–23; was permanent critic of books and art for the newspaper *Proía* (*Morning News*), 1933–40; wrote similar articles for the newspaper *Freedom*, 1956–57; has been a regular contributor to the magazine *Néa Estía* (*New Hearth*) since 1957; has written more than 3,100 articles for the *Great Greek Encyclopedia* on literature and the fine arts, and similar articles for the *Enciclopedia die Personaggi*, Milan. His active membership in a variety of organizations indicates his extraordinary capacities: vice-president of the board of the National Theater, 1955–65; board member of the National Art Gallery, 1938–67; member of the Federation of International Journalists and Authors of Travel, of the International Association of Art Critics, of the Astronautical Society of Greece, of the Group of Twelve, of the Society of European Writers, of the Literary Association of Parnassos; on the administration board of the Society for the Publication of Useful Books and that of the Athenaeum Education Circle, for which he has given twenty lectures a year for sixteen years. In addition to his books of poetry, Panayotópoulos has written six novels (*The Seven Sleeping Children* won the First State Prize, 1956), four collections of short stories (*The Contemporary Man*, First State Prize, 1966); an *Introduction to Modern Greek Literature;* nine volumes of articles and literary criticism (*Kostís Palamás* was given the Palamás award jointly with George Seféris, 1947); two travel books on Greece and others on Egypt, Europe, the East, China and Russia, Cyprus and Eastern Africa (First State Prize, 1963). He has a son from his first marriage, 1926–32, and a son and daughter from his second marriage, 1938.

POETRY. *Miranda's Book*, 1924. *Lyrical Sketches*, 1933. *Alcyone*, 1950. *The Zodiac*, 1952. *The World's Window*, 1962.

NOTES

EUMENIDES. The Furies were avenging spirits who brought retribution on those who violated the laws of hospitality, natural piety, etc., or were guilty of perjury or homicide. Originally they were probably the vengeful ghosts of the slain, or vague embodiments of the avenging powers of nature, pursuing the offenders and inflicting madness. In Athens, following the traditions established by Aeschylos in his play *The Eumenides*, they were believed to have altered their character after the trial of Orestes for killing his mother Clytemnestra, ceasing to pursue with torments that guilt with which no moral fault was associated. In this milder character they were known to Athenians as *Eumenides*, or "gracious goddesses." This poem was written during and about the German-Italian occupation of Greece. ENDYMION: In one version the handsome young prince (or shepherd, or huntsman) Endymion, hunting on Mt. Latmos in Caria, Asia Minor, lay down to rest in a cool grotto, and then fell asleep. Selene, goddess of the moon, captivated by his beauty, stole a kiss while he slept. Zeus granted him immortality and eternal youth on condition that he remain eternally asleep. Selene came faithfully night after night to caress her sleeping lover. CYCLOPEAN ROCK: The Cyclops were a race of giants having but one eye, in the middle of their foreheads. They were credited with building the "Cyclopean" walls of Mycenae and other prehistoric cities, walls constructed of huge irregular blocks without mortar. HECATE: An ancient chthonian goddess with resemblances to Artemis and Selene. She is associated with sorcery, ghosts, and black magic. DEMETER: See note to Karélli's poem "Persephone," p. 711. CASTALIA: See note to "Castalian waters" in Vrettákos' poem "Saying Farewell," p. 759. EUROTAS: River near Sparta whose banks are overgrown with reeds. ARGIVE: Of or pertaining to the Achaean city of Argos or the surrounding territory of Argolis and hence, from the prominence of the Argive king Agamemnon, of or pertaining to the Greeks in general. TEGEA, ARTEMIS: Tegea was an ancient town in the southeastern Arcadian plain. Arcadia has several associations with Artemis, goddess of forest and the chase, twin sister of Apollo. Artemis is often identified with Hecate and Selene.

APOLOGY OF THE SMALL FAUN. GANYMEDE: See note on "Beloved's bucket" in Papatsónis' poem "Ode to Aquarius," p. 729. APHRODITE . . . FOAM: See note to "Cyprian" in Karélli's poem "Persephone," p. 711. LACONIA: Province of the southern Peloponnesos of which Sparta is the capital. PHAEACIAN SHORES . . . SIN: Pertaining to the country of the Phaeacians, fabulous seafaring people who inhabited the lovely island of Scheria (probably Corfu), where Odysseus was cast up naked after being shipwrecked, and where he was thus found by the princess of the island, Nausicaä.

THE FROZEN MOON, IV. From a poem in eight parts. MADONNA . . . TINOS: See note to "Virgin Mary . . . fiesta" in Elýtis' poem "Half-Sunken Boats," p. 697. I LAID ME DOWN AND SLEPT: Psalm 3.

THE FROZEN MOON, VIII. DOG BOUND: Reference to Aeschylos' play *Prometheus Bound*.

SUNDAY OF THE AEGEAN. KHIOS: One of the Cycladic islands. MT. IDA: Near the site of ancient Troy.

HELEN. PROTEUS: A prophetic sea god who, when seized, would assume different shapes to avoid prophesying.

THE NIGHTMARE. TONKIN: Part of French Indochina when this poem was written, now part of Vietnam. MARQUESAS ISLANDS: In the South Pacific Ocean where Gauguin lived and painted for a while. MAORI: The Polynesians. NOA-NOA: Book written and illustrated by Gauguin. WHAT ARE WE . . . GOING: A large painting by Gauguin of Tahitian figures, idols, and landscape entitled "Whence Come We? What Are We? Where Go We?" now in the Boston Museum of Fine Arts. SEVERED EAR . . . ARLES: Van Gogh had settled in Arles, in the south of France, where he was visited for a while by Gauguin. After a violent quarrel with Gauguin, van Gogh went to his room, cut off an ear (some say only the lobe), wrapped it up, and delivered it to one of the girls in a brothel he had frequented with Gauguin.

Tákis Papatsónis

Tákis (Panayótis) Papatsónis was born on January 30, 1895, in Athens, where he completed his early education. He received his degree in law and political science from the University of Athens in 1922, and took courses in finance at the University of Geneva in 1927. He had joined the Ministry of Economics in 1918 and has since served there in various capacities—first as Secretary and Chief of Section, later as Director of Tariffs and Treaties, General Director, Counselor of the High Court, Special Counselor for Economics, and finally, 1954–55, as Secretary General. He has also held many other posts—General Secretary in the Under Secretariat of the Press in the Ministry of Foreign Affairs, 1955–56; vice-president of the board of the National Theater, 1955–64; chairman of the board of the National Art Gallery, 1953–67. He participated as a representative of Greece at many financial conferences—at Geneva, 1927; the League of Nations, 1930; Prague, 1930; and yearly as Permanent Member of the Committee of Greek-German Trade Treaties in Berlin, 1930–39. He attended the International Conference for the Havana Charter, Cuba, 1948–49; the General Agreement of Trade and Traffic (GATT) in Annecy, France, 1949; a similar conference in Torquay, England, 1950; and yearly conferences, 1951–55. From 1945 to the present day he has been deputy chairman of the Commercial Bank of Greece. He attended the meeting of the Organization of the European Economic Cooperation in Paris, 1954. He is a member of the board of the Greek Society of Aesthetics, of which he became vice-president, and participated in the Fourth International Conference in Athens, and the Fifth in Amsterdam, 1964. Since 1947 he has been a member of the board of the Y.M.C.A. in Athens. He was a member of the Group of Twelve. In 1967 he was elected a member of the Athens Academy. He holds the following decorations: Commander of the Order of George I, Greece; of the Order of St. Sabba, Yugoslavia; of the Order of the Polonia Restituta; of the Crown of Italy; and Knight of the League of Honor, France. It is evident from his career that Papatsónis has traveled widely in the Western world; he has visited the United States on three different occasions, spending about a year and a half all told. He married in 1933 and has a daughter.

Papatsónis began writing in 1914, and since then his career in literature has run parallel to his political life. Though receptive to avant-garde movements, his particular fondness is for ancient and medieval Greek and Latin, and he is also proficient in English, French, Italian, Spanish and German. In many periodicals and newspapers he has published poetry, translations, and articles on travel, criticism, aesthetics and economics. In book form he has published *Spiritual Exercises on Mount Athos*, 1963; *Mythical Moldavia*, 1965; *The Four Corners of the World, Vol. I: Exercises in Regions of Criticism, Aesthetics, and Adoration*, 1966; and translations of Hölderlin, Claudel, Aragon, Saint-John Perse, Poe. In periodicals he has published translations of poems by Christina Rossetti and Eliot's *The Waste Land*.

POETRY. *Selections I*, 1934. *Ursa Minor*, 1944. *Selections I, Ursa Minor*, 1962. *Selections II* (First State Prize), 1962.

NOTES

BEFORE THE ADVENT. The period including the four Sundays before Christmas.

TO A YOUNG GIRL BROUGHT UP IN A NUNNERY. SALVE, SANCTA VIRGO: "Help us, Holy Virgin," in imitation of similar pleas in the Catholic jaculatorium.

A MONDAY OF THE YEAR. QUANDO . . . DATUR: "When the Queen of Sheba gives herself to Solomon." The legend is the author's. IN DEREN . . . GEFAHR: "And in their sweetness there is always present bitterness, play, and peril" (from Nietzsche's *Thus Spake Zarathustra*).

RAPE OF THE SABINES. The Sabines were an ancient people of central Italy who lived chiefly in the Apennines to the northeast of Rome. An ancient story tells how Romulus, the legendary founder of Rome, to secure wives for his settlers, arranged some public games, invited the Sabines and other tribes, then during the races seized the Sabine women and drove off the Sabine men.

THE UNLOOKED-FOR THEME. DE PROFUNDIS: Beginning of Psalm 130 in its Latin version: "Out of the depths I cried unto thee, O Lord"—that is, out of the depths of misery.

SUMMER TOURISTS GO TO MASS. HOURS . . . CANONS: See note to "The Dependence," below.

OUTLINE OF ERROR. IN PLATEIS OPPIDI: "In the squares of the city." Lamentations of Jeremiah (2:11) deals with the miseries of Jerusalem—"Mine eyes do fail with tears, my bowels are troubled, my liver is poured upon the earth, for the destruction of the daughter of my people; because the children and the sucklings swoon in the streets of the city."

THE SLUGGISH OF MIND. MEA CULPA: "My fault," from the confession given in the Roman Catholic Church—"I confess to God omnipotent, to the Blessed Virgin Mary, to the Blessed Archangel Michael, to the Holy Apostles Peter and Paul. I confess that I have sinned much in mind, in speech, and in deed. My fault, my fault, my greatest fault."

THE DEPENDENCE. TERCE . . . TENEBRAE: The Canonical Hours, or the eight offices of the day which form the Divine Office of the Roman Catholic Church. Two of these Hours are called "Tenebrae."

THE INNS. CENSUS OF CAESAR AUGUSTUS: "And it came to pass in those days, that there went out a decree from Caesar Augustus, that all the world should be taxed. (And this taxing was first made when Cyrenius was governor of Syria.) And all went to be taxed, every one into his own city. And Joseph also went up from Galilee, out of the city of Nazareth, into Judaea, unto the city of David, which is called Bethlehem; (because he was of the house and lineage of David:) To be taxed with Mary his espoused wife, being great with child. And so it was, that, while they were there, the days were accomplished that she should be delivered. And she brought forth her firstborn son, and wrapped him in swaddling clothes, and laid him in a manger; because there was no room for them at the inn." (Luke 2:1-7)

THE OLD MAN'S LOG OF WOOD. AGNES . . . BODY: Saint Agnes was a young Roman virgin who refused to marry a rich man, for she wished to remain virginal. She crawled naked through the streets of Rome to a brothel and there converted the prostitutes to Christianity. When flames would not touch her at the stake, she was beheaded, at the age of thirteen, under the persecutions of Diocletian, who reigned from 284 to 305.

I SING THE WRATH. An adaptation of the opening line of Homer's *Iliad*, wherein Homer bids the Muse sing of the wrath of Achilles. DODONIAN WILL: Dodona was the seat of the famous oracle of Zeus on Mt. Tomaros in Épiros. ILLYRIAN MOUNTAINEERS AND WESTERN HORDES: The Albanians and Italians who invaded Greece in 1941 at the Greek-Albanian border in Épiros and were shamefully defeated before the German forces overran Greece. ACHAEANS: Broadly, the ancient Greeks, so named in Homer. FATHER ANCHISES . . . BEAR FRUIT: During the sack of Troy, Aeneas, the son of Anchises and Aphrodite, and the son-in-law of Priam, king of Troy, carried his father to safety on his back. Virgil's

Aeneid tells of his wanderings from Troy to Thrace, Crete, Épiros, Carthage, and finally Italy, where his descendant, Romulus, suckled by a she-wolf in infancy, was fabled to have founded the Roman Empire. SIBYL: The priestess of Apollo at Cumae (near the present Naples) helped Aeneas descend to the underworld to see the future greatness of his race, and to learn what Rome's moral mission would be. DREPANUM: The present province of Trapani, where Aeneas landed and where his father Anchises died. HESTIA: Goddess of the hearth, whether of home or city. GALEAZZO: Count Ciano, Mussolini's son-in-law and foreign minister.

THE BONFIRES OF SAINT JOHN. On the eve of June 24, Saint John the Baptist's birthday, bonfires are lit in the streets or on the fields at sunset. After dancing around the flames, the celebrants leap over the bonfire, saying various wishes and prayers. When the fire has gone out, village women scoop up a handful of ashes to take home for divinatory purposes.

THIS CUP. In Gethsemane, thinking on his coming crucifixion, Jesus prays to God: "And he went a little farther, and fell on his face, and prayed, saying, O my Father, if it be possible, let this cup pass from me: nevertheless not as I will, but as thou wilt" (Matthew, 26:39). WHITE-GARMENTED . . . DEEDS: From a Byzantine *tropárion*, or hymn.

CROSSWAYS. ARMENIAN DEACON . . . FEATHERS: A deacon, in the Byzantine church, assists the priests or bishops as curate. The Armenians have a special, very ancient and picturesque ritual according to which, during the consecration of the bread and the wine, two deacons lightly fan the officiating priest or bishop and the Holy Sacraments of the Mass with two large peacock feathers in a demonstration of extreme reverence toward the sacraments.

IN THE KEY OF RESURRECTION. DEATH . . . FUTILE: Part of the matutinal service of the Greek Orthodox Church during Lent. THE VEIL . . . CANDLES ONE BY ONE: "Now from the sixth hour there was darkness over all the land unto the ninth hour. . . . And straightway one of them ran, and took a sponge, and filled it with vinegar, and put it on a reed, and gave him to drink. . . . And, behold, the veil of the temple was rent in twain from the top to the bottom; and the earth did quake, and the rocks rent" (Matthew 27:45–51). LET . . . DEAD: "Jesus said unto him, Let the dead bury their dead: but go thou and preach the kingdom of God" (Luke 9:60). ALL THE FELLOWSHIP . . . HELLENES: From a Byzantine psalm or *tropárion*. STUMBLING BLOCK AND FOOLISH-NESS: "But we preach Christ crucified, unto the Jews a stumblingblock, and unto the Greeks foolishness" (I Corinthians 1:25).

THE THREAD. CENSUS: See note to "The Inns," p. 728.

ATTIC SHAPES. The title and motto were suggested by the translator; the original title is "Attic Things."

ODE TO AQUARIUS. To Eva. MANY WATERS . . . DROWN IT: From The Song of Solomon 8:7. BELOVED'S BUCKET: Ganymede, son of King Tros, the most beautiful youth in antiquity, was abducted by Zeus in the guise of an eagle to become his beloved and the cupbearer of the gods, pouring for them wine and water. Zeus set his image among the stars as Aquarius, the water carrier; the eagle became the constellation Aquila. In primitive times Ganymede seems to have been conceived as the deity responsible for sprinkling the earth with heaven's rain. Aquarius is represented as the figure of a man pouring water from a vase. MINOR WATERS: Very small stars, barely visible, representing the last droplets of water poured out by Aquarius.

Níkos Pappás

Níkos Pappás was born on January 26, 1906, in the town of Tríkala, Thessaly, of well-to-do parents. He completed his early education in his home town, then went to Athens in 1923 and took his degree in law from the University of Athens in 1927, traveling in the meantime to Austria and Germany. During 1927–29 he worked in his father's law office in Tríkala, but had no sooner passed his bar examinations than he fell seriously ill of a spasmodic tick, spending three and a half years in bed, eight months of these in a clinic in Athens. During the winter of 1930–31 he underwent analysis with Sigmund Freud in Vienna. In 1931 he edited the magazine *The Province*, and in 1933, well at length, continued his career as lawyer. In 1936 he married the poetess Ríta Boúmi. During 1935–40 he was literary critic for the newspaper *Kathimeriní* (*Daily News*), later wrote political articles for several progressive newspapers, and in 1951 ran unsuccefully for deputy on a progressive ticket. During 1940–45 he was employed as a lawyer by the Greek government, and in 1947–50 defended some fifty Greek Resistance fighters in military trials, obtaining some degree of fame as a fiery and eloquent lawyer. With his wife, at the invitation of writers' societies, he visited East Germany in 1958, Bulgaria in 1963, Rumania in 1964, and Czechoslovakia in 1965. He retired from the practice of law in 1968. He has edited a selection of Greek folk songs, and together with his wife compiled and in part translated an anthology of world poetry in two volumes.

POETRY. *Futile Words*, Tríkala, 1930. *Blood of the Innocent*, 1944. *Night of Four Years*, 1946. *Legends of the Sleepwalkers*, 1948. *The Captive Angels*, 1957. *The Diary of a Barbarian*, 1957. *12 & 5* (Second State Prize), 1959. *Monolith Without Crack*, 1961.

Signals from a Tempest, 1962. *The Hands,* 1963. *The Heroic Rose* (First State Prize), 1964. *With Everyone and with No One,* 1965. *Legal Entity,* 1966.

NOTES

FOR A GROUP OF AMERICAN POETS. MURDOCK: The author remembers reading about some American poet with this name who toured the United States lecturing and criticizing the present state of Christianity. HAUSHOFER: Albrecht Haushofer, Professor of Political Geography at the University of Berlin, took part in the unsuccessful plot of July 20, 1944, against Hitler, was jailed and then executed in 1945. In prison he wrote the now famous *Morbid Sonnets,* published posthumously in 1946.
BECAUSE OF THIS POETRY. TSITSÁNIS: Yánnis Tsitsánis, writer and player of *bouzóuki* songs and music.
EMMET TILL. The poet had read in a newspaper that a Negro boy of fourteen had been abducted and killed in the South because the day before he had dared to whistle at a white woman in admiration of her beauty. KALAMÁKI, ZÁPPION, KASTÉLLA: Kalamáki is a suburb of Athens by the sea; the Záppion Gardens are adjacent to the National Gardens in the heart of Athens; Kastélla is a hilly district of Piraeus overlooking the harbor of Turkolimáni. THE VISIONARY: See Introduction, p. 27.
AGHLAIA ATHEMIADHOU. ROÚMELI: Part of Central Greece. MORÉA: Medieval name for the Peloponnesos.
DEMOLITION. ATRIDAE: Family of Atreus, king of Mycenae, father of Agamemnon and Menelaos. PAPADHIAMÁNDIS: Alexander Papadhiamándis, 1851–1911, one of the best short-story writers of Greece. MELAHRINÓS: Apóstolos Melahrinós, 1883–1952, symbolist poet.

Níkos Ghavriil Pendzíkis

Níkos Ghavriíl Pendzíkis was born on October 30, 1908, in Thessaloníki. At first, like his sister Zoë Karélli, he was tutored at home, then in Thessaloníki completed the last year of grade school and was later graduated from a public high school. He spent 1926–28 at the University of Paris, from which he received a degree in optical physiology; and 1928–29 at the University of Strasbourg, from which he received a degree in pharmacy. He also traveled in Yugoslavia, Austria, Germany, Switzerland and Italy. Inheriting the oldest pharmacy in Thessaloníki, founded by his father in 1887, he ran it until he sold it in 1959. At the same time, however, he was also the representative for Northern Greece of the Swiss pharmaceutical firm Jir. Geigy, and remained with this firm in its various transformations until he retired in 1969 on a pension. He was married in 1948 and has a son. In addition to his poetry, Pendzíkis has published in book form meditations and ruminations of an extremely original mind, studies of painters and writers, and four "novels" which fall into the category of poetry as well as of prose. In periodicals, he has published many articles on literary and religious subjects. As a painter, he has shown his work in six Panhellenic Exhibitions, in group shows in Athens, Thessaloníki and Kavála, and has had one-man shows in Thessaloníki, 1951, 1952, and in Athens, 1958.

POETRY. *Images*, Thessaloníki, 1944. *Transfer of Relics*, Thessaloníki, 1961.

PROSE. *Andréas Dhimakoúdhis*, Thessaloníki, 1935. *The Dead Man and Resurrection*, 1944, 1970. *Architecture of Scattered Life*, 1963. *The Novel of Mrs. Érsi*, 1966. *Mother Thessaloníki*, 1969. *Retinue*, 1970. *Toward High Mass*, Thessaloníki, 1970.

NOTES

THE MONK AT THE FOUNTAIN. Published in the periodical *Kokhlías*, Thessaloníki, November, 1947. VIRGIN'S GARDEN: Name for Mt. Athos and its monasteries.

DOES IT FLY? DOES IT FLY? Two Greek children play a game called "It flies, it flies!" One of them flaps his arms as though in flight, and cries out, "It flies, it flies, the swallow flies" (or names any other bird or insect). He might try to fool his companion, however, by calling out some creature that cannot fly, as "It flies, it flies, the dog flies!" The second child must take care to flap his own arms if some flying creature is called out, and not be fooled into flapping them when a creature that cannot fly is called out. KARAGIÓZIS: Name of the comical hero of the Greek shadow theater, much beloved by Greek children. MT. HORTIÁTIS: Near Thessaloníki.

SCATTERED LEAVES. OPENED THE CELESTIAL HEAVENS: According to Greek folk tradition, it is believed that any wish made at the Epiphany (January 6) will come true, for on the eve of that day the heavens open their gates, and the wish may thus be heard. NEAPOLIS: The ancient name of the present Kavála. Because it was here that Paul first disembarked to preach Christianity in Europe, it was later also named Christoúpolis. BUT I . . . NO HOPE: First Epistle to the Thessalonians 4:13. MARDONIOS: Brilliant young general and son-in-law of Darius, whose Persian fleet was wrecked off Mt. Athos. The myth about the treasure is to be found in a short story by the Greek writer Alexander Papadhiamándis, 1851–1911. TAKE US . . . BLOW: Barcarole of the early twentieth century, here printed in inverted fashion, beginning with the last line and proceeding to the first, as appropriate to the dead who sing it.

SEASIDE THOUGHTS. In the singular, the Greek word for fish, ἰχθύς, is an acrostic for "Jesus Christ, Son of God, Savior." Since ancient times the fish has been a symbol of life, but after Christ it became the special and secret symbol of Christianity, because some of the Apostles were fishermen, and because Christ performed the miracle of the loaves and the fishes. EMBODIMENT . . . MOISTURE: Plotinos and Porphyry wrote that the soul cannot manifest itself unless water is present. WELL THEN . . . SINS FALLEN: In 830 Euphrosíni, mother of Emperor Theóphilos, invited the most beautiful maidens of Byzantium to the palace and directed her son to give a golden apple to the one he wanted for wife. Theóphilos wanted to give the apple to Kassianí, the most beautiful of the maidens, but in order to test her intelligence asked her, "Do all the vices of the world originate in women?" (meaning Eve). Kassianí answered, "But all good things also have their source in woman" (meaning the Virgin Mary). Theóphilos found her answer so provoking that he gave the apple instead to Theodhóra, though he never ceased loving Kassianí. In bitterness, Kassianí became a nun and wrote the famous *tropárion* (hymn) sung on Holy Tuesday of Easter Week. The poet has changed the opening line of the *tropárion*, "The woman who had fallen into many sins," into the first person.

CONSTANT COMPANY. RODHOLÍVOS: A mountain village of Thrace near Kavála.

DOCUMENTARY. From *Mother Thessaloníki*. SHE WOULD PLACE THE SOAP . . . FROM THERE: According to popular superstition, soap received from another in the normal way would lead to a quarrel.

Pandelis Prevelákis

Pandelís Prevelákis was born on March 2, 1909, in Réthimnon, Crete, where he completed his early education. After three years of study in the School of Philosophy at the University of Athens, he went to Paris, where he took his degree in art and archeology from the Sorbonne in 1933. On his return to Greece, he took his doctorate on a thesis about El Greco from the University of Thessaloníki in 1935. During 1937–41 he was Director of the Departments of Fine Arts in the Ministry of National Education, and since 1939 he has been professor of the history of art in the College of Fine Arts in Athens. In his career as art historian, Prevelákis has written three books on El Greco and four books on painting. His introduction to the Greek literary scene was as a poet, and he has since directed his poetic energies into the writing of four poetic dramas and the translations, mostly into meter, of the poetic drama of Calderón, Benavente, Molière, Claudel, Montherlant, and the *Medea* and *Bacchae* of Euripides, all of which have been produced. Primarily, however, he has made his reputation as a novelist, having written ten novels, which have been translated into many languages. Two of these, *The Sun of Death* and *The Bread of Angels*, were awarded First State Prizes for 1959 and 1966. An acquaintance with Níkos Kazantzákis when Prevelákis was seventeen led to a lifelong friendship. He has translated into Greek Kazantzákis' novel *Le Jardin des Rochers* (*The Rock Garden*, originally written in French), has published a study of Kazantzákis' *The Odyssey* (Group of Twelve Award, 1958), and in 1965 published *Four Hundred Letters from Kazantzákis to Prevelákis, and Forty Other Autographs, with Notes and an Outline of the Inner Biography and Chronology of the Life of Níkos Kazantzákis.* He is a member of the Society of Greek Writers, the Pen Club, the European Society of Writers, the Association of International Art Critics. He has a knowledge of ancient Greek, French, Spanish, Italian, and English. He has been made Commander of the Order of George I by Greece, and Commander of the Order of the Italian Crown.

POETRY. *Soldiers*, 1928. *The Nude Poetry*, 1939. *The Nudest Poetry*, 1941.

POETIC DRAMA. *The Sacrificial Victim* (produced by the National Theater, Athens), 1952. *Lazarus*, 1954. *The Hands of the Living God* (produced by the National Theater, Athens), 1955. *The Volcano* (First State Prize; produced in an outdoor theater in Réthimnon on the centennial of the Cretan Insurrection of 1866), 1963.

IN ENGLISH. *Nikos Kazantzákis and His Odyssey: A Study of the Poet and the Poem*, translated by Philip Sherrard, with a Preface by Kimon Friar (New York: Simon and Schuster, 1961). *Fire in Painting and in Poetry*, translated by Philip Sherrard (Athens, 1963). *The Sun of Death*, translated by Abbott Rick, with a Preface by Henry Miller (New York: Simon and Schuster, 1964); translated by Philip Sherrard (London: John Murray, 1965).

NOTES

IN THIS UPPER JERUSALEM. In a hymn sung on the evening of Palm Sunday in the Greek Orthodox Church, Jesus says to his Apostles, on his way to be crucified: "I go now, not to the earthly Jerusalem to suffer, but unto My Father and your Father, and My God and your God, and I will raise you up into the upper Jerusalem, in the Kingdom of Heaven."

I KNEW WITH YOU THOSE QUIET HOURS. PRIAM . . . SON: Priam, king of Troy, lamented the death of his son Hector, whom Achilles killed in battle and then dragged around the walls of Troy tied to his chariot.

BARCAROLE. DIONYSIAN FESTIVAL OF FLOWERS: Early in the month Anthesterion (mid-February), when the crops were ripening, the vines were being pruned, and the spring flowers were appearing, the Anthesteria, or Festival of Flowers, was held in honor of Dionysos as the god of spring.

Yánnis Rítsos

Yánnis Rítsos was born on May 14, 1909, in the town of Monemvasía, in the southern Peloponnesos, of a family of landowners. He completed his high-school education in the seaside town of Yíthion nearby, then went to Athens in 1925 and enrolled in the university there. At the age of eighteen, however, he fell ill with tuberculosis, returned to his home town for a brief stay, then spent the years 1927–29 in sanatoriums in and around Athens, and 1929–31 in a sanatorium in Crete. His heritage is a tragic one, for both his mother and elder brother died of tuberculosis, his father died in the Municipal Insane Asylum, where a sister also spent several years. Shortly after Metaxás came into power as dictator, in August of 1936, Rítsos' poem "Epitáphios," the lament of a mother over her son killed by army and police in a workers' strike, was publicly burnt, with other books, by the Temple of Zeus of Olympos. A short relapse sent him to another sanatorium near Athens during 1937–38. At various intervals during 1936–56 he worked in a publishing firm. Haunted by thoughts of madness and suicide during these years, Rítsos turned for salvation to poetry and the revolutionary ideal.

During the German-Italian occupation of Greece, he joined the Resistance movement and became a member of the central committee of a crypto-Communist party known as EDA, or Union of the Democratic Left. After the collapse of the Left in 1944, he went into hiding, entrusting to his friends, who later burnt them in panic and fright, a great quantity of his unpublished poetry, correspondence, essays, photographs, and the only novel he has written. Apprehended in July, 1948, toward the end of the Civil War, he was incarcerated until August, 1952, in various detention camps on the islands of Lémnos, Makrónisos, and St. Strátis, where, nevertheless, he managed secretly to write a great deal of poetry, and two as yet unpublished plays, on scraps of paper which he hid in bottles buried in the earth. Shortly after his release, he married, in 1954, the doctor Yaroufaliá Yeoryiádou, with whom he has a daughter.

It was not until 1956 that Rítsos was permitted to travel abroad; then, on the invitation of various cultural associations, he visited Bulgaria, Rumania, Czechoslovakia, the Soviet Union, France, and Cuba in 1966. Although subsequently he had not taken active part in political affairs, he was again arrested immediately after the military coup of April 21, 1967, sent to the detention camp on the island of Yéros, and soon after to Léros. In 1968, suffering from a variety of ailments, he was permitted to be hospitalized in Athens, during August and September, and then, after a month in Léros again, he was permitted to live in exile with his wife in the village of Karlóvasi in Sámos. The great outcry throughout Europe against his detention induced the military regime to offer him a passport if he would refrain from criticism, and allowed him to come to Athens, again for medical reasons, from January to April of 1970. When he refused to accept their terms, he was again exiled to Sámos. Throughout his life, and especially during his incarcerations, Rítsos has painted on whatever material he could obtain, on paper, stones, pebbles, bone, bits of wood or glass. Some of these are of great beauty.

Rítsos has translated the poetry of Éluard, Volkner, Bezrouts, Nezval and Michaux, and has published book translations of Vladimir Mayakovsky, Alexander Blok, Attila Yiosef, Nasim Hikmet, Nikolas Guillen, Ilya Ehrenburg, Dora Gabé, and anthologies of Rumanian and Czechoslovakian poetry.

POETRY. *Tractor*, 1934. *Pyramids*, 1935. *Epitáphios*, 1936. *The Song of My Sister*, 1937. *Spring Symphony*, 1938. *The Ocean's Musical March*, 1940. *Old Mazurka to the Rhythm of Rain*, 1943. *Test*, 1943. *Our Comrade*, 1945. *The Man with the Carnation*, 1952. *Vigilance*, 1954. *Morning Star*, 1955. *Moonlight Sonata* (First State Prize), 1956; revised edition, 1966. *Chronicle*, 1957. *Saying Goodbye*, 1957. *Water Jug*, 1957. *Winter Clarity*, 1957. *Stone Year*, 1957. *The World's Neighborhoods*, 1957. *When the Stranger Comes*, 1958. *Unsubdued City*, 1958. *The Architecture of Trees*, 1958. *The Old Women and the Sea*, 1959. *The Window*, 1960. *The Bridge*, 1960. *The Black Saint*, 1961. *Poems, Vol. 1*, 1961. *Poems, Vol. II*, 1961. *The Dead House*, 1962. *Under the Mountain's Shadow*, 1962. *The Prison Tree and the Women*, 1963. *12 Poems for Caváfis*, 1963. *Testimonies, I*, 1963. *Poems, Vol. III*, 1964. *Games of the Sky and Water*, 1964. *Philoctetos*, 1965. *Romiosíni*, 1966. *Orestes*, 1966. *Testimonies, II*, 1966. *Ostrava.*, 1967. *Stones, Repetitions, Railings*, 1972. *Helen*, 1972.

POETIC DRAMA. *Beyond the Shadow of Cypress Trees*, 1958. *A Woman Beside the Sea*, 1959.

IN ENGLISH: *Poems*. In an English version by Alan Page (Oxford: the Review, No. 21, part 3, 1969). *Romiosíni*. Translation by O. Laos. Introduction by Dan Georgakas. With drawings by Gary Elder (Paradise, Calif.: Dustbooks, 1969). *Selected Poems* (New York: Smyrna Press, 1969). *Gestures and Other Poems*. Translated from the Greek by Níkos Stángos, with illustrations by the poet. (London: Cape Goliard Press, 1971.)

IN SOME MAJOR LANGUAGES. FRENCH: *L'Homme à la fleur* (Éditions Grèce Nouvelle, 1952). *Quatrième Dimension* (Éditions Pierre Seghers, Collection "Autour de Monde," No. 47, 1958). *L'Arbre de la prison et les femmes* (Édition Revue d'Art, 1963). *Témoignages* (Paris: Éditions Pierre Seghers, Collection "Autour de Monde," No. 86, 1966). *La Maison est à louer* (Paris: Les Éditeurs Français Réunis, 1967). *Yánnis Rítsos*, étude, choix de textes et bibliographie par Chrýsa Papandréou, dessins, portraits, fac-similés (Paris: Éditions Pierre Seghers, Collection "Poètes d'aujourd'hui," No. 178, 1968). *Grécité* (Paris: Éditions Fata Morgana, Collection "Discours," 1968). *Pierres, Répétitions, Barreaux* (Édition Bilingue. Poèmes traduits du grec par Chrysa

Propopaki, Antoine Vitz, Gérard Pierrat. Preface d'Aragon
(Paris: Gallimand, Collection "Poètes du Monde Entier," 1970).
Grécité, Après l'épreuve. Traduits par Jacques Lacarrière avec un
frontispice de Matta (Montpellier: Édition Fata Morgana, Collec-
tion "Discours," 1971). *Sophocle, Electre. Parenthèses de Yannis
Ritsos.* Traduction du grec et montage par Antoine Vites. Les
Parenthèses de Yannis Ritsos en collaboration avec Chrysa Proko-
paki (Paris: Les Éditeurs Français Réunis, 1971). *La maison morte.*
Traduction Gérard Pierrat (Paris: Éditions Maspero, 1972).
GERMAN: *Gedichte.* Aus dem Neugriechischen von Vagelis
Tsakiridis (Berlin: Verlag Klaus Wagenbach, "Quarthefte," 1968).
Zeugenaussagen. [*Testimonies,* I, bilingual edition] Griechisch-
Deutsch. Übersetzung und Nachwort von Günter Dietz (Frank-
furt am Main: Verlag Horst Heiderhoff, 1968). *Zeugenaussagen*
[Testimonies, II, bilingual edition] Auswahl und Übersetzung aus
dem Griechischen A. N. Sfountouris. Mit einer Vorbemerkung
von Eleni N. Kazantzaki und einer Einleitung von Max Frisch
(Frankfurt am Main: Verlag Horst Heiderhoff, 1968). *Die
Wurzeln der Welt.* Nachgedichtet von Bernd Jentzsch und Klaus-
Dieter Sommer (Berlin: Verlag Volk und Welt, 1970).
ITALIAN: *Poesie.* Tradotte da Filippo Maria Pontani (Milano:
Pesce d'oro, 1969). *Epitaffio e Makronissos* [Bilingual edition]
Traduzione di Nicola Crocetti e Dimitri Makris. Prefazione di
Giorgio Gatos (Parma: Guanda, 1970). RUSSIAN: *Poems* (Mos-
cow: Foreign Literature, 1959). SPANISH: *Sonata al Claro de
Luna.* Musica Manuel Angulo, prologo José Hierro, grabados
Dimitri (Madrid: Boj, 1966–1967). SWEDISH: *Åborder.* Dikter
i svensk tolkning av Theodor Kallifatides och Östen Sjöstrand.
Inledning av Bengt Holmquist (Stockholm: Wahlström & Wid-
strand, 1971. *Greklands folk.* Dikter, Översattning av Theodor
Kallifatides och Björn Ranung (Stockholm: Wahlström & Wid-
strand, 1968). Translations in book form also in Bulgarian, Chi-
nese, Czechoslovakian, Danish, Finnish, Hungarian, Icelandic,
Norwegian, Rumanian, Slavic and Ukrainian.

NOTES

ROMIOSINI. The very essence of being Greek. See p. 4. of Intro-
duction. MONEVASIÁ: See p. 704. I am indebted for some felicitous
phrases to Níkos Germanácos.

STONES. NIKE: Goddess of victory. ARTEMIS: Goddess of the hunt.
PATROCLOS: In Homer's *Iliad,* the friend of Achilles, slain by Hector.

THE FIRST SENSUAL DELIGHT. KALLIDROMON, OETA, OTHRYS: Mountains in Thessaly, Achilles' native land.

THE PEACOCKS OF PYRILAMPES. Pyrilampes was Charmides' maternal uncle. He married Plato's mother, Periktione, after her first husband had died. He was famous for his embassies to the court of the Persian kings, and to other courts of Asia Minor. Plutarch says that he was the friend of Perikles, who named him "bird breeder" because he brought peacocks from Persia to Greece and bred them.

GRADATIONS. In Book VIII of Homer's *Odyssey*, King Alcinoüs of the Phaeacians proclaims athletic contests and a feast in honor of his guest, Odysseus. Odysseus is invited by the king's son Laodamus to take part in the games, but Odysseus excuses himself, pleading exhaustion from his many adventures. Euryalus, a young Phaeacian, sees fit to insult him: "You are quite right, sir. I should never have taken you for an athlete such as one is accustomed to meet in the world. But rather for some skipper of a merchant crew, who spends his life on a hulking tramp, worrying about his outward freight, or keeping a sharp eye on the cargo, when he comes home with the profits he has snatched. No; one can see you are no sportsman." Odysseus, enraged, "leapt to his feet, and not even troubling to remove his cloak, picked up the biggest disk of all, a huge weight, more massive by far than those used in their regular matches. With one swing he launched it from his mighty hand, and the stone hummed on its course. The Phaeacians, lords of the sea and champions of the long oar, cowered down as it hurtled through the air; and so lightly did it fly from his hand that it overshot the marks of all the other throws. Athene, pretending to be one of the crowd, marked the distance of the cast, and saluted the thrower."—Tr. by E. V. Rieu.

MEMORIAL SERVICES. WHEAT: Refers to a confection made of boiled grains of wheat, raisins, almonds, walnuts, pomegranate seeds, and sugar, offered to the dead at memorial services. AUNT LAHÓ: Rítsos' demotic version of Lachesis, one of the three Fates whose duty it was to determine the life span of each individual.

George Sarandáris

George Sarandáris was born in Constantinople on April 29, 1907, but between the ages of two and twenty-four lived in Italy, where his father's business took him. He completed his early education in Bologna, enrolled in the School of Law at the university there, and between 1929 and 1931 lived in Montaponne and then in Macerata, at whose university he took his degree in law. While in Italy he wrote most of his poetry in Italian, and some in Greek and French, and translated Italian poets into Greek and Greek poets into Italian. He came to Greece in 1931 for his military service and remained there, with infrequent trips to Italy, until his death on February 26, 1941, at the age of thirty-four, from hardships suffered as a common soldier in the Albanian War. He never practiced law but, living on a small income, gave himself completely to poetry and philosophy. During his lifetime he published four small volumes of poetry, a book of prose poems, *Letter to a Woman*, 1936, and three books of "philosophy": *Advice on a Philosophy of Existence*, 1937; *The Appearance of Man*, 1938; and *Essay on Logic as a Theory of the Absolute and the Nonabsolute*, 1939. Many poems in Greek, Italian, and French still remain unpublished.

POETRY. *Loves of the Year*, 1933. *Celestial*, 1934. *The Stars*, 1935. *To Friends of Another Joy*, 1940. *Poems*, edited by George Marinákis, 1961. *Poems in Italian and French*, edited by George Marinákis, 1961. *Inediti Italiani di Serandaris*, edited by Filippo Maria Pontani, Rome, 1965.

NOTES

THREE POEMS OF THE SEA. LA DANSE . . . L'ENFANT: "The dance within the dance / Everyone becomes a child."
I HAVE SEEN ETERNITY IN THE FOREST. FUSTANELLA: The pleated white skirt of the Greek national costume and of the Royal Guards.

George Seféris

George Seféris (Seferiádhis) was born on March 13, 1900, in Smyrna, Turkey. When the First World War broke out in 1914, his family moved to Athens, where he completed his high-school education. In July, 1918, he accompanied his mother to Paris to join his father, who was working there as a lawyer. (At the end of that same year Mr. Seferiádhis was appointed professor of international law at the University of Athens, of which he later became president; and there he published translations from Byron and Sophocles.) Seféris studied literature at, and took a degree in law from, the University of Paris, 1918–24, spending the summer of 1924 and most of 1925 in England. He then returned to Athens, and in 1926 was appointed to the Royal Greek Ministry of Foreign Affairs, where he worked until 1931. He then served in the General Consulate in London, 1931–34; resided in Athens, 1934–

36; served as consul in Koritsa, Albania, 1936–38; as press officer in the Department of Press and Information, Athens, 1938; and visited Rumania in 1939. He married Maria Zánnos in 1941. On the occupation of Greece by German and Italian forces, he accompanied the Greek government in exile to Crete, to Egypt, and finally to South Africa, where he served in the Greek Embassy at Pretoria until 1942, and as press officer to the Greek government in Cairo, 1942–44. He accompanied the government to Italy in 1944, and on October 23 of that year returned to liberated Greece. He then served as Director of the Political Bureau of the Regent Archbishop Dhamaskinós, 1945–46; in the Ministry of Foreign Affairs, 1946–48; as counselor of the Embassy in Ankara, Turkey, 1948–50; as counselor of the Embassy in London, 1951–52; as ambassador to Lebanon, Syria, Jordan, and Iraq, 1953–56; and visited Cyprus in 1953, 1954, and 1955. He then served as Director of the Second Political Bureau of the Ministry of Foreign Affairs in Athens, 1956–57; as a member of the Greek delegation to the United Nations in New York during the discussion of the Cyprus question; and finally served as ambassador to Great Britain, 1957–62. He then retired from diplomatic service in 1962 and settled in Athens. The fall of 1968 he spent as a member of the Institute of Advanced Studies at Princeton, and read his poetry at various institutions and universities in the United States. He has been granted an honorary Doctor of Letters degree by the universities of Cambridge, Oxford and Princeton, an honorary Doctor of Philosophy degree by the University of Thessaloníki, has been elected an Honorary Foreign Member of the American Academy of Arts and Sciences, and an Honorary Fellow of the Modern Language Association. In 1947 he was granted a joint Palamás Award in Athens, in 1961 the William Foyle Prize in Poetry in London, and in 1963 the Nobel Prize for Literature. In addition to writing his own prose and poetry, Seféris has translated Eliot's *Murder in the Cathedral, The Waste Land,* "The Hollow Men, I," "Marina," "Difficulties of a Statesman," and poetry by Pound, Yeats, MacLeish, Auden, Durrell, Keyes, D. H. Lawrence, Marianne Moore, Cecil Day Lewis, Gide, Valéry, Jouve, Éluard, and Michaux, and also the Song of Songs and The Apocalypse of St. John. He died in Athens on September 20, 1971.

POETRY. *Turning Point,* 1931. *The Cistern,* 1932. *Myth of Our History,* 1935. *Notebook of Exercises,* 1940. *Logbook I,* 1940.

Poems I, 1940. *Logbook II*, Alexandria, Egypt, 1944; Athens, 1945. *Thrush*, 1947. *Poems 1924–1946*, 1950. *Logbook III* (under the title *Cyprus . . . Where He Prophesied That I*), 1955. *Poems*, 1962. *Three Secret Poems*, 1966.

IN ENGLISH
POETRY. Lawrence Durrell, *Six Poems from the Greek of Sikelianós and Seféris* (Rhodes, 1946). Bernard Spencer, Nános Valaorítis, Lawrence Durrell, *The King of Asine and Other Poems*, with an Introduction by Rex Warner (London: John Lehman, 1948). Rex Warner, *Poems* (London: The Bodley Head, 1960; Boston: Little, Brown, 1960). Edmund Keeley and Philip Sherrard, *Poems 1924–1955*, bilingual edition (Princeton, N.J.: Princeton University Press, 1967; London: Jonathan Cape, 1969); supplemented edition and paperback edition (Princeton, N.J.: Princeton University Press, 1969 and 1971). Walter Kaiser, *Three Secret Poems*, bilingual edition (Cambridge, Mass.: Harvard University Press, 1969).

PROSE. "Letter to a Foreign Friend," in *T. S. Eliot: A Symposium* (London: Editions Poetry, 1948). "The Cantos, A Note Appended to His Translation of Three Cantos," in *Ezra Pound*, edited by Peter Russell (London: Peter Nevill, Ltd., 1950). *Delphi*, translated by Philip Sherrard, with sixteen color prints and twenty black-and-white prints taken by Herbert Kreft (Munich and Ahrbeck/Hanover: Knorr und Hirth Verlag, 1963). *On the Greek Style, Selected Essays in Poetry and Hellenism*, translated by Rex Warner and Th. Frangópoulos (Boston: Atlantic-Little, Brown, 1966).

OTHER MAJOR LANGUAGES
POETRY. FRENCH: Robert Levesque, *Séféris* (Athens, 1945). Jacques Lacarrière, *Poèmes* (Paris, 1964). GERMAN: Christian Enzenberger, *Poesie* (Frankfurt am Main, 1962). ITALIAN: Filippo Maria Pontani, *Poesie* (Milan, 1963). SWEDISH: Börje Knös and Johannes Edfelt, *Dikter* (Stockholm, 1963). Hjalmar Gullberg, *Stenarnas Dictare Tolkningar* (Stockholm, 1963). SPANISH: Lysandro Z. D. Galtier, *"El Zorzal" y ostros Poemas* (Buenos Aires, 1966).

NOTES

MYTH OF OUR HISTORY. The Greek title is *Mithistórima*, composed
of the words *myth* and *history*, meaning a "novel," a "romance."
In a note to this poem Seféris writes: "I have chosen this word because of its
two component parts—*myth* in that I have employed with sufficient
clarity a defined mythology; *history*, in that I have tried to express with
some coherence a condition as independent of me as the characters of a
novel." I am indebted for the rendering of this title to the English
translation of Seféris by Bernard Spencer, Nanos Valaorítis and Law-
rence Durrell. SI J'AI . . . PIERRES: "If there is anything I care for, it is
only for earth and stones" ("Hunger" in *A Season in Hell*).

IV. THE ARGONAUTS: Sailors and heroes of the ship Argo who sailed to
   Colchis with their leader Jason to fetch the Golden Fleece. AND IF
   . . . THE SOUL: Plato, *Alcibiades*, 133 B. Socrates is telling Alcibiades
   that the soul must look especially at that part of herself in
   which she resembles the divine—"And if the soul, my dear
   Alcibiades, is ever to know herself, must she not look at the soul;
   and especially at that part of the soul in which her virtue resides
   and to any other which is like this?" (Jowett's translation) Seféris
   in his poem quotes the ancient Greek, and in a note comments:
   "These words once gave me a feeling which I related closely to
   these verses of Baudelaire from 'The Death of Lovers'—'Our two
   hearts shall be two huge torches / which shall reflect their double
   lights / in the twin mirrors of our two spirits.'" THE SEA THAT LEADS
   INTO THE OTHER SEA: The Sea of Marmara, which leads from the
   Bosporus into the Black Sea, where Colchis was located. ALEXANDER
   THE GREAT: According to Greek popular tradition, a mermaid will
   grasp a ship and ask, "Where is Alexander the Great?" If the
   sailors do not reply "He lives and reigns," she will rouse a great
   storm and wreck them. THEIR OARS . . . JUSTICE: In Homer's *Odys-
   sey*, Elpenor falls off the roof of Circe's palace and breaks his neck.
   In their haste, Odysseus and his companions leave him unburied.
   When Odysseus later descends into Hades to ask his way home of
   Tiresias, the first shade to address him is that of Elpenor: "Burn me
   with my armor, all that is mine, and heap up a mound for me on the
   shore of the gray sea, in memory of an unhappy man, that men yet
   to be may learn of me. Fulfill this prayer of mine, and fix upon my
   mound my oar with which I rowed in life when I was among my
   companions." (*Odyssey*, XI, 75ff. Translated by A. T. Murray,
   Loeb Classical Library.)

XII. YOUNGEST: "There was one called Elpenor, the youngest of the
   party, not much of a fighting man nor very strong in the head"
   (Homer, *Odyssey*, X, 552). This and all subsequent translations
   from the *Odyssey* are by E. V. Rieu, Penguin Classics.

XV. QUID . . . OPACISSIMUS: "what of the shady plane tree grove?" in
   Pliny the Younger's letter to Caninius Rufus (*Letters*, I, 3)—"How

stands Comum, that favorite scene of yours and mine? What becomes of the pleasant villa, the ever-vernal Portico, the shady plane-tree grove, the crystal Canal so agreeably winding along its flowery banks, together with the charming Lake below, that serves at once the purpose of use and beauty? (Translation by William Melmoth, Loeb Classics)

XVI. ὄνομα δ' Ὀρέστης: "By the name of Orestes." A herald describes to Clytemnestra how Orestes won in the foot race at the Delphic games: "An Argive wins, by the name of Orestes, the son of Agamemnon, King of men, who led the hosts of Hellas" (Sophocles, *Electra*, 694). He then goes on to give a false report of Orestes' death during his participation in the chariot races.

XVII. ASTYANAX: The son of Hector and Andromache. He was very young when the Greeks besieged Troy, and when the city was taken, his mother saved him from the flames, but he was either killed by Odysseus, or flung from the walls of Troy by Neoptolemus to prevent him from ever restoring the kingdom.

XXIV. FEEBLE SOULS . . . ASPHODELS: After Odysseus slays the suitors of Penelope, Hermes leads them to Hades: "Past Ocean Stream, past the White Rock, past the Gates of the Sun and the land of dreams they went, and before long they reached the meadow of asphodel, which is the dwelling place of souls, the disembodied wraiths of men." (Homer, *Odyssey*, XXIV, opening.) TURN . . . EREBUS: "Erebus" means "darkness" and is applied to the dark space through which shades must pass into Hades. Circe instructs Odysseus on how to call up the spirits of the dead in Hades—"When you have finished your invocation to the glorious fellowship of the dead, sacrifice a young ram and a black ewe, holding their heads down toward Erebus while you turn your own aside, as though about to recross the River of Ocean. Then the souls of the dead and departed will come up in their multitude." (*Odyssey*, X, 526ff.)

IN THE MANNER OF G. S. G. S.: George Seféris. MT. PELION . . . CENTAUR: The most wise and just of the centaurs, Chiron, lived on Pelion, a range of mountains in Thessaly where the timber was felled with which the ship Argo was built. Chiron was the teacher of many Greek heroes and was accidentally struck by Heracles with a poisoned arrow. Although immortal, he chose not to live, according to one legend, and bequeathed his immortality to Prometheus. Zeus placed him among the stars as Sagittarius. The word "shirt" connects this passage with another centaur, Nessos, who in carrying Deianira, wife of Heracles, across a river, tried to outrage her. Heracles shot him with an arrow. The dying centaur told Deianira to take some of his blood with her as a certain means of preserving the love of her husband. Fearing that she might one day be supplanted, Deianira steeped a garment of Heracles in the blood. But the blood had been poisoned by the arrow, and the poison penetrated into Heracles' limbs when he wore the garment. He wrenched it off, but it stuck to his flesh and with it he tore away whole pieces from his body. THE INN . . . MENELAUS: Such an inn actually

BIOGRAPHY: GEORGE SEFÉRIS | 745

exists on the approach to Mycenae. SPÉTSES, PÓROS, MÝKONOS: The first
two are islands in the Aegean near the Peloponnesos coast. Mýkonos is
one of the Cyclades. HAIL . . . CONSTITUTION SQUARE: Concord Square
is, roughly, the Times Square or Piccadilly Circus of Athens. Constitu-
tion Square is the main square of the city surrounded and environed by
the House of Parliament, various embassies, the best hotels and smart
shops. Seféris has his characters speak partly in the purist language, and
he comments on how such ragtags of elegant expression have been taken
over by the common people in their daily diction. SUGARED ALMONDS:
At Greek weddings and baptisms, sugar-covered almonds are always
passed out to the guests. AMVRÁKIKOS: Named after the Amvrakian Gulf,
now the Gulf of Árta, part of the Ionian Sea, between Épiros and
Acarnanía. AG ONY: The letters are so separated in the poem to indicate
how they were painted on either side of the prow. Also the first two
letters in Greek, ΑΓ, comprise the abbreviation for "saint." Most Greek
ships are named after a patron saint.

A WORD FOR SUMMER. SYNGROÚ AVENUE: A wide avenue in Athens
that runs from the Temple of Olympian Zeus to Fáliron and the sea.
Seféris has written another poem, "Syngroú Avenue 1939" which he
dedicated to "George Theotokás, who discovered it." Theotokás (1905–
1966) was a novelist and dear friend of Seféris. In his book *Free Spirit*
he wrote: "Day and night, toward the Fáliron shore, Syngroú Avenue
carries the newly born and still unexpressed rhythms of a powerful
lyricism that calls for powerful poets."

THE KING OF ASINE. Ἀσίνην τε: "And Asine." The phrase occurs in
the catalogue where Homer lists the heroes and ships which set out for
Troy. "And they that held Argos and Tiryns, famed for its walls, and
Hermione and Asine, that enfold the deep gulf, Troezen and Eïonae
and vine-clad Epidaurus" (*Iliad*, 560). CASTLE: The ruined akropolis of
Asine, close to the modern village of Tolón on the coast of the Argolid.
AND FROM . . . BAT: After Odysseus had slain the suitors of Penelope,
Hermes led them to Hades—"They obeyed his summons, gibbering like
bats that squeak and flutter in the depths of some mysterious cave when
one of them has fallen from the rocky roof, losing his hold on his
clustered friends. With such shrill discord the company set out in
Hermes' charge, following the Deliverer down the dark paths of decay."
(*Odyssey*, XXIV, opening.) Then follows the line quoted in the first
note to poem XXIV, "Myth of Our History," p. 744.

LAST STOP. NOW THAT . . . AND IDLE: The phrase "now that I sit idle"
comes from the Introduction to General Yánnis Makriyánnis' *Memoirs*.
Makriyánnis was one of the great heroes of the Greek War of Inde-
pendence, and his *Memoirs* have become a model of demotic prose for
many contemporary writers. See "Makriyánnis" in Seféris' *On the
Greek Style*. AMICA SILENTIA LUNAE: Virgil describes how the ships of
the Greeks were sailing "amid the friendly silence of the peaceful
moon" (*Aeneid*, II, 255). KOMMAGENE: A small independent state of
northern Syria in 64 B.C. It had several kings named Antiochos, and was
finally incorporated into the Roman Empire in A.D. 72. A reference also

to Caváfis' poem "Epitaph of Antiochos, King of Kommagene," and to the lines "And the Ephesian sophist Kallistratos—who lived / Often in the small state of Kommagene." SIMPLY BAD HABITS . . . DECEIT: "And now we find justice in no one; all is fraud and deceit" (Makriyánnis, *Memoirs*, II, 258). A TIME . . . IS PLANTED: Ecclesiastes 3:2. PAIN . . . SLEEP: In the beginning of Aeschylos' *Agamemnon*, the Chorus of Argive Elders does not credit the tiding of Agamemnon's homecoming. In an invocation to Zeus "who has established as a fixed ordinance that wisdom comes by suffering," they conclude: "But even as trouble, bringing memory of pain, drips over the mind in sleep, so to those who would not does wisdom come."

HELEN. After the title of this poem, Seféris has placed the following from Euripides' *Helen*: "TEUCER: . . . for the sea-girt land / of Cyprus, where Apollo prophesied that I / should found and name New Salamis from my island home . . . HELEN: It was an image of me. I never went to Troy. . . . MESSENGER: . . . you mean / it was for a cloud, for nothing, we did all that work?" (Lines 148–50, 582, 705–706; these lines and all subsequent lines from *Helen* are translated by Richmond Lattimore.) According to an ancient legend, Helen was not abducted to Troy at all. Aphrodite had promised Helen to Paris because he had given her the golden apple for beauty in preference to Hera or Athena. To avenge herself for the slight, Hera formed an image of Helen out of pure air with which she duped Paris, and spirited away the real Helen to Egypt, where she remained chaste and untouched until her husband Menelaus found her there after the Trojan War. Ancient writers are unanimous in asserting that the port of Salamis in Cyprus was founded by Teucer (son of Telamon, king of the famous island of Salamis in Greece) on his return from the Trojan War. NIGHTINGALES: For various references to nightingales, and especially for "tearful bird" see the Chorus in *Helen* (107ff.)—"To you, who deep forested, choired in the growth / of singing wood, hide nested, / to you I utter my outcry, / to you, beyond all other birds sweet in your singing, / O nightingale of the sorrows / come, with brown beak shaken, / to the beat of your melody, come / with song to my sad singing / as I mourn for the hard sorrows / of Helen, for all the suffering, / all the tears of the daughters of Troy / from spears held by Achaeans." PLATRES: Chief summer resort of wealthy Cypriots and visitors from abroad. BLIND VOICE: Compare with Milton's "Blind mouths" ("Lycidas," 119). THAT'S HOW THE GODS WILLED IT and THE ANCIENT DECEIT OF THE GODS: Helen is speaking: "Wretched men of Troy / and all you Achaeans who, day after day, went on / dying for me beside Scamander, by Hera's craft" (608–10), and "it was by the arts of gods / that they were ruined" (930–31). INTO THE JAWS . . . OF THE EARTH: From a mural painting in a church at Asíni, Cyprus. DOWN OF A SWAN: Helen was the daughter of Leda and Zeus, who made love to her in the form of a swan. WHAT IS A GOD . . . BETWEEN THE TWO: From *Helen*, 1137.

ENKOMI. A village to the northwest of Famagusta, Cyprus. SUDDENLY . . . AN ASSUMPTION: Compare with the vision of Joseph as he sought for a midwife to assist Mary in her birth of Christ—"Now I Joseph was walking, and I walked not. And I looked up to the air and saw the air in amazement. And I looked up unto the pole of the heaven and saw it standing still, and the fowls of the heaven without motion. And I looked upon the earth and saw a dish set, and workmen lying *by it*, and their hands were in the dish: and they that were chewing chewed not, and they that were lifting *the food* lifted it not, and they that put it to their mouth put it not thereto, but the faces of all of them were looking upward. And behold there were sheep being driven, and they went not forward but stood still; and the shepherd lifted his hand to smite them with his staff, and his hand remained up. And I looked upon the stream of the river and saw the mouths of the kids upon *the water* and they drank not. And of a sudden all things moved onward in their course." (Book of James, or Protevangelium 18:2, in *The Apocryphal New Testament*, translated by Montague Rhodes James; Oxford, Clarendon Press, 1955.) Seféris has changed "shepherd" to "plowman."

Ángelos Sikelianós

Ángelos Sikelianós was born March 27, 1884, on the Ionian island of Lefkádha, where he completed his early education. He enrolled in the Law School at the University of Athens in 1900, but abandoned his studies after two years. On a visit to his brother in Libya in 1907 he wrote his first book of poetry, *The Visionary*, and on his return that same year left for Paris with Miss Evelyn Palmer of Bar Harbor, and then for the United States, where they were married late in 1907. After a few months, they returned to Lefkádha, where their son Ghláfkos (Glaúkos) was born in 1909. In 1910 Sikelianós left for a year's stay in Rome, and after returning and completing his military service as a common soldier, settled with his wife in Athens. But for a brief trip to Palestine, Sikelianós never went abroad again, but traveled throughout Greece, confirming thus his knowledge and mastery of Greek tradition and the demotic tongue. After their work on the Delphic Festivals of 1927 and 1930, the Athens Academy cited Ángelos and Eva Sikelianós jointly for their efforts. In 1939 he was awarded the State Prize in Poetry for the whole of his work.

Eva Sikelianós parted from her husband in 1933 and went to live in the United States, supporting him financially, nevertheless, until his death. Because she had never been converted to the Greek Orthodox Church, their marriage was annulled, and in

1940 Sikelianós married Anna Kambanáris in the inner sanctum at Eleusis by the Unlaughing Stone, where Demeter once sat to weep the loss of her daughter Persephone. In honor of Sikelianós, the Council of Europe in 1955 founded a Pan-European Delphic Festival, but this was later changed in 1966 to a European Spiritual Center. In 1951 he inadvertently drank some Lysol, which had accidentally been bought for him instead of Nujol, a medicine, and after lingering for five days, he died of acute inflammation of the lungs on June 9. Eva Sikelianós returned to Greece in April, 1952, and saw Delphi for the last time before she died on June 4 and was buried there.

POETRY. *The Visionary*, 1909. *Prologue to Life: The Consciousness of My Earth*, 1915. *Prologue to Life: The Consciousness of My Race*, 1915. *Prologue to Life: The Consciousness of Woman*, 1916. *Prologue to Life: The Consciousness of Faith*, 1917. *Verses*, 1921. *Delphic Speech: Dedication*, 1927. *Songs of the Border Guards* [*Akritiká*], written by hand and illustrated with woodcuts by Spíros Vasilíou, privately circulated, 1942; reproduced in offset, Cairo, Egypt, 1944. *Mother of God*, Greek text with French translation by Robert Levesque, 1944. *Lyric Life* [*Collected Poems*], Vols. I, II, 1946; Vol. III, 1947. *Consecrated Bread: Selected Poems*, 1943. *Lyric Life*, edited by G. P. Savídhis, Vol. I, 1965; Vols. II, III, 1966; Vol. IV, 1967; Vol. V, 1968; Vol. VI, 1969—of a projected eleven volumes.

POETIC DRAMA. *The Dithyramb of the Rose*, 1932. *Daedalos in Crete*, 1943. *Sibyl*, 1944. *Christ in Rome*, Greek text, with translation by Robert Levesque, 1946. *Christ Unbound; or the Death of Dhiyenís*, 1947. *Thiméli* [sacrificial altar in the orchestra of the ancient Greek theater], in three volumes—Vol. I, *The Dithyramb of the Rose, Daedalos in Crete* and *Sibyl* (1950); Vol. II, *Christ Unbound or The Death of Dhiyenís* (1954); Vol. III, *Asklepiós* (1954).

IN ENGLISH. Lawrence Durrell, *Six Poems from the Greek of Sikelianós and Seféris* (Rhodes, 1946). *The Dithyramb of the Rose*, translated by Frances Sikelianós, with an Introduction by Ted Shawn (privately printed for Ted Shawn in the United

States, 1959). *Akritan Songs* [*Akritiká*], Greek text, with English translation by Paul Nord (New York: The Spap Company, 1944).

IN FRENCH. *Ángelos Sikelianós, Mater Dei,* texte Grec avec traduction et introduction de Robert Levesque, 1944. Robert Levesque, *Sikelianós,* introduction, choix de Poèmes, avant-propos de Paul Éluard, 1946. *Sikélianós, Poèmes Akritiques; La Mort de Digenis,* tragedie, adaptation française par Octave Merlier, bois de Spyro Vassiliou, 1960.

NOTES

SPARTA. "The old husband of a young woman was permitted to introduce her to a handsome young man, and to recognize the offspring of their generous blood as his own" (Plutarch, "Life of Lycurgus," in *The Life of the Noble Grecians and Romans*).

PAN. KINÉTAS: A beach on the road from Athens to Corinth, a former haunt of Pan.

PENTARKIS. Pentarkis was a young athlete from Elis, near Olympia, who won in the children's contests in the Olympic Games of 437, and of whom Pausanius writes that as a youth he won in wrestling and chariot racing. The poet describes Olympia at the foot of Mt. Kronion, and then the sculptor Phidias at night in his workshop at Olympia (the remains of which still stand) working on his chryselphantine statue of Zeus, and portraying Pentarkis on the throne of the statue. ὁ παῖς καλός: "The handsome young man"; καλός in Ancient Greek equally means "good" and "virtuous" as well as "beautiful." ALPHEOS: A stream that flows through Arcadia and Elis. ARCHER OF AEGINA: The archaic statue of Heracles as a kneeling archer, from the East pediment of the Temple of Aphaia at Aegina, *c.* 500–480 B.C., now at the Glyptothek in Munich.

ANADYOMENE. "Anadyomene" means "risen from the sea," and is an epithet applied to Aphrodite because she was said to have risen from the sea at birth. See note to "Cyprian" in Karélli's poem "Persephone," p. 711. In this poem Sikelianós probably had in mind the front of a three-sided relief known as the "Ludovisi Throne" (*c.* 470–460 B.C., Terme Museum, Rome). Two female figures, the Nereids of the poem, are helping a woman who appears to be rising out of the sea. WIND-SWIFT, SEAGREEN: The etymological meaning of Sikelianós' Kymothoe and Glauke, two Nereids of the fifty daughters of the sea god Nereus.

THE MOTHER OF DANTE. The section in quotation marks is adapted from Boccaccio's *Life of Dante,* Chapter XXV.

THALERO. A town near Corinth. The word also means "blossoming" or "verdant."

THE SACRED ROAD. The road from Athens to Eleusis on which the Eleusian procession passed in worship of Demeter, Persephone and Iacchos (a mystic name for Dionysos) in rites involving fertility, purification and the future life. ALKMENE: The mother of Heracles by Zeus. Heracles is a Christ-figure because, after his death, consumed by fire, he was transported to Olympos among the Immortals. REHEARSAL FOR DEATH. The title in Greek, ΜΕΛΕΤΗ ΘΑΝΑΤΟΥ, is taken from Plato's *Phaedo*. A. E. Taylor, in his *Plato: The Man and His Work*, 5th edition (London, Methuen, 1948, p. 179), says of the phrase: "*Not* 'meditation' of death. Μελέτη means the repeated practice by which we prepare ourselves for a performance. It is used of the 'practicing' of a man training for an athletic contest, and again of the 'learning by heart' of such a thing as a speech. . . . No doubt, then, it was also used for an actor's study of his 'part.' . . . The thought is that 'death' is like a play for which the philosopher's life has been a daily rehearsal. His business is to be perfect in his part when the curtain goes up." In the *Phaedo*, Sokrates says: "Ordinary people seem not to realize that those who really apply themselves in the right way to philosophy are directly and of their own accord preparing themselves for death and dying. If this be true, and they have actually been looking to death all their lives, it would of course be absurd to be troubled when the thing comes for which they have so long been preparing and looking forward. . . . If at its release the soul is pure and carries with it no contamination of the body, because it has never willingly associated with it in life, but has shunned it and kept itself separate as its regular practice—in other words, if it has pursued philosophy in the right way and really practiced how to face death easily—this is what 'practicing death' means, isn't it? . . . If this is its condition, then it departs to that place which is, like itself, invisible, divine, immortal, and wise, where, on its arrival, happiness awaits it, and release from uncertainty and uncontrolled desires, and all other human evils, and where, as they say of the initiates of the Mysteries, it really spends the rest of time with God." (Translation by Hugh Tredennick in *Plato, The Collected Dialogues*, edited by Edith Hamilton and Huntington Cairns, New York, Pantheon Books, 1961.) ASTARTE: A Phoenician goddess of fertility and sexual love, akin to Aphrodite. In the cult of the great Mother Goddess and her dying and reviving partner belong Astarte and Adonis in Syria, Ishtar and Tammuz in Mesopotamia, Isis and Osiris in Egypt, Cybele and Attis in Anatolia, Demeter and her daughter Persephone in Greece. "The people of Mesopotamia like to tell how Ishtar had gone in search of Tammuz 'to the land from which there is no returning,' and how in her absence all love had ceased among men and animals, and life was in danger of extinction. As she descended into the underworld she was required gradually to remove her garments until finally she stood naked before Eresh-Kigal, the queen of the dead, who reluctantly responded to appeals from the gods of heaven and allowed Tammuz to be sprinkled with the water of life and set free." (Henry B. Parker, *Gods and Men, The Origins of Western Culture*, London, Routledge and Kegan Paul, 1960, p. 45.) SHUNAMMITE: Sikelianós has "Shulamite," confused in Greek popular tradition with "Shunammite," a woman who appears in the *Song of Solomon* and in *Leviticus* but who had nothing to do with David. See I Kings, 1–4. MYSTIC TRIREME: Dionysos was once abducted by Tyrrhenian pirates and held for ransom, for they mistook him for a prince. They tied him with heavy cords, but these fell to the deck, and a series of marvels occurred. A fragrant and delicious wine flowed around the ship, a vine attached its branches to the sails, ivy wound around the masts, and the god himself turned into a savage lion. In terror, the pirates leaped into the sea and were changed to dolphins. See also a black-figured cup from Vulci by Exekias, c. 353 B.C., now in the Museum Antiker Kleinkunst, Munich. TRAMPLING ON DEATH WITH DEATH: A refrain from the Easter Sunday service—"Christ has risen from death, trampling on death with death, and has bestowed life to those in the tombs. LET THERE BE: Opening of Genesis—"And God said, Let there be light: and there was light . . ."

"HAUTE ACTUALITÉ": "Higher Actuality." The French phrase for Upper Egypt is "Haute Egypte." APIS: A sacred bull supposed by the Egyptians to be an embodiment of Ptah, father of gods and men. His soul passed to the underworld as Osiris-Apis, from which the Greek population of Egypt developed the deity Serapis, worshiped throughout the Roman world. OSIRIS . . . TYPHON: Osiris was the Egyptian god of the underworld, judge of the dead, and one of the fertility gods. He was slain by his brother Set, represented with the head of a beast with high square ears and a pointed snout, and whom the ancient Greeks identified with their mythical monster Typhon. Isis, Osiris' wife, placed his body in a coffin, but Set dismembered and scattered it. Isis then searched out and buried each part of the body, later resurrecting it with the warmth of her love. Osiris is commonly represented as a mummied figure wearing the crown of Upper Egypt. Some authorities regard the Osirian rites as the source of the Eleusinian mysteries. BOOK OF THE DEAD: A collection of formulae, prayers and hymns, knowledge of which was supposed to enable the soul, in its journey into Amenti, the realm of the dead, to pass successfully the foes set to impede its progress, to call upon the helpful gods, and to answer properly the forty-two assessors, or judges, in the hall of Osiris.

UNRECORDED. The title refers to those anecdotes about Christ not admitted into the New Testament or the Apocrypha. Sikelianós may have been thinking of Baudelaire's poem "The Carrion," but he took the incident directly from Goethe's translation in West-East Divan of a moral fable quoted by the Persian poet Nizami (1141–1203): "Jesus and his disciples were passing by a market place, and suddenly, at some distance from the street, they saw the carcass of a dog with a crowd of curious people about it. One said, 'This stench drives me insane,' and another, 'Refusal to bury this will only bring misfortune.' Jesus also observed the carcass and said, 'The teeth are beautiful, like white pearls.' His glance remained on the only thing that was beautiful amid the rot, on the teeth's whiteness. And all blushed with shame, for they had learned only to see what was evil and ugly."

GREEK SUPPER FOR THE DEAD. After a funeral, the mourners gather in the home of the bereaved and partake of food, with the exception of meat, a custom deriving from ancient times. DIONYSOS-HADES: In some versions of the Dionysos myth, Hades fathered Dionysos on Demeter or Persephone. AGATHODEMON: "Good Spirit," or "Good Demon," an ancient god of cornfield and vineyard, protective demon of individuals and the State. The ancient Greeks drank a cup of wine in his honor at the end of every meal.

ATTIC. ROAD TO ELEUSIS: See note to "The Sacred Road," pp. 749–50.

THE SUPREME LESSON. The title is taken from Plato's *Republic*, Book VI, 504–505, where Sokrates says that men of the highest spiritual quality and morality must pass through the trials of the "supreme lesson" (or "highest knowledge" as Jowett translates the phrase). When Glaucon asks him what the highest knowledge is, Sokrates replies: "You have often been told that the idea of the good is the highest knowledge, and that all other things become useful or advantageous only by their use of this. . . . Do you think that the possession of all other things is of any value if we do not possess the good? or the knowledge of all other things if we have no knowledge of beauty and goodness?" ARIADNE: Ariadne was the daughter of Minos and Pasiphae of Crete. She fell in love with Theseus, gave him a ball of thread by which he found his way out of the Labyrinth after he had killed the Minotaur. Theseus in return promised to marry her, but on their arrival in the island of Náxos she was killed by Artemis. This is the Homeric account; it was only after her death that Dionysos married her. The more common tradition relates that she was deserted by Theseus in Náxos where she was found by Dionysos, who made her his wife and set Thetis' crown upon her head. The crown, which Dionysos later set among the stars as the Corona Borealis, was made by Hephaestos of fiery gold and red Indian gems, set in the shape of roses. In this poem Sikelianós uses the body of Ariadne as a symbol of that Form which prefigures eternity; of the idea of the true, the good, and the beautiful; of the knowledge of a mystical and eternal life through death. That part of the poem where Dionysos addresses the sleeping form of Ariadne refers to an ancient dithyrambic worship of springtime at Náxos, relating the sleeping form of Ariadne to the long sleep of winter. HOLY MEN: The priests of Dionysos. THE SACRED MOUNTAIN: Mt. Drio, in Náxos, where according to tradition, Dionysos and Ariadne disappeared. IO, ARGOS: Io was loved by Zeus and metamorphosed by him, through fear of his wife Hera, into a heifer. The goddess then sent hundred-eyed Argos to pursue and watch her. SLEEP MY BELOVÈD: The speech of Dionysos begins here. GATE: Reminiscent of the Great Gate of Apollo's temple at Náxos, still standing.

George Thémelis

George Thémelis was born on September 5, 1900, in the town of Mýtilíni on the island of Sámos. He completed his grade-school education there and his high-school education in the capital of Sámos, Vathí. During 1919–22, he took part in the disastrous

Asia Minor campaign, reaching almost as far as Ankara, Turkey, with the Greek army. He then studied literature at the University of Athens, took his degree in 1925, and began teaching Greek language and literature in various high schools, first on the island of Ikaría, 1926–30, and then in Thessaloníki, where he has lived ever since. During 1934–49, he taught in The Experimental School at the University of Thessaloníki. He married in 1928 and has two sons and three daughters. During 1961–64 he served on the organizing committee and also on the advisory committee of the State Theater of Northern Greece in Thessaloníki, where two of his plays have been produced. In addition to writing his own poetry, he has translated Char, Alberti, Claudel, Aeschylos' *Prometheus Bound* and Sophocles' *Oedipus the King;* has published several scholarly works, particularly on the Greek language and literature; has written one book on Papadhiamándis, and three important books of literary criticism about his fellow poets and poetry in general: *Our Newest Poetry* (1963); *The Extreme Crisis* (1965); and *Our Newest Poetry*, Vol. II (1967), published in Thessaloníki.

POETRY. (All listed works published in Thessaloníki.) *Naked Window*, 1945. *Men and Birds*, 1947. *Odes by Which to Remember Heroes*, 1949. *Escort*, 1950. *Conversations*, 1953. *Orchard* (Joint Second State Prize), 1955. *The Face and the Image*, 1959. *Chiaroscuro* (First State Prize), 1961. *Mona Playing*, 1961. *The Soul Net*, 1965. *Poems* (Collected), 2 volumes, 1969. *Helioscope*, 1971.

IN ITALIAN. Giorgio Themelis, *Poesie*, A curo di Cristino e Dino Sangiglio (Roma: Istituto Editoriale del Mediterraneo, 1968). IN FRENCH. George Themélis, *Choix de Poèmes* (Paris: Éditions Caractères, 1972).

NOTES

THE KING OF VOYAGES. QUANTUM MUTATUS: "How changed he was." Aeneas, in relating the fall of Troy to Dido, Queen of Carthage, tells how Hector came to him in a dream, urging him to flee the doomed city and to find a new home for the gods and people of Troy: "I dreamt, I seemed to behold our Hector standing before me / Most woe-begone and shedding great tears, just as he'd looked once / In death, after being dragged by the chariot, black with the dirt / And blood, his swollen feet pierced where the thongs had been threaded. / Ah, god! what a sight he was! how terribly changed from the Hector / Who once came back arrayed in the armor of Achilles, / Who came back from bombarding the Greek navy with fire! / Now his beard is matted, clotted with blood his hair, / He exhibits the many wounds received while defending his country / In combat around the walls." (Virgil, *The Aeneid*, II, 270–79; translation by Cecil Day Lewis; Doubleday Anchor Books, 1953.)

PLAYING AT CARDS. Part IV of a poem *Orchard* in ten parts. The title has been supplied by the poet. FACE TO FACE and also THROUGH A GLASS: "For now we see through a glass, darkly; but then face to face: now I know in part; but then shall I know even as also I am known" (I Corinthians 13:12). MORE . . . DREAMS: From the funeral service of the Greek Orthodox Church: "All things are more infirm than shadow, more deceitful than dreams, because when death comes all these shall vanish."

THE BODY. Part V of *Orchard*. The title has been supplied by the poet. LET US LOVE . . . IN CONCORD. From the Sunday liturgy by Saint Chrysostom in the Greek Orthodox Church: "Let us love one another, that we may in concord confess: The Father, Son, and Holy Spirit, Trinity, one in substance and undivided."

DE RERUM NATURA. Parts VII, VIII, XII of a poem by the same title in twelve parts. The title is that of the epic poem by Lucretius, *c.* 99–55 B.C., *On the Nature of Things*. BEHOLD . . . GOD: "Then came Jesus forth, wearing the crown of thorns, and the purple robe. And Pilate saith unto them, Behold the man!" (John 19:5)

G. T. Vafópoulos

George Thomás Vafópoulos was born on September 6, 1903, in Gevgelija, now on the Yugoslavian side of the Greek-Yugoslavian border, but at that time under Turkish domination. At the outbreak of the First World War, when Gevgelija became a field of military operations, the family moved to Thessaloníki, where Vafópoulos completed his grade-school and his high-school education. In the fall of 1922 he went to Athens and studied mathematics at the university there, but was compelled to leave in 1924 because of financial difficulties. In 1924 he edited the periodical *Macedonian Letters*. In 1931 he was appointed Secretary to the City Council of Thessaloníki, and in 1939 took the initiative and established the Municipal Library there, which he directed until his retirement in 1963. In his capacity as City Librarian, he was invited in 1951 by the British Council to visit Great Britain for three months in order to study the British Library System. In 1957 he was invited by the Department of State to visit the United States for two months, where he traveled a good deal and studied the libraries in many large and small cities. He has also made extensive visits to France, Belgium, Holland, Luxembourg, Germany, Austria, Switzerland, Italy, Yugoslavia, Rumania and Bulgaria. In 1963 he was awarded the Medal of the Municipality of Thessaloníki for his contribution to the cultural advancement of that city. From 1964 to 1967 he was on the governing board of the State Theater of Northern Greece in Thessaloníki. His first wife, the poetess Anthoúla Stathopoúlou, whom he married in 1932, died in 1935. In 1946 he married Anastásia Yerakopoúlou, a graduate of Durham University, England, and director of the Vafópoulos Institute of English in Thessaloníki. He has published two of a projected three-volume *Pages of an Autobiography*, covering the years 1917–67: *The Passion*, 1970, and *The Resurrection*, 1971.

POETRY. *The Roses of Myrtale*, Thessaloníki, 1931. *The Offering*, Thessaloníki, 1938. *The Offering and Songs of Resurrection*, Thessaloníki, 1948. *The Floor and Other Poems*, Thessaloníki, 1951. *The Vast Night and the Window*, 1959. *Death Songs and Satires* (First State Prize), 1966.

POETIC DRAMA. *Esther*, Thessaloníki, 1934.

NOTES

THE MASK. DR. WAGNER: The assistant in Goethe's *Faust*, symbolizing the pedantic man who interprets all things logically. Here too, as in *Faust*, he knocks on the door and enters.

TIME AND THE FISH. The poet writes ironically of modern poets who, in imitation of Eliot's *Four Quartets*, have written torturously about the problem of time. TABLE . . . TEA: See Eliot's "The Love Song of J. Alfred Prufrock"—"There will be time to murder and create, / And time for all the works of days and hands / That lift and drop a question on your plate; / Time for you and time for me, / And time yet for a hundred indecisions, / And for a hundred visions and revisions, / Before the taking of a toast and tea." TIME PRESENT . . . TIME PAST: The opening of Eliot's "Burnt Norton" in *Four Quartets*.

ADMONITIONS. PIERIA . . . MELPOMENE: Mnemosyne was the goddess of Memory and mother of the Nine Muses, fathered by Zeus. Pieria, an ancient Thracian country, was one of the earliest seats of worship of the Muses. Melpomene was the Muse of Tragedy and Music. ARIADNE: See note to "Ariadne" in Sikelianós' poem "The Supreme Lesson," p. 752. LETTERS . . . RILKE: Particularly Rilke's *Letters to a Young Poet.*

Kóstas Várnalis

Kóstas Várnalis was born of Greek parentage on February 27, 1884, in Pírghos, Bulgaria. He completed his grade-school education there and the first year of high school, and finished his secondary studies in Philippoúpolis (now Plóvdiv), Bulgaria. In 1903 he enrolled in the School of Philosophy at the University of Athens, and took his degree in 1908. From 1909 to 1911 he taught Greek language and literature in Greek high schools in Bulgaria and in a high school in Alamliádha, the Peloponnesos; became a director of secondary schools in various parts of Greece, 1911–17; a professor of secondary education in a high school in Piraeus, 1918–25, taking time off in 1919 to study literature, philosophy and sociology for a year at the Sorbonne on a scholarship. In 1925 he also taught modern Greek literature at the Pedagogic Academy in Athens; but in that year he was fired, under the dictatorship of Pángalos, for his left-wing activities. Since then he has made his living as a journalist, free-lance writer, and translator. In 1929 he married the poetess and writer Dora Moátsou. In 1958 he was awarded the Lenin Peace Prize. In addition to writing his poetry, he has written a book of short stories, two books on Solomós, six books of biographical, satirical, critical and aesthetic essays, and some children's fairy tales. He has translated into meter Aristophanes' *Clouds, Pluto, Peace, Lysistrata* and *Knights,* Euripides' *Bacchae* and *Heracles,* Molière's *Misanthrope* and *School for Women,* Corneilles' *Le Cid* and *Les Précieuses Ridicule,* and Musset's *Le Chandelier.* All these plays have been produced by various Greek theaters.

POETRY. *Honeycombs,* 1905. *The Burning Light* (under the pseudonym of Dhímos Tanálias), Alexandria, Egypt, 1922; Athens, 1933, 1945. *The Slaves Besieged,* 1927. *Selections,* 1954. *Poems,* 1956. *Poetic,* 1964. *The Free World,* 1965.

NOTES

APHRODITE. Homer relates (*Odyssey*, VIII, 266–367) how Aphrodite and Ares, making love in bed, were entangled in a fine mesh net which her husband, Hephaestos, had prepared. He then called in all the male gods (the goddesses stayed home in shame) to witness their plight, and the gods laughed at them and ridiculed them. When released, Aphrodite went to Paphos, in Cyprus, where a famous shrine was dedicated to her. There the Graces bathed and anointed her with immortal oil.

THE CHOSEN ONE. FEAST OF FLOWERS: See note to Prevelákis' poem "Barcarole," p. 735.

ALCIBIADES. *c*. 450–404 B.C. Athenian statesman and general, extremely wealthy, charming, handsome, self-willed, capricious, and a natural leader of men. Once he sent seven chariots to the Olympian Games, where his entries carried away the first, second, and fourth prizes. He was accused of mutilating the sacred Hermae, marble or bronze pillars surmounted by a bust, usually of the god Hermes, and given a human semblance by the addition of erect penuses. They stood in large numbers in the streets and squares of the cities. In joint command with Nicias, Alcibiades was sent with a fleet to conquer Sicily, but he plotted against the Athenians. Nicias was defeated and killed, and the surviving Athenians were sent to die at hard labor in the marble quarries of Sicily. Those able to recite from the plays of Euripides were set free.

MY SUN. ASPHODELS . . . MEADOWS: See first note to Seféris' poem No. XXIV of *Myth of Our History*, p. 744. SOLOMOS' . . . LIBERTY: See note to "Hymn" in Elýtis' "Psalm II," p. 700.

THE 4 MISTAKES OF "THE UNKNOWN SOLDIER." GRAND CROSSES: War decorations of high merit.

Nikiphóros Vrettákos

Nikiphóros Vrettákos was born on January 1, 1912, in the town of Krokéas, near Sparta. He spent his childhood on his father's farm in the region of Ploúmitsa, near the seaside town of Yíthion, completed his grade-school education in Krokéas and his high-school education in Yíthion. In 1929 he went to Athens and studied at the university there, but dropped out after a year and a half and worked as a clerk in various small businesses until 1937, returning at intervals to the farm in Ploúmitsa. He married in 1934 and has a son and daughter. During 1938–47 he worked as a civil servant in the Ministry of Labor; in 1950 was elected Advisor to the National Progressive Union of the Center under General Plastíras; during 1951–64 he worked as a customs official in Piraeus, and during 1954–55 served as Municipal Counselor to the mayor of Piraeus. Since 1947 he also worked as a journalist and translator for about five different newspapers and periodicals, and for a while in 1949 he edited the periodical *Free Letters*. He visited Hungary on the invitation of the Writers' Society there and the Soviet Union on the invitation of its government. He was sent to Yugoslavia by the Greek Ministry of the Exterior to attend a literary conference, and he has also visited Italy, Austria, France and England. In addition to his poetry he has written four novels, an impression of his trip to the Soviet Union, a biography in relation to the German-Italian occupation, lyric essays on peace, and *Nikos Kazantzakis; His Agony and His Work*, 1960. In October of 1967 he was invited to Switzerland by his German translator and has lived there since, spending some time in Italy and England, living partly on his royalties and his work as a journalist.

POETRY. *Under Shadows and Lights*, 1929. *Descending to the Silence of the Centuries*, 1933. *Man's Grimaces*, 1935. *The War*, 1935. *The Swan's Letter*, 1937. *Voyage of the Archangel*, 1938; 1941. *Margharíta—Sunset Images*, 1939. *Man's Grimaces* (all the previous books, State Prize), 1940. *The Zenith of Fire*, 1940. *Heroic Symphony*, 1945. *33 Days*, 1945. *The Legendary Country*, 1947. *Margharíta's Book*, 1949. *Taíyetos and Silence*, 1949. *The Turbid Rivers*, 1950. *Exodus on Horseback*, 1952. *Ploúmitsa*, 1951. *To Robert Oppenheimer*, 1954. *The Poems, 1929–1951* (First State Prize), 1955. *Time and the River*, 1957. *My Mother in Church*, 1957. *Royal Oak*, 1961. *Autobiography*, 1961. *Selections*, 1965.

NOTES

ELEGY OF FLOWERING FIRE. ταíΥΕΤΟΣ: Mountain range near Sparta.
ELEGY ON THE TOMB OF A YOUNG WARRIOR. BORDER GUARD: See first note to Cálas' poem "Dhiyenís," p. 687.
BOY WITH HARMONICA. CONSTITUTION SQUARE: In the heart of Athens, surrounded by the better-class hotels, by the Parliament building with its Tomb of the Unknown Warrior.
RETURN FROM DELPHI. This translation is an extensively revised version of one by Konstandínos Lárdas published in the first number of *The Charioteer*, Summer 1960, then edited by Kimon Friar. CHARIOTEER: Bronze statue, *c.* 475–470 B.C., now in the museum at Delphi. PHAEDRIADES: Two precipitous rocks on Mt. Parnassos above the Castalian Spring at

Delphi. PYTHIAN APOLLO: Immediately after birth, or four days after, the infant Apollo slew with his arrows the dragon serpent Python at her lair in Delphi, on Mt. Parnassos, which later became his most famous shrine and where his priestess, Pythia, in an ecstatic trance under the influence of the god, uttered oracles famous throughout antiquity.

SAYING FAREWELL. CASTALIAN WATERS: Spring on Mt. Parnassos famous for its silver purity. The Latin poets made it the favorite resting spot of Apollo and the Muses, and endowed its waters with the magic of poetic inspiration.

A SELECT GENERAL
BIBLIOGRAPHY

Listed below are selected books and periodicals wherein appear two or more of the poets presented in this anthology. The arrangement is chronological.

In English

POETRY ANTHOLOGIES IN BOOK FORM

"Five Modern Greek Poems," translation and commentary by Kimon Friar, in *New Direction in Prose and Poetry*, No. 13 (New York: New Directions Press, 1951). Kazantzákis, Sikelianós, Seféris, Engonópoulos, Gátsos.

Six Poets of Modern Greece; chosen, translated, and introduced by Edmund Keeley and Philip Sherrard (London: Thames and Hudson, 1960; New York: Alfred A. Knopf, 1961). Caváfis, Sikelianós, Seféris, Antoníou, Elýtis, Gátsos.

Four Greek Poets; chosen and translated from the Greek by Edmund Keeley and Philip Sherrard (Harmondsworth, Middlesex, England: Penguin Books, 1966). Caváfis, Seféris, Elýtis, Gátsos.

"Greek Poetry," edited and translated by Kimon Friar, with an Introduction, in *Modern European Poetry*, Willis Barnstone, ed. (New York: Bantam Books, 1966). Sikelianós, Kazantzákis, Seféris, Thémelis, Antoníou, Rítsos, Mátsas, Engonópoulos, Elýtis, Gátsos, and others.

Nine Greek Poets, translations by John A. Goumas (Athens: Athens Publishing Center, 1968). Báras, Embirícos, Engonópoulos, Sarandáris, and others.

"Poetry," edited and translated by Kimon Friar, in *Modern Greek Literature*, edited and prose selections translated by Mary Gianos (New York: Twayne Publications, 1969). Caváfis, Sikelianós, Kazantzákis, Ouránis, Papatsónis, Kariotákis, Seféris, Thémelis,

763

Karélli, Embirícos, Vafópoulos, Báras, Sarandáris, Melissánthi, Rítsos, Engonópoulos, Mátsas, Elýtis, Vrettákos, Gátsos.
Modern Greek Poetry, translated and edited by Rae Dalven. Second edition, revised and enlarged (New York: Russell and Russell, 1972). Extremely inaccurate translations.

CRITICAL WORKS

PHILIP SHERRARD, *The Marble Threshing Floor: Studies in Modern Greek Poetry* (London: Valentine, Mitchell, 1956). Essays and translation: Solomós, Palamás, Caváfis, Sikelianós, Seféris.

GEORGE THOMSON, *The Greek Language* (Cambridge: W. Heffer & Sons, 1960).

"Kazantzákis," in Colin Wilson, *The Strength to Dream* (London: Gollancz, 1962).

"Kazantzákis' *Odyssey*," by Frederic Will, in *Hereditas*, Seven Essays on the Modern Experience of the Classical, edited by Frederic Will (Austin: University of Texas Press, 1964).

NICHOLAS BACHTIN, *Introduction to the Study of Modern Greek* (Birmingham, no date).

PETER BIEN, *Kazantzákis and the Linguistic Revolution in Greek Literature* (Princeton, N.J.: Princeton Unviersity Press, 1972).

———, *Níkos Kazantzákis* (New York: Columbia University Press, 1972).

EDMUND KEELEY AND PETER BIEN, editors, *Modern Greek Writers* (Princeton, N.J.: Princeton University Press, 1972). Essays by various critics on Kazantzákis, Solomós, Kálvos, Mátesis, Palamás, Caváfis, Seféris, Elýtis.

BASIL G. MANDILARÁS, *Studies in the Greek Language*, Some Aspects of the Development of the Greek Language up to the Present Day (Athens, 1972). Contains two chapters on "Kazantzákis and Language" and "The Language of Kazantzákis."

PERIODICALS

"The Surrealist Painters and Poets of Greece," *Athene*, Chicago, Summer, 1947. Translations by Kimon Friar: Engonópoulos, Embirícos, and others.
Portfolio VI, designed and edited by Caresse Crosby, Paris, 1948. Translations by Elsa Barker, Eva Sikelianós, and Derek Patmore: Sikelianós, Engonópoulos; also Vrettákos and Rítsos in French.
"Kimon Friar: New Greek Poetry, An Anthology and Commentary," *Poetry*, Chicago, June, 1951. Sikelianós, Seféris, Kazantzákis, Papatsónis, Embirícos, Antoníou, Vrettákos, Engonópoulos, Elýtis, Gátsos, and others.

Wake No. 12, Boston, Winter, 1953. Translations by Kimon Friar: Kazantzákis, Seféris, Papatsónis, Elýtis.

"Greek Number," *Poetry*, Chicago, October, 1954. Translated by Edmund Keeley and George Savídhis, Ruth Whitman: Elýtis, Gátsos, Seféris.

Folder, New York, Vol. 2, No. I, 1954–55. Translations by Kimon Friar: Seféris, Karélli, and others.

"Perspective of Greece," edited by Kimon Friar and Ronald Freelander, *Atlantic Monthly*, Boston, June, 1955. Translations by Kimon Friar: Papatsónis, Kazantzákis, Embirícos, Elýtis, Sikelianós, Seféris, Palamás.

"Eleven Poems from Greece," *The London Magazine*, London, October, 1965. Translations by Philip Sherrard, C. Tachtsis, Kay Cicellis. Caváfis, Embirícos, Elýtis, and others.

Fulbright Review. Vol. II. Athens, Fall, 1965. Translations by Kimon Friar: Elýtis, Embirícos, Mátsas, Vrettákos, and others.

"Greece," *Modern Poetry in Translation*, London, New York, Grossman Publishers, in association with Cape Goliard, 1968. Translations by Paul Merchant: Seféris, Embirícos, Elýtis, Rítsos, and others.

"Thirteen Poets from Salonika," *The Charioteer*, No. 10, New York, 1968. "An Introduction to the Salonika Poets," by George Odysseus. Translations by Kimon Friar: Thémelis, Karélli, Vafópoulos, Pendzíkis, and others.

"Greek Poetry Special Issue," edited by Peter Levi, S.J., *Agenda*, London, Winter 1969. Translations by Peter Levi of Seféris, Antoníou; by Edmund Keeley and George Savídhis of Elýtis.

Mundus Artium, Winter 1970. Translations by Kimon Friar of Rítsos, Elýtis; by J. C. Stathátos of Rítsos.

Contemporary Literature in Translation, Vancouver, Canada, Winter 1970. Painting by Engonópoulos on cover, and translations by Kimon Friar of Embirícos and Engonópoulos.

Omphalos, A Mediterranean Review, Vol. I, No. 1, Athens, March, 1972. Translations by Peter Dreyer, N. C. Germanácos, and Peter Mackridge of Seféris, Rítsos, Caváfis.

Interested readers may find much poetry in translation in the following magazines:

Athene, edited by Demetrios A. Michalaros, Chicago, 1941–1967. These contain a great many poems translated from the modern Greek, but of extremely uneven choice and quality.

The Charioteer. A Quarterly Review of Modern Greek Culture, New York, 1960–. The first three issues were edited by Kimon Friar, the others by Andonis Decavalles and Bebe Spanos.

Greek Heritage, An American Quarterly of Greek Culture, edited by Kimon Friar. Six issues, from the Summer of 1963 through Vol. 11, No. 6, 1965. The first two issues were published in Chicago, the last four in Athens.

IN FOREIGN LANGUAGES

BOOK ANTHOLOGIES

Domaine Grèce (1930–1946). Robert Levesque. Geneva and Paris: Éditions des Trois Collines, 1947.
Griechische Lyric der Gegenwart; Übertragen von Otto Stainingir. Linz: J. Wimmer, 1960.
Panorama Moderner Lyrik. Sigbert Mohn Verlag, 1960.
Trittico neogreco: Porfiras–Kavafis–Sikelianos; presentati e tradotti da Bruno Lavagnini. Athens: Edizioni dello Istituto Italiano di Atene, 1954.
Poesia greca del '900. Con testo a fronte presentata e tradotta da Mario Vitti. Parma: Ugo Guanda Editore, 1957; revised, 1966.
Arodafnusa. Poeti neogreci (1880–1940). Athens, 1957. Greek texts, and translations into Italian of 32 poets by Bruno Lavagnini.

CRITICAL WORKS

S. BAUD-BOVY, *Poésie de la Grèce Moderne.* Lausanne, 1946.
GEORGES SPYRIDAKI, *La Grèce et la Poésie Moderne.* Paris, 1954.
BRUNO LAVAGNINI, *Storia della letteratura neoellenica.* Milano, 1955.
MARIO VITTI, *Orientamento della Grecia, nel suo risorgimento letterario.* Roma, 1955.
———, *Storia della letteratura neo-greca.* Roma, 1971.

IN GREEK

ANTHOLOGIES

Medieval and Modern Greek Poetry; edited with an Introduction in English by C. A. Trypanis. Oxford: Clarendon Press, 1951.
Anthology of Cyprian Poetry; edited by Andréas S. Ioánnou. 1951.
Anthology, 1708–1952; edited by I. N. Apostolídhis. 1933; expanded and reissued, 1956.
Anthology of Post-War Poetry; edited by Dínos Yorghoúdhis and K. Yennatás; Introduction by Aléxandros Aryiríou. 1957.
Supplement to the Anthology; edited by I. N. Apostolídhis. 1959.

Contemporary Poetry; edited by Pános N. Panayotoúnis and Pávlos N. Nathanaíl. 1961.

Greek Poetry Anthologized; 5 vols.; edited by M. Avyéris, V. Rótas, T. Stávros, and M. M. Papaïoánnou. 1958–1961. From ancient to modern times.

Anthology of Contemporary Greek Poetry (1930–1960); edited by A. Dhiktéos and F. Barlás. 1961.

Anthology of Poetry; edited by Panayótis K. Pános. 1963.

Anthology of Poetry (1453–1964); 3 vols.; edited by Mihaíl Peránthis. No date.

Cyprian Anthology; edited by Andréas Hristophídhis. 1965.

Poetry Anthology, from 1453 to the Present Time; 7 vols.; edited by Línos Polítis. 1965.

Anthology of Neo-Hellenic Literature. Poetry, Erudite and Demotic from the Medieval Ages to Our Day; edited by Rénos Apostolídhis. 3 vols., 1970–1971.

The Penguin Book of Greek Verse; introduced and edited by Constantine A. Trypanis with plain prose translations of each poem. Harmondsworth, Middlesex: Penguin Books, 1971. From Homer to Elýtis.

CRITICAL WORKS

K. V. Paráskhos, *Greek Lyric Poets.* 1953.

S. Spandhonídhis, *The Newest Poetry in Greece.* 1955.

Andréas Karandónis, *Introduction to Modern Poetry.* 1958.

M. G. Meraklís, *Our Poetry, Disagreement, Midpoint. Kalamáta,* 1959.

Yánnis Kordhátos, *History of Neo-Hellenic Literature (1453–1961).* 2 vols., 1962.

Áres Dhiktéos, *Theory of Poetry.* 1962.

——, *Search for Poetic Personality.* 1963.

George Thémelis, *Our Newest Poetry,* Vol. I. First and Second Circle, 1963.

Dhimítris A. Yérontas, *Comparisons: Neo-Hellenic and Western Modes of Speech.* 1963.

George Thémelis, *The Extreme Crisis.* 1964.

Pános K. Thasítis, *Round About Poetry.* Thessaloníki, 1966.

Andréas Karandónis, *Physiognomies.* 1966.

George Thémelis, *Our Newest Poetry,* Vol. II. *General Aspects.* 1967.

Kóstas Steryópoulos. *From Symbolism to the "New Poetry."* 1967.

K. T. Dhimarás, *History of Neo-Hellenic Literature. From Its First Roots to Our Epoch,* 4th ed. 1968.

LÍNOS POLÍTIS, *History of Greek Literature* (2d ed., supplemented). Thessaloníki, 1969.

P. PAPATHANASÓPOULOS, *Encounters in the Region of Our Newest Poetry,* 1971.

RECORDS

A series of recordings, primarily of poets reading their own poetry, have been brought out by Lýra-Diónysos, Athens—*Seféris Reads Seféris, Rítsos Reads Rítsos, Elýtis Reads Elýtis, Engonópoulos Reads Engonópoulos, Embirícos Reads Embirícos, Várnalis Reads Várnalis, George Savídhis Reads Caváfis, George Katsímbalis Reads Palamás* (with a few poems read by Palamás himself). Also: *Lady of the Vineyards.* Read by Yánnis Rítsos; with music by Ákis Limoúres. Strofés.

The following poems have been adapted and set to music:

Áxion Estí, by Odysseus Elýtis; set to music by Míkis Theodhorákis; sung by Ghrighóris Bithikótsis, T. Dhimítrief; narrated by Mános Katrákis; with the Small Athens Orchestra and the Mixed Chorus of Thália Vizantíou; orchestra and chorus conducted by the composer. His Master's Voice.

Small Cyclades, by Odysseus Elýtis; set to music by Míkis Theodhorákis; sung by Dora Yannakópoulos. His Master's Voice. Sung by Soúla Birbílis, Lýra-Diónysos.

Sun the First, by Odysseus Elýtis; set to music by Yánnis Markópoulos; sung by Méri Dhimitriádhis and Stávros Pasparákis; narrated by Yánnis Fértis; with members of the Enian Choral Orchestra; conducted by the composer. Phillips.

Heroic and Elegiac Song for the Lost Lieutenant of the Albanian Campaign, by Odysseus Elýtis; set to music by Nótis Mavroïdhís; sung by Renáta Karenárou, Pétros Pandhís, Petrí Salpéa, and chorus; narrated by Hrístos Tsangás; orchestra and chorus conducted by the composer. Lýra-Diónysos.

The R of Eros, by Odysseus Elýtis; set to music by Línos Kókotos; sung by Réna Koumyóti and Mihális Violáris. Lýra.

Bolívar: A Greek Poem, by Níkos Engonópoulos; set to music by Níkos Mamangákis in the form of folk cantatas; sung by George Zoghráfos; orchestra and chorus conducted by the composer. Lýra-Diónysos.

Epitáphios, by Yánnis Rítsos; set to music by Míkis Theodhorákis. (1) Sung by Naná Moúskhouri; orchestra directed by Mános Hadzidhákis. Fidelity. (2) Sung by Ghrighóris Bithikótsis and

Kéti Thími; Manólis Hiótis and his orchestra. Columbia. (3) Recited by Kákia Panaghótou; Fine Arts Chorus of Tríkala directed by Terpsihóri Papastefánou. RCA Victor. (4) Sung by Méri Línda and Manólis Hiótis. Columbia. *Romiosíni*, by Yánnis Rítsos; set to music by Míkis Theodhorákis. (1) Sung by Ghrighóris Bithikótsis; Folk Orchestra directed by Míkis Theodhorákis. His Master's Voice. (2) *The Ballad of a Free People*. Broadside Records, Album No. BR307, New York. Also: Recited by Giánnis Rítsos. Fassett Recording Studio, Boston.

TAPES

Tapes of poems read by the poets or by others may be found in the Poetry Room of the Lamont Library at Harvard University. The spelling is that used in their catalogue: Athanasoúlis, Bárnales, Brettákos, Caracásis, Caváfis (read by Geórges Katsímpales), Decaválles, Diktaíos, Dimákis, Elýtes, Eongonópoulos, Empeiríkos, Geralís, Karoúzos, Kótsiras, Kabáphes (read by Geórgios Pánou Sabbídes), Krandiótis, Mátsas, Palamás (reads five of his poems, the rest by G. Katsímpales), Papadítsas, Papatsónes, Rítsos, Sachtoúres, Seféris, Sinópoulos, Stergiópoulos, Thémelis, Vakaló, Vavitsiótis, and selections from modern Greek poetry read by Katsímpales and Trypánes.

ACKNOWLEDGMENTS

My greatest debt is to the living poets themselves with whom I made the first transcriptions of each poem (with the exception of only a few poems), and who then patiently checked with me my various versions throughout the years, and the final form each poem took. I am also indebted to them for supplying me with biographical and bibliographical information, with checking these for me, and for writing me, in many instances, a Credo of their work to aid me in understanding. My thanks also to the wives of three poets, Mrs. Anna Sikelianós, Mrs. Dora Várnalis, and Mrs. Soúla Vafópoulos; to Mr. George Marinákis, editor and biographer of George Sarandáris, and to Mr. Pétros Markákis, editor and biographer of Kóstas Ouránis. In my publication of Níkos Kazantzákis' *The Odyssey: A Modern Sequel,* I have already thanked those who have aided me in the translation of that epic. In particular now I wish to thank Mr. Níkos Gátsos who, over the years, has helped me immeasurably with my translations, discussing with me and clarifying for me, when the poet himself was not available, many difficult passages and interpretations. I am indebted for similar assistance to Professor Andónis Decávalles, Mr. Pandelís Prevelákis, Mr. Nános Valaorítis, and to friends who have also helped me to interpret, to check on sources, or to gather notes, to Miss Nélly Andrikópoulos, Miss Katerína Angeláki-Rooke, Mr. Pétros Efthimíou, Mr. Níkos Germanácos, Mr. Andréas Karandónis, Miss Olympía Karáyorghas, Professor Edmund Keeley, Mr. Yánnis Mítsios, Professor Demétrios Moútsos, Miss Athiná Sahínis, Mrs. Hébe Skandalákis, Mr. Kóstas Steryópoulos, Mr. Strátis Tsírkas, Mr. Násos Vayanás, and to many anonymous friends. Mr. Níkos Gátsos, Dr. Elías Kapetanópoulos, Mr. Aléxis Dhiamandópoulos, Mr. Peter Mackridge, Mr. Násos Vayanás and Professor Charles Mitsákis, who were so kind as to read my Introduction, make suggestions, and correct errors, although I am solely responsible for whatever errors may remain. Last of all, my thanks to my publishers who never hurried me all these years, in particular to the late Max Lincoln Schuster, who initially encouraged me, and to my editor, Mr. Michael Korda. Readers of my work will notice that I have incorporated here and there throughout my text comments about several poets and themes which I have published elsewhere, hoping to give them here their final form. Some of these translations have been published in the following:

BOOKS: *Introduction to Modern Greek Literature*, Mary Gianos, ed. (Twayne Publishers); *A Little Treasury of World Poetry*, Hubert Creekmore, ed. (Scribner's); *Modern European Poetry*, Willis Barnstone, ed. (Bantam Books); *New Directions No. 13*, James Laughlin, ed. (New Directions Press); *New World Writing 2*, Arabel J. Porter, ed. (New American Library); *Zero Anthology No. 8*, Themistocles Hoetis, ed.

PERIODICALS: *Accent, Arizona Quarterly, Athene, Atlantic Monthly, The Charioteer, Chicago Review, Folder, Fulbright Review, Greek Heritage, Mundus Artium, New York Times Book Review, Poetry* (Chicago), *Quarterly Review of Literature, Shenandoah, Wake No. 12.*

INDEX
OF POEMS AND POETS